Thirteenth Canadian Edition

Human Resources
Management
in Canada

Thirteenth Canadian Edition

Human Resources Management in Canada

in Canada

Gary Dessler
Florida International University

Nita Chhinzer
University of Guelph

PEARSON

Toronto

Editorial Director: Claudine O'Donnell
Acquisitions Editor: Carolin Sweig
Marketing Manager: Lisa Gillis
Program Manager: Karen Townsend
Project Manager: Jessica Hellen
Manager of Content Development: Suzanne Schaan
Developmental Editor: Jennifer Murray
Media Editor: Kamilah Reid-Burrell
Media Developer: Kelli Cadet
Production Services: Integra
Permissions Project Manager: Joanne Tang
Photo Permissions Research: Melody English, Integra
Text Permissions Research: Renae Horstman, Integra
Interior and Cover Designer: Anthony Leung
Cover Image: © Hero Images/Getty Images
Vice-President, Cross Media and Publishing Services: Gary Bennett

Credits and acknowledgments for material borrowed from other sources and reproduced, with permission, in this textbook appear on the appropriate page within the text.

If you purchased this book outside the United States or Canada, you should be aware that it has been imported without the approval of the publisher or the author.

7   18

Library and Archives Canada Cataloguing in Publication
Dessler, Gary, 1942-, author
   Human resources management in Canada / Gary Dessler
and Nita Chhinzer.—Canadian 13th edition.
   Includes bibliographical references and index.
   ISBN 978-0-13-400544-7 (paperback)
   1. Personnel management—Textbooks.   2.   Personnel management—Canada—Textbooks.
I. Chhinzer, Nita, author   II. Title.
   HF5549.D49   2016   658.3   C2015-907842-3

ISBN 978-0-13-400544-7

Dedication

To my mother

—G.D.

I would like to dedicate this book to those students who consistently demonstrate the ability to integrate, analyse and transfer knowledge, both within the classroom and outside of it. Your excellence keeps me inspired.

—N.N.C.

Brief Contents

Table of Contents

Human resources continue to provide a source of competitive advantage for organizations in a hyper-competitive, global environment. The thirteenth edition of *Human Resources Management in Canada* demonstrates how human resources are among the most important assets in organizations today. This book is designed to provide a complete, comprehensive review of human resources management (HRM) concepts and techniques in a highly readable and understandable form for a wide audience: students specializing in HRM and those in business programs, supervisory/managerial staff, and small-business owners. Accordingly, this book exposes readers to both a breadth and depth of core issues, processes, and strategic elements of how the human resources at work contribute to organizational success. The strategic importance of HRM activities is emphasized throughout the book, using recent examples from the Canadian employment landscape.

As in previous editions, the Canadian thirteenth edition provides extensive coverage of all HRM topics, such as job analysis, HR planning, recruitment, selection, orientation and training, career development, compensation and benefits, performance appraisal, health and safety, and labour relations. The scientific/academic contributions to the world of human resources are embedded throughout the book and highlighted with *Evidence-Based HR* icons in the margins. *Hints to Ensure Legal Compliance* are also highlighted, and *Ethical Dilemmas* are presented for discussion.

NEW TO THE CANADIAN THIRTEENTH EDITION

Alignment with new HR competencies requirements for the new national level certifications in HR (CHRP, CHRL, CHRE)

- In 2015, the national level Canadian Council of Human Resources Association (CCHRA) replaced the previous Required Professional Competencies (RPCs) with 44 newly formed HR competencies. The new competency list aligns with the move away from the Certified Human Resource Professional (CHRP) and Senior Human Resource Professional (SHRP) designations to a three-tier designation process, as discussed in detail in Chapter 1 (Certified Human Resource Practitioner, Certified Human Resource Leader, and Certified Human Resource Executive.) This book is updated to reflect the new set of required HR competencies associated with the new designations for Human Resource experts in Canada.

- While most provincial/territorial HR bodies have expanded on the baseline 44 HR competencies to reflect a range of expected expertise in each competency (e.g., Ontario), other provincial/territorial HR bodies are in the process of determining how these will be implemented. Accordingly, this textbook has been updated to delete the old RPCs and include the baseline 44 HR competencies developed by the CCHRA, highlighting where they are applied.

Expert Opinion Boxes

- **Expert Opinion Industry Viewpoint.** Practitioners such as the President of Unifor, Executives from Loblaw and Labatt, HR representatives from the Government of Yukon, and a series of small-business leaders provide insight into relevant and current industry perspectives for each chapter. This provides the reader with valuable insight regarding critical issues according to industry experts, and first hand knowledge in terms of how these issues impact Canadian workplaces.

- **Expert Opinion Academic Viewpoint.** Canada Research Chairs from across Canadian universities in a wide variety of associated disciplines like Human Resource Management, Organizational Behaviour, Psychology, Economics, Social Science, and other disciplines answer questions related to critical issues in the world of work from both HR and non-HR perspectives. These evidence-based discussions are aligned with key subtopics in each chapter and bring the reader into the academic discussions between and across reputable academic experts in Canada.

HR in the News

- **Each chapter includes at least one HR in the News** section aimed at maximizing the relevance and transferability of what students are learning. These are strategically placed in the text to align with the core content and highlight the theory versus practice differences that may be applicable. This contribution helps mazimize the transferability of learning from each chapter by highlighting significant Canadian topics and experiences associated with employee and employer relationships.

HR by the Numbers

- **Each chapter also includes an HR by the Numbers** section, a new visual that highlights the impact and trends of core concepts. These provide succinct and clear metrics associated with the concepts presented in each chapter, identifying practical issues within the framework of the theory or ideals presented in the text. These are all relevant, current, thought-provoking, and visually appealing. This aligns with the focus on evidence-based HR.

KEY FEATURES OF THE CANADIAN THIRTEENTH EDITION

An evidence-based HR approach: The authors assume an evidence-based approach to the breadth of topics in the book, incorporating research from peer-reviewed academic journals to provide valid and reliable information to guide decision-making. This approach attempts to bridge the research–user gap and build confidence in the relevance, quality, and applicability of research findings.

Bridging research and practice: Consistent with the evidence-based approach to HR, each chapter introduces expert opinions (as stand-alone boxes) from researcher experts (specifically, Canada Research Chairs) addressing research contributions associated with a subtopic in each chapter. To complement this, a wide range of industry expert opinions are also included in each chapter (as stand-alone boxes), bringing the reader into current and relevant perspectives of the topics from a wide range of practitioners. These opinions are presented in the book and contrasted in the student-based technology-enabled activities (discussed below).

Additional Features

Learning Outcomes. Specific learning goals are defined on each chapter-opening page.

HR Competencies. The associated HR competencies with each chapter are presented in the chapter opening and icons are inserted throughout the chapter, highlighting where each HR competency is addressed/developed.

Key Terms. Key terms appear in boldface within the text, are defined in the margins, and are listed at the end of each chapter and in the index.

Current Examples. Numerous real-world examples of HRM policies, procedures, and practices at a wide variety of organizations, ranging from small service providers to huge global corporations, can b a e found throughout the text.

Full-Colour Figures, Tables, and Photographs. Throughout each chapter, key concepts and applications are illustrated with strong, full-colour visual materials.

Web Links. Helpful Internet sites are provided throughout the text and are featured in the margins.

Integrated Chapters. Rather than approaching topics as isolated silos, the book highlights areas of overlap in order to present HRM as an integrated set of topics.

Boxed Features. The four boxed features—*Workforce Diversity, Strategic HR, Entrepreneurs and HR*, and *Global HRM*—have been updated and revised in all chapters.

End-of-Chapter Summaries. At the end of each chapter, the summary reviews key points related to each of the learning outcomes.

End-of-Chapter Review and Discussion Questions. Each chapter contains a set of review and discussion questions.

Critical Thinking Questions. Each chapter contains end-of-chapter questions designed to provoke critical thinking and stimulate discussion.

Experiential Exercises. Each chapter includes a number of individual and group-based experiential exercises that provide learners with the opportunity to apply the text material and develop some hands-on skills.

Running Case. The running case at the end of each chapter illustrates the types of HRM challenges confronted by small-business owners and front-line supervisors. It is accompanied by critical thinking questions, which provide an opportunity to discuss and apply the text material.

Case Incidents. Case incidents can be found at the end of each chapter. These cases present current HRM issues in a real-life setting and are followed by questions designed to encourage discussion and promote the use of problem-solving skills.

Highlighted Themes

WORKFORCE DIVERSITY

The Evolution of Thought on Sexual Harassment in Canada

In August 1982, two young women named Dianne Janzen and Tracy Govereau secured waitressing jobs at Pharos Restaurant in Winnipeg, Manitoba. The women hardly knew each other and rarely worked together. The cook, Tommy Grammas, started groping the women and making sexual advances during each woman's shift at work. As the women resisted the sexual advances, Tommy told them to "shut up or be fired."

Janzen tried to make it clear to Grammas that his actions were inappropriate, which did not stop the unwanted behaviour. When Janzen approached the owner, Philip Anastasiadis, he commented that she "needed to get laid." Feeling unsupported and embarrassed, Janzen continued working for two months before eventually quitting the job to remove herself from the continually hostile environment. Govereau was soon fired from her job, because of her "attitude."

Both women filed complaints under the Manitoba Human Rights Code. They claimed that only females ran the risk of

being harassed at Pharos, since none of the male waiters, cashiers, or busboys had ever been harassed; thus, sexual harassment was a form of discrimination based on sex.

After a series of appeals, in 1989 the case was reviewed by the Supreme Court of Canada. In this historic case, the Supreme Court agreed that the women were sexually harassed at work, that sexual harassment is a form of sex discrimination (and is therefore illegal), and that employers are responsible for their employees' actions.

Up until the ruling, the terms of sexual harassment were not defined and the application of the law was unclear. The real impact of the precedent that this ruling set was that it gave employers and employees an unrestricted definition of sexual harassment that has since been instrumental in capturing a broader level of unwelcomed behaviours at work.

Source: Summarized from Stephen Hammond of Harassment Solutions Inc., "The Historic Fight Against Sexual Harassment," Canadian HR Reporter, 24, no. 14 (August 15, 2011), p. 33. Used with permission from Stephen Hammond, Harassment Solutions Inc.; Harassment is a Form of Discrimination, www.chrc-ccdp.ca/en/timeportals/milestones/125mile.asp, Canadian Human Rights Commission, 1989. Reproduced with the permission of the Minister of Public Works and Government Services Canada, 2012.

• **Workforce Diversity.** The Workforce Diversity boxes describe some of the issues and challenges involved in managing the diverse workforce found in Canadian organizations. The broad range of types of diversity addressed include generational/age, ethnic, gender, racial, and religious.

STRATEGIC HR

Pumping Up People Supply

Building an aortic pericardial heart valve is no easy task. The intricate medical device, measuring mere millimetres, requires highly specialized skills in its production and engineering. Therefore, there is a very small talent pool available to Burnaby, BC-based Sorin Group Canada. They hire engineers who focus on custom-engineered machinery and equipment, quality assurance experts who ensure that regulations are followed, and production technicians who hand-sew and hand-suture the heart valves.

According to Judith Thompson, senior manager of HR at Sorin Group, "Canada isn't well-known for its biomedical engineers so even when we hire now, to ask for medical device experience, we wouldn't get it. So we hire an engineer or scientist and train on the rest of it." The company has come to realize the benefits, and necessity, of new immigrants as a major source of talent. "Our culture is very diverse. About 90 percent of our staff speak English as a second language,

from production people to vice-presidents, so we don't look for Canadian-born, Canadian-educated, Canadian experience because in these economic times that would set us back," she says. "I would never have filled 60 positions last year with those criteria."

Training is extensive, as it takes three or four months before workers, wearing gowns and gloves in a super-clean environment, can make a product that is usable. And even then they can only make a certain number of valves or components per week—it takes another six months to ramp up to regular production, says Thompson. Sorin supports its employees with in-house English-language training, through a partnership with immigration services, and provides subsidies to foreign-trained engineers who want to pursue an engineering degree in British Columbia.

Source: Adapted from S. Dobson, "Pumping Up People Supply at Sorin Group Canada to Build Heart Valves," Canadian HR Reporter, February 23, 2009.

• **Strategic HR.** These boxes provide examples that illustrate the ways in which organizations are using effective HRM policies and practices to achieve their strategic goals.

ENTREPRENEURS and HR

Succession Planning and Family Businesses

In the second quarter of 2010, small businesses created 35 549 jobs, while large firms created only 728 jobs. During that period, small businesses in the construction sector alone accounted for 23 014 new jobs, while those in the healthcare and social assistance sectors introduced 9755 new jobs.

Multigenerational family-controlled businesses often struggle with succession planning. Only one-third of family-owned businesses survive the transition to the second generation. And of these, only one-third survive the transition to the third generation.[14]

There are many reasons for these failures.

1. Determining who will inherit the business and how ownership will be determined among children can be a source of immense stress for family business owners. Therefore, many choose to ignore the issue of succession planning altogether.

2. Second, a family business is a great source of pride for the business owner and is often their single largest asset. The concept of retirement or walking away can be incomprehensible to those who built the business.

3. There may not be a qualified or interested successor within the family.

While these are difficult issues to deal with, family businesses must begin to take an informed and strategic approach to these issues.

• **Entrepreneurs and HR.** Suggestions, examples, and practical hints are provided to assist those in smaller businesses who have limited time and resources to implement effective HRM policies and procedures.

GLOBAL HRM

Successful Integration of Immigrants in Canada

There are many examples of innovative, forward-thinking companies that have developed initiatives to aid in the successful integration of immigrants into their workforce. The result is a competitive advantage and ability to recognize and recruit strong talent.

• RBC requires recruiters and managers to be trained in cross-cultural awareness to help interpret and understand past experiences related to the job. This represents a two-way mutual understanding approach to recruitment.

• Assiniboine Credit Union assumes an organic approach by training managers and employees on diversity and

cultural awareness, offering a mentorship or buddy program, and regularly soliciting and communicating feedback from the programs, which then aids in modifying the programs.

• Manulife offers paid internships (of 4 to 12 months) and formalizes the process by having clear indications of who is eligible for the programs offered (must be in Canada less than three years, have at least three years of foreign experience, and so on).

Source: Based on G. Lirse and G. Tillman, "Valorizing Immigrants' Non-Canadian Work Experience" (Ottawa, ON: Work and Learning Knowledge Centre, 2009).

• **Global HRM.** In recognition of the increasing impact of globalization, topics highlighted in the Global HRM boxes include cultural issues in retirement plans, employment contracts in Europe, and the importance of personal relationships for business success in China.

Supplements

MyManagementLab

We have created an outstanding supplements package for *Human Resources Management in Canada*, Thirteenth Canadian edition. In particular, we have provided access to MyManagementLab, which provides students with an assortment of tools to help enrich and expedite learning. MyManagementLab is an online study tool for students and an online homework and assessment tool for faculty. MyManagementLab lets students assess their understanding through auto-graded tests and assignments, develop a personalized study plan to address areas of weakness, and practise a variety of learning tools to master management principles. New and updated MyManagementLab resources include the following:

- **New Personal Inventory Assessment (PIA).** Students learn better when they can connect what they are learning to their personal experience. PIA is a collection of online exercises designed to promote self-reflection and engagement in students, enhancing their ability to connect with concepts taught in principles of management, organizational behaviour, and human resource management classes. Assessments can be assigned by instructors, who can then track students' completions. Student results include a written explanation along with a graphic display that shows how their results compare to the class as a whole. Instructors will also have access to this graphic representation of results to promote classroom discussion.

- **New Personalized Study Plan.** As students work through MyManagementLab's new Study Plan, they can clearly see which topics they have mastered—and, more importantly, which they need to work on. Each question has been carefully written to match the concepts, language, and focus of the text, so students can get an accurate sense of how well they've understood the chapter content.

- **New Video Library & Exercises.** Robust video library with over 1000 videos that include easy-to-assign assessments. The video library also includes the ability for instructors to add YouTube or other video sources, allows for students to upload video submissions, and has polling and teamwork functions. Engaging videos explore business topics related to the theory students are learning in class; quizzes then assess students' comprehension of the concepts covered in each video.

- **New Learning Catalytics.** Learning Catalytics is a "bring your own device" student engagement, assessment, and classroom intelligence system. It allows instructors to engage students in class with a variety of question types designed to gauge student understanding.

- **Assignable Mini-Cases and Video Cases.** Instructors have access to a variety of case-based assessment material that can be assigned to students, with multiple-choice quizzes or written-response format in MyManagementLab's new Writing Space.

- **Pearson eText.** The Pearson eText gives students access to their textbook anytime, anywhere. In addition to note taking, highlighting, and bookmarking, the Pearson eText offers interactive and sharing features. Rich media options may include videos, animations, interactive figures, and built-in assessments, all embedded in the text. Instructors can share their comments or highlights, and students can add their own, creating a tight community of learners within the class.

  The Pearson eText may include a responsive design for easy viewing on smartphones and tablets. Many of our eTexts now have configurable reading settings, including resizable type and night reading mode.

- **Glossary Flashcards.** This study aid is useful for students' review of key concepts.

- **Simulations.** Simulations help students analyze and make decisions in common business situations; the simulations assess student choices and include reinforcement quizzes, outlines, and glossaries.

Instructor Supplements

Most of these instructor supplements are available for download from a password-protected section of Pearson Canada's online catalogue (www.pearsoncanada.ca/highered). Navigate to your textbook's catalogue page to view a list of those supplements that are available. See your local sales representative for details and access.

- **Instructor's Manual.** This comprehensive guide contains a detailed lecture outline of each chapter, descriptions of the discussion boxes, answers to review and critical thinking questions, answers to the case questions, and hints regarding the experiential exercises.

- **Test Item File.** This comprehensive test bank contains more than 1500 multiple-choice, true/false, and short essay questions.

- **PowerPoint® Lecture Slides.** This practical set of PowerPoint lecture slides outlines key concepts discussed in the text, and includes selected tables and figures from the text.

- **Computerized Test Bank.** Pearson's computerized test banks allow instructors to filter and select questions to create quizzes, tests, or homework. Instructors can revise questions or add their own, and may be able to choose print or online options. The test bank for *Human Resources Management in Canada*, Thirteenth Edition, includes more than 1500 multiple-choice, true/false, and short essay questions.

- **Image Gallery.** This package provides instructors with images to enhance their teaching.

- **Learning Solutions Managers.** Pearson's Learning Solutions Managers work with faculty and campus course designers to ensure that Pearson technology products, assessment tools, and online course materials are tailored to meet your specific needs. This highly qualified team is dedicated to helping schools take full advantage of a wide range of educational resources, by assisting in the integration of a variety of instructional materials and media formats. Your local Pearson Education sales representative can provide you with more details on this service program.

ACKNOWLEDGEMENTS

Over the editions, this manuscript was reviewed at various stages of its development by a number of peers across Canada, and we want to thank those who shared their insights and constructive criticism.

Stan Arnold, Humber College

David Berrington, Sauder School of Business, UBC

Anna Bortolon, Conestoga College

Elizabeth Clipsham, Capilano University

Katrina Di Gravio, University of Waterloo

Thomas Foard, University of Guelph-Humber

Sarah Holding, Vancouver Island University

Helen MacDonald, Nova Scotia Community College

Cheryl Meheden, University of Lethbridge

James O'Brien, University of Western Ontario

Melanie Peacock, Mount Royal University

Chet Robie, Wilfrid Laurier University

Aaron Schat, McMaster University

Andrew Templer, University of Windsor

Bryan Webber, Vancouver Island University

We are very grateful to many people at Pearson Canada: Carolin Sweig, Senior Acquisitions Editor; Jessica McInnis, Marketing Manager; Karen Townsend, Program Manager; Jennifer Murray, Developmental Editor; Jessica Hellen, Project Manager; and all the other people behind the scenes who have helped make this edition possible.

A special note of thanks is extended to research assistant Kristen Piggott.

Gary Dessler
Florida International University

Nita N. Chhinzer
University of Guelph

Dr. Nita N. Chhinzer

Dr. Nita N. Chhinzer is an Associate Professor of Human Resources at the Department of Management, University of Guelph. Her research is concentrated on Strategic Human Resources Management, with a strong focus on downsizing practices, procedures, and ethics. Her program of research includes securing a stronger understanding of downsizing activity in the Canadian context, with an aim to affect public policy and legislation regarding layoffs. She has gained international recognition with conference participation including Athens, Greece; Paris, France; Dubai, UAE; and many North American speaking engagements. From May 2012–2017, Dr. Chhinzer is the recipient of the prestigious Fellowship in Leadership, HRM and Work.

CHAPTER

1

The Strategic Role of Human Resources Management

LEARNING OUTCOMES

AFTER STUDYING THIS CHAPTER, YOU SHOULD BE ABLE TO,

DEFINE human resources management (HRM) and **ANALYZE** the strategic significance of human resources management.

DESCRIBE the value of HR expertise to non–HR managers and entrepreneurs.

DESCRIBE the stages in the evolution of HRM.

EXPLAIN how HRM has changed over recent years to include a higher-level advisory role.

DESCRIBE the competencies and recognition of growing professionalism of the HRM function.

DISCUSS the internal and external environmental factors affecting human resources management policies and practices, and **EXPLAIN** their impact.

REQUIRED HR COMPETENCIES

10100: Impact the organization and human resources practices by bringing to bear a strategic perspective that is informed by economic, societal, technological, political, and demographic trends to enhance the value of human resources.

10200: Develop an understanding of the application of governance principles and methods by keeping current with the leading practices to contribute to and implement approved strategy.

10300: Provide effective leadership for human resources, with due recognition of the roles and responsibilities of the governing body and the organization's leadership and their relationships with other stakeholders, to implement the business plan and manage risk.

10400: Contribute to the organization's vision, mission, values, and goals, demonstrating business acumen and participating in the strategic planning process, to support organizational objectives.

10600: Align human resources practices by translating organizational strategy into human resources objectives and priorities to achieve the organization's plan.

20200: Adhere to ethical standards for human resources professionals by modelling appropriate behaviour to balance the interests of all stakeholders.

20500: Foster the advancement of the human resources profession by participating in professional activities and advocating for the profession to enhance the value of human resources in the workplace.

20600: Promote an evidence-based approach to the development of human resources policies and practices using current professional resources to provide a sound basis for human resources decision-making.

THE STRATEGIC ROLE OF HUMAN RESOURCES MANAGEMENT

human resources management (HRM) The management of people in organizations to drive successful organizational performance and achievement of the organization's strategic goals.

Human resources management (HRM) refers to the management of people in organizations. Human resources professionals are responsible for ensuring that the organization attracts, retains, and engages the diverse talent required to meet operational and performance commitments made to customers and shareholders. Their job is to ensure that the organization finds and hires the best individuals available, develops their talent, creates a productive work environment, and continually builds and monitors these human assets. They have the primary responsibility for managing the workforce that drives organizational performance and achieves the organization's strategic goals.[1]

More specifically, HRM involves formulating and implementing HRM systems (such as recruitment, performance appraisal, and compensation) that are aligned with the organization's strategy to ensure that the workforce has the competencies and behaviours required to achieve the organization's strategic objectives. It is crucial that the HR strategy be aligned with the company's strategic plan (see **Figure 1.1**).

HR Competency

10100

Just as important as the financial capital that is required for an organization to operate, the knowledge, education, training, skills, and expertise of a firm's workers represent its increasingly valuable **human capital**. More and more organizations are awakening to the importance of human capital as the next competitive advantage.[2]

human capital The knowledge, education, training, skills, and expertise of an organization's workforce.

Research studies over the past two decades have confirmed that effective HR practices are related to better organizational performance.[3] Organizational benefits range from employee empowerment to extensive training that affects the productivity of employees.[4] The resource-based view of the firm suggests that human resource practices contribute to the development of embedded knowledge of a firm's culture, history, processes, and context, which are non-imitable.[5]

HR Competency

10200

EVIDENCE-BASED HR

More specifically, three HR practices (profit sharing, results-oriented performance appraisal, and employment security) have strong relationships with important accounting measures of performance (return on assets and return on equity).[6] High-performance HR practices (comprehensive employee recruitment and selection procedures, incentive

FIGURE 1.1   Linking Company-Wide and HR Strategies

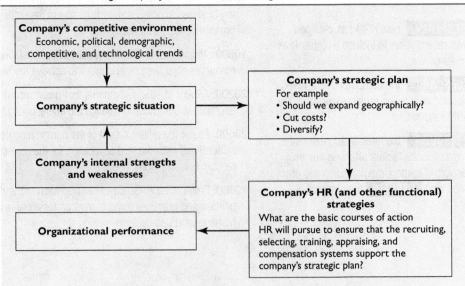

Source: © Gary Dessler, Ph.D., 2007.

compensation and performance management systems, and extensive employee involvement and training) have a positive relationship with turnover, productivity, and corporate financial performance (gross rate of return on capital).[7]

Why Is Human Resource Management Important to All Managers?

Perhaps it's easiest to answer this by listing some mistakes managers *don't* want to make. For example, no manager wants to:

hire the wrong person for the job

experience high turnover

have employees work below performance expectations

waste time with useless interviews

have the company taken to court because of discriminatory actions

have the company cited under federal occupational safety laws for unsafe practices

have some employees think their salaries are unfair relative to others in the organization

allow a lack of training to undermine a department's effectiveness

commit any unfair labour practices

In addition, throughout one's career, he or she may spend time as a HR manager. About one-third of the top HR managers in Fortune 100 companies moved to HR from other functional areas.[8] Reasons given include the fact that such people may give the firm's HR efforts a more strategic emphasis, and the possibility that they're sometimes better equipped to integrate the firm's human resource efforts with the rest of the business.[9] For example, Pearson Corporation (which publishes this book) promoted the head of one of its publishing divisions to the role of Chief Human Resource executive at its corporate headquarters.

HR is critical in large and small organizations. More than two in every three people working in the private sector in Canada as of 2012—about 7.7 million out of 11.3 million—work for small firms.[10] Statistically speaking, therefore, most people graduating from university, college, or private training programs in the next few years either will work for small businesses or will create new small businesses of their own, usually without a designated HR department. Thus, entrepreneurs, employees, and managers in small businesses should know the nuts and bolts of human resource management.

A BRIEF HISTORY OF HRM

HRM has changed dramatically over time and has assumed an increasingly strategic role. The demands on HR staff and expectations regarding their role have evolved as HRM has changed. HR practices have been shaped by society's prevailing beliefs and attitudes about workers and their rights, which have evolved in three stages.

Scientific Management: Concern for Production

scientific management The process of "scientifically" analyzing manufacturing processes, reducing production costs, and compensating employees based on their performance levels.

Frederick Taylor was the driving force behind **scientific management**, the process of "scientifically" analyzing manufacturing processes, reducing production costs, and compensating employees based on their performance.[11] As a result, management practices in the late 1800s and early 1900s emphasized task simplification and performance-based pay. Such incentives were expected to lead to higher wages for workers, increased profits for the organization, and workplace harmony. Taylor's views were not accepted by all management theorists. For example, Mary Parker Follett, a writer ahead of her time, advocated the use of self-management, cross-functional cooperation, empowerment, and managers as leaders, not dictators.[12]

The Human Resources Movement: Concern for People and Productivity

human resources movement
A management philosophy focusing on concern for people and productivity.

HRM is currently based on the theoretical assumptions of the **human resources movement**. Arriving at this joint focus on people and productivity involved four evolutionary phases.[13]

Phase 1

In the early 1900s, HRM—or personnel administration, as it was then called—played a very minor or non-existent role. During this era, personnel administrators assumed responsibility for hiring and firing (a duty formerly looked after by first-line supervisors), ran the payroll department, and administered benefits. Their job consisted largely of ensuring that procedures were followed.

Phase 2

As the *scientific management movement* gained momentum, operational efficiency increased but wage increases did not keep up, causing workers to distrust management. The resulting increase in unionization led to personnel departments serving as the primary contact for union representatives. Following the depression of the 1930s, various pieces of legislation were enacted, including a minimum wage act, an unemployment insurance program, and protection of workers' right to belong to unions. Legal compliance was subsequently added to the responsibilities of personnel managers. During the 1940s and 1950s, personnel managers were also involved in dealing with the impact of the *human relations movement*. Orientation, performance appraisal, and employee relations responsibilities were added to their job.

Phase 3

The third major phase in personnel management was a direct result of government legislation passed during the 1960s, 1970s, and 1980s that affected employees' human rights, wages and benefits, working conditions, health and safety, and established penalties for failure to meet them. The role of personnel departments expanded dramatically. They continued to provide expertise in such areas as compensation, recruitment, and training, but in an expanded capacity.

outsourcing The practice of contracting with outside vendors to handle specified business functions on a permanent basis.

Technological advances resulted in outsourcing much of the operational HR activities. **Outsourcing** involves contracting with outside vendors to handle specified business functions on a permanent basis. Although using outside experts to provide employee counselling and payroll services has been common for many years, the outsourcing of other specific HR functions, including pension and benefits administration, recruitment, management development, and training, has become increasingly common.[14]

For example, Air Canada, CIBC, BMO Financial Group, Hewlett-Packard Canada, IBM Canada, Calgary Health, and TELUS have all outsourced part or all of their administrative HR functions. During the latter part of this era, the term "human resources management" emerged. This change represented a shift in emphasis—from maintenance and administration to corporate contribution, proactive management, and initiation of change.[15]

Phase 4

The fourth phase of HRM is the current phase, where the role of HR departments has evolved to that of helping their organization achieve its strategic objectives.[16] HR activities have become ubiquitous, where not only the HR department but also every line manager has responsibilities related to employees as they move through the stages of the human-capital life cycle: selection and assimilation into the organization, development of capabilities while working in the organization, and transition out of the organization. **Figure 1.2** highlights core job requirements that are found in non-HR roles that were traditionally limited to the HR department, thus providing further evidence for the permeation of HR skills throughout the organization. Thus, to succeed in their respective roles all potential managers must be aware of the basics of HR.

HR professionals often serve as subject-matter experts or in-house consultants to line managers, offering advice on HR-related matters, formulating HR policies and procedures, and providing a wide range of HR services.

HR Competency

20500

FIGURE 1.2   Traditional HR Responsibilities in Non-HR Roles

Chief Executives

- direct human resources activities, including the approval of human resource plans or activities, the selection of directors or other high-level staff, or establishment or organization of major departments

Information Technology Project Managers

- develop or update project plans for information technology projects, including information such as project objectives, technologies, systems, information specifications, schedules, funding, and staffing
- confer with project personnel to identify and resolve problems
- direct or coordinate activities of project personnel

General and Operational Managers

- determine staffing requirements, and interview, hire, and train new employees, or oversee those personnel processes
- manage staff, preparing work schedules and assigning specific duties

Registered Nurse

- direct or supervise less-skilled nursing or healthcare personnel, or supervise a particular unit

First-Line Supervisors of Police and Detectives

- inform personnel of changes in regulations and policies, implications of new or amended laws, and new techniques of police work
- train staff in proper police work procedures
- monitor and evaluate the job performance of subordinates, and authorize promotions and transfers

Chefs and Head Cooks

- monitor sanitation practices to ensure that employees follow standards and regulations
- determine production schedules and staff requirements necessary to ensure timely delivery of services
- instruct cooks or other workers in the preparation, cooking, garnishing, or presentation of food

Source: O*NET OnLine, www.onetonline.org, U.S. Department of Labour. (accessed March 2, 2015).

Operational and Strategic Aspects of Human Resource Management

All managers are, in a sense, human resource managers, because they all get involved in recruiting, interviewing, selecting, and training their employees. Yet most firms also have a human resource department with its own top manager. How do the duties of this human resource manager and department relate to the human resource duties of sales and production and other managers? Answering this requires a short definition of line versus staff authority. **Authority** is the right to make decisions, to direct the work of others, and to give orders. Managers usually distinguish between line authority and staff authority.

In organizations, having what managers call **line authority** traditionally gives managers the right to *issue orders* to other managers or employees. Line authority therefore creates a superior (order giver)–subordinate (order receiver) relationship. When the Vice-President of sales tells his or her sales director to "get the sales presentation ready by Tuesday," he or she are exercising line authority. **Staff authority** gives a manager the right to *advise* other managers or employees. It creates an advisory relationship. When the human resource manager suggests that the plant manager use a particular selection test, he or she is exercising staff authority.

On the organization chart, managers with line authority are **line managers**. Those with staff (advisory) authority are **staff managers**. In popular usage, people tend to associate line managers with managing departments (like sales or production) that are crucial for the company's survival. Staff managers generally run departments that are advisory or supportive (like purchasing and human resource management). Human resource managers are usually staff managers. They assist and advise line managers in areas like recruiting, hiring, and compensation.

In small organizations, line managers may carry out all these personnel tasks unassisted. But as the organization grows, line managers need the assistance, specialized knowledge, and advice of a separate human resource staff. The human resource department provides this specialized assistance.

authority The right to make decisions, direct others' work, and give orders.

line authority The authority exerted by an HR manager by directing the activities of the people in his or her own business unit, department, or service area.

staff authority Staff authority gives the manager the right (authority) to advise other managers or employees.

line manager A manager who is authorized to direct the work of subordinates and is responsible for accomplishing the organization's tasks.

staff manager A manager who assists and advises line managers.

Human Resource Manager's Duties

A recent national survey of HR professionals identified five critical pieces of knowledge required by HR professionals today. Presented in priority order, they are business acumen, an understanding of employment law and legislation, talent management, broad HR knowledge, and employee–labour relations knowledge.[17]

The results align with an overall trend of increased expectations of HR professionals, suggesting that there are core capabilities that those responsible for HR activities (within the HRM department and outside of it) must secure to help deliver value to the organization.

Credible Activist   A core HR contribution is that of being both credible (respected, listened to, trusted) and active (takes a position, challenges assumptions). Both of these qualities are required to help an organization optimize the value added from its human resources.

The activist role is shared with non-HR positions as well. For example, a recent study conducted by Monster.com found that 73 percent of CEOs spent more than 25 percent of their time on talent-related activities, with three in every five identifying employee satisfaction/engagement as a key goal for their job, and three of every four identifying retention of high-performing employees as one of their goals.[18]

EVIDENCE-BASED **HR**

HR Competency
10600

EVIDENCE-BASED **HR**

HR IN THE NEWS

Superhero Employees

In September 2014, 542 Nexen employees got dressed in Batman costumes not only to kick off a fundraiser for United Way, but also to earn them a spot in the Guinness Book of World Records. Employees felt that it was really fun and provided an opportunity to show strong commitment and community spirit. In 2011, the company set a record for the most individuals dressed up as Superman in support of their United Way contribution.[19]

PERSONAL INVENTORY ASSESSMENT

Learn About Yourself
Leading Positive Change

PERSONAL INVENTORY ASSESSMENT

Learn About Yourself
Effective Empowerment and Enagagement

employee engagement The emotional and intellectual involvement of employees in their work, such as intensity, focus, and involvement in his or her job and organization.

EVIDENCE-BASED HR

Culture and Change Steward   The ability to appreciate, help shape, and articulate an organization's corporate culture includes understanding, guiding, and reacting to both internal and external stakeholder expectations. HR staff has a responsibility to shape and support a culture of change as well as develop programs, strategies, or projects to embed desired change throughout the organization.

Intense global competition and the need for more responsiveness to environmental changes put a premium on **employee engagement**, the emotional and intellectual involvement of employees in their work, such as intensity, focus, and involvement in their job and organization. Engaged employees drive desired organizational outcomes—they go beyond what is required; understand and share the values and goals of the organization; perceive that there are opportunities for growth, development, and advancement; enjoy collegial relationships with managers and co-workers; trust their leaders; and regard the success of the organization as their success.[20] According to an analysis of a Hewitt Associates database (over 4 million employees from almost 1500 companies), there is a strong positive relationship between engagement and organizational performance (sales growth and total shareholder return).[21]

Talent Manager and Organizational Designer   As traditional linear career paths change, the importance of an HR professional's ability to effectively manage human resources has become more critical as employees enter, exit, or move up, down, or across the organization. In this vein, HR specialists must embed theory, research, and practice into the processes, policies, and structures of an organization.

HR professionals and line managers play a pivotal role in *lowering labour costs*, the single largest operating expense in many organizations, particularly in the service sector. Doing so might involve introducing strategies to reduce turnover, absenteeism, and the rate of incidence of occupational illnesses and injuries. It could also mean adopting more effective recruitment, selection, and training

"What if we don't change at all ... and something magical just happens?"

cartoonresource/Fotolia

programs. At one international tire manufacturing firm, adopting a behaviour-based interview strategy as the basis for selection of entry-level engineers resulted in savings of $500 000 in three years. These savings were due to lower turnover, lower training costs, and improved capabilities of the engineering staff because of a better fit.[22]

Strategy Architect   HR professionals significantly contribute to strategy by integrating internal stakeholder and external stakeholder expectations. Through identifying, forecasting, and facilitating organizational responses to an ever-changing internal workforce and often volatile external pressures, HR plays an active role in the establishment and execution of overall strategy.

Traditionally, **strategy**—the company's plan for how it will balance its internal strengths and weaknesses with external opportunities and threats to maintain a competitive advantage—was formulated without HR input. But today HR professionals are increasingly involved in both formulating and implementing organizational strategy. A survey of over 1100 corporate managers in Canada found that three-quarters of them strongly believe that the HR function contributes significantly to the overall success of their company and view having an HR professional on staff as a strategic advantage.[23]

Operational Executor   Leading HR researcher Brian Becker says, "It isn't the content of the strategy that differentiates the winners and losers, it is the ability to execute."[24] HR specialists are expected to be **change agents** who lead the organization and its employees through organizational change. Making the enterprise more responsive to product or service innovations and technological change is the objective of many management strategies. Flattening the pyramid, empowering employees, and organizing around teams are ways in which HRM can help an organization respond quickly to its customers' needs and competitors' challenges.

Policy drafting, adaption, and implementation, as well as employees' administrative needs, were traditional roles that HR fulfilled. In recent years the efficiency in dealing with operational issues has significantly improved through the use of technology, shared services, or outsourcing. However, much of the expertise in operational aspects of employee-related policies remains largely within the HR professional's realm of responsibility.

Business Ally   Organizational goal setting and development of business objectives is highly dependent on external opportunities or threats. HR professionals, together with other organizational managers, play a role in what strategic planners call **environmental scanning**, which involves identifying and analyzing *external* opportunities and threats that may be crucial to the organization's success. These managers can also supply competitive intelligence that may be useful as the company formulates its strategic plans. Details regarding a successful incentive plan being used by a competitor, impending labour shortages, and information about pending legislative changes are examples.

HR professionals can also add value to the strategy formulation process by supplying information regarding the company's *internal* strengths and weaknesses, particularly as they relate to the organization's workforce. HR professionals not only understand the value and social context of the business, but they are also increasingly relied on to determine how an organization should be structured and how work can be integrated to ensure financial success.

REORGANIZING THE HRM FUNCTION

The evolution of HR is far from done. HR's transformation has been underway for several years, but progress has been somewhat inconsistent because of lack of senior management support and the fact that many non-HR managers still view HR as a cost

---

strategy The company's plan for how it will balance its internal strengths and weaknesses with external opportunities and threats to maintain a competitive advantage.

EVIDENCE-BASED HR

change agents Specialists who lead the organization and its employees through organizational change.

PERSONAL INVENTORY ASSESSMENT

Learn About Yourself
Comfort with Change Scale

environmental scanning
Identifying and analyzing external opportunities and threats that may be crucial to the organization's success.

expert opinion
academic viewpoint

Dr. Rick Hackett

Identification: Dr. Rick Hackett, Professor and Canadian Research Chair in Organizational Behaviour and Human Performance, and Fellow of Canadian Psychological Association

Affiliation: DeGroote School of Business, McMaster University

Focus: Executive/managerial assessment, leadership, HR recruitment, testing, selection, work attitudes, absenteeism, and performance assessment.

1. In your expert opinion, who is responsible for managing the added value associated with human resources (employees) in an organization?

    My one-word answer: Everyone. Responsibility for managing employees in an organization might start at the executive level (executives develop the mission and vision that essentially drive the organizational strategy), but all stakeholders (employees, managers, specialists) facilitate the execution of that vision or mission. We rely on people to express the values required to meet the goals and objectives of the organization, which involves alignment of culture, incentives, process, and practices that often permeate through HR.

2. What are some of the hot topics being researched in the world of HRM now, which existing and future managers should know about?

    I.   Data Analytics: In recent years there has been a lot of discussion of big data, specifically about how we can harness the volume of data accessible through HR systems. Big data in HR changes in real time, it's dynamic, with constantly changing algorithms.

    II. Technology for Performance Management: This is linked with data analytics, but addresses how we harness technology to make HR more effective. For example, HRIS requires packages tailored to the needs of specialized workers.

    III. Contingent Workforce: Organizations have a smaller core workforce with an increasing use of contingent workers. The issues of what this means for retention, information security, intellectual property, and the impact on the labour force composition requires consideration.

    IV. Intrepreneurship: Innovation within the organization requires an exploration of what kinds of infrastructure we need in place to support new information and innovation.

3. Why should those who manage human resources in an organization use academic articles in peer-reviewed journals to inform their decisions?

    Pressing demands of the day-to-day job requirements make it hard for practitioners to manage information overload. Instead, researchers should work with media teams at their research centres (e.g., universities, government agencies) or develop industry-oriented papers to communicate information in a meaningful way outside of the research community. Recent research grant applications have started asking about plans for research dissemination, but we can also build in incentive systems to recognize research communicated in practitioner forums.

Source: Reprinted by permission from Dr. Rick Hackett.

centre. Many HR professionals need to acquire more broad-based business knowledge and skill sets to be considered and respected as equal business partners by other executives in the company.[25] In a few organizations HR remains locked in an operational mode, processing forms and requests, administering compensation and benefits, managing policies and programs, and overseeing hiring and training.[26] Many HR experts (industry and academic) realize the changing face of HR. Dr. Rick Hackett's perspectives of the profession and hot topics for the future are highlighted in the Expert Opinion box above.

Many employers are changing how they organize their human resource functions. For one thing, the traditional human resource organization tends to divide HR activities into separate "silos" such as recruitment, training, and employee relations for the whole company. IBM split its 330 000 employees into three segments for HR purposes: executive and technical employees, managers, and rank and file employees. Separate human resource management teams (consisting of recruitment, training, and pay specialists, for instance) focus on each employee segment. This helps to ensure that the employees in each segment get the specialized testing, training, and rewards they require.[27]

There are other configurations as well.[28] For example, some employers create *transactional HR teams*. These teams provide specialized support in day-to-day HR activities (such as changing benefits plans), usually through centralized call centres and through outside vendors (such as benefits advisors). Specialized *corporate HR teams* assist top management in top-level issues such as developing the personnel aspects of the company's long-term strategic plan. *Embedded HR teams* have HR generalists (also known as "relationship managers" or "HR business partners") assigned to functional departments like sales and production. They provide the selection and other assistance the departments need. *Centres of expertise* are like specialized HR consulting firms within the company. For example, one might provide specialized advice in organizational change to the company's department managers.

<aside>
HR Competency

10300
</aside>

Evidence-Based Human Resource Management

<aside>
evidence-based HRM use of data, facts, analytics, scientific rigor, critical evaluation, and critically evaluated research/case studies to support human resource management proposals, decisions, practices, and conclusions.
</aside>

A major contribution of HRM is making decisions based on **evidence-based HRM**. This is the use of data, facts, analytics, scientific rigour, critical evaluation, and critically evaluated research/case studies to support human resource management proposals, decisions, practices, and conclusions.[29] Put simply, evidence-based human resource management means using the best-available evidence in making decisions about the human resource management practices you are focusing on.[30] The evidence may come from *actual measurements* (such as, how did the trainees like this program?). It may come from *existing data* (such as, what happened to company profits after we installed this training program?). Or, it may come from published *research studies* (such as, what does the research literature conclude about the best way to ensure that trainees remember what they learn?). Throughout this book, we will show you how managers can use evidence to make better human resource management decisions, by highlighting areas of research that are instrumental to the HRM realm. This is identified in the margins where needed.

<aside>
HR Competency

20600
</aside>

Measuring the Value of HR: Metrics

<aside>
metrics Statistics used to measure activities and results.
</aside>

Today's HR professionals need to be able to measure the value and impact of their organization's human capital and HRM practices. The use of various **metrics**, or statistics, to measure the activities and results of HR is now quite common. Traditional operational measures focused on the amount of activity and the costs of the HR function (such as number of job candidates interviewed per month, cost per hire, and so on), but today's measures need to reflect the quality of people and the effectiveness of HRM initiatives that build workforce capability. These new measures provide critical information that can be linked to organizational outcomes like productivity, product or service quality, sales, market share, and profits. For example, the percentage of first-choice job candidates accepting an offer to hire indicates the strength of the organization's employment brand in the marketplace and directly affects the quality of the workforce.[31]

<aside>
EVIDENCE-BASED HR

balanced scorecard A measurement system that translates an organization's strategy into a comprehensive set of performance measures.
</aside>

Many organizations are using the **balanced scorecard** system that includes measures of the impact of HRM on organizational outcomes. The balanced scorecard approach translates an organization's strategy into a comprehensive set of performance measures. It includes financial measures that tell the results of actions already taken. It complements the financial measures with operational measures of organizational, business unit, or department success that will drive future performance. It balances long-term and short-term actions and measures of success relating to financial results, customers, internal business processes, and human capital management.[32] For example, one measure relating to HRM is the percentage of senior management positions with fully job-ready successors ready to move up.

GROWING PROFESSIONALISM IN HRM

Today, HR practitioners must be professionals in terms of both performance and qualifications.[33] Every profession has several characteristics: (1) a common body of knowledge; (2) benchmarked performance standards; (3) a representative professional association; (4) an external perception as a profession; (5) a code of ethics; (6) required training credentials for entry and career mobility; (7) an ongoing need for skill development; and (8) a need to ensure professional competence is maintained and put to socially responsible uses.

certification Recognition for having met certain professional standards.

The Canadian Council of Human Resources Associations (CCHRA) is a national/federal-level organization with over 40 000 members that manages **certification** for human resource professionals. The CCHRA is a national body through which all provincial HR associations are affiliated (certification is administered through provincial HR associations), and is in turn a member of the World Federation of People Management Associations (WFPMA). In addition, there is an International Personnel Management Association of Canada (IPMA-C), which is a national association for public-sector and quasi-public-sector HR professionals.

HR Competency

20500

Canadian Council of Human Resources Associations
www.chrp.ca

World Federation of People Management Associations
www.wfpma.com

Similar to other professional designations, such as Chartered Accountant (CA) and Professional Engineer (P.Eng.), there are three different levels of certification in human resources in Canada: Level 1—Certified Human Resource Professional (CHRP), Level 2—Certified Human Resource Leader (CHRL), and Level 3—Certified Human Resource Executive (CHRE) (See **Figure 1.3**). This three-level structure of certification is relatively new (2015) and replaces a two-level certification model. The CCHRA governs provincial HR associations (which manage these certifications) to ensure national consistency of the certifications. The Expert Opinion box on the next page highlights the professionalization of HR, from the perspective of the vice-president of regulatory affairs at the Human Resources Professionals Association (HRPA).

HR Competency

10300

The old model evaluated expertise based on 187 required professional capabilities (called RPCs), while the new model evaluates expertise in nine different function areas (see **Figure 1.4** for a complete list) *plus* five enabling competencies (Strategic and Systems Thinking, Professional and Ethical Practice, Critical Problem-Solving and Analytical Decision Making, Change Management and Cultural Transformation, and Communication, Conflict Resolution, and Relationship Management).

FIGURE 1.3   HR Professional Certifications

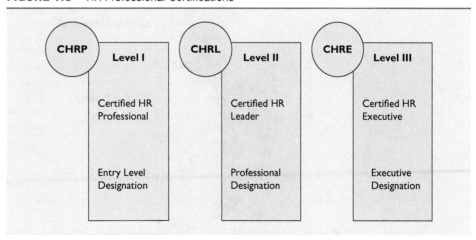

Source: Based on HRPA's CHRP Designations, www.hrdesignations.ca.

expert opinion
industry viewpoint

Dr. Claude Balthazard

Identification: Claude Balthazard (Ph.D., C.Psych., CHRP), Vice-President of Regulatory Affairs at the Human Resources Professionals Association (HRPA)

Focus: HRPA's Privacy Officer, plus ensuring registration and certification processes at HRPA meet regulatory and technical standards

1. **What do you consider key elements to the professionalization of a discipline?**

    I. An occupation has to have the potential to be a true profession. Work done by it must be sufficiently important to society, require advanced knowledge to do it well, and have perceived risk or consequences to the organization or stakeholders when individuals in the profession do not have the required competencies.

    II. The professional has to act as part of a profession, which involves both developing the institutions and identities of a profession, as well as convincing the public that this is the vase. This is an iterative process.

2. **What are the benefits of professionalization at an individual level?**

    There are self-serving motivations, as well as self-actualization benefits. For the self-serving motivations, there is evidence that earning potential increases, career trajectories change or accelerate, and perceived status (self) increases with professionalization. From a more self-actualization perspective, people want to maximize their contributions to society and an organization through applying a higher level of professionalism or expertise.

3. **What are the challenges HR professionals need to be aware of and how can we overcome these weaknesses?**

    Internally, we are not as disciplined as we need to be, and, externally, we haven't convinced others (e.g., executives) that there is a unique body of knowledge required to succeed in this profession. This is not a challenge unique to the HR profession, but we can overcome this by having an emphasis on a strong academic foundation of knowledge.

    We don't want to trade experience for a critical, holistic, and analytical understanding of the HRM realm. In engineering or law, for example, one cannot become a professional based on experience alone. The fact that the old process (last updated in 2001) had a single level for certification was also problematic. The recent changes with three levels of certification help reflect the full breadth and scope of HR's contribution to an organization and our society.

Source: Reprinted by permission from Claude Balthazard.

FIGURE 1.4   HR Competency Model: Nine Functional Areas

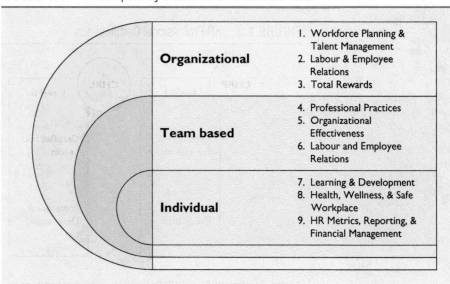

Organizational	1. Workforce Planning & Talent Management 2. Labour & Employee Relations 3. Total Rewards
Team based	4. Professional Practices 5. Organizational Effectiveness 6. Labour and Employee Relations
Individual	7. Learning & Development 8. Health, Wellness, & Safe Workplace 9. HR Metrics, Reporting, & Financial Management

Source: Based on HRPA's Competency Framework, www.hrdesignations.ca.

TABLE 1.1   Median Pay for All HR Titles: Comparison by Major Cities

City and Province	Median Pay without CHRP ($,000)	Median Pay with CHRP ($,000)	Financial Difference (as a % of non-CHRP salary)
Vancouver, BC	48.9	64.1	31.1%
Calgary, AB	53.9	75.6	40.3%
Winnipeg, MB	49.9	62.1	24.4%
Toronto, ON	50.4	64.7	28.4%
Montreal, QC	51.6	67.5	30.8%

Source: "Fuel for HR Careers—The 2013 Market Value of CHRP Certification." *PayScale.* Retrieved from http://www.hrpa.ca/documents/chrp_2013_infographic_lg.pdf, Human Resources Management Association.

Overall, it appears that the labour market rewards professionalism and designations (including, but not limited to the CHRP designation). Information regarding differences in pay for CHRP and non-CHRP HR jobs in Canada is provided in **Table 1.1**.

Other important associations for HR specialists include the Canadian Industrial Relations Association; WorldatWork, for compensation and rewards issues; health and safety associations, such as the Industrial Accident Prevention Association, the Construction Safety Association, and Safe Communities Canada; and the Canadian Society for Training and Development.

In addition to the international- and national-level broad HR designations, a series of more specialized or specific professional designations in Canada allows those who may be interested in specialized areas to gain recognition for a deeper level of subject-matter expertise, as per **Table 1.2**. The Association of Professional Recruiters offers a Registered Professional Recruiter designation (RPR). The Board of Canadian Registered Safety Professionals offers a Canadian Registered Safety Professional designation (CRSP). The Canadian Management Professional Association offers a Canadian Management Professional designation (CMP). The Canadian Payroll Association offers the Payroll Compliance Practitioner (PCP) and Certified Payroll Manager (CPM) designations. The National Institute of Disability Management and Research offers the Certified Return to Work Co-ordinator (CRTWC) and Certified Disability Management Professional (CDMP) designations.[34] This list is not exhaustive, but it does demonstrate the professionalism and recognition of certification in the HR discipline.

HR Competency

10300

Simulate on MyManagementLab

Management and Ethics

HR Competency

20200

PERSONAL INVENTORY ASSESSMENT

Learn About Yourself
Ethical Leadership Assessment

Ethics

The professionalization of HRM has created the need for a uniform code of ethics, as agreement to abide by the code of ethics is one of the requirements of maintaining professional status. Since what is ethical or unethical is generally open to debate (except in a few very clear-cut cases such as wilful misrepresentation), most codes do not tell employees what they should do. Rather, they provide a guide to help employees discover the best course of action by themselves.[35] Increasingly, HR departments are being given a greater role in providing ethics training and monitoring to ensure compliance with the code of ethics. Some organizations have such a commitment to ethics that they have a full-time ethics officer. On the other hand, a 2008 survey of Ontario HR professionals found that 78.2 percent had been coerced into doing something morally or legally ambiguous at least once in their careers.[36]

TABLE 1.2 Professional HR Designations in Canada (as of 2006)

Designation	Designation Holders in Canada
Certified Human Resources Professional (CHRP)	18 000
Group Benefits Associate (GBA)	1430
Registered Professional Recruiter (RPR)	1200
Certified Payroll Manager (CPM)	1200
Certified Employee Benefits Specialist (CEBS)	896
Payroll Compliance Practitioner (PCP)	850
Certified Compensation Professional (CCP)	734
Retirement Plans Associate (RPA)	652
Canadian Management Professional (CMP)	550
International Personnel Management Association (IPMA) – Certified Practitioner	266
Registered Assessment Specialist (RAS)	250
Certified Training and Development Professional (CTDP)	250
Registered Professional Trainer (RPT)	200
Compensation Management Specialist (CMS)	174
Global Remuneration Professional (GPR)	37
Senior Professional in HR (SPHR)	37

Source: Reprinted by permission of Canadian HR Reporter. © Copyright Thomson Reuters Canada Ltd.,2009, Toronto, Ontario

An Ethical Dilemma

Can or should an employee reveal information that was disclosed in confidence about a troubled co-worker, and if so, under what circumstances?

EVIDENCE-BASED **HR**

social responsibility The implied, enforced, or felt obligation of managers, acting in their official capacities, to serve or protect the interests of groups other than themselves.

The most prevalent ethical issues confronting Canadian organizations today pertain to security of information, employee and client privacy, environmental issues, governance, and conflicts of interest.[37] The major reasons for the failure of ethics programs to achieve the desired results are lack of effective leadership and inadequate training. Positive outcomes associated with properly implemented ethics programs include increased confidence among stakeholders, such as clients, partners, and employees; greater client/customer and employee loyalty; decreased vulnerability to crime; reduced losses due to internal theft; and increased public trust.[38]

In recent years, the concept of **social responsibility** has frequently been discussed as an important manifestation of ethics. A company that exercises social responsibility attempts to balance its commitments, not only to its investors but also to its employees and customers, other businesses, and the community or communities in which it operates. Mountain Equipment Co-op (MEC) is an example of a company that considers socially responsible approaches to all aspects of its business—selecting and designing products, manufacturing MEC-brand products, transporting products and people, greening operations, engaging employees, equipping members, supporting the community, driving economic performance, and governing the co-operative. It examines every aspect of a product's life cycle from a social responsibility perspective, from the resources that go into making and shipping it, to the satisfaction of the employees and the members who take the products home.[39]

ENVIRONMENTAL INFLUENCES ON HRM

HR Competency

10100

There are numerous external and internal environmental influences that drive the strategic focus of HRM. To be effective, all managers, including those with responsibility for HR, must monitor the environment on an ongoing basis, assess the impact of any changes, and be proactive in responding to such challenges. **Table 1.3** illustrates the major external and internal environmental influences on HRM.

External Environment Influences

Six major external environmental influences on HRM will be discussed: economic conditions, labour market issues, technology, government, globalization, and environmental concerns.

Economic Conditions

Economic conditions affect supply and demand for products and services, which, in turn, have a dramatic impact on the number and types of employees required as well as on an employer's ability to pay wages and provide benefits. When the economy is healthy, companies often hire more workers as demand for products and services increases. Consequently, unemployment rates fall, there is more competition for qualified employees, and training and retention strategies increase in importance. Conversely, during an economic downturn, some firms reduce pay and benefits to maintain workers' jobs. Other employers are forced to downsize by offering attractive early retirement and early leave programs or by laying off or terminating employees. Unemployment rates rise and employers are often overwhelmed with applicants when vacancies are advertised.

productivity The ratio of an organization's outputs (goods and services) to its inputs (people, capital, energy, and materials).

    Productivity refers to the ratio of an organization's outputs (goods and services) to its inputs (people, capital, energy, and materials). Canada's relatively low productivity growth rate is of concern because of increasing global competition. To improve

TABLE 1.3   External and Internal Environmental Influences on HRM

External	Internal
Economic Conditions: affect supply and demand for products, impacting quantity and quality of employees required and ability to pay/give benefits.	**Organizational Culture:** values, beliefs, and norms of organizational members.
Labour Diversity: protected groups (visible/ethnic minorities, women, Aboriginal, disabled) and generational differences (traditionalists, baby boomers, Gen X-ers, Gen Y-ers).	**Organizational Climate:** the atmosphere's impact on employee motivation, job performance, and productivity.
Technology: controlling data and privacy.	**Management Practices:** organizational structure and employee empowerment.
Government: abiding by provincial and national standards.	
Globalization: managing the workforce in an intense, hypercompetitive global economy.	
Environment: managing sustainability and corporate social responsibility.	

primary sector Jobs in agriculture, fishing and trapping, forestry, and mining.

secondary sector Jobs in manufacturing and construction.

tertiary or service sector Jobs in public administration, personal and business services, finance, trade, public utilities, and transportation/communications.

productivity, managers must find ways to produce more outputs with current input levels or use fewer resources to maintain current output levels. In most organizations today, productivity improvement is essential for long-term success.

Employment trends in Canada have been experiencing dramatic change. The **primary sector**, which includes agriculture, fishing and trapping, forestry, and mining, now represents only 4 percent of jobs. Employment in the **secondary sector** (manufacturing and construction) has decreased to 19 percent of jobs. The sector that has grown to represent 77 percent of jobs, dominating the Canadian economy, is the **tertiary or service sector**, which includes public administration, personal and business services, finance, trade, public utilities, and transportation/communications.

Since all jobs in the service sector involve the provision of services by employees to individual customers, effectively managing and motivating human resources is critical. Although there are some lesser-skilled jobs (in housekeeping and food services, for example), many service-sector jobs demand highly knowledgeable employees.

HR by the Numbers

Workforce Diversity in Canada

Visible and Ethnic Minorities

200 the number of different ethnic origins reported in 2011 in Canada[41]

6.3 m the approximate number of people who identified themselves as a visible minority in 2011[42]

Women

31% the percentage of women in Canada who are now the primary breadwinner in dual-earner couples[43]

11.8 m the number of women between the working ages of 15 to 65 in Canada[44]

Aboriginals

18.2% the percentage of Aboriginals in Canada who are youths between the ages of 15 to 24[45]

20.1% the increase in the Aboriginal population between 2006 to 2011[46]

Persons with Disabilities

50% the higher unemployment rate experienced by disabled persons compared to the able-bodied population[47]

17% the lower income experienced by disabled persons compared to the able-bodied population[48]

◄●┤Simulate on MyManagementLab

Human Resources & Diversity

Labour Market Issues

Increasing Workforce Diversity   Canada's workforce is among the most diverse in the world. *Diversity* refers to the attributes that humans are likely to use to tell themselves, "that person is different from me." These attributes include demographic factors (such as race, gender, and age) as well as values and cultural norms.[40] The HR by the Numbers box above demonstrates the diversity in Canada's workforce and focuses on the four protected groups: visible and ethnic minorities, women, Aboriginals, and persons with disabilities.

Generational Issues   Another aspect of diversity is generational differences. There are four generations in the workplace, and nearly half of all Canadians say they have experienced a clash with workers older or younger than themselves. On the other hand, about one-quarter of workers say they don't notice age differences, and another one-quarter think this situation provides an excellent learning opportunity. **Table 1.4** outlines attitudes, key characteristics, and expectations of the four generations.

Education   Approximately 54 percent of Canada's population has some post-secondary education (trades, college, or university).[49] Given the higher expectations of the better-educated labour force, managers are expected to ensure that the talents and capabilities of employees are fully utilized and that opportunities are provided for career growth.

On the other hand, a startlingly high proportion of Canadians (26 percent) have only marginal literacy skills, meaning their ability to understand and use printed and written documents in daily activities to achieve goals and to develop knowledge and potential is limited. A frightening reality is that inadequate reading and writing skills have replaced lack of experience as the major reason for rejecting entry-level candidates.[50] **Figure 1.5** provides a recent breakdown of literacy levels in Canada. Functional illiteracy is exacting a toll not only on individual social and economic opportunities, but also on organizations' accident rates and productivity levels.

EVIDENCE-BASED HR

TABLE 1.4 The Four Generations

	Traditionalists 1922–1945	**Baby Boomers 1946–1964**	**Generation X-ers 1965–1980**	**Generation Y-ers 1981–2000**
Notes	Grew up in an era of hardship, including a war and the Great Depression.	The largest group in the workforce. Grew up in a time of major optimism and change amidst the moon landing and the women's movement.	This group grew up as divorce rates skyrocketed. First technology-literate generation.	Beginning to enter the workforce. Expect to change jobs frequently.
Attitudes, Values, and Expectations	• Loyalty • Respect for authority • Dedication • Sacrifice • Conformity • Honour • Privacy • Stability • Economic conservatism	• Optimism • Involvement • Team oriented • Personal growth and gratification • Youthfulness • Equality • Career focused	• Independence • Self-reliance • Pragmatism • Skepticism • Informality • Balance	• Confidence • Diversity • Civic duty • Optimism • Immediate access to information and services
Key Characteristics	• Compliant • Detail oriented • Hard-working • Fiscally frugal • Trustworthy • Risk averse • Long-term focused	• Driven to succeed • Team player • Relationship focused • Eager to add value • Politically savvy in the workplace • Competitive	• Flexible and adaptable • Creative • Entrepreneurial • Multitasker • Results driven • Individualistic	• Collective action • Expressive and tolerant of differences • Eager to accept challenges • Innovative and creative

Source: Loyalty Unplugged: How to Get, Keep & Grow All Four Generations. Reprinted by permission from Adwoa K Buahene.

FIGURE 1.5   Literary Levels of Canadians (16–64 years old)

Level 1: 14.6% of Canadians

This level represents individuals with very low levels of literacy skills. They may be unable to follow written instructions at work or determine correct measurements required for task completion.

Level 2: 27.3% of Canadians

This level includes individuals who can comprehend material that is is simple and straightforward. While they can read, they generally score poorly on tests involving reading. They can cope on a non-complex, daily level, but face difficulty with more complex demands, such as learning new job skills.

Level 3: 38.6% of Canadians

The majority of Canadians are at the level 3 literacy level. This skill level involves the ability to integrate multiple sources of information, or solve complex problems.

Level 4 & 5: 19.5% of Canadians

This is the highest literacy level. Individuals at this level have higher-order information processing skills.

Source: Adapted from The Conference Board of Canada, "All Signs Point to Yes: Literacy's Impact on Workplace Health and Safety," September 2008, p. 4.

**contingent/non-standard
workers** Workers who do not have
regular full-time employment status.

Non-Standard or Contingent Workers The labour market has undergone major structural changes with the growth of **contingent (or "non-standard") workers**, that is, workers who do not fit the traditional definition of permanent, full-time employment with the same employer on an indeterminate basis. These non-traditional workers are often used by companies to provide flexible, on-demand labour, without the same guarantees for continued employment, employee development, or benefits that regular full-time employees are given.

An Ethical Dilemma

The maintenance department supervisor has just come to you, the HR manager, voicing concern about the safety of two of her reporting employees whom she recently discovered to be functionally illiterate. What are your responsibilities to these employees, if any?

The forms of employment involving part-time, fixed-term, temporary, home, and standby workers; those who have more than one job; and the self-employed have become so significant numerically that they now affect about one-third of the workforce. More women fall into this category than men.[51] Non-standard work is often poorly paid, offers little or no job security, and is generally not covered by employment legislation. The HR by the Numbers box below identifies some core metrics associated with the use of contingent workers in Canada.

HR by the Numbers

Increased Use of Contract Workers[52]

377 readers of *HR Reporter* and members of HRPA polled

63% have seen an increase in the use of contract workers in their organization in the last five years

51.2% identify that contract workers in their company receive no benefits at all

23.6% feel company does not have well-defined processes in place to manage contract workers

Technology

From Twitter to Facebook to videoconferencing setups that make it seem like everyone is in the same room, there is a wide range of technology available to organizations today. All of this technology can make working in and managing a dispersed workforce easier and can enable people to work anywhere and everywhere. The workplace of today includes "hotels, cafes and conference venues, as well as public areas of lounges and airports."[53] However, it has also brought new concerns as the line between work and family time has become blurred.[54]

Questions concerning data control, accuracy, the right to privacy, and ethics are at the core of a growing controversy brought about by the new information technologies. Sophisticated computerized control systems are used to monitor employee speed, accuracy, and efficiency in some firms. More firms are also monitoring employee email, voice mail, telephone conversations, and computer usage, and some now monitor employee behaviour using video surveillance.[55]

Government

Various laws enacted by governments have had and will continue to have a dramatic impact on the employer–employee relationship in Canada. One of the factors that makes employment law in Canada so challenging is that there are 14 different jurisdictions involved. Each of the ten provinces and three territories has its own human rights, employment standards, labour relations, health and safety, and workers' compensation legislation. In addition, about 10 percent of the workforce (including employees of the federal government and Crown corporations, chartered banks, airlines, national railways, and the Canadian Armed Forces) is covered by federal employment legislation.

Although there is some commonality across jurisdictions, there is also considerable variation. Minimum wage, overtime pay requirements, vacation entitlement, and grounds protected under human rights legislation, for example, vary from one province/territory to another. Furthermore, some jurisdictions have pay equity and employment

Hints TO ENSURE LEGAL COMPLIANCE

equity legislation while others do not. This means that companies with employees in more than one jurisdiction have different rules applying to different employees. There are, however, certain laws that apply to all employers and employees across Canada, such as employment insurance and the Canada/Quebec Pension Plan.

Globalization

globalization The emergence of a single global market for most products and services.

The term **globalization** refers to the emergence of a single global market for most products and services. This growing integration of the world economy into a single, huge marketplace is increasing the intensity of competition and leading most organizations to expand their operations around the world.[56] Firms in other parts of the world are also seeing human resources as a source of competitive advantage.

There are increasing numbers of multinational corporations—firms that conduct a large part of their business outside the country in which they are headquartered and that locate a significant percentage of their physical facilities and human resources in other countries. For example, Toyota has a large market share in the United States, Europe, and Africa, and is the market leader in Australia. Toyota has factories all over the world, manufacturing or assembling vehicles like the Corolla for local markets. Notably, Toyota has manufacturing or assembly plants in the United States, Japan, Australia, Canada, Indonesia, Poland, South Africa, Turkey, the United Kingdom, France, and Brazil, and has recently added plants in Pakistan, India, Argentina, the Czech Republic, Mexico, Malaysia, Thailand, China, and Venezuela.[57]

HR Competency

20200

Globalization means that HR professionals need to become familiar with employment legislation in other countries and need to manage ethical dilemmas when labour standards are substantially lower than those in Canada. Companies doing business in sub-Saharan Africa, for example, have to deal with a high death rate among employees with AIDS. Some are paying for antiretroviral drugs to keep their employees alive.[58]

Environmental Concerns

Environmental concerns have suddenly (some might say finally) emerged as an issue for people, particularly the younger generations.[59] Sustainability, climate change, global warming, pollution, carbon footprints, extinction of wildlife species, ecosystem fragility, and other related issues are increasingly important to people around the world. There is increasing evidence that interest in environmental issues is motivating the behaviour of employees, and that they are concerned about whether they work for environmentally responsible companies. Companies like Fairmont Hotels have made environmental stewardship a priority for almost 20 years. They have found that developing a reputation as an environmental leader and demonstrating corporate social responsibility have not only helped them to gain market share, but have also been a strong employee retention tool.[60]

Internal Environment Influences

How a firm deals with the three internal environmental influences of organizational culture, organizational climate, and management practices has a major impact on its ability to meet its objectives.

Organizational Culture

organizational culture The core values, beliefs, and assumptions that are widely shared by members of an organization.

Organizational culture consists of the core values, beliefs, and assumptions that are widely shared by members of an organization. Culture is often conveyed through an organization's mission statement, as well as through stories, myths, symbols, and ceremonies. It serves a variety of purposes:

- communicating what the organization "believes in" and "stands for"
- providing employees with a sense of direction and expected behaviour (norms)
- shaping employees' attitudes about themselves, the organization, and their roles
- creating a sense of identity, orderliness, and consistency
- fostering employee loyalty and commitment

All managers with HR responsibilities play an important role in creating and maintaining the type of organizational culture desired. For example, they may organize recognition ceremonies for high-performing employees and be involved in decisions regarding symbols, such as a logo or the design of new company premises. Having a positive culture has a positive impact on employer branding, recruitment, retention, and productivity.

Employees in fast-food establishments are taught how to provide courteous, efficient customer service.

organizational climate The prevailing atmosphere that exists in an organization and its impact on employees.

empowerment Providing workers with the skills and authority to make decisions that would traditionally be made by managers.

Organizational Climate

Organizational climate refers to the prevailing atmosphere, or "internal weather," that exists in an organization and its impact on employees.[61] It can be friendly or unfriendly, open or secretive, rigid or flexible, innovative or stagnant. The major factors influencing the climate are management's leadership style, HR policies and practices, and the amount and style of organizational communication. The type of climate that exists is generally reflected in the level of employee motivation, job satisfaction, performance, and productivity. HR professionals play a key role in helping managers throughout the firm establish and maintain a positive organizational climate.

Management Practices

Management practices have changed considerably over the past decade, with many HRM implications. For example, the traditional bureaucratic structure with many levels of management is being replaced by flatter organizational forms using cross-functional teams and improved communication. Since managers have more people reporting to them in flat structures, they cannot supervise their employees as closely and employee **empowerment** has greatly increased.

CHAPTER SUMMARY

1. Human resources management (HRM) refers to the management of people in organizations. Strategic HRM involves linking HRM with strategic goals and objectives to improve business performance. In more and more firms, HR professionals are becoming strategic partners in strategy formulation and execution.

2. The major stages in the evolution of management thinking about workers were (1) personnel administration, which was administrative and task oriented, (2) scientific management, which focused on production, and (3) the human resources movement, in which HRM provided expertise on a wide range of issues in house, while

task-based work became increasingly outsourced, and (4) human resource partnership, in which it was recognized that organizational success is linked to operational and strategic management of labour.

3. Activities of employee management, empowerment, training, and guidance are often shared between managers in the organization (executive and line managers) and HR professionals. Therefore, managers, executives, and HR personnel are all influential in effective human resources management.

4. Human resources activities are now being seen as falling into two categories. The first is the traditional operational (administrative) category, where HR hires and maintains employees and then manages employee separations. The second is the more recent strategic category, where HR is focused on ensuring that the organization is staffed with the most effective human capital to achieve its strategic goals.

5. There are numerous professional designations that will boost a career trajectory in human resources. The most basic of these is the Canadian Human Resources Professional (CHRP). However, additional designations exist that are important and may be influential in building expertise and careers in management or human resources management.

6. A number of external factors have an impact on HRM, including economic factors, labour market issues, technology, government, globalization, and environmental concerns.

MyManagementLab

Study, practise, and explore real business situations with these helpful resources:

- **Interactive Lesson Presentations:** Work through interactive presentations and assessments to test your knowledge of management concepts.
- **PIA (Personal Inventory Assessments):** Enhance your ability to connect with key concepts through these engaging self-reflection assessments.

PIA PERSONAL INVENTORY ASSESSMENT

- **Study Plan:** Check your understanding of chapter concepts with self-study quizzes.
- **Videos:** Learn more about the management practices and strategies of real companies.
- **Simulations:** Practise decision-making in simulated management environments.

KEY TERMS

authority *(p. 6)*
Baby Boomers *(p. 17)*
balanced scorecard *(p. 10)*
certification *(p. 11)*
change agents *(p. 8)*
contingent/non-standard workers *(p. 18)*
employee engagement *(p. 7)*
empowerment *(p. 20)*
environmental scanning *(p. 8)*
evidence-based HRM *(p. 10)*
Generation X-ers *(p. 17)*
Generation Y-ers *(p. 17)*
globalization *(p. 19)*
human capital *(p. 2)*
human resources management (HRM) *(p. 2)*
human resources movement *(p. 4)*

line authority *(p. 6)*
line manager *(p. 6)*
metrics *(p. 10)*
organizational climate *(p. 20)*
organizational culture *(p. 19)*
outsourcing *(p. 4)*
primary sector *(p. 16)*
productivity *(p. 15)*
scientific management *(p. 3)*
secondary sector *(p. 16)*
social responsibility *(p. 14)*
staff authority *(p. 6)*
staff manager *(p. 6)*
strategy *(p. 8)*
tertiary or service sector *(p. 16)*
Traditionalists *(p. 17)*

REVIEW AND DISCUSSION QUESTIONS

1. Describe the transformation that HR underwent over the years. Discuss how changes in internal and external factors contributed to the evolution in HR.

2. Describe the role of HR in strategy formulation and strategy implementation.

3. Describe how the external environment influences HR.

4. Differentiate between organizational culture and organizational climate.

5. Describe the multiple jurisdictions related to employment legislation affecting HRM in Canada.

6. Give examples of how HR management concepts and techniques can be of use to all managers.

7. Explain how HR has become professionalized and describe the value of this professionalization.

CRITICAL THINKING QUESTIONS

1. Working individually or in groups, develop outlines showing how trends like workforce diversity, technological innovation, globalization, and changes in the nature of work have affected the college or university you are attending now. Present in class.

2. Explain how changing economic and competitive pressures have had an impact on the organization in which you are working or one in which you have worked. How has your business responded to these pressures?

3. A firm has requested your assistance in ensuring that its multigenerational workforce functions effectively as a team. What strategies or programs would you recommend? Why?

4. Choose a non-HR role you have had in your previous jobs. Identify how you used the core competencies of HR professionals in that role and how it affected your job performance.

EXPERIENTIAL EXERCISES

1. Working alone or with a small group of classmates, interview an HR manager and prepare a short essay regarding his or her role in strategy formulation and implementation.

2. Review job ads for five senior HR roles on job posting websites or corporate websites. Identify common competencies required for those roles as per the ads. Contrast these required competencies (both implied and explicit) with the core HR professional competencies highlighted in this chapter. Discuss the most consistently required competency and the impact of that competency on organizational success.

3. Review job ads for five executive roles (such as CEO, vice-president, or president) on job posting websites or corporate websites. Identify common

competencies required for those roles as per the ads. Contrast these required competencies (both implied and explicit) with the core HR professional competencies highlighted in this chapter. Discuss the most consistently required competency and how it is important in non–HR roles.

4. According to a 2013 study of the world's most attractive firms (released by Universum), the top 10 employers for career seekers with a business background were (in priority order): Google, Ernst & Young, Goldman Sachs, PricewaterhouseCoopers, Microsoft, Apple, Deloitte, KPMG, Coca-Cola, and Proctor & Gamble. In groups, review the company websites of these organizations to determine the corporate strategy, objectives, and markets that these

organizations target. As a team, discuss the similarities and differences among the strategies, objectives, and markets of these 10 employers. Explain how these factors might affect Generation Y-ers perceiving these companies as desirable employers.

5. Using the sample balanced scorecard template provided by your professor, in pairs develop a balanced scorecard measure for a hypothetical company in the retail urban clothing sector. This company has many stores in large and small cities in your province. Be sure to take into consideration current economic conditions as you develop your measures.

6. Exchange your completed set of measures with another pair. Compare and contrast your measures. Is one set "better" than the other? Why or why not? Debrief as instructed.

RUNNING CASE

Running Case: LearnInMotion.com

Introduction

The main theme of this book is that HRM—activities like recruiting, selecting, training, and rewarding employees—is not just the job of a central HR group, but rather one in which every manager must engage. Perhaps nowhere is this more apparent than in the typical small service business, where the owner–manager usually has no HR staff to rely on. However, the success of such an enterprise often depends largely on the effectiveness with which workers are recruited, hired, trained, evaluated, and rewarded. To help illustrate and emphasize the front-line manager's HR role, throughout this book we will use a continuing ("running") case based on an actual small business in Ottawa's high-tech region. Each segment will illustrate how the case's main players—owner–managers Jennifer Lau and Pierre LeBlanc—confront and solve HRM problems each day by applying the concepts and techniques presented in that particular chapter. Here is some background information you'll need to answer questions that arise in subsequent chapters.

LearnInMotion.com: A Profile

Jennifer and Pierre graduated from university as business majors in June 2015 and got the idea for LearnInMotion. com as a result of a project they worked on together in their entrepreneurship class during their last semester. The professor had divided the students into two- or three-person teams and asked them to "create a business plan for a high-tech company." The idea the two came up with was LearnInMotion.com. The basic idea of the website was to list a vast array of web-based, CD-ROM-based, or textbook-based continuing education–type business courses for working people who wanted to take a course from the comfort of their own homes. Users could come to the website to find and then take a course in one of several ways. Some courses could be completed interactively online via the site; others were in a form that was downloadable directly to the user's computer; others (which were either textbook or CD-ROM-based) could be ordered and delivered (in several major metropolitan areas) by independent contractor delivery people. Their business mission was "to provide work-related learning when, where, and how you need it."

Based on their research, they knew the market for work-related learning was booming. At the same time, professional development activities like these were increasingly Internet-based. Tens of thousands of online and offline training firms, universities, associations, and other content providers were trying to reach their target customers via the Internet. Jennifer and Pierre understandably thought they were in the right place at the right time.

Jennifer's father had some unused loft space in Kanata, Ontario, and so with about $45 000 of accumulated savings, Jennifer and Pierre incorporated and were in business. They retained the services of an independent programmer and hired two people—a web designer to create the graphics for the site (which would then be programmed by the programmer) and a content manager whose job was to enter information onto the site as it came in from content providers. By the end of 2008, they also completed upgrading their business plan into a form they could show to prospective venture capitalists. They sent the first version to three Canadian venture capitalists. Then they waited.

And then they waited some more. They never heard back from the first three venture capitalists, so they sent their plan to five more. They still got no response. But

Pierre and Jennifer pressed on. By day they called customers to get people to place ads on their site, to get content providers to list their available courses, and to get someone—anyone—to deliver textbook- and CD-ROM-based courses, as needed, across Canada. By May 2016 they had about 30 content providers offering courses and content through LearnInMotion.com. In the summer, they got their first serious nibble from a venture capital firm. They negotiated with this company through much of the summer, came to terms in the early fall, and closed the deal—getting just over $1 million in venture funding—in November 2016.

After a stunning total of $75 000 in legal fees (they had to pay both their firm's and the venture capital firm's lawyers to navigate the voluminous disclosure documents and agreements), they had just over $900 000 to spend. The funding, according to the business plan, was to go toward

accomplishing five main goals: redesigning and expanding the website; hiring about seven more employees; moving to a larger office; designing and implementing a personal information manager (PIM)/calendar (users and content providers could use the calendar to interactively keep track of their personal and business schedules); and last but not least, driving up sales. LearnInMotion.com was off and running.

QUESTIONS

1   What is human resources management and does it have a role to play in this organization? If so, in what ways specifically?
2   What environmental influences will affect the role that human resources management could play within this organization?

CASE INCIDENT

Jack Nelson's Problem

As a new member of the board of directors for a local bank, Jack Nelson was being introduced to all the employees in the home office. When he was introduced to Ruth Johnson he was curious about her work and asked her what the machine she was using did. Johnson replied that she really did not know what the machine was called or what it did. She explained that she had only been working there for two months. She did, however, know precisely how to operate the machine. According to her supervisor, she was an excellent employee.

At one of the branch offices, the supervisor in charge spoke to Nelson confidentially, telling him that "something was wrong," but she didn't know what. For one thing, she explained, employee turnover was too high, and no sooner had one employee been put on the job than another one resigned. With customers to see and loans to be made, she continued, she had little time to work with the new employees as they came and went.

All branch supervisors hired their own employees without communication with the home office or other branches. When an opening developed, the supervisor tried to find a suitable employee to replace the worker who had quit.

After touring the 22 branches and finding similar problems in many of them, Nelson wondered what the home office should do or what action he should take. The banking firm was generally regarded as a well-run institution that had grown from 27 to 191 employees in the past eight years. The more he thought about the matter, the more puzzled Nelson became. He couldn't quite put his finger on the problem, and he didn't know whether to report his findings to the president.

QUESTIONS

1   What do you think is causing some of the problems in the bank's branches?
2   Do you think setting up an HR unit in the main office would help?
3   What specific functions should an HR unit carry out? What HR functions would then be carried out by supervisors and other line managers? What role should the Internet play in the new HR organization?

Source: George, Claude. (1985). *Supervision in Action: Art Managing Others,* 4th Ed. Pearson Education.

Orange Line Media/Shutterstock

CHAPTER

2

The Changing Legal Emphasis

Compliance and Impact on Canadian Workplaces

LEARNING OUTCOMES

AFTER STUDYING THIS CHAPTER, YOU SHOULD BE ABLE TO

EXPLAIN how employment-related issues are governed in Canada.

DISCUSS at least five prohibited grounds for discrimination under human rights legislation, and **DESCRIBE** the requirements for reasonable accommodation.

DESCRIBE behaviour that could constitute harassment, and **EXPLAIN** the employers' responsibilities regarding harassment.

DESCRIBE the role of minimums established in employment standards legislation and the enforcement process.

REQUIRED HR COMPETENCIES

20100: Conduct human resources responsibilities and build productive relationships consistent with standards of practice with due diligence and integrity to balance the interests of all parties.

20300: Adhere to legal requirements as they pertain to human resources policies and practices to promote organizational values and manage risk.

20400: Recommend ethical solutions to the organization's leadership by analyzing the variety of issues and options to ensure responsible corporate governance and manage risk.

20600: Promote an evidence-based approach to the development of human resources policies and practices using current professional resources to provide a sound basis for human resources decision-making.

50200: Interpret legislation, collective agreements (where applicable), and policies consistent with legal requirements and organizational values to treat employees in a fair and consistent manner and manage the risk of litigation and conflict.

90400: Manage human resources information in compliance with legal requirements using appropriate tools and procedures in order to support decision-making and inform leaders about progress toward organizational objectives.

THE LEGAL FRAMEWORK FOR EMPLOYMENT LAW IN CANADA

A 2011 survey conducted by Queen's University in partnership with the Human Resources Institute of Alberta (HRIA) and the International Personnel Management Association (IPMA) asked 451 HR professionals to identify the top five critical pieces of knowledge required in their roles. While business acumen was identified as the most critical piece of knowledge, employment law/legislative awareness and talent management were tied for second position.[1] While HR professionals are expected to provide guidance, training, programs, and policy developments that are legally defensible, the actions of supervisors and managers as agents of the organization must also abide by

industry **viewpoint**

Lauren Bernardi

Identification: Ms. Lauren Bernardi (LLB)
Principal at Bernardi Human Resource Law and author of *Powerful Employment Policies*, published by Canada Law Book

1. **While the focus of employment law in Canada is to protect both employer and employees rights, most of what we read or hear is focused on protecting employees. What are some of the core legal obligations employees have to their employers?**

Most employee obligations come through common law rather than legislation. There is an expected duty of loyalty. Employers contract employees to work, which requires being honest and productive (e.g., don't spend work hours texting). In addition, the employee is expected to not engage in a conflict of interest, which means the employee cannot steal company information, start a

new business, or take that information to competitors.

2. **In your opinion, who is responsible for compliance with employment laws within an organization?**

Everybody. Some laws affect employees, such as health and safety (the employee has a responsibility to comply) or human rights laws (the employee cannot engage in discriminatory behaviour). Management has the responsibility to enforce and apply the law. Human resource teams are also responsible for compliance, but they also serve an advisory role.

The leadership and the owners of the business have to take a top-down approach to compliance, and they genuinely need to care about their employees. They can be the avenue HR uses for buy-in by championing the value of adherence to legally sound best business practices. The leadership team should also recognize the business opportunity proactive and compliant business practices provide (e.g., progressive discipline results in more productive employees).

3. **Based on your experience, what areas of concern are most overlooked by employers?**

I. The impact of the negative work environment, which can be formed when management and employers disregard harassment claims or toxic workplaces. These affect the bottom line through decreased

productivity, and increased turnover and absenteeism.

II. Rather than appreciating the strategic and business benefits of managing HR issues, employers often use the legal system to reactively investigate a complaint. Employers need to consider a more proactive approach to developing policies, procedures, and decision-making within the legal framework.

III. Psychosocial factors that affect the health of the organization and its employees as well as the bottom line are often neglected. Recently, an initiative by the Mental Health Commission of Canada was created aimed at bringing awareness to these factors. The initiative suggests that we have to consider physical health and safety laws, and we also need to consider psychosocial factors, such as respect, engagement, and leadership. Consideration of psychosocial factors is voluntary. However, there is a Canada-wide case study project currently operating in which participating organizations are introducing measures to improve psychological health and safety in their workplaces. I'm working on this initiative because Bernardi Human Resource Law is the only law firm in Canada participating in the case study project.

Source: Reprinted by permission from Lauren Bernardi.

HR Competency

20300

EVIDENCE-BASED HR

legislated rules and regulations. The risk of expensive lawsuits and their impact on employer branding or reputation requires an awareness of employment law within the organization that extends well beyond just the HR professionals.

There are a number of distinct sets of responsibilities that exist between the employee and employer, including formal and informal expectations. There is a mutual expectation of each party to maintain the employment relationship by fulfilling their own responsibilities within the relationship. For example, there may be an implied, informal expectation from an employee's point of view that as long as they attend work for the scheduled number of hours, they can expect job security and continued employment from the employer. Such informal and personalized expectations are difficult to manage and correct if one party feels that the other has violated the expectations within the mutual relationship. As a result, the influence and impact of formal expectations (largely established through legislation and the interpretation of it) play a significant role in the Canadian workplace.

The primary objective of most employment legislation in Canada is to prevent employers from exploiting paid workers, assuming that an implicit power imbalance exists in the employment relationship (in favour of the employer).[2] While employers have a right to modify employee work terms and arrangements according to legitimate business needs, employees have a right to be protected from harmful business practices. In this regard, the government's role is to balance employee and employer needs through the development and maintenance of employment legislation, as highlighted in **Figure 2.1**. While there is a large focus on legislation protecting employees, the legislation also protects employers, as outlined in the Expert Opinion box from the perspective of a leading employment law lawyer and author. The judicial system provides a forum for interpreting legislation according to the precedents that past judicial rulings have established.

HR Competency

20100

FIGURE 2.1 Government's Role in Balancing Employer and Employee Needs

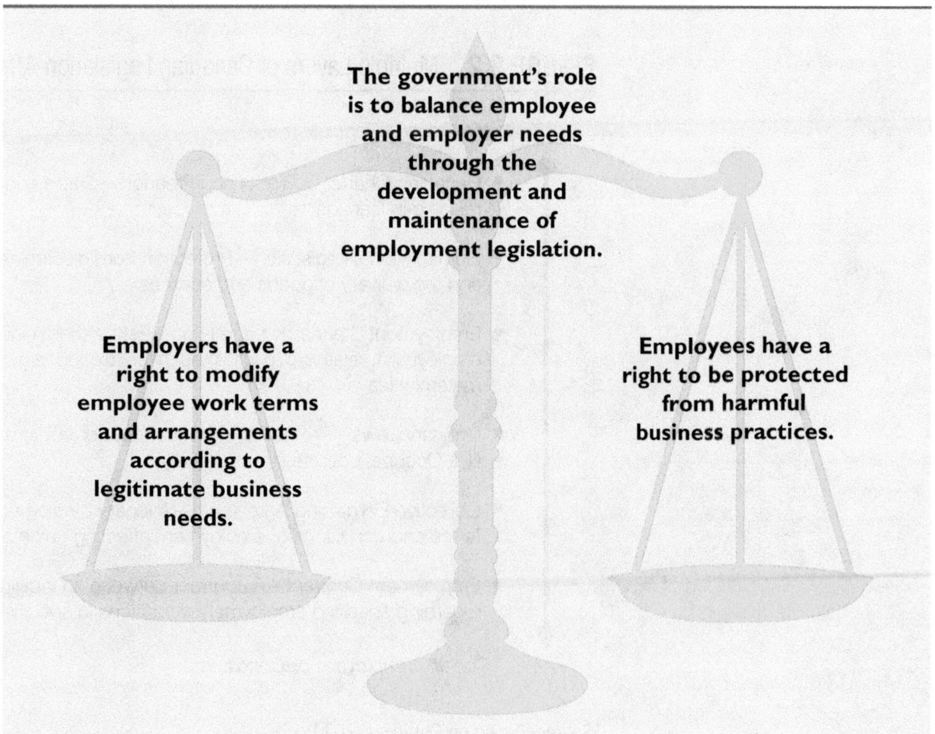

The government's role is to balance employee and employer needs through the development and maintenance of employment legislation.

Employers have a right to modify employee work terms and arrangements according to legitimate business needs.

Employees have a right to be protected from harmful business practices.

Source: Data from Chhinzer, N. (2013).

Hierarchy of Employment Legislation in Canada

1. As highlighted in **Figure** 2.2, at the broadest level all persons residing in Canada are guaranteed protection under constitutional law, particularly the Charter of Rights and Freedoms. The regulations set forth in the Charter are not employment specific, but all employers must abide by them because they are fundamental, guaranteed rights to all persons residing in Canada.

2. Provincial/Territorial human rights codes ensure that the rights of every Canadian are protected and that all persons are treated with equality and respect. Discrimination based on protected grounds highlighted in the legislation is prohibited in not only the employment relationship but also the delivery of goods and services. Therefore, while the application of the Charter of Rights and Freedoms and human rights codes extends beyond just the employment relationship, they both have a significant impact on workplace practices.

3. In Canada, employers and employees must abide by a series of employment-specific legislation, such as employment standards acts, which vary slightly by jurisdiction. There is a great deal of commonality to the legislation across jurisdictions, but there are also some differences. For example, vacations, statutory holidays, and minimum wage standards are provided by all jurisdictions, but specific entitlements may vary from one jurisdiction to the next. Therefore, a company with employees in more than one province/territory must monitor the legislation in each of those jurisdictions and remain current as legislation changes. Ensuring legality across multiple jurisdictions can be complex, since it is possible for a policy, practice, or procedure to be legal in one jurisdiction yet illegal in others.

4. There are laws that specifically regulate some areas of HRM—occupational health and safety (occupational health and safety acts are reviewed in Chapter 14), union relations (labour relations acts are reviewed in Chapter 16), as well as pensions

FIGURE 2.2 Multiple Layers of Canadian Legislation Affecting Workplace Practices

Affects the General Population

- Canadian Charter of Rights and Freedom—Basic rights guaranteed to all persons residing in Canada

- Human Rights Legislation—Protection from discrimination in employment relationships and the delivery of goods and services

- Employment Standards Legislation—Establishes minimum terms and conditions of the employment relationship within each jurisdiction (e.g., minimum wages, hours of work, maternity leave)

- Ordinary Laws—Protection under context- or content-specific laws affecting workplaces (like Occupational Health and Safety)

- Collective Bargaining Agreement—A legally binding agreement establishing minimum terms and conditions of employment affecting unionized positions

- Employment Contract—A contract between an individual employee and their employer regarding specified employment conditions in specified roles

Affects Specific Employees or Conditions

Source: Based on Chhinzer, 2011.

and compensation (pay equity acts, the Income Tax Act, and others are discussed briefly in Chapters 11–12).

5. Even more specific is the issue of contract law, which governs collective agreements and individual employment contracts. Contract law imposes specific requirements and constraints on management and employee policies, procedures, and practices. For example, a collective bargaining agreement is a contract regarding the terms and conditions of employment that both employees and employers must abide by legally. In non-unionized situations, individual employment contracts are often signed prior to the commencement of the employment relationship and constitute individualized legal agreements that employees and employers must abide by.

Tort Law

tort law Primarily judge-based law, whereby the precedent and jurisprudences set by one judge through his or her assessment of a case establishes how similar cases will be interpreted.

In addition to the legislation above, Canada has also inherited the English system of tort law. **Tort law** is primarily judge-based law, whereby the precedent and jurisprudences set by one judge through his or her assessment of a case establishes how similar cases will be interpreted. Tort law is often separated into two categories: intentional torts (for example, assault, battery, trespass, intentional affliction of mental distress) and unintentional torts (for example, negligence based on events in which harm is caused by carelessness).

To avoid flooding the courts with complaints and the prosecutions of relatively minor infractions, the government in each jurisdiction creates special regulatory bodies to enforce compliance with the law and aid in its interpretation. Such bodies, which include human rights commissions and ministries of labour, develop legally binding rules called **regulations** and evaluate complaints.

Hints : TO ENSURE LEGAL
        COMPLIANCE

regulations Legally binding rules established by special regulatory bodies created to enforce compliance with the law and aid in its interpretation.

Within these various levels of legislation there is a sense of hierarchy, as per Figure 2.2. The more general the impact of the legislation, the more it supersedes lower levels of legislation. For example, a collective bargaining agreement cannot agree to wages less than the minimum wage established in the applicable provincial employment standards act. Likewise, an employment standards act cannot violate the minimums set forth in the Charter of Rights and Freedoms.

There are two opposing interpretations of Canadian legislation. Employees often choose to view the regulations as a statutory floor and expect to receive higher than the minimum requirements (more than the minimum wage, minimum entitlement for vacation days, minimum entitlement for severance pay, and so on). In contrast, employers often prefer to view legislated guidelines as a contractual ceiling and align maximum commitment levels to the minimums established in the guidelines. HR professionals play a critical role in balancing these divergent sets of expectations, with obligations toward both the employees and employers.

LEGISLATION PROTECTING THE GENERAL POPULATION

HR Competency

90400

Human rights legislation makes it illegal to discriminate, even unintentionally, against various groups. Reactive (complaint driven) in nature, the focus of such legislation is on the types of acts in which employers should *not* engage. Included in this category are:

1. the *Charter of Rights and Freedoms*, federal legislation that is the cornerstone of human rights in Canada, and

2. *human rights legislation*, which is present in every jurisdiction.

The freedom of religion is protected under the Charter of Rights and Freedoms and applies to all levels of government.

Charter of Rights and Freedoms
Federal law enacted in 1982 that guarantees fundamental freedoms to all Canadians.

Supreme Court of Canada
www.scc-csc.gc.ca

equality rights Found in Section 15 of the Charter of Rights and Freedoms, which guarantees the right to equal protection and benefit of the law without discrimination.

human rights legislation
Jurisdiction-specific legislation that prohibits intentional and unintentional discrimination in employment situations and in the delivery of goods and services.

The Charter of Rights and Freedoms

The cornerstone of Canada's legislation pertaining to issues of human rights is the Constitution Act, which contains the **Charter of Rights and Freedoms**. The Charter applies to the actions of all levels of government (federal, provincial/territorial, and municipal) and agencies under their jurisdiction as they go about their work of creating laws. The Charter takes precedence over all other laws, which means that all legislation must meet Charter standards; thus, it is quite far-reaching in scope.

There are two notable exceptions to this generalization. The Charter allows laws to infringe on Charter rights if they can be demonstrably justified as reasonable limits in a "free and democratic society." Since "demonstrably justified" and "reasonable" are open to interpretation, many issues challenged under the Charter eventually end up before the Supreme Court of Canada, the Charter's ultimate interpreter. The second exception occurs when a legislative body invokes the "notwithstanding" provision, which allows the legislation to be exempted from challenge under the Charter.

The Charter provides the following fundamental rights and freedoms to every Canadian, including but not limited to:

1. freedom of conscience and religion
2. freedom of thought, belief, opinion, and expression, including freedom of the press and other communication media
3. freedom of peaceful assembly
4. freedom of association

In addition, the Charter provides Canadian multicultural heritage rights, First Nations' rights, minority language education rights, equality rights, the right to live and work anywhere in Canada, the right to due process in criminal proceedings, and the right to democracy.[3]

Section 15—**equality rights**—provides the basis for human rights legislation, because it guarantees the right to equal protection and benefit of the law without discrimination, in particular without discrimination based on race, national or ethnic origin, colour, religion, sex, age, or mental or physical disability.[4]

Human Rights Legislation

Every person residing in Canada is protected by **human rights legislation**, which prohibits intentional and unintentional discrimination in employment situations and the delivery of goods and services. Human rights legislation is extremely broad in scope, affecting almost all aspects of HRM when applied to the employment relationship. An important feature of human rights legislation is that it supersedes the terms of any employment contract or collective agreement.[5] For these reasons, supervisors and managers must be thoroughly familiar with the human rights legislation of their jurisdiction and their legal obligations and responsibilities specified therein.

Human rights legislation prohibits discrimination against all Canadians in a number of areas, including employment. To review individual provincial and territorial human rights laws would be confusing because of the many but generally minor differences among them, often only in terminology (for example, some provinces use the term

FIGURE 2.3   Prohibited Grounds of Discrimination in Employment by Jurisdiction

Prohibited Grounds of Discrimination	Federal	Alta.	B.C.	Man.	N.B.	N.L.	N.S.	Ont.	P.E.I.	Que.	Sask.	N.W.T.	Y.T.	Nunavut
Race	♦	♦	♦	♦	♦	♦	♦	♦	♦	♦	♦	♦	♦	♦
Colour	♦	♦	♦	♦	♦	♦	♦	♦	♦	♦	♦	♦	♦	♦
Creed or religion	♦	♦	♦	♦	♦	♦	♦	♦	♦	♦	♦	♦	♦	♦
Sex	♦	♦	♦	♦	♦	♦	♦	♦	♦	♦	♦	♦	♦	♦
Marital status	♦	♦	♦	♦	♦	♦	♦	♦	♦	♦	♦	♦	♦	♦
Age	♦	♦	♦	♦	♦	♦	♦	♦	♦	♦	♦	♦	♦	♦
		18+	19–65			19–65		18+			18–64			
Mental & physical disability	♦	♦	♦	♦	♦	♦	♦	♦	♦	♦	♦	♦	♦	♦
Sexual orientation	♦	♦	♦	♦	♦	♦	♦	♦	♦	♦	♦	♦	♦	♦
National or ethnic origin	♦				♦	♦	♦	♦			♦	♦	♦	♦
Family status	♦	♦		♦			♦	♦	♦	♦	♦	♦	♦	♦
Ancestry or place of origin		♦	♦	♦	♦			♦			♦		♦	♦
Political belief			♦	♦	♦	♦	♦		♦	♦			♦	
Association				♦	♦		♦	♦					♦	♦
Source of income		♦		♦				♦		♦	♦	♦		
Social condition or origin					♦	♦				♦			♦	
Language										♦	♦		♦	
Pardoned conviction	♦											♦	♦	♦
Record of criminal conviction										♦			♦	
Assignment, attachment, or seizure of pay						♦								

Source: Prohibited Grounds of Discrimination in Canada. Canadian Human Rights Commission, 2006.

Government of Canada
http://canada.gc.ca

Canadian Human Rights Tribunal
www.chrt-tcdp.gc.ca

discrimination As used in the context of human rights in employment, a distinction, exclusion, or preference based on any of the prohibited grounds and has the effect of nullifying or impairing the right of a person to full and equal recognition and exercise of his or her human rights and freedoms.

"creed," others "religion"). As indicated in **Figure 2.3**, most provincial/territorial laws are similar to the federal statute in terms of scope, interpretation, and application. All jurisdictions prohibit discrimination on the grounds of race, colour, religion/creed, sex, marital status, age, disability, and sexual orientation. Some, but not all, jurisdictions further prohibit discrimination on the basis of family status, nationality or ethnic origin, and various other grounds.

Discrimination Defined

Central to human rights laws is the concept of **discrimination**. When someone is accused of discrimination, it generally means that he or she is perceived to be acting in an unfair or prejudiced manner within the context of prohibited grounds for discrimination. For example, if an employee was discriminated against based on his or her initials or if they wore a black top to work that day, this would fall outside the scope of human rights legislation. The law prohibits unfair discrimination—making choices on the basis of perceived but inaccurate differences to the detriment of specific individuals or groups. Standards pertaining to unfair discrimination have changed over time. Both intentional and unintentional discrimination is prohibited.

Intentional Discrimination

Except in specific circumstances that will be described later, intentional discrimination is prohibited. An employer cannot discriminate *directly* by deliberately refusing to hire, train, or promote an individual, for example, on any of the prohibited grounds. It is important to realize that deliberate discrimination is not necessarily overt. In fact, overt (blatant) discrimination is relatively rare today. But subtle, indirect discrimination can be difficult to prove. For example, if a 60-year-old applicant is not selected for a job and is told that there was a better-qualified candidate, it is often difficult for the rejected job seeker to determine if someone else truly did more closely match the firm's specifications or if the employer discriminated on the basis of age.

An employer is also prohibited from intentional discrimination in the form of **differential or unequal treatment**. No individuals or groups may be treated differently in any aspect of terms and conditions of employment based on any of the prohibited grounds. For example, it is illegal for an employer to request that only female applicants for a factory job demonstrate their lifting skills or to insist that any candidates with a physical disability undergo a pre-employment medical exam, unless all applicants are being asked to do so.

It is also illegal for an employer to engage in intentional discrimination *indirectly* through another party. This means that an employer may not ask someone else to discriminate on his or her behalf. For example, an employer cannot request that an employment agency refer only male candidates for consideration as management trainees or instruct supervisors that racial minorities are to be excluded from consideration for promotions.

Discrimination because of association is another possible type of intentional discrimination listed specifically as a prohibited ground in the legislation of several Canadian jurisdictions. It involves the denial of rights because of friendship or other relationship with a protected group member. An example would be the refusal of a firm to promote a highly qualified male into senior management on the basis of the assumption that his wife, who was recently diagnosed with multiple sclerosis, will require too much of his time and attention and that her needs may restrict his willingness to travel on company business.

Unintentional Discrimination

Unintentional discrimination (also known as constructive or systemic discrimination) is the most difficult to detect and combat. Typically, it is embedded in policies and practices that appear neutral on the surface and that are implemented impartially, but have an adverse impact on specific groups of people for reasons that are not job related or required for the safe and efficient operation of the business. Examples are shown in **Figure 2.4**.

The Expert Opinion box below highlights recent dialogue regarding gender-based unintentional discrimination in the workplace and the complex role and impact of legislation, from the perspective of a Canada Research Chair in Global Womens Issues.

---

differential or unequal treatment Treating an individual differently in any aspect of terms and conditions of employment based on any of the prohibited grounds.

discrimination because of association Denial of rights because of friendship or other relationship with a protected group member.

unintentional/constructive/systemic discrimination Discrimination that is embedded in policies and practices that appear neutral on the surface and are implemented impartially, but have an adverse impact on specific groups of people for reasons that are not job related or required for the safe and efficient operation of the business.

HR Competency
20100

FIGURE 2.4 Examples of Systemic Discrimination

- Minimum height and weight requirements, which screen out dispropor-tionate numbers of women and people from Asia, who tend to be shorter in stature.
- Internal hiring policies or word-of-mouth hiring in workplaces that have not embraced diversity.
- Limited accessibility to company premises, which poses a barrier to persons with mobility limitations.
- Culturally biased or non-job-related employment tests, which discriminate against specific groups.
- Job evaluation systems that are not gender-neutral; that is, they under-value traditional female-dominated jobs.
- Promotions based exclusively on seniority or experience in firms that have a history of being white-male-dominated.
- Lack of a harassment policy or guidelines, or an organizational climate in which certain groups feel unwelcome and uncomfortable.

Source: Based on material provided by the Ontario Women's Directorate and the Canadian Human Rights Commission.

Permissible Discrimination via Bona Fide Occupational Requirements

bona fide occupational requirement (BFOR) A justifiable reason for discrimination based on business necessity (that is, required for the safe and efficient operation of the organization) or a requirement that can be clearly defended as intrinsically required by the tasks an employee is expected to perform.

Employers are permitted to discriminate if employment preferences are based on a **bona fide occupational requirement (BFOR)**, defined as a justifiable reason for discrimination based on business necessity, such as the requirement for the safe and efficient operation of the organization (for example, a person who is blind cannot be employed as a truck driver or bus driver). In some cases, a BFOR exception to human rights protection is fairly obvious. For example, when casting in the theatre, there may be specific roles that justify using age, sex, or national origin as a recruitment and selection criterion.

The *Meiorin* case (Supreme Court of Canada, 1999) established three criteria that are now used to assess if the discrimination qualifies as a BFOR:

1. Question of rationale: Was the policy or procedure that resulted in the discrimina-tion based on a legitimate, work–related purpose?

2. Question of good faith: Did the decision makers or other agents of the organiza-tion honestly believe that the requirement was necessary to fulfill the requirements of the role?

3. Question of reasonable necessity: Was it impossible to accommodate those who have been discriminated against without imposing undue hardship on the employer?

HR Competency

90400

EVIDENCE-BASED HR

The issue of BFORs gets more complicated in situations in which the occupational requirement is less obvious; the onus of proof is then placed on the employer. There are a number of instances in which BFORs have been established. For example, adherence to the tenets of the Roman Catholic Church has been deemed a BFOR when selecting faculty to teach in a Roman Catholic school.[6] The Royal Canadian Mounted Police has a requirement that guards be of the same sex as prisoners being guarded, which was also ruled to be a BFOR.[7]

Dr. Bipasha Baruah

Identification: Bipasha Baruah (PhD), Associate Professor and Canada Research Chair in Global Women's Issues

Affiliation: Department of Women's Studies and Feminist Research, University of Western Ontario

1. **How have women traditionally been disenfranchised in the workplace?**

   Pre-industrialization, there was a collective farm system, and everyone contributed to work. However, with the Industrial Revolution and urbanization, gender-based roles within the family and work were redefined. Through the feminist movement, individual necessity, economic times, or at times of war, women returned to work. In addition, females committed to education as a tool to advance their careers. Now, women are the primary breadwinner in 30 percent of the households in Canada, and 40 percent in the USA.

   However, research has shown that women still bear the primary responsibility for caregiving within a family unit, and they continue to be penalized for employment interruptions.

   Men are also victims of gender stereotyping. Some men feel significant stress or pressure associated with being the dominant breadwinner, while others feel that their desires for work–life balance or paternity leave might be rejected. Generally, we need societal perceptions to shift to help lift prejudice from both male and female perspectives.

2. **Why do we need legislation to protect women in the workplace?**

   The broader point is that we can always fine-tune policy, and even if we get it to be near perfect, there are certain groups that have enjoyed so much accumulated privilege that even the most equal, perfect policy may be co-opted to continue to benefit those who traditionally have benefited. Even at the university level, only one out of every four Canada Research Chair positions is filled by a woman. Only one out of the 22 Canada Excellence Research Chairs is a female. Research into this situation has shown that reference letters from women included statements such as referring to the candidate as a wife, lady, or mother, and using gender stereotype–based descriptors such as referring to women as agreeable, maternal, or sympathetic. Among the most educated, the discussion of personal qualities dominates references for women rather than focusing on their accomplishments, expertise, or competency.

3. **How has the workplace failed at securing equal opportunities or wages for women?**

   Legislation cannot be the sole vehicle for gender equality because pro-women legislation is largely symbolic when it comes to altering roles and entitlement hierarchies within the family and within society at large. We need the right combination of progressive policy AND consciousness-raising initiatives that raise awareness among women as well as men about the benefits of greater gender equity. The consciousness-raising piece is as crucial as policy reforms and state actions that protect women's interests and facilitate their agency.

Source: Reprinted by permission from Bipasha Baruah.

Reasonable Accommodation

reasonable accommodation
The adjustment of employment policies and practices that an employer may be expected to make so that no individual is denied benefits, disadvantaged in employment, or prevented from carrying out the essential components of a job because of grounds prohibited in human rights legislation.

undue hardship The point to which employers are expected to accommodate employees under human rights legislative requirements.

An important feature of human rights legislation is the requirement for **reasonable accommodation**. Employers are required to adjust employment policies and practices so that no individual is prevented from doing his or her job on the basis of prohibited grounds for discrimination. Accommodation may involve scheduling adjustments to accommodate religious beliefs or workstation redesign to enable an individual with a physical disability to perform a particular task.

Employers are expected to accommodate to the point of **undue hardship**, meaning that the financial cost of the accommodation (even with outside sources of funding) or health and safety risks to the individual concerned or other employees would make accommodation impossible.[8] Failure to make every reasonable effort to accommodate employees is a violation of human rights legislation in all Canadian jurisdictions. The term "reasonable" is relatively vague and open to interpretation, which can be found in the precedent that has been established in the legal system. The Supreme Court of Canada recently clarified the scope of the duty to accommodate by stating that it does

The Job Accommodation Network
http://askjan.org/

Alberta Human Rights Commission
www.albertahumanrights.ab.ca

BC Human Rights Tribunal
www.bchrt.bc.ca

Manitoba Human Rights Commission
www.gov.mb.ca/hrc

New Brunswick Human
Rights Commission
**www.gnb.ca/
hrc-cdp/index-e.asp**

Newfoundland and Labrador
Human Rights Commission
www.justice.gov.nl.ca/hrc

Northwest Territories Human
Rights Commission
www.nwthumanrights.ca

Nova Scotia Human Rights
Commission
 www.gov.ns.ca/humanrights

Nunavut Human Rights Tribunal
www.nhrt.ca

Ontario Human Rights Commission
www.ohrc.on.ca

Prince Edward Island Human
Rights Commission
www.gov.pe.ca/humanrights/

Québec Commission des droits
de la personne et des droits de la
jeunesse
www.cdpdj.qc.ca

Saskatchewan Human Rights
Commission
www.shrc.gov.sk.ca

Yukon Human Rights Commission
www.yhrc.yk.ca

not require an employer to completely alter the essence of the employment contract, whereby the employee has a duty to perform work in exchange for remuneration. For example, if the characteristics of an illness are such that the employee remains unable to work for the foreseeable future, even though the employer has tried to accommodate the employee, the employer will have satisfied the test of undue hardship.[9]

Human Rights Case Examples

In claims of discrimination, it does not matter if the protected grounds were the primary or heaviest weighted factor in the decision being challenged, or if it was one of many considerations made in the decision. If there were 20 criteria used to make a decision, and even one of those criteria violated protection against discrimination as per the applicable human rights legislation, then the entire decision made by the employer can be deemed illegal. **Figure 2.5** provides clarity as to the distribution of case type encountered by human rights commissions.

Disability

Claims of discrimination based on disability make up almost half of all human rights claims. A disability in human rights legislation includes a wide range of conditions, some which are visible and some which are not. In general, a distinction can be drawn between a physical disability and a mental one. A disability may be present from birth, caused by an accident, or develop over time and may include (depending on the jurisdiction) physical, mental, and learning disabilities; mental disorders; hearing or vision disabilities; epilepsy; drug and alcohol dependencies; environmental sensitivities; as well as other conditions. Temporary illnesses are generally not considered to be disabilities under human rights legislation (unless related to a workplace safety claim), but mental disorders, even temporary ones, are included in the definition of a disability. The intent of providing protection from discrimination based on past, present, or perceived disabilities is largely based on the principle of having an inclusive society with a barrier-free design and equal participation of persons with varying levels of ability.[10] Because employers set standards or requirements, they therefore "owe an obligation to be aware of both the differences between individuals, and differences that characterize groups of individuals. They must build conceptions of equality into workplace [or other] standards."[11]

FIGURE 2.5   Types of Cases Encountered by Provincial/Territorial Human Rights Commissions

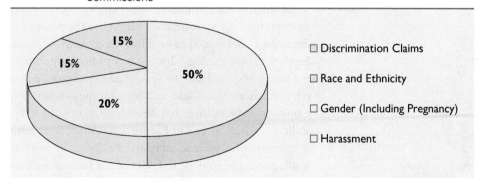

Source: According to Raj Anand, partner with WeirFoulds LLP and former chief commissioner of the Ontario Human Rights Commission. Presentation on "Equity, Diversity and Accommodation" at Osgoode Hall Law School, April 7, 2011.

According to the Supreme Court of Canada, the focus of a disability is not simply the presence of it, but the effect of the disability. In a case heard by the Supreme Court of Canada in 2000 against the City of Boisbriand and Communauté urbaine de Montréal, the city had dismissed an employee, Palmerino Troilo, from his position as a police officer because he suffered from Crohn's disease. Medical evidence presented in the case indicated that Troilo could perform normal functions of his job, but the city argued that the illness was permanent and could be interpreted subjectively as an indication of future job-related challenges. The judge found that the illness did not actually result in any functional limitations and held that Troilo had been a victim of discriminatory exclusion.[12] In this case, it was not the presence of a disability that was of concern to employment-related legislation, but the impact of that disability on creating job-related functional limitations.

The Supreme Court of Canada has suggested three broad inquiries to determine if discrimination has taken place:

1. Differential treatment: Was there substantively differential treatment due to a distinction, exclusion, or preference or because of a failure to take into account the complainant's already disadvantaged position within Canadian society?

2. An enumerated ground (a condition or clause that is explicitly protected by legislation): Was the differential treatment based on an enumerated ground?

3. Discrimination in a substantive sense: Does the differential treatment discriminate by imposing a burden upon or withholding a benefit from a person? Does the differential treatment amount to discrimination because it makes distinctions that are offensive to human dignity?

HR Competency

20300

EVIDENCE-BASED   HR

Accommodation   Although each situation is unique, there are general principles for accommodating persons with disabilities.

First, providing equal access to employment is largely based on removal of physical, attitudinal, and systemic barriers. These accommodations should be provided in a manner that most respects the dignity of the person, including an awareness of privacy, confidentiality, autonomy, individuality, and self-esteem. Each person's needs are unique and must be considered independently when an accommodation request is made. Persons with disabilities have the fundamental right to integration and full participation; therefore, barriers should be removed to the point of undue hardship. Workplace programs and policies should be designed by inclusion to combat "social handicapping," in which societal attitudes and actions create non-inclusive thinking against people who have no or few limitations. Providing equal access to employment is largely based on the removal of physical, attitudinal, and systemic barriers. Even when all of these factors are considered, there might still be a need for accommodation.

Second, if discrimination does exist, the company must demonstrate individualized attempts to accommodate the disability to the point of undue hardship. The *Meiorin* test discussed earlier is used to establish if the company reached the point of undue hardship. Employers have the legal duty to accommodate persons with disability, and the employees have a responsibility to seek accommodation, co-operate in the process, exchange relevant information, and explore accommodation solutions together.[13] Examples of employer and employee responsibilities associated with the duty to accommodate disabilities are highlighted in **Figure 2.6**. Often, accommodations can be made easily and at minimal cost, such as increased flexibility in work hours or break times; providing reading material in digitized, Braille, or large print formats; installing automatic doors and making washrooms accessible; or job restructuring, retraining, or assignment to an alternative position within the company.

FIGURE 2.6 Duty to Accommodate Disabilities: Shared Responsibilities

As a person with a disability	As an employer or union
• Tell your employer or union what your disability-related needs are as they relate to your job duties. • Provide supporting information about your disability-related needs, including medical or other expert opinions where necessary. • Participate in exploring possible accommodation solutions.	• Accept requests for accommodation from employees in good faith. • Request only information that is required to provide the accommodation. For example, you need to know that an employee's loss of vision prevents them from using printed material, but you do not need to know they have diabetes. • Take an active role in examining accommodation solutions that meet individual needs. • Deal with accommodation requests as quickly as possible, even if it means creating a temporary solution while a long-term one is developed. • Maximize confidentiality for the person seeking accommodation and be respectful of his or her dignity. • Cover the costs of accommodations, including any necessary medical or other expert opinion or documentation.

Source: © Queen's Printer for Ontario, 2000. Reproduced with permission.

Third, the duty to accommodate requires the most appropriate accommodation to be undertaken to the point of undue hardship. The principle underlying this condition is that accommodations are unique, numerous, part of a process, and a matter of degree. Rather than an all-or-nothing approach, there may be many options available to accommodate an employee's disability with varying degrees of complexity, resource demands, and effects on work processes. An accommodation can be considered appropriate if it results in equal opportunity to attain the same level of performance, benefits, and privileges others experience, or if it is adopted for the purpose of achieving equal opportunity and meets the individual's disability-related needs. In cases where alternative options preserve the same level of dignity and respect, employers are entitled to select the less expensive or less disruptive option.

Accommodation of employees with "invisible" disabilities, such as chronic fatigue syndrome, fibromyalgia, and mental illnesses, is becoming more common. An employee with bipolar disorder was terminated when he began to exhibit pre-manic symptoms after waiting for a response from management regarding his request for accommodation. A human rights tribunal in 2008 found that the company had not investigated the nature of his condition or possible accommodations and awarded the employee over $80 000 in damages.[14]

Harassment

The most historic battle for protection against harassment was initiated in 1982, at a time when it was largely interpreted that sexual harassment was not a form of sex discrimination (therefore, not illegal) and it was perceived that employers were not responsible for the actions of their employees. As indicated in the Workforce Diversity

Gina Sanders/Fotolia

The Supreme Court of Canada has determined that sexual harassment at work is a form of sex discrimination (and is therefore illegal), and that employers are responsible for their employees' actions.

harassment Unwelcome behaviour that demeans, humiliates, or embarrasses a person and that a reasonable person should have known would be unwelcome.

HR Competency

50200

box on next page, perspectives on sexual harassment and employers' responsibilities toward protecting employees from sexual harassment have shifted significantly over the last three decades, largely due to a Supreme Court ruling on a case initiated by two young waitresses.

Some jurisdictions prohibit harassment on all prescribed grounds, while others only expressly ban sexual harassment. **Harassment** includes unwelcome behaviour that demeans, humiliates, or embarrasses a person and that a reasonable person should have known would be unwelcome.[15] Examples of harassment are included in **Figure 2.7**. Minority women often experience harassment based on both sex and race.[16]

One type of intentional harassment that is receiving increasing attention is bullying, which involves repeated and deliberate incidents of negative behaviour that cumulatively undermine a person's self-image. This psychological form of harassment is much more prevalent and pervasive in workplaces than physical violence.[17] In 2004, a Quebec law prohibiting workplace psychological harassment came into effect with the intent of ending bullying in the workplace. In the first year, more than 2500 complaints were received, surpassing expectations to such a degree that the number of investigators was increased from 10 to 34.[18] Saskatchewan also prohibits psychological harassment, in its occupational health and safety legislation.[19]

Employer Responsibility   The Supreme Court has made it clear that protecting employees from harassment is part of an employer's responsibility to provide a safe and healthy working environment. If harassment is occurring and employers are aware or ought to have been aware, they can be charged as well as the alleged harasser.[20] Employer responsibility also includes employee harassment by clients or customers once it has been reported. In an Ontario case, Bell Mobility was ordered

FIGURE 2.7   Examples of Harassment

Some examples of harassment include:

- unwelcome remarks, slurs, jokes, taunts, or suggestions about a person's body, clothing, race, national or ethnic origin, colour, religion, age, sex, marital status, family status, physical or mental disability, sexual orientation, pardoned conviction, or other personal characteristics;
- unwelcome sexual remarks, invitations, or requests (including persistent, unwanted contact after the end of a relationship);
- display of sexually explicit, sexist, racist, or other offensive or derogatory material;
- written or verbal abuse or threats;
- practical jokes that embarrass or insult someone;
- leering (suggestive staring) or other offensive gestures;
- unwelcome physical contact, such as patting, touching, pinching, hitting;
- patronizing or condescending behaviour;
- humiliating an employee in front of co-workers;
- abuse of authority that undermines someone's performance or threatens his or her career;
- vandalism of personal property; and
- physical or sexual assault.

Source: Anti-Harassment Policies for the Workforce: An Employer's Guide, www.chrc-ccdp.ca/pdf/AHPoliciesWorkplace_en.pdf, Canadian Human Rights Commission, 2006.

WORKFORCE DIVERSITY

The Evolution of Thought on Sexual Harassment in Canada

In August 1982, two young women named Dianna Janzen and Tracy Govereau secured waitressing jobs at Pharos Restaurant in Winnipeg, Manitoba. The women hardly knew each other and rarely worked together. The cook, Tommy Grammas, started groping the women and making sexual advances during each woman's shift at work. As the women resisted the sexual advances, Tommy told them to "shut up or be fired."

Janzen tried to make it clear to Grammas that his actions were inappropriate, which did not stop the unwanted behaviour. When Janzen approached the owner, Philip Anastasiadis, he commented that she "needed to get laid." Feeling unsupported and embarrassed, Janzen continued working for two months before eventually quitting the job to remove herself from the continually hostile environment. Govereau was soon fired from her job, because of her "attitude."

Both women filed complaints under the Manitoba Human Rights Code. They claimed that only females ran the risk of being harassed at Pharos, since none of the male waiters, cashiers, or busboys had ever been harassed; thus, sexual harassment was a form of discrimination based on sex.

After a series of appeals, in 1989 the case was reviewed by the Supreme Court of Canada. In this historic case, the Supreme Court agreed that the women were sexually harassed at work, that sexual harassment is a form of sex discrimination (and is therefore illegal), and that employers are responsible for their employees' actions.

Up until the ruling, the terms of sexual harassment were not defined and the application of the law was unclear. The real impact of the precedent that this ruling set was that it gave employers and employees an unrestricted definition of sexual harassment that has since been instrumental in capturing a broader level of unwelcomed behaviours at work.

Source: Summarized from Stephen Hammond of Harassment Solutions Inc., "The Historic Fight Against Sexual Harassment," *Canadian HR Reporter*, 24, no. 14 (August 15, 2011), p. 33. Harassment is a Form of Discrimination, www.chrc-ccdp.ca/en/timeportals/milestones/125mile.asp, Canadian Human Rights Commission, 1989.

Sexual Harassment: Your Rights and Responsibilities
www.ohrc.on.ca/en/sexual-and-gender-based-harassment-know-your-rights

sexual harassment Offensive or humiliating behaviour that is related to a person's sex, as well as behaviour of a sexual nature that creates an intimidating, unwelcome, hostile, or offensive work environment or that could reasonably be thought to put sexual conditions on a person's job or employment opportunities.

sexual coercion Harassment of a sexual nature that results in some direct consequence to the worker's employment status or some gain in or loss of tangible job benefits.

sexual annoyance Sexually related conduct that is hostile, intimidating, or offensive to the employee but has no direct link to tangible job benefits or loss thereof.

to pay an employee more than $500 000 after a supervisor assaulted her in the office and she developed post-traumatic stress disorder. The company was found vicariously liable for the supervisor's aggressive behaviours and was found to have breached its duty of care to provide a safe and harassment-free working environment.[21]

Sexual Harassment   The type of harassment that has attracted the most attention in the workplace is **sexual harassment**. Sexual harassment is offensive or humiliating behaviour that is related to a person's sex, as well as behaviour of a sexual nature that creates an intimidating, unwelcome, hostile, or offensive work environment or that could reasonably be thought to put sexual conditions on a person's job or employment opportunities.

Sexual harassment can be divided into two categories: sexual coercion and sexual annoyance.[22] **Sexual coercion** involves harassment of a sexual nature that results in some direct consequence to the worker's employment status or some gain in or loss of tangible job benefits. Typically, this involves a supervisor using control over employment, pay, performance appraisal results, or promotion to attempt to coerce an employee to grant sexual favours. If the worker agrees to the request, tangible job benefits follow; if the worker refuses, job benefits are denied or taken away.

Sexual annoyance is sexually related conduct that is hostile, intimidating, or offensive to the employee but has no direct link to tangible job benefits or loss thereof. Rather, a "poisoned work environment" is created for the employee, the tolerance of which effectively becomes a term or condition of employment. An Alberta court upheld the dismissal of a male employee who had used profane language, sexually infused talk and jokes, and displayed pornographic and graphically violent images. The employee claimed that he was a misunderstood jokester who had never worked with a

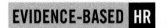

female engineer before and blamed the company for not training him on appropriate conduct. However, the court found that the company had embarked on a campaign to recruit women into trade positions many years earlier and that all employees had been provided with diversity training. In addition, the company had also implemented and widely publicized an antiharassment policy.[23]

Harassment Policies To reduce liability, employers should establish sound harassment policies, communicate such policies to all employees, enforce the policies in a fair and consistent manner, and take an active role in maintaining a working environment that is free of harassment. Effective harassment policies should include:

1. an antiharassment policy statement, stating the organization's commitment to a safe and respectful work environment and specifying that harassment is against the law;

2. information for victims (for example, identifying and defining harassment);

3. employees' rights and responsibilities (for example, respecting others, speaking up, reporting harassment);

4. employers' and managers' responsibilities (for example, putting a stop to harassment, being aware, listening to employees);

5. antiharassment policy procedures (what to do if you are being harassed, what to do if you are accused of harassment, what to do if you are a third-party employee, investigation guidelines, remedies for the victim and corrective action for harassers, guidelines for handling unsubstantiated complaints and complaints made in bad faith, confidentiality);

6. penalties for retaliation against a complainant;

7. guidelines for appeals;

8. other options such as union grievance procedures and human rights complaints; and

9. how the policy will be monitored and adjusted.[24]

Race and Colour

Discrimination on the basis of race and colour is illegal in every Canadian jurisdiction. For example, the B C Human Rights Tribunal found that two construction companies had discriminated against 38 Latin American workers brought in to work on a public transit project; the Latin Americans were treated differently than workers brought in from European countries in that they were paid lower wages and provided with inferior accommodation. As a result, the Tribunal awarded each worker $100 000.[25]

Religion

Discrimination on the basis of religion can take many forms in Canada's multicultural society. For example, it is a violation of human rights laws across Canada to deny time to pray or to prohibit clothing recognized as religiously required (for example, a hijab for Muslim women or a turban for Sikh men). According to a recent survey in Toronto, discriminatory hiring practices and workplace racism toward Muslim women are quite common. Of the 32 women surveyed, 29 said that their employer had commented on their hijab, and 13 said they were told that they would have to stop wearing their hijab if they wanted the job.[26]

A well-recognized case on religion involved Canadian National Railway (CN). An employee, Mr. Bhinder, worked as a maintenance electrician in the Toronto coach yard. As a practising Sikh, he wore a turban both on and off work premises. Four years after Bhinder first started working for CN, the company introduced a rule requiring all employees working in the coach yard to wear a hard hat, citing safety reasons. Bhinder informed management that he was unable to wear the hard hat since his faith prohibited him from wearing anything other than the turban and there was no way he could wear anything under or over it. He was fired and subsequently launched a discrimination case against CN. In 1995, the Supreme Court of Canada found that the rule discriminated against Bhinder on religious grounds, but that the requirement was bona fide. Therefore, it was not considered to be a discriminatory process and CN did not have a duty to accommodate Bhinder.

An Ethical Dilemma

Your company president tells you not to hire any gay or lesbian employees to work as part of his office staff because it would make him uncomfortable. What would you do?

HR Competency

20400

Sexual Orientation

Discrimination on the basis of sexual orientation is prohibited in all jurisdictions in Canada. As a result of lawsuits by same-sex couples, the Supreme Court ruled that all laws must define "common-law partners" to include both same-sex and opposite-sex couples.[27] In a recent federal case, a lesbian employee alleged that she was harassed by a co-worker. She made a complaint to her supervisors but felt the complaint was not investigated properly. She alleged that she was given a poor performance review because of her complaint and that her request for a transfer to another work site was denied. The Canadian Human Rights Commission ordered her employer to provide a letter of apology, financial compensation for pain and suffering, and a transfer to another work site. The Commission also ordered a meeting with the employer's harassment coordinator to talk about the complainant's experiences with the internal complaint process.[28]

Age

Many employers believe that it is justifiable to specify minimum or maximum ages for certain jobs. In actual fact, evidence is rarely available to support the position that age is an accurate indicator of a person's ability to perform a particular type of work.[29] For example, because of an economic downturn, an Ontario company was forced to lay off staff. The complainant, a foreman, had worked for the company for more than 32 years and was 57 at the time he was selected for termination along with another foreman who was aged 56. Both were offered a generous retirement package. The two foremen who remained were younger than the two released. The vice-president had prepared a note indicating that the two older workers who were terminated were told of the need to reduce people and that they "hoped to keep people with career potential." The Ontario Human Rights Tribunal found that the company engaged in age discrimination on the basis of the good employment record of the complainant, the ages of those selected for layoff compared with those retained, and the vice-president's statement, which was found to be a "euphemism; its meaning concerns age."[30]

Enforcement

Enforcement of human rights acts is the responsibility of the human rights commission in each jurisdiction. It should be noted that all costs are borne by the commission, not by the complainant, which makes the process accessible to all employees, regardless of financial means. The commission itself can initiate a complaint if it has reasonable grounds to assume that a party is engaging in a discriminatory practice.

Challenges of human rights legislation are heard by the human rights tribunal. The tribunal's primary role is to provide a speedy and accessible process to help parties affected by discrimination claims resolve the conflict through mediation. Once a claim is filed with the human rights commission or tribunal, the organization is notified and given a relatively short period of time (for example, 30 calendar days) to prepare its case. Regardless of whether a formal complaint or an informal accusation has been filed against a company, the employer has a duty to investigate claims of discrimination. Fulfilling the duty to investigate starts with the selection of an appropriate investigator. A checklist to be reviewed when selecting an investigator is provided in **Figure 2.8**.

An employer's obligations include the following:

1. demonstrating an awareness of the issues of discrimination or harassment, including having an antidiscrimination/antiharassment policy in place, a complaint mechanism, and training available for employees

2. fulfilling post-complaint actions, including assessing the seriousness of the complaint, launching an investigation promptly, focusing on employee welfare, and taking actions based on the complaint

3. resolving the complaint by demonstrating reasonable resolution and communication

If discrimination is found, two forms of remedies can be imposed. **Systemic remedies** (forward looking) require the respondent to take positive steps to ensure compliance with legislation, both in respect to the current complaint and with respect to any future practices. If a pattern of discrimination is detected, the employer will be ordered to cease such practices and may be required to attend a training session or hold regular human rights workshops. **Restitutional remedies** include monetary compensation for the complainant to put him or her back to the position he or she would be in if the discrimination had not occurred (this includes compensation for injury to dignity and self-respect). A written letter of apology may also be required.

HR Competency

20100

EVIDENCE-BASED HR

systemic remedies Forward-looking solutions to discrimination that require respondents to take positive steps to ensure compliance with legislation, both in respect to the current complaint and any future practices.

restitutional remedies Monetary compensation for the complainant to put him or her back to the position he or she would be in if the discrimination had not occurred (this includes compensation for injury to dignity and self-respect), and may include an apology letter.

FIGURE 2.8 A Checklist for Employers when Selecting a Workplace Investigator

❏ **Internal or external investigators:** Many employers select trained internal HR experts to conduct workplace investigations, while others rely on external investigators. Selection is dependent on the resources (time and money) of the firm, the complexities of the case (potential conflicts of interest), the expertise of the in-house staff, and the severity of the case.

❏ **One investigator or two:** The nature of the case may warrant the need for more than one investigator (e.g., one male and one female in the case of a sexual harassment claim).

❏ **Respecting the mandate:** Investigators should be able to maintain the role within the mandate of the task they have been assigned (e.g., fact finder or adviser) and not stray too far off track. Assigned investigators are perceived as agents of the organization; therefore, the organization can be held partially accountable for investigator actions.

❏ **Impartiality or neutrality:** Investigators should have no conflict of interest vested in the conditions, persons, or context of the case they are handling.

❏ **Reliable, thorough, and professional:** Although these qualities should go without saying, an investigator is expected to be a competent, effective, and professional communicator throughout the investigation, and must be capable of making credible assessments.

❏ **Quality of the written report:** The details and word selection in the written report can become evidence in a case. Therefore, a high-quality report details "what happened" and assists counsel in their defence.

❏ **Respects confidentiality:** The investigator should only discuss the investigation when required and respect the confidentiality of all parties affected by the investigation.

Source: Chhinzer, N., summary from Module 4 at the HR Law Certificate Program at Osgoode Hall Law School, 2011.

FIGURE 2.9   Common Remedies Issued by Human Rights Tribunals

Systemic Remedies (forward looking)	Restitution Remedies (penalties for past events)
• cease and desist the discriminatory practice • change a program to eliminate discriminatory elements, such as offering same-sex benefits under an employee benefit plan • make physical modifications to work places as mandated • develop non-discriminatory action plans • develop employment equity plans • post notices regarding provisions and protection offered to employees under the human rights code • develop information-sharing practices for future programs to allow monitoring of progress toward antidiscrimination goals	• payment of retroactive benefits • reinstatement of employment • payment for lost wages • compensation for insult to dignity, mental anguish, or infringement of rights under the human rights code • a public apology

Source: Raj Anand, "Human Rights and the Professional Regulator in the 21st Century," pp. 17–18, November 4, 2011. Used with permission from Raj Anand, Partner, WeirFoulds LLP.

The most common reason for restitutional remedies is compensation for lost wages; others include compensation for general damages, complainant expenses, and pain and humiliation. The violator is generally asked to restore the rights, opportunities, and privileges denied the victim, such as employment or promotion. The total compensation received by the complainant is generally between $0 and $20 000, with a general range of $10 000 to $20 000 for cases where evidence confirmed discrimination occurred and a restitution was ordered. **Figure 2.9** highlights examples of common remedies issued by human rights tribunals.

LEGISLATION SPECIFIC TO THE WORKPLACE

occupational segregation
The existence of certain occupations that have traditionally been male dominated and others that have been female dominated.

glass ceiling An invisible barrier, caused by attitudinal or organizational bias, that limits the advancement opportunities of qualified designated group members.

The Charter of Rights and Freedoms legalizes employment equity initiatives, which go beyond human rights laws in that they are proactive programs developed by employers to remedy past discrimination or prevent future discrimination. Human rights laws focus on prohibiting various kinds of discrimination; however, over time it became obvious that there were certain groups for whom this complaint-based, reactive approach was insufficient. Investigation revealed that four identifiable groups— women, Aboriginal people, persons with disabilities, and visible minorities—had been subjected to pervasive patterns of differential treatment by employers, as evidenced by lower pay on average, occupational segregation, higher rates of unemployment, underemployment, and concentration in low-status jobs with little potential for career growth. An example of **occupational segregation** is that the majority of women worked in a very small number of jobs, such as nursing, teaching, sales, and secretarial/clerical work. Advancement of women and other designated group members into senior management positions has been hindered by the existence of a **glass ceiling**, an "invisible" barrier caused by attitudinal or organizational bias

FIGURE 2.10 The Catalyst Pyramid—Canadian Women in Business

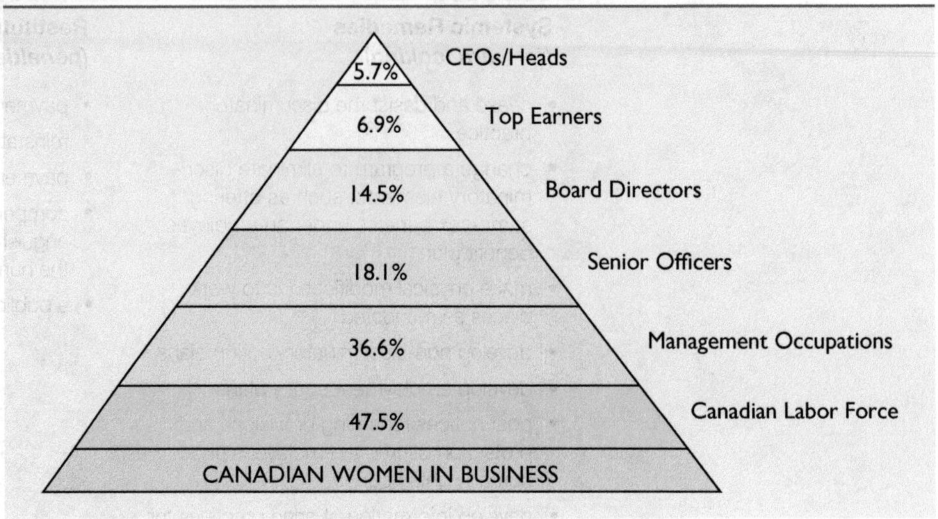
5.7%
CEOs/Heads
6.9%
Top Earners
14.5%
Board Directors
18.1%
Senior Officers
36.6%
Management Occupations
47.5%
Canadian Labor Force
CANADIAN WOMEN IN BUSINESS

Source: Catalyst Pyramid: Canadian Women in Business. New York: Catalyst, 2013

that limits the advancement opportunities of qualified individuals. As you can see in **Figure 2.10**, a survey from 2012 confirmed that the glass ceiling is still intact.

Employment equity legislation is intended to remove employment barriers and promote equality for the members of the four designated groups. Employers under federal jurisdiction must prepare an annual plan with specific goals to achieve better representation of the designated group members at all levels of the organization and timetables for goal implementation. Employers must also submit an annual report on the company's progress in meeting its goals, indicating the representation of designated group members by occupational groups and salary ranges, and providing information on those hired, promoted, and terminated. In addition, the Federal Contractors Program requires firms bidding on federal contracts of $200 000 or more to implement an employment equity plan.

In contrast, mandatory employment equity programs are virtually non-existent in provincial and territorial jurisdictions. Some provinces have employment equity policies that encourage employment equity plans in provincial departments and ministries. Quebec has a contract compliance program under which employers in receipt of more than $100 000 in provincial funding must implement an employment equity plan.[31]

employment equity program
A detailed plan designed to identify and correct existing discrimination, redress past discrimination, and achieve a balanced representation of designated group members in the organization.

An **employment equity program** is designed to achieve a balanced representation of designated group members in the organization. It is a major management exercise because existing employees must become comfortable working with others from diverse backgrounds, cultures, religions, and so on, and this represents a major change in the work environment. A deliberately structured process is involved, which can be tailored to suit the unique needs of the firm. The employment equity process usually takes six months. The first step is the demonstration of senior management commitment and support, which leads to data collection and analysis of the current workforce demographics. Following that, there is an employment systems review, which leads to plan development and eventual plan implementation. The last step is monitoring, evaluating, and revising the plan.

Although embracing employee equity or diversity offers opportunities to enhance organizational effectiveness, transforming an organizational culture presents a set of challenges that must be handled properly. Diversity initiatives should be undertaken slowly, since they involve a complex change process. Resistance to change may have to be overcome, along with stereotyped beliefs or prejudices and employee resentment.

cartoonresource/Fotolia

"See that dark spot? That's potential litigation."

Canadian Association of
Administrators of Labour Legislation
www.caall-acalo.org

Workplace Standards
**www.workplace.ca/laws/
employ_standard_comp.html**

equal pay for equal work
Specifies that an employer cannot
pay male and female employees
differently if they are performing the
same or substantially similar work.

EVIDENCE-BASED HR

The Plight of the Four Designated Groups

Women

Women accounted for 47 percent of the employed workforce in 2012.[32] Two-thirds of all employed women were working in teaching, nursing and related health occupations, clerical or other administrative positions, or sales and service occupations. There has been virtually no change in the proportion of women employed in these traditionally female-dominated occupations over the past decade. Women continue to be under-represented in engineering, natural sciences, and mathematics, a trend unlikely to change in the near future because women are still under-represented in university programs in these fields.[33]

Every jurisdiction in Canada has legislation incorporating the principle of *equal pay for equal work*. In most jurisdictions, this entitlement is found in the employment (labour) standards legislation; otherwise, it is in the human rights legislation. **Equal pay for equal work** specifies that an employer cannot pay male and female employees differently if they are performing the same or substantially similar work. Pay differences based on a valid merit or seniority system or employee productivity are permitted; it is only sex-based discrimination that is prohibited. This principle makes it illegal, for example, for the Canadian government to employ nurses (mostly women) as "program administrators" and doctors (mainly men) as "health professionals" to do the same job adjudicating Canada Pension Plan disability claims and pay the men twice as much.[34]

Aboriginals

Most Aboriginal employees in the workforce are concentrated in low-skill, low-paid jobs such as trades helpers. The unemployment rate for Aboriginal people is significantly higher than the rate among non-Aboriginals, and their income is significantly lower.[35]

People with Disabilities

About 45 percent of people with disabilities are in the labour force, compared with almost 80 percent of the non-disabled population. Although 63 percent of people with a mild disability are in the workforce, only 28 percent of those with a severe to very severe disability are working. The median employment income of workers with disabilities is 83 percent of that of other Canadian workers.[36]

Visible Minorities

According to the federal Employment Equity Act, a visible minority is defined as "persons, other than Aboriginal peoples, who are non-Caucasian in race or non-white in colour." Often the terms "visible minority" and "immigrant" are used interchangeably, but these two terms are actually distinct. An immigrant represents a person who was not born in Canada, but resides in Canada for the purpose of settlement. In the 2011 Canadian census, there were almost 6.2 million immigrants in the Canadian population. There were almost 6.8 million persons who self-identified as visible minorities, with the largest representation among South Asians and Chinese, followed by persons who self-identified as black, Filipino, and Latin American.[37] In 1981, 55.5 percent of new immigrants to Canada were visible minorities, but by 2001 that proportion reached 72.9 percent.[38] This suggests that almost three out of every ten

HR IN THE NEWS

Recruiter Pays for Series of Abusive Texts to Applicant

An applicant was denied employment in June 2013 through a series of abusive text messages, including recruiter texts to the applicant saying the company "only hires white men" and "I don't hire foreners (sic)". The manager who sent the text claimed his texts were non-discriminatory stating "it's called freedom of speech" (referring to the constitutional law). The Human Rights Tribunal disagreed, and found the text exchange included multiple violations of the Human Rights Act, ordering the Ottawa-based Valley Cleaning and Restoration company to pay $8000 plus interest to the applicant.[39]

KSAs Knowledge, skills, and abilities.

underemployment Being employed in a job that does not fully utilize one's knowledge, skills, and abilities (KSAs).

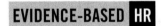
EVIDENCE-BASED HR

immigrants in the last decade were not visible minorities, while there are millions of people born in Canada who are visible minorities, but not immigrants.

Traditionally, visible minorities were typically unable to obtain employment that took full advantage of their knowledge, skills, and abilities (**KSAs**), and thus faced **underemployment**. As a result, visible minorities were included as a designated group. A recent study on diversity in the Greater Toronto Area (GTA) highlighted the continuing disadvantaged status of visible minorities. The study looked at 3257 leaders in the GTA in all sectors and found that just 13 percent were visible minorities (even though visible minorities make up half of the GTA population).[40]

EMPLOYMENT/LABOUR STANDARDS LEGISLATION

employment (labour) standards legislation Laws present in every Canadian jurisdiction that establish minimum employee entitlements and set a limit on the maximum number of hours of work permitted per day or week.

All employers and employees in Canada, including unionized employees, are covered by **employment (labour) standards legislation**. The intent of an employment standards act (ESA) is to establish minimum terms and conditions for workplaces pertaining to such issues as wages; paid holidays and vacations; maternity, parental, or adoption leave (or some mix thereof); bereavement leave; compassionate care leave; termination notice; and overtime pay. They also set the maximum number of hours of work permitted per day or week; overtime pay is required for any work in excess of the maximum.

While employer and employee agreements or practices can exceed minimums established in an ESA, neither party can choose to opt out of or waive the rights established in the applicable ESA. For example, if the ESA minimum requirement establishes a minimum vacation rate of 4 percent of pay, an employment agreement cannot have a provision for only 3 percent of pay as vacation pay, even if both parties consent.

HR IN THE NEWS

Who is Earning Minimum Wage?

The number of workers in Canada making minimum wage has increased over the last two decades. In 1997, 5 percent of all employees in Canada were paid the minimum wage.

In 2013, this proportion rose to 6.7 percent. Women are 25 percent more likely to be earning minimum wage than men. Overall, those earning minimum wage continue to be younger, less-educated, and employed in the service sector.[41]

In contrast, the minimums established in an ESA can be exceeded in employment contracts, through collective bargaining agreements (in unionized positions), or based on common law (precedent established by the judicial system). The HR in the News box above highlights metrics associated with minimum wage pay in Canada. An employer or employee can agree to 5 percent of pay as vacation pay without violating the ESA, for example.

If there is a conflict between the applicable ESA and another contract, the principle of greater benefit is applied. For example, an employment policy or contract is communicated to employees stating that in the case of a layoff, employees will be provided with one month notice for every year that they worked if they are laid off. The applicable ESA minimum requires the provision of only one week notice per year that an employee worked, up to an eight-week maximum. In this example, an employee who worked for 10 years would be given the greater benefit (10 months of notice before a layoff), not the minimum under the ESA, to preserve the greater benefit to the employee.

While ESAs provide minimum terms and conditions of employment, they are not totally inclusive. Often, students on work exchange programs, inmates on work projects, police officers, independent officers, and others are explicitly excluded from protection under an ESA. In addition, regulations for specific occupations such as doctors, lawyers, managers, architects, and specific types of salespersons modify the applicability of certain sections of ESAs.

Enforcement of ESAs

Governed by federal, provincial, or territorial employment standards acts (ESAs), enforcement is complaint based, and violators can be fined. This occurs through the filing of a formal written or electronic complaint against the violator to the appropriate authorities (often the provincial or territorial ministry of labour). A person, union, or corporation can file a complaint with the ministry for violations, given that ESAs have an interest in mitigating the employment relationships between employee and employers.

HR by the Numbers

Challenges with a Jurisdiction Based Approach to Employment Law in Canada ◄42

2.5% of business sector employers operated in more than one jurisdiction in Canada in 2011

40% of business sector workers were employed in multijurisdictional enterprises in Canada in 2011

25% of multijurisdictional enterprises were active in 6 or more jurisdictions

80% of multi-jurisdictional enterprises had more than 500 employees

Employees are required to give up their rights to sue an employer in civil court once a claim is filed with the ministry of labour. This protects employers from dual proceedings on the same issue, and protects courts from being overwhelmed with duplicate cases. There are also strict limitation periods, establishing the maximum amount of time that can elapse between the violation and the filing of a complaint, with these limits differing based on the violation (unpaid wages, vacation pay, and so on). There is also a general maximum claim limit (for example, $10 000 under the Ontario ESA) for unpaid wages. Under ESAs, employees have been awarded compensation for actual unpaid wages and direct earnings losses, time required to find a new job and expenses to seek a new job, benefit plan entitlements, severance pay, and loss of "reasonable expectation" of continued employment.

Enforcement of employment standards legislation and human rights legislation (both of which are jurisdictional) can be especially challenging in Canada, as a number of organizations operate in multiple jurisdictions. Therefore, these organizations are subject to multiple and sometimes varying human rights legislation rules (as highlighted in the HR by the Numbers box).

RESPECTING EMPLOYEE PRIVACY

Today's employers are grappling with the problem of how to balance employee privacy rights with their need to monitor the use of technology-related tools in the workplace. Employers must maintain the ability to effectively manage their employees and prevent liability to the company, which can be held legally liable for the actions of its employees.[43] They want to eliminate time wasted (on surfing the web, playing computer games, and so on) and abuse of company resources (such as use of the Internet and email at work for personal and possibly illegal uses, such as gambling or visiting pornographic sites).[44] For example, one employee used workplace computers to access hundreds of pornographic websites, to surf Internet dating sites for hours at a time, and to maintain personal files with sexually explicit images. The employee was dismissed and an arbitrator upheld the dismissal, stating that the employee had engaged in serious culpable misconduct.[45] Another concern is employee blogging, as a posting intended to be seen by a few friends that includes confidential company information or comments about management can easily make its way to a national media outlet without the author even knowing it.[46]

HR Competency

20600

Privacy Commissioner of Canada
www.priv.gc.ca

Personal Information Protection and Electronic Documents Act (PIPEDA) legislation that governs the collection, use, and disclosure of personal information across Canada, including employers' collection and dissemination of personal information about employees

Employees are concerned with privacy—their control over information about themselves and their freedom from unjustifiable interference in their personal life. The **Personal Information Protection and Electronic Documents Act (PIPEDA)** governs the collection, use, and disclosure of personal information across Canada, including employers' collection and dissemination of personal information about employees. Any information beyond name, title, business address, and telephone number is regarded as personal and private, including health-related information provided to insurers. Employers must obtain consent from employees whenever personal information is collected, used, or disclosed.[47]

Some employers have resorted to electronic monitoring, which is becoming easier and less expensive as new software is developed, that can track websites visited by

Hints **TO ENSURE LEGAL COMPLIANCE**

workers and the time spent on each.[48] In general, courts in Canada have permitted electronic surveillance as long as there is proper balancing of opposing interests. Employers are given substantial leeway in monitoring their employees' use of the internet and email, and they are in an even stronger position if there is a written policy in place. The policy should be updated regularly to reflect changes in technology and should address the use of all company technological equipment away from the employer's premises, including laptops, smartphones, tablets, and so on.

Video Surveillance

Some employers install video surveillance equipment to prevent employee theft and vandalism and to monitor productivity. Employees must be made aware of the surveillance. Unions often file grievances against video surveillance, and arbitrators have been reluctant to support such surveillance because of privacy concerns. Courts typically assess whether the surveillance was reasonable and whether there were reasonable alternatives available. Generally, they have decided that video surveillance is not reasonable and that other means could be used.[49]

An Ethical Dilemma

Is it ethical to use video surveillance of employees? Do you think employees need to be told of surveillance tools if they are used?

CHAPTER SUMMARY

1. The legal framework in Canada attempts to balance employee and employer rights using multiple overlapping legislative pieces, including legislation aimed at protecting the general public (the Charter of Rights and Freedoms, human rights legislation) as well as more specific legislation (employment equity legislation, employment standards acts, and privacy legislation).

2. The responsibility for employment-related law resides with the provinces and territories; however, employees of the federal civil service, Crown corporations and agencies, and businesses engaged in transportation, banking, and communications are federally regulated. So there are 14 jurisdictions for employment law in Canada—ten provinces, three territories, and the federal jurisdiction. Ninety percent of Canadians are covered by provincial/territorial employment legislation, and 10 percent are covered by federal employment legislation.

3. Harassment includes a wide range of behaviours that a reasonable person *ought to know* are unwelcome. Employers and managers have a responsibility to provide a safe and healthy working environment. If harassment is occurring and they are aware or ought to have been aware, they can be charged along with the alleged harasser. To reduce liability, employers should establish harassment policies, communicate these to employees,

enforce the policies, and play an active role in maintaining a work environment free of harassment.

4. All jurisdictions prohibit discrimination on the grounds of race, colour, sexual orientation, religion/ creed, physical and mental disability, sex, age, and marital status. Employers are required to make reasonable accommodation for employees by adjusting employment policies and practices, so that no one is disadvantaged in employment on any of the prohibited grounds, to the point of undue hardship. Employers are allowed to put in conditions related to employment that may discriminate, provided that these conditions are bona fide occupational requirements.

5. Employment standards legislation establishes minimum terms and conditions for workplaces in each jurisdiction, and violations of these terms are identified in a complaint-based process, whereby the ministry of labour will investigate violations once an employee files a complaint.

6. Privacy legislation focuses on how to balance employee privacy rights with an employer's need to monitor the use of technology-related tools in the workplace. The Personal Information Protection and Electronic Documents Act (PIPEDA) governs the collection, use, and disclosure of personal information across Canada.

MyManagementLab

Study, practise, and explore real business situations with these helpful resources:

- **Interactive Lesson Presentations:** Work through interactive presentations and assessments to test your knowledge of management concepts.
- **PIA (Personal Inventory Assessments):** Enhance your ability to connect with key concepts through these engaging self-reflection assessments. **P I A** PERSONAL INVENTORY ASSESSMENT
- **Study Plan:** Check your understanding of chapter concepts with self-study quizzes.
- **Videos:** Learn more about the management practices and strategies of real companies.
- **Simulations:** Practise decision-making in simulated management environments.

KEY TERMS

bona fide occupational requirement (BFOR) *(p. 33)*
Charter of Rights and Freedoms *(p. 30)*
differential or unequal treatment *(p. 32)*
discrimination *(p. 31)*
discrimination because of association *(p. 32)*
employment equity program *(p. 44)*
employment (labour) standards legislation *(p. 46)*
equality rights *(p. 30)*
equal pay for equal work *(p. 45)*
glass ceiling *(p. 43)*
harassment *(p. 38)*
human rights legislation *(p. 30)*
KSAs *(p. 46)*
occupational segregation *(p. 43)*

Personal Information Protection and Electronic Documents Act (PIPEDA) *(p. 48)*
reasonable accommodation *(p. 34)*
regulations *(p. 29)*
restitutional remedies *(p. 42)*
sexual annoyance *(p. 39)*
sexual coercion *(p. 39)*
sexual harassment *(p. 39)*
systemic remedies *(p. 42)*
tort law *(p. 29)*
underemployment *(p. 46)*
undue hardship *(p. 34)*
unintentional/constructive/systemic discrimination *(p. 32)*

REVIEW AND DISCUSSION QUESTIONS

1. Describe the impact of the Charter of Rights and Freedoms on HRM.

2. Differentiate among the following types of discrimination and provide one example of each: direct, differential treatment, indirect, because of association, and systemic.

3. Provide five examples of prohibited grounds for discrimination in employment in Canadian jurisdictions.

4. Explain the purpose of employment standards legislation, and the concept of "the greater good" when assessing these minimums.

5. Define "sexual harassment" and describe five types of behaviour that could constitute such harassment.

6. Define the concepts of occupational segregation, underemployment, and the glass ceiling.

7. What is the test to define if a bona fide occupational requirement exists? What are the three elements of this test?

8. What is the role of privacy legislation in Canada? Describe the act that protects employees' privacy.

CRITICAL THINKING QUESTIONS

1. Go to your provincial or territorial employment (labour) standards website and determine the following:
   - minimum legal age to work in this jurisdiction
   - minimum hourly wages

   - maximum number of hours that can be worked in a week before overtime must be paid

   How does this information apply to you and your friends and family? Did you notice anything else that caught your interest that you were previously unaware of?

2. Prepare a report outlining legally acceptable questions that may be asked at a selection interview with a young female engineer applying for the job of engineering project manager at an oil field in rural northern Alberta with an otherwise all-male group. (Refer to Appendix 7.1 on page 179 for help.)

3. Working with a small group of classmates, search the web for a company in your community that has an antidiscriminatory employment program. Contact the company's HR manager and request more information on the program. Prepare a brief report summarizing its key features.

4. The organization you are working for is relatively new and growing and has no HR department. They have asked you to prepare a briefing about what can and cannot be asked during an employment interview. Given that it is a small organization, management usually conducts interviews. You notice a number of managers huffing about how the law doesn't apply to them and their actions can't result in a lawsuit. In addition to preparing a briefing about the types of questions that can and cannot be asked in an interview, prepare a response to the perception that the law does not apply to the managers in this situation.

EXPERIENTIAL EXERCISES

1. While organizations can hold employees responsible for behaviour in the workplace, the perception that employees are not accountable for their social media presence outside of the workplace is changing. For example, a crane operator at Tenaris Algoma Tubes Inc. posted about a co-worker (a "stocker"), making suggestions of a physically aggressive act and a violent and humiliating sex act that the crane operator claimed could be inflicted on the stocker. When the stocker heard about the comments, she contacted the company, who investigated the matter and subsequently dismissed the crane operator. The union grieved the dismissal, but an Ontario arbitrator upheld the dismissal, highlighting that the act was in violation of workplace policies and a form of workplace harassment. Research this case and highlight what other companies can learn from this. What policies should organizations consider given this experience? What challenges would an organization have to overcome in order to make the policies you recommend realistic, fair, and legally defensible?

2. An employee who has been off for two months with a stress-related ailment has just contacted you indicating that she would like to return to work next week but won't be able to work full time for another month or so. How would you handle this?

3. A supervisor has just approached you to indicate a concern she has with an employee. The supervisor indicates that the employee is often surfing the Internet while at work and fears that not only is this affecting productivity negatively, but it is also a violation of the company's rules for Internet surfing using a company computer. The supervisor would like you to ask the IT team to investigate how many hours a day are logged to non-work-related activities for that employee and also asks for a list of websites that the employee visits. What is the role of privacy legislation from both the employer and the employee perspectives? What additional information would you need to make a decision about next steps? What recommendations can you make to the supervisor to deal with the situation in the short term?

RUNNING CASE

Running Case: LearnInMotion.com

Legal Issues

One of the problems that Jennifer and Pierre are facing at LearnInMotion.com concerns the inadequacies of the firm's current human resources management practices and procedures. The previous year had been a swirl of activity—creating and testing the business model, launching the site, writing and rewriting the business plan, and finally getting venture funding. And it would be accurate to say that in all that time, they put absolutely no time into employee manuals, HR policies, or other HR-related matters. Even the 25-page business plan has no information in this regard. The plan provided considerable detail regarding budgetary projections, competition, market growth, and business strategy. However, it was silent when it came to HR, except for containing short bios of the current employees and projections of the types of positions that would have to be staffed in the first two years.

Almost from the beginning, it was apparent to both Jennifer and Pierre that they were (as Pierre put it) "out of [their] depth" when it came to the letter and spirit of equal employment opportunity laws. Having both been through business school, they were familiar with the general requirements, such as not asking applicants their age during interviews. However, those general guidelines weren't always easy to translate into practice during the actual applicant interviews. Two incidents particularly concerned them. One of the applicants for a sales position was in his 50s, which made him about twice as old as any other applicant. Although Pierre didn't mean to be discriminatory, he found himself asking this candidate such questions as "Do you think you'll be able to get up to speed selling an Internet product?" and "You know, we'll be working very long hours here; are you up to that?"—questions that he did not ask the other, younger candidates. There was also a problem with a candidate for the content manager position. The candidate was a single mother with two children, and Pierre asked her quite pointed questions, such as "What are your children's ages and what childcare arrangements do you have?" and "This job involves quite a bit of overtime and weekend work. Are you sure your kids won't get in the way of that?" Jennifer thought questions like these were probably okay, but she wasn't sure.

There was also a disturbing incident in the office. There were already two content management employees,

Maya and Dan, whose job it was to actually place the course and other educational content on the website. Dan, along with Alex, the web surfer, occasionally used vulgarity, for instance, when referring to the problems the firm was having getting the computer supplier to come to the office and repair a chronic problem with the firm's server. Pierre's attitude was that "boys will be boys." However, Jennifer and Maya cringed several times when "the boys" were having one of these exchanges and felt strongly that this behaviour had to stop. However, Jennifer was not sure language like this constituted harassment under the law, although she did feel that at a minimum it was uncivil. The two owners decided it was time to institute and implement some HR policies that would ensure their company and its employees adhered to the letter and the spirit of the various employment laws. Now they want you, their management consultant, to help them actually do it.

Questions

1 Is the Employment Standards Act applicable to this employer, as they are situated in Ontario? As Learn-InMotion.com's management consultant, what areas of the act do you feel Jennifer and Pierre need to be aware of in regards to their current employee relations issues? Specifically, what areas would you recommend they include in their new human resource policy manual?

2 Should Pierre and Jennifer put a "respectful workplace policy" in place? If so, develop a draft of this type of policy using the web resources listed throughout this chapter.

CASE INCIDENT

A New HR Professional's First Workplace Dilemma

Laura, a recent graduate from a human resources diploma program from a local community college, has just landed her first role as a human resources coordinator at a small bottling company. Upper management has made it clear that they want Laura to make the updating of the current human resources manual her first priority. During her second week on the job, Laura was strolling down the hallway toward the break room to get herself a cup of coffee when she passed the director of marketing's office. As she passed she noticed an inappropriate picture of a woman visible on his computer. Shocked at what she had just seen, Laura continued down the hall, not sure what to do

next. Upon returning to her office, Laura decided the best way to start revising the manual was to introduce a policy on appropriate computer use. She felt this would address the problem as she didn't want to start her new job on a negative note by reporting the director of marketing to the CEO without a clear policy in place.

Questions

1 Do you agree with how Laura handled this situation? If so, why? If not, what would you have done differently?

2 Is it important for this company to have such a policy in place? If so, how can the employment (labour) standards act in your province/territory help in drafting a policy on appropriate computer use?[49]

Ambrophoto/Shutterstock

CHAPTER

3

Human Resources Management and Technology

LEARNING OUTCOMES

AFTER STUDYING THIS CHAPTER, YOU SHOULD BE ABLE TO

EXPLAIN trends in the nature of work and the relationship these have with technology or automation.

DISCUSS the strategic importance of technology in HRM.

DESCRIBE the impact that HR technology has on the role of the HR professional and the seven core competencies that have emerged.

EXPLAIN the key functions of a human resource information system (HRIS) and its strategic importance.

DEFINE HRIS and **DESCRIBE** its main components.

ANALYZE the use of HR audits and metrics to assess talent management issues.

DESCRIBE the three-step process involved in selecting and implementing an HRIS.

DISCUSS what is meant by e-HR and the benefits of web-enabled service applications.

REQUIRED HR COMPETENCIES

20600: Promote an evidence-based approach to the development of human resources policies and practices using current professional resources to provide a sound basis for human resources decision-making.

20700: Research business information and global and technological trends using credible sources to incorporate appropriate technologies and ideas into the practice of human resources.

90100: Make informed business decisions using financial and operating information to align human resources with business strategy.

90200: Conduct comprehensive human resources audits by sampling policies, procedures, programs, and systems to identify strengths and areas for improvement and to ensure compliance.

90300: Specify the requirements for a human resources information system that captures data and generates reports to inform leaders of trends to achieve organizational objectives.

90400: Manage human resources information in compliance with legal requirements using appropriate tools and procedures in order to support decision-making and inform leaders about progress toward organizational objectives.

90500: Report on the effectiveness of human capital investments with respect to key performance indicators using appropriate measures and metrics to monitor trends and promote the organization's progress toward its objectives.

TRENDS IN THE NATURE OF WORK

Technology has affected how people work, and it therefore impacts the skills and training today's workers need. This includes automation as well as information and communication technology (ICT). These technological shifts have led to an increased awareness of and demand for knowledge work in human capital.

Automation

Automation reduces the need for manual labour. For example, after an 18-week training course, a skilled mechanic works as a team leader in a plant where about 40 percent of the machines are automated. In older plants, machinists would manually control machines that cut chunks of metal into things like engine parts. Today, the mechanic and his team spend much of their time keying commands into computerized machines that create precision parts for products, including water pumps.[1]

Technology has been driving the shift in Canada from "brawn to brain," as shift to a service-based economy. From 2003–2013, goods-producing industries experienced 1.1 percent job loss (with growth concentrated in Alberta), while services-producing industries experienced almost 18 percent job growth.[2] According to the Department of Finance Canada, high skilled, high wage, and private sector employment has been the main source of job creation post 2008.[3]

EVIDENCE-BASED HR

Several things account for this. With global competition, more manufacturing jobs have moved to low-wage countries. Kellogg's, Heinz, and Daimler moved manufacturing operations out of the country.[4] Furthermore, higher productivity enables manufacturers to produce more with fewer workers. Just-in-time manufacturing techniques link daily manufacturing schedules more precisely to customer demand, reducing inventory needs. As manufacturers integrate Internet-based customer ordering with just-in-time manufacturing, scheduling becomes more precise.

For example, when a customer orders a Dell computer, the same Internet message that informs Dell's factory to produce the order also signals the screen and keyboard makers to prepare for a courier to pick up their parts. The net effect is that manufacturers have been squeezing slack and inefficiencies out of production, enabling companies to produce more products with fewer employees. In North America and much of Europe, manufacturing jobs are down, service jobs up, and the manufacturing jobs that remain are increasingly high technology oriented.

Information and Communication Technology (ICT)

The use of computers and the Internet is present in all sectors of the economy in Canada, transforming businesses in the way in which work is completed. Canada spends about 6 percent of its GDP on ICT, which triples the world average.[5] Various research studies demonstrate the positive impact of computer technology productivity of the employee within the firm, although the magnitude of the impact varies by study.

ICT increases workers' flexibility, and the degree of integration between various functional areas. It also decreases the degree of centralization in the organization, resulting in a flattening of organizational structures. This decentralization is perceived to increase efficiency. In addition, computer use provides management with up-to-date information about products, processes, and market conditions, enabling quick decision-making and a focus on quality.

However, not all use of technology in the workplace is positive. Employees can receive interruptions every day, from instant messages, texts, emails, phone, and Skype, which can be distracting for some employees, thereby reducing productivity and resulting in longer hours of work. These distractions may be work based or personal. A survey conducted by salary.com found that 64 percent of respondents admitted to wasting time at work on a daily basis. The Internet was the biggest time waster, including accessing personal websites while at work, new sites, social media, online shopping, or other nonwork-related websites. Respondents of the survey identified that they wasted time due to a lack of incentive, job dissatisfaction, or sheer boredom.[6]

There has been a large focus also on work–life balance in Canada, given that technology has blurred the lines between personal and professional space. Employees may be expected to work remotely, respond to emails immediately outside of regular

HR Competency

90500

---

expert
opinion
academic viewpoint

Dr. Jorge Niosi

Identification: Dr. Jorge Niosi (PhD, FRSC), Professor and Canada Research Chair on the Management of Technology

Affiliation: Department of Management and Technology, Université du Québec à Montréal

1. Where are the IT clusters in Canada today? What are some common attributes of these clusters?

There are four major clusters (Greater Toronto Area, Montréal, Ottawa, Vancouver metropolitan regions) and some smaller ones. The Toronto and Montréal clusters are less specialized, serving multiple industries. The smaller clusters like Hamilton, Calgary, Québec City, Edmonton, Saskatchewan, Regina, and Victoria are focused on specific industries such as oil and gas, ICT, machinery, biotech, or finance software. Combined, the major IT clusters account for 80 percent of

Canadian industrial research and development spending.

2. Given that universities, government labs, and innovative firms are considered the core of a National System of Innovation (NSI), what are innovative firms and/or government agencies doing to develop talent pipelines from the Universities?

The government has introduced several incentives and policies to assist with the development of talent. Some policies are horizontal, such as tax breaks for research and development (R&D), which allow the company to spend the R&D funding more liberally; however, Revenue Canada Inspectors can audit expenses associated with R&D. Other government programs (like the Strategic Aerospace and Defense Initiative plan for at least $500 million a year) are focused largely on industry-specific issues. There are also non-reimbursable loans available to small and medium enterprises (SMEs). There is the National Research Council (NRC), a set of government institutes in Ottawa and other cities. If a SME has an idea for a new process or product, they can work with the NRC to develop the product and/or process, then access support via funds or expertise required to bring the innovation to the market.

There also university grants available for things such as biotech, or nanotech or software. These grants focus on what's done in a university environment and help transfer or commercialize the new research.

In addition, there are a number of incentives available for student development, including government and industry support for programs and transfer of graduates to careers within industry.

3. What internal factors are required to enable organizational adaption to technological changes?

The technical competency of an organization is critical to success in regard to technical change. They must understand what's going on outside of the organization to help build networks with governments, and universities, and incorporate technical change. In order to succeed, they must be able to appreciate the language of the networks, and build bridges or ask questions or know who to contact to request more information. The concept of seeing technology as being bigger than just an organizational issue triggers a recognition of the need to cooperate, organize networks, and request government funding, where appropriate.

The ideal candidate usually has one or two academic degrees (usually in engineering, science, or technology), they can understand technical terms sufficiently, and they keep track to technical trends in industry. A good manager should also be able to find information and use it correctly, often partnering within Canada or outside Canada when needed.

Source: Reprinted by permission from Dr. Jorge Niosi.

working hours, or have no clarity as to what regular working hours might be. As we will discuss in the Occupational Health & Safety chapter, work–life balance is a major stressor that impacts employees' short-term and long-term productivity. Technology is a major catalyst in people feeling that expectations are unrealistic, high levels of job stress, and frustration with the employer, as highlighted in the Expert Opinion box, as per the perspective from the Canada Research Chair on the Management of Technology.[7]

Knowledge Work and Human Capital

In general, therefore, jobs require more education and more skills. For example, we saw that automation and just-in-time manufacturing mean that even manufacturing jobs require more reading, math, and communication skills.[8]

human capital The knowledge, education, training, skills, and expertise of a firm's workers.

For employers, this means relying more on knowledge workers and therefore on *human capital*.[9] **Human capital** refers to the knowledge, skills, and abilities of a firm's workers.[10] Today, as management guru Peter Drucker predicted years ago, "the center of gravity in employment is moving fast from manual and clerical workers to knowledge workers."[11] Human resource managers now list "critical thinking/problem solving" and "information technology application" as the two skills most likely to increase in importance over the next few years.[12]

HUMAN RESOURCES MANAGEMENT AND TECHNOLOGY

When new employees are hired, they are required to provide information such as first and last name, address, emergency contacts, banking information, beneficiary information for pension and benefits, marital status, and social insurance number on a variety of HR and employment-related forms. The HR by the Numbers box highlights the prevalence and use of technology-enabled delivery of HR.

HR by the Numbers

Technology Enabled Delivery of HR[14]

10% of companies in a 32 country, 1025 company survey identify that they use mobile HR applications

59% of the 1025 companies surveyed offer an HR portal to employees

106 000 additional workers will be required in the Information and Communications Technology (ICT) sector from 2011–2016, according to the Information Technology Association of Canada

40% of research and development (R&D) spending by Canada's business sector is spent on activities associated with ICT

4% forecasted increase in ICT spending in Canada annually

75% of the ICT workforce is male

These are data, and HR has always been the custodian of this data. How the data are used, the type of data collected, how the data are updated, where the data are stored, and the type of system used to collect the data has changed over time, but the need to collect the information relating to hiring, promoting, and terminating employees has not changed. However, the systems that HR uses to capture this data and the importance that HR now places on technology have fundamentally changed. According to a report from Towers Perrin, even in today's uncertain economic times, a third of global organizations are increasing their investments in HR technology while half have maintained their budgets.[13]

This chapter starts with explaining the strategic importance of technology in HRM. Changes to the role of HR professionals because of their increasing use of technology and the new key competencies that HR professionals must exhibit to deliver superior service to employees will be discussed. Then the role of human resources information systems in managing the human capital of an organization will be reviewed, including web-based electronic HR. Finally, trends in HR and technology will be discussed.

Technology permeates business life today.

Rawpixel/Fotolia

THE STRATEGIC IMPORTANCE OF TECHNOLOGY IN HRM

HR technology can be defined as any technology that is used to attract, hire, retain and maintain talent, support workforce administration, and optimize workforce management.[15] This technology can be found in different types of human resource information systems (HRIS), can be used by various stakeholders, such as managers, employees, and HR professionals, and can be accessed in different ways, such as via the company intranet.

HR technology Any technology that is used to attract, hire, retain and maintain talent, support workforce administration, and optimize workforce management.

There is no doubt that technology has made it easier and faster to gather, collate, and deliver information and to communicate with employees. More importantly, it has the potential to reduce the administrative burden on the HR department members so they are able to focus on more meaningful HR activities, such as providing line managers with the appropriate decision-making tools that will enable managers to make more effective HR-related decisions.[16] Research indicates that companies who use technology effectively to manage their HR functions are more effective than those that do not.[17] Perhaps not surprisingly, Google is using technology in an innovative way to help manage employee retention, as discussed in the Strategic HR box.

Over the next decade, there will be significant pressures on the HR department to manage costs and deliver effective and efficient services. Being responsive and providing service 24/7, 365 days a year across an organization's global networks is the new norm.[18]

A strong strategic relationship between HR and technology will enable HR to achieve three key objectives:

1. *strategic alignment* with business objectives
2. *business intelligence*—providing users with relevant data
3. *effectiveness and efficiency*—changing how HR work is performed by reducing lead times and costs, and increasing service levels[19]

STRATEGIC HR

Google Tackles Retention Issues with "Predictive Attrition"

Google has worked hard to keep its employees happy. But it is facing some retention challenges as several senior people reportedly have departed in the past year. In response, Google has intensified its efforts in the area of "predictive attrition" to "find situations that may increase the likelihood of some Googlers leaving the company so that managers and HR staff can work on avoiding those very situations," said Wendy Rozeluk of global communications and public affairs at Google Canada in Toronto.

Google is not providing specific details about its analysis, but the algorithm looks at data from employees who have left the company, studying factors such as where people work, team size, and compensation. The tool analyzes less obvious factors that may contribute to the decision to leave the company but identifies groups versus specific people at risk of leaving. For example, are tenured, high-performing engineers in North America more likely to stay or leave than junior ones in Europe?

"As anyone who has observed Google over the years knows, we're serious about keeping our employees happy," said Rozeluk. "What we were looking for was general trends that might indicate an increased likelihood that someone might leave."

The expectations are high for HR. Achievement of these objectives will require HR professionals to be very effective at leveraging technology to reduce the time spent on administrative and legal compliance work so that it can focus on delivering strategic services.[20] Demonstrating that HR is adding value to the bottom line continues to be a major challenge for HR. A Mercer survey suggested that over 60 percent of chief financial officers continue to view HR as a cost centre that focuses primarily on executing administrative and compliance functions, and that only 15 percent of them reported that HR was focused on strategic activities.[21]

HR Competency

90100

THE IMPACT OF TECHNOLOGY ON THE ROLE OF HR

The impact of technology has fundamentally changed the HR role. It has enabled HR to decrease its involvement in transactional (administrative) activities and to increase its focus on how to improve its delivery of strategic services. As a result, seven core competencies have emerged that are critical to the development of the HR professional, as shown in **Figure 3.1**. Wayne Brockbank and David Ulrich from the University of Michigan Business School identified five key competencies for HR,[22] and a study by Mercer highlighted two additional competencies.[23] These competencies are mastery of HR technology, strategic contribution, business knowledge, personal credibility, data management, financial management, and HR service delivery.

HR Competency

20700

The traditional HR role has changed in three major ways as a result of the technologically enabled environment: (1) deceased transactional activities, (2) increased client/customer focus, and (3) increased delivery of strategic services.

FIGURE 3.1 Emerging Role of the HR Professional: Seven Key Competencies

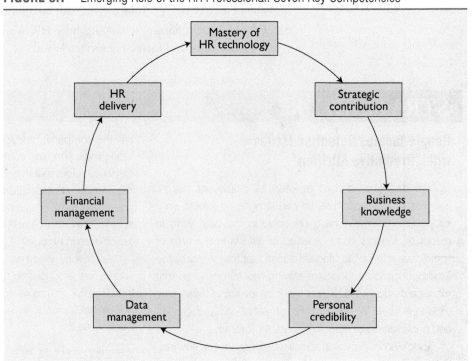

Source: Julie Bulmash, 2009.

Decreased Transactional Activities

Technology enables the reduction of the administrative burden, resulting in lowering basic transaction costs. Proactive HR professionals leverage technology to improve the design and delivery of basic HR services. In order to do so, HR professionals develop business knowledge with respect to the key drivers of organizational productivity and become cognizant of costs associated with enhancing efficiencies and effectiveness of the workforce. Reducing administrative and compliance activities through automation is considered necessary if HR is going to liberate itself from these day-to-day activities. Selecting the appropriate technology and ensuring that it is deployed appropriately are very important activities to ensure the organization can meet its goals. A survey published by the Society of Human Resource Management indicated that technical skills such as software and Internet literacy, as well as database skills, are considered most important for the HR specialist to develop.[24]

Increased Client/Customer Focus

In organizations, HR deals with many internal customers, including managers, employees, and all the other departments in the organization. These customers expect HR to understand and respond to their requests quickly, reduce bureaucracy, and provide information that is meaningful, useful, and accurate. In today's economic climate, there is a significant need for HR professionals to understand the financial side of organizations, in particular how to help the organization control its people costs.

Managers expect HR to understand their key business issues and to provide relevant and meaningful information to help them make better decisions. For example, managers are responsible for creating and maintaining their staffing budgets. Information about the number of employees who quit or were terminated or the numbers of maternity and other planned leaves is important to help the manager plan more effectively.

Today's employees expect responsiveness, flexibility, and access to information 24/7. To be effective, HR must understand how technology can best meet the needs of their customers. When these stakeholders become more comfortable with the fact that HR is listening and cares about their needs, they will gain respect for HR and trust HR. This trust will lead them to sharing their concerns to a greater degree and trusting HR with their data requirements.

A significant partner of HR is the information technology (IT) department. The next section will focus on how HR can develop a good working relationship with this critical group.

HR and the IT Department: Developing Good Working Relationships

If HR is going to gain credibility with the IT department and work effectively, it must demonstrate its knowledge of and respect for the IT discipline. Specifically, it is important for HR to exhibit knowledge of different types of HR systems, technology delivery methods, best practices of other organizations, and the types of technology enhancements that set these organizations apart. For example, when AT&T long distance services decided to implement an HR/payroll system, HR met with several different vendors to explore the functionalities of the different systems and worked with a team of IT professionals to help them make an informed decision.

In order for HR to build this technological knowledge, they can seek out learning opportunities such as trade shows, meetings with software vendors, formal courses in IT, and reading material about technological trends and issues. Not only will HR practitioners be able to speak the language of IT, but they will also gain a greater understanding of the IT discipline and the challenges facing IT professionals.[25]

HUMAN RESOURCES INFORMATION SYSTEMS (HRIS)

There are over 140 human resources information systems being offered by over a hundred vendors in the United States and Canada.[26] The costs of implementing such a system range from $1000 to $12 million.[27] Licensing fees cost anywhere from three to eight times the cost of the software licence for implementation costs.[28]

Not all companies have the latest and greatest technology, nor do all companies need the most advanced technology. However, all companies do have HR-related information needs. The information needs of a small company with 40 employees may only require the use of a simple Microsoft Word or Microsoft Excel file to keep basic employee data. A company with 3000 employees manages a greater volume of data, which can be daunting without a more sophisticated tool to store and retrieve data.

human resources information system (HRIS) Integrated systems used to gather, store, and analyze information regarding an organization's human resources.

Also referred to as human resources management systems (HRMS) in the literature,[29] **human resources information systems (HRIS)** can be defined as integrated systems used to gather, store, and analyze information regarding an organization's human resources.[30] These systems consist of software applications that work in conjunction with an electronic database.[31] HRIS enable HR professionals to collaborate with the organization to ensure efficiency and effectiveness of the workforce, become more customer focused, and align their activities to the business plan, thus contributing to the bottom line. Using HRIS technology can help HR automate and simplify tasks, reduce administration and record keeping, and provide management with data and resources.

All these systems have different functionalities (or capabilities) and some are much more complex than others, but they all provide a repository for information/data to be stored and maintained. HRIS possess varying degrees of reporting capability. However, the system must transform basic data into information that is meaningful to managers. This is a challenge facing HR departments today and will ultimately determine whether HR is able to deliver strategic HR services. Much of the data now available to HR comes from a **data warehouse**—a specialized type of database that is optimized for reporting and analysis and is the raw material for managers' decision support.[32]

data warehouse A specialized type of database that is optimized for reporting and analysis and is the raw material for managers' decision support.

HR Competency
90300

The Relationship between HRM and HRIS

HRIS is the composite of databases, computer applications, hardware, and software necessary to collect, record, store, manage, deliver, manipulate, and present data regarding human resources.[33] It is primarily a transaction processor, editor, and record keeper, maintaining employee, organizational, and HR-related data.[34] Its primary function is to provide information to its clients, such as employees, managers, payroll staff, and HR professionals. It is important to note that the term "systems" refers not just to the technical hardware and software. From an HR perspective, "systems" is about the people, policies, procedures, and data required to manage the HR function. In reality, computer technology is not the key to being successful at managing HR information; what it does do well is provide a very useful tool for "operationalizing" the information, making it easier to obtain and disseminate information and ensuring that the information is specific to the organization's HR policies and practices.[35]

An HRIS must allow for the assimilation and integration of HR policies and procedures in addition to operating the computer hardware and software applications.[36] For example, a simple business rule—promotional raises are not to exceed 8 percent of salary—can easily be programmed into the system.

Enhancing Decision-Making: Decision Support Systems

The ability to extract data from the HRIS and use this data not just for information purposes but to improve the quality of decisions made by managers and HR professionals has become important in the effective management of human capital.[37] It is not only a matter of interpreting the data but also using the data within a meaningful context to help managers and HR professionals make effective business decisions.

It is not uncommon for managers to request reports from the HRIS. For example, a manager might be responsible for his or her own salary budget and, when it comes time for annual increases, managers are typically asked to recommend appropriate salary increases for their employees based on their budgets. In order to make a quality decision, the manager might need to confirm each employee's current salary, look at the history of salary increases, review compensation policies, and review the employees' performance history. To make the most informed decision, the manager needs information that is relevant, useful, timely, and accurate.

metrics (workforce analytics)
Statistical measures of the impact of HRM practices on the performance of an organization's human capital.

Metrics, also known as **workforce analytics**, are statistical measures of the impact of HRM practices on the performance of an organization's human capital. An example of a metric is the cost of the HR department per employee, calculated as the total cost of the HR department for a given period of time divided by the total number of employees employed during that time. Metrics can help managers identify opportunities to improve performance and control costs. There are many possible metrics to use, and they are chosen by identifying key HR issues, gathering data from HR and other areas, setting applicable standards for rigour, and ensuring relevance.[38] Leading-edge organizations have adopted metrics/workforce analytics and are using sophisticated HRIS capabilities to generate relevant and high-quality data. An example in the area of health and safety is obtaining HRIS data on the number of accidents and injuries and also on the causes of these injuries. Knowing the causes will enable HR to develop the applicable policies and practices to reduce the number of health and safety problems.[39]

HR Competency
90500

Effective HR departments use precision data analysis to aid managers in effective decision-making. This ability to contribute to decisions has enabled HR to demonstrate that the effective management of human capital can have a significant and measurable impact on a company's bottom line.[40] **Figure 3.2** summarizes the main user groups for the HRIS and the key information provided to each group.

FIGURE 3.2 HRIS Users

	Employee*	Manager	HR
Record and maintain	✓	✓	✓
Compliance			✓
Forecasting and planning		✓	✓
Talent management/ knowledge management	✓	✓	✓
Strategic		✓	✓
Decision making	✓	✓	✓

*Employee is only able to record and maintain data in the HRIS if it is web-enabled.

Source: Julie Bulmash, 2009.

Strategic Alignment

Information from the system can help organizations align more effectively with their strategic plans. For example, if an organization's plan was to enter into a new market and it required a certain number and type of employees, the data from the system can provide the manager with a barometer as to whether the organization is moving toward the goal and the manager can leverage the information on the skills employees possess to help the organization effectively obtain the goal.

Strategy and Strategy-Based Metrics   Benchmarking provides only one perspective on how your company's human resource management system is performing.[41] It shows how your human resource management system's performance compares to the competition. However, it may *not* reveal the extent to which your firm's HR practices are supporting its strategic goals. For example, if the strategy calls for doubling profits by improving customer service, to what extent are your new training practices helping to improve customer service?

Managers use *strategy-based metrics* to answer such questions. **Strategy-based metrics** focus on measuring the activities that contribute to achieving a company's strategic aims.[42] Thus, for a hotel, the strategic HR metrics might include 100 percent employee testing, 80 percent guest returns, incentive pay as a percent of total salaries, and sales up 50 percent. If changes in HR practices such as increased training and better incentives have their intended effects, then strategic metrics like guest returns and guest compliments should also rise.

Such analyses often employ data-mining techniques. Data mining sifts through huge amounts of employee data to identify correlations that employers then use to improve their employee selection and other practices. **Data mining** is "the set of activities used to find new, hidden, or unexpected patterns in data."[43] Data-mining systems use tools like statistical analysis to sift through data looking for relationships. Department stores often use data mining.

strategy-based metrics Metrics that specifically focus on measuring the activities that contribute to achieving a company's strategic aims.

EVIDENCE-BASED **HR**

Data mining Algorithmic assessment of vast amounts of employee data to identify correlations that employers then use to improve their employee-selection and other practices.

HR Competency

90200

THE MAJOR COMPONENTS OF AN HRIS

There are several different generic subsystems that comprise an HRIS[44] administration, recruitment, time and attendance, training and development, pension administration, employment equity, performance evaluation, compensation and benefit administration, organization management, health and safety, labour relations, and payroll, as shown in **Figure 3.3**.

HR Administration

The day-to-day minutiae of maintaining and updating employee records take an enormous amount of time. One study found that 71 percent of HR employees' time was devoted to transactional tasks like checking leave balances, maintaining address records, and monitoring employee benefits distributions.[45] HRIS packages substitute powerful computerized processing for a wide range of the firm's HR transactions.

HR information systems also facilitate employee self-processing. For example, at Provident Bank, the benefits system Benelogic lets employees self-enroll in all their desired benefits programs over the Internet at a secure site. It also "support[s] employees' quest for 'what if' information relating to, for example, the impact on their take-home pay of various benefits options."[46] That's all work that HR employees would previously have had to do for Provident's employees.

FIGURE 3.3   HRIS Subsystems

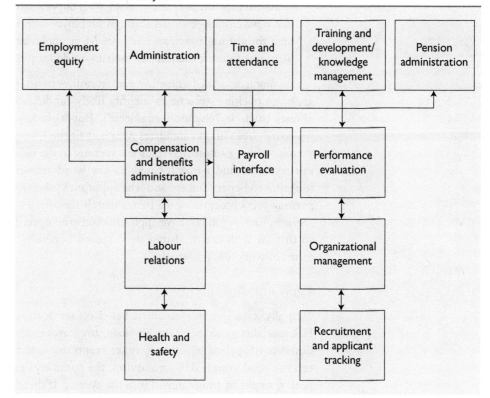

Source: Julie Bulmash, 2006.

HR Competency

HR Competency
20600

HR Competency
90400

narstudio/Fotolia

HRIS can provide information regarding metrics, but transferring the metrics and information to actionable HR activities is an essential function of the HR team.

By integrating numerous individual HR tasks (training records, appraisals, employee personal data, and so on), the HRIS improves HR's reporting capabilities. For example, reports might be available (company-wide and by department) for healthcare cost per employee, pay and benefits as a percent of operating expense, cost per hire, report on training, volunteer turnover rates, turnover costs, time to fill jobs, and return on human capital invested (in terms of training and education fees, for instance).

Recruitment and Applicant Tracking

As an example of why to use metrics, consider that most employers spend thousands of dollars (or more) recruiting employees, without measuring which hiring source produces the best candidates. The logical solution is to assess recruitment effectiveness using measures or metrics. Metrics here might include quality of new hires and which recruitment sources produce the most new hires.[47]

One way to track and analyze such data is by using a computerized **applicant tracking system** (ATS). ATS vendors include Authoria, PeopleFilter, Wonderlic, eContinuum, and PeopleClick. Regardless of the vendor, analyzing recruitment effectiveness using ATS software involves two basic steps:

applicant tracking systems (ATS) Online systems that help employers attract, gather, screen, compile, and manage applicants.

- First, the employer (and vendor) decides how to measure the performance of new hires. For example, with Authoria's system, hiring managers input their evaluations of each new hire at the end of the employee's first 90 days, using a 1-to-5 scale.[48]

- Second, the applicant tracking system then enables the employer to track the recruitment sources that correlate with superior hires. It may show, for instance, that new employees hired through employee referrals stay longer and work better than those from newspaper ads do. Most applicant tracking systems enable hiring managers to track such hiring metrics on desktop dashboards.

Intelligent automated resumé screening is another trend. Employers have long used online applicant tracking software to identify likely candidates based on resumé key words or phrases (such as "chemical engineer"). But basic key word screens like these won't necessarily zero in on candidates who best fit the hiring employer and job. Vendors are therefore taking automated resumé screening to the next level. For example, rather than just trying to find a match based on key words, monster.com's 6Sense resumé search tool aims to better "understand" the applicant's job preferences (based on things like the person's job history) so as to better match the applicant with the available job. Other services, such as Jobfox, have applicants and employers complete detailed questionnaires so that (as with online dating sites) there's hopefully a better match, for instance in terms of work–life preferences.

Time and Attendance

Typically, vacation entitlement is based on service. To calculate this information the HR specialist would need the hire date, any leaves of absence (paid or unpaid), termination date (if applicable), and any other events that interrupted service. This information can be found in an HRIS. In addition, the company's policy (such as a "use it or lose it" policy) might be programmed into the system. If there are any special rules, this information is also programmed into the system; for example, employees often continue to accumulate vacation on certain types of leaves.

Other data that can be found with respect to time and attendance include information on absenteeism (the number of days an employee was absent), leaves of absence, whether these leaves were sabbatical or personal, parental leaves, and the dates the employee started and ended the leave. Policy details would be programmed; for example, some companies have a policy that states that, if an employee is absent for more than a certain number of days, his or her pay is decreased by a certain amount. **Figure 3.4** shows a related screen from a popular HRIS from PeopleSoft, whose subsystem is called the Enterprise Time and Labour system.

FIGURE 3.4 PeopleSoft Enterprise Time and Labour Screen

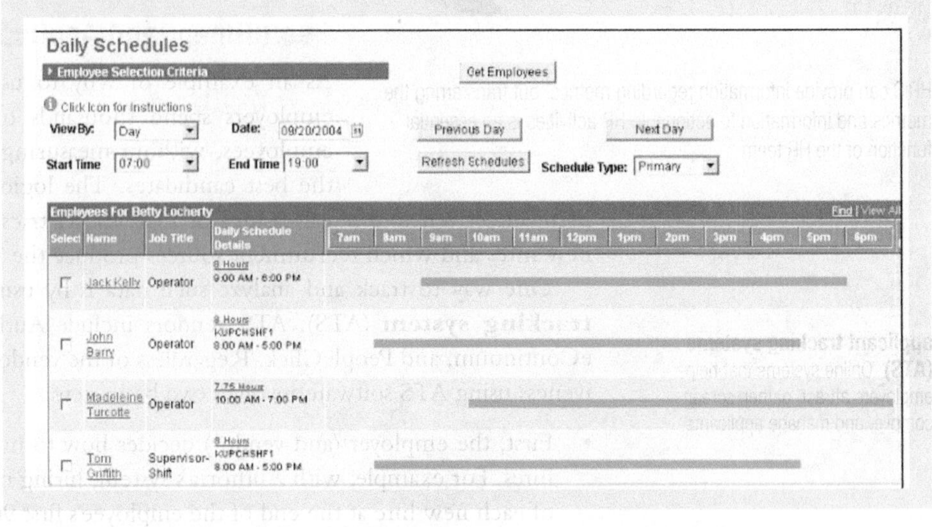

Source: Reproduced with permission of Oracle.

Training and Development/Knowledge Management

Employers use Internet-based learning to deliver almost all the types of training. A **learning portal** is a section of an employer's website that offers employees online access to training courses. Many employers arrange to have an online training vendor make its courses available via the employer's portal. Most often, the employer contracts with applications service providers (ASPs). Here, when employees go to their firm's learning portal, they actually access the menu of training courses that the ASP offers for the employer. A Google search for e-learning companies reveals many, such as SkillSoft, Plateau Systems, and Employment Law Learning Technologies.

Learning management systems (LMS) are special software tools that support Internet training by helping employers identify training needs, and to schedule, deliver, assess, and manage the online training itself. Blackboard and WebCT are two familiar college-oriented learning management systems. General Motors uses a LMS to help its dealers in Africa and the Middle East deliver training. The Internet-based LMS includes a course catalog, supervisor approved self-enrollment, and pre- and post-course tests. The system automatically schedules the individual's training.[49]

Many employers integrate the LMS with the company's talent management systems. That way, skills inventories and succession plans automatically update as employees complete their training.[50] Online learning doesn't necessarily teach individuals faster or better. In one review, web-based instruction was a bit more effective than classroom instruction for teaching memory of facts and principles; web-based instruction and classroom instruction were equally effective for teaching information about how to perform a task or action.[51] But, of course, the need to teach large numbers of students remotely, or to enable trainees to study at their leisure, often makes e-learning the logical choice.[52]

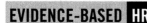

Pension Administration

For organizations that sponsor retirement plans for their employees, information necessary to produce annual pension statements will be recorded. This data includes date of plan entry, normal retirement date, employee elections regarding contributions, and the annual company contribution.

Employment Equity Information

Federally regulated organizations are responsible for annual reporting of their employment equity information to the government. Ensuring data integrity and accuracy is very important and a key responsibility of the HR professional. For example, organizations that are subject to employment equity legislation are required to file an annual report. These reports can be generated with ease if this information has been recorded and maintained appropriately. Some HRIS software interfaces directly with the Workplace Equity Information Management System (WEIMS) provided by the government.[53] In this case, the information from the HRIS can be downloaded directly into the required reporting system.

Performance Evaluation

Employers increasingly use computerized or Internet-based appraisal systems. These enable managers to compile computerized notes on subordinates during the year, and then to merge these with ratings for the employee on several performance traits. The software presents written examples to support part of the appraisal. Most such appraisals combine several appraisal methods, usually graphic ratings anchored by critical incidents.[54]

For example, Employee Appraiser (developed by the Austin-Hayne Corporation, San Mateo, California) presents a menu of evaluation dimensions, including dependability, initiative, communication, decision-making, leadership, judgment, and planning and productivity.[55] Within each dimension (such as "Communication") are separate performance factors for things like writing, verbal communication, and receptivity to criticism. When the user clicks on a performance factor, he or she is presented with a graphic rating scale. However, instead of numerical ratings, "Employee Appraiser" uses behaviourally anchored examples. Thus, for *verbal communication* there are six choices, ranging from "presents ideas clearly" to "lacks structure." The manager chooses the phrase that most accurately describes the worker. Then "Employee Appraiser" generates an appraisal with sample text.

Compensation and Benefits Administration

The HRIS includes information regarding the company's compensation and benefits plans and its policies relating to these plans. For example, information can include the pay increase associated with a promotion, data regarding pay grades and ranges for each position, the bonus structure, and which positions are entitled to a bonus. In addition, information can be entered regarding the type of benefit plans, whether there is a cost-sharing arrangement, and how it would change if an employee took an unpaid leave. A survey of over 182 companies by Watson Wyatt found that one in five expect to change their HR service delivery systems. The most commonly planned changes are implementing a healthcare portal that provides employees with health improvement information (73 percent) and offering total compensation information to employees via the web (65 percent).[56]

Organization Management

This subsystem identifies the organizational structure and stores job descriptions for each position in the structure. It can also link the positions/jobs to specific workers. It may also have a field to enter the National Occupational Classification (NOC) codes. Department managers or owners of smaller firms often use manual devices to track employee qualifications. Thus, a *personnel inventory and development record form* compiles qualifications information on each employee. The information includes education, company-sponsored courses taken, career and development interests, languages, desired assignments, and skills. **Personnel replacement charts** are another option, particularly for the firm's top positions. They show the present performance and promotability for each position's potential replacement. As an alternative, you can develop a **position replacement card**. For this you create a card for each position, showing possible replacements as well as their present performance, promotion potential, and training.

Health and Safety

Managers should routinely inspect for problems using safety audit/ checklists as aids. Also, investigate all accidents and "near misses." Set up employee safety committees to evaluate safety adequacy, conduct and monitor safety audits, and suggest ways for improving safety.[57] Managers expedite safety audits by using personal digital assistants.[58] For example, Process and Performance Measurement (PPM) is a Windows application for designing and completing safety audit questionnaires. To use this application, the manager gives the safety audit a name, enters the audit questions, and lists possible answers. Typical questions for a fire extinguisher audit might include, "Are fire extinguishers clearly identified and accessible?" and "Are only

"According to these advanced formulas ... we are way underpaid."

cartoonresource/Fotolia

HR IN THE NEWS

Payroll Hero Expands Internationally

British Columbia, Canada and Manila, the Philippines–based PayrollHero announced that Krispy Kreme donuts will be using its HRIS system to track attendance, scheduling, analytics, and payroll in more than 40 of its locations. During the 2008 financial crisis, the company explored the Philippines for outsourcing of customer service, when it realized the business opportunity to automate HR functions abroad. In 2014, half of the company's clients were in the Philippines.[59]

approved fire extinguishers used in the workplace?"[60] The supervisor or employee then uses his or her PDA to record the audit and transmit it to the firm's safety office.

Evidence-based safety and security-related metrics to audit would include, for instance, injury and illness rates, workers' compensation cost per employee, at-risk behaviour reduction, and safety training exercises.[61] To ensure that the audit results in improvements, *trend the audit data* (for instance, to see if accident rates are rising or falling or steady) and *track the corrective actions* through to completion.[62]

HR Competency

20600

Labour Relations

Information such as union membership, seniority lists, grievances, and resolutions can be found in this subsystem.

Payroll Interface

Payroll administration is one of the first functions most employers computerize or outsource, and for good reason. Administering the payroll system—keeping track of each employee's worker status, wage rate, dependents, benefits, overtime, tax status, and so on; computing each paycheck; and then directing the actual printing of checks or direct deposits—is a time-consuming task, one complicated by the need to comply with many different employment law and jurisdictions. The HR in the News box highlights a Canadian-based payroll company that recently experienced success with international expansion.

WHAT ARE HR AUDITS?

HR audit An analysis by which an organization measures where it currently stands and determines what it has to accomplish to improve its HR functions.

Human resource managers often collect data on matters such as employee turnover and safety via *human resource audits*. One practitioner calls an **HR audit** "an analysis by which an organization measures where it currently stands and determines what it has to accomplish to improve its HR function."[63] The HR audit generally involves reviewing the company's human resource functions (recruiting, testing, training, and so on), usually using a checklist, as well as ensuring that the firm is adhering to regulations, laws, and company policies.

In conducting the HR audit, managers often benchmark their results to those of comparable companies. Sample measures (metrics) might include the ratio of HR professionals per 100 company employees. HR audits vary in scope and focus. Typical areas audited include:[64]

1. roles and headcount (including job descriptions, and employees categorized by exempt/nonexempt and full- or part-time)

2. compliance with federal, state, and local employment-related legislation

3. recruitment and selection (including use of selection tools, background checks, and so on)

4. compensation (policies, incentives, survey procedures, and so on)

5. employee relations (union agreements, performance management, disciplinary procedures, employee recognition)

6. mandated benefits (Social Security, unemployment insurance, workers' compensation, and so on)

7. group benefits (insurance, time off, flexible benefits, and so on)

8. payroll (such as legal compliance)

9. documentation and record keeping; for example, do our files contain information including résumés and applications, offer letters, job descriptions, performance evaluations, benefit enrollment forms, payroll change notices, and documentation related to personnel actions such as employee handbook acknowledgments?[65]

10. training and development (new employee orientation, workforce development, technical and safety, career planning, and so on)

11. employee communications (employee handbook, newsletter, recognition programs)

12. termination and transition policies and practices

Talent Management

Managers use special workforce (or talent) analytics software tools to convert their workforce data into actionable information. Analytics improves performance. For example, human resource consulting firms such as Aon Hewitt will compile a client's employee data. Its analytics engine then analyzes this data and presents it to the client through a web-based portal. Dashboards then enable managers to identify workforce trends, and to answer questions such as "Are there trends we should further analyze in the turnover data?"

A talent analytics team at Google analyzed data on employee backgrounds, capabilities, and performance.[66] The team was able to identify the factors (such as an employee feeling underutilized) likely to lead to the employee leaving. In a similar project, Google analyzed data on things like employee survey feedback to identify the attributes of successful Google managers. Microsoft identified correlations among the schools and companies that the employees arrived from and the employees' subsequent performance. This enabled Microsoft to improve its recruitment and selection practices.[67] Software company SAS's employee-retention program sifts through employee data on traits like skills, tenure, performance, education, and friendships. The program can predict which high-value employees are more likely to quit in the near future.[68]

Alliant Techsystems created a "flight risk model" to calculate the probability an employee would leave. This enabled it to predict high turnover and to take corrective action.[69] IBM uses workforce analytics to identify employees who are "idea leaders" to whom other employees frequently turn for advice (for instance, based on e "mentions" by colleagues).[70] One study compared high- and low-performance organizations' use of HR analytics. Eighty-one percent of the high-performing organizations gave HR leaders such workforce data, compared with 33 percent of the low-performing ones.[71]

Employers are using talent analytics to answer six types of talent management questions:[72]

Human capital facts. For example, "What are the key indicators of my organization's overall health?" JetBlue found that one such key indicator was employee engagement, in that it correlated with financial performance.

Analytical HR. For example, "Which units, departments, or individuals need attention?" Lockheed Martin collects performance data in order to identify units needing improvement.

Human capital investment analysis. For example, "Which actions have the greatest impact on my business?" By monitoring employee satisfaction levels, Cisco was able to improve its employee-retention rate from 65 percent to 85 percent, saving the company nearly US$50 million in recruitment, selection, and training costs.

Workforce forecasts. Dow Chemical uses a computerized model. This predicts future required headcount for each business unit based on predictions for things like sales trends.

Talent value model. For example, "Why do employees choose to stay with—or leave—my company?" For instance, Google was able to anticipate when an employee felt underutilized and was preparing to quit, thus reducing turnover costs.

Talent supply chain. For example, "How should my workforce needs adapt to changes in the business environment?" Thus, retail companies can use special analytical models to predict daily store volume and release hourly employees early.

SELECTING AND IMPLEMENTING AN HRIS

Organizations can choose from many different systems in all sorts of sizes and with varying degrees of functionality and sophistication. The choice of technology revolves around two basic questions: (1) What is the desired amount of customization? and (2) What type of system is required/preferred? Organizations can decide whether they want to purchase a standard system and adapt their internal processes to align with the system, develop a proprietary system, or customize a modular software system to fit the organization's existing processes. Some of the criteria that may affect this decision are the cost of the system, the number of employees, the degree of efficiency, and the company's existing hardware and software. Regardless of the type of system selected, the key reasons for purchase are generally cost savings, faster processing of information, and access to relevant information that will help the organization achieve its goals.[73]

Types of HRIS

An effective HRIS matches its technical capabilities with the needs of the organization. These needs typically increase with the size of the organization.[74] Smaller firms might use very generic software applications such as Microsoft Excel and Access. These firms might only require payroll and benefits administration, time and attendance reporting, and an employee scheduling function.

Mid-sized firms typically require compliance tracking and reporting, health claims administration, payroll, and compensation and benefits administration. Managers may require information on performance appraisal, time and attendance, succession planning, skills testing, and employee scheduling. Employees may use the system to aid in career development. Mid-sized firms require greater data integration, and the systems will have better backup and recovery capability. They will also allow for many users. In mid-sized systems, all HRIS functions typically flow through one single system so data redundancies can be identified and eliminated.

Large organizations typically require greater functionality than mid-sized firms. In addition to those functions mentioned above, these firms will require employee screening, résumé processing and tracking, and additional compliance and reporting requirements like employment equity. They may also require self-service options, which are web-based applications that enable managers and employees to access and manage information directly without having to go through HR or the manager.

The type of HRIS they might require can be part of a larger **enterprise-wide or enterprise resource planning (ERP) system** that supports enterprise-wide or cross-functional requirements rather than a single department within the organization.[75] These systems originated from software that integrated information from the organization's functional areas (finance, marketing, operations, and so on) into one universal database so that financial information could be linked to marketing information and so on. An enterprise-wide system typically includes several HR modules, such as a payroll module and a training and development module. These systems vary with respect to cost, functionality, and robustness, so depending on the organization's requirements, some systems will be more appropriate than others.

HR technology can also be provided by a **stand-alone system**, meaning a self-contained system that does not rely on other systems to operate. These systems are not enterprise-wide, but they do perform specific HR-related functions. Examples include Halogen Software Inc. and Sage HRMS Inc.[76]

Typically, organizations follow a three-step process to choose an HRIS. The three steps are (1) adoption phase, (2) implementation phase, and (3) integration (institutionalization) phase.[77]

Phase 1: Adoption—Determining the Need

In this phase, organizations typically engage in a needs analysis to determine what type of system they will purchase. A needs analysis helps the organization decide on what the system should be capable of doing and what the technical specifications will be. There are several main areas to be considered: company background, management considerations, technical considerations, HR considerations, and cost considerations.[78]

> *Company Background*: The industry, the size of the company, and the projected growth are important elements to consider. Typically, organizations require HR software after they reach 100 employees.
>
> *Management Considerations*: Normally, management would have some preconceived views regarding what they want the system to do and the type of software that might be required. They may want a complex system with enterprise-wide capabilities or a stand-alone system.
>
> *Technical Considerations*: Elements such as hardware, operating systems, networking, databases, and telecommunications all need to be considered. It is important to understand the kind of technology the company currently has and is able to support.

enterprise-wide system/ enterprise resource planning (ERP) system A system that supports enterprise-wide or cross-functional requirements rather than a single department within the organization.

stand-alone system A self-contained system that does not rely on other systems to operate.

HR Competency

90300

HR Considerations: The HR department must consider its own needs. What type of daily requests and which employee transactions would make the most sense to automate? What types of forms, reports, or listings are maintained? The needs assessment would identify the types of data required to produce reports, where these data can be found, and how reliable the data are. HR would look at the manual reports currently being maintained and decide how these can be automated.

Cost Considerations: Factored into the price that an organization can afford are considerations such as additional hardware purchases required, the number of additional staff needed during the implementation phase, training costs, and ongoing support costs.

Once the needs analysis is complete, companies send out a **request for proposal (RFP)** to a number of vendors requesting details of how the implementation of their particular HRIS will meet the organization's needs. Then demonstrations of the various systems are scheduled and the system that most closely aligns with the organization's needs is selected.

At this point, the adoption phase is complete, and the organization will move into the implementation phase.

EVIDENCE-BASED HR

request for proposal (RFP)
A document requesting that vendors provide a proposal detailing how the implementation of their particular HRIS will meet the organization's needs.

Phase 2: Implementation

In this phase, the company selects a project team that typically includes outside consultants who have knowledge and expertise on the technical side and expertise in change management to help the organization with the implementation. In addition to the outside consultants, there is usually a senior project manager who leads the team, subject matter experts from HR and payroll, and management from the various functional areas across the organization. These managers will be using the system, so it is important for them to ensure that the system is implemented effectively and that their requirements are clearly understood.

The activities involved in this phase focus on getting the system "up and running" within a controlled environment so that the system can be tested to ensure that it is functioning in the way the organization requires. The existing data are "converted" into the new system, meaning that the old system data are transformed to be made compatible with the new system. The software is tested and the users are expected to provide feedback before the system goes live. "Going live" means disengaging any previous HRIS and providing users access to the new system only. In this phase, security profiles are established for the users.

Privacy and Security

There are major privacy concerns when setting up an HRIS because of the sensitive personal nature of much of the data stored there, such as medical claims. Careful decisions must be made regarding who will have access to the computer hardware, software, and databases, and who will be able to modify the databases.[79] Establishing security profiles is a very important activity when implementing an HRIS. The staff members who will be working with the HRIS must be identified and security profiles established. These profiles specify which staff members have access to each screen, which data elements (fields) each staff member can have access to, and which staff members can enter or change data. Security profiles are typically attached to positions in the organization rather than to individuals.

For example, the profile for an HR administrator who enters employee information into the system and who is the point of contact for all changes that employees make to their "tombstone data" would include viewing, entering, and changing data. A line manager's profile typically includes viewing information relating to his or her employees, but not confidential data that is irrelevant to the work situation, and the profile would not include changing employee records.

A final, critical piece of HRIS security is making sure the system users clearly understand and adhere to the company confidentiality policy and code of ethics. All users need to understand that they must not share passwords, post them in view of others, or compromise them in any way.

Phase 3: Integration

The final step in implementing an HRIS is to train the users on the system. The organization's goal is for the stakeholders to use the system and reap the benefits identified through the needs analysis. However, many difficulties can arise with the implementation of a new system and, as with any change, people need to become comfortable with it. People often have difficulties transitioning to an HRIS, so the organization can experience inertia.[80]

Employees need to be trained, but even after training they may not feel fully competent and might not use the system. With any new system, stakeholders can underestimate its complexity.

HR Competency
20700

ELECTRONIC HR

electronic HR (e-HR) A form of technology that enables HR professionals to integrate an organization's HR strategies, processes, and human capital to improve overall HR service delivery.

HR portal A single Internet access point for customized and personalized HR services.

employee self-service (ESS) Enables employees to access and manage their personal information directly.

Electronic HR (e-HR) enables HR professionals to integrate an organization's HR strategies, processes, and human capital to improve overall HR service delivery.[81] By the mid-1990s, organizations were beginning to embrace ways in which to incorporate electronic and computer functions into their HR strategies.[82] Companies continue to look for better ways to manage costs, provide better service, and effectively manage their human capital. e-HR has become integral to helping organizations achieve these goals.

The most significant development in HR technology that enables direct employee access to HR applications is the web-based **HR portal**, which provides users with a single Internet access point for customized and personalized HR services.[83]

The two most popular web-based applications enable HR self-service and therefore save time and reduce paperwork for HR staff.[84] These applications have allowed companies to shift responsibility for viewing and updating records onto employees and managers and have fundamentally changed the manner in which employees acquire information and interact with their HR departments.

Employee self-service (ESS) systems enable employees to access and manage their personal information directly on a 24/7 basis without having to go through their HR departments or their managers. Employees often access ESS systems via the Internet, sometimes using a portal on the company's secure intranet site.

Some common ESS options allow employees to update personal information, such as address, phone number, emergency contact name and number; revise banking information; enroll in benefits programs; research benefit options; view payroll information like salary deductions; record vacation time and sick days; record travel expenses; access HR policies; participate in training delivered via the web; and access company communications and newsletters issued by the HR department. For example, an

Rawpixel/Fotolia

Advances in technology allow users to gain access to their employment-related health and benefits information quickly and conveniently.

"Bad news, Stevens. While monitoring your email I discovered that you're monitoring my email."

Fotolia

management self-service (MSS) Enables managers to access a range of information about themselves and the employees who report to them and to process HR-related paperwork that pertains to their staff.

HR Competency

90400

HR Competency

20600

employee who recently separated from his or her spouse can log on through the company's intranet site, click on the HR portal, and make all the required changes to emergency contact name, beneficiary information, and other benefit details that list the former spouse's name, all from the convenience and privacy of the employee's own home. ESS systems can be very effective. A study by *HR Focus* found that HR generalist workloads were reduced by an average of 15 percent after the introduction of an ESS.[85]

Management self-service (MSS) systems allow managers to access a range of information about themselves and the employees who report to them. MSS systems also give managers the opportunity to process HR-related paperwork that pertains to their staff. Managers can view résumés that are on file, view merit reviews, submit position requisitions, view employee salaries, and keep track of employee performance and training histories. Typically, this type of system offers a broader range of services than is available to non-managerial staff. In addition to providing HR-related information, MSS systems often provide managers with additional tools to help them with tasks such as budget reviews, report writing, and authorization of expense reimbursements.

Research indicates that when used properly, MSS systems reduce the workload of HR generalists by more than 21 percent because they are not spending that time on planning annual compensation increases, viewing employee histories, initiating requests for positions, or posting jobs.[86]

Cautions Regarding e-HR

Surveys of ESS and MSS system users indicate that although 80 percent of respondents agreed that web-based self-service systems can lower HR operation costs, only 40 percent believe that their company is actually achieving this result. Two-thirds of those surveyed agree that web-based self-service systems can effectively support the transformation of the HR department into a more strategic partner by redirecting some of their responsibilities onto employees, but only 37 percent actually felt there was a change.[87] The Expert Opinion box highlights current discussion regarding how HR systems can be developed and integrated effectively.

Why does this discrepancy exist? Could it be that employees and managers view this new technology as the "work of HR" and therefore are resistant to using it? Perhaps the technology is not as user-friendly as it should be. The usefulness of this technology will depend on whether the content is considered beneficial and relevant, on how easy the system is to navigate, and on its cultural fit with the organization. Realizing the potential of any new technology means that processes associated with the technology must be changed. People need to use the system in the right way. Only then will they reap the expected benefits.[88]

Another interesting issue to consider is how HR has responded to this new technology. As was mentioned earlier, with these technological developments in place the traditional transactional HR activities are no longer required and, as a result, HR may feel disenfranchised. Implementation of HR technology does not necessarily mean a reduction in the number of HR staff—in fact, the number of staff either increased or remained the same after e-HR was launched.[89] e-HR is about redistributing administrative HR work to provide HR professionals with more time to focus on the strategic activities that add value to the bottom line. The expectations are high for HR in terms of what it is expected to deliver to sustain innovation.[90]

Surinder Singh

Identification: Mr. Surinder Singh, President, NorthCloud Inc.

Focus: Providing technology solutions for digital agencies, e-commerce, retailers, startups and corporations

1. How do technology systems benefit employees in a firm?

One of the biggest advantages with technology-based systems is that the automation of business processes or systems do not heavily rely on human contributions to cycle information through the system. Knowledge workers do not want to be constrained with how to move information from point A to B. Rather, they focus on the more macro issues of content. Automation helps streamline their work to become more strategic.

Additionally, the automation of systems often opens up lines of communication, creating visibility and transparency regarding tasks, projects, and potential roadblocks that might emerge during the project plan. For example, an employee who is critical to success of the project might have had plans to be away at the point in the project that he or she is leading. This transparency can help proactively manage the project successfully. There are also clear lines of accountability and expectations built into work plans that are transparent to the members of the team.

People generally have a basic technological competency quite early in their careers and are comfortable using new technology. In addition, employees often receive support through training and involvement in new processes in the workplace.

2. What is a key challenge associated with incorporating new technology-enabled systems in the workplace?

When developing new systems, working with a limited or isolated group of executives or users can be problematic. Project leaders who are too eager to make decisions without first conducting a complete needs assessment may not understand the full scope of how a technology-based solution can solve the breadth of issues that need consideration. This can lead to software solutions that are mismatched with the actual problems or issues in the organization.

In my experience, getting users and employees involved in the design process or specification process is critical to success of the project. Key users can speak on behalf of employees who complete the work, and can recognize issues or problems that impact their work. Involvement of users is essential to the development of successful solutions.

3. As an entrepreneur in the technology industry in Canada, what are you looking for when scouting talent?

A smart person who is motivated can find a path to success. For example, in interviews, I often ask candidates what they have recently learned and ask them to debrief me on that topic. In this dynamic environment, the ability to learn is fundamental to long-term job success. A candidate's experience with software today quickly can become dated. Instead, we focus on lifelong learners.

Accordingly, we have a team-based developmental approach in the organization. Person-to-organization fit is critical in dynamic or entrepreneurial organizations, which often leads me to consider: Can we spend 12 hours a day with this individual? For full-time employees, there is also a consideration regarding the balance of competencies and personalities across the team, thus reflecting on how the individual fits within the team is important.

The software industry has community sites where individuals can showcase their portfolio of work. We evaluate software engineering projects that candidates have shared as evidence of their work quality and contribution, and often discuss their portfolio before the interview.

Source: Used by permission from Surinder Singh

Today's HR professionals must be technically savvy and be able to "speak the language of business." They must understand the business environment and the major drivers relating to workforce productivity as determined by management. The use of HR metrics will be increasingly important to assess whether HR is providing services that provide value to the organization.

HR departments today are faced with significant challenges if they are going to contribute to organizational effectiveness. How HR uses technology to evaluate its own effectiveness and leverages emerging technologies to drive productivity and the management of human capital will make the difference between an HR department that just plays a supporting role and one that is truly a business partner.

CHAPTER SUMMARY

1. Technology has the potential to reduce the administrative burden on the HR department so they are able to focus on more meaningful HR activities, such as providing managers with the appropriate decision-making tools that will enable them to make more effective HR-related decisions. Companies who use technology appropriately to manage their HR functions will be more effective than those that do not. Enhancing the relationship between HR and technology will enable HR to achieve three key objectives: (1) strategic alignment with the business objectives, (2) business intelligence—providing users with relevant data, and (3) effectiveness and efficiency—changing how the work is performed by reducing lead times and costs and increasing service levels.

2. The role of the HR professional has changed fundamentally as a result of technology. It has enabled HR to decrease its involvement in transactional (administrative) activities and to increase its focus on how to increase its delivery of strategic services. The core competencies that have developed are mastery of HR technology, strategic contribution, business knowledge, personal credibility, data management, HR delivery, and financial management.

3. An HRIS is a group of integrated systems used to gather, store, and analyze information regarding an organization's human resources. Its main components are administration, recruitment, compensation and benefit administration, payroll, time and attendance, employment equity, performance evaluation, and health and safety.

4. The key functions of an HRIS are to create and maintain employee records, ensure legal compliance, enable managers to forecast and plan their staffing requirements, enable managers and HR to manage knowledge and talent through career and succession planning, ensure the organization is aligned more effectively with its strategic plan, and assist managers with decision-making by providing the relevant data required to make effective and informed decisions. The key stakeholders include employees, managers, and HR/payroll professionals.

5. A critical issue in HRIS is the use of metrics to enable decision-making. Through the use of an HR audit, an organization can measure the effectiveness and status of its HR functions. The data extracted from the HRIS should be used to align and evaluate how the human resources aid in helping the organization achieve its strategic vision.

6. The three steps in the process of selecting and implementing an HRIS are (1) the adoption phase, where organizations carry out a needs analysis to determine requirements; (2) the implementation phase, where project teams are created, the software is tested, and privacy and security concerns are addressed; and (3) the integration phase, where training and change management activities are conducted.

7. Electronic HR (e-HR) refers to a form of technology that enables HR professionals to integrate an organization's HR strategies, processes, and human capital to improve overall HR service delivery. Examples include the migration of HRIS applications onto an intranet, the use of web-based HR portals that provide users with a single Internet access point for customized and personalized HR services, and the use of web-based applications such as employee self-service (ESS) and management self-service (MSS) to enhance HR services.

MyManagementLab

Study, practise, and explore real business situations with these helpful resources:
- **Interactive Lesson Presentations:** Work through interactive presentations and assessments to test your knowledge of management concepts.
- **PIA (Personal Inventory Assessments):** Enhance your ability to connect with key concepts through these engaging self-reflection assessments.
- **Study Plan:** Check your understanding of chapter concepts with self-study quizzes.
- **Videos:** Learn more about the management practices and strategies of real companies.
- **Simulations:** Practise decision-making in simulated management environments.

PIA — PERSONAL INVENTORY ASSESSMENT

KEY TERMS

applicant tracking systems (ATS) *(p. 63)*

data mining *(p. 62)*

data warehouse *(p. 60)*

electronic HR (e-HR) *(p. 72)*

employee self-service (ESS) *(p. 72)*

enterprise-wide system/enterprise resource planning (ERP) system *(p. 70)*

HR audit *(p. 67)*

HR portal *(p. 72)*

HR technology *(p. 57)*

human capital *(p. 56)*

human resources information system (HRIS) *(p. 60)*

learning management system *(p. 65)*

learning portal *(p. 65)*

management self-service (MSS) *(p. 73)*

metrics (workforce analytics) *(p. 61)*

personnel replacement charts *(p. 66)*

position replacement card *(p. 66)*

request for proposal (RFP) *(p. 71)*

stand-alone system *(p. 70)*

strategy-based metrics (p. 62)

REVIEW AND DISCUSSION QUESTIONS

1. Explain how automation, ICT, and knowledge work impact the use of technology in the workplace.

2. Describe the role of technology in enabling HR to help the organization achieve its strategic objectives.

3. Discuss the six key functions of an HRIS and the subsystem components that reside in an HRIS.

4. Describe several technological trends that HR must be aware of in order to offer value-added technology solutions.

5. Explain what an HR audit is and why it is important.

6. Describe the three steps involved in selecting and implementing an HRIS.

7. What is e-HR, and its associated risks and benefits?

CRITICAL THINKING QUESTIONS

1. In order for HR to demonstrate that it is a strategic partner with the business, it must be aware of its customer requirements. In terms of technology, what actions and initiatives would HR have to take to demonstrate this awareness?

2. The role of HR has fundamentally changed as a result of technology. How will HR deliver service in the future? What delivery mechanisms will work best?

3. Do you think that it is important for all types of organizations to have an HRIS? Why or why not?

4. Compare and contrast the costs and benefits of being a member of an HRIS implementation team.

5. Do you think that maintaining the security of an HRIS is a major concern for HR technology professionals? What security issues are most important today?

6. How does HR technology help organizations deliver transactional HR activities in a more efficient way?

7. In today's economic climate, organizations are concerned with talent management. How can HR technology be used to ease these concerns?

EXPERIENTIAL EXERCISES

1. Explore two vendors who offer technology-related solutions for talent management such as Taleo (www.taleo.com) and Halogen Software (www.halogensoftware.com). Consider how these programs can contribute to organizational effectiveness. How will they help managers manage more effectively? How will they aid HR in delivering strategic services?

2. Go to www.workopolis.com or www.monster.ca. Find a job posting for an HRIS manager and HRIS analyst/administrator. How are the jobs different? What types of activities does each role carry out?

3. Investigate what workers are saying about how the web has helped them work more effectively.

Go to www.GigaOM.com/collaboration. What types of issues are being discussed there? Are there some trends?

4. To accommodate a diverse workforce, HR must consider various types of delivery methods to communicate HR information. Explore the difference between video and audio podcasts, interactive voice response (IVR), and a company intranet. Describe these methods of delivery and how they can be used to deliver HR information. (Some interesting HR-related podcasts—such as the Harvard Business Review Idea Cast—can be found at www.apple.com by accessing the iTunes store.)

RUNNING CASE

Does LearnInMotion.com Need an HRIS?

Jennifer was getting frustrated. With only a few employees, the company kept a paper-based file for each employee with personal information, benefits forms, and so on. She and Pierre had decided to outsource payroll, but she still had to spend several hours every two weeks gathering payroll information, such as regular hours, overtime hours, vacation time and sick time that had been taken, and so on to send to the payroll company. The benefits information and calculations were supposed to be carried out by the payroll company, but there had been several instances where mistakes had been made.

Jennifer and Pierre discussed the issue and decided that, as a high-tech company, they should investigate

the possibility of computerizing their employee files and information. Even with a very small number of employees, they both thought it might be easier for them to use some sort of HRIS. They have asked you, their management consultant, to provide answers to the following questions.

QUESTIONS

1. What data should be stored for each employee? How would the company use these data?
2. Conduct an HRIS needs analysis for the company. What are the results?
3. Would you recommend an HRIS to Jennifer and Pierre? If so, what kind of system?

CASE INCIDENT

Integration and Transfer of HR Functions Using HRIS

Jack Newman had recently been appointed regional director of Boomerang Water Corporation, a major service utility in Australia. Jack's previous appointment was with a large manufacturing company in the United States, where he had made a reputation for himself as a visionary specializing in customer service and performance management.

Jack was the youngest person and only non-Australian ever to be appointed as a director at Boomerang Water Corporation. This particular region of the utility employed approximately 2000 workers engaged in the customer service and maintenance provision side of the business. These employees operated in groups of about 30 workers. One supervisor managed each work group. These groups were located in five departments across the region, with each department specializing in a particular customer service or maintenance function. The region serviced about 500 000 customers.

A central division controlled the human resource management functions for the region. This division was located in the region's main town. Elaine MacVain headed the HR division. Elaine had been with the utility for nearly 25 years and over these years had developed a reputation for running a strong, controlled division that provided the customer service and maintenance department with a diversity of HR services. Elaine considered the main focus of the division to be to process day-to-day HR transactions and maintain employee records. Elaine managed a staff of 10 HR professionals who processed employee data that included workers' pay, leave entitlements and requests, and shift work entitlements. The HR department was responsible for recruitment and selection, the performance management system, occupational health and safety records, and career planning. Ron Locat, a member of Elaine's division, had developed a stand-alone HRIS to maintain the HR department's records. Ron had little formal IT training but had undergone in-house training in the use of Microsoft Access and had used Access to create the division's database system. Elaine and the other members of the HR division did not have a high level of IT literacy, but they could operate the Access system that Ron had developed. Elaine was grateful for the work Ron had put into the database system and felt indebted to him for the support that he gave to the HR staff.

A major focus of the utility was training the customer service and maintenance employees. The utility had a promotion system based on the employee's level of technical skills. Employees were promoted to higher levels of competency and pay scales on completion of skills training. Peter Noall, who had been with the utility for about four years, headed the training division, which had three staff in addition to Peter. One staff member was an ex-technical college teacher, and two had been technical supervisors in the organization. Due to the small size of the training division, Peter was forced to outsource much of the organization's training needs. Work safety was a major responsibility of Peter's, and he was very proud of the organization's safety record. Peter had contracted the purchase of an expensive, dedicated training database system to support the organization's training function. The system provided the training division with a powerful tool with which to profile the total skills base of the organization, identify present and future training needs, track employees' competency levels, and evaluate training outcomes in relation to productivity gains. The training division was

proud of its use of high-level technology to support strategic training initiatives.

On commencing his appointment, Jack Newman decided his immediate focus was on improving the organization's customer service. He engaged the Fast Track—Immediate Success consultancy group to run a number of focus groups and conduct a strategic analysis related to the delivery of customer service. Eddie Wanton from Fast Track organized focus groups within the HR division and the training division and ran three focus groups of 20 randomly selected supervisors. Eddie's report to Jack Newman included the following concerns and recommendations aimed to improve customer service.

Report from Fast Track

Concern 1: At present, customer complaints are directed to work group supervisors.

Recommendation: Introduce a new division dedicated to customer service quality.

Concern 2: Customer service is not supported by an integration of customer feedback, work group practices, training, and HR strategies.

Recommendation: Link the new customer service quality division to HR, training, and work group supervision.

Concern 3: At present, the HR division has sole responsibility for performance management, not the training division or work group supervisors.

Recommendation: Link performance management responsibilities to work group supervisors via training plans and HR recruitment strategies.

Concern 4: Communications among the HR division, training division, and work group supervisors are low level and infrequent.

Recommendation: Introduce an organization structure that seamlessly integrates and promotes strategic communication between HR, training, and work group supervision.

Concern 5: The HR division and the training division have created tightly controlled centres of knowledge that do not directly inform work group supervisors.

Recommendation: Introduce the transfer of targeted HR and training responsibilities directly to work group supervisors.

Eddie Wanton's Recommended Strategy

Introduce a database information system that will seamlessly integrate HR functions, training functions, and customer service functions. Use the information system to develop strategic links between these functions. Use the new information system to break down information channel barriers between the HR and training divisions. Use the system to devolve appropriate HR and training operations to work group supervisors. Create a new customer service quality division and use the new IT system to integrate it with the other divisions and work group supervisors. In short, change the organization's communication and information architecture to promote the integration of cross-divisional information sharing, decision-making, and control.

QUESTIONS

1   How can the assignment of a champion facilitate the introduction of the new HRIS? Is Jack Newman the best person to act as champion?

2   Why have the HR and training divisions built quite different database systems? What are the difficulties involved in integrating the functions of these divisions?

3   What are the advantages of integrating the functions of the HR division, training division, and those of the work group supervisors?

4   What are the advantages and disadvantages of the Boomerang Water Corporation buying an off-the-shelf integrated HR database system?

5   In what ways may the transfer of some HR functions to work group supervisors improve the efficiency of the HR division? In what ways may work group supervisors be advantaged or disadvantaged by the transfer of HR functions?

Source: G. Dessler, J. Griffiths, and B. Lloyd-Walker, *Human Resources Management*, 2nd ed. (Frenchs Forest, New South Wales: Pearson Education Australia, 2004), pp. 97–99. Reprinted with permission of the publisher.

CHAPTER

4

Alexander Raths/Fotolia

Designing and Analyzing Jobs

LEARNING OUTCOMES

**AFTER STUDYING THIS CHAPTER, YOU
SHOULD BE ABLE TO**

EXPLAIN multiple uses of job
analysis in HR decisions

IDENTIFY the steps in job analysis,
and **DESCRIBE** the evolution of job
analysis.

DEFINE job design and **EXPLAIN**
the difference between a job and a
position.

DESCRIBE the evolution of job design
and how organizational structure influences job design.

EXPLAIN the three reasons why
competency-based job analysis has
become more common.

DESCRIBE and **EVALUATE** multiple
methods of collecting job analysis
information.

EXPLAIN the difference between a
job description and a job specification.

REQUIRED HR COMPETENCIES

10600: Align human resources practices by translating organizational strategy into human
resources objectives and priorities to achieve the organization's plan.

20600: Promote an evidence-based approach to the development of human resources
policies and practices using current professional resources to provide a sound basis for
human resources decision-making.

40200: Increase the attractiveness of the employer to desirable potential employees
by identifying and shaping the organization's employee value proposition to build a
high-quality workforce.

FUNDAMENTALS OF JOB ANALYSIS

Job analysis is a process by which information about jobs is systematically gathered and organized. Job analysis is sometimes called the cornerstone of HRM.

job A group of related activities and duties, held by a single employee or a number of incumbents.

A **job** consists of a group of related activities and duties. Ideally, the duties of a job should be clear and distinct from those of other jobs, and they should involve natural units of work that are similar and related. This approach helps to minimize conflict and enhance employee performance. A job may be held by a single employee or may have a number of incumbents. The collection of tasks and responsibilities performed by one person is known as a **position**. To clarify, there are 45 positions and 4 jobs in a department with 1 supervisor, 1 clerk, 40 assemblers, and 3 tow-motor operators.

position The collection of tasks and responsibilities performed by one person.

Uses of Job Analysis Information

job analysis The procedure for determining the tasks, duties, and responsibilities of each job, and the human attributes (in terms of knowledge, skills, and abilities) required to perform it.

Job analysis is the procedure firms use to determine the tasks, duties, and responsibilities of each job, and the human attributes (in terms of knowledge, skills, and abilities) required to perform it. Once this information has been gathered it is used for developing job descriptions (what the job entails) and job specifications (what the human requirements are). As illustrated in **Figure 4.1**, the information gathered, evaluated, and summarized through job analysis is the basis for a number of interrelated HRM activities.

HR Competency
20600

Human Resources Planning

Knowing the actual requirements of an organization's various jobs is essential for planning future staffing needs. When this information is combined with knowledge about the skills and qualifications of current employees, it is possible to determine which jobs can be filled internally and which will require external recruitment.

Recruitment and Selection

The job description and job specification information should be used to decide what sort of person to recruit and hire. Identifying bona fide occupational requirements

FIGURE 4.1 Uses of Job Analysis Information

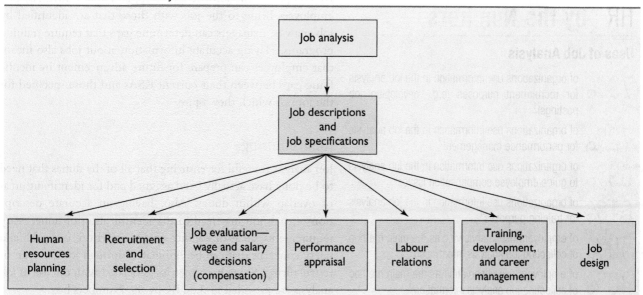

and ensuring that all activities related to recruitment and selection (such as advertising, screening, and testing) are based on these requirements is necessary for legal compliance in all Canadian jurisdictions.

Compensation

Job analysis information is also essential for determining the relative value of and appropriate compensation for each job. Job evaluation should be based on the required skills, physical and mental demands, responsibilities, and working conditions—all assessed through job analysis. The relative value of jobs is one of the key factors used to determine appropriate compensation and justify pay differences if challenged under human rights or pay equity legislation. Information about the actual job duties is also necessary to determine whether a job qualifies for overtime pay and for maximum-hours purposes, as specified in employment standards legislation.

Performance Management

To be legally defensible, the criteria used to assess employee performance must be directly related to the duties and responsibilities identified through job analysis. For many jobs involving routine tasks, especially those of a quantifiable nature, performance standards are determined through job analysis. For more complex jobs, performance standards are often jointly established by employees and their supervisors. To be realistic and achievable, such standards should be based on actual job requirements as identified through job analysis.

Labour Relations

In unionized environments, the job descriptions developed from the job analysis information are generally subject to union approval before being finalized. Such union-approved job descriptions then become the basis for classifying jobs and bargaining over wages, performance criteria, and working conditions. Once approved, significant changes to job descriptions may have to be negotiated.

Training, Development, and Career Management

By comparing the knowledge, skills, and abilities (KSAs) that employees bring to the job with those that are identified by job analysis, managers can determine gaps that require training programs. Having accurate information about jobs also means that employees can prepare for future advancement by identifying gaps between their current KSAs and those specified for the jobs to which they aspire.

Restructuring

Job analysis is useful for ensuring that all of the duties that need to be done have actually been assigned and for identifying areas of overlap within duties. Also, having an accurate description of each job may lead to the identification of unnecessary requirements, areas of conflict or dissatisfaction, or health and safety concerns that can be eliminated through job redesign or restructuring. Some basic metrics associated with the use of job analysis are provided in the HR by the Numbers box.

HR | by the Numbers

Uses of Job Analysis

73% of organizations use information in the job analysis for recruitment purposes (e.g., developing job postings)[1]

72% of organizations use information in the job analysis for performance management[2]

69% of organizations use information in the job analysis to guide employee compensation issues[3]

61% of organizations use information in the job analysis for training purposes[4]

50% of employers use interviewing as the main method of collecting job analysis information[5]

30% of employers use observation as the main method of collecting job analysis information[6]

Steps in Job Analysis

There are six critical steps involved in analyzing jobs. Organizations collect details about jobs on a relatively continuous basis for many uses, such as the ones outlined above (planning, recruitment and selection, performance management, compensation, and so on). Traditionally, organizations would first determine the intended use of job analysis information, since this determined the types of data that should be collected and the techniques used. However, this preliminary step has been largely abolished in practice given the diverse uses of job analysis information and the continual need for such information.

The six steps involved in job analysis are as follows:

1. Relevant organizational information is reviewed.
2. Jobs are selected to be analyzed.
3. Using one or more job analysis techniques, data are collected on job activities.
4. The information collected in Step 3 is then verified and modified, if required.
5. Job descriptions and specifications are developed based on the verified information.
6. The information is then communicated and updated on an as-needed basis.

The structure of this chapter aligns with the six steps of job analysis.

STEP 1: REVIEW RELEVANT BACKGROUND INFORMATION

PERSONAL INVENTORY ASSESSMENT

Learn About Yourself
Organizational Structure
Assessment

organizational structure The formal relationships among jobs in an organization.

organization chart A "snapshot" of the firm, depicting the organization's structure in chart form at a particular point in time.

HR Competency

10600

An organization consists of one or more employees who perform various tasks. The relationships between people and tasks must be structured so that the organization achieves its strategic goals in an efficient and effective manner through a motivated and engaged workforce. There are many ways to distribute work among employees, and careful consideration of how this is done can provide a strategic advantage over competitors.

Organizational structure refers to the formal relationships among jobs in an organization. An **organization chart** is often used to depict the structure. As illustrated in **Figure 4.2**, the chart indicates the types of departments established and the title of each manager's job. By means of connecting lines, it clarifies the chain of command and shows who is accountable to whom. An organization chart presents a "snapshot" of the firm at a particular point in time, but it does not provide details about actual communication patterns, degree of supervision, amount of power and authority, or specific duties and responsibilities. In the example provided in Figure 4.2, there may be the expectation that Auditor Plant A will have to report some information to Manager Plant A. Often an organizational chart will exclude this information or identify secondary reporting responsibilities using a dotted line.

Designing an organization involves choosing a structure that is appropriate given the company's strategic goals. **Figure 4.3** depicts three common types of organizational structure: bureaucratic, flat, and matrix. In flatter organizations, managers have increased spans of control (the number of employees reporting to them) and thus less time to manage each one. Therefore, employees' jobs involve more responsibility. In organizations using self-managed work teams, employees' jobs change daily, so management intentionally avoids having employees view their jobs as a specific, narrow set of responsibilities. The focus is on defining the job at hand in terms of the overall best interests of the organization.

FIGURE 4.2 A Sample Organization Chart

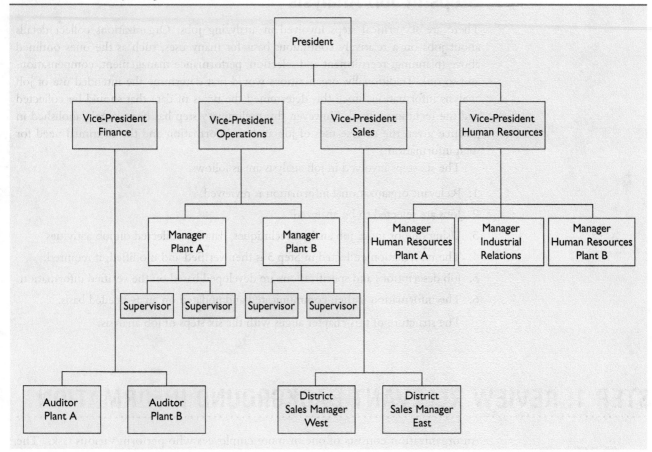

process chart A diagram showing
the flow of inputs to and outputs from
the job under study.

Step 1 includes the review of relevant background information, such as organization charts, process charts, and existing job descriptions.[7] A **process chart** (like the one in **Figure 4.4**) shows the flow of inputs to and outputs from the job under study. (In Figure 4.4, the inventory control clerk is expected to receive inventory from suppliers, take requests for inventory from the two plant managers, provide requested inventory to these managers, and give information to the plant accountant on the status of in-stock inventories.)

STEP 2: SELECT JOBS TO BE ANALYZED

The next step involves the selection of representative positions and jobs to be analyzed. This selection is necessary when there are many incumbents in a single job and when a number of similar jobs are to be analyzed because it would be too time-consuming to analyze every position and job.

job design The process of
systematically organizing work into
tasks that are required to perform a
specific job.

Job design is the process of systematically organizing work into the tasks that are required to perform a specific job. An organization's strategy and structure influence the ways in which jobs are designed. In bureaucratic organizations, for example, because a hierarchical division of labour exists, jobs are generally highly specialized. In addition, effective job design also takes into consideration human and technological factors.

FIGURE 4.3   Bureaucratic, Flat, and Matrix Organizational Structures

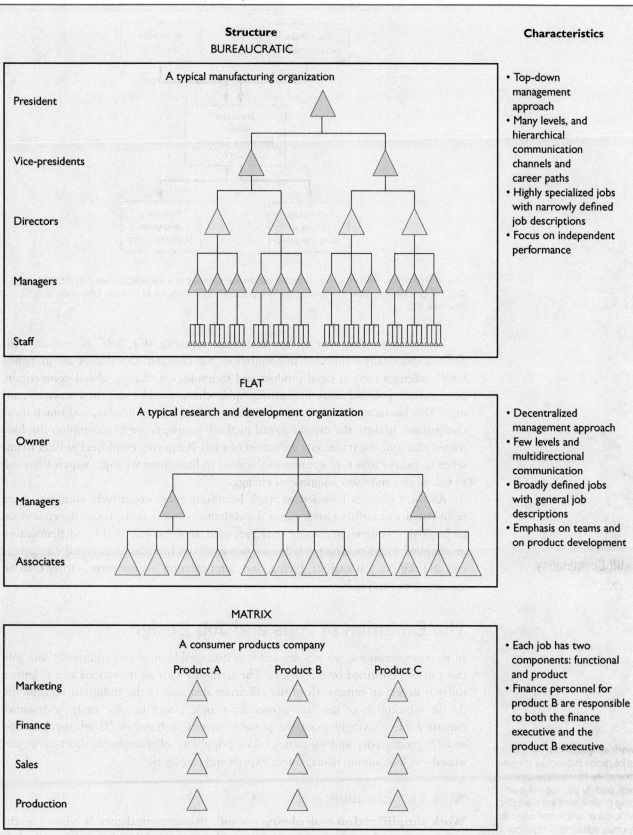

FIGURE 4.4   Process Chart for Analyzing a Job's Workflow

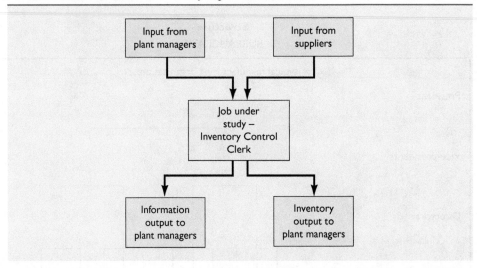

Source: Henderson, Richard I. (ed.), *Compensation Management in a Knowledge-based World*, 10th ed., © 2006, p. 114. Reprinted and Electronically reproduced by permission of Pearson Education, Inc., New York, NY.

In the twenty-first century, the traditional meaning of a "job" as a set of well-defined and clearly delineated responsibilities has changed. Companies are grappling with challenges such as rapid product and technological change, global competition, deregulation, political instability, demographic changes, and a shift to a service economy. This has increased the need for firms to be responsive, flexible, and much more competitive. In turn, the organizational methods managers use to accomplish this have started changing the traditional definition of a job. Requiring employees to limit themselves to narrow jobs runs counter to the need to have them willingly switch from task to task as jobs and team assignments change.

All these changes have led to work becoming more cognitively complex, more team-based and collaborative, more dependent on social skills, more dependent on technological competence, more time pressured, more mobile, and less dependent on geography.[8] This situation has led some organizations to focus on personal competencies and skills in job analysis, hiring, and compensation management, rather than on specific duties and tasks.

The Evolution of Jobs and Job Design

In most organizations, work is divided into manageable units and, ultimately, into jobs that can be performed by employees. The term job with no quotations as it is known today is largely an outgrowth of the efficiency demands of the Industrial Revolution. As the substitution of machine power for people power became more widespread, experts wrote glowingly about the positive correlation between (1) job specialization and (2) productivity and efficiency.[9] The popularity of specialized, short-cycle jobs soared—at least among management experts and managers.

Work Simplification

work simplification An approach to job design that involves assigning most of the administrative aspects of work (such as planning and organizing) to supervisors and managers, while giving lower-level employees narrowly defined tasks to perform according to methods established and specified by management.

Work simplification evolved from scientific management theory. It is based on the premise that work can be broken down into clearly defined, highly specialized, repetitive tasks to maximize efficiency. This approach to job design involves assigning most of the administrative aspects of work (such as planning and organizing) to supervisors and managers, while giving lower-level employees narrowly defined tasks to perform according to methods established and specified by management.

Work simplification can increase operating efficiency in a stable environment and may be very appropriate in settings employing individuals with intellectual disabilities or those lacking education and training (as in some operations in the developing world); it is not effective, however, in a changing environment in which customers/clients demand custom-designed products and/or high-quality services, or one in which employees want challenging work. Moreover, among educated employees, simplified jobs often lead to lower satisfaction, higher rates of absenteeism and turnover, and sometimes to a demand for premium pay to compensate for the repetitive nature of the work.

industrial engineering A field of study concerned with analyzing work methods; making work cycles more efficient by modifying, combining, rearranging, or eliminating tasks; and establishing time standards.

Industrial Engineering

Another important contribution of scientific management was the study of work. **Industrial engineering**, which evolved with this movement, is concerned with analyzing work methods and establishing time standards to improve efficiency. Industrial engineers systematically identify, analyze, and time the elements of each job's work cycle and determine which, if any, elements can be modified, combined, rearranged, or eliminated to reduce the time needed to complete the cycle.

Too much emphasis on the concerns of industrial engineering—improving efficiency and simplifying work methods—may result in human considerations being neglected or downplayed. For example, an assembly line, with its simplified and repetitive tasks, embodies the principles of industrial engineering but may lead to repetitive strain injuries, high turnover, and low satisfaction because of the lack of psychological fulfillment. Thus, to be effective, job design must also satisfy human psychological and physiological needs.

Industrial engineering improves efficiency and simplifies work methods but neglects human considerations, such as repetitive strain and lack of psychological fulfillment.

Job Enlargement (Horizontal Loading)

By the mid-1900s, reacting to what they viewed as the "dehumanizing" aspects of highly repetitive and specialized jobs, various management theorists proposed ways of broadening the activities engaged in by employees. **Job enlargement,** also known as **horizontal loading**, involves assigning workers additional tasks at the same level of responsibility to increase the number of tasks they have to perform. Thus, if the work was assembling chairs, the worker who previously only bolted the seat to the legs might take on the additional tasks of assembling the legs and attaching the back as well. Job enlargement reduces monotony and fatigue by expanding the job cycle and drawing on a wider range of employee skills.

job enlargement (horizontal loading) A technique to relieve monotony and boredom that involves assigning workers additional tasks at the same level of responsibility to increase the number of tasks they have to perform.

Job Rotation

job rotation A technique to relieve monotony and employee boredom that involves systematically moving employees from one job to another.

Another technique to relieve monotony and employee boredom is **job rotation**. This involves systematically moving employees from one job to another. Although the jobs themselves don't change, workers experience more task variety, motivation, and productivity. The company gains by having more versatile, multiskilled employees who can cover for one another efficiently.

Job Enrichment

job enrichment (vertical loading) Any effort that makes an employee's job more rewarding or satisfying by adding more meaningful tasks and duties.

It has also been suggested that the best way to motivate workers is to build opportunities for challenge and achievement into jobs through **job enrichment**, also known as **vertical loading**.[10] This is defined as any effort that makes an employee's job more rewarding or satisfying by adding more meaningful tasks and duties. Job enrichment involves increasing autonomy and responsibility by allowing employees to assume a greater role in the decision-making process.

Enriching a job can be accomplished through activities such as

- increasing the level of difficulty and responsibility of the job;
- assigning workers more authority and control over outcomes;
- providing feedback about individual or unit job performance directly to employees;
- adding new tasks requiring training, thereby providing an opportunity for growth; and
- assigning individuals entire tasks or responsibility for performing a whole job rather than only parts of it, such as conducting an entire background check rather than just checking educational credentials.

Job enrichment is not always the best approach. It is more successful in some jobs and settings than in others; for example, not all employees want additional responsibilities and challenges. Some people prefer routine jobs and may resist job redesign efforts. In addition, job redesign efforts almost always fail when employees lack the physical or mental skills, abilities, or education needed to perform the additional tasks required post job enrichment.

EVIDENCE-BASED HR

ergonomics An interdisciplinary approach that seeks to integrate and accommodate the physical needs of workers into the design of jobs. It aims to adapt the entire job system— the work, environment, machines, equipment, and processes—to match human characteristics.

Ergonomics

In addition to considering psychological needs, effective job design also requires taking physiological needs and health and safety issues into account. **Ergonomics** seeks to integrate and accommodate the physical needs of workers into the design of jobs. It aims to adapt the entire job system—the work, environment, machines, equipment, and processes—to match human characteristics. Doing so results in eliminating or minimizing product defects, damage to equipment, and worker injuries or illnesses caused by poor work design.

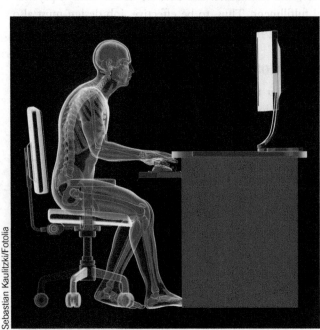

Ergonomics considerations apply to manual and knowledge workers alike, and aim at adapting job aspects to physical aspects in a sustainable way.

Competency-Based Job Analysis

Not coincidentally, many employers and job analysis experts say traditional job analysis procedures can't go on playing a central role in HR management.[11] Their basic concern is this: In high-performance work environments in which employers need workers to seamlessly move from job to job and exercise self-control, job descriptions based on lists of job-specific duties may actually inhibit (or fail to encourage) the flexible behaviour companies need. Employers are therefore shifting toward newer approaches for describing jobs, such as competency-based analysis. The Expert Opinion box provides an example of how entrepreneurial, dynamic or innovative firms approach job description.

Scott Dolson

Identification: Mr. Scott Dolson, People Operations Specialist at Miovision Technologies

1. How do you think job descriptions are different in entrepreneurial firms or dynamic firms than in larger, more structured organizations?

Job descriptions that are tasked based, job specific, and static in nature can be constraining or narrowing in dynamic firms. Instead, we look at how the role helps the organization achieve its goals, and compose a few bullet points of core competencies required for each position where vacancy comes up. Rather than calling these job descriptions, we refer to these as the operating plans. Each of the 75 employees in the organization has an individualized operating plan that is embedded in the large organizational operating plan. There's a large focus on cultural alignment and the business focus on the competencies. So rather than aligning an individual to a specific position, we focus on larger, but alignment with the organization's operating plan.

2. What challenges do you face when trying to identify the core requirements for a job in an innovative firm?

First, there is a very competitive labour market for technical competencies, so the use of networking and the ability to move quickly on opportunities as they're presented is critical to filling vacancies and growing the firm.

Second, with a high speed of change, it is critical that we maintain clarity on the main projects the individual will be involved in, and share that information with candidates in order to look for synergies and identify what knowledge is needed to be successful.

Third, we are also a very engineering-centric company, and we take a lot of direction from the engineers in everything from operations to project management. In order to help open up lines of communication and make sure that we're understanding the situation correctly, we include the engineering hiring manager in multiple traditional human resource processes such as recruitment, selection, training, development, and career planning.

3. Within your company, how do you provide clarity as to employees' job responsibilities while maintaining flexibility to alter the job requirements as the market and organization changes?

Rather than creating and then shelving job descriptions until annual performance review times, we treat our operating plan and employee job descriptions as live documents. Accordingly, we update our version of the job description on a monthly basis. This process involves both employee and manager input and consensus.

Parallel to this is the culture of continuous feedback in order to identify opportunities for growth and help provide clarity on career trajectory options. Essentially, in organizations that are dynamic, you need lots of communication platforms for the employee to learn about company projects, share information, learn about new initiatives, etc. as well as full transparency as to where they fit in the organization. We provide this by giving access to operating plans of all others in the organization.

Source: Reprinted by permission from Scott Dolson

---

competencies Demonstrable characteristics of a person that enable performance of a job.

competency-based job analysis Describing a job in terms of the measurable, observable behavioural competencies an employee must exhibit to do a job well.

Competency-based job analysis basically means writing job descriptions based on competencies rather than job duties. It emphasizes what the employee must be capable of doing, rather than a list of the duties he or she must perform. **Competencies** are demonstrable characteristics of a person that enable performance. Job competencies are always observable and measurable behaviours that comprise part of a job. The job's required competencies can be identified by simply completing this sentence: "In order to perform this job competently, the employee should be able to..."

Competency-based job analysis means describing the job in terms of the measurable, observable behavioural competencies (knowledge, skills, or behaviours) that an employee doing that job must exhibit to do the job well. This contrasts with the traditional way of describing a job in terms of job duties and responsibilities. Traditional job analysis focuses on "what" is accomplished—on duties and responsibilities. Competency-based analysis focuses more on "how" the worker meets the job's

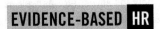

Simulate on MyManagementLab

Individual Behaviour

objectives or actually accomplishes the work. Traditional job analysis is thus job focused; competency-based analysis is worker focused—specifically, what must he or she be competent to do?

Three Reasons to Use Competency Analysis

There are three reasons to describe jobs in terms of competencies rather than duties. Giving someone a job description with a list of specific duties may simply breed a "that's-not-my-job" attitude by pigeonholing workers too narrowly.

1. Traditional job descriptions (with their lists of specific duties) may actually backfire if a *high-performance work system* is the goal. The whole thrust of these systems is to encourage employees to work in a self-motivated way by organizing the work around teams, encouraging team members to rotate freely among jobs (each with its own skill set), pushing more responsibility for things like day-to-day supervision down to the workers, and organizing work around projects or processes in which jobs may blend or overlap. Employees here must be enthusiastic about learning and moving among jobs.

2. Describing the job in terms of the skills, knowledge, and competencies the worker needs is *more strategic*. For example, a company with a strategic emphasis on miniaturization and precision manufacturing should encourage some employees to develop their expertise in these two strategically crucial areas.

3. Measurable skills, knowledge, and competencies support the employer's *performance management process*. Training, appraisals, and rewards should be based on fostering and rewarding the skills and competencies required to achieve work goals. Describing the job in terms of skills and competencies facilitates understanding of those required competencies.

Examples of Competencies

In practice, managers often write paragraph-length competencies for jobs and organize these into two or three clusters. For example, the job's required competencies might include *general or core competencies* (such as reading, writing, and mathematical reasoning), *leadership competencies* (such as leadership, strategic thinking, and teaching others), and *technical/task/functional competencies* (which focus on the specific technical competencies required for specific types of jobs or occupations).

EVIDENCE-BASED HR

So, some technical competencies for the job of systems engineer might include the following:

- Design complex software applications, establish protocols, and create prototypes.

- Establish the necessary platform requirements to efficiently and completely coordinate data transfer.

- Prepare comprehensive and complete documentation including specifications, flow diagrams, process patrols, and budgets.[12]

Similarly, for a corporate treasurer, technical competencies might include the following:

- Formulate trade recommendations by studying several computer models for currency trends and using various quantitative techniques to determine the financial impact of certain financial trades.

ndoeljindoel/Fotolia

At a Nissan factory in Tokyo, Japan, workers meet at a productivity session, surrounded by unfinished car frames hanging along the assembly line. Work teams like this are part of the trend toward a multiskilled, cross-functional, self-directed team organization that allows workers greater autonomy in meeting goals. In plants like these, broadly described jobs that emphasize employees' required competencies are replacing narrowly defined jobs.

- Recommend specific trades and when to make them.
- Present recommendations and persuade others to follow the recommended course of action.[13] (Note: Exhibiting this competency presumes the treasurer has certain knowledge and skills that one could measure.)

Comparing Traditional versus Competency-Based Job Analysis

In practice, in almost any job description today some of the job's listed duties and responsibilities are competency-based, while most are not. For example, consider the typical duties you might find in a marketing manager's job description. Which of the duties would complete this phrase: "In order to perform this job competently, the employee should be able to..."?

Some familiar duties and responsibilities would not easily fit these requirements. For example, "works with writers and artists and oversees copywriting, design, layout, and production of promotional materials" is not particularly measurable. How can the extent to which the employee "works with writers and artists" or "oversees copywriting, design, and layout" be measured? Put another way, in analyzing this job, how would one determine whether the person had been adequately trained to work with writers and artists? In fact, what sort of training would that duty and responsibility even imply? It's not clear at all.

On the other hand, some of the job's typical duties and responsibilities are more easily expressed as competencies. For example, the phrase "to perform this job competently, the employee should be able to..." could easily be completed with "conduct marketing surveys on current and new-product concepts, prepare marketing activity reports, and develop and execute marketing plans and programs."

Team-Based Job Designs

A logical outgrowth of job enrichment and the job characteristics model has been the increasing use of **team-based job designs**, which focus on giving a **team**, rather than an individual, a whole and meaningful piece of work to do. Team members are empowered to decide among themselves how to accomplish the work.[14] Often they are cross-trained and then rotated through different tasks. Team-based designs are best suited to flat and matrix organization structures. Increasingly, organizations are using "virtual teams"—people working together effectively and efficiently across boundaries of time and space and using software to make team meetings more productive.[15]

STEP 3: COLLECTING JOB ANALYSIS INFORMATION

Various qualitative and quantitative techniques are used to collect information about the duties, responsibilities, and requirements of the job; the most important ones will be discussed in this section. In practice, when the information is being used for multiple purposes, ranging from developing recruitment criteria to compensation decisions, several techniques may be used in combination.

Collecting job analysis data usually involves a joint effort by an HR specialist, the incumbent, and the jobholder's supervisor. The HR specialist (an HR manager, job analyst, or consultant) might observe and analyze the work being done and then develop a job description and specification. The supervisor and incumbent generally also get involved, perhaps by filling out questionnaires. The supervisor and incumbent typically review and verify the job analyst's conclusions regarding the job's duties, responsibilities, and requirements.

The interview is probably the most widely used method for determining the duties and responsibilities of a job. Three types of interviews are used to collect job analysis data:

1. *individual interviews* with each employee;
2. *group interviews* with employees who have the same job; and
3. *supervisory interviews* with one or more supervisors who are thoroughly knowledgeable about the job being analyzed.

The group interview is used when a large number of employees are performing similar or identical work, and it can be a quick and inexpensive way of learning about the job. As a rule, the immediate supervisor attends the group session; if not, the supervisor should be interviewed separately to get that person's perspective on the duties and responsibilities of the job.

expert
▲opinion
academic viewpoint

Dr. Arla Day

Identification: Dr. Arla Day (PhD), Canada Research Chair in Industrial/Organizational Psychology

Affiliation: Department of Psychology, Saint Mary's University

1. Some of your research focuses on uses of Information and Communication Technology (ICT) on the workplace and the impact that has on perceptions of stress. Why did you focus on ICT?

We've seen how communication technology is a source of stress for people at work (cell phones, pagers, computer crashes, etc.). However, there is very little research exploring outcomes of communication technology on the workforce: specifically well-being, productivity, and stress. I was interested in examining the prevalence of ICT in the workplace to make both the work and the workplace better for individuals and organizations; to what extent can information communication technology actually help the individual, make lives more stressful, and what can organizations do to support ICT in the workplace?

Individuals who use more technology feel increased expectations to be more available, to stay current, and to learn more programs. Casual users of technology don't have the same expectations. As a result, I focused my research on ICT in the workplace.

2. Your research uses the Job Demands–Resources Model. What is the difference between a job resource and a job demand, and how does ICT affect both?

Technology as a job resource can help people do jobs better, with the ultimate aim to improve well-being. In contrast, technology as a job demand suggests that there are associated costs to the individual, with expectations of time and resource commitments for personal growth and development.

Interestingly, ICT can act as a demand and a resource. As a resource, ICT can help individuals complete job tasks, make the job easier, and can act as a collaboration tool. In addition, ICT is a demand based on how it is you. For example, employees with cell phones might feel pressure to have phones turned on all the time and immediately respond to requests. This can act as a source of stress, which can lead to exhaustion or burn out.

3. What can organizations do to reduce levels of stress associated with use of ICT in the workplace?

I. The level of control an employee has over the use of ICT can mitigate negative outcomes, because it empowers the employees to make choices about context and use. This has also been shown to improve the job function and reduce stress.

II. Employees need ICT support, not only in regards to how, when, and why the technology is used, but also trusting the employee to use the technology for a variety of reasons (e.g., checking Facebook at lunch).

III. Support the technology well, making sure that it is updated and that the product works as intended. Troubleshoot problems. So day-to-day functions of the software, and ensuring that the software is compatible with the desired uses. Ensure that employees are given an opportunity to be trained on the use of each adaptation.

Source: Reprinted by permission from Dr. Arla Day.

The most fruitful interviews follow a structured or checklist format. A job analysis questionnaire may be used to interview job incumbents or may be filled out by them. It includes a series of detailed questions regarding such matters as the general purpose of the job; responsibilities and duties; the education, experience, and skills required; physical and mental demands; and working conditions. The Expert Opinion box discusses job demands and the impact research associated with job demands and stress.

Interview Guidelines

When conducting a job analysis interview, supervisors and job analysts should keep several things in mind:

1. The job analyst and supervisor should work together to identify the employees who know the job best and those who might be expected to be the most objective in describing their duties and responsibilities.

2. Rapport should be established quickly with the interviewee by using the individual's name, speaking in easily understood language, briefly reviewing the purpose of the interview (job analysis, not performance appraisal), and explaining how the person came to be chosen.

3. A structured guide or checklist that lists questions and provides spaces for answers should be used. Using a form ensures that crucial questions are identified ahead of time, that complete and accurate information is gathered, and that all interviewers (if there is more than one) glean the same types of data, thereby helping to ensure comparability of results. However, leeway should also be permitted by including some open-ended questions, such as "Is there anything that we didn't cover with our questions?"

4. When duties are not performed in a regular manner—for instance, when the **incumbent** doesn't perform the same tasks or jobs over and over again many times a day—the incumbent should be asked to list his or her duties *in order of importance and frequency of occurrence*. This will ensure that crucial activities that occur infrequently—like a nurse's occasional emergency room duties—aren't overlooked.

5. The data should be reviewed and verified by both the interviewee and his or her immediate supervisor.

incumbent Individual currently holding the position.

Questionnaire

Having employees or supervisors fill out questionnaires to describe job-related duties and responsibilities is another good method of obtaining job analysis information. There are two major decisions around a questionnaire: how structured it will be and who will complete it. In practice, a typical job analysis questionnaire often falls between the two extremes of structured and open-ended. **Table 4.1** shows the difference between the two, identifying some of the decisions that should be made when planning a questionnaire.

HR Competency

20600

Position Analysis Questionnaire (PAQ) A questionnaire used to collect quantifiable data concerning the duties and responsibilities of various jobs.

One of the most popular pre-developed, structured job analysis questionnaires is the **Position Analysis Questionnaire (PAQ)**.[16] The PAQ itself is filled in by a job analyst, who should already be acquainted with the particular job to be analyzed. The PAQ contains 194 items, each of which represents a basic element that may or may not play an important role in the job. The job analyst decides whether each item plays a role in the job and, if so, to what extent (using a five-point scale). If, for example, "written

TABLE 4.1   Considerations for Developing Job Analysis Questionnaire

1. How structured is a questionnaire?

Structured	Open-ended
a long list of specific duties or tasks (such as "change and splice wire")	simply describes the major duties of the job
asks whether or not each duty or task is performed	
how much time is normally spent on the task	

2. Who will complete questionnaire?

Employees: may inflate requirements	Supervisors: may be unaware of all components of the job

PAQ Services Inc.
www.paq.com

materials" received a rating of four, this would indicate that materials such as books, reports, and office notes play a considerable role in this job.

The advantage of the PAQ is that it provides a quantitative score or profile of the job in terms of how that job rates on six basic dimensions: (1) information input, (2) mental processes, (3) work output (physical activities and tools), (4) relationships with others, (5) job context (the physical and social environment), and (6) other job characteristics (such as pace and structure). Because it allows for the assignment of a quantitative score to each job based on these six dimensions, the PAQ's real strength is in classifying jobs. Results can be used to compare jobs with one another; this information can then be used to determine appropriate pay levels.[17]

Functional Job Analysis (FJA)
A quantitative method for classifying jobs based on types and amounts of responsibility for data, people, and things. Performance standards and training requirements are also identified.

Functional Job Analysis (FJA) is also a regularly used pre-established questionnaire that rates a job on responsibilities for data, people, and things from simple to complex. For example, working with "things" literally means the physical interaction with tangibles such as desktop equipment (pencils, paper clips, telephone), groceries, luggage, or a bus. Physical involvement with tangibles such as a telephone may not seem very important in tasks primarily concerned with data (such as data analysis) or people (such as nursing), but its importance is quickly apparent for a worker with a disability. This technique also identifies performance standards and training requirements. Thus, FJA allows the analyst to answer the question: "To do this task and meet these standards, what training does the worker require?"[18]

Observations

Observation involves watching employees perform their work and recording the frequency of behaviours or the nature of performance. This can be done using information that is prepared in advance (structured), or in real time with no advance information provided to the observer (unstructured), or a combination of the two.

Direct observation is especially useful when jobs consist mainly of observable physical activities. Jobs like those of a janitor, assembly-line worker, and accounting clerk are examples. Third-party observation focuses more on reality than perception. As a result, third-party observation is often viewed as having more credibility, since there is minimal incentive to distort the results.

A challenge is that observations can influence job behaviour. Additionally, observation is usually not appropriate when the job entails a lot of immeasurable mental activity (e.g., lawyers or design engineers). Nor is it useful if the employee engages in important activities that might occur only occasionally, such as compiling year-end reports. Often, direct observation and interviewing are used together.

Participant Diary/Log

diary/log Daily listings made by employees of every activity in which they engage, along with the time each activity takes.

Another technique involves asking employees to keep a **diary/log** or list of what they do during the day. Each employee records every activity in which he or she is involved (along with the time spent) in a log. This can produce a very complete picture of the job, especially when supplemented with subsequent interviews with the employee and his or her supervisor. The employee might, of course, try to exaggerate some activities and underplay others. However, the detailed, chronological nature of the log tends to minimize this problem.

The National Occupational Classification

National Occupational Classification (NOC) A reference tool for writing job descriptions and job specifications. Compiled by the federal government, it contains comprehensive, standardized descriptions of about 40 000 occupations and the requirements for each.

The **National Occupational Classification (NOC)**, the product of systematic, field-based research by Human Resources and Skills Development Canada (HRSDC), is an excellent source of standardized job information. It was updated and revised in 2011 and contains comprehensive descriptions of approximately 40 000 occupations and the requirements for each. To illustrate the types of information included, the NOC listing for specialists in human resources is shown in **Figure 4.5**.

Organizations can readily access information regarding the required activities, requirements, competencies, and so on by job title. However, it is highly recommended that companies who use external sources such as the NOC:

1. adjust information based on their organizational strategy and structure;

2. update information as required (for example, the term "personnel" is used in reference to educational attainment; while this was an appropriate term in the late 1990s when the data was collected, the evolution of HR has made this term obsolete); and

3. engage in the verification techniques in detail as per Step 4 (which we will discuss shortly).

occupation A collection of jobs that share some or all of a set of main duties.

The NOC and its counselling component, the *Career Handbook* (2nd ed.), both focus on occupations rather than jobs. An **occupation** is defined as a collection of jobs that share some or all of a set of main duties. The list of examples of job titles within each of the 520 Unit Groups in the NOC provides a frame of reference for the boundaries of that occupational group. The jobs within each group are characterized by similar skills.

Occupational Information Network **www.job-analysis.net**

To provide a complete representation of work in the Canadian economy, the NOC classifies occupations into Major Groups based on two key dimensions—skill level and skill type. The Major Groups, which are identified by two-digit numbers, are then broken down further into Minor Groups, with a third digit added, and Unit Groups, at which level a fourth digit is added. Within these three levels of classification, a Unit Group provides the actual profile of an occupation.[19] For example:

Major Group 31—Professional Occupations in Health

Minor Group 311—Physicians, Dentists, and Veterinarians

Unit Group 3113—Dentists

FIGURE 4.5   NOC Job Description for Specialists in Human Resources

1121 Human resources professionals

- Human resources professionals develop, implement, and evaluate human resources and labour relations policies, programs, and procedures and advise managers and employers on human resource matters. Human resources professionals are employed throughout the private and public sectors, or they may be self-employed.
- *Example Titles*
  - business agent, labour organization
  - classification officer - human resources
  - classification specialist
  - compensation research analyst
  - conciliator
  (*more available online*)

Main Duties

- Human resources professionals perform some or all of the following duties:
  - Plan, develop, implement, & evaluate human resources and labour relations strategies including policies, programs, and procedures to address an organization's human resources requirements
  - Advise managers and employees on the interpretation of human resources policies, compensation and benefit programs, and collective agreements
  - Negotiate collective agreements on behalf of employers or workers, mediate labour disputes & grievances, and provide advice on employee and labour relations
  - Research and prepare occupational classifications, job descriptions, salary scales, and competency appraisal measures and systems
  (*more available online*)

Employment Requirements

- A university degree or college diploma in human resources management or a related field, such as business administration, industrial relations, commerce, or psychology or completion of a professional development program in human resources administration is required.
- Some employers may require human resources professionals to hold a Ceritified Human Resources Professional (CHRP) designation

Additional Information

- Progression to management positions is possible with experience
- Classified elsewhere
  - *Human resources and recruitment officers (1223)*
  - *Human resources managers (0112)*
  - *Personnel clerks (1415)*
  - *Professional occupations in business management consulting (1122)*
  - *Training officers and instructors (in 4021 College & other vocational instructors)*

Source: Title: Human Resources and Skills Development Canada, National Occupational Classification, 2011 URL: http://www5.hrsdc.gc.ca/noc/2011/QuickSearch.aspx?val65=1121 Employment and Social Development Canada, 2015. Reproduced with the permission of the Minister of Employment and Social Development Canada, 2015.

Using Multiple Sources of Job Analysis Information

Job analysis information can be obtained from individual workers, groups, supervisors, or observers. Interviews, observations, or questionnaires can be used. Some firms use a single approach, but one study suggests that using just one source is not wise because

An Ethical Dilemma

If a job analyst is on the other side of the world from an employee who completed a web-based job analysis questionnaire, should another method of job analysis also be used to confirm the accuracy of the information?

each approach has drawbacks. For example, in a group interview, some group members may feel pressure to go along with the group's consensus, or an individual employee may be careless about how he or she completes a questionnaire. Thus, collecting job analysis data from only one source may lead to inaccurate conclusions, so when possible, job analysis data should be collected from several sources.

STEP 4: VERIFYING INFORMATION

cartoonresource/Fotolia

"The Big Book of Information Overload just came in."

The job analysis information should be verified with any workers performing the job and with the immediate supervisor. This corroboration will help to confirm that the information is factually correct and complete, and it can also help gain the employees' acceptance of the job analysis data.

The knowledge that information will be verified increases the reliability and validity of the results in two ways. First, areas of inconsistency or concern can be further probed to develop awareness as to why the inconsistency exists and what should be done about it. Second, participants in the data collection techniques will be more honest and consistent knowing that they may later be held accountable for their contributions.

STEP 5: WRITING JOB DESCRIPTIONS AND JOB SPECIFICATIONS

cartoonresource/Fotolia

"We need a columnist whose political analysis is cogent and articulate. You game?"

Job Descriptions

A **job description** is a written statement of *what* the jobholder actually does, *how* he or she does it, and *under what conditions* the job is performed. The description is quite comprehensive and includes such essential elements as job identification, summary, and duties and responsibilities, as well as the human qualifications for the job.

No standard format is used in writing job descriptions, but most include the following types of information: job identification, job summary, relationships, duties and responsibilities, authority of incumbent, performance standards, and working conditions. As mentioned previously, job specifications (human qualifications) may also be included. Recently, some organizations have experimented with job titles, allowing employees an opportunity to be involved in establishing their own job titles, based largely on the results of the job analysis. The HR in the News box highlights the results of recent research in the area of job titles.

job description A list of the duties, responsibilities, reporting relationships, and working conditions of a job—one product of a job analysis.

Job Identification

The job identification section generally contains several categories of information. The *position title* specifies the title of the job, such as vice-president, marketing manager,

HR IN THE NEWS

Experimenting with Job Titles

Given that job titles carry important meaning, organizations that allow employees to participate in defining their job titles (e.g., Yahoo, IBM, Google, Quicken Loans) attempt to bridge employees' desire for identity expression with an organizational desire or need for control. Researchers at the Wharton School and the London School of Business studied the impact of the recent experimental practice of allowing employees to participate in creating their own job titles (called self-reflective

job titles). Such job titles provide meaning to employees both at work (often as the first piece of information communicated to others) and off the job (as a vehicle for identity expression and image construction), and thus are critical in how employees present and view themselves in the world. The results of the studies, which are published in the *Academy of Management Journal*, identify three significant findings that managers can benefit from.

1. Self-reflective job titles can help employees cope with emotional exhaustion, by allowing

employees to focus on the positive aspects of their contributions to work.

2. Involving employees in their job title development can help employees see the "we" in the organization, allowing them to establish how they are distinctive in the larger established organizational framework and structure.

3. Rather than viewing job titles as a symbol of organizational bureaucracy (thus a source of frustration), self-reflective job titles are effective in employee stress reduction.[20]

recruiter, or inventory control clerk. The *department* and *location* are also indicated, along with the title of the immediate supervisor—in this case under the heading *reports to*.

Job Summary

The *job summary* describes the general nature of the job, listing only its major functions or activities. For the job of materials manager, the summary might state that he or she will "purchase economically, regulate deliveries of, store, and distribute all materials necessary on the production line," while the summary for a mailroom supervisor might indicate that he or she will "receive, sort, and deliver all incoming mail properly, and he or she will handle all outgoing mail, including the accurate and timely posting of such mail."[21]

An Ethical Dilemma

In view of the fact that job descriptions are not required by law and that some organizations have found them no longer relevant, would abolishing job descriptions raise any moral or legal concerns?

Relationships

The *relationships* section indicates the jobholder's relationships with others inside and outside the organization Others directly and indirectly supervised are included, along with peers, superiors, and outsiders relevant to the job.

Duties and Responsibilities

This section presents a detailed list of the job's major duties and responsibilities. Each of the job's major duties should be listed separately and described in a few sentences.

For instance, the duties of the vice-president of human resources might include developing and recommending HRM strategies, policies, and practices; providing policy guidance; and identifying, analyzing, and interpreting internal and external environmental changes. Typical duties of other jobs might include maintaining balanced and controlled inventories, making accurate postings to accounts payable, maintaining favourable purchase price variances, or repairing production line tools and equipment.

HR Competency

10600

Most experts state unequivocally that "one item frequently found that should *never* be included in a job description is a 'cop-out clause' like 'other duties, as assigned.'" This phrase leaves open the nature of the job and the people needed to staff it, and it can be subject to abuse.[22]

Authority

This section of a job description should define the limits of the jobholder's authority, including his or her decision-making authority, direct supervision of other employees, and budgetary limitations. For example, the vice-president of human resources may have the authority to approve all budgeted non-capital expenditures and budgeted capital expenditures up to $100 000; approve expense accounts for subordinates; hire and fire subordinates; and exercise line authority over direct reporting positions.

Performance Standards/Indicators

Some job descriptions also contain a performance standards/indicators section, which indicates the standards the employee is expected to achieve in each of the job description's main duties and responsibilities.

Setting standards is never easy. Most managers soon learn, however, that just telling employees to "do their best" doesn't provide enough guidance to ensure top performance. One straightforward way of setting standards is to finish the statement: "I will be completely satisfied with your work when..." This sentence, if completed for each duty listed in the job description, should result in a usable set of performance standards.[23] Some examples would include the following:

Duty: Accurately Posting Accounts Payable

- All invoices received are posted within the same working day.
- All invoices are routed to the proper department managers for approval no later than the day following receipt.
- No more than three posting errors per month occur, on average.
- The posting ledger is balanced by the end of the third working day of each month.

Duty: Meeting Daily Production Schedule

- Work group produces no fewer than 426 units per working day.
- No more than 2 percent of units are rejected at the next workstation, on average.
- Work is completed with no more than 5 percent overtime per week, on average.

Working Conditions and Physical Environment

The job description should also list the general working conditions involved in the job. This section generally includes information about noise level, temperature, lighting, degree of privacy, frequency of interruptions, hours of work, amount of travel, and hazards to which the incumbent may be exposed.

Special guidelines for entrepreneurial and small businesses are provided in the Entrepreneurs and HR box.

Job Descriptions and Human Rights Legislation

Human rights legislation requires employers to ensure that there is no discrimination on any of the prohibited grounds in any aspect of the terms and conditions of employment. To ensure that job descriptions comply with this legislation, a few key points should be kept in mind:

- Job descriptions are not legally required but are highly advisable.

- Essential job duties should be clearly identified in the job description. Indicating the percentage of time spent on each duty or listing duties in order of importance are strategies used to differentiate between essential and non-essential tasks and responsibilities.

- When assessing suitability for employment, training program enrollment, and transfers or promotions, and when appraising performance, the only criteria examined should be the knowledge, skills, and abilities (KSAs) required for the essential duties of the job.

- When an employee cannot perform one or more of the essential duties because of reasons related to a prohibited ground, such as a physical disability or religion, reasonable accommodation to the point of undue hardship is required.

Job Specifications

job specification A list of the "human requirements," that is, the requisite knowledge, skills, and abilities needed to perform the job—another product of a job analysis.

Writing the **job specification** involves examining the duties and responsibilities of the job and answering the question, "What human traits and experience are required to do this job?" Much of this information can be obtained from the job analysis questionnaire. The job specification clarifies what kind of person to recruit and which qualities that person should be tested for. It is sometimes included with the job description.

Complying with human rights legislation means keeping a few pointers in mind:

- All listed qualifications are bona fide occupational requirements (BFORs) based on the current job duties and responsibilities.

- Unjustifiably high educational or lengthy experience requirements can lead to systemic discrimination.

- The qualifications of the current incumbent should not be confused with the minimum requirements, since he or she might be underqualified or overqualified.

- For entry-level jobs, identifying the actual physical and mental demands is critical. For example, if the job requires detailed manipulation on a circuit-board assembly line, finger dexterity is extremely important and is something for which candidates should be tested. A **physical demands analysis**—which identifies the senses used and the type, frequency, and amount of physical effort involved in the job—is often used to supplement the job specification. Having such detailed information is particularly beneficial when determining accommodation requirements. The mental and emotional demands of a job are typically missing from job analysis information. They should be specified so that the mental and emotional competencies of job applicants can be assessed and any need for accommodation can be identified.

Hints TO ENSURE LEGAL COMPLIANCE

physical demands analysis Identification of the senses used and the type, frequency, and amount of physical effort involved in a job.

HR Competency

20600

ENTREPRENEURS and HR

A Practical Approach to Job Analysis and Job Descriptions

Without their own job analysts or even their own HR managers, many small-business owners need a more streamlined approach to job analysis. A resource that includes all of the possible positions that they might encounter, with a detailed listing of the duties normally assigned to these positions, exists in the National Occupational Classification (NOC) mentioned earlier. The practical approach to job analysis for small-business owners presented next is built around this invaluable reference tool.

Step 1: Develop an Organization Chart

Drawing up the organization chart of the present structure comes first. Then, depending on how far in advance planning is being done, a chart can be produced that shows how the organization should look in the immediate future (say, in two months), as well as two or three other charts showing how the organization is likely to evolve over the next two or three years.

Step 2: Use a Job Analysis Questionnaire

Next, a job analysis questionnaire can be used to determine what each job entails. A shorter version of one of the more comprehensive job analysis questionnaires may be useful for collecting job analysis data. An example of a job summary for a customer service clerk follows:

Answers inquiries and gives directions to customers, authorizes cashing of customers' cheques, records and returns lost credit cards, sorts and reviews new credit applications, and works at the customer service desk.

Step 3: Obtain a Copy of the National Occupational Classification (NOC) and Related Publications for Reference

Next, standardized examples of the job descriptions needed should be obtained from the NOC website at www5.hrsdc.gc.ca/NOC/English/NOC/2011/Welcome.aspx. A related publication entitled *Job Descriptions: An Employers' Handbook* is also available for downloading from the NOC website atwww5.hrsdc.gc.ca/NOC/English/NOC/2011/EmployersHandbook.aspx.

Step 4: Choose Appropriate Job Titles and Job Descriptions and Copy Them for Reference

For each department, the NOC job titles and job descriptions that are believed to be appropriate should be chosen. The NOC definition will provide a firm foundation for the job description being created. It will provide a standardized list and constant reminder of the specific duties that should be included.

Step 5: Complete the Job Description

An appropriate job description for the job under consideration can then be written. The job analysis information, together with the information from the NOC, can be used to create a complete listing of the tasks and duties of each of the jobs. The working conditions section can be completed once all of the tasks and duties have been specified.

An Ethical Dilemma

Are personality traits really part of the KSAs and bona fide occupational requirements/essential duties of a job?

Identifying the human requirements for a job can be accomplished through a judgmental approach (based on educated guesses of job incumbents, supervisors, and HR managers) or statistical analysis (based on the relationship between some human trait or skill and some criterion of job effectiveness). Basing job specifications on statistical analysis is more legally defensible. For example, the Personality-Related Position Requirements Form (PPRF) is a survey instrument designed to assist managers in identifying potential personality-related traits that may be important in a job. Identifying personality dimensions is difficult when using most job analysis techniques, because they tend to be much better suited to unearthing human aptitudes and skills—like manual dexterity. The PPRF uses questionnaire items to assess the relevance of such basic personality dimensions as agreeableness, conscientiousness, and emotional stability to the job under study. The relevance of these personality traits can then be assessed through statistical analysis.[24]

Completing the Job Specification Form

Once the required human characteristics have been determined, whether using statistical analysis or a judgmental approach, a job specification form should be completed.

Writing Competency-Based Job Descriptions

Defining the job's competencies and writing them up involves a process that is similar in most respects to traditional job analysis. In other words, the manager will interview job incumbents and their supervisors, ask open-ended questions regarding job responsibilities and activities, and perhaps identify critical incidents that pinpoint success on the job. These job descriptions can be particularly useful in organizations that use competency-based pay, as discussed in Chapter 11.

STEP 6: COMMUNICATION AND PREPARATIONS FOR REVISIONS

HR Competency

40200

Organizations are often affected by internal and external factors, as described in Chapter 1, that influence organizational strategy, structure, or processes. Most organizations adopt strategies with a three- to five-year target, and many are forced to adjust according to environmental factors much sooner. Significant organizational changes like restructuring, new product development, technological changes, and competition modify the nature of how work is done, resulting in a need for revisions to the existing job descriptions and specifications. A 2013 study by the Conference Board of Canada highlights that the reasons for conducting a job analysis vary (as per **Table 4.2**), thus communication of the results of job analysis may vary.

Job analysis must be structured enough to allow for modifications as required while still providing current and future employees with an understanding of what they are expected to do. Once a system is developed to collect data, an organization may

TABLE 4.2 Job Evaluation: Why Do We Do It? What Do We Use It For?

Why do we do it?		What do we use it for?	
Reason	(%)	Use	(%)
Internal equity	94	Career paths/ladders	59
Market competitiveness validation	72	Performance management standards/expectations	55
Good practice	66	Recruitment protocols	49
Compliance with pay equity legislation	58	Variable pay differentials	41
Other (e.g., required in collective agreement)	5	Competency standards/levels	37
		Training and Development budgets	14
		Other (e.g., org. design)	4

Source: Stewart, Nicole. *Job Evaluation and Classification: A State of Practice in Canadian Organizations.* Ottawa: The Conference Board of Canada, 2014.

choose to (1) regularly update the data collected in a proactive manner, (2) develop systems to collect data on an ongoing basis, or (3) adjust job analysis activities in a reactive manner after a significant organizational change is initiated.

Information provided from the job analysis must be communicated to all relevant stakeholders. For example, employees must be aware of the core job requirements to help drive desired performance. Line managers must be aware of information provided in the job analysis to help align expectations of various jobs, manage performance, and manage HR planning activities. Recruiters use this information to determine and assess the desired knowledge, skills, abilities, and other characteristics (KSAOs) of potential candidates and to develop job ads. Compensation specialists can use this information to develop or modify pay scales according to job-related activities. Overall, the job analysis process is a fundamental component of HRM and a cornerstone that is critical to other organizational activities related to labour and work processes.

CHAPTER SUMMARY

1. In any organization, work has to be divided into manageable units and ultimately into jobs that can be performed by employees. The process of organizing work into tasks that are required to perform a specific job is known as job design. The term "job" means a group of tasks and duties, and several employees may have the same job. The collection of tasks and responsibilities performed by one person is known as a "position."

2. Job analysis involves six steps: (1) collect background information, (2) select the representative positions and jobs to be analyzed, (3) collect data, (4) review the information collected with the incumbents and their supervisors, (5) develop job descriptions and job specifications, and (6) communicate and review on an ongoing basis.

3. Techniques used to gather job analysis data include interviews, questionnaires (including the PAQ and FJA), direct observation, participant diaries/logs, and the National Occupational Classification (NOC), to list just a few.

4. Competency-based job analysis, focusing on how the job is done (the behaviours required) more than on task requirements, has become more common for three reasons. First, traditional job descriptions may not be appropriate in organizations with flexible jobs. Second, describing the job in terms of the skills, knowledge, and competencies the worker needs is more strategic. Third, competency-based job analysis supports the employer's performance management process.

5. A job description is a written statement of what the jobholder actually does, how he or she does it, and under what conditions the job is performed. The job specification involves examining the duties and responsibilities and answering this question: "What human traits and experience are required to do this job?"

MyManagementLab

Study, practise, and explore real business situations with these helpful resources:
- **Interactive Lesson Presentations:** Work through interactive presentations and assessments to test your knowledge of management concepts.
- **PIA (Personal Inventory Assessments):** Enhance your ability to connect with key concepts through these engaging self-reflection assessments.
- **Study Plan:** Check your understanding of chapter concepts with self-study quizzes.
- **Videos:** Learn more about the management practices and strategies of real companies.
- **Simulations:** Practise decision-making in simulated management environments.

P I A PERSONAL INVENTORY ASSESSMENT

KEY TERMS

competencies *(p. 89)*
competency-based job analysis *(p. 89)*
diary/log *(p. 95)*
ergonomics *(p. 88)*
Functional Job Analysis (FJA) *(p. 94)*
incumbent *(p. 93)*
industrial engineering *(p. 87)*
job *(p. 81)*
job analysis *(p. 81)*
job description *(p. 97)*
job design *(p. 84)*
job enlargement (horizontal loading) *(p. 87)*
job enrichment (vertical loading) *(p. 88)*

job rotation *(p. 87)*
job specification *(p. 100)*
National Occupational Classification (NOC) *(p. 95)*
occupation *(p. 95)*
organization chart *(p. 83)*
organizational structure *(p. 83)*
physical demands analysis *(p. 100)*
position *(p. 81)*
Position Analysis Questionnaire (PAQ) *(p. 93)*
process chart *(p. 84)*
team *(p. 91)*
team-based job designs *(p. 91)*
work simplification *(p. 86)*

REVIEW AND DISCUSSION QUESTIONS

1. Explain how job analysis provides important information that is required for at least three different functions of HRM.

2. Differentiate among job enlargement, job rotation, and job enrichment, and provide an example of each.

3. Why is ergonomic job design becoming increasingly important?

4. Several methods for collecting job analysis data are available—interviews, the Position Analysis Questionnaire, and so on. Compare and contrast four of these methods, explaining what each is useful for and listing the pros and cons of each.

5. Although not legally required, having job descriptions is highly advisable. Why? How can firms ensure that their job specifications are legally defensible?

6. What are competencies? Why are companies starting to use competency-based job analysis? How is this approach different from the traditional approach?

7. In a company with only 25 employees, is there less need for job descriptions? Why or why not?

CRITICAL THINKING QUESTIONS

1. Why isn't it always desirable or appropriate to use job enrichment when designing jobs? How would you determine how enriched an individual employee's job should be?

2. Assume that you are the job analyst at a bicycle manufacturing company in British Columbia and have been assigned responsibility for preparing job descriptions (including specifications) for all the

supervisory and managerial positions. One of the production managers has just indicated that he will not complete the job analysis questionnaire you have developed.

a. How would you handle this situation?

b. What arguments would you use to attempt to persuade him to change his mind?

c. If your persuasion efforts failed, how would you go about obtaining the job analysis information you need to develop the job description for his position?

3. Because the top job in a firm (such as president, executive director, or CEO) is by nature more strategic and broader in scope than any other job, is competency-based job analysis more appropriate? Is there less need for a job description for the president? Why or why not?

4. If you were designing a job for a new marketing and sales representative for a small entrepreneurial company that is experiencing rapid growth, what approach would you take? Explain why you would take this approach. How would you go about determining job specifications?

5. If a supervisor reviews the job analysis information provided by an employee and says that the job duties and responsibilities have been inflated, but the employee says that the supervisor does not really know what the job entails, how can a decision be made about what information is accurate?

EXPERIENTIAL EXERCISES

1. Use organization chart software to draw an organization chart that accurately depicts the structure of the organization in which you are currently employed or one with which you are thoroughly familiar. Once you have completed this task, form a group with several of your classmates. Taking turns, have each member show his or her organization chart to the group, briefly describe the structure depicted, explain whether or not the structure seems to be appropriate, and identify several advantages and disadvantages he or she experienced working within this structure.

2. Working individually or in groups and using the HRSDC website, find the National Occupational Classification (NOC) job descriptions for both a university professor and a college professor. Compare the two descriptions, noting similarities and differences. Using the NOC descriptions and your own observations of people in this role, create a competency profile for each job. How similar are they? Why do you think this is so? Compare and discuss your results with other individual students or groups.

3. Working individually, prepare a job description (including job specifications) for a position that you know well, using the job analysis questionnaire in this chapter. Once you have done so, exchange job descriptions with someone else in the class. Critique your colleague's job description and provide specific suggestions regarding any additions/deletions/revisions that you would recommend to ensure that the job description accurately reflects the job and is legally defensible.

4. Working in groups of three or four, identify the jobs that have been or are held by students in your group. Select one job to analyze. Use the job analysis questionnaire provided in the chapter to conduct a job analysis interview and document a job description and specifications. Compare and critique your work with the work done by another group.

RUNNING CASE

Running Case: LearnInMotion.com

Who Do We Have to Hire?

As the excitement surrounding the move into their new offices wound down, the two principal owners of LearnInMotion.com, Pierre and Jennifer, turned to the task of hiring new employees. In their business plan they'd specified several basic goals for the venture capital funds they'd just received, and hiring a team topped the list. They knew their other goals—boosting sales and expanding the website, for instance—would be unreachable without the right team.

They were just about to place their ads when Pierre asked a question that brought them to a stop: "What kind of people do we want to hire?" It seemed they hadn't really considered this. They knew the answer in general terms, of course. For example, they knew they needed at least two salespeople, a programmer, a web designer, and several content management people to transform the incoming material into content they could post on their site. But it was obvious that job titles alone really didn't provide enough guidance. For example, if they couldn't specify the exact duties of these positions, how could they decide whether they needed experienced employees? How could they decide exactly what sorts of experiences and skills they had to look for in their candidates if they didn't know exactly what these candidates would have to do? They wouldn't even know what questions to ask.

And that wasn't all. For example, there were other tasks to do that weren't necessarily included in the sorts of things that salespeople, programmers, web designers, or content management people typically do. Who was going to answer the phones? (Jennifer and Pierre had originally assumed they'd put in one of those fancy automated call directory and voicemail systems—until they found out it

would cost close to $10 000.) As a practical matter, they knew they had to have someone answering the phones and directing callers to the proper extensions. Who was going to keep track of the monthly expenses and compile them for the accountants, who'd then produce monthly reports for the venture capitalist? Would the salespeople generate their own leads? Or would LearnInMotion.com have to hire web surfers to search and find the names of people for the sales staff to call or email? What would happen when the company had to purchase supplies, such as fax paper or printer ink? Would the owners have to do this themselves, or should they have someone in-house do it for them? The list, it seemed, went on and on.

It was obvious, in other words, that the owners had to get their managerial act together and draw up the sorts of documents they'd read about as business majors—job descriptions, job specifications, and so forth. The trouble was, it had all seemed a lot easier when they read the textbook. Now they want you, their management consultant, to help them actually do it.

QUESTIONS

1 To assist Pierre and Jennifer in developing much-needed job descriptions, follow the steps outlined in the job analysis process and design a job description for the positions of web designer, salesperson, and receptionist.

2 As part of the job analysis process you will follow in question 1, evaluate the methods of collecting job analysis information and discuss which ones you would recommend (including why) to Pierre and Jennifer as part of developing the job descriptions.

3 As their management consultant, would you recommend they use quantitative or qualitative methods, or both? Why?

CASE INCIDENT

What Is a Human Resources Consultant to Do?

Anthony LePage is the owner of a local recruitment agency that has an established presence in the northern Ontario market. He is looking to expand its service offerings to include consulting services to small businesses. A recent marketing blitz advertising this new service has led to a new partnership with a large local manufacturing business.

After the meeting with the owner of the manufacturing business, the mandate is clear that the owner is seeking the agency's assistance in creating and writing job descriptions for all of the positions within the company. Some of these positions include administrative assistants, sales, engineering, and skilled trades, along with many others. There are more than 100 descriptions to write. The owner would like to see a sample job description within one week before he signs the contract to complete the remainder of the job descriptions.

Anthony LePage has just hired you as the human resources consultant in charge of producing this job description sample for his new client and has asked you to answer the following questions.

QUESTIONS

1   Outline what the crucial differences are between a job description and a job specification.

2   The owner of the business has heard that qualitative methods produce the best job descriptions. Would you attempt to persuade him otherwise?

3   Develop a sample job description for the position of administrative assistant for the owner and explain why you included the various sections that you did.

4   The owner has heard from some of his colleagues about the use of competencies. He wants to know what they are and if these should be incorporated into the job descriptions he requires.

CHAPTER
5

Pavel L Photo and Video/Shutterstock

Human Resources Planning

LEARNING OUTCOMES

AFTER STUDYING THIS CHAPTER, YOU SHOULD BE ABLE TO

DEFINE human resources planning (HRP) and **DISCUSS** its strategic importance.

DESCRIBE four quantitative and two qualitative techniques used to forecast human resources demand.

DISCUSS briefly the four strategies used to forecast internal human resources supply and four types of market conditions assessed when forecasting external human resources supply.

DESCRIBE the ways in which a surplus of human resources can be handled.

EXPLAIN how organizations deal with a shortage of human resources.

REQUIRED HR COMPETENCIES

10100: Impact the organization and human resources practices by bringing to bear a strategic perspective that is informed by economic, societal, technological, political, and demographic trends to enhance the value of human resources.

10400: Contribute to the organization's vision, mission, values, and goals, demonstrating business acumen and participating in the strategic planning process, to support organizational objectives.

10600: Align human resources practices by translating organizational strategy into human resources objectives and priorities to achieve the organization's plan.

20600: Promote an evidence-based approach to the development of human resources policies and practices using current professional resources to provide a sound basis for human resources decision-making.

40100: Create a workforce plan by identifying current and future talent needs to support the organization's goals and objectives.

40200: Increase the attractiveness of the employer to desirable potential employees by identifying and shaping the organization's employee value proposition to build a high quality workforce.

90100: Make informed business decisions using financial and operating information to align human resources with business strategy.

90200: Conduct comprehensive human resources audits by sampling policies, procedures, programs, and systems to identify strengths and areas for improvement and to ensure compliance.

90300: Specify the requirements for a human resources information system that captures data and generates reports to inform leaders of trends to achieve organizational objectives.

THE STRATEGIC IMPORTANCE OF HUMAN RESOURCES PLANNING

human resources planning (HRP) The process of forecasting future human resources requirements to ensure that the organization will have the required number of employees with the necessary skills to meet its strategic objectives.

Human resources planning (HRP) is the process of forecasting future human resources requirements to ensure that the organization will have the required number of employees with the necessary skills to meet its strategic objectives. HRP is a proactive process, which both anticipates and influences an organization's future by systematically forecasting the supply of and demand for employees under changing conditions and by developing plans and activities to satisfy these needs. Effective HRP helps an organization achieve its strategic goals and objectives, achieve economies in hiring new workers, make major labour market demands more successfully, anticipate and avoid shortages and surpluses of human resources, as well as control or reduce labour costs.

HRP has recently become a key strategic priority not just for HR departments but for strategic business planners as well. Currently, Canada is in the beginning stages of a major labour shortage. The existing labour shortage in Canada is forecast to increase to 1 million workers over the next 15 years.[1] As the baby boom generation begins to retire, there are not enough candidates to fill vacant positions.[2] On average, two out of every three job openings over the next decade will be focused on replacing retiring workers. In addition, fertility rates in Canada continue to decline, resulting in fewer possible workers for the future labour force. Combined, these conditions create a situation of fierce labour competition, further increasing the importance of effective HRP. HRP will be absolutely essential for successful strategy implementation.[3]

As illustrated in **Figure 5.1**, key steps in the HRP process include analyzing forecasted labour supply, forecasting labour demands, and then planning and implementing HR programs to balance supply and demand.

HR Competency

10100

FIGURE 5.1 Human Resources Planning Model

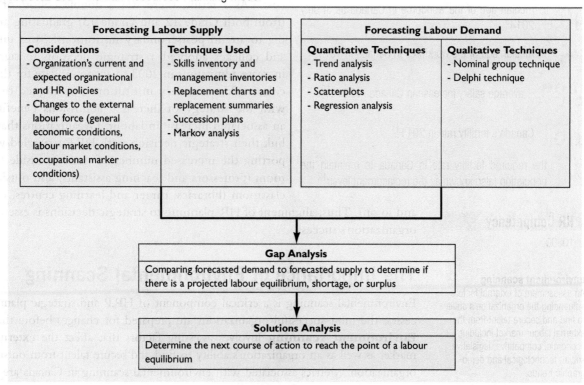

Forecasting Labour Supply		Forecasting Labour Demand	
Considerations	**Techniques Used**	**Quantitative Techniques**	**Qualitative Techniques**
- Organization's current and expected organizational and HR policies - Changes to the external labour force (general economic conditions, labour market conditions, occupational marker conditions)	- Skills inventory and management inventories - Replacement charts and replacement summaries - Succession plans - Markov analysis	- Trend analysis - Ratio analysis - Scatterplots - Regression analysis	- Nominal group technique - Delphi technique

Gap Analysis

Comparing forecasted demand to forecasted supply to determine if there is a projected labour equilibrium, shortage, or surplus

Solutions Analysis

Determine the next course of action to reach the point of a labour equilibrium

Lack of or inadequate human resources planning within an organization can result in significant costs when unstaffed positions create costly inefficiencies and when severance pay is required for large numbers of employees being laid off. It can also create situations in which one department is laying off employees while another is hiring individuals with similar skills, which can reduce morale or productivity and can often result in turnover. The greater concern is that ineffective HRP can lead to an organization's inability to accomplish short-term operational plans or long-range strategic plans.

HR by the Numbers

Strategic Workforce Planning in Canada

53% of organizations surveyed identify that their strategic workforce plan supports their organization's long-term business strategy objectives[4]

29% of organizations surveyed identify that they use a robust workforce planning process[5]

66% the labour force participation rate in Canada in 2013, defined as the percent of the population over 15 years of age that were able and willing to work (regardless of if they were employed or unemployed)[6]

80% of organizations report challenges with recruiting candidates who have required critical skills[7]

40.4 median age of the workforce in Canada as of July 2014[8]

26.2 median age of the workforce in Canada in 1971[9]

2.8% average salary increase in Canada in 2014[10]

1.61 Canada's fertility rate in 2011[11]

2.1 the required fertility rate in Canada to maintain the population (also known as the replacement level)[12]

HR Competency

10600

environment scanning
An assessment of external factors influencing the organization's ability to find and secure talent from the external labour market including economic, competitive, legislative, social, technological and demographic trends.

The Relationship between HRP and Strategic Planning

An HR plan (HRP) does not occur independently of the other departments within an organization (such as finance, marketing, and research and development). The HRP must align with the overall goals of the organization as well as both the long-term and short-term strategic plans set by the organization. Fundamental to the business planning process is the impact and alignment of HRP (as discussed in detail in Chapter 1). An organization's strategic decision to expand, redirect, diverge, divest, partner, or merge will have an associated effect on the HR expectations and plans of the organization.

Failure to integrate HRP and strategic planning can have very serious consequences. For example, in Ontario, a fifth year of high school called the Ontario Academic Credit (OAC) year (often referred to as Grade 13) was abolished in 2003 as an effort to cut provincial government costs. As a result, there was a double cohort of students (from both Grade 12 and Grade 13) graduating and wanting to attend postsecondary institutions. Most universities and colleges adopted a strategic decision to significantly increase admissions in 2003 to accommodate for the double cohort. Postsecondary institutions that aligned their HRP with the strategy of increased admissions benefited from an associated increase in labour. Organizations that did not link their strategic decision with HRP struggled with supporting the increased number of students inside the classroom (professors and teaching assistants) and outside of the classroom (libraries, career and learning centres, cafeterias, and so on). Thus, alignment of HR planning to strategic decisions is essential to an organization's success.

The Importance of Environmental Scanning

Environmental scanning is a critical component of HRP and strategic planning processes; the most successful organizations are prepared for changes before they occur. **Environment scanning** involves assessing factors that affect the external labour market as well as an organization's ability to find and secure talent from outside of the organization. Metrics associated with environmental scanning in Canada are provided

Tyler Olson/Fotolia

A trend toward higher education can reduce the size of the available external workforce in the short run.

in the HR by the Numbers box. The external environmental factors most frequently monitored include

- economic conditions (local, regional, national, international); for example, if the unemployment rate in a region is low, an organization would have to be more aggressive in recruiting talent, as selection may be more scarce

- market and competitive trends; for example, compensation policies that lag behind competitors' policies may result in higher turnover or more difficulties in attracting talent

- new or revised laws and the decisions of courts and quasi-judicial bodies; for example, a raise in the minimum wage rate can inflate the cost of labour in an organization, therefore creating budgetary pressure to reduce labour expenses

- social concerns such as healthcare, childcare, and educational priorities; for example, a trend toward securing higher education can reduce the size of the available external workforce in the short run, but in the longer run can result in retaining applicants with more specialized training

- technological changes affecting processes, products, and people; for example, a new technology developed at a local university can be implemented in the organization and significantly reduce labour demands through automation of a previously labour-intensive process

- demographic trends of an internal and external labour force; for example, if an organization is situated in a community largely inhabited by senior citizens, it may face difficulties securing a diverse or full-time workforce from the local area

HR Competency

10100

Steps in Human Resources Planning

HRP is critical to an organization's success as it aligns forecasted labour supply (provided by the human resources department) with the predicted labour demands of the organization (such as the number of employees needed and the skill sets required). An element of HR planning that is often taken for granted is the availability and accuracy of information regarding the current HR situation. Understanding the internal labour force in the present is the basis for a number of demand and supply estimates. Therefore, before embarking on an HR planning exercise, current HR levels must be assessed.

There are numerous sources of information for identifying existing talent and human resources in an organization. An organization chart can provide HR planners and managers with an understanding of the organizational structure, business units, and possible career paths. This macro-level information can be linked to more micro-level information, such as how many employees the company currently has at each level, what existing skill sets the employees have, as well as the demographic information and job-related information about the existing employee base.

An organization must forecast future HR demand (the number of employees and the skill sets needed in the future) and forecast future HR supply (internal availability of workers). These two forecasts can occur simultaneously or one after the other depending on the resources available (time, money, people, and so on). Only after demand and supply is forecast can an organization identify potential labour imbalance issues, which leads to the development and implementation of plans to balance HR.

HR Competency

40100

FORECASTING THE AVAILABILITY OF CANDIDATES (SUPPLY)

Short-term and long-range HR demand forecasts only provide half of the staffing equation by answering the question, "How many employees will we need?" The next major concern is how projected openings will be filled. There are two sources of supply:

1. *Internal*—present employees who can be trained, transferred, or promoted to meet anticipated needs
2. *External*—people in the labour market not currently working for the organization, including those who are employed elsewhere and those who are unemployed who can be expected to join the organization to meet anticipated needs

Forecasting the Supply of Internal Candidates

Before estimating how many external candidates will need to be recruited and hired, management must determine how many candidates for projected openings will likely come from within the firm. This is the purpose of forecasting the supply of internal candidates.

EVIDENCE-BASED HR

Skills Inventories and Management Inventories

skills inventories Manual or computerized records summarizing employees' education, experience, interests, skills, and so on, which are used to identify internal candidates eligible for transfer or promotion.

Skills inventories contain comprehensive information about the capabilities of current employees. Data gathered for each employee include name, age, date of employment, current position, present duties and responsibilities, educational background, previous work history, skills, abilities, and interests. Information about current performance and readiness for promotion is generally included as well. Data pertaining to managerial staff are compiled in **management inventories**. Records summarizing the background, qualifications, interests, and skills of management employees, as well as information about managerial responsibilities and management training, are used to identify internal candidates eligible for promotion or transfer opportunities.

management inventories Records summarizing the qualifications, interests, and skills of management employees, along with the number and types of employees supervised, duties of such employees, total budget managed, previous managerial duties and responsibilities, and managerial training received.

To be useful, skills and management inventories must be updated regularly. Failure to do so can lead to present employees being overlooked for job openings. Updating every two years is generally adequate if employees are encouraged to report significant qualifications changes (such as new skills learned or courses completed) to the HR department as they occur.

Replacement Charts and Replacement Summaries

replacement charts Visual representations of who will replace whom in the event of a job opening. Likely internal candidates are listed, along with their age, present performance rating, and promotability status.

Replacement charts are typically used to keep track of potential internal candidates for the firm's most critical positions. It assumes that the organization chart will remain static for a long period of time and usually identifies three potential candidates for a top-level position, should it become vacant. Such charts typically indicate the age of potential internal candidates (which cannot be used as a criterion in making selection or promotion decisions but is necessary to project retirement dates), the current performance level of the employee, and his or her promotion potential. The latter is based on the employee's future career aspirations and a supervisory assessment of readiness for promotion.

To provide a more objective estimate of future potential, this information may be supplemented by results of psychological tests, interviews with HR specialists, and other selection techniques.

FIGURE 5.2 Personnel Replacement Chart Showing Development Needs of Potential Future Divisional Vice-Presidents

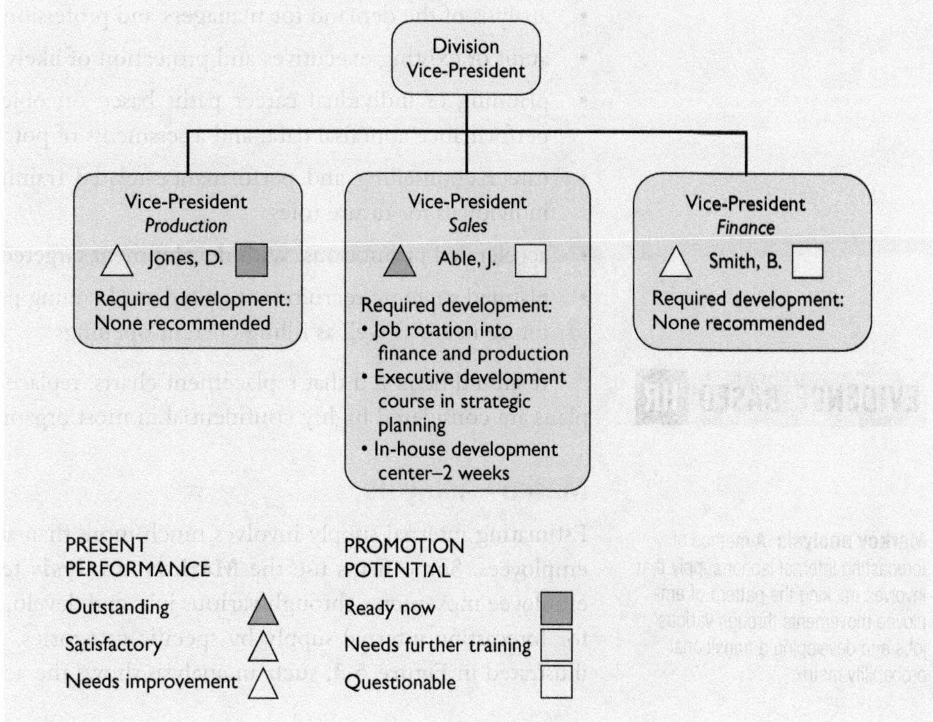

Although replacement charts provide an excellent quick reference tool, they contain very little information. For that reason, many firms prefer to use **replacement summaries**. Such summaries list likely replacements for each position and their relative strengths and weaknesses, as well as information about current position, performance, promotability, age, and experience. These additional data can be extremely helpful to decision makers, although caution must be taken to ensure that no discrimination occurs on the basis of age, sex, and so on.

replacement summaries Lists of likely replacements for each position and their relative strengths and weaknesses, as well as information about current position, performance, promotability, age, and experience.

Succession Plans

Forecasting the availability of inside candidates is particularly important in succession planning. In a nutshell, **succession planning** refers to the plans a company makes to fill its most important executive positions. It extends beyond the replacement chart by focusing on developing people rather than simply identifying potential replacements. As a result, there is a stronger focus on skills development for a specific list of potential successors within an organization.

succession planning The process of ensuring a suitable supply of successors for current and future senior or key jobs so that the careers of individuals can be effectively planned and managed.

In the days when companies were hierarchical and employees tended to remain with a firm for years, executive succession was often straightforward: Staff climbed the ladder one rung at a time, and it wasn't unusual for someone to start on the shop floor and end up in the president's office. Although that kind of ascent is still possible, employee turnover and flatter structures mean that the lines of succession are no longer as direct. For example, potential successors for top positions might be routed through the top jobs at several key divisions, as well as overseas, and sent through a university graduate-level, advanced management program.

Succession planning is extremely important today, affecting both large and small organizations. The Entrepreneurs and HR Box highlights some of the challenges that entrepreneurial organizations often face with succession planning. Because succession planning requires balancing the organization's top management needs with the potential career aspirations of available candidates, succession should include these activities:

- analysis of the demand for managers and professionals in the company
- audit of existing executives and projection of likely future supply
- planning of individual career paths based on objective estimates of future needs, performance appraisal data, and assessments of potential
- career counselling and performance-related training and development to prepare individuals for future roles
- accelerated promotions, with development targeted at future business needs
- planned strategic recruitment aimed at obtaining people with the potential to meet future needs as well as filling current openings[13]

It should be noted that replacement charts, replacement summaries, and succession plans are considered highly confidential in most organizations.

EVIDENCE-BASED HR

Markov Analysis

Markov analysis A method of forecasting internal labour supply that involves tracking the pattern of employee movements through various jobs and developing a transitional probability matrix.

Estimating internal supply involves much more than simply calculating the number of employees. Some firms use the **Markov analysis** technique to track the pattern of employee movements through various jobs and develop a transitional probability matrix for forecasting internal supply by specific categories, such as position and gender. As illustrated in **Figure 5.3**, such an analysis shows the actual number (and percentage) of

FIGURE 5.3　Hypothetical Markov Analysis for a Manufacturing Operation

2013 ＼ 2014	Plant Manager	Foreperson	Team Leader	Production Worker	Exit
Plant Manager (n = 5)	80% / 4				20% / 1
Foreperson (n = 35)	8% / 3	82% / 28			10% / 4
Team Leader (n = 110)		11% / 12	70% / 77	7% / 8	12% / 13
Production Worker (n = 861)			6% / 52	72% / 620	22% / 189
Projected Supply	7	40	129	628	

Percentages represent transitions (previous year's actuals).
Actual numbers of employees are shown as whole numbers in each block
(projections for 2014 based on current staffing).

ENTREPRENEURS and HR

Succession Planning and Family Businesses

In the second quarter of 2010, small businesses created 35 549 jobs, while large firms created only 728 jobs. During that period, small businesses in the construction sector alone accounted for 23 014 new jobs, while those in the healthcare and social assistance sectors introduced 9755 new jobs.

Multigenerational family-controlled businesses often struggle with succession planning. Only one-third of family-owned businesses survive the transition to the second generation. And of these, only one-third survive the transition to the third generation.[14]

There are many reasons for these failures.

1. Determining who will inherit the business and how ownership will be determined among children can be a source of immense stress for family business owners. Therefore, many choose to ignore the issue of succession planning altogether.

2. Second, a family business is a great source of pride for the business owner and is often their single largest asset. The concept of retirement or walking away can be incomprehensible to those who built the business.

3. There may not be a qualified or interested successor within the family.

While these are difficult issues to deal with, family businesses must begin to take an informed and strategic approach to these issues.

HR Competency

90300

employees who remain in each job from one year to the next, as well as the proportions promoted, demoted, transferred, and leaving the organization. These proportions (probabilities) are used to forecast human resources supply.

In the example provided, there were 35 employees in the foreperson occupation in 2013. Out of these, 82 percent (28 employees) are expected to remain in that position next year (based on past levels of activity). The organization can anticipate that 8 percent of the foreperson population (which would be 3 out of the 35 employees in 2013) would be promotable to the role of plant manager. In addition, the past trends show that 10 percent of employees at this level are lost to turnover (representing four employees who are expected to leave the organization before the start of next year). In addition, out of the 110 team leaders (the level below), 11 percent (12 employees) would be eligible for promotion to a foreperson position. Therefore, next year's projected supply of forepersons would be the 28 from this year who are projected to stay in that role plus the 12 team leaders who are projected to be eligible for promotion over the year, for a total supply of 40 forepersons.

In addition to such quantitative data, the skills and capabilities of current employees must be assessed and skills inventories prepared. From this information, replacement charts or summaries and succession plans can be developed.

Forecasting the Supply of External Candidates

Some jobs cannot be filled with internal candidates because no current employees are qualified (such as entry-level jobs) or they are jobs that experience significant growth. In these situations, the firm looks for external candidates. Employer growth is primarily responsible for the number of entry-level openings. A key factor in determining the number of positions that must be filled externally is the effectiveness of the organization's training, development, and career-planning initiatives. If employees are not encouraged to expand their capabilities, they may not be ready to fill vacancies as they arise, and external sources must be tapped.

HR Competency

90300

To project the supply of outside candidates, employers assess general economic conditions, labour market conditions, and occupational market conditions.

General Economic Conditions

General economic conditions refer to the impact of natural fluctuations in economic activity, which impacts all businesses. These include factors such as interest rates, wage rates, rate of inflation, and unemployment rates. In general terms, the lower the rate of unemployment, the smaller the labour supply and the more difficult it will be to recruit employees. It is important to note that unemployment rates vary by occupation and geographic location and can result in an organization's inability to fill certain positions.

Labour Market Conditions

Labour market conditions refer to the demographics of those in the population, such as education levels, age, gender, marital status, and so on. Demographic conditions remain stable and can be forecast with a relatively high degree of accuracy. Fortunately, a wealth of national labour market information is available from Statistics Canada and other government or private sources. Regional chambers of commerce and provincial/local development and planning agencies can be excellent sources of local labour market information.

Statistics Canada
www.statcan.gc.ca

A crucial reality is that a large portion of the population is expected to retire over the next decade, significantly decreasing the size of the labour force. Graduating students (from any level of education) who are just joining the workforce are projected to account for 550 000 new entrants to the labour market a year.[15] In contrast, new immigrants are expected to account for 131 500 new entrants to the labour market a year. An example of a company that has come to realize the benefits of new immigrants as a major source of talent is provided in the Strategic HR box.

Occupational Market Conditions

In addition to looking at the overall labour market, organizations also generally want to forecast the availability of potential candidates in specific occupations (engineers, drill

STRATEGIC HR

Pumping Up People Supply

Building an aortic pericardial heart valve is no easy task. The intricate medical device, measuring mere millimetres, requires highly specialized skills in its production and engineering. Therefore, there is a very small talent pool available to Burnaby, BC–based Sorin Group Canada. They hire engineers who focus on custom-engineered machinery and equipment, quality assurance experts who ensure that regulations are followed, and production technicians who hand-sew and hand-suture the heart valves.

According to Judith Thompson, senior manager of HR at Sorin Group, "Canada isn't well-known for its biomedical engineers so even when we hire now, to ask for medical device experience, we wouldn't get it. So we hire an engineer or scientist and train on the rest of it." The company has come to realize the benefits, and necessity, of new immigrants as a major source of talent. "Our culture is very diverse. About

90 percent of our staff speak English as a second language, from production people to vice-presidents, so we don't look for Canadian-born, Canadian-educated, Canadian experience because in these economic times that would set us back," she says. "I would never have filled 60 positions last year with those criteria."

Training is extensive, as it takes three or four months before workers, wearing gowns and gloves in a super-clean environment, can make a product that is usable. And even then they can only make a certain number of valves or components per week—it takes another six months to ramp up to regular production, says Thompson. Sorin supports its employees with in-house English-language training, through a partnership with immigration services, and provides subsidies to foreign-trained engineers who want to pursue an engineering degree in British Columbia.

Source: Reprinted by permission of Canadian HR Reporter. © Copyright Thomson Reuters Canada Ltd.,2009, Toronto, Ontario.

HR IN THE NEWS

No Easy Solution to the Canadian Military Pilots Shortage

In the 1990s, the Canadian government reduced military personnel by about one-third and instituted a hiring freeze. More recently, civilian airlines have heavily recruited military fliers, and there has been a mass exodus of baby boomers due to retirement. As a result, the Royal Canadian Air Force (RCAF) struggle to find and retain enough military pilots for fighter jets, search-and-rescue aircrafts, and helicopters is magnified. Thus, the RCAF has been recruiting retired RCAF pilots and laid-off British military aviators to help ease the shortage.

Some are dissatisfied with the solutions used by the RCAF to manage the severe labour shortage. There is media buzz around the hiring of pilots who do not meet the minimum medical requirements (hearing and vision), suggesting that the practice of allowing waivers for requirements is dangerous and can have catastrophic effects if a crash or accident were to happen. There is also an ongoing debate around hiring foreigners for pilot positions in the RCAF, suggesting that the organization is attempting to shrink its responsibility toward training employees, thereby saving training money.[16]

Tomasz Zajda/Fotolia

In recent years, the information, communication, and technology (ICT) sectors have suffered from a significant skills shortage, where the demand for ICT workers exceeds the supply. This shortage is expected to continue until 2016.

press operators, accountants, and so on) for which they will be recruiting. A few years ago, Alberta faced a severe labour shortage of workers in the oil and gas sector.[17] Furthermore, the mining industry, the construction industry, the electricity industry, the manufacturing industry, as well as the non–profit sector are also experiencing significant labour shortages.[18] A shortage of information technology workers is projected to cost the Canadian economy $10 billion per year until it is resolved.[19] Shortages of civil service workers, accountants, lawyers, engineers, meteorologists, funeral directors (to bury the baby boomers), and hospitality industry workers are also expected.[20] Some decisions to adjust for occupational market conditions attempt to make the best of a bad situation, but often lead to debate and public scrutiny, as highlighted in the HR in the News box.

FORECASTING FUTURE HUMAN RESOURCES NEEDS (DEMAND)

A key component of HRP is forecasting the number and type of people needed to meet organizational objectives. Managers should consider several factors when forecasting such requirements. From a practical point of view, the demand for the organization's product or service is paramount. Thus, in a manufacturing firm, sales are projected first. Then the volume of production required to meet these sales requirements is determined.

Finally, the staff needed to maintain this volume of output is estimated. In addition to this "basic requirement" for staff, several other factors should be considered, including

1. *projected turnover* as a result of resignations or terminations
2. *quality and nature of employees* in relation to what management sees as the changing needs of the organization
3. *decisions to upgrade* the quality of products or services *or enter into new markets,* which might change the required employee skill mix
4. *planned technological and administrative changes aimed at increasing productivity and reducing employee head count,* such as the installation of new equipment or introduction of a financial incentive plan
5. the *financial resources* available to each department; for example, a budget increase may enable managers to pay higher wages or hire more people; conversely, a budget crunch might result in wage freezes or layoffs

HR Competency
90100

In large organizations, needs forecasting is primarily quantitative in nature and is the responsibility of highly trained specialists. *Quantitative techniques* for determining human resources requirements include trend analysis, ratio analysis, scatter plot analysis, and regression analysis. These are often viewed as numerically or mathematically grounded, and therefore more objective in nature. *Qualitative approaches* to forecasting range from sophisticated analytical models to informal expert opinions about future needs, often involving subjective interpretations or estimates, such as the nominal group technique or the Delphi technique.

Quantitative Approaches

Trend Analysis

trend analysis The study of a firm's past employment levels over a period of years to predict future needs.

Trend analysis involves studying the firm's employment levels over the last three to five years to predict future needs. The purpose is to identify employment trends that might continue into the future, assuming that the past is a strong predictor of the future. Trend analysis is valuable as an initial estimate only, since employment levels rarely depend solely on the passage of time. Other factors (like changes in sales volume and productivity) will also affect future staffing needs.

Ratio Analysis

ratio analysis A forecasting technique for determining future staff needs by using ratios between some causal factor (such as sales volume) and the number of employees needed.

Ratio analysis involves making forecasts based on the ratio between some causal factor (such as sales volume) and the number of employees required (for example, the number of salespeople). Ratio analysis can also be used to help forecast other employee requirements. Like trend analysis, ratio analysis assumes that productivity remains about the same. For example, suppose a salesperson traditionally generates $500 000 in sales and that plans call for increasing the firm's sales by $3 million next year. Then, if the sales revenue–salespeople ratio remains the same, six new salespeople would be required (each of whom produces an extra $500 000 in sales).

The Scatter Plot

scatter plot A graphical method used to help identify the relationship between two variables.

Scatter plots can be used to determine whether two factors—a measure of business activity and staffing levels—are related. If they are, then when the measure of business activity is forecast, HR requirements can also be estimated.

An example to illustrate follows. Legislative changes to the healthcare system require that two 500-bed Canadian hospitals be amalgamated. Both previously had responsibility for acute, chronic, and long-term care. The government's plan is for Hospital

A to specialize in acute care while Hospital B assumes responsibility for chronic and long-term care. In general, providing acute care requires staffing with registered nurses (RNs), while chronic and long-term care facilities can be staffed primarily with registered practical nurses (RPNs).

By the end of the calendar year, 200 beds at Hospital A must be converted from chronic and long-term care beds to facilities for acute patients. At the same time, Hospital A's 200 chronic and long-term patients must be transferred to Hospital B. In a joint meeting, the directors of nursing and HR decide that a good starting point in the planning process would be to calculate the relationship between hospital size (in terms of number of acute beds) and the number of RNs required. After placing telephone calls to their counterparts at eight hospitals in larger centres across the country, they obtain the following information:

Size of Hospital (Number of Acute Beds)	Number of Registered Nurses
200	240
300	260
400	470
500	500
600	620
700	660
800	820
900	860

To determine how many RNs would be needed, they use the data obtained to draw the scatter plot shown in **Figure 5.4**, in which hospital size is shown on the horizontal axis and number of RNs is shown on the vertical axis. If the two factors are related, then the points will tend to fall along a straight line, as they do in this case. Carefully drawing a line that minimizes the distances between the line and each of the plotted

FIGURE 5.4   Determining the Relationship between Hospital Size and Number of Registered Nurses

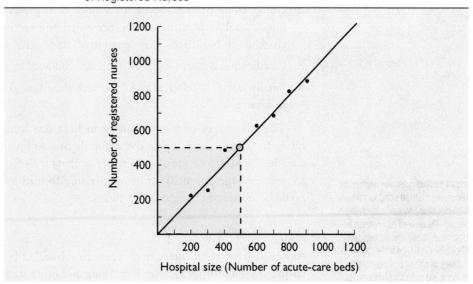

Note: After fitting the line, the number of employees needed, given the projected volume, can be extrapolated (projected).

points (the line of best fit) permits an estimate of the number of nurses required for hospitals of various sizes. Thus, since Hospital A will now have 500 acute-care beds, the estimated number of RNs needed is 500.

Regression Analysis

regression analysis A statistical technique involving the use of a mathematical formula to project future demands based on an established relationship between an organization's employment level (dependent variable) and some measurable factor of output (independent variable).

Regression analysis is a more sophisticated statistical technique to determine the line of best fit, often involving multiple variables (rather than just two, as per the example above). As a statistical tool used to investigate the effect of one variable on another, the investigator is able to determine the magnitude and direction of the relationship between variables to develop future predictions. In the context of HRP, it involves the use of a mathematical formula to project future demands based on an established relationship between an organization's employment level (dependent variable) and some measurable factors of output (independent variables), such as revenue, sales, or production level.

Qualitative Approaches

In contrast to quantitative approaches, which use statistical formulas, qualitative techniques rely solely on expert judgments. Two approaches used to forecast human resources demand (or supply) are the nominal group and Delphi techniques. Although managerial judgment is central to qualitative forecasting, it also plays a key role when quantitative techniques are used. It's rare that any historical trend, ratio, or relationship will continue unchanged into the future. Judgment is therefore needed to modify the forecast based on anticipated changes.

EVIDENCE-BASED HR

Nominal Group Technique

nominal group technique A decision-making technique that involves a group of experts meeting face to face. Steps include independent idea generation, clarification and open discussion, and private assessment.

The **nominal group technique** involves a group of experts (such as first-line supervisors and managers) meeting face to face. Although one of its uses is human resources demand forecasting, this technique is used to deal with issues and problems ranging from identifying training needs to determining safety program incentives. The steps involved are as follows:[21]

1. Each member of the group independently writes down his or her ideas on the problem or issue (in this case, estimates of demand).

2. Going around the table, each member then presents one idea. This process continues until all ideas have been presented and recorded, typically on a flipchart or chalkboard. No discussion is permitted during this step.

3. Clarification is then sought, as necessary, followed by group discussion and evaluation.

4. Finally, each member is asked to rank the ideas. This is done independently and in silence.

The advantages of this technique include involvement of key decision makers, a future focus, and the fact that the group discussion involved in the third step can facilitate the exchange of ideas and greater acceptance of results. Drawbacks include subjectivity and the potential for group pressure to lead to a less accurate assessment than could be obtained through other means.

Delphi Technique

Delphi technique A judgmental forecasting method used to arrive at a group decision, typically involving outside experts as well as organizational employees. Ideas are exchanged without face-to-face interaction and feedback is provided and used to fine-tune independent judgments until a consensus is reached.

Although short-term forecasting is generally handled by managers, the **Delphi technique** is useful for long-range forecasting and other strategic planning issues. It typically involves outside experts as well as company employees, based on the premise that outsiders may be able to assess changes in economic, demographic, governmental, technological, and social conditions, and their potential impact, more objectively, The Delphi technique involves the following steps:[22]

1. The problem is identified (in this case, estimates of demand) and each group member is requested to submit a potential solution by completing a carefully designed questionnaire. Direct face-to-face contact is not permitted.

2. After each member independently and anonymously completes the initial questionnaire, the results are compiled at a centralized location.

3. Each group member is then given a copy of the results.

4. If there are differences in opinion, each individual uses the feedback from other experts to fine-tune his or her independent assessment.

5. The third and fourth steps are repeated as often as necessary until a consensus is reached.

As with the nominal group technique, the advantages of the Delphi technique include involvement of key decision makers and a future focus; in addition, though, it permits the group to critically evaluate a wider range of views. Drawbacks include the fact that judgments may not efficiently use objective data, the time and costs involved, and the potential difficulty in integrating diverse opinions.

HR Competency

40200

PLANNING AND IMPLEMENTING HR PROGRAMS TO BALANCE SUPPLY AND DEMAND

Once the supply and demand of human resources have been estimated, program planning and implementation begin. The end result of the forecasting process is an estimate of short-term and long-range HR requirements. Long-range plans are general statements of potential staffing needs and may not include specific numbers.

staffing table A pictorial representation of all jobs within the organization, along with the number of current incumbents and future employment requirements (monthly or yearly) for each.

Short-term plans—although still approximations—are more specific and are often depicted in a staffing table. A **staffing table** is a pictorial representation of all jobs within the organization, along with the number of current incumbents and future employment requirements (monthly or yearly) for each.

To successfully fill positions internally, organizations must manage performance and careers. Performance is managed through effectively designing jobs and quality-of-working-life initiatives; establishing performance standards and goals; coaching, measuring, and evaluating; and implementing a suitable reward structure (compensation and benefits).

To manage careers effectively, policies and systems must be established for recruitment, selection and placement (including transfer, promotion, retirement, and termination), and training and development. Policies and systems are also required for job analysis, individual employee assessment, replacement and succession planning, and career tracking, as well as career planning and development.

Specific strategies must be formulated to balance supply and demand considerations. As illustrated in **Figure 5.5**, there are three possible scenarios:

1. projected labour demand matches projected labour supply (equilibrium)

2. projected labour supply exceeds projected demand (surplus)

3. projected labour demand exceeds projected supply (shortage)

FIGURE 5.5   Balancing Supply and Demand Considerations

Conditions	Possible Solutions
Labour Equilibrium (when labour demand equals labour supply)	• Vacancies are filled internally through training, transfers, or promotions or externally through hiring
Labour Surplus (when labour demand is less than labour supply)	• Hiring freeze: reassign current workers to job openings • Attrition: standard employee resignation, retirement, or death • Early retirement buyout programs: entice those close to retirement to retire early with a buyout program, access to full or reduced pension, and/or continuation of benefits • Job sharing, work sharing, or reduced workweek programs: reducing work from the standard full-time workload to a less than full-time work • Layoff: temporary or permanent withdrawal of employment due to business or economic reasons • Termination: permanent separation from the organization because of job performance reasons • Leave of absence: voluntary, temporary withdrawal of employment with guaranteed job upon return
Labour Shortage (when labour demand is greater than labour supply)	• Scheduling overtime hours • Hiring temporary workers • Subcontracting work • External recruitment • Internal promotions or transfers

Labour Equilibrium

Although it is extremely rare to have a labour equilibrium, when the expected supply matches the actual demand organizations do not need to change their course of action. Existing plans to replace outgoing employees should be maintained by promoting or transferring internal members of the organization as well as recruiting external labourers.

Labour Surplus

hiring freeze A common initial response to an employee surplus; openings are filled by reassigning current employees and no outsiders are hired.

attrition The normal separation of employees from an organization because of resignation, retirement, or death.

early retirement buyout programs Strategies used to accelerate attrition that involve offering attractive buyout packages or the opportunity to retire on full pension with an attractive benefits package.

A labour surplus exists when the internal supply of employees exceeds the organization's demand. Most employers respond initially by instituting a **hiring freeze**, which means that openings are filled by reassigning current employees and no outsiders are hired. The surplus is slowly reduced through **attrition**, which is the normal separation of employees because of resignation, retirement, or death. When employees leave, the ensuing vacancies are not filled and the staffing level decreases gradually without any involuntary terminations. In addition to the time it takes, a major drawback of this approach is that the firm has no control over who stays and who leaves.

Some organizations attempt to accelerate attrition by offering incentives to employees to leave, such as **early retirement buyout programs**. Staffing levels are reduced and internal job openings created by offering attractive buyout packages or the opportunity to retire on full pension with an attractive benefits package at a relatively early age (often 50 or 55). To be successful, buyouts must be handled carefully. Selection criteria should be established to ensure that key people who cannot be easily replaced do not leave the firm.

job sharing A strategy that involves dividing the duties of a single position between two or more employees.

work sharing Employees work three or four days a week and receive EI benefits on their non-workday(s).

reduced workweek Employees work fewer hours and receive less pay.

EVIDENCE-BASED HR

layoff The temporary or permanent withdrawal of employment to workers for economic or business reasons.

termination Permanent separation from the organization for any reason.

leave of absence Allows those who may be interested in taking time away from work for a variety of reasons (e.g., personal, educational, etc.) to have a set period of time away from their position without pay, but with a guarantee that their job will be available upon their return.

EVIDENCE-BASED HR

A drawback of buyouts and early retirement packages is that they often require a great deal of money upfront. Care must also be taken to ensure that early retirement is voluntary, since forced early retirement is a contravention of human rights legislation.

Another strategy used to deal with an employee surplus involves reducing the total number of hours worked. **Job sharing** involves dividing the duties of a single position between two or more employees. Reducing full-time positions to *part-time work* is sometimes more effective, especially if there are peak demand periods. Creating a job-share position or offering part-time employment can be win–win strategies, since layoffs can be avoided. Although the employees involved work fewer hours and thus have less pay, they are still employed, and they may enjoy having more free time at their disposal; the organization benefits by retaining good employees.

25 years ago, the federal government introduced a **work-sharing** scheme, a layoff-avoidance strategy that involves employees working three or four days a week and receiving employment insurance (EI) benefits on their non-workday(s). The program was temporarily extended to provide 52 weeks of benefits from February 1, 2009 to April 3, 2010, during the recent economic slowdown.[23] Similar to work sharing, but without a formal arrangement with the government regarding EI benefits, is a **reduced workweek**. Employees simply work fewer hours and receive less pay. The organization retains a skilled workforce, lessens the financial and emotional impact of a full layoff, and reduces production costs. One potential drawback is that it is sometimes difficult to predict in advance, with any degree of accuracy, how many hours of work should be scheduled each week. A significant number of organizations use alternative work arrangements other than the traditional Monday to Friday 9–5 schedule, as highlighted in the Expert Opinion box.

Another strategy used to manage employee surplus is a **layoff**; the temporary withdrawal of employment to workers for economic or business reasons. Layoffs may be short in duration (for example, when a plant closes for brief periods in order to adjust inventory levels or to retool for a new product line), but can last months or even years at a time if the organization is negatively affected by a major change in the business cycle. However, layoffs are often permanent in nature. Layoffs are not easy for managers, who have to reduce the number of employees to the required level, or for workers, but are usually necessary to ultimately reduce the impact of the organization's economic downturn. Layoffs and terminations are discussed in depth in Chapter 15.

Termination is a broad term that encompasses permanent separation of the worker from the organization. Termination is often triggered by a management decision to sever the employment relationship due to reasons that are related to job performance. Purging poorly performing employees is often an ongoing activity in any organization, regardless of any projected labour surpluses; however, the rate of termination may increase if there is a projected surplus of labour.

The option of a voluntary **leave of absence** can also be used if the labour surplus is temporary in nature. A leave of absence allows those who may be interested in time off for personal, educational, or other reasons to have a set period of time away from their position, with a guarantee that their job will be available upon their return. A leave of absence can be paid or unpaid, but often seniority and benefits remain intact. Terms of the leave and expected return must be clearly outlined, including potential conflicts of interest and mutual expectations from each party.

Easing the Pain of Labour Surplus Management

Although restructuring initiatives, ranging from layoffs to mergers and acquisitions, were prevalent in the last two decades, organizations that engaged in layoffs were not consistently achieving the desired goals or financial benefits of their

expert.
opinion
industry viewpoint

Renee Paquin

Identification: Ms. Renee Paquin, Director, Corporate Human Resources & Diversity Services Yukon Public Service Commission

1. What is the government of Yukon's approach to employees' use of flex time?

There are a number of flexible arrangements available for employees. We can average hours over two weeks or one month terms, use traditional flex time, allow compressed work weeks, job sharing and part-time positions, and some seasonal or auxiliary positions are usually limited to spring and summer (e.g., firefighters, campground crews).

This works best when clients want flexibility, and when the nature of work is one such that we can allow some flexibility. We recognize that candidates choose employers on a number of issues including the job, the work environment, and some nonwork considerations such as the local community and climate. A number of our employees enjoy physical activity associated with the region, and flexible arrangements can allow people to engage in activities that support work–life balance and that they are passionate about. We believe that our employees should live healthy and fulfilling lives, for overall physical and mental well-being. In addition, there are a number of employees who require flex time in order to care for others such as dependents and aging parents.

2. What benefits has this employer experienced through flex time options?

We have noticed an increase in interest of individuals outside of Yukon for a job, so there is a recruitment benefit. We also see a retention benefit, given that these arrangements help keep us competitive with local external employers. Initially, some new hires believe they will be here for one to two years, but stayed because they love the nature of the work and the options for work–life balance.

3. What obstacles have you experienced when implementing flexible work arrangements, and how can these be overcome?

I. At times, we can have up to 100 percent of our staff in a specific unit on a compressed work week. We have to modify the days that employees can take off, in order to ensure that we're staffed to appropriate levels throughout the week. We learn to create clear decision rules around why or how to move requested days off, and also use a written agreement to approve flexible hours on an individual basis.

II. Internal mobility can be a challenge at times. An employee currently on flex time may apply for a job somewhere else in the organization that may not have flex time options. In this case, we are careful to communicate which positions allow flex time and which ones do not.

III. Locally, there is a demand for teleworking, but the technology infrastructure doesn't exist to support teleworking consistently. This creates an external limitation that prevents the use of teleworking regularly, although we still allow it on days with severe weather.

Source: Renee Paquin, Director, Corporate Human Resources & Diversity Services Yukon Public Service Commission. Reprinted by permission.

HR Competency

20600

survivor syndrome A range of negative emotions experienced by employees remaining after a major restructuring initiative, which can include feelings of betrayal or violation, guilt, or detachment, and can result in stress symptoms, including depression, increased errors, and reduced performance.

supplemental unemployment benefits (SUBs) A top-up of EI benefits to bring income levels closer to what an employee would receive if on the job.

decisions. In a study of 6418 workforce reductions in Fortune 500 firms over 18 years, researchers found no consistent evidence that downsizing led to improved financial performance.[24]

A primary reason for this is the high cost associated with **survivor syndrome**, a range of emotions that can include feelings of betrayal or violation, guilt, or detachment. The remaining employees, anxious about the next round of terminations, often suffer stress symptoms, including depression, increased errors, and reduced performance.

To ease the financial burden of layoffs, some organizations offer **supplemental unemployment benefits (SUBs)**, which are a top-up of EI benefits to bring income levels of temporarily laid-off workers closer to their regular, on-the-job pay. SUB programs are generally negotiated through collective bargaining between the employee and employer. Benefits are payable until the pool of funds set aside has been exhausted.

A **severance package** is typically provided when employees are being terminated through no fault of their own in order to avoid wrongful dismissal lawsuits. Severance pay is legally required in certain situations, such as mass layoffs.

An Ethical Dilemma

How much time, effort, and money should firms devote to helping "surviving" employees deal with downsizing? With mergers and acquisitions?

---

severance package A lump-sum payment, continuation of benefits for a specified period of time, or other benefits that are provided to employees who are being terminated.

Hints : TO ENSURE LEGAL COMPLIANCE

HR Competency

20600

---

transfer Movement of an employee from one job to another that is relatively equal in pay, responsibility, or organizational level.

promotion Movement of an employee from one job to another that is higher in pay, responsibility, or organizational level, usually based on merit, seniority, or a combination of both.

"How could anyone think that this department is under staffed?"

cartoonresource/Fotolia

In addition to pay, severance packages often include the continuation of benefits for a specified period. In determining the appropriate package, employers should take salary, years of service, the employee's age, and his or her likelihood of obtaining another job into consideration.[25] Executives may be protected by a *golden parachute clause* in their contract of employment, which is a guarantee by the employer to pay specified compensation and benefits in the case of termination because of downsizing or restructuring. To soften the blow of termination, *outplacement assistance*, generally offered by an outside agency, can assist affected employees in finding employment elsewhere. The issues and processes related to managing a labour surplus legally and fairly are provided in significant detail in Chapter 15 (managing employee terminations).

Labour Shortage

A labour shortage exists when the internal supply of human resources cannot meet the organization's needs. Scheduling overtime hours is often the initial response. Employers may also subcontract work on a temporary or permanent basis. Another short-term solution is to hire temporary employees. The use of contingent workers to address short and medium term labour shortages has been increasing in Canada (as discussed in Chapter 1), however the treatment of temporary workers when compared with permanent workers is often an issue to consider, as discussed in the Expert Opinion box.

As vacancies are created within the firm, opportunities are generally provided for employee transfers and promotions, which necessitate performance management, training (and retraining), and career development. Of course, internal movement does not eliminate a shortage, which means that recruitment will be required. It is hoped, though, that resultant vacancies will be for entry-level jobs, which can be filled more easily externally.

Internal Solutions to a Labour Shortage

A **transfer** involves a lateral movement from one job to another that is relatively equal in pay, responsibility, or organizational level. Transfers can lead to more effective use of human resources, broaden an employee's skills and perspectives, and help make him or her a better candidate for future promotions. Transfers also offer additional technical and interpersonal challenges and increased variety of work, which may enhance job satisfaction and motivation.

A **promotion** involves the movement of an employee from one job to another that is higher in pay, responsibility, or organizational level. Such a move may be based on merit, seniority, or a combination of both. Merit-based promotions are awarded in recognition of a person's outstanding performance in his or her present job or as an assessment of his or her future potential.

A focus on employee retention initiatives can also mitigate potential labour shortages. The HRP process often highlights challenges the organization is having with turnover or retention at specific levels. This may warrant further investigation into why employees are leaving and which types of employees are leaving. Rather than a broad focus on retention, organizations can benefit from focusing on retaining key employees or employees with strong job performance. A discussion of career planning to assist with internal solutions regarding a labour shortage is provided in Chapters 9 and 10 (career development and performance management).

expert opinion
academic viewpoint

Dr. Catherine Connelly

Identification: Dr. Catherine Connelly (PhD), Canada Research Chair in Organizational Behaviour

Affiliation: College of New Scholars, Artists and Scientist of the Royal Society of Canada, Social Science & Humanities, McMaster University

1. Based on research, how do temporary workers get treated differently in an organization when compared to full-time workers?

That depends on what kind of temporary work the employee is engaging in. By definition, independent contractors have to be treated differently. For example, an organization is not responsible for the training and development of contractors.

In contrast, temporary workers hired through an agency are more likely to be assigned tasks that are less interdependent than full-time workers. This is somewhat understandable, given the temporary nature of the employment, but these temporary workers can also be excluded from social interactions or suffer from social injustice (e.g., they may be told that there is an opportunity for permanent employment, when there may or may not be; they may be misled about work hours or the nature of work).

At a macro-level, these employees are more vulnerable, so they sometimes put up with a lot. The temporary workers who seem to be treated best are the ones who are working their way into an organization or permanent situation, such as apprentices, co-op students, or public school supply teachers. In these cases, fellow employees have experienced a similar rite of passage, and are more considerate toward those in the situation.

2. Extending on the previous question, how is behaviour toward the organization different for temporary workers than full-time workers?

Research identifies that contingent workers who are treated well will have higher levels of organizational citizenship behaviour, partially motivated by their desire for a career in the organization. If they are treated poorly, they will have higher counterproductive behaviours. There is also evidence regarding temporary workers who work for employment agencies that suggests that if the agency treats the worker poorly, the worker might retaliate against the organization they are assigned to at the moment, or vice versa. This is highly dependent on the amount of visibility the worker has to the organization or the agency. The theoretical foundation for this reaction is based on social exchange theory and equity theory.

3. What do you think the future of non-standard workers in Canada will look like?

Legislatively, a major factor to be considered is the change in the temporary foreign workers program. This started in the spring of 2013, with tightening regulations, limited eligibility, and increased costs associated with employing foreign workers.

The future also will include expanded concepts of contingent workers. For example, "astronaut workers" is a term that is used with increasing frequency to reflect those who move/reside for months at a time at one location for employment (e.g., Alberta) and returned back to home for part of the year (e.g., New Brunswick).

Additionally, there is more research to be done regarding the underground economy, which has been discussed at some level by US researchers, but remains relatively unexplored by Canadian academics.

Source: Reprinted by Permission from Dr. Catherine Connelly.

External Solutions to a Labour Shortage

External solutions to managing a labour shortage involve recruiting the right quality and quantity of talent needed in an organization to meet the long-term goals and strategy of the company. The next chapter (Chapter 6) extensively discusses the recruitment process, methods of recruitment, and strategies of determining recruitment targets. Options for recruitment and selection related to managing a labour shortage are provided in Chapters 6 and 7 (recruitment and selection).

CHAPTER SUMMARY

1. Human resources planning (HRP) is the process of reviewing HR requirements to ensure that the organization has the required number of employees with the necessary skills to meet its strategic goals. Forecasting future labour demand and supply is a critical element of the strategic planning process. HRP and strategic planning become effective when a reciprocal and interdependent relationship exists between them.

2. Four quantitative techniques for forecasting future HR demand are trend analysis, ratio analysis, scatter plots, and regression analysis. Two qualitative techniques used to forecast demand are the nominal group technique and the Delphi technique.

3. Four strategies used to forecast internal HR supply are Markov analysis, skills and management inventories, replacement charts and summaries, and succession planning. Forecasting external HR supply requires an assessment of general economic conditions, labour market conditions, and occupational labour conditions.

4. Strategies to manage a labour surplus include a hiring freeze; downsizing through attrition; early retirement buyout programs; reduced hours through job sharing, part-time work, work sharing, or reduced workweeks; leaves of absence; and termination of employment.

5. Strategies to manage a human resources shortage include internal and external solutions, such as hiring employees, employee transfers and promotions, and retention programs.

MyManagementLab

Study, practise, and explore real business situations with these helpful resources:

- **Interactive Lesson Presentations:** Work through interactive presentations and assessments to test your knowledge of management concepts.
- **PIA (Personal Inventory Assessments):** Enhance your ability to connect with key concepts through these engaging self-reflection assessments.
- **Study Plan:** Check your understanding of chapter concepts with self-study quizzes.
- **Videos:** Learn more about the management practices and strategies of real companies.
- **Simulations:** Practise decision-making in simulated management environments.

KEY TERMS

attrition *(p. 122)*
Delphi technique *(p. 120)*
early retirement buyout programs *(p. 122)*
environment scanning *(p. 110)*
hiring freeze *(p. 122)*
human resources planning (HRP) *(p. 109)*
job sharing *(p. 123)*
layoff *(p. 123)*
leave of absence *(p. 123)*
management inventories *(p. 112)*
Markov analysis *(p. 114)*
nominal group technique *(p. 120)*
promotion *(p. 125)*
ratio analysis *(p. 118)*
reduced workweek *(p. 123)*

regression analysis *(p. 120)*
replacement charts *(p. 112)*
replacement summaries *(p. 113)*
scatter plot *(p. 118)*
severance package *(p. 125)*
skills inventories *(p. 112)*
staffing table *(p. 121)*
succession planning *(p. 113)*
supplemental unemployment benefits (SUBs) *(p. 124)*
survivor syndrome *(p. 124)*
termination *(p. 123)*
transfer *(p. 125)*
trend analysis *(p. 118)*
work sharing *(p. 123)*

REVIEW AND DISCUSSION QUESTIONS

1. Describe the costs associated with a lack of or inadequate HRP.

2. After analyzing the human resources implications of an organization's strategic plans, what are the three subsequent processes involved in HRP?

3. Discuss the pros and cons of five of the approaches to dealing with a labour surplus from both the organization and employee perspective.

4. Differentiate between replacement charts and succession plans, and explain in which situation each is preferred.

5. Discuss various methods of easing the burden of a layoff or termination.

CRITICAL THINKING QUESTIONS

1. A number of quantitative and qualitative techniques for forecasting human resources demand were discussed in this chapter. Working in groups, identify which strategies would be most appropriate for (a) small versus large companies, (b) industries undergoing rapid change, and (c) businesses/industries in which there are seasonal variations in HR requirements.

2. Suppose that it has just been projected that, because of a number of technological innovations, your firm will need 20 percent fewer clerical employees within the next three years. There are currently 122 clerical positions in the company, split between three departments of equal size. Retirements at this level are projected to be roughly 2 percent per year. Annual voluntary turnover and involuntary turnover for Department A is 2 percent and 5 percent, respectively; Department B is 3 percent and 3 percent; and Department C is 5 percent and 0 percent. Do you project a labour shortage or surplus in the next three years for clerical positions? What actions would you take in this situation?

3. Suppose that you are the HR manager at a firm at which a hiring freeze has just been declared. The plan is to downsize through attrition. What steps would you take to ensure that you reap the advantages of this strategy while minimizing the disadvantages?

4. You were recently asked to identify one employee you manage as a top performer to align with a new company program offering top performers intensive management skills training. The employee you identified for this role is unaware of the program. This morning, she confided in you that she just applied for graduate school and will find out if she has been accepted five months from now, with the intent to start the program one month after that. Would you change the identification of who was the top performer in your team based on this information? Why or why not?

EXPERIENTIAL EXERCISES

1. Develop a realistic, hypothetical staffing table for a department or organization that you are familiar with.

2. Contact the HR manager at a firm in your area and find out whether the firm uses any of the following: (a) skills/management inventories, (b) replacement charts or summaries, and (c) a succession plan. Prepare a brief summary of the information gathered. Once you have completed these tasks, form a group with several of your classmates. Share your findings with the group members. Were there similarities across firms? Did company size seem to make a difference in terms of strategies used for forecasting the supply of internal candidates? Can you identify any other factors that seem to play a role in the choice of forecasting techniques used?

3. This assignment requires working in teams of five or six. Half of each team is to assume the role of management at a firm that is about to undergo major downsizing. The other half of each team is to assume the role of employees—some who will be affected and others who will remain. Each management team is paired with an employee team and must prepare and role-play a realistic meeting of the two parties. Managers should work toward minimizing

the negative impact on those who will be affected as well as on those who will remain. Individuals in employee roles should envision what their thoughts and feelings would be (if they have never actually been in this situation, that is) and to portray them as realistically as possible.

4. Form teams of three or four people. Your instructor will assign you a position on the following statement: "All employees in an organization should be aware of their personal standing with respect to replacement charts and succession planning." Formulate your arguments to support your assigned position and then debate the statement with an opposing team, as instructed.

5. With a partner, research "survivor syndrome" and what specific companies have done to successfully mitigate this response and regain full employee commitment. Prepare a brief (two to three minute, maximum) oral presentation to share what you have learned.

RUNNING CASE

Running Case: LearnInMotion.com

To Plan or Not to Plan?

One aspect of HRM that Jennifer and Pierre studied at university was HR planning. Their professor emphasized its importance, especially for large organizations. Although LearnInMotion.com was certainly small at this point, with only a few employees, they were planning to expand, and it seemed that detailed HRP should be an essential part of their plans. There was no succession plan—after all, they have just started the business! But they both knew that the market for technology workers, in general, was competitive. Jennifer and Pierre have asked for some assistance with the following questions.

QUESTIONS

1 What is human resources planning and how will it help LearnInMotion.com's strategic plans?
2 Describe the steps in the human resources planning process and discuss the important elements within each that will benefit LearnInMotion.com.

CASE INCIDENT

How to Downsize Successfully While Using HRP Fundamentals

A successful franchise owner of a prestigious sporting goods chain is feeling the effects of technology, with more and more online sales and less and less customers in the shops. Locally there are three stores, and typically each store needs the following positions staffed for optimum profitability and success: a store manager, an assistant manager, five department managers, and 20 customer service representatives, averaging $1 200 000 in annual revenue. However, there has been a trend of 20 percent sales decline in stores, with an increase of 30 percent sales online (last year the online revenue stream was $300 000). The franchise owner was able to handle all of the online sales with a team of five full-time remote workers (working from home) last year.

The owner wants each store to maintain their productivity, which he measures as the revenue per employee. He also thinks that there is potential to grow the online business.

Please help the owner by answering the following questions.

QUESTIONS

1 Using your HR planning expertise, forecast the demand of labour in the stores and the online environment over the next three years.
2 Assuming an annual 15 percent turnover level of in-store workers and a 30 percent turnover level of online-focused employees, determine HR supply estimates over the next three years.
3 Do you forecast a labour shortage or surplus? Develop a clear plan to help address the forecasted labour shortage or surplus.

CHAPTER

6

Gemenacom/Shutterstock

Recruitment

LEARNING OUTCOMES

AFTER STUDYING THIS CHAPTER, YOU SHOULD BE ABLE TO

DEFINE recruitment and discuss the increasing use of employer branding.

EXPLAIN the recruitment process.

EXPLAIN the importance of application forms

ANALYZE the roles of job posting, human resources records, and skills inventories in recruiting from within.

IDENTIFY at least 10 methods used for external recruitment.

EXPLAIN two strategies used to recruit non-permanent staff.

DISCUSS strategies for recruiting a more diverse workforce.

REQUIRED HR COMPETENCIES

10600: Align human resources practices by translating organizational strategy into human resources objectives and priorities to achieve the organization's plan.

20600: Promote an evidence-based approach to the development of human resources policies and practices using current professional resources to provide a sound basis for human resources decision-making.

40200: Increase the attractiveness of the employer to desirable potential employees by identifying and shaping the organization's employee value proposition to build a high-quality workforce.

40300: Execute a workforce plan by sourcing, selecting, hiring, onboarding, and developing people to address competency needs and retain qualified talent aligned with the organization's strategic objectives.

THE STRATEGIC IMPORTANCE OF RECRUITMENT

recruitment The process of searching out and attracting qualified job applicants, which begins with the identification of a position that requires staffing and is completed when résumés or completed application forms are received from an adequate number of applicants.

EVIDENCE-BASED HR

recruiter A specialist in recruitment whose job is to find and attract capable candidates.

Recruitment is the process of searching out and attracting qualified job applicants. It begins with the identification of a position that requires staffing and is completed when résumés or completed application forms are received from an adequate number of applicants. A Watson Wyatt study found that organizations with superior recruiting practices financially outperform those with less effective programs and that successful recruiting is a strong indicator of higher shareholder value.[1]

Authority for recruitment is generally delegated to HR staff members, except in small businesses where line managers usually recruit their own staff. In large organizations where recruiting is done on a continual basis, the HR team typically includes specialists, known as **recruiters**, whose job is to find and attract qualified applicants. Recruiters are becoming increasingly critical to achieving an organization's strategic objectives as competition for the employees necessary for strategy implementation increases due to the growing talent shortage.

Organizations are increasingly seeking the high profile given to an "employer of choice," such as those included in lists such as Mediacorp's "Top 100 Employers," the Hewitt Associates "50 Best Employers," and the *Financial Post*'s "Ten Best Companies to Work for." Employers such as Royal Bank of Canada, Enerflex, Microsoft Canada, and many others are also applying the marketing concept of branding to strengthen their recruitment activities.[2]

Employer Branding

Gabriel Bouchard, founder of the Monster Canada online job board, says, "In an increasingly tight job market, employers must remain permanently visible to potential employees, establishing and maintaining relationships with potential candidates before they even begin pursuing a new job. This is particularly crucial when it comes to hard-to-fill or mission-critical positions."[3] Proactive employers are trying to obtain a competitive advantage in recruitment by establishing themselves as employers of choice through employer branding. The purpose of an employer brand is to attract people to apply to work at the organization and to earn the loyalty of current employees.

employer branding The image or impression of an organization as an employer based on the benefits of being employed by the organization.

Employer branding is the image or impression of an organization as an employer based on the perceived benefits of being employed by the organization. It is the experience of an employee when working for a company, based on feelings, emotions, senses, realities, and benefits (functional benefits such as personal development, economic benefits such as monetary rewards, and psychological benefits such as feelings of purpose, belonging, and recognition). It is essentially a promise made to employees and their perception of how well that promise is delivered.[4] Employer branding involves three steps as summarized in **Table 6.1**.

McDonald's used focus groups to identify the interests of one of their target markets for recruitment (young people). The results of the focus groups suggest that this target market is interested in balancing their own freedom and goals with making money. As a result, McDonald's offered flexible hours, uniform choices, scholarships, and discount cards to support its value proposition slogan, "We take care of our employees." This value proposition was also communicated through television ads and a recruiting website. Following the introduction of this branding initiative, McDonald's saw a surge in the number of young people who recognized McDonald's as a great place to work.[5] With the right branding strategy, job seekers line up to apply for jobs. A successful brand results in job seekers saying "I'd like to work there."[6]

TABLE 6.1   Employer Branding Steps

Step	Example
1. Define the target audience	The target group may be one of the four generations in today's workforce, the underemployed, or the four employment equity groups.
2. Develop the employee value proposition	Loblaw and Fairmont Hotels offer potential employees the opportunity to participate in "green" environmental initiatives.[7] At PCL Construction of Alberta, 80 percent of employees own stock in the company.[8]
3. Reinforce value proposition in communication	An integrated marketing approach to internal and external communication should use various channels, such as television, radio, print, websites, social media, and so on.[9]

THE RECRUITMENT PROCESS

As illustrated in **Figure 6.1**, the recruitment process has a number of steps:

1. Job openings are identified through HR planning (based on the organization's strategic plan) or manager request. HR plans play a vital role in the identification process, because they indicate present and future openings and specify which should be filled internally and which externally. Openings do arise unexpectedly, though, when managers request that a new employee be hired.

2. The job requirements are determined. This step involves reviewing the job description and the job specifications and updating them, if necessary. Chapter 4 included a discussion of job analysis, which outlined how job analysis describes how to collect and interpret job descriptions and specifications.

3. Appropriate recruiting source(s) and method(s) are chosen. The major decision here is whether to start with internal or external recruiting. There is no single, best recruiting technique, and the most appropriate for any given position depends on a number of factors, which will be discussed in the next section.

4. A pool of qualified recruits is generated. The requirements of employment equity legislation (if any) and the organization's diversity goals should be reflected in the applicant pool.

A recruiter must be aware of constraints affecting the recruitment process to be successful in his or her job. Constraints arise from organizational policies, such as

FIGURE 6.1   An Overview of the Recruitment Process

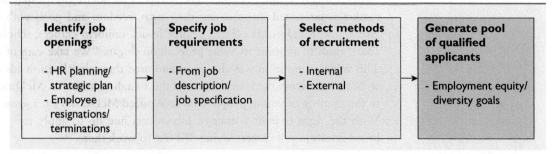

Identify job openings	Specify job requirements	Select methods of recruitment	Generate pool of qualified applicants
- HR planning/ strategic plan - Employee resignations/ terminations	- From job description/ job specification	- Internal - External	- Employment equity/ diversity goals

promote-from-within policies, which mean that a recruiter cannot start recruiting externally for a specified period, even if he or she is aware that there are no suitable internal candidates. Constraints also arise from compensation policies, since they influence the attractiveness of the job to potential applicants. If there is an employment equity plan, it will specify goals for increasing recruitment from the designated groups. Monetary and non-monetary inducements offered by competitors impose a constraint, since recruiters must try to meet the prevailing standards of the company or use alternative inducements.

Perhaps the biggest constraint on recruiting activity at this time is the current labour shortage, which makes recruiting more difficult. One survey by Hewitt Associates found that recruitment practices will have to undergo "enormous change" over the next several years.[10]

DEVELOPING AND USING APPLICATION FORMS

For most employers, completion of an application form or uploading a résumé into an applicant tracking system that codes and logs data is a critical step in the recruitment process (as described in Chapter 3). These provide an efficient means of collecting verifiable historical data from each candidate in a standardized format; it usually includes information about education, prior work history, and other job-related skills. The use of online applications significantly reduces the risk of lost applications, increases the exposure level of the job ad (global reach), and minimizes the likelihood of biases associated with other forms of face-to-face recruitment. However, online application forms can also result in a large number of applications (for example, Google receives over 3000 per day[11]), thus putting pressure on staff to manage the high volume.

HRIS (Human Resources Information System) software can be extremely useful here for automatically coding and storing applications, thus allowing HR professionals to search through the applications using specified search functions. The HRIS can also pre-screen applicants against predetermined criteria, providing an automated shortlist of qualified candidates. This significantly reduces the need for HR staff to screen résumés, but increases the importance of the content of the résumés and the validity of the pre-screening criteria.

Due to the convenience and ubiquity of web browsers, application forms are increasingly being used online to allow applicants to build a profile and submit information directly or indirectly to potential employers. This offers around-the-clock convenience, since applicants can create and submit applications or résumés on an ongoing, real-time basis. Even when detailed résumés have been submitted, most firms also request that a standardized company application form be completed. There are many reasons for this practice:

EVIDENCE-BASED HR

- Candidate comparison is facilitated because information is collected in a uniform manner.

- The information that the company requires is specifically requested, rather than just what the candidate wants to reveal.

- Candidates are typically asked to complete an application form while on the company premises, and thus it is a sample of the candidate's own work (obtaining assistance with résumés is common, given that many job boards offer online résumé-building options).

- Application forms typically ask the candidate to provide written authorization for reference checking.

- Candidates are asked to acknowledge that the information provided is true and accurate, which protects the company from applicants who falsify their credentials.
- Many application forms today have an optional section regarding designated group member status. The data collected are used for employment equity tracking purposes.

biographical information blank (BIB) A detailed job application form requesting biographical data found to be predictive of success on the job, pertaining to background, experiences, and preferences. Responses are scored.

One type of application form that can be used to predict performance is a **biographical information blank (BIB)**, also known as a biodata form. Essentially, it is a more detailed version of an application form, focusing on biographical data found to be predictive of job success. Questions relating to age, gender, race, or other grounds prohibited under human rights legislation cannot be used. Candidates respond to a series of questions about their background, experiences, and preferences, including willingness to travel and leisure activities. Because biographical questions rarely have right or wrong answers, BIBs are difficult to fake. The development of a BIB requires that the items that are valid predictors of job success be identified and that scores be established for different responses to these items. By totalling the scores for each item, it is possible to obtain a composite score for each applicant.

RECRUITMENT AVENUES: RECRUITING FROM WITHIN THE ORGANIZATION

human capital theory The accumulation of firm-specific knowledge and experience involves a joint investment by both the employee and employer; therefore, both parties benefit from maintaining a long-term relationship.

Although recruiting often brings job boards and employment agencies to mind, current employees are generally the largest source of recruits. Filling open positions with inside candidates has several advantages. According to **human capital theory**, the accumulation of firm-specific knowledge and experience involves a joint investment by both the employee and employer; therefore, both parties benefit from maintaining a long-term relationship. Employees see that competence is rewarded, thus enhancing their commitment, morale, and performance. Having already been with the firm for some time, insiders may be more committed to the company's goals and less likely to leave. Managers (as agents of the organization) are provided with a longer-term perspective when making business decisions. It is generally safer to promote from within, because the firm is likely to have a more accurate assessment of the person's skills and performance level than would otherwise be the case. In addition, inside candidates require less orientation than outsiders do.

HR Competency

40200

Recruiting from within also has a number of drawbacks. Employees who apply for jobs and don't get them may experience discontentment (informing unsuccessful applicants as to why they were rejected and what remedial action they might take to be more successful in the future is thus essential).[12] Managers may be required to post all job openings and interview all inside candidates, even when they already know whom they want to hire, thus wasting considerable time and creating false hope on the part of those employees not genuinely being considered. Employees may be less satisfied with and accepting of a boss appointed from within their own ranks than they would be with a newcomer; it is sometimes difficult for a newly chosen leader to adjust to no longer being "one of the gang."[13] There is also a possibility of "inbreeding." When an entire management team has been brought up through the ranks, they may have a tendency to make decisions "by the book" and to maintain the status quo when a new and innovative direction is needed.

EVIDENCE-BASED HR

Recruiting from within can be accomplished by using job posting, human resources records, and skills inventories.

Job Posting

job posting The process of notifying current employees about vacant positions.

Job posting is a process of notifying current employees about vacant positions. Most companies now use computerized job-posting systems, where information about job vacancies can be found on the company's intranet. This involves a notice outlining the job title, duties (as listed in the job description), qualifications (taken from the job specification), hours of work, pay range, posting date, and closing date. Not all firms use intranets. Some post jobs on bulletin boards or in employee publications. As illustrated in **Figure 6.2**, there are advantages and disadvantages to using job postings to facilitate the transfer and promotion of qualified internal candidates.

An Ethical Dilemma

Suppose a manager has already made up his or her mind about who will be selected for an internal position. An internal job posting and subsequent interviews have shown another equally qualified candidate. Who should be offered the position?

Human Resources Records

Human resources records are often consulted to ensure that qualified individuals are notified, individually, of vacant positions. An examination of employee files, including résumés and application forms, may uncover employees who are working in jobs below their education or skill levels, people who already have the requisite KSAs, or individuals with the potential to move into the vacant position if given some additional training.

Skills Inventories

Skills inventories are a useful recruitment tool. Although such inventories may be used instead of job postings, they are more often used as a supplement. Whether computerized or manual, referring to such inventories ensures that qualified internal candidates are identified and considered for transfer or promotion when opportunities arise.

Limitations of Recruiting from Within

It is rarely possible to fill all non-entry-level jobs with current employees. Middle- and upper-level jobs may be vacated unexpectedly, with no internal replacements yet qualified or ready for transfer or promotion; or the jobs may require such specialized training and experience that there are no potential internal replacements. Even in firms with a policy of promoting from within, potential external candidates are increasingly being

FIGURE 6.2 Advantages and Disadvantages of Job Posting

Advantages

- Provides every qualified employee with a chance for a transfer or promotion.
- Reduces the likelihood of special deals and favouritism.
- Demonstrates the organization's commitment to career growth and development.
- Communicates to employees the organization's policies and guidelines regarding promotions and transfers.
- Provides equal opportunity to all qualified employees.

Disadvantages

- Unsuccessful job candidates may become demotivated, demoralized, discontented, and unhappy if feedback is not communicated in a timely and sensitive manner.
- Tensions may rise if it appears that a qualified internal candidate was passed over for an equally qualified or less qualified external candidate.
- The decision about which candidate to select may be more difficult if there are two or more equally qualified candidates.

considered to meet strategic objectives. Hiring someone from outside may be preferable in order to acquire the latest knowledge and expertise or to gain new ideas and revitalize the department or organization.[14]

RECRUITMENT AVENUES: RECRUITING FROM OUTSIDE THE ORGANIZATION

"Diversity is good. Pass it down."

Unless there is a workforce reduction, even in firms with a promote-from-within policy, a replacement from outside must eventually be found to fill the job left vacant once all eligible employees have been given the opportunity for transfer or promotion. In addition, most entry-level positions must be filled by external candidates. The advantages of external recruitment include the following:

- access to a larger pool of qualified candidates, which may have a positive impact on the quality of the selection decision

- availability of a more diverse applicant pool, which can assist in meeting employment equity goals and timetables

- acquisition of skills or knowledge not currently available within the organization or the introduction of new ideas and creative problem-solving techniques

- elimination of rivalry and competition caused by employees jockeying for transfers and promotions, which can hinder interpersonal and interdepartmental cooperation

- potential cost savings resulting from hiring individuals who already have the required skills, rather than providing extensive training

Planning External Recruitment

When choosing the external recruitment method(s), several factors should be considered in addition to the constraints mentioned earlier. The type of job to be filled has a major impact on the recruitment method selected. For example, most firms normally rely on professional search firms for recruiting executive-level employees. In contrast, Internet advertising is commonly used for recruiting other salaried employees. Some job ads can be creative, while others are informative, as highlighted in the HR in the News box.

Yield ratios help to indicate which recruitment methods are the most effective at producing qualified job candidates. A **yield ratio** is the percentage of applicants that proceed to the next stage of the selection process. A recruiting yield pyramid, such as that shown in **Figure 6.3**, can be devised for each method by calculating the yield ratio for each step in the selection process.

The hypothetical firm in Figure 6.3 typically hires 50 entry-level accountants each year. Given these ratios, the firm knows that using this particular recruitment method, 1200 leads must be generated to hire 50 new accountants. While this example identifies how yields are calculated and used, each organization typically determines their own desired yields based on industry, position, size, and resources of the organization to determine their own internal yield targets.

The average number of days from when the company initiates a recruitment method to when the successful candidate begins to work is called *time-lapse data*. Assume that

yield ratio The percentage of applicants that proceed to the next stage of the selection process.

HR IN THE NEWS

Creative Job Ads

Job advertisements give a meaningful message about the company and what it values, as highlighted in these creative help wanted ads.

HR Competency

20600

EVIDENCE-BASED HR

the accounting company in the above example found the following scenario: Six days elapsed between submission of application forms and résumés to invitation for an interview; five days then passed from invitation to actual interview; five days from interview to job offer; six days from job offer to acceptance; and 23 days from acceptance of job offer to commencement of work. These data indicate that, using on-campus recruiting, the firm must initiate recruitment efforts at least 45 days before the anticipated job opening date. Calculating time-lapse data for each recruitment method means that the amount of lead time available can be taken into account when deciding which strategy or strategies would be most appropriate.

Many methods of recruiting from the external labour market are in use. A 2010 study of 5858 job seekers by Right Management found that the most successful way to find a job was through traditional networking, followed by online job boards. The results of the study are highlighted in **Figure 6.4**.

Traditional networking includes cold calls, print advertising, employee referrals, and former employees who have remained in contact with the organization. Organizations can gain access to large pools of candidates through relationships formed during open houses and job fairs, professional and trade associations, labour organizations, and military personnel. Online recruitment includes Internet-based job boards, corporate websites, and social networking sites. Agency recruitment includes HRSDC, executive search firms, and private employment agencies. Recruitment of non-permanent staff can come from temporary help agencies and contract workers.

FIGURE 6.3   Recruiting Yield Pyramid

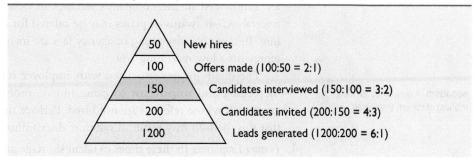

50	New hires
100	Offers made (100:50 = 2:1)
150	Candidates interviewed (150:100 = 3:2)
200	Candidates invited (200:150 = 4:3)
1200	Leads generated (1200:200 = 6:1)

FIGURE 6.4   Most Successful Ways to Find a Job in Canada, 2010

Respondents were asked to identify only one tool that they used to find their most recent job.

1. Networking (35 percent)
2. Online Job Boards (24 percent)
3. Agencies or Recruiters (13 percent)
4. Cold Calls (10 percent)
5. Online Networks (5 percent)
6. Newspapers or Classified Ads (3 percent)

Source: Based on Survey by Right Management, published in "Networking Gets the Job Done," *Canadian HR Reporter* (August 15, 2011), p. 4.

Traditional Networking

1. *Cold Calls: Walk-Ins and Write-Ins* Individuals who go to organizations in person to apply for jobs without referral or invitation are called walk-ins. People who submit unsolicited résumés to organizations are known as write-ins. Walk-ins and write-ins are an inexpensive recruitment method. Their résumés are generally screened by the HR department and if an applicant is considered suitable, his or her résumé is retained on file for three to six months or passed on to the relevant department manager if there is an immediate or upcoming opening for which the applicant is qualified.

    Some organizations, such as RBC Financial Group, are using computer databases to store the information found on the résumés and application forms of walk-in and write-in candidates. Whether the original document is paper based or submitted online, it can be scanned and stored in databases for fast, easy access using a few key words.[15]

2. *Print Advertising* To achieve optimum results from an advertisement, the following four-point guide should be kept in mind as the ad is being constructed: attract attention, develop interest, create desire, instigate action. There are two general types of newspaper advertisements: **want ads** and **blind ads**. Want ads describe the job and its specifications, the compensation package, and the hiring employer. Although the content pertaining to the job, specifications, and compensation is identical in blind ads, such ads omit the identity and address of the hiring employer.

    Although many job seekers do not like responding to blind ads because there is always the danger of unknowingly sending a résumé to the firm at which they are currently employed, such ads do result in the opening remaining confidential.

3. *Employee Referrals* Some organizations encourage applications from friends and relatives of current employees by mounting an employee referral campaign. Openings are announced in the company's intranet or newsletter along with a request for referrals. Cash awards or prizes may be offered for referrals that culminate in a new hire. Because no advertising or agency fees are involved, paying referral rewards still represents a low recruiting cost.

    The disadvantages associated with employee referrals include the potential for inbreeding and **nepotism** to cause morale problems and dissatisfaction among employees whose referrals are not hired. Perhaps the biggest drawback, however, is that this method may result in systemic discrimination.

4. *Former Employees* In these times of talent shortage and diminishing employee loyalty, some organizations are making efforts to keep in touch with former employees who

want ad A recruitment ad describing the job and its specifications, the compensation package, and the hiring employer. The address to which applications or résumés should be submitted is also provided.

blind ad A recruitment ad in which the identity and address of the employer are omitted.

nepotism A preference for hiring relatives of current employees.

may be interested in rejoining the organization in future. Organizations such as Microsoft, Ernst & Young, and Procter & Gamble established alumni networks that offer benefits such as healthcare, job boards, and alumni parties. About 25 percent of hires at the manager level and above at Microsoft are returning employees, known as "boomerangs."[16]

5. *Educational Institutions* Recruiting at educational institutions is extremely effective when candidates require formal training but need relatively little full-time work experience. Most high schools, colleges, and universities have counselling centres that provide job-search assistance to students through such activities as skills assessment testing and workshops on résumé preparation and interview strategies. High schools can provide recruits for entry-level jobs. Colleges and universities often host career fairs at multiple points throughout the academic year; some are generic in nature while others are more focused (e.g., a hospitality career fair).

Cooperative (co-op) education and field placement programs have become increasingly popular in Canada. These programs require students to spend a specified amount of time working in organizations as an integral part of the academic program, thereby gaining some hands-on skills in an actual work setting. Co-op programs are offered in some high schools, as well as in colleges and universities. A core consideration is the academic life to work life transition for new graduates, as highlighted in the Expert Opinion box.

Summer internship programs hire college or university students to complete summer projects between their second-last and final year of study. Their performance is assessed, and those who are judged to be superior are offered permanent positions following graduation. Other firms offer internship opportunities to graduates, thereby enabling them to acquire hands-on skills to supplement their education. As with student internships, outstanding performers are often offered full-time employment at the end of the program. It is now possible for firms to recruit graduate interns online through Career Edge, an organization committed to helping university, college, and high school graduates gain essential career-related experience through internships. Career Edge uses the Internet as its sole means of bringing companies and youth together. More than 12 000 young Canadians have started their careers through the program in more than 1000 organizations.[17] Within a few months of completing their internship, nearly 80 percent of interns have found permanent employment with competitive salaries, and nearly 60 percent of the interns are hired by host organizations on a full-time basis.[18]

Internship, co-op, and field placement programs can produce a win–win result. The employer is provided with an inexpensive opportunity to assess potential employees while benefiting from the current knowledge and enthusiasm of bright, talented individuals. Because co-op students and interns have been exposed to the organization, they are less likely to leave shortly after permanent hire than recruits with no previous exposure to the firm.[19] Recognizing these benefits has made such programs a major recruitment method in many organizations. Recently, there has been media coverage regarding the risks of unpaid internships, which are problematic in that these employees do not secure

HR by the Numbers

Value of Internships

66% of HR professionals in Ontario view unpaid internships that without an educational or training value should be considered illegal[20]

66% of unpaid internships are part of an education or training program[21]

59% of HR professionals surveyed feel that the government should amend legislation to address the issue of unpaid internships[22]

100 000–300 000 the estimate of the number of people working in unpaid internships in Canada at a given time; there is no reporting required to measure the number and contribution of unpaid interns in Canada[23]

22 the age of Andy Ferguson when he had a fatal car accident during his 1-hour commute home from an unpaid internship; he had worked 16 out of the 24 hours prior to the accident, at Astral Media in Alberta[24]

72 the number of hours in a row 21-year-old Moritz Erhardt worked at Merrill Lynch prior to experiencing a fatal epileptic seizure; the coroner's inquest found that exhaustion from work could not be definitely linked to the intern's death[25]

Dr. José Domene

Identification: Dr. José F. Domene (PhD), Canada Research Chair in School to Work Transition and a licensed psychologist who works with university students experiencing career and mental health concerns

Affiliation: Social Science & Humanities, University of New Brunswick

1. **What kind of mental or physical impact does failure to complete school and secure long-term full-time employment generally have on young people?**

When we talk about securing long-term full-time employment, we contrast it with unemployment (those who are looking for paid work but are unemployed) and underemployment (contingent workers and those in jobs outside of their field or skill level). Research shows the mental and physical negative impact of both can be similar at this age, such as decreased self-esteem, increased depressive symptoms, increased stress and anxiety, and even an increase in substance use. These individuals perceive facing delays in achieving goals in other areas of life, such as paying debts, moving to an independent living situation, or the timing of getting married and having children.

Data shows that job satisfaction is critical, even for underemployed individuals. An increase in job satisfaction may mitigate the negative mental health consequences associated with the condition of underemployment, based on recent research of young adults' initial transition into the workforce.

2. **Based on your research, what are some of the most effective ways to ensure successful school-to-work transition?**

Youth unemployment rates in Canada are higher than those of the population, so even if an individual does everything right, it might not guarantee a desirable employment situation. With that said, there is a joint responsibility between the educational institute and the individual, with things they should do and things they should avoid.

Individual

- Do have a sense of what you want in your career trajectory before embarking on post-secondary education, and select education accordingly.
- Do consider taking a leave from education if you are not sure why you are there, but have a concrete timeline for returning and a specific plan for how you will spend that time to figure out your interests.
- Do begin networking while in school (e.g., co-op, internship, volunteer). Real world experience makes connections for employment, acts as a competitive advantage in the labour market, and helps identify person–job fit.

- Don't drop out of school altogether, because research reveals that, on average, people with university or community college credentials have better lifetime earning potential and career progression opportunities than people with only a high school diploma.
- Don't wait until the final year of school to use campus-based career and counselling services: The earlier you begin, the more time you have to implement the assistance that they can provide.

Educational Institute

- Do increase collaboration between career services and faculty advisors.
- Do recognize that job readiness and opportunities for employment are one of the reasons why students attend university.

- Don't focus only on specific or narrowly defined job skills. Instead, recognize the value of general work/life competencies and transferable skills that can be developed in many different programs of study (e.g., communication, critical thinking).

Source: Reprinted by Permission from Dr. José F. Domene.

employment-related health and safety benefits, may not receive training or educational benefits, or may be working beyond legislated maximum hours (as highlighted in the HR by the Numbers box).

Accessing Candidate Pools

HR Competency

40300

There are multiple methods of organizing, meeting, networking with, and collecting information regarding large pools of external candidates, including open houses, job fairs, professional and trade associations, labour organizations, and military personnel.

1. *Open Houses and Job Fairs* Another popular recruitment method involves holding an open house. The Halifax Career Fair, a partnership among Nova Scotia's universities and colleges, is the foremost recruiting event in Atlantic Canada. The event attracts about 150 companies from across the country and 2000 students.[26]

    Common in retail firms looking to staff a new store from the ground up, open houses have also been the choice of corporations trying to draw out scarce talent in an ultra-tight job market. A similar recruitment method involves holding a job fair onsite. At such events, recruiters share information about the organization and job opportunities with those attending in an informal, relaxed setting. Some organizations are now holding job fairs online (known as virtual job fairs) to connect with a wider geographical audience. Top prospects are invited to visit the firm or to return at a later date for a more in-depth assessment.

2. *Professional and Trade Associations* Professional and trade associations can be extremely helpful when recruiters are seeking individuals with specialized skills in such fields as IT, engineering, HR, and accounting, particularly if experience is a job requirement. Many such associations conduct ongoing placement activities on behalf of their members, and most regularly send their members newsletters or magazines in which organizations can place job advertisements.

    Such advertising may attract individuals who hadn't previously thought about changing jobs, as well as those actively seeking employment. It may also assist with ensuring that the candidates meet the required skills sets and professional capabilities of their profession, as highlighted by the case of the employer looking for a personal physician in the Expert Opinion box.

    For example, the Human Resources Professionals Association (HRPA) in Ontario has an employment service called the Hire Authority. For a nominal fee, employers can post HR-related employment opportunities on the HRPA website, where they can be viewed by HRPA members. These job postings are also emailed to members of the HRPA once a week. Additionally, employers can pay for access to an online database of member résumés and can search, sort, and pre-screen qualified candidates for vacant positions.[27]

3. *Labour Organizations* Some firms, particularly in the construction industry, obtain recruits through union hiring halls. The union maintains a roster of members (typically skilled trades people, such as carpenters, pipe fitters, welders, plumbers, and electricians), whom it sends out on assignment as requests from employers are received. Once the

Internships, co-ops, and field placements allow interns the opportunity to acquire hands-on skills to supplement their education and offer employers the opportunity to assess the performance of potential recruits.

auremar/Fotolia

expert opinion
industry viewpoint

Myles Harding

Identification: Mr. Myles Harding, Managing Director at Inline Reference Check

1. Why are employers interested in conducting pre-hire screening and background checks?

Candidates' experiences or credentials are acclaimed until they are verified. Organizations assume liability for their employees, and thereby need to verify these claims. Verification is often job specific. For example, a company figurehead's public presence is critical, so social media checks are useful.

A benefit of pre-hire screening and background checks is that it provides information which can aid the individual and the organization going forward. By identifying areas where the candidate requires additional support (e.g., management of Facebook settings, IT training, Project Management Training, etc.), additional considerations can be made to aid in the onboarding process and retention.

2. What is the benefit of having a third party conduct the reference check?

I. Contacting representatives and following up takes time, and a third party has dedicated staff, which reduces transition time between tasks.

II. Using a third party reduces the liability of the hiring organization. Third party screeners have additional liability insurance for errors and omissions.

III. A third party is a great source of knowledge, current advice on legislation, and acceptable practices. Third party screeners know what background checks are allowed for which positions, resulting in less violation of privacy. For example, credit checks are not allowed for candidates applying for non-finance related roles.

IV. Access to certain information requires specialization or certification, which a reputable third party screener should have. For example, access to credit checks requires the organization to be certified, engage in audit checks, and report on certain metrics.

V. A neutral third party advisory perspective reduces the potential for conflict of interest or bias. Hiring managers might have an escalation of commitment to their desired candidate, but a third party screener is less biased by this information.

3. In your experience, what surprises employers once a full candidate background is provided?

I. Asking critical follow-up questions in a phone interview with a referee discloses areas of challenge and areas for improvement. Some hiring teams are surprised when references are not positive.

II. Some candidates omit awards or recognition earned, which is beneficial in the assessment.

III. When a criminal record check is positive, hiring managers are often surprised. Very few organizations have a policy in place to deal with unfavourable references, or to determine what will disqualify a person from a job based on a positive criminal record check, or other detrimental verification.

IV. One of my most memorable experiences was with a client who was financially healthy, but physically ill and searching for a personal physician. The client engaged in the full recruitment selection process, and when he shortlisted his candidate, he asked us to complete the background check. Our investigation revealed that the candidate was in no way a medical professional and did not have any designations or degrees, training or education in the field. He was actually a hairdresser by trade.

Source: Reprinted by permission from Myles Harding.

union members have completed their contracted work at one firm, they notify the union of their availability for another assignment.

4. *Military Personnel* Military reservists are also potential recruits. The Canadian Forces Liaison Council (CFLC) is responsible for promoting the hiring of reservists by civilian employers. The CFLC also encourages civilian employers to give reservists time off for military training. Reserve force training develops skills and attributes sought after in the civilian workforce, such as leadership, planning, coordination, and teamwork.[28] The CFLC's Reserve Employment Assistance Program (REAP) allows employers to place job postings for skilled personnel at more than 300 military units across the country at no charge.[29]

Online Recruiting

The majority of companies now use *online recruitment*, and a majority of Canadian workers use the Internet to research prospective employers, review job postings, complete online applications, and post their résumés. The Internet provides recruiters with a large audience for job postings and a vast talent pool. Online recruiting can involve accessing one or more Internet job boards, using a corporate website, or using social networking sites.

1. *Internet Job Boards* Online job boards are fast, easy, and convenient and allow recruiters to search for candidates for positions in two ways. First, companies can post a job opening online (often for a fee) and customize it by using corporate logos and adding details about the company benefits and culture. Job seekers can search through the job postings, often by job type, region, or other criterion, and apply for the position online through the job board. The popularity of Internet job boards among job seekers is high because of the number of job postings available on one site.

   Second, job seekers can post their résumés on job boards, and firms can search the database. Canada has hundreds of job boards, ranging from the two largest, Workopolis and Monster, to many smaller job boards serving specific fields from tourism to medicine.[30] Job board meta-crawlers enable job seekers to search multiple job boards with one query.

   The advantages of job boards include candidate assistance with self-assessment and résumé writing, and pre-screening assistance for recruiters. One problem with Internet job boards is their vulnerability to privacy breaches. Fake job postings can lead to identity theft from submitted résumés, and résumés are sometimes copied onto competing job boards or other sites.[31] As a result, job boards are now providing tips for job seekers on maintaining privacy and confidentiality.[32]

2. *Corporate Websites* With the overabundance of applicants found on most online job boards, employers are now using their own corporate websites to recruit. Career pages provide a single platform for recruitment that promotes the employer brand, educates the applicant about the company, captures data about the applicant, and provides an important link to job boards where a company's positions may be advertised.[33] Virtual workplace tours using video can be provided to attract top talent aligned with the employer brand.[34] Corporate websites also help the company create a pool of candidates who have already expressed interest in the organization.[35]

   Using pre-screening strategies is essential, however. The volume of résumés definitely does not diminish when the firm accepts them online. At Hewlett-Packard, for example, more than 1 million online applications are received each year.[36] One way of coping with this volume is to generate automatic replies acknowledging receipt of applications.[37] Applicant tracking software is available to help recruiters track individual candidates through the recruitment and selection processes and to enable candidates to keep their profiles up to date.

   Active job seekers are not the only potential future employees who visit corporate websites. Customers, investors, and competitors also visit them.[38] Many of those visiting career websites are "happily employed" individuals (known as "passive" job seekers) who are likely to arrive at the career site after browsing the company's main pages for other reasons, such as research into products or services. Therefore, it is important that a firm have a prominently positioned link on the homepage leading directly to the careers section to make it easy for passive job seekers to pursue job opportunities within the company.[39]

3. *Online Networking Sites* Many organizations are turning to social networking sites like Facebook to find young, tech-savvy recruits. Some create virtual recruitment booths and others create a company profile where they can post jobs and publicize their employer brand. Other users seeking jobs can become "friends" of potential employers and upload their profiles, which contain more information than résumés. Ernst & Young is one firm that has used this approach—it has even established its own company social networking site for employees and alumni.[40]

The advantage of using social networking for recruitment purposes is the opportunity to connect with millions of other users at little or no cost. One disadvantage is the possibility of unhappy employees or customers posting negative comments on the site.[41]

Agency Recruiters

1. *Human Resources and Skills Development Canada (HRSDC)* Through various programs, including those for youth, Aboriginals, and persons with disabilities, HRSDC helps unemployed individuals find suitable jobs and helps employers locate qualified candidates to meet their needs—at no cost to either party. There is a stigma of being unemployed, as highlighted in the HR by the Numbers box, that can be overcome by assistance programs that aim to minimize time to reemployment.

The Job Bank is the largest web-based network of job postings available to Canadian employers free of charge, and it provides access to 700 000 new jobs each year, with more than 40 000 jobs at any given time and up to 2000 new jobs posted every day. HRSDC also operates Job Match, a web-based recruitment tool that can match employers' skill requirements with individuals' skill sets. Job seekers receive a list of employers with a matching job vacancy and employers receive a list of qualified candidates.[42]

2. *Executive Search Firms* Employers use executive search firms to fill critical positions in a firm, usually middle- to senior-level professional and managerial positions. Such firms often specialize in a particular type of talent, such as executives, sales, scientific, or middle-management employees. They typically know and understand the marketplace, have many contacts, and are especially adept at contacting qualified candidates who are employed and not actively looking to change jobs (which is why they have been given the nickname "headhunters"). Generally, one-third of the fee is payable as a retainer at the outset. Compared with the value of the time savings realized by the client firm's executive team, however, such a fee often turns out to be insignificant.

Using this recruitment method has some potential pitfalls.[44] Executive search firms cannot do an effective job if they are given inaccurate or incomplete information about the job or the firm. It is therefore essential for employers to explain in detail the type of candidate required—and why. A few headhunters are more salespeople than professionals, and they are more interested in persuading the employer to hire a candidate than in finding one who really meets the job specifications. Some firms have also been known to present an unpromising candidate to a client simply to make their one or two other prospects look that much better. The Association of Canadian Search, Employment, and Staffing Services (ACSESS) sponsors the Certified Personnel Consultant (CPC) designation, which signifies that recruiters have met specific

HR | by the Numbers

The Stigma of Being Unemployed

47 HR managers assessed comparable résumés for a marketing position (study 1)

10–15% lower score on both a competency scale and hireability scale given to résumés of currently unemployed applicants over employed applicants (study 1)

12 000 fake résumés sent out for jobs posted online (study 2)

4.7% call-back rate of applicants (study 2)

45% lower chance that those being invited for an interview if unemployed for eight months versus one month[43]

educational and testing requirements and confirms an individual's commitment to best industry practices.[45]

3. *Private Employment Agencies* Private employment agencies are often called on to provide assistance to employers seeking clerical staff, functional specialists, and technical employees. The "staffing" business has grown into a $6 billion industry that places hundreds of thousands of job seekers each year.[46] Generally, it is the employer who pays the agency fee. It is not uncommon for employers to be charged a fee equal to 15 to 30 percent of the first year's salary of the individual hired through agency referral. This percentage may vary depending on the volume of business provided by the client and the type of employee sought.

These agencies take an employer's request for recruits and then solicit job seekers, relying primarily on Internet job boards, advertising, and walk-ins/write-ins. Employment agencies serve two basic functions: (1) expanding the applicant pool and (2) performing preliminary interviewing and screening.

Specific situations in which an employment agency might be used for recruiting include the following:

- The organization does not have an HR department or does not have anyone with the requisite time and/or expertise.

- The firm has previously experienced difficulty in generating a pool of qualified candidates for the position or a similar type of position.

- A particular opening must be filled quickly.

- There is a desire to recruit a greater number of designated group members than the firm has been able to attract on its own.

- The recruitment effort is aimed at reaching individuals who are currently employed and might therefore feel more comfortable answering ads placed by an employment agency and subsequently dealing with one.

It should be noted, however, that the amount of service provided varies widely, as does the level of professionalism and the calibre of staff. Although most agencies screen applicants carefully, some simply provide a stream of applicants and let the client's HR department staff do the screening. Agency staff is usually paid on a commission basis, and their desire to earn a commission may occasionally compromise their professionalism (for example, encouraging job seekers to accept jobs for which they are neither qualified nor suited).

Recruiting Non-Permanent Staff

In recent years, many companies have increased their use of contingent workers to attain labour flexibility and acquire employees with special skills on an as needed basis. In these firms, recruiters are spending more time seeking temporary (term, seasonal, casual) and contract workers and less time recruiting permanent staff.[47] Two common sources of non-permanent staff are temporary help agencies and contract workers.

HR Competency

40300

1. *Temporary Help Agencies* Temporary help agencies, such as Kelly Services and Office Overload, exist in major cities in Canada. They specialize in providing temporary workers to cover for employees who are ill, on vacation, or on a leave of absence. Firms also use temporary employees to handle seasonal work, peak workloads, and special projects for which no current employees have the time or expertise. Temporary workers (temps) are agency employees and are reassigned to another employer when their services are no longer required.

Milles Studio/Fotolia

The number of temporary and freelance workers is increasing all over the world. Freelancing allows employers to match their job needs to independent workers who complete tasks on an as needed basis.

contract workers Employees who develop work relationships directly with the employer for a specific type of work or period of time.

EVIDENCE-BASED HR

An Ethical Dilemma

Is it ethical to keep extending the contracts of contract workers rather than hiring them as permanent employees to avoid the cost of employee benefits?

Temps provide employers with three major benefits:

i. They cost much less than permanent employees, as they generally receive less compensation than permanent staff. There are also savings related to the hiring and training costs associated with permanent employees. In fact, training has become the central investment in the business strategy of many temporary employment agencies. For example, Accountemps invests in the skills and training of employees after they have worked for a specified amount of time. This training includes online tutoring in software they may use on the job and tuition reimbursement for skills training.[48]

ii. If a temp performs unsatisfactorily, a substitute can be requested immediately. Generally, a suitable replacement is sent to the firm within one business day.

iii. Individuals working as temps who are seeking full-time employment are often highly motivated, knowing that many firms choose full-time employees from the ranks of their top-performing temps.

2. **Contract workers** Some employees develop work relationships directly with the employer for a specific type of work or period of time.[49] For example, Parc Aviation is a major supplier of contract workers to the airline industry. Airline organizations benefit from the services of contract engineers by having them cover seasonal or unplanned peaks in business, carry out special tasks or projects, and reduce the necessity for airlines to downsize permanent staff during cyclical downturns.[50]

Many professionals with specialized skills become contract workers, including project managers, accountants, and lawyers. Some have consciously made a decision to work for themselves; others have been unable to obtain full-time employment in their field of expertise or have found themselves out of a full-time job because of cutbacks. Thus, some want to remain self-employed; others work a contract while hoping to obtain a full-time position eventually. Some firms hire former employees (such as retirees) on a contract basis.

RECRUITING A MORE DIVERSE WORKFORCE

Recruiting a diverse workforce is not just socially responsible—it's a necessity. As noted previously, the composition of Canada's workforce is changing dramatically. Trends of particular significance include the increasing necessity of hiring older employees, a decrease in the availability of young workers, and an increase in the number of women, visible minorities, Aboriginal people, and persons with disabilities in the workforce.

Attracting Older Workers

Many employers, recognizing the fact that the workforce is aging, are encouraging retirement-age employees to stay with the company or are actively recruiting employees who are at or beyond retirement age. For example, 20 percent of Home Depot Canada's workforce is over the age of 50.[51] Hiring and retaining older employees has significant benefits. These workers typically have high job satisfaction, a strong sense of loyalty and organizational commitment, a strong work ethic, good people skills, and a willingness to work in a variety of roles, including part time.[52]

STRATEGIC HR

Attracting the Younger Generation

The younger generation aims to take advantage of every form of technology to make their job search successful and easier. Certain key words attract these individuals to an organization's ads when they do online searches. The younger generation likes short, snappy copy that gets right to the point of what they will be doing. But of equal or more importance, the ad needs to advertise the culture of the organization as it relates to the values of this generation. The ads should include statements such as "fast-paced environment," "individual contribution," "work–life balance," "do it your way," "opportunity to grow," "no rules," and "state-of-the-art technology." Of course, organizations should list these kinds of features in the ads only if they truly offer them.

Source: Based on R. Throckmorton and L. Gravett, "Attracting the Younger Generation," *Canadian HR Reporter* (April 23, 2007).

To make a company attractive to older workers, it is important to deal with stereotypical attitudes toward older workers through education, ensure that HR policies do not discourage recruitment of older workers, develop flexible work arrangements, and redesign jobs to accommodate decreased dexterity and strength. A Conference Board of Canada study found that the most common recruitment strategy for older workers was rehiring former employees and retirees. Less than 20 percent were using recruitment campaigns directed specifically at mature workers.[53]

Attracting Younger Employees

Many firms are taking steps to address the pending shortage of younger employees. Younger members of the workforce are part of the Generation X and Generation Y cohorts. To appeal to Generation X-ers, it is important for the company to stress that employees will be able to work independently and that work–life balance will be supported, as outlined in the Strategic HR box.

Recruiting Designated Group Members

PERSONAL INVENTORY ASSESSMENT

Learn About Yourself
Multicultural Awareness Scale

Most of the recruitment methods already discussed can be used to attract members of designated groups (Aboriginal people, women, visible minorities, and persons with disabilities), provided that the employer's commitment to equality and diversity is made clear to all involved in the recruitment process—whether it is employees who are asked for referrals or private employment agencies. This can also be stressed in all recruitment advertising. Alternative publications targeted at designated group members should be considered for advertising, and linkages can be formed with organizations and agencies specializing in assisting designated group members. Specific examples follow.

The Aboriginal Human Resource Council, headquartered in Saskatoon, Saskatchewan, sponsors the Aboriginal Inclusion Network, which offers a job board, résumé database, and other tools to hire, retain, and promote Aboriginal talent. The Inclusion Network is linked to 350 Aboriginal employment centres across Canada, and the number of job seekers on the network increased 70 percent from 2009 to 2011.[54]

The Society for Canadian Women in Science and Technology (SCWIST) is a not-for-profit, volunteer organization aimed at improving attitudes and stereotypes about and assisting women in scientific, technological, and engineering careers. Employers can access valuable resources such as websites, employment agencies, and publications to attract professional women for employment opportunities in industries where they generally have a low representation.[55]

WORKink is Canada's most powerful online career development and employment portal for Canadians with disabilities. The WORKink site offers a full complement of employment and recruitment resources and services for job seekers with disabilities and for employers looking to create an inclusive workplace. WORKink is sponsored by the Canadian Council on Rehabilitation and Work. Employers can post job openings free of charge, browse résumés of people with disabilities, or access information on how to adapt the work environment to accommodate people with disabilities in their region.[56]

The Ontario Ministry of Community and Social Services sponsors a program called Paths to Equal Opportunity intended to provide links to information on removing and preventing barriers so that people with disabilities can work, learn, and play to their fullest potential. In conjunction with the Canadian Abilities Foundation, the program publishes a resource booklet called *Abilities @ Work*, which provides specific information to employers who want to find out about recruiting, interviewing, hiring, and working with people with disabilities. It also provides information to employees and job seekers with disabilities who want information on looking for work, accommodation in the workplace, and maintaining employment.

HR Competency

20600

Another useful tool is the guidebook *Tapping the Talents of People with Disabilities: A Guidebook for Employers*, which is available through the Conference Board of Canada.

CHAPTER SUMMARY

1. Recruitment is the process of searching out and attracting qualified job applicants. It begins with the identification of a position that requires staffing and is completed when résumés or completed application forms are received. In order to manage the increasing talent shortage, proactive employers are trying to obtain a competitive advantage in recruitment by establishing themselves as employers of choice through employer branding.

2. The recruitment process has four steps. First, job openings are identified through HR planning or manager request. Second, the job description and job specifications are reviewed to determine the job requirements. Third, appropriate recruiting source(s) and method(s) are chosen. Fourth, using these strategies, a pool of qualified candidates is generated.

3. Application forms have been largely replaced by online applications, where candidates provide information on education and experience, a brief overview of past career progress, and other information that can be used to predict whether an applicant will succeed on the job.

4. Internal recruitment methods include job posting, mining human resources records, or using skills inventories.

5. External recruitment can be multifaceted. Traditional networking includes cold calls, print advertising, employee referrals, and former employees who have remained in contact with the organization. Organizations can gain access to large pools of candidates through relationships formed during open houses and job fairs, professional and trade associations, labour organizations, and military personnel. Online recruitment includes Internet-based job boards, corporate websites and social networking sites. Agency recruitment includes HRSDC, executive search firms and private employment agencies. Recruitment of non-permanent staff can come from temporary help agencies and contract workers.

6. Recruiting a diverse workforce is a necessity, given the shrinking labour force. In particular, recruiters are trying to attract older workers, younger workers, women, visible minorities, Aboriginal people, and people with disabilities.

MyManagementLab

Study, practise, and explore real business situations with these helpful resources:

- **Interactive Lesson Presentations:** Work through interactive presentations and assessments to test your knowledge of management concepts.
- **PIA (Personal Inventory Assessments):** Enhance your ability to connect with key concepts through these engaging self-reflection assessments.
- **Study Plan:** Check your understanding of chapter concepts with self-study quizzes.
- **Videos:** Learn more about the management practices and strategies of real companies.
- **Simulations:** Practise decision-making in simulated management environments.

KEY TERMS

biographical information blank (BIB) *(p. 134)*
blind ad *(p. 138)*
contract workers *(p. 146)*
employer branding *(p. 131)*
human capital theory *(p. 134)*
job posting *(p. 135)*

nepotism *(p. 138)*
recruiter *(p. 131)*
recruitment *(p. 131)*
want ad *(p. 138)*
yield ratio *(p. 136)*

REVIEW AND DISCUSSION QUESTIONS

1. Discuss the advantages and disadvantages of recruiting from within the organization. Identify and describe the three tools that are used in this process.

2. Brainstorm the advantages of external recruitment. Discuss the risks associated with external recruiting.

3. Explain the difference between an Internet job board and a corporate career website.

4. Under what circumstances should a private employment agency be used?

5. Describe the advantages of using online application forms or résumé repositories as part of the recruitment process.

CRITICAL THINKING QUESTIONS

1. What potential problems may result if the employer branding value proposition presented during the recruitment process is not reinforced once the new recruit is working for the organization? What could organizations do to avoid this situation?

2. What potential problems could be created by offering referral bonuses to existing employees?

3. Working individually or in groups, find at least five employment ads, either on the Internet or in a local newspaper, that suggest that the company is family friendly and should appeal to women, minorities, older workers, and single parents. Discuss what they're doing to be family friendly.

4. As the labour supply gets tighter and tighter, would you be in favour of loosening requirements for foreign-trained professionals (for example, doctors, professors, accountants, engineers) to become immediately qualified in Canada? Why or why not? Identify the underlying assumptions in the position you took.

5. What are some of the specific reservations that a 30-year-old candidate might have about applying for a job that requires managing a workforce that is on average 10 years older than he or she is?

6. Assume you are the HR manager in a highly homogenous company that now wants to better reflect the diversity of the target client group in its employee population. What must you consider as you think about implementing your new recruitment strategy?

EXPERIENTIAL EXERCISES

1. Go to your university's or college's career centre and gather information on all the services they provide. How many companies come to recruit students through the centre each year? What services does the centre provide to employers seeking to hire graduating students? Employers seeking to hire summer students? Employers seeking to hire students for internships?

2. Working individually or in groups, interview a manager between the ages of 25 and 35 at a local business who manages employees age 40 or older. Ask the manager to describe three or four of his or her most challenging experiences managing older employees.

3. Considering the current economic situation and using the following list of jobs, identify all of the sources that could be used to recruit qualified applicants:

   - Registered nurses (RN) to work in the critical care unit of a new regional hospital

   - carpenters to work on a new home building project

   - Chief financial officer (CFO) for an international engineering firm with a head office located in Vancouver

   - retail sales associates to work in an urban clothing chain

   - customer service representatives to work in a bank branch

   - bilingual administrative assistants for a Canadian financial services company operating internationally

RUNNING CASE

Running Case: LearnInMotion.com

Getting Better Applicants

If Jennifer and Pierre were asked what the main problem was in running their business, their answer would be quick and short: hiring good people. They were simply astonished at how hard it was to attract and hire good candidates. After much debate, they decided to post openings for seven positions: two salespeople, one web designer, two content management people, one office manager, and one web surfer.

Their first approach was to design and place a large display ad in two local newspapers. The display ad listed all the positions available. Jennifer and Pierre assumed that by placing a large ad with the name of the company prominently displayed and a bold border around the ad, it would draw attention and therefore generate applicants.

For two consecutive weekends, the ad cost the fledgling company close to $1000, but it produced only a handful of applicants. After speaking with them by phone, Jennifer and Pierre rejected three outright, two said they weren't interested, and two scheduled interviews but never showed up.

The owners therefore decided to change their approach. They used different recruiting methods for each position. In the paper, they placed ads for the salespeople under "Sales" and for the office manager under "Administrative."

They advertised for a web designer by placing an ad on Monster.ca. And for the content managers and web surfer they placed neatly typed help wanted ads in the career placement offices of a technical college and a community college about 10 minutes away from their office. They also used this job posting approach to find independent contractors they could use to physically deliver courses to users' homes or offices.

The results were disappointing. Over a typical weekend, literally dozens of want ads for experienced salespeople appear, as well as almost as many for office managers. The ad for salespeople generated three calls, one of whom Jennifer and Pierre felt might be a viable candidate, although the person wanted a much higher salary than they had planned to pay. One possible candidate emerged for the office manager position.

They decided to change the positioning of the sales ad in the newspaper from "Salespersons Wanted" to "Phone Sales," which is a separate category (because the job involved entirely inside phone sales). Many of the calls they got (not all of them, but many) were from salespeople who were used to working in what some people called "boiler-room" operations. In other words, they sit at the phone all day making cold calls from lists provided by their employers, selling anything from burglar alarms to investments, all under very high-pressure conditions. They weren't interested in LearnInMotion.com, nor was LearnInMotion.com interested in them.

They fared a little better with the web designer ad, which produced four possible applicants. They got no phone calls from the local college job postings; when they

called to ask the placement offices why, they were told that their posted salary of $8 per hour was "much too low." They went back and replaced the job postings with $10 hourly rates.

"I just don't understand it," Jennifer finally said. Especially for the sales job, Jennifer and Pierre felt that they were offering perfectly acceptable compensation packages, so the lack of applicants surprised them. "Maybe a lot of people just don't want to work for dot-coms anymore," said Pierre, thinking out loud. "When the bottom fell out of the dot-com market, a lot of good people were hurt by working for a series of two or three failed dot-coms. Maybe they've just had enough of the wired world."

QUESTIONS

1 Describe how the recruitment process (including all of the steps) outlined in Figure 6.1 will be of assistance to Jennifer and Pierre to solve their recruitment problems.

2 Draft a new job posting for each of the seven positions discussed in the case. Then discuss how you put the job postings together and why, using Figure 6.2 and Figure 6.3 as examples.

CASE INCIDENT

Solving a Potential Recruitment Dilemma

Rachel Lucas is the human resources manager of a prestigious accounting firm. Rachel recently attended a local human resources professionals' association meeting where recruitment was the topic up for discussion. At this meeting all aspects of the recruitment process, including recruitment methods and how to increase diversity through the use of application forms, were to be discussed. Rachel couldn't wait to apply what she learned at this meeting to her job.

While listening to the scheduled speaker for the evening, Rachel started to think about the current recruitment initiatives she was dealing with at work. The firm was entering its traditional busy season where many clients would need tax returns completed. This time every year she needed to source and hire quality, qualified candidates to fill 50 tax preparer positions. The partners were relying heavily on her this year to get higher quality candidates because of the complex returns that would have to be completed, and to have them in place within three weeks.

As the speaker was finishing his presentation, Rachel wondered what recruitment process and techniques she should use. What would be the best decisions for the firm?

QUESTIONS

1 Should Rachel use internal or external recruitment techniques to staff these 50 positions?

2 Rachel is hoping to recruit qualified candidates from a variety of diverse demographics. Will she have to use different recruitment techniques to do this? If so, what ones are the most effective to attract these candidates (older workers, designated group members, and so on)?

3 Rachel plans on hiring recruiters to assist her in staffing these 50 positions. Knowing the company will require the recruiters to adhere to the concept of employer branding, describe what steps Rachel should take to orient the new recruiters to the branding process.

Fotolia

Selection

LEARNING OUTCOMES

AFTER STUDYING THIS CHAPTER, YOU SHOULD BE ABLE TO

DEFINE selection and **DISCUSS** its strategic importance.

DEFINE reliability and validity and **EXPLAIN** their importance in selection techniques.

DESCRIBE at least four types of testing used in selection and **ANALYZE** the conflicting legal concerns related to alcohol and drug testing.

DESCRIBE the major types of selection interviews by degree of structure, type of content, and manner of administration.

EXPLAIN the importance of reference checking, **DESCRIBE** strategies to make such checking effective, and **ANALYZE** the legal issues involved.

REQUIRED HR COMPETENCIES

20100: Conduct human resources responsibilities and build productive relationships consistent with standards of practice with due diligence and integrity to balance the interests of all parties.

20300: Adhere to legal requirements as they pertain to human resources policies and practices to promote organizational values and manage risk.

20600: Promote an evidence-based approach to the development of human resources policies and practices using current professional resources to provide a sound basis for human resources decision-making.

40300: Execute a workforce plan by sourcing, selecting, hiring, onboarding, and developing people to address competency needs and retain qualified talent aligned with the organization's strategic objectives.

50200: Interpret legislation, collective agreements (where applicable), and policies consistent with legal requirements and organizational values to treat employees in a fair and consistent manner and manage the risk of litigation and conflict.

90500: Report on the effectiveness of human capital investments with respect to key performance indicators using appropriate measures and metrics to monitor trends and promote the organization's progress toward its objectives.

THE STRATEGIC IMPORTANCE OF EMPLOYEE SELECTION

selection The process of choosing among individuals who have been recruited to fill existing or projected job openings.

Selection is the process of choosing among individuals who have been recruited to fill existing or projected job openings. Whether considering current employees for a transfer or promotion or outside candidates for a first-time position with the firm, information about the applicants must be collected and evaluated. Selection begins when a pool of applicants has submitted their résumés or completed application forms as a result of the recruiting process.

The selection process has important strategic significance. More and more managers have realized that the quality of the company's human resources is often the single most important factor in determining whether the firm is going to survive and be successful in reaching the objectives specified in its strategic plan. Those individuals selected will be implementing strategic decisions and, in some cases, creating strategic plans. Thus, successful candidates must fit with the strategic direction of the organization. For example, if the organization is planning to expand internationally, language skills and international experience will become important selection criteria.

When a poor selection decision is made and the individual selected for the job is not capable of acceptable performance in the job, strategic objectives will not be met. In addition, when an unsuccessful employee must be terminated, the recruitment and selection process must begin all over again, and the successor must be properly oriented and trained. The "hidden" costs are frequently even higher, including internal disorganization and disruption and customer alienation. Recent research (as summarized in the HR by the Numbers box) identifies that while ideally selection should involve a clear process, in reality, the adoption and use of an appropriate selection process (as summarized in this chapter) may be problematic in many organization, often resulting in a number of hiring mistakes.

HR by the Numbers

Hiring Mistakes

14% of new hires are considered unsuccessful by the employer[1]

3 times the annual salary is the estimated cost of turnover from a position[2]

49% of new hires regret accepting the job offer[3]

88% of new hires feel they did not receive an accurate description of the job[4]

31% of employers who feel new hire was unsuccessful blame overreliance on hiring manager's evaluations[5]

21% of employers who feel new hire was unsuccessful blame employee for overselling skills[6]

Supply Challenges

Although it is desirable to have a large, qualified pool of recruits from which to select applicants, this is not always possible. Certain vacant positions may be subject to a labour shortage (based on job requirements, location, work environment, and so on), while other simultaneous vacant positions may be subject to a labour surplus (due to external environment factors, training and education levels, immigration patterns, and so on). A **selection ratio** is the ratio of the number of applicants hired to the total number of applicants available, as follows:

selection ratio The ratio of the number of applicants hired to the total number of applicants.

Number of Applicants Hired ÷ Total Number of Applicants = Selection Ratio

A small selection ratio, such as 1:2, may be indicative of a limited number of applicants from which to select, and it may also mean low-quality recruits. If this is the case, it is generally better to start the recruitment process over again, even if it means a hiring delay, rather than taking the risk of hiring an employee who will be a marginal performer at best.

A large selection ratio, such as 1:400, may be indicative that the job ad is too vague, that the organization's HR team may need to automate the screening process, or that there is a need for more resources to find the right job candidate among the high number of applicants.

The Selection Process

multiple-hurdle strategy
An approach to selection involving a series of successive steps or hurdles. Only candidates clearing the hurdle are permitted to move on to the next step.

Most firms use a sequential selection system involving a series of successive steps—a **multiple-hurdle strategy**. Only candidates clearing a "hurdle" (selection techniques including pre-screening, testing, interviewing, and background/reference checking) are permitted to move on to the next step. Clearing the hurdle requires meeting or exceeding the minimum requirements established for that hurdle. Thus, only candidates who have cleared all of the previous hurdles remain in contention for the position at the time that the hiring decision is being made.

HR Competency
50200

To assess each applicant's potential for success on the job, organizations typically rely on a number of sources of information. The number of steps in the selection process and their sequence vary with the organization. The types of selection instruments and screening devices used are also not standardized across organizations. Even within a firm, the number and sequence of steps often vary with the type and level of the job, as well as the source and method of recruitment. **Figure 7.1** illustrates the steps commonly involved.

At each step in the selection process, carefully chosen selection criteria must be used to determine which applicants will move on to the next step. It is through job analysis that the duties, responsibilities, and human requirements for each job are identified. By basing selection criteria on these requirements, firms can create a legally defensible hiring system.[7] Individuals hired after thorough screening against these carefully developed selection criteria (based directly on the job description and job specifications) learn their jobs readily, are productive, and generally adjust to their jobs with a minimum of difficulty.

Designing an effective selection process involves composing a series of job-related questions to be asked of all applicants for a particular job. There are also a few job-related, candidate-specific questions. Doing so involves the following five steps, the first two of which should occur before recruitment:[8]

1. Decide who will be involved in the selection process and *develop selection criteria*. Specifying selection criteria involves clarifying and weighting the information in the job description and job specifications and holding discussions among the interview team members, especially those most familiar with the job and co-workers.

must criteria Requirements that are absolutely essential for the job, include a measurable standard of acceptability, or are absolute and can be screened initially on paper.

2. *Specify musts and wants and weight the wants.* Once agreed on, the selection criteria should be divided into the two categories: musts and wants.[9] **Must criteria** are those that are absolutely essential for the job, include a measurable standard of acceptability, or are absolute. There are often only two musts: a specific level of

FIGURE 7.1   Six Typical Hurdles in the Selection Process

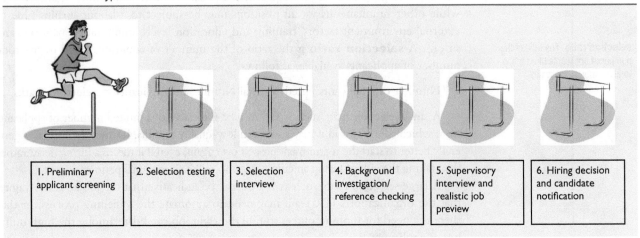

| 1. Preliminary applicant screening | 2. Selection testing | 3. Selection interview | 4. Background investigation/ reference checking | 5. Supervisory interview and realistic job preview | 6. Hiring decision and candidate notification |

want criteria Those criteria that represent qualifications that cannot be screened on paper or are not readily measurable, as well as those that are highly desirable but not critical.

HR Competency

20100

EVIDENCE-BASED **HR**

Hints **TO ENSURE LEGAL COMPLIANCE**

HR Competency

20300

peshkova/Fotolia

More and more HR professionals are improving the initial screening process with the use of technology.

education (or equivalent combination of education and work experience) and a minimum amount of prior work experience. These criteria can be initially screened, based on the applicants' résumés or applications. The **want criteria** include skills and abilities that cannot be screened on paper (such as verbal skills) or are not readily measurable (such as leadership ability, teamwork skills, and enthusiasm), as well as qualifications that are desirable but not critical.

3. Determine assessment strategies and *develop an evaluation form*. Once the must and want criteria have been identified, appropriate strategies for learning about each should be specified. For some qualifications, especially those that are critically important, the team may decide to use several assessment strategies. For example, leadership skills might be assessed through behavioural questions, situational questions, a written test, and an assessment centre. Once all want criteria have been agreed on and weighted, it becomes the basis for candidate comparison and evaluation.

4. *Develop interview questions* to be asked of all candidates. Questions should be developed for each KSA to be assessed during the interview. *Job-knowledge questions* and *worker-requirements questions* to gauge the applicants' motivation and willingness to perform under prevailing working conditions, such as shift work or travel, should also be included.

5. *Develop candidate-specific questions.* A few open-ended, job-related questions that are candidate specific should be planned, based on each candidate's résumé and application form.

Acquiring Employees and the Law

The entire recruitment and selection procedure must comply with human rights legislation. All information collected from the time an ad is posted to the time that the selection decision is made must be free from questions that would directly or indirectly classify candidates on the basis of any of the prohibited grounds under human rights legislation; potential employers cannot ask for a photograph, information about illnesses, disabilities or workers' compensation claims, or information that could lead to direct, intentional discrimination, such as age, gender, sexual orientation, marital status, maiden name, date of birth, place of origin, number of dependents, and so on.

If the process collects any information that is considered a prohibited ground for discrimination, an unsuccessful candidate may challenge the legality of the entire recruitment and selection processes. In such cases, the burden of proof is on the employer. Thus, taking human rights legislation requirements into consideration when designing effective recruitment and selection procedures is imperative. *A Guide to Screening and Selection in Employment* in Appendix 7.1 provides helpful hints. Specific guidelines regarding questions that can and cannot be asked on application forms are available through the human rights commissions in each jurisdiction.

Managing the process in a legally defensible way involves keeping the following guidelines in mind:

1. Ensure that all selection criteria and strategies are based on the job description and the job specifications.

2. Do not ask questions that would violate human rights legislation, either directly or indirectly. Questions cannot be asked about candidates' marital status, childcare arrangements, ethnic background, or workers' compensation history, for example.

3. Obtain written authorization for reference checking from prospective employees, and check references carefully.

4. Save all records and information obtained about the applicant during each stage of the selection process.

5. Reject applicants who make false statements on their application forms or résumés.

STEP 1: PRELIMINARY APPLICANT SCREENING

Initial applicant screening is generally performed by members of the HR department. Application forms and résumés are reviewed, and those candidates not meeting the essential selection criteria are eliminated first. Then, the remaining applications are examined and those candidates who most closely match the remaining job specifications are identified and given further consideration.

The use of technology is becoming increasingly popular to help HR professionals improve the initial screening process. Almost all large firms or firms with high turnover use technological applications to help screen large numbers of candidates and generate short lists of individuals who will move on to the next step in the selection process. Technology can be used to aid in the screening process, as highlighted in the Expert Opinion box.

HR Competency

20600

Crowdsourcing

Google found a way to foster the employee interaction its success depends on by using "crowdsourcing" for screening decisions.[10] When a prospective employee applies for a job, his or her information (such as school and previous employers) goes into Google's applicant-tracking system.[11] The ATS then matches the applicant's information with that of current Google employees. When it finds a match, it asks those Google employees to comment on the applicant's suitability for the position. This gives Google recruiters a valuable insight into how the employees actually doing the work think the applicant will do at Google. It also fosters a sense of community and interaction among Google employees.

STEP 2: SELECTION TESTING

Selection testing is a common screening device used by approximately two-thirds of Canadian organizations to assess specific job-related skills as well as general intelligence, personality characteristics, mental abilities, interests, and preferences.[12] Testing techniques provide efficient, standardized procedures for screening large numbers of applicants. Several thousand psychological and personality tests are on the market.[13]

The Importance of Reliability and Validity

EVIDENCE-BASED HR

Tests and other selection techniques are only useful if they provide reliable and valid measures.[14] All reputable tests will provide information to users about the reliability and validity of the test.

reliability The degree to which interviews, tests, and other selection procedures yield comparable data over time; in other words, the degree of dependability, consistency, or stability of the measures used.

Reliability

The degree to which interviews, tests, and other selection procedures yield comparable data over time is known as **reliability**. Reliability is the degree of dependability,

Dr. Benjamin Taylor

Identification: Dr. Benjamin Taylor (PhD) is the Chief Data Scientist for HireVue.

1. How has HireVue used technology to change the recruitment and selection process?

HireVue pioneered digital on-demand interviewing. Most employers have been limited to traditional screening procedures, with fixed duration/schedule. Decisions were often made based on artificial thresholds (e.g., minimum education) which were not based on data, but based on individual biases or competitiveness of the applicant pool. Our service allows organizations to pre-establish interview questions and access a large pool of candidates who respond to the questions via video interviews.

We made it easier to view and share interviews remotely, at any pace. In addition, we allow multiple raters to score applicants and we can assess reliability of these scores. This saves money and time associated with transportation and accommodation of applicants for face-to-face screening. Similarly, applicants benefit from low barriers of entry, as they can easily access multiple jobs, upload interviews at their convenience, and keep a single profile current.

2. How does HireVue use technology to make evidence-based decisions?

We collect over 15 000 numerical features used to evaluate each interview. We use this data to predict which candidate will be a top performer in the interview. Beyond that, if a company has used our service more than once, we can tailor decision criteria based on previous use of the service and largely automate the shortlisting process.

The range of interview questions that companies want to use is from 5 to 30, so we assume an evidence-based approach to suggest how many questions would be ideal and how long a candidate should be given to think about or answer a question. Data collected demonstrates that minimal incremental predictive value is added when more than 15 well-crafted, intelligent questions are used. We have also used the information to identify accuracy level of recruiters, which is a metric most organizations find useful.

3. So far, we have spoken largely about external hires. Could a system like this be used for both internal and external hires?

One of the largest airlines in the US uses our system for internal and external screening of applicants (in addition to referrals). Although they use the same platform to test internal and external candidates, the questions asked for internal candidates have a different focus, leading to different decision models. For example, the issue of organizational or industry alignment has less variability among internal candidates. Internal candidates are more concerned with getting feedback regarding why they were not selected. Our system can use the metrics we collect to validate decisions made, increasing awareness of internal candidate selection choices (e.g., those offered the job scored higher on certain factors).

Source: Reprinted by permission from Benjamin Taylor.

consistency, or stability of the measures used. For example, a test that results in widely variable scores (for example, if the same candidate completes the test three times and secures scores of 60 percent, 82 percent, and 71 percent) when it is administered on different occasions to the same individual is unreliable. Reliability also refers to the extent to which two or more methods yield the same results or are consistent. For example, applicants with high scores on personality tests for impulsivity or lack of self-control are correlated with the likelihood of failing background checks due to criminal behaviour.[15] Reliability also means the extent to which there is agreement between two or more raters (inter-rater reliability).

When dealing with tests, another measure of reliability that is taken into account is internal consistency. For example, suppose a vocational interest test has 10 items, all of which were supposed to measure, in one way or another, the person's interest in working outdoors. To assess internal reliability, the degree to which responses to those 10 items vary together would be statistically analyzed (which is one reason that tests often include questions that appear rather repetitive). Reliability can be diminished when questions are answered randomly, when the test setting is noisy or uncomfortable, and when the applicant is tired or unwell.

Validity

validity The accuracy with which a predictor measures what it is intended to measure.

Validity, in the context of selection, is an indicator of the extent to which data from a selection technique, such as a test or interview, are related to or predictive of subsequent performance on the job. For example, high impulsivity is correlated with low productivity.[16] Separate validation studies of selection techniques should be conducted for different subgroups, such as visible minorities and women, to assess **differential validity**. In some cases, the technique may be a valid predictor of job success for one group (such as white males) but not for other applicants, thereby leading to systemic discrimination. Three types of validity are particularly relevant to selection: criterion-related, content, and construct validity.

differential validity Confirmation that the selection tool accurately predicts the performance of all possible employee subgroups, including white males, women, visible minorities, persons with disabilities, and Aboriginal people.

Criterion-Related Validity   The extent to which a selection tool predicts or significantly correlates with important elements of work behaviour is known as **criterion-related validity**. Demonstrating criterion-related validity requires proving that those who exhibit strong sales ability on a test or in an interview, for example, also have high sales on the job, and that those individuals who do poorly on the test or in the interview have poor sales results.

criterion-related validity The extent to which a selection tool predicts or significantly correlates with important elements of work behaviour.

Content Validity   When a selection instrument, such as a test, adequately samples the knowledge and skills needed to perform the job, **content validity** is assumed to exist. The closer the content of the selection instrument is to actual samples of work or work behaviour, the greater the content validity. For example, asking a candidate for a secretarial position to demonstrate word processing skills, as required on the job, has high content validity.

content validity The extent to which a selection instrument, such as a test, adequately samples the knowledge and skills needed to perform the job.

Construct Validity   The extent to which a selection tool measures a theoretical construct or trait deemed necessary to perform the job successfully is known as **construct validity**. Intelligence, verbal skills, analytical ability, and leadership skills are all examples of constructs. Measuring construct validity requires demonstrating that the psychological trait or attribute is related to satisfactory job performance, as well as showing that the test or other selection tool used accurately measures the psychological trait or attribute. As an example of poor construct validity, an accounting firm was selecting applicants for auditor positions based on a test for high extroversion, when the job in fact required working alone with data. A test to select applicants with high introversion would have had higher construct validity and would have helped to avoid the high turnover rate the firm was experiencing.[17]

construct validity The extent to which a selection tool measures a theoretical construct or trait deemed necessary to perform the job successfully.

Professional standards for psychologists require that tests be used as supplements to other techniques, such as interviews and background checks; that tests be validated in the organization where they will be used; that a certified psychologist be used to choose, validate, administer, and interpret tests; and that private, quiet, well-lit, and well-ventilated settings be provided to all applicants taking the tests.[18]

Tests of Cognitive Abilities

Ensuring validity of selection tools when assessing candidates with disabilities may require accommodation of the disability. Included in the category of tests of cognitive abilities are tests of general reasoning ability (intelligence), tests of emotional intelligence, and tests of specific cognitive abilities, like memory and inductive reasoning.

Intelligence Tests

Intelligence (IQ) tests are tests of general intellectual abilities (also referred to as general mental abilities or GMA) and have been used since the end of World War I.[19] They measure not a single "intelligence" trait, but rather a number of abilities, including memory, vocabulary, verbal fluency, and numerical ability. An IQ score is actually a *derived* score, reflecting the extent to which the person is above or below the "average" adult's intelligence score. Empirical research suggests that general mental ability is the strongest general predictor of job performance at one's chosen occupation.[20] Intelligence is often measured with individually administered tests, such as the Stanford-Binet test or the Wechsler test. Other IQ tests, such as the Wonderlic Personnel Test, can be administered to groups of people. These are relatively quick pen and paper or online tests that can be accessed for a nominal fee.

EVIDENCE-BASED HR

Emotional Intelligence Tests

Emotional intelligence (EI) tests measure a person's ability to monitor his or her own emotions and the emotions of others and to use that knowledge to guide thoughts and actions. Someone with a high emotional quotient (EQ) is self-aware, can control his or her impulses, is self-motivated, and demonstrates empathy and social awareness. Many people believe that EQ, which can be modified through conscious effort and practice, is actually a more important determinant of success than a high IQ. However, there is extremely limited and highly controversial empirical evidence to support the importance of EQ in the workplace.[21] Self-assessment tests include the Emotional Quotient Inventory (EQ-i), the EQ Map, the Mayer-Salovey-Caruso Emotional Intelligence Test (MSCEIT), and the Emotional Intelligence Questionnaire (EIQ). The Emotional Competence Inventory (ECI) is a 360-degree assessment in which several individuals evaluate one person to get a more complete picture of the individual's emotional competencies.[22]

PERSONAL INVENTORY ASSESSMENT

Learn About Yourself
Emotional Intelligence
Assessment

Emotional Intelligence Consortium
www.eiconsortium.org

PERSONAL INVENTORY ASSESSMENT

Learn About Yourself
Cognitive Style Indicator

Specific Cognitive Abilities

There are also measures of specific thinking skills, such as inductive and deductive reasoning, verbal comprehension, memory, and numerical ability. Tests in this category are often called **aptitude tests**, since they purport to measure the applicant's aptitude for the job in question, that is, the applicant's potential to perform the job once given proper training. An example is the test of mechanical comprehension illustrated in **Figure 7.2**. It tests the applicant's understanding of basic mechanical principles. It may therefore reflect a person's aptitude for jobs—like that of machinist or engineer—that require mechanical comprehension. Multidimensional aptitude tests commonly used in applicant selection include the General Aptitude Test Battery (GATB).

Hints TO ENSURE LEGAL COMPLIANCE

FIGURE 7.2   Test of Mechanical Comprehension

Based on the figure below, please identify how much weight is required to balance the lever.

5 Kg

3 m   1 m

Tests of Motor and Physical Abilities

There are many *motor abilities* that a firm might want to measure. These include finger dexterity, manual dexterity, speed of arm movement, and reaction time. Motor abilities tests measure the speed and accuracy of simple judgment, as well as the speed of finger, hand, and arm movements. Tests include the Crawford Small Parts Dexterity Test, the Stromberg Dexterity Test, the Minnesota Rate of Manipulation Test, and the Purdue Pegboard.

Tests of physical abilities may also be required.[23] For example, some firms are now using functional abilities evaluations (FAE) to assist with placement decisions. An FAE, which measures a whole series of physical abilities—ranging from lifting, to pulling and pushing, sitting, squatting, climbing, and carrying—is particularly useful for positions with a multitude of physical demands, such as a firefighter or police officer.[24] Ensuring that physical abilities tests do not violate human rights legislation requires basing such tests on job duties identified through job analysis and a physical demands analysis, ensuring that the tests duplicate the actual physical requirements of the job, developing and imposing such tests honestly and in good faith, ensuring that those administering the tests are properly trained and administer the tests in a consistent manner, and ensuring that testing standards are objectively related to job performance.[25]

Measuring Personality and Interests

A person's mental and physical abilities are seldom sufficient to explain his or her job performance. Other factors, such as the person's motivation and interpersonal skills, are important too. Personality and interest inventories are sometimes used as predictors of such intangibles.

Personality tests can measure basic aspects of an applicant's personality, such as introversion, stability, and motivation. The use of such tests for selection assumes that it is possible to find a relationship between a measurable personality trait (such as conscientiousness) and success on the job.[26] Many of these tests are *projective*. In the Thematic Apperception Test, an ambiguous stimulus (like an inkblot or clouded picture) is presented to the test taker, and he or she is asked to interpret or react to it. Because the pictures are ambiguous, the person's interpretation must come from within—the viewer supposedly *projects* into the picture his or her own emotional attitudes about life. Thus, a security-oriented person might have a very different description of what he or she sees compared to someone who is not.

The Myers-Briggs Type Indicator instrument, which has been in use for more than 50 years, is believed to be the most widely used personality inventory in the world. More than 2 million assessments are administered annually in the United States alone.[27] Another example of a common personality test is the Minnesota Multiphasic Personality Inventory (MMPI), which measures traits like hypochondria and paranoia.

Research studies confirm that personality tests can help companies hire more effective workers. For example, industrial psychologists often talk in terms of

PERSONAL INVENTORY ASSESSMENT

Learn About Yourself
Are You a Type A Personality?

personality tests Instruments used to measure basic aspects of personality, such as introversion, stability, motivation, neurotic tendency, self-confidence, self-sufficiency, and sociability.

Tests and inventories can be done in standardized formats, often using pen and paper tests or online environments to collect information.

the "Big Five" personality dimensions as they apply to employment testing: *extroversion, emotional stability, agreeableness, conscientiousness,* and *openness to experience.*[28] These dimensions can be measured using the NEO Five-Factor Inventory (NEO-FFI) and similar tests. One study focused on the extent to which these dimensions predicted performance (in terms of job and training proficiency, for example) for professionals, police officers, managers, sales workers, and skilled/semi-skilled workers. Conscientiousness showed a consistent relationship with all performance criteria for every occupation. Extroversion was a valid predictor of performance for managers and sales employees—the two occupations involving the most social interaction. Both openness to experience and extroversion predicted training proficiency for all occupations.[29]

There has been an ongoing debate in the research world on whether personality can be faked. In a test of 77 experienced assessors, over 70 percent agreed that "faking is a serious threat to the validity of personality inventory in the assessment process."[30] Evidence supports two specific trends in personality tests and faking: (1) people can fake personality inventories when they are motivated to do so, and (2) individual differences exist in the ability to fake.[31]

Interest inventories compare a candidate's interests with those of people in various occupations. Thus, a person taking the Strong-Campbell Interest Inventory would receive a report comparing his or her interests with those of people already in occupations such as accountant, engineer, manager, or medical technologist. Interest inventories have many uses. One is career planning, since people generally do better in jobs involving activities in which they have an interest. Another is selection. If the firm can select people whose interests are roughly the same as those of high-performing incumbents in the jobs for which it is hiring, the new employees are more likely to be successful.[32]

Achievement Tests

An **achievement test** is basically a measure of what a person has learned. Most of the tests taken in school are achievement tests. They measure knowledge or proficiency in such areas as economics, marketing, or HRM. Achievement tests are also widely used in selection. For example, the Purdue Test for Machinists and Machine Operators tests the job knowledge of experienced machinists with such questions as "What is meant by 'tolerance'?" Other tests are available for electricians, welders, carpenters, and so forth. In addition to job knowledge, achievement tests measure the applicant's abilities; a keyboarding test is one example.

Work Sampling

Work samples focus on measuring job performance directly and thus are among the best predictors of job performance. In developing a work-sampling test, experts first list all the possible tasks that jobholders would be required to perform. Then, by listing the frequency of performance and relative importance of each task, key tasks are identified. Each applicant then performs the key tasks, and his or her work is monitored by the test administrator, who records the approach taken. Finally, the work-sampling test is validated by determining the relationship between the applicants' scores on the work samples and their actual performance on the job. Once it is shown that the work sample is a valid predictor of job success, the employer can begin using it for selection.[33]

interest inventories Tests that compare a candidate's interests with those of people in various occupations.

HR Competency

40300

achievement tests Tests used to measure knowledge or proficiency acquired through education, training, or experience.

Learn About Yourself
Personal Assessment of
Management Skills (PAMS)

management assessment centre A comprehensive, systematic procedure used to assess candidates' management potential that uses a combination of realistic exercises, management games, objective testing, presentations, and interviews.

A management game or simulation is a typical component in a management assessment centre.

situational tests Tests in which candidates are presented with hypothetical situations representative of the job for which they are applying and are evaluated on their responses.

EVIDENCE-BASED HR

Management Assessment Centres

In a **management assessment centre**, the management potential of 10 or 12 candidates is assessed by expert appraisers who observe them performing realistic management tasks. The centre may be a plain conference room, but it is often a special room with a one-way mirror to facilitate unobtrusive observations. Examples of the types of activities and exercises involved include the following:

1. *An in-basket exercise.* Each candidate is faced with an accumulation of reports, memos, messages from incoming phone calls, letters, and other materials collected in the in-basket of the simulated job that he or she is to take over and is required to take appropriate action. For example, he or she must write letters, return phone calls, and prepare meeting agendas. The trained evaluators then review the results.

2. *A leaderless group discussion.* A leaderless group is given a discussion question and told to arrive at a group decision. The raters evaluate each candidate's interpersonal skills, acceptance by the group, leadership ability, and individual influence.

3. *Management games.* Participants engage in realistic problem solving, usually as members of two or more simulated companies that are competing in the marketplace. Decisions might have to be made about issues such as how to advertise and manufacture and how much inventory to keep in stock.

4. *Individual presentations.* During oral presentations on an assigned topic, each participant's communication skills and persuasiveness are evaluated.

5. *Objective tests.* Candidates may be asked to complete paper and pencil or computer-based personality, aptitude, interest, or achievement tests.

6. *An interview.* Most centres also require an interview between at least one of the expert assessors and each participant to evaluate interests, background, past performance, and motivation.

Situational Testing

In **situational tests**, candidates are presented with hypothetical situations representative of the job for which they are applying (often on video) and are evaluated on their responses.[34] Several of the assessment centre exercises described above are examples of situational tests. In a typical test, a number of realistic scenarios are presented and each is followed by a multiple-choice question with several possible courses of action, from which candidates are asked to select the "best" response, in their opinion.[35] The level of each candidate's skills is then evaluated, and an assessment report can be easily generated, making the simulation easier and less expensive to administer than other screening tools. Simulations also provide a realistic job preview by exposing candidates to the types of activities they will encounter on the job.

A research study of situational testing on 160 civil service employees demonstrated the validity of the situational test in predicting overall job performance as well as three performance dimensions: core technical proficiency, job dedication, and interpersonal facilitation. The situational test provided valid predictive information over and above cognitive ability tests, personality tests, and job experience.[36]

Micro-Assessments

micro-assessment A series of verbal, paper-based, or computer-based questions and exercises that a candidate is required to complete, covering the range of activities required on the job for which he or she is applying.

An entirely performance-based testing strategy that focuses on individual performance is a **micro-assessment**. In a micro-assessment, each applicant completes a series of verbal, paper-based, or computer-based questions and exercises that cover the range of activities required on the job for which he or she is applying. In addition to technical exercises, participants are required to solve a set of work-related problems that demonstrate their ability to perform well within the confines of a certain department or corporate culture. Exercises are simple to develop because they are taken directly from the job.

Physical Examination, Substance Abuse Testing, and Polygraph Tests

The use of medical examinations in selection has decreased, in part because of the loss of physically demanding manufacturing and natural resource jobs. Before 1980, 25 percent of new hires underwent a medical exam, but by 2001, only 11 percent were required to do so.[37] Three main reasons that firms may include a medical examination as a step in the selection process are as follows:

1. To determine that the applicant *qualifies for the physical requirements* of the position and, if not, to document any *accommodation requirements*;

2. To establish a *record* and *baseline* of the applicant's health for the purpose of future insurance or compensation claims; and

3. To *reduce absenteeism* and *accidents* by identifying any health issues or concerns that need to be addressed, including communicable diseases of which the applicant may have been unaware. Medical exams are permitted only after a written offer of employment has been extended (except in the case of bona fide occupational requirements, as for food handlers).

The purpose of pre-employment substance abuse testing is to avoid hiring employees who would pose unnecessary risks to themselves and others or perform below expectations. However, in Canada, employers are not permitted to screen candidates for substance abuse. Alcohol and drug addiction is considered to be a disability under human rights codes (see Chapter 2), and an employee cannot be discriminated against during the selection process based on a disability.[38]

A polygraph test (also referred to as a lie detector test) involves using a series of controlled questions while simultaneously assessing physiological conditions of individuals such as blood pressure, pulse, respiration, and skin conductivity, with the assumption that deceptive responses produce different physiological responses than truthful responses. Such tests have been widely rejected by the scientific community since they have failed to produce valid or reliable results. In Ontario, the Employment Standards Act specifically prohibits use of polygraphs in pre-employment selection. Validated tests of honesty or integrity are more useful and reliable in the selection process.

Data Analytics

Data or workforce analysis is revolutionizing the employee selection process.[39] New numbers-crunching data analysis software enables employers to dig through their existing employee data to better identify what types of people succeed or fail, and also lets employers test more candidates more quickly on more aspects of their personal lives. For example, department store chain Bon-Ton Stores Inc. had very high turnover among its cosmetics sales associates. To analyze the problem, management worked with Kenexa, which supplies assessment tools.

They chose 450 current cosmetics associates, who filled out anonymous surveys aimed at identifying employee traits. By using data mining techniques to analyze this and other data, the company identified cosmetics associates' traits that correlated with performance and tenure. Bon-Ton had assumed that the best associates were friendly and enthusiastic about cosmetics. However, the best were actually problem solvers. They take information about what the customer wants and needs, and solve the problem.[40] This helped Bon-Ton formulate better selection tools.

Similarly, in staffing its call centres, Xerox Corp. long assumed that applicants with call centre experience made the best candidates, but instead it turned out to be personality; creative personalities were successful, while inquisitive ones were not. Xerox now relies on its computerized software to hire for its almost 40 000 call centre jobs.

Employers using such automated screening systems should remember that they are dealing with human beings. Ensure the rejection standards are valid, and respond quickly to applicants regarding their status.[41]

STEP 3: THE SELECTION INTERVIEW

selection interview A procedure designed to predict future job performance on the basis of applicants' oral responses to oral inquiries.

The interview is used by virtually all organizations for selecting job applicants. The **selection interview**, which involves a process of two-way communication between the interviewee and the interviewer, can be defined as "a procedure designed to predict future job performance on the basis of applicants' oral responses to oral inquiries."[42]

Interviews are considered to be one of the most important aspects of the selection process and generally have a major impact on both applicants and interviewers. Interviews significantly influence applicants' views about the job and organization, enable employers to fill in any gaps in the information provided on application forms and résumés, and supplement the results of any tests administered. They may also reveal entirely new types of information.

A major reason for the popularity of selection interviews is that they meet a number of the objectives of both the interviewer and interviewee. Interviewer objectives include assessing applicants' qualifications and observing relevant aspects of applicants' behaviour, such as verbal communication skills, degree of self-confidence, and interpersonal skills; providing candidates with information about the job and expected duties and responsibilities; promoting the organization and highlighting its attractiveness; and determining how well the applicants would fit into the organization. Typical objectives of job applicants include presenting a positive image of themselves, selling their skills and marketing their positive attributes to the interviewer(s), and gathering information about the job and the organization so that they can make an informed decision about the job, career opportunities in the firm, and the work environment.[43] This issue is also highlighted in the Expert Opinion box, which discusses the nature and impact of snap judgments we make of those we meet.

PERSONAL INVENTORY ASSESSMENT

Learn About Yourself
Communication Styles

Types of Interviews

Selection interviews can be classified according to the degree of structure, their content, and the way in which the interview is administered.

expert opinion
academic viewpoint

Dr. Nicholas Rule

Identification: Dr. Nicholas Rule (PhD), Canada Research Chair in Social Perception and Cognition

Affiliation: Department of Psychology and Joseph L. Rotman School of Management, University of Toronto

1. Our first impression of someone is essentially a snap judgment we make about them. Based on research, what aspects do we assess in our first impression?

Inherently, people make judgments of race, age, sexual orientation, and attractiveness when they see someone. Accuracy varies, though: perceptions of race are 99.2 percent accurate, while perceptions of sexual orientation are 64.5 percent accurate. The correlation between perception of age and actual age is close to 0.80, which is quite high. These snap judgments lead to perceptions of other attributes. For example, perceptions of greater physical attractiveness are associated with higher ratings of intelligence, social competence, and emotional stability. These evaluations happen almost automatically, within 1/20th of a second after we see a person's face.

2. Do we get treated differently based on others' first impressions of us?

Research embedded in empirical data suggests that we do. Recent research on perceptions of sexual orientation shows that we use this information in decision-making. For example, when interviewing for a position as a nurse (a stereotypically feminine occupation), data suggest that gay men have an advantage over straight men, but the advantage is reversed when seeking a job as an engineer (a stereotypically masculine profession). Notably, this is without explicit disclosure of sexual orientation. The judgments depend on the perceivers' stereotypes about how effective each person would be for the job.

Other research shows some blockbuster effects associated with perceptions of attractiveness: attractive people secure higher salaries, enjoy greater career success, and are even more likely to live longer ... to a point. Often, others resent people who are considered to be too attractive.

3. Does research suggest that first impressions of competency levels vary or that there is general consensus in how we are perceived?

This depends. It varies from one domain to another. For example, leadership as a competency is difficult to measure, as is political savvy. Instead, business leaders are evaluated based on their ability to make money for stockholders. Evidence identifies that judgments of leadership (at the CEO level) are associated with stock price performance, even when we control for industry and the CEO's tenure at the organization. Within North America and Europe, there is some consistency in what "looking competent" means, but this varies globally.

Source: Reprinted by permission from Dr. Nicholas Rule.

The Structure of the Interview

unstructured interview An unstructured, conversational-style interview. The interviewer pursues points of interest as they come up in response to questions.

structured interview An interview following a set sequence of questions.

First, interviews can be classified according to the degree to which they are structured. In an **unstructured interview**, questions are asked as they come to mind. Thus, interviewees for the same job may or may not be asked the same or similar questions, and the interview's unstructured nature allows the interviewer to ask questions based on the candidate's last statements and to pursue points of interest as they develop. Unstructured interviews generally have low reliability and validity.[44]

The interview can also be structured. In the classic **structured interview**, the questions and acceptable responses are specified in advance and the responses are rated for appropriateness of content.[45] In practice, however, most structured interviews do not involve specifying and rating responses in advance. Instead, each candidate is asked a series of predetermined, job-related questions based on the job description and specifications. Such interviews are generally high in validity and reliability. However, a totally structured interview does not provide the flexibility to pursue points of interest as they develop, which may result in an interview that seems quite mechanical to all concerned.

mixed (semi-structured) interview An interview format that combines the structured and unstructured techniques.

HR | by the Numbers

Growing Use of Electronic Mediums for Selection[46]

76% of interviewers prefer face-to-face over video conferencing

16.1% higher rating secured by women compared to men in semi-structured face-to-face interviews

68% of interviewers felt that video conferencing added no additional benefits over face-to-face interviews

40% of interviewers felt that video conferencing made it hard to read nonverbal cues (e.g., facial expression, fidgeting)

17.4% higher rating secured by women compared to men in semi-structured video conferences

7.5% average higher rating secured for interviews using video conferencing over face-to-face methods

Between these two extremes is the **mixed (semi-structured) interview**, which involves a combination of pre-set, structured questions based on the job description and specification, and a series of candidate-specific, job-related questions based on information provided on the application form or résumé. The questions asked of all candidates facilitate candidate comparison, while the job-related, candidate-specific questions make the interview more conversational. A realistic approach that yields comparable answers and in-depth insights, the mixed interview format is extremely popular, as highlighted in the HR by the Numbers box.

A study of 92 employment interviews found that the interviewers using high levels of structure in the interview process evaluated applicants less favourably than those who used semi-structured or unstructured interviews, and those applicants who were evaluated using a semi-structured interview were rated slightly higher than those evaluated by unstructured interviews. Additionally, the study found that significant differences occur in the way that female and male interviewers evaluate their applicants. Although male interviewers' ratings were unaffected by the interview structure, female interviewers' ratings were substantially higher in unstructured and semi-structured interviews than in highly structured interviews.[47]

EVIDENCE-BASED HR

situational interview A series of job-related questions that focus on how the candidate would behave in a given situation.

The Content of the Interview

Interviews can also be classified according to the content of their questions. A **situational interview** is one in which the questions focus on the individual's ability to project what his or her *future* behaviour would be in a given situation.[48] The underlying premise is that intentions predict behaviour. For example, a candidate for a supervisory position might be asked how he or she would respond to an employee coming to work late three days in a row. The interview can be both *structured* and *situational*, with predetermined questions requiring the candidate to project what his or her behaviour would be. In a structured situational interview, the applicant could be evaluated, say, on whether he or she would try to determine if the employee was experiencing some difficulty in getting to work on time or would simply issue a verbal or written warning to the employee.

behavioural interview or behaviour description interview (BDI) A series of job-related questions that focus on relevant past job-related behaviours.

The **behavioural interview**, also known as a **behaviour description interview (BDI)**, involves describing various situations and asking interviewees how they behaved *in the past* in such situations.[49] The underlying assumption is that the best predictor of future performance is past performance in similar circumstances.

Administering the Interview

Interviews can also be classified based on how they are administered:

- one-on-one or by a panel of interviewers
- sequentially or all at once
- face-to-face or technology-aided (such as videoconferencing or by phone)

The majority of interviews are sequential, face-to-face, and one-on-one. In a *sequential* interview, the applicant is interviewed by several persons in sequence

HR IN THE NEWS

Recruiters Reveal Real Interview Failures

While the selection process is focused on selecting the best candidate for the position, some interviews leave recruiters with memorable moments, such as:

- An interviewee who highlighted that the loss of the previous job was based on the previous company owner's wife being jealous of the way the interviewee wore skimpy clothes and was flirtatious.[51]
- A candidate who delayed starting her interview because she was in the middle of a game of solitaire that she believed she could win.[52]
- A recent college graduate who was asked to name the last professional book that she read, to which she quickly replied *50 Shades of Grey*.[53]
- When a candidate was asked what he did to relieve stress, he simply shrugged his shoulders and said "I drank heavily."[54]
- Some candidates don't even need a formal interview to leave an impression. Aleksey Vayner's self-directed mock interview video entitled "Impossible is Nothing" went viral and became a quick cautionary note about how carefully one should portray their image to potential employers.

---

panel interview An interview in which a group of interviewers questions the applicant.

mass interview an interview process in which a panel of interviewers simultaneously interviews several candidates.

before a selection decision is made. In an *unstructured sequential* interview, each interviewer may look at the applicant from his or her own point of view, ask different questions, and form an independent opinion of the candidate. Conversely, in a *structured sequential* (or serialized) interview, each interviewer rates the candidate on a standard evaluation form, and the ratings are compared before the hiring decision is made.[50]

A **panel interview** involves the candidate being interviewed simultaneously by a group (or panel) of interviewers, including an HR representative, the hiring manager, and potential co-workers, superiors, or reporting employees. The key advantages associated with this technique are the increased likelihood that the information provided will be heard and recorded accurately; varied questions pertaining to each interviewer's area of expertise; minimized time and travel/accommodation expenses as each interviewee only attends one interview; reduced likelihood of human rights/employment equity violations since an HR representative is present; and less likelihood of interviewer error, because of advanced planning and preparation.

A more stressful variant of the panel interview is the **mass interview**. The panel poses a problem to be solved and then sits back and watches which candidate takes the lead in formulating an answer. The HR in the News box reveals real interview failures to learn from.

nyul/Fotolia

A panel interview is an efficient and cost-effective way of permitting a number of qualified persons to assess a candidate's KSAs.

Common Interviewing Mistakes

Several common interviewing errors that can undermine the usefulness of interviews are discussed in the following section. These interviewer errors can be reduced by properly planning and training interviewers on the process, as well as educating interviewers about these risks.

1. *Poor Planning* Many selection interviews are simply not carefully planned and may be conducted without having prepared written questions in advance. Lack of planning often leads to a relatively unstructured interview, in which whatever comes up is discussed. The end result may be little or no cross-candidate job-related information. The less structured the interview is, the less reliable and valid the evaluation of each candidate will be.[55]

2. *Snap Judgments* One of the most consistent literature findings is that interviewers tend to jump to conclusions—make snap judgments—during the first few minutes of the interview or even before the interview begins based on the candidates' test scores or résumé data. Thus, candidates feel pressure to start off on the right foot with the interviewer. However, snap judgments are not accurate or reliable in the selection process and should be avoided.

3. *Negative Emphasis* Many interviewers seem to have a consistent negative bias. They are generally more influenced by unfavourable than favourable information about the candidate. Also, their impressions are much more likely to change from favourable to unfavourable than vice versa. Providing information about the value or weight of criteria in the selection process can ensure that the interviewer assesses the criteria accordingly.

4. *Halo Effect* It is also possible for a positive initial impression to distort an interviewer's rating of a candidate, because subsequent information is judged with a positive bias. This is known as the **halo effect**. Having gained a positive impression of the candidate on one or more factors, the interviewer may not seek contradictory information when listening to the candidate's answers to the questions posed or may interpret/frame all responses positively.

5. *Poor Knowledge of the Job* Interviewers who do not know precisely what the job entails and what sort of candidate is best suited for it usually make their decisions based on incorrect stereotypes about what a good applicant is. Interviewers who have a clear understanding of what the job entails conduct more effective interviews.

6. *Contrast (Candidate-Order) Error* **Contrast or candidate-order error** means that the order in which applicants are seen can affect how they are rated. In one study, managers were asked to evaluate a candidate who was "just average" after first evaluating several "unfavourable" candidates. The average candidate was evaluated more favourably than he or she might otherwise have been because, in contrast to the unfavourable candidates, the average one looked better than he or she actually was.

7. *Influence of Nonverbal Behaviour* Interviewers are also influenced by the applicant's nonverbal behaviour, and the more eye contact, head moving, smiling, and other similar nonverbal behaviours, the higher the ratings. These nonverbal behaviours often account for more than 80 percent of the applicant's rating. This finding is of particular concern since nonverbal behaviour is tied to ethnicity and cultural background.

8. *Leading* Some interviewers are so anxious to fill a job that they help the applicants to respond correctly to their questions by asking leading questions or guiding the candidate to the expected

halo effect A positive initial impression that distorts an interviewer's rating of a candidate because subsequent information is judged with a positive bias.

contrast or candidate-order error An error of judgment on the part of the interviewer because of interviewing one or more very good or very bad candidates just before the interview in question.

"Was the interview too early for you?"

cartoonresource/Fotolia

answer. An obvious example might be a question like: "This job calls for handling a lot of stress. You can do that, right?" The leading is not always so obvious. Subtle cues regarding the preferred response, such as a smile or nod, are also forms of leading.[56]

9. *Too Much / Too Little Talking* If the applicant is permitted to dominate the interview, the interviewer may not have a chance to ask his or her prepared questions and often learns very little about the candidate's job-related skills. At the other extreme, some interviewers talk so much that the interviewee is not given enough time to answer questions. One expert suggests using the 30/70 rule: During a selection interview, encourage the candidate to speak 70 percent of the time, and restrict the interviewer speaking to just 30 percent of the time.[57]

10. *Similar-to-Me Bias* Interviewers tend to provide more favourable ratings to candidates who possess demographic, personality, and attitudinal characteristics similar to their own, regardless of the value of those characteristics to the job.[58] The result can be a lack of diversity in the organization and a poor fit with the job if secured.

Designing an Effective Interview

Problems like those just described can be avoided by designing and conducting an effective interview. Combining several of the interview formats previously discussed enables interviewers to capitalize on the advantages of each.[59] To allow for probing and to prevent the interview from becoming too mechanical in nature, a semi-structured format is recommended. Given their higher validity in predicting job performance, the focus should be on situational and behavioural questions.

CONDUCTING AN EFFECTIVE INTERVIEW

Although the following discussion focuses on a semi-structured panel interview, the steps described apply to all selection interviews.[60]

Planning the Interview

Before the first interview, agreement should be reached on the procedure that will be followed. Sometimes all members of the team ask a question in turn; in other situations, only one member of the team asks questions and the others serve as observers. Sitting around a large table in a conference room is much more appropriate and far less stressful than having all panel members seated across from the candidate behind a table or desk, which forms both a physical and a psychological barrier. As noted earlier, special planning is required when assessing candidates with disabilities.

Establishing Rapport

The main purpose of an interview is to find out as much as possible about the candidate's fit with the job specifications, something that is difficult to do if the individual is tense and nervous. The candidate should be greeted in a friendly manner and put at ease.

Asking Questions

The questions written in advance should then be asked in order. Interviewers should listen carefully, encourage the candidate to express his or her thoughts and ideas fully, and record the candidate's answers briefly but thoroughly. Taking notes increases the validity of the interview process, since doing so (1) reduces the likelihood of forgetting job-relevant information and subsequently reconstructing forgotten information in accordance with biases and stereotypes; (2) reduces the likelihood of making a snap judgment and helps to prevent the halo effect, negative emphasis, and candidate-order errors; and (3) helps to ensure that all candidates are assessed on the same criteria.[61] Below are some examples of appropriate interview questions:

- Knowledge and experience factor: Situational questions such as "How would you organize such a sales effort?" or "How would you design that kind of website?" can probe for information on this factor.

- Intellectual factor: Here, such things as complexity of tasks the person has performed, grades in school, test results (including scholastic aptitude tests and so on), and how the person organizes his or her thoughts and communicates are assessed.

- Motivation factor: The person's likes and dislikes (for each task, what he or she liked or disliked about it), aspirations (including the validity of each goal in terms of the person's reasoning about why he or she chose it), and energy level should be probed, perhaps by asking what he or she does on, say, a "typical Tuesday."

- Personality factor: Questions probing for self-defeating behaviours (aggressiveness, compulsive fidgeting, and so on) and exploring the person's past interpersonal relationships should be asked. Additional questions about the person's past interactions (working in a group at school, working with fraternity brothers or sorority sisters, leading the work team on the last job, and so on) should also be asked. A judgment about the person's behaviour in the interview itself can also be made—is the candidate personable? Shy? Outgoing?

Closing the Interview

Toward the end of the interview, time should be allocated to answer any questions that the candidate may have and, if appropriate, to advocate for the firm and position. It is useful to also inform the candidate about the next steps and timelines that the organization will follow at this point.

Evaluating the Candidate

Immediately following each interview, the applicant's interview performance should be rated by each panel member independently, based on a review of his or her notes or an observation form. Because interviews are only one step in the process, and because a final decision cannot be reached until all assessments (including reference checking) have been completed, these evaluations should not be shared at this time.

STEP 4: BACKGROUND INVESTIGATION/ REFERENCE CHECKING

Background investigation and reference checking are used to verify the accuracy of the information provided by candidates on their application forms and résumés. In an ideal world, every applicant's story would be completely accurate, but in real life this is often not the case, as highlighted in the HR in the News box. At least one-third of applicants lie—overstating qualifications or achievements, attempting to hide negative

HR IN THE NEWS

Skeletons in the closet: Be careful about lying on your résumé!

1. Walmart hired David Tovar in 2006, who worked his way up to the role of the company's chief spokesman by 2014. As he went up for another promotion, third-party screeners (a.k.a. reference checkers) found that Mr. Tovar had lied on his application and had never completed his degree from the University of Delaware as he had claimed on his résumé. This information was discussed at length in the media and Mr. Tovar soon resigned from Walmart.[64]

2. After just four months on the job, it was discovered that Yahoo CEO Scott Thompson padded his résumé and had never completed the computer science degree on his résumé. He soon resigned, but blamed the error on a headhunting firm he used a decade earlier.[65]

3. Upon receiving an anonymous email, Veritas Software launched an internal investigation which revealed that their chief financial officer, Kenneth E. Lonchar, did not hold an MBA from Stanford University or an accounting degree from Arizona State University as he had claimed. He soon resigned from the company.[66]

information, or being deliberately evasive or untruthful.[62] The HR in the News box demonstrates that lying on a résumé has significant repercussions.

Unfortunately, some employers do not check references, which can have grave consequences. Background checks are thus necessary to avoid negligent hiring lawsuits when others are placed in situations of unnecessary and avoidable risk.[63] Cases in Canada have included a nurse who practised in a Toronto hospital for almost two years without a registered nurse qualification, a manufacturing plant payroll officer who embezzled almost $2 million, and a teacher arrested for possessing child pornography.[67] Other problems can also be addressed through background checks. Loblaw recently took action to reduce its $1 billion disappearing goods problem by making criminal record checks mandatory for all prospective employees. As a result, 7.5 percent of prospective hires have been eliminated because of criminal records.[68]

Surveys indicate that at least 90 percent of Canadian organizations conduct background checks.[69] Many firms use reference-checking services or hire a consultant to perform this task. Obtaining such assistance may be a small price to pay to avoid the time and legal costs associated with the consequences of failing to do a thorough background check.

Information to Be Verified

A basic background check includes a criminal record check, independent verification of educational qualifications, and verification of at least five years' employment, together with checks of three performance-related references from past supervisors. For financially sensitive positions, a credit check may also be included.

FIGURE 7.3 Online Postings by Job Candidates that Concern Hiring Managers

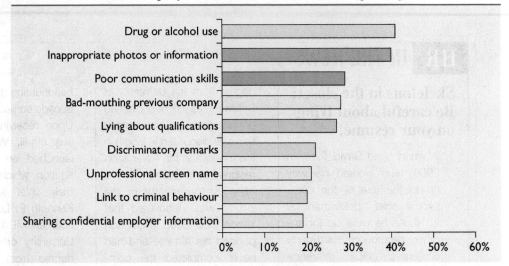

Source: Data from R. Zupek, "Is Your Future Boss Researching You Online?" CareerBuilder.ca, www.careerbuilder. ca/blog/2008/10/09/cb-is-your-future-boss-researching-you-online (accessed May 24, 2009).

Obtaining Written Permission

As a legal protection for all concerned, applicants should be asked to indicate, in writing, their willingness for the firm to check with current or former employers and other references. There is generally a section on the application form for this purpose. Many employers will not give out any reference information until they have received a copy of such written authorization. Because background checks may provide information on age or other prohibited grounds for discrimination, some employers do not conduct background checks until a conditional offer of employment has been extended.[70]

However, other employers do not hesitate to seek out information in the public domain at any time, without permission. A recent survey found that almost one-quarter of employers are using social networking sites like Facebook to gather information on job applicants. A third of those employers find enough negative information (such as the items listed in **Figure 7.3**) to eliminate a candidate from further consideration, and one-quarter of them find favourable content that supports the candidate's application.[71]

Providing References

In providing reference information, the concept of *qualified privilege* is important. Generally speaking, if comments are made in confidence for a public purpose, without malice, and are honestly believed, the defence of qualified privilege exists. Thus, if honest, fair, and candid references are given by an individual who is asked to provide confidential information about the performance of a job applicant, then the doctrine of qualified privilege generally protects the reference giver, even if negative information is imparted about the candidate.[72] An overly positive reference, however, describing an employee dismissed for theft as "trustworthy," for example, can be considered *negligent misrepresentation* if the former employee steals from a new

"Everything on your resume is true ... right?"

cartoonresource/Fotolia

employer.[73] Due to concerns about the possibility of civil litigation, some Canadian companies have adopted a "no reference" policy regarding previous employees or are only willing to confirm the position held and dates of employment—especially in the case of discharged employees.[74]

STEP 5: SUPERVISORY INTERVIEW AND REALISTIC JOB PREVIEW

realistic job preview (RJP) A strategy used to provide applicants with realistic information—both positive and negative—about the job demands, the organization's expectations, and the work environment.

The two or three top candidates typically return for an interview with the immediate supervisor, who usually makes the final selection decision. The supervisory interview is important because the supervisor knows the technical aspects of the job, is most qualified to assess the applicants' job knowledge and skills, and is best equipped to answer any job-specific questions from the candidate. Also, the immediate supervisor generally has to work closely with the selected individual and must feel comfortable with that person. The selected individual must fit with the current members of the hiring department, something that the supervisor is often best able to assess. When a supervisor makes a hiring recommendation, he or she is usually committed to the new employee's success and will try to provide assistance and guidance. If the new hire is not successful, the supervisor is more likely to accept some of the responsibility.

A **realistic job preview (RJP)** should be provided at the time of the supervisory interview. The purpose of an RJP is to create appropriate expectations about the job by presenting realistic information about the job demands, the organization's expectations, and the work environment.[75] Studies have reported that RJPs lead to improved employee job satisfaction, reduced voluntary turnover, and enhanced communication.[76] Although some candidates may choose not to accept employment with the firm after an RJP, those individuals probably would not have remained with the firm long had they accepted the job offer.[77]

STEP 6: HIRING DECISION AND CANDIDATE NOTIFICATION

EVIDENCE-BASED HR

statistical strategy A more objective technique used to determine whom the job should be offered to; involves identifying the most valid predictors and weighting them through statistical methods, such as multiple regression.

To make the hiring decision, information from the multiple selection techniques used must be combined, and the applicant who is the best fit with the selection criteria must be identified. HR department staff members generally play a major role in compiling all the data. It is the immediate supervisor who is usually responsible for making the final hiring decision, though. Firms generally make a subjective evaluation of all the information gleaned about each candidate and arrive at an overall judgment. The validity and reliability of these judgments can be improved by using tests that are objectively scored and by devising a candidate-rating sheet based on the weighted want criteria.

Another approach involves combining all the pieces of information according to a formula and giving the job to the candidate with the highest score. Research studies have indicated that this approach, called a **statistical strategy**, is generally more reliable and valid than is a subjective evaluation.[78]

Regardless of collection methodology, all information used in making the selection decision should be kept in a file, including interview notes, test results, reference-checking information, and so on. In the event of a human rights challenge, negligent hiring charge, or union grievance about the selection decision, such data are critical.

Once the selection decision has been made, a job offer is extended to the successful candidate. Often, the initial offer is made by telephone, but it should be followed up with a written employment offer that clearly specifies important terms and conditions of employment, such as starting date, starting salary, probation period, and so on.

An Ethical Dilemma

As the HR manager, how much feedback should you provide to those individuals not selected for a position?

Candidates should be given a reasonable length of time in which to think about the offer and not be pressured into making an immediate decision. If there are two candidates who are both excellent and the first-choice candidate declines the offer, the runner-up can then be offered the job.

CHAPTER SUMMARY

1. Selection is the process of choosing among individuals who have been recruited to fill existing or projected job openings. The purpose of selection is to find the "best" candidate. Because the quality of the company's human resources is often a competitive advantage in achieving the company's strategic objectives, selection of employees has considerable strategic importance. Those individuals selected will be implementing strategic decisions and, in some cases, creating strategic plans. Thus, the successful candidates must fit with the strategic direction of the organization.

2. Reliability (the degree to which selection techniques are dependable, consistent, and stable) and validity (which relates to accuracy) of selection tests and interviews are critically important for effective selection of the best candidate and to satisfy legal requirements.

3. The different types of tests used for selection include intelligence tests, emotional intelligence tests, aptitude tests, tests of motor and physical abilities, personality tests, interest inventories, achievement tests, the work-sampling technique, management assessment centres, situational testing, micro-assessments, and

medical examinations. Pre-employment substance abuse testing is not permitted under human rights legislation in Canada.

4. Selection interviewing can be unstructured, structured, or semi-structured. The content varies between situational interviews (focus on future behaviour) and behavioural interviews (focus on past behaviour). Interviews can be administered on a one-on-one basis, sequentially, or by using a panel.

5. Reference checking is an important source of information about job candidates. Failure to check references can lead to negligent or wrongful-hiring lawsuits. When providing references, the legal concept of qualified privilege means that if honest, fair, and candid references are given, the reference giver is protected from litigation, even if negative information is imparted about the candidate. Providing falsely positive references can lead to charges of negligent misrepresentation by subsequent employers. Fear of civil litigation has led some Canadian companies to adopt a policy of "no references" or to only confirm a former employee's position and dates of employment.

MyManagementLab

Study, practise, and explore real business situations with these helpful resources:

- **Interactive Lesson Presentations:** Work through interactive presentations and assessments to test your knowledge of management concepts.
- **PIA (Personal Inventory Assessments):** Enhance your ability to connect with key concepts through these engaging self-reflection assessments.
- **Study Plan:** Check your understanding of chapter concepts with self-study quizzes.
- **Videos:** Learn more about the management practices and strategies of real companies.
- **Simulations:** Practise decision-making in simulated management environments.

PIA PERSONAL INVENTORY ASSESSMENT

KEY TERMS

achievement tests *(p. 161)*
aptitude tests *(p. 159)*
behavioural interview or behaviour description
    interview (BDI) *(p. 166)*
construct validity *(p. 158)*
content validity *(p. 158)*
contrast or candidate-order error *(p. 168)*
criterion-related validity *(p. 158)*
differential validity *(p. 158)*
emotional intelligence (EI) tests *(p. 159)*
halo effect *(p. 168)*
intelligence (IQ) tests *(p. 159)*
interest inventories *(p. 161)*
management assessment centre *(p. 162)*
micro-assessment *(p. 163)*
mixed (semi-structured) interview *(p. 166)*
mass interview *(p. 167)*

multiple-hurdle strategy *(p. 154)*
must criteria *(p. 154)*
panel interview *(p. 167)*
personality tests *(p. 160)*
realistic job preview (RJP) *(p. 173)*
reliability *(p. 156)*
selection *(p. 153)*
selection interview *(p. 164)*
selection ratio *(p. 153)*
situational interview *(p. 166)*
situational tests *(p. 162)*
statistical strategy *(p. 173)*
structured interview *(p. 165)*
unstructured interview *(p. 165)*
validity *(p. 158)*
want criteria *(p. 155)*

REVIEW AND DISCUSSION QUESTIONS

1. Explain the differences among criterion-related valid-ity, content validity, and construct validity.

2. Describe five different types of testing that may be used in the selection process and give an example of each.

3. Describe any four activities involved in a management assessment centre.

4. Name and describe the pros and cons of the three different types of interview structures.

5. Explain the difference between situational and behavioural interviews. Give examples of situational and behavioural interview questions.

6. Briefly discuss any five common interviewing mistakes and explain how such errors can be avoided.

7. Why is the supervisory interview important in the selection process?

CRITICAL THINKING QUESTIONS

1. If you were asked to design an effective selection process for retail sales representatives working on a 100 percent commission basis, which of the steps described in this chapter would you include and why? Justify the omission of any steps and explain why the quality of the selection decision will not be compromised by their elimination.

2. Assume that you have just been hired as the employment manager in a small manufacturing firm that has never done any selection testing. Write a memorandum to the CEO describing the types of tests that you would recommend the firm consider using in the future. Also list some of the legal and ethical concerns pertaining to such testing and how such concerns can be overcome, and the benefits to the firm for using the recommended testing.

3. Describe strategies that you could use to (a) establish rapport with an extremely nervous candidate, (b) get an interviewee who is rambling "back on track," (c) clarify a statement made by an applicant during an interview, and (d) obtain detailed reference information from an individual who seems reluctant to say much.

4. Alberta oil and gas companies are using pre-employment substance abuse testing even though it is prohibited. Their argument is that, because they have multibillion-dollar projects underway with a lot of potential for accidents, environmental damage, and so on, they want to be sure that they are not hiring employees who have substance abuse problems. They know that their young, transient, and relatively wealthy oil sands workforce commonly abuses drugs and alcohol. How could this situation be resolved in the spirit of the law on accommodating disabilities?

5. After reviewing candidate résumés for characteristics and credentials that align with job requirements, the company you are working for invites candidates for a semi-structured interview. However, during the interview, you notice that no one is taking notes and there is no standard marking guide. The discussion that follows the interviews often involves the debriefing, which includes interviewers discussing their gut feel. Given that you are new to the organization, and a selection expert, they asked you what they could do to improve the selection process. What recommendations would you make? How can they increase the validity and reliability of their results?

EXPERIENTIAL EXERCISES

1. Design a semi-structured interview questionnaire for a position with which you are extremely familiar, basing the candidate-specific questions on your own résumé. Ensure that behavioural, situational, job-knowledge, and worker-requirements questions are included. Once you have done so, select a partner. Role-play two selection interviews—one based on your questionnaire and the other based on your partner's questionnaire. The individual who wrote the questions is to play the role of interviewee, with his or her partner serving as the interviewer. Do not forget to build rapport, ask the questions in order, take effective notes, and bring the interview to a close. Once you have completed the two role-plays, critically evaluate each interview questionnaire.

2. Create an offer of employment for a successful customer service representative at a call centre, outlining the terms and conditions of employment. Keep in mind that a copy of the letter should be signed and returned by the new hire and that a signed letter of offer becomes an employment contract.

3. Using the NOC job description and the competency job analysis you created earlier in the course for either a university or college professor, develop two situational and two behavioural interview questions for either a college or university professor along with an outline of a "good" answer for each that you expect from the interviewees. Share and critique both questions and answers. Discuss how taking the time to complete this activity can help in candidate selection.

4. In groups, discuss and compile examples of the worst interview experiences you've had. What was it about these interviews that made them so bad? How does that align with your learnings in this chapter? If time permits, discuss in class.

RUNNING CASE

Running Case: LearnInMotion.com

The Better Interview

Like virtually all the other HR-related activities at LearnInMotion.com, the company has no organized approach to interviewing job candidates. Three people, Jennifer, Pierre, and Greg (from the board of directors), interview each candidate, and the three then get together for a discussion. Unfortunately, they usually reach strikingly different conclusions. For example, Greg thought a particular candidate was "stellar" and would not only be able to sell but also eventually assume various administrative responsibilities to take the load off Jennifer and Pierre. Pierre thought this particular candidate was hopeless: "I've been selling for eight years and have hired many salespeople, and there's no way this person's going to be a closer," he said. Jennifer, noting that a friend of her mother had recommended this particular candidate, was willing to take a wait-and-see attitude: "Let's hire her and see how she does," she said. Pierre replied that this was no way to hire a salesperson, and, in any case, hiring another administrator was pretty far down their priority list. "I wish Greg would stick to the problem at hand, namely hiring a 100 percent salesperson."

Jennifer was sure that inadequate formal interviewing practices, procedures, and training accounted for at least some of the problems they were having in hiring and keeping good salespeople. They did hire one salesperson whom they thought was going to be terrific, based on the praise provided by her references and on what they understood her previous sales experience had been; she stayed for a month and a half, sold hardly anything, cost the company almost $10 000 of its precious cash, and then left for another job.

The problem wasn't just with the salespeople. They also hired a programmer largely based on his assertion that he was expert in various web-related programming languages, including HTML, XML, and JavaScript. They followed up with one of his references, who was neutral regarding the candidate's programming abilities. But, being desperate, Jennifer and Pierre hired him anyway—only to have him leave three weeks later, more or less by mutual consent.

"This is a total disaster," said Jennifer, and Pierre could only agree. It was obvious that in some respects their interviews were worse than not interviewing at all. For example, if they didn't have interviews, perhaps they would have used more caution in following up with the candidates' references. In any case, they now want you, their management consultant, to tell them what to do.

QUESTIONS

1 How would you restructure LearnInMotion.com's selection process?
2 Should Pierre and Jennifer use the multiple-hurdle strategy? Why or why not?
3 What are some of the legal implications of a new selection process that Jennifer and Pierre need to be aware of?

CASE INCIDENT

The Case of What Should Have Been Known

Sunrise Academy, a privately run technical college, has been operating now for four successful years. Executive Director Ron Phillips is responsible for overseeing the college. He has just been reviewing the latest enrollment figures and is pleasantly surprised again by the projected number for the upcoming school year. This will mean that a new professor will be needed in the business administration program. Ron picks up the phone and calls the director of human resources to start the process for drafting a job posting to advertise the position both internally and externally.

A week goes by and HR calls Ron to indicate that they have many applications available to be reviewed for potential interviews. Ron reviews the applicants and a short list is developed and called for interviews. After a round of four "okay, but not spectacular" interviews, Ron was beginning to think they would never find a good candidate. However, the last interviewee, Rita Miller, turned out to be the successful choice and was subsequently offered the position. HR checked two references prior to offering Rita the position in writing. HR also asked Rita to bring an original copy of her Masters of Business Administration degree once it was received, as this degree was a requirement in the professor posting.

Rita brought a copy of her degree to HR within a week of being offered the position. HR's policy is also to call the issuing institution to verify degrees. Things became busy in the department so it was nearly two months later when someone finally checked Rita's degree. The results indicated Rita's degree was forged. HR called Ron with the news, and Ron has asked you to come in to help him decide what to do next.

QUESTIONS

1   Are there any legal implications to be aware of as a result of this selection decision?
2   What should have been done differently in the selection process?
3   How should the background-checking process be improved at Sunrise Academy?

Subject	Avoid Asking	Preferred	Comment
Name	about name change: whether it was changed by court order, marriage, or other reason maiden name		ask after selection if needed to check on previously held jobs or educational credentials
Address	for addresses outside Canada	ask place and duration of current or recent address	
Age	for birth certificates, baptismal records, or about age in general	ask applicants whether they are eligible to work under Canadian laws regarding age restrictions	if precise age is required for benefits plans or other legitimate purposes, it can be determined after selection
Sex	males or females to fill in different applications about pregnancy, childbearing plans, or childcare arrangements	ask applicant if the attendance requirements can be met	during the interview or after selection, the applicant, for purposes of courtesy, may be asked which of Dr., Mr., Mrs., Miss, or Ms. is preferred
Marital Status	whether the applicant is single, married, divorced, engaged, separated, widowed, or living common law whether an applicant's spouse may be transferred about spouse's employment	if transfer or travel is part of the job, the applicant can be asked if he or she can meet these requirements ask whether there are any circumstances that might prevent completion of a minimum service commitment	information on dependants can be determined after selection if necessary
Family Status	number of children or dependants about childcare arrangements	if the applicant would be able to work the required hours and, where applicable, overtime	contacts for emergencies and/or details on dependants can be determined after selection
National or Ethnic Origin	about birthplace, nationality of ancestors, spouse, or other relatives whether born in Canada for proof of citizenship	since those who are entitled to work in Canada must be citizens, permanent residents, or holders of valid work permits, applicants can be asked if they are legally entitled to work in Canada	documentation of eligibility to work (papers, visas, etc.) can be requested after selection
Military Service	about military service in other countries	inquire about Canadian military service where employment preference is given to veterans by law	
Language	mother tongue where language skills obtained	ask whether applicant understands, reads, writes, or speaks languages required for the job	testing or scoring applicants for language proficiency is not permitted unless it is job related
Race or Colour	about race or colour, including colour of eyes, skin, or hair		
Photographs	for photo to be attached to applications or sent to interviewer before interview		photos for security passes or company files can be taken after selection
Religion	whether applicant will work a specific religious holiday about religious affiliation, church membership, frequency of church attendance for references from clergy or religious leader	explain the required work shift, asking whether such a schedule poses problems for the applicant	reasonable accommodation of an employee's religious beliefs is the employer's duty *(continued)*

Subject	Avoid Asking	Preferred	Comment
Height and Weight			no inquiry unless there is evidence that they are genuine occupational requirements
Disability	for list of all disabilities, limitations, or health problems whether applicant drinks or uses drugs whether applicant has ever received psychiatric care or been hospitalized for emotional problems whether applicant has received workers' compensation		the employer should: – disclose any information on medically related requirements or standards early in the application process – then ask whether the applicant has any condition that could affect his or her ability to do the job, preferably during a pre-employment medical examination a disability is only relevant to job ability if it: – threatens the safety or property of others – prevents the applicant from safe and adequate job performance even when reasonable efforts are made to accommodate the disability
Medical Information	whether currently under a physician's care name of family doctor whether receiving counselling or therapy		medical exams should be conducted after selection and only if an employee's condition is related to job duties offers of employment can be made conditional on successful completion of a medical exam
Pardoned Conviction	whether applicant has ever been convicted whether applicant has ever been arrested whether applicant has a criminal record	if bonding is a job requirement, ask whether the applicant is eligible	inquiries about criminal records or convictions are discouraged unless related to job duties
Sexual Orientation	about the applicant's sexual orientation		contacts for emergencies and/or details on dependants can be determined after selection
References			the same restrictions that apply to questions asked of applicants apply when asking for employment references

Source: A Guide to Screening and Selection in Employment, www.chrc-ccdp.ca/publications/screening_employment-en.asp. Canadian Human Rights Commission.

CHAPTER

8

Goodluz/Shutterstock

Onboarding and Training

LEARNING OUTCOMES

AFTER STUDYING THIS CHAPTER, YOU SHOULD BE ABLE TO

DISCUSS the concept of a learning organization and its benefits.

EXPLAIN how to develop an onboarding program.

DESCRIBE the five-step training process.

DISCUSS two techniques used for assessing training needs.

EVALUATE at least five traditional training techniques.

DESCRIBE the three types of e-learning.

DESCRIBE how to evaluate the training effort.

EXPLAIN several common types of training for special purposes.

REQUIRED HR COMPETENCIES

10600: Align human resources practices by translating organizational strategy into human resources objectives and priorities to achieve the organization's plan.

20600: Promote an evidence-based approach to the development of human resources policies and practices using current professional resources to provide a sound basis for human resources decision-making.

30200: Develop initiatives through which leaders align culture, values, and work groups to increase the productivity and engagement of employees.

40300: Execute a workforce plan by sourcing, selecting, hiring, onboarding, and developing people to address competency needs and retain qualified talent aligned with the organization's strategic objectives.

70100: Identify organizational learning priorities aligned with the business strategy using key stakeholder involvement to ensure appropriate learning and optimal return on investment.

70200: Develop opportunities for employees to learn and grow professionally by maximizing their potential aligned with business strategy to contribute effectively to organizational objectives.

70300: Implement learning and development programs in accordance with adult learning principles to build competency and ensure relevance and effectiveness.

70400: Evaluate learning and development priorities and programs in accordance with sound measurement principles to document attainment and progress toward organizational objectives.

70500: Develop an organizational culture where learning occurs at different levels by making learning a part of everyday work activity to enhance individual, team, and organizational effectiveness.

BECOME A LEARNING ORGANIZATION

learning organization An organization skilled at creating, acquiring, and transferring knowledge and at modifying its behaviour to reflect new knowledge and insights.

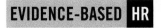

Learning is a survival technique for both individuals and organizations. Today, employees at all levels know that they must engage in lifelong learning to remain employable and have a satisfying career. A **learning organization** is an organization skilled at creating, acquiring, and transferring knowledge and at modifying its behaviour to reflect new knowledge and insights. Research identifies that learning organizations in Canada invest more in learning and development of their employees, and thereby realize greater returns on investment. Overall, these organizations report superior employee performance, levels of customer satisfaction, and quality metrics when compared with organizations that do not prioritize the learning culture.

The HR department is often the driving force behind ensuring that the training and development opportunities necessary to create a learning organization are in place, particularly in transferring knowledge, learning from experience, experimentation through searching for and testing new knowledge, learning from others, and systematic problem solving.

According to a Conference Board of Canada 2014 study, the average organization in Canada spends $705 on learning and development per employee and the average employee undergoes 28 hours of training and development a year.[1] However, expenditures on learning and development are significantly less than our American comparators. In addition, learning and development expenses in Canada are split largely between external providers, internal providers, and third-party (e.g., university) providers, indicating a focus on both job or organization-specific training and general training or skills development.

Considerations

The terms "orientation" and "training" are associated, but actually represent slightly different variations of employee assimilation efforts. Orientation refers to a long-term, continuous socialization process in which employee and employer expectations or obligations are considered. With a focus on organization-specific topics, orientation attempts to transfer learning into behaviour using disciplined, consistent efforts.[2] In comparison, training refers to short-term, discrete efforts in which organizations impart information and instructions in an effort to help the recipient gain the required skills or knowledge to perform the job at adequate levels. Given that training often occurs after the orientation process, this chapter first reviews the process of orienting/onboarding employees, followed by a review of the training process.

ONBOARDING & ORIENTATION OF NEW EMPLOYEES

Once employees have been recruited and selected, the next step is orienting or onboarding them to their new company and their new job. The terminology used to reflect this process is changing, with increasing use of the term onboarding rather than orientation. Thus, we will use the terms interchangeably. A strategic approach to recruitment and retention of employees includes a well-integrated orientation program, both before and after hiring.[3] New employees need a clear understanding of company policies, expectations regarding their performance, and operating procedures. In the long term, a comprehensive orientation program can lead to reductions in turnover, increased morale, fewer instances of corrective discipline, and fewer employee grievances. It can also reduce the number of workplace injuries, particularly for young workers.[4]

Purpose of Onboarding Programs

employee onboarding (orientation) A procedure for providing new employees with basic background information about the firm and the job.

socialization The ongoing process of instilling in all employees the prevailing attitudes, standards, values, and patterns of behaviour that are expected by the organization.

Employee onboarding (orientation) provides new employees with basic background information about the employer and specific information that they need to perform their jobs satisfactorily. At the Law Society of Upper Canada, any time a new employee walks through the door the organization acts quickly to help the person get started on the right foot. The Law Society views orientation as an investment in the retention of talent. The essence of the orientation program is to introduce people to the culture, give them a common bond, teach the importance of teamwork in the workplace, and provide the tools and information to be successful at the Law Society.[5]

Orientation is actually one component of the employer's new-employee socialization process. **Socialization** is the ongoing process of instilling in all employees the prevailing attitudes, standards, values, and patterns of behaviour that are expected by the organization.[6] During the time required for socialization to occur, a new employee is less than fully productive. A strong onboarding program can speed up the socialization process and result in the new employee achieving full productivity as quickly as possible. The Expert Opinion box highlights the some critical issues associated with social inclusion to be considered when establishing goals of the orientation process.

---

expert opinion
academic viewpoint

Dr. Ann Beaton

Identification: Dr. Ann Beaton (PhD), Canada Research Chair in Intergroup Relations

Affiliation: Social Science & Humanities, Université de Moncton

1. **Your research focuses on social exclusion and inclusion. Can you briefly explain those concepts?**

   Social inclusion is a social vision. It involves the need to belong, as well as the reality of belonging. In this sense, individuals need to feel that they're contributing to society or the organization, and the organization needs to have the structures in place to promote mutual value. This includes policies, programs, and management styles that foster a sense of belonging. In order to be inclusionary, we should not view diversity management as merely a moral obligation, but rather as a core element or value of the organization.

   On the other hand, social exclusion is embedded more in the social/economic/political context. When we experience exclusion we disengage, which is linked with an increase in depression symptoms and a decrease in self-esteem. In some organizations, they don't have the structures to work proactively to eliminate social exclusion. For example, there's no mechanism to stop exclusionary behaviour or support change.

2. **There is a lot of discussion about the need for diversity in organizations. What are some of the major benefits inclusive organizations experience?**

   There is evidence that suggests having an inclusionary environment helps employers attract and retain employees. For example, seeing women in leadership roles promotes others to recognize the paradigm shift of the company. However, there is power in numbers, so an organization has to be careful that there is not a token female executive. An increased level of diversity in an organization reduces the sense of threat felt among the minority group. Research also indicates a reduced incidence of mental health symptomology and increased well-being (e.g., self-esteem). Combined, these efforts can reduce turnover, thereby saving cost associated with turnover.

3. **What are some of the things that an organization can do to adopt an inclusive approach to recruiting?**

   I.   A proactive and effective recruitment strategy focused on diversity should avoid tokenism.

   II. Avoid framing the increased diversity as a zero-sum game between the majority and the minority. We need to be careful that the majority group does not view personal or group threat. This can be done through effective communication, clear decision rules, and focus on competencies in an inclusive environment.

   III. Organizations need to build a multicultural framework of values and celebrate diversity. This helps foster social cohesion, creating a sense of appreciation and knowledge regarding the differences in the workplace and in the workers. This can make a contact between groups harmonious and productive, rather than self-focused.

Source: Reprinted by permission from Dr. Ann Beaton.

Orientation helps the employee to perform better by providing necessary information about company rules and practices. It helps to clarify the organization's expectations of an employee regarding his or her job, thus helping to reduce the new employee's first-day jitters and **reality shock** (also referred to as **cognitive dissonance**)—the discrepancy between what the new employee expected from his or her new job and its realities.

An important part of any effective orientation program is sitting down and deciding on work-related goals with the new employee. These goals provide the basis for early feedback and establish a foundation for ongoing performance management.[7] Orientation is the first step in helping the new employee manage the learning curve; it helps new employees become productive more quickly than they might otherwise.

Some organizations commence orientation activity before the first day of employment. At Ernst & Young, the firm keeps in touch with people who have been hired but have not yet started work by sending them internal newsletters, inviting them to drop by for chats, and hosting dinners for them.[8] Others use orientation as an ongoing "new-hire development process" and extend it in stages throughout the first year of employment to improve retention levels and reduce the overall costs of recruitment.[9]

Online onboarding systems that can be provided to new employees as soon as they accept the job offer are increasingly being used to engage employees more quickly and accelerate employee performance.[10] Online onboarding provides strategic benefits starting with building the brand as an employer of choice. This approach engages new hires in a personalized way and accelerates their time-to-productivity by completing benefits decisions, payroll forms, new-hire data, introduction of policies and procedures, and preliminary socialization using videos and graphics before the first day on the job, leading to a productive day one.[11]

reality shock (cognitive dissonance) The state that results from the discrepancy between what the new employee expected from his or her new job and the realities of it.

EVIDENCE-BASED HR

Content of Orientation Programs

Orientation programs range from brief, informal introductions to lengthy, formal programs. In the latter, the new employee is usually given (over an extended period of time) the following:

- internal publications, including employee handbooks that cover matters such as company history, current mission, activities, products, and people

- facility tour and staff introductions

- job-related documents, including an explanation of job procedures, duties and responsibilities, working hours, and attendance expectations; vacations and holidays; payroll, employee benefits, and pensions; and work regulations and policies such as personal use of company technology

- expected training to be received (when and why)

- performance appraisal criteria, including the estimated time to achieve full productivity

 **Hints** TO ENSURE LEGAL COMPLIANCE

Note that some courts have found employee handbook contents to represent a contract with the employee. Therefore, disclaimers should be included that make it clear that statements of company policies, benefits, and regulations do not constitute the terms and conditions of an employment contract, either express or implied. Firms should think twice before including such statements in the handbook as "No employee will be terminated without just cause," or statements that imply or state that employees have tenure; these could be viewed as legal and binding commitments.

Responsibility for Orientation

The orientation process is a continuous, long-term process aimed at moulding desired behaviours and aligning values of the employee and the organization. As such, there is a *formal* component of orientation that often occurs when a new employee first joins the organization. There is also an ongoing *informal* orientation process, with the aim to build a strong employee bond with organizational values, history, and tradition. This can include staff involvement such as mentoring, management guidance (by using high-level staff, firms communicate the importance of messages and experiences in a more meaningful way), and through employee empowerment (indoctrination of values and information to guide workplace behaviour).

The first day of the orientation usually starts with the HR specialist, who explains such matters as working hours and vacation. The employee is then introduced to his or her new supervisor, who continues the orientation by explaining the exact nature of the job, introducing the person to his or her new colleagues, and familiarizing the new employee with the workplace. Sometimes, another employee at a peer level will be assigned as a "buddy" or mentor for the newly hired employee for the first few weeks or months of employment.[12] It is a good idea for the HR department to follow up with each new employee about three months after the initial orientation to address any remaining questions.

Executive Integration

Newly hired or promoted executives typically do not participate in formal orientation activities, and there is little planning regarding how they will be integrated into their new position and company. The common assumption is that the new executive is a professional and will know what to do, but full executive integration can take up to 18 months.[13] To make things even more difficult, executives are often brought in as change agents, in which case they can expect to face considerable resistance. Thus, a lack of attention to executive integration can result in serious problems with assimilation and work effectiveness. It is common to perceive executive integration as an orientation issue, but integration at senior levels in the organization requires an ongoing process that can continue for months as the new executive learns about the unspoken dynamics of the organization that are not covered in orientation programs, such as how decisions are really made and who holds what type of power.[14]

An Ethical Dilemma

Is it ethical to withhold information from an incoming executive about critical problems that he or she will face?

Executive integration is of critical importance to a productive relationship between a new executive and his or her organization, and it is important to review previous successes and failures at executive integration on an ongoing basis. Key aspects of the integration process include the following:

- identifying position specifications (particularly the ability to deal with and overcome jealousy)
- providing realistic information to job candidates and providing support regarding reality shock
- assessing each candidate's previous record at making organizational transitions
- announcing the hiring with enthusiasm
- stressing the importance of listening as well as demonstrating competency, and promoting more time spent talking with the boss
- assisting new executives who are balancing their work to change cultural norms while they themselves are part of the culture itself[15]

Problems with Orientation Programs

A number of potential problems can arise with orientation programs. Often, *too much information* is provided in a short time (usually one day) and the new employee is overwhelmed. New employees commonly find themselves inundated with forms to fill out for payroll, benefits, pensions, and so on. Another problem is that *little or no orientation* is provided, which means that new employees must personally seek answers to each question that arises and work without a good understanding of what is expected of them. This is a common problem for part-time and contract workers. Finally, the orientation information provided by the HR department can be *too broad* to be meaningful to a new employee, especially on the first day, whereas the orientation information provided by the immediate supervisor may be *too detailed* to realistically be remembered by the new employee.

Evaluation of Orientation Programs

Orientation programs should be evaluated to assess whether they are providing timely, useful information to new employees in a timely and cost-effective manner. Three approaches to evaluating orientation programs are as follows:

1. *Employee reaction.* Interview or survey new employees for their opinion on the usefulness of the orientation program. Also, evaluate job performance within specified time periods to assess transference of learning and behaviours where possible.
2. *Socialization effects.* Review new employees at regular intervals to assess progress toward understanding and acceptance of the beliefs, values, and norms of the organization.
3. *Cost/benefit analysis.* Compare (1) orientation costs, such as printing handbooks and time spent orienting new employees by HR staff and immediate supervisors, with (2) benefits of orientation, including reduction in errors, rate of productivity, efficiency levels, and so on.

THE TRAINING PROCESS

training The process of teaching employees the basic skills/competencies that they need to perform their jobs.

Training employees involves a learning process in which workers are provided with the information and skills that they need to successfully perform their jobs. Training might mean showing a new production worker how to operate a machine, a new salesperson how to sell the firm's product, or a new supervisor how to interview and appraise employees. Whereas *training* focuses on skills and competencies needed to perform employees' current jobs, *development* is training of a long-term nature. Its aim is to prepare current employees for future jobs within the organization. Training is the primary focus of this chapter, while development is the primary focus of the next chapter.

It is important to ensure that business and training goals are aligned and that training is part of an organization's strategic plan.[16] A training professional in today's business world has to understand the organization's business, speak its language, and demonstrate the business value of training investment.[17] In today's service-based economy, highly knowledgeable workers can be the company's most important assets. Thus, it is important to treat training as a strategic investment in human capital.[18]

Canadian Society for Training and Development (CSTD)
www.cstd.ca

HR IN THE NEWS

Ontario Manufacturing Learning Consortium

Given the shortage of people entering the skilled trades occupations, projected retirements of the existing trade workers, and tighter rules on bringing in temporary foreign workers, Canadian companies are struggling to find skilled tradespersons. A cluster of Canadian companies have

assumed a relatively unique approach to talent management, beginning an initiative called the Ontario Manufacturing Learning Consortium, viewable at www. omlc.ca. This includes companies in various industries, as well as four industry associations (aerospace, tooling and machining, nuclear, and the manufacturing sector).

This consortium hires youth without the desired skill level

but trains these paid workers in a skilled trade via a six-month-long mix of classroom and on-the-job training. The employees are paid for the training period ($12–15/hr) and are under no contractual obligation to stay with the employer. The companies spend between $15 000 to $20 000 per trainee, and therefore are hopeful that this investment in the employee will lead to a good person–job match.

The Necessity of Training

A recent federal government report concluded that Canada's ability to remain globally competitive and manage technological change effectively is highly contingent on our ability to upgrade and renew the skills of our labour force. The assumption that youth workers alone hold the responsibility for skills development is no longer valid, and older workers must also adopt a lifelong learning approach.[19] In 2009, approximately one in every three adult Canadians engaged in some form of non-formal job-related education.[20]

Already, a skills crisis has arisen in the manufacturing sector, where lack of qualified workers is a major problem. Skills in greatest need of improvement are problem solving, communications, and teamwork.[21] Training is therefore moving to centre stage as a necessity for improving employers' competitiveness. The federal government has called for businesses to increase spending on training, and business has asked the government to expand programs for professional immigrants to get Canadian qualifications in their fields. In response, the Canadian Council on Learning was created by the federal government to promote best practices in workplace learning. For example, the Quebec government has legislated that all firms with a payroll of more than $1 million must spend 1 percent of payroll on employee training (or else pay a tax in the same amount).[22]

EVIDENCE-BASED HR

Another benefit of increased training is the fact that training can strengthen employee commitment. It implies faith in the future of the company and of the individual employee. Few things can better illustrate a firm's commitment to its employees than continuing developmental opportunities to improve themselves, and such commitment is usually reciprocated.[23] This loyalty is one reason that a high-commitment firm like the Bank of Montreal provides all employees with seven days of training per year at a cost of $1800 per employee—more than double the national average.[24] Today's young employees view learning and growth as the pathway to a successful and secure future and are attracted to organizations that have a commitment to keeping and growing their talent.[25] An example of a unique approach is found in the HR in the News box.

Training and Learning

Training is essentially a learning process. To train employees, therefore, it is useful to know something about how people learn. For example, people have three main learning styles: **auditory**, learning through talking and listening; **visual**, learning through pictures and print; and **kinesthetic**, tactile learning through a whole-body experience. Training effectiveness can be enhanced by identifying learning styles and personalizing the training accordingly.[26] The following four guidelines help trainers maximize the effectiveness of the training process:

1. At the start of training, provide the trainees with an overall picture of the material to be presented. When presenting material, use as many visual aids as possible and a variety of familiar examples. Organize the material so that it is presented in a logical manner and in meaningful units. Try to use terms and concepts that are already familiar to trainees.

2. Maximize the similarity between the training situation and the work situation and provide adequate training practice. Give trainees the chance to use their new skills immediately on their return to work. Train managers first and employees second to send a message about the importance of the training, and control contingencies by planning rewards for trainees who successfully complete and integrate the new training.[27]

3. Motivation affects training outcomes independently of any increase in cognitive ability. Training motivation is affected by individual characteristics like conscientiousness and by the training climate.[28] Therefore, it is important to try to provide as much realistic practice as possible. Trainees learn best at their own pace and when correct responses are immediately reinforced, perhaps with a quick "Well done." For many younger employees, the use of technology can motivate learning. Simulations, games, virtual worlds, and online networking are revolutionizing how people learn and how learning experiences are designed and delivered. Learners who are immersed in deep experiential learning in highly visual and interactive environments become intellectually engaged in the experience.[29]

4. Research shows that the trainee's pre-training preparation is a crucial step in the training process. It is important to create a perceived need for training in the minds of participants.[30] Also, provide preparatory information that will help to set the trainees' expectations about the events and consequences of actions that are likely to occur in the training environment (and, eventually, on the job). For example, trainees learning to become first-line supervisors may face stressful situations, high workloads, and difficult employees. Studies suggest that the negative impact of such conditions can be reduced by letting trainees know ahead of time what might occur.[31]

Legal Aspects of Training

Under human rights and employment equity legislation, several aspects of employee training programs must be assessed with an eye toward the program's impact on designated group members.[32] For example, if relatively few women or visible minorities are selected

---

HR Competency

40300

auditory learning through talking and listening.

visual learning through pictures and print.

kinesthetic tactile learning through a whole-body experience.

PERSONAL INVENTORY ASSESSMENT

Learn About Yourself
Work Motivation Indicator

EVIDENCE-BASED HR

Hints TO ENSURE LEGAL COMPLIANCE

FIGURE 8.1 The Five Steps in the Training and Development Process

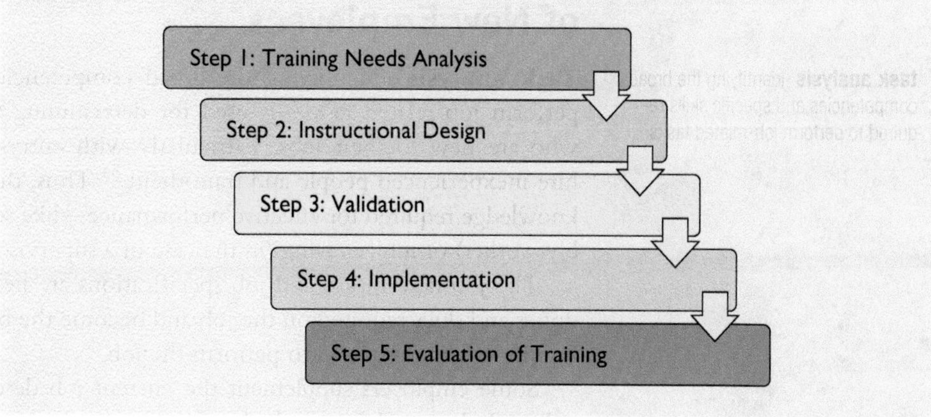

for the training program, there may be a requirement to show that the admissions procedures are valid—that they predict performance on the job for which the person is being trained. It could turn out that the reading level of the training manuals is too advanced for many trainees for whom English is not their first language, which results in their doing poorly in the program, quite aside from their aptitude for the jobs for which they are being trained. The training program might then be found to be unfairly discriminatory. On the other hand, employees who refuse a lawful and reasonable order to attend a training program may be considered to have abandoned their position.[33]

Negligent training is another potential problem. **Negligent training** occurs when an employer fails to train adequately, and an employee subsequently harms a third party. Also, employees who are dismissed for poor performance or disciplined for safety infractions may claim that the employer was negligent in that the employee's training was inadequate.

negligent training Occurs when an employer fails to adequately train an employee who subsequently harms a third party.

The Five-Step Training Process

A typical training program consists of five steps, as summarized in **Figure 8.1**. The purpose of the *needs analysis* step is to identify the specific job performance skills needed; to analyze the skills and needs of the prospective trainees; and to develop specific, measurable knowledge and performance objectives. Managers must make sure that the performance deficiency is amenable to training rather than caused by, say, poor morale because of low salaries. In the second step, *instructional design*, the actual content of the training program is compiled and produced, including workbooks, exercises, and activities. The third step is *validation*, in which the bugs are worked out of the training program by presenting it to a small, representative audience. Fourth, the training program is *implemented*, using techniques like those discussed in this chapter and the next (such as on-the-job training and programmed learning). Fifth, there should be an *evaluation* and follow-up step in which the program's successes or failures are assessed.

HR Competency
70400

STEP 1: TRAINING NEEDS ANALYSIS

The first step in training is to determine what training is required, if any. The main challenge in assessing the training needs of new employees is to determine what the job entails and to break it down into subtasks, each of which is then taught to the new employee. Task analysis and performance analysis are the two main techniques for identifying training needs.

HR Competency
20600

Task Analysis: Assessing the Training Needs of New Employees

task analysis Identifying the broad competencies and specific skills required to perform job-related tasks.

Task analysis—identifying the broad competencies and specific skills required to perform job-related tasks—is used for determining the training needs of employees who are new to their jobs. Particularly with entry-level workers, it is common to hire inexperienced people and train them.[34] Thus, the aim is to develop the skills and knowledge required for effective performance—like soldering (in the case of an assembly worker) or interviewing (in the case of a supervisor).

The job description and job specifications are helpful here. These list the specific duties and skills required on the job and become the basic reference point in determining the training required to perform the job.

Some employers supplement the current job description and specification with a task analysis record form, which typically contains six types of information:

1. list of job's main tasks and subtasks
2. indication of frequency of tasks and subtasks
3. measurable description of performance standards for each task and subtask, for instance, "tolerance of 0.007 inches" or "within two days of receiving the order"
4. conditions under which task is performed
5. the competencies and specific skills or knowledge required for each task and subtask, specifying exactly what knowledge or skills must be taught
6. the decision as to whether the task is best learned on or off the job, based on several considerations such as training objectives, methods, and resources (for example, prospective jet pilots must learn something about the plane off the job in a simulator before actually getting behind the controls)

Once the essential skills involved in doing the job are determined, new employees' proficiency in these skills can be assessed and training needs identified for each individual.

Performance Analysis: Determining the Training Needs of Current Employees

"It's important to note we really did try hard."

Performance analysis means verifying whether there is a significant performance deficiency and, if so, determining whether that deficiency should be rectified through training or some other means (such as transferring the employee). The first step is to appraise the employee's performance because, to improve it, the firm must first compare the person's current performance with what it should be. Examples of specific performance deficiencies follow:

> "Salespeople are expected to make ten new contacts per week, but John averages only six."

> "Other plants our size average no more than two serious accidents per month; we are averaging five."

Distinguishing between *can't do* and *won't do* problems is at the heart of performance analysis. First, the firm must determine whether it is a *can't do* problem and, if so, its specific causes.

For example, the employees do not know what to do or what the standards are; there are obstacles in the system (such as a lack of tools or supplies); job aids are needed; poor selection has resulted in hiring people who do not have the skills to do the job; or training is inadequate. Conversely, it might be a *won't do* problem. In this case, employees *could* do a good job if they wanted to. If so, the reward system might have to be changed, perhaps by implementing an incentive program.

Establish Training Objectives

Once training needs have been identified, training objectives can be established, which should be concrete and measurable. Objectives specify what the trainee should be able to accomplish after successfully completing the training program. They thus provide a focus for the efforts of both the trainee and the trainer and provide a benchmark for evaluating the success of the training program. A training program can then be developed and implemented with the intent to achieve these objectives. These objectives must be accomplished within the organization's training budget.

STEP 2: INSTRUCTIONAL DESIGN

HR

After the employees' training needs have been determined and training objectives have been set, the training program can be designed. There are two major considerations in developing the instructional design: First, will learning be programmed or informal? Second, what is the medium for training? While a large portion of training occurs in the workplace (on-the-job training and apprenticeships), the option of assisted or third-party learning allows organizations to gain expertise not available in house and may offer significant cost reductions through the benefits of economies of scale.

Programmed Learning

programmed learning A systematic method for teaching job skills that involves presenting questions or facts, allowing the person to respond, and giving the learner immediate feedback on the accuracy of his or her answers.

Whether the programmed instruction device is a textbook or a computer, **programmed learning** consists of three components:

1. presenting questions, facts, or problems to the learner
2. allowing the person to respond
3. providing feedback on the accuracy of his or her answers

The main advantage of programmed learning is that it reduces training time by about one-third.[35] Programmed instruction can also facilitate learning because it lets trainees learn at their own pace, provides immediate feedback, and (from the learner's point of view) reduces the risk of error. However, trainees do not learn much more from programmed learning than they would from a traditional textbook. Therefore, the cost of developing the manuals or software for programmed instruction has to be weighed against the accelerated but not improved learning that should occur.

EVIDENCE-BASED HR

Informal Learning

About two-thirds of industrial training is not formal at all but rather results from day-to-day unplanned interactions between the new worker and his or her colleagues. Informal learning may be defined as "any learning that occurs in which the learning process is not determined or designed by the organization."[36]

Traditional Training Techniques

Classroom Training Classroom training continues to be the primary method of providing corporate training in Canada, and lectures are a widely used method of classroom training delivery. Lecturing has several advantages. It is a quick and simple way of providing knowledge to large groups of trainees, as when the sales force must be taught the special features of a new product. The HR by the Numbers box highlights metrics associated with the impact of education on wages and their return on investment.

Classroom learning has evolved to maintain its relevance in the technological age. With features such as wikis, blogs, and podcasts, learning opportunities must reflect employees' new abilities and needs.

Blended Learning Blended learning, using a combination of instructor-led training and online e-learning, has been found to provide better learning results and higher learner engagement and enthusiasm than expected. In blended learning, the in-class training becomes tightly integrated with the online experience, and the relevance to the learner is vastly improved. Thus, the classroom has evolved to include interactions with remote colleagues and instructors, e-learning in many forms, coaching, assessment, and feedback.[42]

On-the-Job Training

On-the-job training (OJT) involves having a person learn a job by actually performing it. Virtually every employee—from mailroom clerk to company president—gets some on-the-job training when he or she joins a firm. In many companies, OJT is the only type of training available. It usually involves assigning new employees to experienced workers or supervisors who then do the actual training.[43]

OJT has several advantages: it is relatively inexpensive, trainees learn while producing, and there is no need for expensive off-job facilities like classrooms or manuals. The method also facilitates learning, since trainees learn by actually doing the job and get quick feedback about the quality of their performance.

Apprenticeship Training Apprenticeship training basically involves having the learner/apprentice study under the tutelage of a master craftsperson. Apprenticeship training is critical today, as more than half of skilled tradespeople are expecting to retire by 2020. Federal, provincial, and territorial governments are increasing their funding of apprenticeship training programs to meet this growing need for more tradespeople.[44]

Apprentices become skilled workers through a combination of classroom instruction and on-the-job training. Apprenticeships are widely used to train individuals for many occupations, including those of electrician and plumber. In Canada, close to 170 established trades have recognized apprenticeship programs.[45]

Job Instruction Training Many jobs consist of a logical sequence of steps and are best taught step by step. This step-by-step process is called **job instruction training (JIT)**. To begin, all necessary steps in the job are listed, each in its proper sequence. Alongside each step, a corresponding "key point" (if any) should

HR | by the Numbers

Formal Post-Secondary Education in Canada

2 M the number of Canadians enrolled in full-time and part-time education for the 2012–2013 academic year[37]

10% of students in Canada's post-secondary educational institutes are international students or new immigrants[38]

10% the return on investment each additional year of education produces[39]

8–13% range of positive earnings effect (wage increase) women experience for every additional year of post-secondary education (period studied: 2002–2007)[40]

$24.3 B estimated foregone GDP in Ontario alone, based on the skills gap, as estimated by the Conference Board of Canada

40% of unemployment in Ontario in the manufacturing, health care, financial services and professional, scientific and technical services can be attributed to the skills gap[41]

highwaystarz/Fotolia

On-the-job training is structured and concrete. Here, a supervisor teaches an employee to fix a central heating boiler.

job instruction training (JIT) The listing of each job's basic tasks along with key points to provide step-by-step training for employees.

be noted. The steps show what is to be done, while the key points show how it is to be done and why. In today's service economy, job instruction training for step-by-step manual work is being superseded by behaviour modelling for service workers.

Technology-Enabled Training Techniques

E-Learning Electronic-dependent or web-based training is now commonly used by Canadian organizations. It is generally estimated that online training costs about 50 percent less than traditional classroom-based training. Also, online learning is ideal for adults, who learn what they want, when they want, and where they want. Online training is often the best solution for highly specialized business professionals who have little time available for ongoing education. Further, online training is ideal for global organizations that want consistent training for all employees worldwide. Alcan Inc. is using this approach to standardize its training programs for 72 000 employees in 55 countries.[46]

However, critics point out that content management, sound educational strategy, learner support, and system administration should receive more attention, as they are often the critical determining factors in successful training outcomes. In the last few years, "learner content management systems" have been developed to deliver personalized content in small units or modules of learning. These systems complement learning management systems that are focused on the logistics of managing learning. Together, they form a powerful combination for an e-learning platform. This development is considered part of the new phase of e-learning, involving greater standardization and the emergence of norms. However, the freedom of online learning means that unless learners are highly motivated, they may not complete the training. It is estimated that learners don't complete 50 to 90 percent of online courses. In general, it is important to seek blended learning, including both personal interaction and online training tools.[47]

Audiovisual Techniques Audiovisual techniques (CDs, DVDs, computer-based techniques) can be very effective and are widely used. They can be more expensive than conventional lectures to develop, but offer some advantages. Trainers should consider using these when there is a need to illustrate how a certain sequence should be followed over time, there is a need to expose trainees to events not easily demonstrable in live lectures, or the training is going to be used organization-wide.

There are three options when it comes to audiovisual material: buying an existing product, making one, or using a production company. Dozens of businesses issue catalogues that list audiovisual programs on topics ranging from applicant interviewing to zoo management.

The advantages of audiovisual techniques include instructional consistency (computers, unlike human trainers, do not have good days and bad days), mastery of learning (if the trainee does not learn it, he or she generally cannot move on to the next step), flexibility for the trainee, and increased trainee motivation (resulting from the responsive feedback).

video conferencing Connecting two or more distant groups by using audiovisual equipment.

Video conferencing, in which an instructor is televised live to multiple locations, is now a common method for training employees. It has been defined as "a means of joining two or more distant groups using a combination of audio and visual equipment."[48] Video conferencing allows people in one location to communicate live with people in another city or country or with groups in several places at once. It is particularly important to prepare a training guide ahead of time, as most or all of the learners will not be in the same location as the trainer. It is also important for the trainer to arrive early and test all equipment that will be used.

NASA/Johnson Space Center

Vestibule training simulates flight conditions at NASA headquarters.

vestibule or simulated training
Training employees on special off-the-job equipment, as in airplane pilot training, whereby training costs and hazards can be reduced.

electronic performance support systems (EPSS) Computer-based job aids, or sets of computerized tools and displays, that automate training, documentation, and phone support.

Vestibule or simulated training is a technique by which trainees learn on the actual or simulated equipment that they will use on the job, with the training taking place off the job. Therefore, it aims to obtain the advantages of on-the-job training without actually putting the trainee on the job. Vestibule training is virtually a necessity when it is too costly or dangerous to train employees on the job. Putting new assembly-line workers right to work could slow production, for instance, and when safety is a concern—as with pilots—vestibule training may be the only practical alternative.

Vestibule training may consist of simply placing a trainee in a separate room with the equipment that he or she will actually be using on the job; however, it often involves the use of equipment simulators. In pilot training, for instance, the main advantages of flight simulators are safety, learning efficiency, and cost savings (on maintenance costs, pilot cost, fuel cost, and the cost of not having the aircraft in regular service).[49]

A new generation of simulations has been developed to simulate role-play situations designed to teach behavioural skills and emotional intelligence. Body language, facial expressions, and subtle nuances are programmed in. These new simulations offer authentic and relevant scenarios involving pressure situations that tap users' emotions and force them to act.[50]

Electronic performance support systems (EPSS) are computer-based job aids, or sets of computerized tools and displays, that automate training, documentation, and phone support. EPSS provides support that is faster, cheaper, and more effective than traditional paper-based job aids, such as manuals. When a customer calls a Dell Computer service representative about a problem with a new computer, for example, the representative is probably asking questions prompted by an EPSS, which takes the service representative and the customer through an analytical sequence, step by step. Without the EPSS, Dell would have to train its service representatives to memorize an unrealistically large number of solutions. Learners say that an EPSS provides significant value in maximizing the impact of training. If a skill is taught but the trainees don't need to use it until several weeks or months later, the learning material is always available through the EPSS.[51]

STEPS 3 AND 4: VALIDATION AND IMPLEMENTATION

Validation of the training program that has been designed is an often-overlooked step in the training process. In order to ensure that the program will accomplish its objectives, it is necessary to conduct a pilot study, or "run through," with a representative group of trainees. The results of the pilot study are used to assess the effectiveness of the training.

Revisions to the program can be made to address any problems encountered by the pilot group of trainees in using the training material and experiences provided to them. Testing at the end of the pilot study can measure whether or not the program is producing the desired improvement in skill level. If the results fall below the level of the training objectives, then more work must be undertaken to strengthen the instructional design.

Once the program has been validated, it is ready to be implemented by professional trainers. In some cases, a train-the-trainer workshop may be required to familiarize trainers with unfamiliar content or with unique and innovative new methods for presenting the training content. The Expert Opinion box provides an example of how a company can implement training.

Kim Woods

Identification: Ms. Kim Woods, Training Manager at Laser Quest, Certified Training and Development Professional (CTDP)

1. The company website for recruitment highlights the use of The Learning Centre (TLC). What is this tool?

At Laser Quest, we have built a company culture that values training and development, and TLC is the department that helps bring that to life. Each location is managed by a General Manager (GM). The TLC's role is to ensure training is effective, despite the difficulty in conducting traditional classroom training due to this geographic dispersion. Laser Quest's training is multifaceted and starts with a minimum two weeks of one-on-one training and continues through the use of online resources, workshops, and in-house created videos.

Throughout the year, we offer the opportunity for employees to gather and learn in a group setting, including meetings with subject matter experts at our home office in Toronto and our annual GM conference. This facilitates teambuilding and encourages participants to learn from each other through conversation, group training, and workshops based around specific organizational priorities, such as the release of new marketing initiatives or technology.

2. Why do you advertise TLC as part of your recruitment effort?

People inherently want more from a job than a paycheque. We hope applicants recognize that Laser Quest is investing in their personal development and truly cares about its employees as human beings. Training and development are ingrained in Laser Quest's culture; this helps with retention, performance, and recruiting. We want our employees (present and future) to know they are valued.

3. What are some of the training challenges LaserQuest faces?

I. Local managers need the resources to train and coach their teams. Not everyone has the training skills of a certified trainer, but they do their best. Training materials need to be as detailed as possible. We offer a Train the Trainer program for those who demonstrate competency and interest in training.

II. Our goal is to provide an exceptional customer experience, no matter where you are. Training programs and content need to reinforce this need for consistency, but be flexible enough to be relevant in all situations, from our busiest location to our newest locations.

III. Although the majority of our part-time staff are high school and university students, turnover levels are below industry standards because of both the targeted selection process used during hiring and the culture we have created. Our preference is to promote from within at the remote locations and the home office, which helps with retention.

Source: Reprinted by permission from Kim Woods.

STEP 5: EVALUATION OF TRAINING

transfer of training Application of the skills acquired during the training program into the work environment and the maintenance of these skills over time.

It is important to assess the return on investment in human capital made through training by determining whether the training actually achieved the objectives. **Transfer of training** is the application of the skills acquired during the training program into the work environment and the maintenance of these skills over time. A number of actions can be taken before, during, and after a training program to enhance transfer of training.[52]

Before training, potential trainees can be assessed on their level of ability, aptitude, and motivation regarding the skill to be taught, and those with higher levels can be selected for the training program. Trainees can be involved in designing the training, and management should provide active support at this stage.

During the training, it is important to provide frequent feedback, opportunities for practice, and positive reinforcement. After the training program, trainees can use goal-setting and relapse-prevention techniques to increase the likelihood of applying what they have learned. Management can enhance transfer of training by providing opportunities to apply new skills and by continuing to provide positive reinforcement of the new skills while being tolerant of errors.

After trainees complete their training (or at planned intervals during the training), the program should be evaluated to see how well its objectives have been met and the extent to which transfer of training has occurred. Thus, if assemblers should be able to solder a junction in 30 seconds, or a photocopier technician repair a machine in 30 minutes, then the program's effectiveness should be measured based on whether these objectives are attained. For example, are trainees learning as *much* as they can? Are they learning as *fast* as they can? Is there a *better method* for training them? These are some of the questions that are answered by properly evaluating training efforts.

Overall, there is little doubt that training and development can be effective. Formal studies of training programs substantiate the potential positive impact of such programs. Profitable companies spend the most on training, and those rated as being among the 100 best companies to work for in Canada spend the most per employee on training.[53]

There are two basic issues to address when evaluating a training program. The first is the design of the evaluation study and, in particular, whether controlled experimentation will be used. The second is the training effect to be measured.

controlled experimentation
Formal methods for testing the effectiveness of a training program, preferably with a control group and with tests before and after training.

Controlled experimentation is the best method to use in evaluating a training program. A controlled experiment uses both a training group and a control group (that receives no training). Data (for example, on quantity of production or quality of soldered junctions) should be obtained both before and after the training effort in the training group, and before and after a corresponding work period in the control group. In this way, it is possible to determine the extent to which any change in performance in the training group resulted from the training itself, rather than from some organization-wide change like a raise in pay, which would likely have affected employees in both groups equally.

Training Effects to Measure

HR Competency

40300

Four basic categories of training outcomes can be measured:[54]

1. *Reaction.* First, evaluate trainees' reactions to the program. Did they like the program? Did they think it worthwhile? An evaluation form can assess employee reaction to the training program.[55]

2. *Learning.* Second, test the trainees to determine whether they learned the principles, skills, and facts that they were supposed to learn.

3. *Behaviour.* Next, ask whether the trainees' behaviour on the job changed because of the training program. For example, are employees in the store's complaint department more courteous toward disgruntled customers than they were previously? These measures determine the degree of transfer of training.

4. *Results.* Last, but probably most important, ask questions such as these: "Did the number of customer complaints about employees drop?" "Did the rejection rate improve?" "Was turnover reduced?" "Are production quotas now being met?" and so on. Improvements in these "metrics"—specific measures of workplace results—are especially important. The training program may succeed in terms of the reactions from trainees, increased learning, and even changes in behaviour, but if the results are not achieved, then in the final analysis the training has not achieved its goals. If so, the problem may be related to inappropriate use of a training program. For example, training is ineffective when environmental factors are the cause of poor performance.

Although the four basic categories are understandable and widely used, there are several things to keep in mind when using them to measure training effects. First, there are usually only modest correlations among the four types of training criteria (that is, scoring "high" on learning does not necessarily mean that behaviour or results will also score "high," and the converse is true as well). Similarly, studies show that "reaction" measures (for example, asking trainees "How well did you like the program?") may provide some insight into how trainees felt about the program, but probably will not provide much insight into what they learned or how they will behave once they are back on the job.

TRAINING FOR SPECIAL PURPOSES

Training increasingly does more than just prepare employees to perform their jobs effectively. Training for special purposes—increasing literacy and adjusting to diversity, for instance—is required too. The following is a sampling of such special-purpose training programs.

Literacy and Essential Skills Training

National Adult Literacy Database
www.nald.ca

Functional illiteracy is a serious problem for many employers. As the Canadian economy shifts from goods to services, there is a corresponding need for workers who are more skilled, more literate, and better able to perform at least basic arithmetic. Not only does enhanced literacy give employees a better chance for success in their careers, but it also improves bottom-line performance of the employer—through time savings, lower costs, and improved quality of work.[56]

In 2008, the Canadian Council on Learning reported that almost half of Canadian adults are below the internationally accepted literacy standard for coping in a modern society.[57] A 2010 update of this research suggests that Canada's largest cities (like Toronto, Vancouver, and Ottawa) will see a substantial increase in the illiteracy rate of the workforce, largely due to the spike in the number of seniors and the growing number of immigrants.[58] Research by University of Ottawa economists for Statistics Canada has shown that investments in essential skills training to improve literacy and numeracy pay off. For every increase of 1 percent in national literacy scores relative to the international average, a country will realize a 2.5 percent gain in productivity and a 1.5 percent increase in per capita GDP over the long term.[59]

EVIDENCE-BASED HR

Employers are responding to this issue in two main ways. Organizations such as diamond mining company BHP Billiton, steel giant Dofasco, the Construction Sector Council, and the Canadian Trucking Human Resources Council have implemented a training strategy with the objective of raising the essential skills of their workforces. Essential skills of workers can be measured with the Test of Workplace Essential Skills (TOWES), developed by Bow Valley College in Calgary. In 2005, the federal government made funding available for training professionals to develop enhanced language training (ELT) to provide job-specific English instruction to help immigrants gain employment in their area of expertise.[60]

HR Competency
10600

Training for Global Business and Diverse Workforces

With increasingly diverse workforces and customers, there is a strong business case for implementing global business and diversity training programs. Research by Healthy Companies International has found that success in the global marketplace is predicted

PERSONAL INVENTORY ASSESSMENT

Learn About Yourself
Intercultural Sensitivity Scale

by developing leaders at all levels of business and by placing a high value on multicultural experience and competencies. The research identified four global literacies, or critical competencies, required to succeed in the global economy:

- personal literacy—understanding and valuing oneself
- social literacy—engaging and challenging other people
- business literacy—focusing and mobilizing the business
- cultural literacy—understanding and leveraging cultural differences[61]

Diversity training enhances cross-cultural sensitivity among supervisors and non-supervisors, with the aim of creating more harmonious working relationships among a firm's employees. It also enhances the abilities of salespeople to provide effective customer service.[62]

Two broad approaches to diversity training are cross-cultural communication training and cultural sensitivity training. *Cross-cultural communication training* focuses on workplace cultural etiquette and interpersonal skills. *Cultural sensitivity training* focuses on sensitizing employees to the views of different cultural groups toward work so that employees from diverse backgrounds can work together more effectively. All employees should be involved in managing diversity, and diversity initiatives should be planned and supported as any other business opportunity would be.[63]

Customer Service Training

More and more retailers are finding it necessary to compete based on the quality of their service, and many are therefore implementing customer service training programs. The basic aim is to train all employees to (1) have excellent product knowledge and (2) treat the company's customers in a courteous and hospitable manner. The saying "The customer is always right" is emphasized by countless service companies today. However, putting the customer first requires employee customer service training.

The Canadian retail industry has struggled in the past with poorly trained workers who were not equipped to provide quality customer service. Retailers now understand that they need to make a serious investment in their employees.[64] The Retail Council of Canada offers a national customer service certification program for retail sales associates and retail first-level managers, based on national occupational standards and essential skills profiles for each group. Certification requires the completion of a workbook, a multiple-choice exam, an in-store evaluation-of-performance interview, and experience (600 hours for sales associates, one year for first-level managers). The certification program for sales associates includes the topics of professionalism, customer service and sales, inventory, store appearance, security and safety, and communication. Topics for first-level managers include professionalism, communication, leadership, human resources, operations, marketing, sales, customer service, administration, and planning.[65]

Training for Teamwork

An Ethical Dilemma

Is it ethical to require employees to participate in weekend and evening training programs if they do not want to because it is going to take time that they would otherwise be spending on personal and family responsibilities?

An increasing number of firms today use work teams to improve their effectiveness. However, many firms find that teamwork does not just happen and that employees must be trained to be good team members.

Some firms use outdoor training—such as Outward Bound programs—to build teamwork. Outdoor training usually

involves taking a group of employees out into rugged terrain, where, by overcoming physical obstacles, they learn team spirit, cooperation, and the need to trust and rely on each other.[66] An example of one activity is the "trust fall." Here, an employee has to slowly lean back and fall backward from a height of, say, three metres into the waiting arms of five or ten team members. The idea is to build trust in one's colleagues.

Not all employees are eager to participate in such activities. Firms like Outward Bound have prospective participants fill out extensive medical evaluations to make sure that participants can safely engage in risky outdoor activities. Others feel that the outdoor activities are too contrived to be applicable back at work. However, they do illustrate the lengths to which employers will go to build teamwork.

Training for First-Time Supervisors/Managers

As Baby Boomers head into retirement, young employees are rising to positions of authority quickly and in large numbers. They are assuming supervisory and managerial roles at much younger ages than their counterparts were only 10 to 15 years ago, with some university graduates being hired into management training programs right after graduation. Along with the steep learning curve that all first-time supervisors/managers face, the latest group faces the challenges of managing employees from previous generations who are still present in the workforce.

New supervisors/managers are often chosen for their technical ability, and their interpersonal and communication skills get overlooked. But it is precisely these skills that will determine success as a manager, which requires networking and the ability to get work done through other people. New managers also need to learn to define their personal management style, how to give and receive feedback, how to motivate others, and how to manage conflict.[67]

The transition demands crucial training because first-time supervisors/managers need to learn a new set of skills. Formal training is required, and higher-level managers need to coach, mentor, and provide performance feedback to new young supervisors.[68] This type of training can be provided by external organizations like the Canadian Management Centre.

CHAPTER SUMMARY

1. A learning organization creates, acquires, and transfers knowledge. Organizations that have a learning culture can gain benefits of productivity and retention. The management of learning within an organization often lies within the HR department.

2. A strategic approach to recruitment and retention of employees includes a well-integrated orientation (onboarding) program both before and after hiring. New employees need a clear understanding of company policies, expectations regarding their performance, and operating procedures. Orientation is part of the socialization process that instills in new employees the prevailing attitudes, standards, values, and patterns of behaviour that

are expected by the organization. Onboarding helps to reduce reality shock—the discrepancy between what the new employee expected from his or her job and its realities.

3. The basic training process consists of five steps: needs analysis, instructional design, validation, implementation, and evaluation.

4. Two techniques for assessing training needs are (1) task analysis to determine the training needs of employees who are new to their jobs, and (2) performance analysis to appraise the performance of current employees to determine whether training could reduce performance problems.

5. Traditional training techniques include on-the-job-training, apprenticeship training, informal learning, job instruction training, classroom training, audiovisual techniques, programmed learning, and vestibule or simulated training.

6. Three types of e-learning are computer-based training, online training, and electronic performance support systems.

7. In evaluating the effectiveness of a training program, four categories of outcomes can be measured: reaction, learning, behaviour, and results.

8. Today's organizations often provide training for special purposes, including literacy training, diversity training, customer service training, training for teamwork, and training for first-time supervisors/ managers.

MyManagementLab

Study, practise, and explore real business situations with these helpful resources:

- **Interactive Lesson Presentations:** Work through interactive presentations and assessments to test your knowledge of management concepts.
- **PIA (Personal Inventory Assessments):** Enhance your ability to connect with key concepts through these engaging self-reflection assessments.
- **Study Plan:** Check your understanding of chapter concepts with self-study quizzes.
- **Videos:** Learn more about the management practices and strategies of real companies.
- **Simulations:** Practise decision-making in simulated management environments.

P I A PERSONAL INVENTORY ASSESSMENT

KEY TERMS

auditory *(p. 188)*
controlled experimentation *(p. 196)*
electronic performance support systems (EPSS) *(p. 194)*
employee onboarding (orientation) *(p. 183)*
job instruction training (JIT) *(p. 192)*
kinesthetic *(p. 188)*
learning organization *(p. 182)*
negligent training *(p. 189)*
programmed learning *(p. 191)*

reality shock (cognitive dissonance) *(p. 184)*
socialization *(p. 183)*
task analysis *(p. 190)*
training *(p. 186)*
transfer of training *(p. 195)*
vestibule or simulated training *(p. 194)*
video conferencing *(p. 193)*
visual *(p. 188)*

REVIEW AND DISCUSSION QUESTIONS

1. Prepare an orientation program checklist for your current or most recent job.

2. Identify and describe three special orientation situations that may be encountered.

3. Choose a task you are familiar with—such as mowing the lawn or using a chat room— and develop a job instruction training sheet for it.

4. Ali Khan is an undergraduate business student majoring in accounting. He has just failed the first accounting course, Accounting 101, and is understandably upset. Explain how you would use

performance analysis to identify what, if any, are Ali's training needs.

5. What are the advantages and disadvantages of e-learning?

6. Think about a job you have had in the past. For this job, identify which training technique was used and reflect on reasons why you think that system was used. Next, select a different training technique from the chapter that you think would have been good to use, providing a justification as to why this would be a suitable technique.

CRITICAL THINKING QUESTIONS

1. "A well-thought-out onboarding program is especially important for employees (like many recent graduates) who have had little or no work experience." Explain why you agree or disagree with this statement.

2. What are some of the typical on-the-job training techniques? What do you think are some of the main drawbacks of relying on informal on-the-job training techniques for onboarding?

3. This chapter points out that one reason for implementing special global training programs is to avoid business loss because of cultural insensitivity. What sort of cultural insensitivity do you think is meant, and how might that translate into lost business?

What sort of training programs would you recommend to avoid such cultural insensitivity?

4. Most training programs are not formally evaluated beyond a reaction measure. Why do you think employers do not measure the impact of training on learning, behaviour, and results more often?

5. Assume that your company president wants to develop a more customer-focused organization. For the past 10 years, the company has focused on cost containment while growing the business. Write a memo to your company president that supports the investment in customer service training as part of the strategic plan.

EXPERIENTIAL EXERCISES

1. Obtain a copy of an employee handbook from your employer or from some other organization. Review it and make recommendations for improvement.

2. Working individually or in groups, follow the steps in Figure 8.1 and prepare a training program for a job that you currently hold or have had in the past.

3. In small groups of four to six students, complete the following exercise:

WestJet has asked you to quickly develop the outline of a training program for its new reservation clerks. Airline reservation clerks obviously need numerous skills to perform their jobs. (You may want to start by listing the job's main duties, using the information provided below.)

Produce the requested training outline, making sure to be very specific about what you want to teach the new clerks and what methods and aids you suggest using to train them.

   Duties of Airline Reservation Clerks:

   Customers contact airline reservation clerks to obtain flight schedules, prices, and itineraries. The reservation clerks look up the requested information on the airline's flight schedule systems, which are updated continuously. The reservation clerk must deal courteously and expeditiously with the customer and be able to quickly find alternative flight arrangements to provide the customer with the itinerary that fits his or her needs. Alternative flights and prices

must be found quickly so that the customer is not kept waiting and so that the reservation operations group maintains its efficiency standards. It is often necessary to look under various routings, since there may be a dozen or more alternative routes between the customer's starting point and destination.

4. Working in groups of four to six students, complete the following exercise:

Determine who in your group knows how to make paper objects such as cranes, boxes, balloons, ninja darts, fortunes, boats, and so on. Select one person who is willing to be a subject matter expert (SME) to assist your group in developing an on-the-job training program to make one product.

   Using the expertise of your SME, develop, document (refer to the sample job instruction template earlier in the chapter), and validate a training plan to make the chosen product. Modify the documented plan as required after your pilot. Ensure that everyone in your group has a copy of the plan and can reliably make the product to standards. Once this is accomplished, each group member will pair up with a member of another group that made a different product. Each person in the resulting pairs will train his or her partner on how to make the products using the training plan and sample he or she created.

   Debrief the exercise as instructed.

RUNNING CASE

Running Case: LearnInMotion.com

The New Training Program

"I just don't understand it," said Pierre. "No one here seems to follow instructions, and no matter how many times I've told them how to do things, they seem to do them their own way." At present, LearnInMotion.com has no formal onboarding or training policies or procedures. Jennifer believes this is one reason why employees generally ignore the standards that she and Pierre would like them to adopt.

Several examples illustrate this problem. One job of the web designer (her name is Maureen) is to take customer copy for banner ads and adapt it for placement on LearnInMotion.com. She has been told several times not to tinker in any way with a customer's logo: Most companies put considerable thought and resources into logo design, and as Pierre has said, "Whether or not Maureen thinks the logo is perfect, it's the customer's logo, and she's to leave it as it is." Yet just a week ago, they almost lost a big customer when Maureen, to "clarify" the customer's logo, modified its design before posting it on LearnInMotion.com.

That's just the tip of the iceberg. As far as Jennifer and Pierre are concerned, it is the sales effort that is completely out of control. For one thing, even after several months on the job, it still seems as if the salespeople don't know what they're talking about. For example, LearnInMotion.com has several co-brand arrangements with websites like Yahoo! This setup allows users on other sites to easily click through to LearnInMotion.com if they are interested in ordering educational courses or CDs. Jennifer has noticed that, during conversations with customers, the two salespeople have no idea which sites co-brand with LearnInMotion.com, or how to get to the LearnInMotion.com site from the partner website. The salespeople also need to know a lot more about the products themselves. For example, one salesperson was trying to sell someone who produces programs on managing call centres on the idea of listing its products under LearnInMotion.com's "communications" community. In fact, the "communications" community is for courses on topics like interpersonal communications and how to be a better listener; it

has nothing to do with managing the sorts of call centres that, for instance, airlines use for handling customer inquiries.

As another example, the web surfer is supposed to get a specific email address with a specific person's name for the salespeople to use; instead he often just comes back with an "information" email address from a website. The list goes on and on.

Jennifer feels the company has had other problems because of the lack of adequate employee training and orientation. For example, a question came up recently when employees found out they weren't paid for the Canada Day holiday. They assumed they would be paid, but they were not. Similarly, when a salesperson left after barely a month on the job, there was considerable debate about whether the person should receive severance pay and accumulated vacation pay. Other matters to cover during an orientation, says Jennifer, include company policy regarding lateness and absences; health and hospitalization benefits (there are none, other than workers' compensation); and matters like maintaining a safe and healthy workplace, personal appearance and cleanliness, personal telephone calls and email, substance abuse, and eating on the job.

Jennifer believes that implementing orientation and training programs would help ensure that employees know how to do their jobs. She and Pierre further believe that it is only when employees understand the right way to do their jobs that there is any hope those jobs will in fact be carried out in the way the owners want them to be. Now they want you, their management consultant, to help them.

QUESTIONS

1 How would you change LearnInMotion.com's orientation program? Should this company rename this process to an onboarding program instead?
2 Should Pierre and Jennifer be involved in the onboarding program to emphasize the importance of this process to their staff?
3 Should management of each department assist in the development and subsequent enforcement of the new onboarding program? Why or why not?

CASE INCIDENT

A Case of Too Little Training Too Late!

It's late Friday afternoon in Thunder Bay, Ontario, and Jeff Hartley, a returning summer student, is looking forward to the end of the workday so that he can join his team from the paint department at the baseball game tonight. At the same time, in the office area adjacent to the plant, Julie Adler is working on the finishing touches to a new training program she will be requiring all new employees to take prior to being hired at Simplas Inc. Julie just completed hiring back all of the summer students who were on staff last year and is anxious to have them attend this required training/onboarding program scheduled for Monday morning.

The company has never had a formal onboarding program before, including no Workplace Hazardous Materials Information System (WHMIS) training regarding chemicals and their effects in the workplace. Julie has been noticing some unsafe behaviours lately and wants to take this opportunity to put appropriate training in place. Another part of Julie's plan for this training is to emphasize the supervisor's role in each department with regard to promoting safe behaviours, especially in the area of proper handling of chemicals in the workplace.

An hour later Julie has put the finishing touches on her new orientation/training program, has confirmed the trainer scheduled to certify everyone in WHMIS on Monday, and has received top management support for her program when she hears screams coming from the paint department. Running down the stairs to the paint department, she sees Jeff Hartley unconscious on the floor. The sound of the arrival of the ambulance erupts into the air. After Jeff is taken to the hospital, Julie is desperate to investigate what happened. She turns to his supervisor and demands to know all the details. Apparently, in his hurry to be done for the day, Jeff did not wear his face mask while he was painting a final part and must have passed out from the paint fumes collecting in the area. Julie sighs and realizes just how much more training will be needed at this company; onboarding is just a start. Please assist Julie by answering the following questions.

QUESTIONS

1   What legal aspects regarding the obvious lack of training in this case will Julie, as HR manager, and the company have to deal with?
2   How can the five-step training process assist in this scenario?
3   Should Julie put together specific training for all summer students?

Sergey Nivens/Shutterstock

Career and Management Development

Sergey Nivens/Shutterstock

LEARNING OUTCOMES

AFTER STUDYING THIS CHAPTER, YOU SHOULD BE ABLE TO

EXPLAIN the strategic importance of career planning and development.

DISCUSS new approaches to career development and **ANALYZE** the factors that affect career choices.

EXPLAIN the roles in career development.

RECOMMEND how to manage transfers and promotions more effectively.

EXPLAIN what management development is and why it is important.

DESCRIBE leadership development and its impact.

REQUIRED HR COMPETENCIES

20600: Promote an evidence-based approach to the development of human resources policies and practices using current professional resources to provide a sound basis for human resources decision-making.

40200: Increase the attractiveness of the employer to desirable potential employees by identifying and shaping the organization's employee value proposition to build a high quality workforce.

40300: Execute a workforce plan by sourcing, selecting, hiring, onboarding, and developing people to address competency needs and retain qualified talent aligned with the organization's strategic objectives.

70100: Identify organizational learning priorities aligned with the business strategy using key stakeholder involvement to ensure appropriate learning and optimal return on investment.

70300: Implement learning and development programs in accordance with adult learning principles to build competency and ensure relevance and effectiveness.

70500: Develop an organizational culture where learning occurs at different levels by making learning a part of everyday work activity to enhance individual, team, and organizational effectiveness.

70600: Develop initiatives through which leaders learn mentoring and coaching skills to support learning and development priorities of employees.

CAREER PLANNING AND DEVELOPMENT

career A series of work-related positions, paid or unpaid, that help a person to grow in job skills, success, and fulfillment.

career development The lifelong series of activities (such as workshops) that contribute to a person's career exploration, establishment, success, and fulfillment.

career planning The deliberate process through which someone becomes aware of personal skills, interests, knowledge, motivations, and other characteristics; acquires information about opportunities and choices; identifies career-related goals; and establishes action plans to attain specific goals.

HRM activities play an important role in **career planning and development**. Career-related programs help HR professionals maintain employee commitment—an employee's identification with and agreement to pursue the company's or the unit's strategic goals. Offering career support is generally a win-win situation. The employees, armed with better insights about their occupational strengths, should be better equipped to serve the company and less likely to leave.[1] The employer should benefit from higher engagement and lower turnover.

A **career** is a series of work-related positions, paid or unpaid, that help a person to grow in job skills, success, and fulfillment. **Career development** is the lifelong series of activities (such as workshops) that contribute to a person's career exploration, establishment, success, and fulfillment. And, as the Workforce Diversity box illustrates, career development for older workers is just as important as it is for younger employees. **Career planning** is the deliberate process through which someone becomes aware of personal skills, interests, knowledge, motivations, and other characteristics; acquires information about opportunities and choices; identifies career-related goals; and establishes action plans to attain specific goals.

NEW APPROACHES TO CAREER DEVELOPMENT

occupational orientation The theory that there are six basic personal orientations that determine the sorts of careers to which people are drawn.

In the early stages of career development research, career patterns were assumed to be stable, predictable, linear, and based on hierarchies. Career stages were seen as influential on the employee's knowledge of and preference for various occupations, and were often associated with the concept that based on an employee's age, their career stage could be established. Later studies, like the Vocational Preference Test (VPT) by John Holland, suggested that a person's personality (including values, motives, and needs) determines his or her **occupational orientation**, which is another important factor in career choices. Based on research with the Vocational Preference Test (VPT), six basic personality types or orientations were identified: realistic, investigative, social, conventional, enterprising, and artistic.

The beginning of the twenty-first century was marked by a new social arrangement and diversification of approaches to work, which have begun to challenge traditional theories of career development. Job transitions are more frequent, therefore occupational prospects and linear career patterns lose definability and predictability.

As a result, a new concept of career development emerged, in which the primary stakeholder of a career is the person, not the organization.[2] Therefore, a more dynamic and holistic approach to career development is emerging, with a focus on lifelong learning, flexibility, and adaptability. As such, a number of individual and organizational considerations need to be made.

Identify Skills and Aptitudes

Successful performance depends not just on motivation, but also on ability. Someone may have a conventional orientation, but whether he or she has the skills to be an accountant, banker, or credit manager will largely determine the specific occupation

PERSONAL INVENTORY ASSESSMENT

Learn About Yourself
Core Self Evaluation Scale

WORKFORCE DIVERSITY

Career Development for Older Workers

While mandatory retirement has been largely abolished in Canada, employers often neglect career development of older workers. The "second middle age" refers to the 20-year period when an individual is between ages 60 and 80. Research has shown that they have lower rates of absenteeism, fewer accidents, higher levels of job satisfaction, and a stronger work ethic.

Here are practical career development strategies that will help keep employees fully engaged during their second middle age:

- *Adopt a new attitude:* Older workers' views are generally grounded in years of experience, but at the same time many of them reflect an open mind, a flexible and forward-thinking attitude, and a willingness to take calculated risks.
- *Provide career counselling:* People want to do work that is consistent with their values, and that taps into their interests, knowledge base, and skill set. These factors may change over the course of an individual's career, and counselling may help address this change.

For example, it may help an older worker realize that returning to an earlier role could be rejuvenating, or that embarking on a completely new endeavour may be a great alternative to retirement.

- *Invest in training and development:* As long as intellectual capability is valued at the workplace, it is easy for older workers to adjust for slower mental pace and occasional memory lapse, which are typical of aging. The workplace should separate signs of aging from capacity in primary mental functions, such as language fluency, numerical ability, and spatial orientation.
- *Honour the need for work–life balance:* Creative work arrangements should be considered. Things such as flexible working hours and sabbaticals enable second middle-agers to spend the necessary time with family, as well as fulfill their professional ambitions and responsibilities.

Source: Based on M. Watters of Optimum Talent/KWA Partners, "Career Development for Employees Heading into Their 'Second Middle Age,'" *Canadian HR Reporter* (February 13, 2006), p. 13.

---

ultimately chosen. Therefore, each individual's skills must be identified based on his or her education and experience. In organizations using competency- or skill-based pay, a formal system for evaluating skills will already be in place.

For career-planning purposes, a person's aptitudes are usually measured with a test battery, such as the general aptitude test battery (GATB). This instrument measures various aptitudes, including intelligence and mathematical ability. Considerable work has been done to relate aptitudes, such as those measured by the GATB, to specific occupations.

◄◉┤**Simulate** on MyManagementLab

Managing Your Career

career anchor A concern or value that a person will not give up if a choice has to be made.

EVIDENCE-BASED HR

Identify Career Anchors

Edgar Schein says that career planning is a continuing process of self-discovery. As a person learns more about him- or herself, a dominant **career anchor** may become apparent. Career anchors, as their name implies, are concerns or values that a person will not give up if a choice has to be made. Schein identified eight career anchors:

1. *Technical/functional:* People who have a strong technical/functional career anchor tend to avoid decisions that would drive them toward general management. Instead, they make decisions that will enable them to remain and grow in their chosen technical or functional fields.

2. *Managerial competence:* Other people show a strong motivation to become managers, and their career experience convinces them that they have the skills and values required to rise to general management positions. A management position of high responsibility is their ultimate goal.

3. *Creativity:* People who become successful entrepreneurs have a need to build or create something that is entirely their own product—a product or process that bears their name, a company of their own, or a personal fortune that reflects their accomplishments.

4. *Autonomy and independence:* Some people seem driven to be on their own, free of the dependence that can arise when a person works in a large organization where promotions, transfers, and salary decisions make them subordinate to others.

5. *Security:* Some people are mostly concerned with long-run career stability and job security. A stable future with one organization that offers a good retirement program and benefits or maintaining similar geographic surroundings may be important.

6. *Service/dedication:* More and more people feel a need to do something meaningful in a larger context. Information technology has made global problems, such as the environment, overpopulation, and poverty, highly visible.

7. *Pure challenge:* A small group of people define their career in terms of overcoming impossible odds, solving unsolved problems, and winning out over competitors.

8. *Lifestyle:* A growing number of people, particularly dual-career couples, define their careers as part of a larger lifestyle, integrating two careers and two sets of personal and family concerns.

FOCUS ON LIFE TRAJECTORIES

Issues of work–life balance are becoming more significant in a person's reflections about their career aspirations. In addition, the growth in the number of people employed in the contingent workforce (temporary, part time, contractual, freelance, casual, and so on) makes managing interactions between work and life domains more critical in career planning.

As a result, career development can be envisioned as a *life trajectory*, in which a person designs and builds his or her career and life simultaneously. This increases the importance of ensuring that employees are empowered decision makers when an organization engages in career planning. As well, the value of career development initiatives must extend beyond adding value to the employer to also include an explicit discussion of the transferability and value of the initiatives to the employee.[3]

The focus on life trajectories requires a shift in thinking about career development, as outlined below:

1. *From traits and states to context:* Research on personality traits and ability factors to guide occupation-driven careers relied on stability and predictability. In the new economy, career patterns should be viewed as professional identities that are dynamic. Understanding the range of factors that are outside of the organization's control is critical to the new approach of career development.

2. *From prescriptive to process:* On average, people up to the age of 36 change their jobs every two years. Traditional career paths involving a single, committed occupational choice are no longer a reality. Instead, career planners must stay informed about all of the job-specific requirements and offer a best fit of career patterns, focusing on adding information and content to enable employees to achieve a range of career ambitions.

3. *From linear to non-linear:* Traditional career development was very deductive in that it assumed past employment patterns were valid predictors of future career ambitions.

HR Competency

40200

PERSONAL INVENTORY ASSESSMENT

Learn About Yourself
Creative Style Assessment

Thus, there is a necessary shift to a more holistic life design for career development, with an awareness of non-linear, often mutually dependant, causalities. Career plans must be frequently re-evaluated and updated involving an iterative strategy between organizational agents and employees.

4. *From scientific facts to narrative evaluations:* The old path of completing all desired education, securing a job, then establishing a family is no longer a reality for many Canadians; there is growing diversity of individual realities. Career development must empower employees to self-assess and interpret their own life experiences (often in the form of a narrative) and assist employees in making sense of their distinct perspective and implementing co-evolution.

5. *From describing to modelling:* Career development must adapt to individual experiences, ambitions, abilities, opportunities, and perspectives. Thus, the use of simple descriptive or scientific statistics alone undermines the complexity of career development. Career forecasting in this sense should develop a number of possible configurations and continuously monitor interacting variables to increase the success of career development.

Roles in Career Development

The individual, the manager, and the employer all have roles in the individual's career development. Ultimately, however, it is the *individual* who must accept responsibility for his or her own career, since workers are often seen as collaborators in the organizations that employ them.[4] This requires an entrepreneurial, goal-oriented approach that uses four key skills: self-motivation, independent learning, effective time and money management, and self-promotion.[5] Younger workers today are increasingly expecting to develop these skills by pursuing a career path that involves moving through multiple organizations.[6] **Networking** is the foundation of active career management and is essential for accessing the most valuable career resource—people. Networking is an organized process whereby the individual arranges and conducts a series of face-to-face meetings with his or her colleagues and contacts, plus individuals that they recommend. Networking does not involve asking for a job and it is not a one-sided encounter where only one individual benefits, but rather is a mutual sharing process. Its objectives are to let people know about background and career goals, and to exchange information, advice, and referrals.[7] A personal networking chart is shown in **Figure 9.1.**

Within the organization, the individual's *manager* plays a role in career development, too. The manager should provide timely and objective performance feedback, offer developmental assignments and support, and participate in career development discussions. The manager acts as a coach, an appraiser, an adviser, and a referral agent by listening to and clarifying the individual's career plans, giving feedback, generating career options, and linking the employee to organizational resources and career options.

Finally, the *employer* also plays a career development role. For example, an organization wanting to retain good employees should provide career-oriented training and development opportunities, offer career information and career programs, and give employees a variety of career options. Most employees will ultimately assess their employers on the extent to which the organization allowed them to excel and to become the people they believed they had the potential to become. How well an employer fulfills this career development role will help determine an employee's overall job satisfaction and commitment to his or her employer.[8]

networking An organized process whereby the individual arranges and conducts a series of face-to-face meetings with his or her colleagues and contacts, plus individuals that they recommend.

HR Competency
20600

HR Competency
40300

FIGURE 9.1   Personal Networking Chart

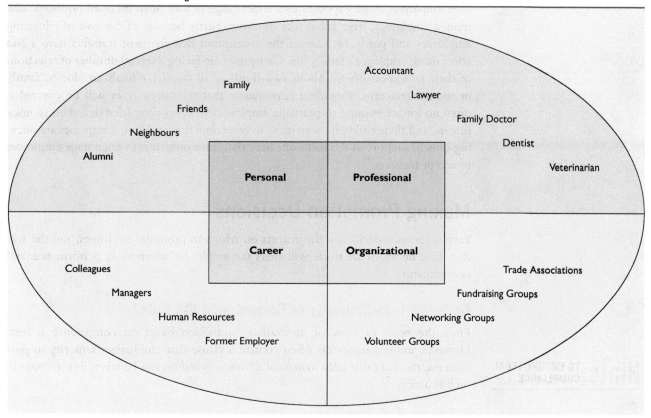

Source: Based on *It's Your Move* by Marge Watters. Published by HarperCollins Publishers Ltd.

EMPLOYEE LIFE-CYCLE AND CAREER MANAGEMENT

An employee life-cycle includes entry, internal movement, and exit from an organization. Transfers, promotions, and retirements are significant career-related decisions made on an ongoing basis. These decisions have important career development implications for the employee and substantial benefits for the organization in terms of creating a pool of potential future managers with broad experience throughout the firm.

Managing Transfers

Employees may seek transfers into jobs that offer greater possibility for career advancement or opportunities for personal enrichment, or into those that are more interesting or more convenient—better hours, location of work, and so on.[9]

Employers may transfer a worker to fill a vacant position or, more generally, to find a better fit for the employee within the firm. Transfers are thus increasingly used as a way to give employees opportunities for diversity of job assignment and, therefore, personal and career growth. Many organizations are recognizing that future leaders will need international experience to effectively manage their organizations in the increasingly globalized world of business, and they are providing international assignments as a career development experience.

Policies of routinely transferring employees from locale to locale, either to give their employees more exposure to a wider range of jobs or to fill open positions with trained employees, have fallen into disfavour, partly because of the cost of relocating employees and partly because of the assumption that frequent transfers have a bad effect on an employee's family life. Companies are facing a record number of rejections of their relocation offers. About two-thirds of all transfer refusals are due to family or spousal concerns. Providing reassurances that relocation costs will be covered is often no longer enough to persuade employees to upset their lifestyles, their spouses' careers, and their children's activities. To overcome this problem, companies are offering spousal support in the form of career transition programs to encourage employees to accept transfers.[10]

Making Promotion Decisions

Employers must decide on the criteria on which to promote employees, and the way that these decisions are made will affect the employees' motivation, performance, and commitment.

Decision 1: Is Seniority or Competence the Rule?

From the point of view of motivation, promotion based on competence is best. However, union agreements often contain a clause that emphasizes seniority in promotions, meaning that only *substantial differences in abilities* can be taken into account in such situations.[11]

Hints **TO ENSURE LEGAL COMPLIANCE**

Decision 2: How is Competence Measured?

If promotion is to be based on competence, how will competence be defined and measured? Defining and measuring *past* performance are relatively straightforward matters, but promotion also requires predicting the person's *potential*; thus, there must be a valid procedure for predicting a candidate's future performance. Tests and assessment centres can be used to evaluate employees and identify those with executive potential.[12]

Decision 3: Is the Process Formal or Informal?

Many employers still depend on an informal system where the availability and requirements of open positions are kept secret. Key managers make promotion decisions among employees whom they know personally and who have impressed them.[13] The problem is that when employees are not made aware of the jobs that are available, the criteria for promotion, and how promotion decisions are made, the link between performance and promotion is severed, thereby diminishing the effectiveness of promotion as a reward. For this reason, many employers establish formal, published promotion policies and procedures that describe the criteria by which promotions are awarded. Skills inventories, replacement charts, and replacement summaries (like those discussed in Chapter 5) can be used to compile detailed information about the qualifications of hundreds or even thousands of employees. The net effect of such actions is twofold: (1) an employer ensures that all

"They make a big deal out of promoting someone around here."

cartoonresource/Fotolia

qualified employees are considered for openings, and (2) promotion becomes more closely linked with performance in the minds of employees, which also increases the legal defensibility of the decision.

Decision 4: Vertical, Horizontal, or Other?

Promotions aren't necessarily upwards. Thus some employees, such as engineers, may have little or no interest in promotion to managerial roles. Several options are available. Some firms create two parallel career paths, one for managers and another for "individual contributors" such as high-performing employees. Another option is to move the person horizontally. For instance, a production employee may move to human resources to develop his or her skills and to test and challenge his or her aptitudes. In a sense, "promotions" are possible even when leaving the person in the same job. For example, you might enrich the job and provide training to enhance the opportunity for assuming more responsibility.

MANAGEMENT DEVELOPMENT

management development Any attempt to improve current or future management performance by imparting knowledge, changing attitudes, or increasing skills.

Management development is any attempt to improve managerial performance by imparting knowledge, changing attitudes, or increasing skills. Management development is particularly important as Baby Boomers enter retirement and the next generation of managers assumes senior management responsibilities. It can also help attract top talent or achieve employer-of-choice status. The ultimate aim of management development programs is to achieve business strategy. For this reason, the management development process consists of (1) assessing the company's human resources needs to achieve its strategic objectives, (2) creating a talent pool, and (3) developing the managers themselves.[14]

Another critical issue in management development is training local managers in other parts of the world to take over from the original expatriate managers first sent out to initiate operations. Many organizations are focusing on management development in the Asia-Pacific region.

succession planning A process through which senior-level and critical strategic job openings are planned for and eventually filled.

HR | by the Numbers

Succession Planning

59% of Canadian companies surveyed identify developing organizational leaders as their number one priority

66% of Canadian companies surveyed identify high potential employees

44% of companies inform their high potential employees that they have been identified as such[17]

2 average number of hours annually that a Board of Directors spends on succession planning

59% of Boards of Directors indicate that they would like to spend more time on succession planning

36% of Boards of Directors identify that they are satisfied with the current succession practices in their organizations[18]

Succession Planning

Most organizations take special measures to plan ahead to develop replacements for senior executives because of their key strategic role. This process is called **succession planning**. Succession planning provides "a significant competitive advantage to companies that take it seriously—and serious risks to those that do not."[15] Although succession planning has traditionally been focused only on management jobs, many organizations today include other strategic positions as well. When an organization loses a top salesperson or a talented engineer, the loss will not make headlines but the impact on the bottom line could still be significant. A vacant position can mean that important decisions are delayed or made by other employees with less knowledge and expertise.[16] The HR by the Numbers box highlights commitment levels and metrics associated with succession planning.

Successful succession planning begins with the following steps:[19]

1. establishing a strategic direction for the organization and jobs that are critical to achieving that strategic direction

2. identifying core skills and competencies needed in jobs that are critical to achieve the strategy

3. identifying people inside the organization who have, or can acquire, those skills and providing them with developmental opportunities (being prepared to recruit externally as well)

Succession planning for senior managers needs to be overseen by the CEO, as it can easily become an emotional issue for ambitious managers and can evoke political behaviour that can only be dealt with at the highest level.[20] HR staff ensure that all the required information for effective succession planning (such as skills inventories) is available, help to ensure objectivity in the process, and provide the development activities required for employees identified in the succession plan.[21] However, a recent survey showed that half of North American companies with succession plans did not actively manage them.[22] Once potential successors have been identified, a *replacement chart* is often prepared. This chart summarizes potential candidates and their development needs for each job in the succession management plan.[23] It is important to ensure that these plans are implemented and carefully managed. In recent years, succession plans have included promotion of relatively inexperienced candidates to C-level positions, as highlighted in the HR in the News box.

Employees should be encouraged to be proactive and accept responsibility for their own careers, including seeking out opportunities for leadership training. Employees who feel empowered and motivated to be the initiators of their own management development process may already be demonstrating leadership potential. Empowering employees in the organization to be part of a mutual succession-planning process increases the potential for its success.[24]

EVIDENCE-BASED HR

HR IN THE NEWS

Fast-tracking to Executive Positions

In recent years, an emerging trend of relatively inexperienced candidates "leapfrogging" positions or "fast-tracking" their careers into CEO positions has been prominent in retail, technology, media, and communication sectors. Companies such as Yahoo, Google, Burger King, General Motors, and Microsoft have appointed CEOs with accelerated paths to the C-suite. These individuals generally have adaptive leadership traits, an understanding of the diverse customer base, an ability to embrace disruptive technologies, and a record of innovation.[25]

Management Development Techniques

HR Competency

70500

Management development can include both on-the-job and off-the-job techniques. On-the-job development techniques are very popular, including developmental job rotation, the coaching/understudy approach, and action learning approach.

Developmental Job Rotation

developmental job rotation
A management training technique that involves moving a trainee from department to department to broaden his or her experience and identify strong and weak points.

Developmental job rotation involves moving management trainees from department to department to broaden their understanding of all parts of the business.[26] The trainee—often a recent college or university graduate—may work for several months in each department; this not only helps to broaden his or her experience, but it also helps the trainee discover which jobs he or she prefers.

In addition to providing a well-rounded training experience for each person, job rotation helps to prevent stagnation through the constant introduction of new points of view in each department. It also tests the trainee and helps to identify the person's strong and weak points.[27] Job rotation is more appropriate for developing general line managers than functional staff experts.

Coaching/Understudy Approach

HR Competency

70600

action learning A training technique by which management trainees are allowed to work full time, analyzing and solving problems in other departments.

In the *coaching/understudy approach*, the trainee works directly with the person that he or she is to replace; the latter is, in turn, responsible for the trainee's coaching. Normally, the trainee relieves the executive of certain responsibilities and learns the job by doing it.[28] This helps to ensure that the employer will have trained managers to assume key positions. To be effective, the executive has to be a good coach and mentor. His or her motivation to train the replacement will depend on the quality of the relationship between them.

Action Learning

Action learning releases managers from their regular duties so that they can work full time on projects, analyzing and solving problems in departments other than their own. The trainees meet periodically with a project group of four or five people with whom their findings and progress are discussed and debated. TD Bank Group and TELUS use this method.[29]

The idea of developing managers in this way has pros and cons. It gives trainees real experience with actual problems, and to that extent it can develop skills like problem analysis and planning. Furthermore, working with the others in the group, the trainees can and do find solutions to major problems. The main drawback is that, in releasing trainees to work on outside projects, the employer loses the full-time services of a competent manager. There are many techniques that are used to develop managers off the job, perhaps in a conference room at headquarters or off the premises entirely at a university or special seminar.

Many organizations offer special seminars and conferences aimed at providing skill-building training for managers. For example, the Niagara Institute in Niagara-on-the-Lake, Ontario, offers programs that develop skills essential for strong leadership; the Canadian Management Professionals Association offers a professional accreditation program leading to the Canadian Management Professional (CMP) designation.[30] Outdoor experiential expeditions, or adventure learning experiences, are sometimes used to enhance leadership skills, team skills, and risk-taking behaviour.[31]

ESLINE/Fotolia

Adventure learning participants enhance their leadership skills, team skills, and risk-taking behaviour.

College/University-Related Programs

Colleges and universities provide three types of management development activities. First, many schools provide *executive development programs* in leadership, marketing, HRM, operations management, and so on. The programs use cases and lectures to provide senior-level managers with the latest management skills, as well as practice in analyzing complex organizational problems. Most of these programs take the executives away from their jobs, putting them in university-run learning environments for their entire stay.

Second, many colleges and universities also offer *individualized courses* in areas like business, management, and healthcare administration. Managers can take these courses to fill gaps in their backgrounds. Thus, a prospective division manager with a gap in experience with accounting controls might sign up for a two-course sequence in managerial accounting.

Finally, many schools also offer *degree programs*, such as the MBA or Executive MBA. The latter is a Master of Business Administration degree program geared especially to middle managers and above, who generally take the courses on weekends and proceed through the program with the same group of colleagues.

The employer usually plays a role in university-related programs.[32] First, many employers offer *tuition refunds* as an incentive for employees to develop job-related skills. Thus, engineers may be encouraged to enroll in technical courses aimed at keeping them abreast of changes in their field. Supervisors may be encouraged to enroll in programs to develop them for higher-level management jobs. Employers are also increasingly granting technical and professional employees extended *sabbaticals*—periods of time off—to attend a college or university to pursue a higher degree or to upgrade skills.

Researchers consistently identify a positive return on investment for the development of human capital, often using formal education as a proxy for competence. The Expert Opinion box highlights evidence identifying that skills acquisition and human capital development involves a multiple-stakeholder approach.

In-House Development Centres

Some employers have **in-house development centres**, also called "corporate universities." These centres usually combine classroom learning (lectures and seminars, for instance) with other techniques, like assessment centres, in-basket exercises, and role-playing, to help develop employees and other managers. The number of corporate universities in North America has grown exponentially over the last several years because of their effectiveness in recruiting and retaining the brightest minds and in developing employee loyalty.[33] In Canada, BMO Financial Group, Canada Post, the City of Richmond, and many others all find that corporate universities can create a competitive advantage.[34]

Behaviour Modelling

From the career-development perspective, learning techniques can assist in the short-term or long-term career development of employees using behaviour modelling.

Behaviour modelling involves (1) showing employees the right (or "model") way of doing something, (2) letting each person practice the right way to do it, and (3) providing feedback regarding each employee's performance.[35] It has been used to train first-line supervisors to better handle common supervisor–employee interactions; this includes giving recognition, disciplining, introducing changes, and improving poor

expert.
opinion
academic **viewpoint**

Dr. Lance Lochner

Identification: Dr. Lance Lochner (PhD), Canada Research Chair in Human Capital and Productivity, Director of the CIBC Centre for Human Capital and Productivity

Affiliation: Social Science & Humanities, University of Western Ontario

1.   Who do you think the stakeholders are in human capital policy development and why?

Everyone has a shared impact or interest in human capital development (workers, parents, children, firms etc.), but the influence on human capital policy development is limited. Voters elect representatives based on political agendas. They can also express their voice to their elected official and influence priorities. Firms influence training and what kinds of programs are offered in the educational system.

2.   Taking an evidence-based approach, what is the economic impact of human capital development?

Evidence on wages is overwhelming. Every additional year of education adds 8–12 percent to worker wages. These wage premiums have gone up in recent years and are dependent on which major the individual completed.

The issue isn't just limited to completion of post-secondary education. Completion of high school is a major milestone as well. Research identifies that increased education attainment decreases criminal activity. Based on evidence from males in the US, there is an additional annual $3000 in benefit to society (e.g. reduced victim costs, cost of incarceration) for every additional year of education completed.

3.   What are the major challenges Canada faces with the development of human capital in the near future?

This is not an individual dilemma, rather the impact is aggregated or macro. Research consistently supports the notion that internationalism and ICT have created less demand for unskilled workers. The result is a bigger decline in the wages of less skilled workers, with growing demand for tech-savvy, highly educated, analytical employees. There is a market-based reward system to incentivize skills acquisition, but there are four main challenges to this:

I.   Difficulty in determining forecasted firm or industry level skill demand. For corrections to be made now, we need to be able to accurately predict skill demands for the next 10–20 years, which is challenging.

II.   Speed at which change is occurring. We need to recognize limits to how quickly we can adjust the Canadian labour skill portfolio. Roughly speaking, only 1 in every 40 members of the labour force is a new graduate, so the short-term impact of the education system is limited.

III.   Education systems focused on post-secondary education for career trajectories and skills development. The issues of developing analytical skills, numeracy, problem-solving skills, and collaboration also need to be addressed in the formative years of kindergarten to high school education. Skills development is not limited exclusively to post-secondary education; it's a lifelong exercise.

IV.   Retraining efforts. One of the most difficult challenges is determining how to train and incentivize displaced workers for retraining. What should we do with those who are later in the careers but working in sectors/industries that are in decline?

Source: Reprinted by permission from Dr. Lance Lochner.

performance. It has also been used to train middle managers to better handle interpersonal situations, such as performance problems and undesirable work habits. Finally, it has been used to train employees and their supervisors to take and give criticism, give and ask for help, and establish mutual trust and respect.

The basic behaviour-modelling procedure can be outlined as follows:

1.   *Modelling:* First, trainees watch films that show model persons behaving effectively in a problem situation. In other words, trainees are shown the right way to behave in a simulated but realistic situation. The film or video might thus show a supervisor effectively disciplining an employee, if teaching how to discipline is the aim of the training program.

2.   *Role-playing:* Next, the trainees are given roles to play in a simulated situation; here they practice and rehearse the effective behaviours demonstrated by the models.

3. *Social reinforcement:* The trainer provides reinforcement in the form of praise and constructive feedback based on how the trainee performs in the role-playing situation.

4. *Transfer of training:* Finally, trainees are encouraged to apply their new skills when they are back on their jobs.

Critical elements of behaviour modelling include case studies, role-playing, management games, and simulations. The **case study method** presents a trainee with a written description of an organizational problem. The person then analyzes the case in private, diagnoses the problem, and presents his or her findings and solutions in a discussion with other trainees.[36] The case study method is aimed at giving trainees realistic experience in identifying and analyzing complex problems in an environment in which their progress can be subtly guided by a trained discussion leader. Through the class discussion of the case, trainees learn that there are usually many ways to approach and solve complex organizational problems. Trainees also learn that their own needs and values often influence their solutions.

The aim of **role-playing** is to create a realistic situation and then have the trainees assume the parts (or roles) of specific people in that situation.[37] When combined with the general instructions for the role-playing exercise, roles like these for all of the participants can trigger a spirited discussion among the role-players, particularly when they all throw themselves into the roles. The idea of the exercise is to solve the problem at hand and thereby develop trainees' skills in areas like leadership and delegation.

In a computerized **management game**, trainees are divided into five- or six-person companies, each of which has to compete with the others in a simulated marketplace. Each company sets a goal (for example, "maximize sales") and is told that it can make several decisions, such as (1) how much to spend on advertising, (2) how much to produce, (3) how much inventory to maintain, and (4) how many of which product to produce. As in the real world, each company usually cannot see what decisions the other firms have made, although these decisions do affect their own sales. Management games can be good development tools. People learn best by getting involved in the activity itself, and the games can be useful for gaining such involvement. They help trainees develop their problem-solving and leadership skills, as well as foster cooperation and teamwork.

Several things can be done to increase the effectiveness of behaviour modelling approaches. If possible, the cases should be actual scenarios from the trainees' own firms; this will help ensure that trainees understand the background of the situation, as well as make it easier for trainees to transfer what they learn to their own jobs and situations. Instructors have to guard against dominating the behaviour modelling sessions and make sure that they remain no more than a catalyst or coach. Finally, they must carefully debrief employees about the intended versus actual behaviour as part of the learning process.[38]

case study method A development method in which a trainee is presented with a written description of an organizational problem to diagnose and solve.

role-playing A training technique in which trainees act the parts of people in a realistic management situation.

management game A computerized development technique in which teams of managers compete with one another by making decisions regarding realistic but simulated companies.

HR Competency

70500

opolja/Fotolia

Trainees participating in a case study discussion

Mentoring

mentoring The use of an experienced individual (the mentor) to teach and train someone (the protégé) with less knowledge in a given area.

Another approach to behaviour modelling includes mentoring. **Mentoring** has traditionally been defined as the use of an experienced individual (the mentor) to teach and train someone (the protégé) with less knowledge in a given area. Through individualized attention, "the mentor transfers needed information, feedback, and encouragement to the protégé," and in that way, the opportunities for the protégé to optimize his or her career success are improved. Effective mentoring builds trust both ways in the mentor–protégé relationship. Mentoring provides benefits to mentors, who demonstrate

HR Competency

70600

enhanced attitudes and job performance, and protégés, who become more self-confident and productive and experience greater career satisfaction and faster career growth.[39]

Organizational mentoring may be formal or informal. Informally, of course, middle- and senior-level managers will often voluntarily take up-and-coming employees under their wings, not only to train them but also to give career advice and to help them steer around political pitfalls. However, many employers also establish formal mentoring programs. Here, employers actively encourage mentoring relationships to take place and may pair protégés with potential mentors.[40] Training may be provided to facilitate the mentoring process and, in particular, to aid both mentor and protégé in understanding their respective responsibilities in the mentoring relationship.

A new development in mentoring is *reverse mentoring* programs, where younger employees provide guidance to senior executives on how to use technology for messaging, buying products and services, finding new business opportunities, and so forth. Procter & Gamble, General Electric, and the Wharton Business School are all using reverse mentoring. The relationship that develops often provides benefits to the young mentor as well when the technology-challenged older manager reciprocates in the form of career advice and guidance. Younger employees can also contribute toward understanding the ever-changing consumer marketplace.[41]

LEADERSHIP DEVELOPMENT

PERSONAL INVENTORY ASSESSMENT

Learn About Yourself
Leadership Style Inventory

Canada is facing a shortage of leadership talent. At the same time, leadership values are evolving. The traditional command-and-control leadership style is losing its effectiveness, and there is a growing need for leaders who can listen to others and tolerate mistakes made in good faith as part of a learning process. Some companies have clearly defined and articulated approaches to leadership development, as highlighted in the Expert Opinion box. Organizations can gain competitive advantage by addressing this leadership gap.[42]

Bob Hedley, former vice-president of People and Leadership at Maple Leaf Foods, says, "Where I lose sleep right now is we still don't have enough bench strength. One of the challenges is to acquire enough talent within the company and grow them fast enough so that we are ready to grow ourselves."[43] Maple Leaf Foods believes that employees' success guarantees the success of the company. They call it the "Leadership Edge"—thousands of high-performing people thriving in a high-performance culture. Employees are provided with ongoing feedback about their performance through a state-of-the-art performance assessment and development process. Employees receive recognition for both their accomplishments and their potential. This feedback is followed up with well-targeted developmental activities to ensure continued growth and development.[44]

At the executive level, 70 percent of learning comes from job experience, 20 percent comes from other individuals such as mentors and coaches, and 10 percent comes from formal training.[45] Many companies are trying to enhance learning from others by providing one-on-one executive coaching by independent coaches as part of the executive development process. In some cases, company managers are being provided with training in coaching skills, indicating the growing interest in developing coaching competencies throughout the management ranks.[46] For example, SaskEnergy created a long-term coaching program for 200 managers from all levels to help them develop successful leadership behaviours and provide skills they could apply to their teams. Coaching goals were tied to organizational strategy and succession planning, and senior management actively supported the program. The success of the program is helping to build leaders and position SaskEnergy for future success.[47]

The leadership development programs at the Banff Centre in Alberta focus on building leadership capability in five crucial areas that make up the leadership system:

HR Competency

70500

EVIDENCE-BASED **HR**

expert opinion
industry viewpoint

Mark Wilson

Identification: Mr. Mark Wilson, SVP Human Resources & Labour Relations at Loblaw

1. What are the core elements of Loblaw's talent development framework?

At Loblaw, we have a relatively structured talent development framework that is aimed at creating a highly effective, high-performing, and engaged workforce. There are two critical inputs that we focus on. The first is the business strategy or objectives, which highlights what the organization expects from our colleagues. The second is the culture and leadership, which highlights what the organization expects the colleagues to know in order to succeed at their job.

These two critical inputs drive five components: the workforce strategy, what is measured and assessed, development plans, talent acquisition, and the execution and assessment process. We have organized a common set of behavioural expectations based on four different levels of leadership, This structure is used throughout the organization, but very slightly adjusted to the target audience (e.g., executive development competencies vary from store-level competencies).

2. Loblaw has a leadership development program. How is it structured?

For leadership development, we have an executive development program for the 225 executives within the organization, which is based on the talent development framework, but allows for a high degree of individualization. For executive and C-suite members, we have clearly detailed descriptors to differentiate the requirements between the two levels and have invested over 1 million dollars to conduct executive assessment and integrate the evaluation of the competencies of this group inclusive of leadership assessments, career achievement discussions, and 360 feedback. This will lead to a detailed individualized report for each of our leadership team members, which is shared in a one-on-one feedback session and results in a plan on how to close the gaps and targeted competency development. This could be used for succession planning, as well as career-mapping purposes. For succession planning, we generally aim to have two or three colleagues on the bench for future vacancies.

3. What kinds of employee challenges are associated with talent development programs?

First, the general approach to talent development needs to be driven by business strategy, but from the self-awareness perspective, the colleague needs to also be invested in their own future and career. The organization has programs in place, provides support, offers leadership commitment or mentoring, and has a total rewards structure that drives the desired behaviour, including rewarding career management to mobility, progression, and job enrichment. Sometimes this means lateral moves or project work to gain breadth of experience before moving vertically and this takes time.

Second, there are times in which we cannot develop internal talent, such as when we get involved in new industries, or require a specialized skill set relatively quickly. For example, we didn't have an apparel focus in the business strategy. Seven years ago we created the Joe Fresh brand by bringing in external talent, because it was not available for development in-house. We still use our talent development program to set expectations and develop on competence throughout the organization, but in some cases, we still have to bring in external talent.

Source: Reprinted by permission from Mark Wilson.

self, team, business unit, organization, and community/society. Leading in increasingly complex situations requires a systematic approach to successfully understand and navigate the interdependencies and linkages among all parts of the system, from the self through to the greater community. For this reason, the Banff Centre uses an integrated approach to develop leaders.[48] The Banff Centre believes that the three basic requirements of successful leadership are knowledge, competency, and character. **Figure 9.2** illustrates the Banff Centre Competency Matrix Model, which is based on six categories of competencies—self-mastery, futuring (vision), sense making (thinking), design of intelligent action, aligning people to action (leading), and adaptive learning.

Today it is critical that leadership development be a strategic priority for organizations to successfully cope with the coming exodus of Baby Boomer executives. Without new executive talent that is trained and ready to assume senior-level responsibilities, Canadian companies will find it difficult to continue to compete successfully in the global economy.

CHAPTER SUMMARY

1. Career planning and development is a critical strategic issue in ensuring that the supply of necessary talent is available. It involves the deliberate process through which a person becomes aware of personal career-related attributes, and the lifelong series of activities that contribute to his or her career fulfillment.

2. New approaches to career development are less focused on stage of life (which was historically largely age based), and more involved in identifying occupational orientation: realistic, investigative, social, conventional, enterprising, and artistic. In addition, skills and aptitudes can be identified, as can career anchors: technical/functional, managerial competence, creativity, autonomy, security, service/dedication, pure challenge, or lifestyle.

3. The focus on life trajectories involves reframing career development from traits and states to context, from prescriptive to process, from linear to non-linear, from scientific to narrative, and from descriptive to modelling. In this evolution, organizations can benefit from becoming learning organizations that use behaviour modelling, including role-playing, simulations, management games, and mentoring opportunities.

4. An employee life-cycle includes entry, internal movement, and exit from an organization. Internal transfers offer an opportunity for personal and career development, but they have become more difficult to manage because of spousal and family concerns. Thus, career-transition programs for spouses are often provided. In making promotion decisions, firms have to (1) decide to promote based on seniority or competence, (2) decide how to measure competence, (3) choose between a formal or informal promotion system, and (4) determine the direction of the movement.

5. Management development is any attempt to improve managerial performance and is aimed at preparing employees for future jobs with the organization. When an executive position needs to be filled, succession planning is often involved. Management development is important because the majority of Canadian companies are facing a leadership shortage at all levels.

6. Managerial on-the-job training methods include developmental job rotation, coaching, and action learning. Basic off-the-job techniques include case studies, management games, outside seminars, college/university-related programs, and in-house development centres.

MyManagementLab

Study, practise, and explore real business situations with these helpful resources:

- **Interactive Lesson Presentations:** Work through interactive presentations and assessments to test your knowledge of management concepts.
- **PIA (Personal Inventory Assessments):** Enhance your ability to connect with key concepts through these engaging self-reflection assessments.
- **Study Plan:** Check your understanding of chapter concepts with self-study quizzes.
- **Videos:** Learn more about the management practices and strategies of real companies.
- **Simulations:** Practise decision-making in simulated management environments.

PERSONAL INVENTORY ASSESSMENT

KEY TERMS

action learning *(p. 213)*
behaviour modelling *(p. 214)*
career *(p. 205)*
career anchor *(p. 206)*
career planning and development *(p. 205)*
case study method *(p. 216)*
developmental job rotation *(p. 213)*
in-house development centre *(p. 214)*

management development *(p. 211)*
management game *(p. 216)*
mentoring *(p. 216)*
networking *(p. 208)*
occupational orientation *(p. 205)*
role-playing *(p. 216)*
succession planning *(p. 211)*

REVIEW AND DISCUSSION QUESTIONS

1. Describe why career planning and development has become more strategically important. Give a brief outline of what organizations are doing to take a more strategic approach in this area.

2. What are the six main types of occupational orientation?

3. What is a career anchor? For each of the five career anchors, explain why you think each is important today.

4. Explain three different ways in which managers can assist in the career development of their employees.

5. Explain the four important decisions to be made in establishing a promotion policy.

6. Explain the three major on-the-job management development techniques.

CRITICAL THINKING QUESTIONS

1. Do you think developmental job rotation is a good method to use for developing management trainees? Why or why not?

2. Would you tell high-potential employees that they are on the "fast track"? How might this knowledge affect their behaviour? How might the behaviour of employees who are disappointed at not being included in management development activities be affected?

3. How do you think employees are going to respond to the new focus on career planning, given the emphasis in recent years on "being in charge of your own career"?

4. What steps could a company take to reduce political behaviour in the succession planning process?

5. Discuss the six competencies in the Competency Matrix Model used at the Banff Centre. Do you think that any one of these is more important than the others? Why or why not? If you were asked to list them in order of importance, what order would you put them in and why?

EXPERIENTIAL EXERCISES

1. Review the website of a provider of management development seminars, such as the Canadian Institute of Management. Obtain copies of recent listings of seminar offerings. At what levels of management are the seminar offerings aimed? What seem to be the most popular types of development programs? Why do you think that is the case?

2. Find a person who is web-challenged (perhaps a family friend or one of your professors who is having trouble setting up a website or getting full use of the email system). Offer to reverse mentor him or her on using the web for a short time (a few weeks) in return for some career mentoring for you. Prepare a short report on the benefits of this experience for both of you.

3. Review all positions you have ever held. Below each position, identify core knowledge, skills, and

abilities that you learned in each position. Next, identify a career you would like to be actively engaged in over the next three years. Under the future career, outline core knowledge, skills, and abilities the position would require. Now reflect on your own career trajectory to highlight your history of skill development and identify any gaps that may exist for you to advance to your desired career in the future.

4. Compare and contrast the approach that a firm you have worked for (paid or unpaid) or have knowledge about is taking with respect to career development for younger and older workers. Based on your comparison, develop a career development policy statement for that organization that reflects the diverse needs of different groups of employees.

RUNNING CASE

Running Case: LearnInMotion.com

What to Do about Succession?

In the second year of operation of LearnInMotion.com, Jennifer was involved in a serious car accident and spent two months in the hospital and another four months in rehabilitation before she was able to return to work. During this six-month period, Pierre had to manage the entire business on his own. It proved to be next to impossible. Despite some new training, the sales effort continued to falter and sales revenues declined by 25 percent. Staff turnover at LearnInMotion.com increased, as employees found it frustrating that it was so difficult to have even a brief conversation with Pierre. Employees who left were not replaced, because the decline in sales meant that costs had to be reduced. Thus, Pierre was spared the difficult job of downsizing—at least for now.

The first day that Jennifer returned to work, Pierre said, "We have to have a succession plan. This business will not survive unless we have other employees who can take over from us temporarily now and permanently in the long term."

Jennifer agreed. "Yes, it was difficult for me being unable to work and knowing that you were overwhelmed with every problem in every part of the company," she said. "And maybe our employees' performance in their current jobs would be enhanced if they knew they had been identified as having management potential and were provided with specific development opportunities. We'll have to establish a management development program as well."

"I agree," said Pierre, "but we can't afford to spend much money on this." So Pierre and Jennifer would like your help in establishing a succession plan and a management development plan.

QUESTIONS

1 Would the process of career and development planning assist Pierre and Jennifer?
2 If Jennifer and Pierre decide to use succession planning, what steps of this process should they follow to put such a program in place? Who should be involved in the process?
3 If they decide to promote from within, how should promotions or transfers be handled?
4 What management development techniques should be developed?

CASE INCIDENT

What Should Wilma and Frank Do?

Frank and Wilma Rogers live in the Toronto area. Frank is a product engineer in the automotive industry and Wilma is a professor for a local community college. Wilma has been working on her doctorate for the last five years and is scheduled to graduate with her Ph.D. in Business Administration shortly. Wilma has just received an interesting telephone call and can't wait to talk to Frank about it.

Over dinner that night Wilma tells Frank about the phone call: a past boss of hers called to tell her about an open position at a university in Nunavut. As Wilma excitedly discusses the associate professor of business position and the opportunities it will bring, Frank is thinking to himself what a great opportunity it is, but that he doesn't find the location appealing. He subsequently tells her this and nothing more is discussed.

A week goes by and Wilma still finds herself yearning to know more about this position and wanting to apply. She calls Frank and explains this to him and he encourages her to apply. Wilma calls her former boss and applies for the position. Eventually she gets an offer. Wilma gives her notice at the college and within the next six months starts her new position. Wilma moves to Nunavut, but Frank stays in Toronto until he can find a job in Nunavut. A few more months go by and Frank has not been able to find a comparable job, so he pressures Wilma to consider moving back to Toronto and leaving her new position. Wilma is torn about what to do as she loves her new job but understands why Frank is frustrated.

QUESTIONS

1 According to Edgar Schein, what career anchors are driving Wilma's and Frank's careers at this point?
2 If Wilma wishes to stay in her new job, how could her employer assist her with this dilemma?
3 Is there anything Frank and Wilma should have done differently in your opinion? If so, what?

Pressmaster/Shutterstock

CHAPTER
10

Performance Management

LEARNING OUTCOMES

AFTER STUDYING THIS CHAPTER, YOU SHOULD BE ABLE TO

EXPLAIN the strategic value and importance of performance management.

DISCUSS the five steps in the performance management process.

DEFINE contextual and task-based performance and how they differ.

DESCRIBE five performance appraisal methods and the pros and cons of each.

DISCUSS the major problems inhibiting effective performance appraisals.

DISCUSS 360-degree appraisal from multiple sources.

DESCRIBE the three types of appraisal interviews.

DISCUSS the future of performance management.

REQUIRED HR COMPETENCIES

10600: Align human resources practices by translating organizational strategy into human resources objectives and priorities to achieve the organization's plan.

20100: Conduct human resources responsibilities and build productive relationships consistent with standards of practice with due diligence and integrity to balance the interests of all parties.

20600: Promote an evidence-based approach to the development of human resources policies and practices using current professional resources to provide a sound basis for human resources decision-making.

30100: Promote engagement, commitment, and motivation of employees by developing, implementing, and evaluating innovative strategies to enhance productivity, morale, and culture.

40300: Execute a workforce plan by sourcing, selecting, hiring, onboarding, and developing people to address competency needs and retain qualified talent aligned with the organization's strategic objectives.

40400: Implement a performance management system by measuring against established goals and expectations to align individual and organizational performance with strategy.

THE STRATEGIC IMPORTANCE OF PERFORMANCE MANAGEMENT

HR Competency

10600

performance management The process encompassing all activities related to improving employee performance, productivity, and effectiveness.

HR Competency

40400

In any organization, achieving strategic objectives requires employee productivity above all else because organizations strive to create a high-performance culture by using a minimum number of employees. Thus, it has been suggested that better performance management represents a largely untapped opportunity to improve company profitability.[1] Many companies are still dealing with the reality that their performance management systems are ineffective—for example, they need to downsize poor performers, but performance appraisal records indicate that all employees are performing adequately.

Performance management is a process encompassing all activities related to improving employee performance, productivity, and effectiveness. It includes *goal setting, pay for performance, training and development, career management*, and *disciplinary action*. The performance management system must provide an integrated network of procedures across the organization that will influence all work behaviour.[2] This involves assessing a number of elements regarding an employee's performance, as highlighted in **Table 10.1**. While individual objectives and goals are elements of performance appraisals in 97 out of 337 companies, significantly less consideration is given to the assessment of values, skills, or team objectives. There are three major purposes of performance management: it aligns employee actions with strategic goals, it is a vehicle for culture change, and it provides input into other HR systems such as development and remuneration.[3]

Effective performance appraisals are the basis for successful performance management. Although performance appraisal is a difficult interpersonal task for managers, it cannot be eliminated.

Managers need some way to review employees' work-related performance. Despite the difficulties involved, performance management is still the basis for fostering and managing employee skills and talents, and it can be a key component of improved organizational effectiveness. Performance management techniques in high- and low-performing organizations are essentially the same, but managers in high-performing organizations tend to conduct and implement appraisals and manage performance on a daily basis more effectively.[4]

Recent research indicates that effective performance management involves

- linking individual goals and business strategy;
- showing leadership and accountability at all levels of the organization;

TABLE 10.1 Elements of Performance Appraisals (used by 337 Canadian Organizations)

Individual objectives/goals	97
Training and professional development	70
Competencies	69
Behaviours	61
Organizational objectives/goals	53
Team objectives/goals	53
Skills enhancement plan	41
Values	35
Other (e.g., self-appraisal, results)	4

Source: The Conference Board of Canada. "Performance Management: Turning Individual Stress to Organizational Strategy," June 2012, p. 2., © 2012.

- ensuring close ties among appraisal results, rewards, and recognition outcomes;
- investing in employee development planning; and
- having an administratively efficient system with sufficient communication support.[5]

The key success factor for effective performance appraisal that will lead to optimum employee performance is the quality of the performance appraisal dialogue between a manager and an employee.[6] Managers need to engage in training on an ongoing basis to ensure that they are in a position to engage in high-quality formal appraisal discussions.

Overall, the solution is to create more effective appraisals, as described in this chapter. Effective appraisals are essential to managing the performance required of an organization's employees to achieve that organization's strategic objectives.

THE PERFORMANCE MANAGEMENT PROCESS

PERSONAL INVENTORY ASSESSMENT

Learn About Yourself
Work Performance Assessment

Performance management is of considerable strategic importance to today's organizations because the most effective way for firms to differentiate themselves in a highly competitive, service-oriented, global marketplace is through the quality of its employees.[7] The performance management process contains five steps,[8] as highlighted in **Figure 10.1**.

Performance appraisals in Canada are legal documents. While they should be used for planning promotions, career development, training, and performance improvement plans, they can also be required in courts when assessing wrongful termination cases. Given the importance of performance appraisals, it is problematic that in a 2012 survey of 746 Human Resource Professional Association members and HR reporter readers, 11 percent of respondents identified that performance appraisals were not mandatory in their organization. Additionally, 42 percent of respondents said that there were no consequences for non-completion of appraisals, and 65 percent of respondents identified that they were somewhat to very satisfied with information obtained from performance reports.[9]

Dr. Robert Thorndike researched performance management processes and suggests that employment decisions (such as a performance appraisal system) must be valid, practical, reliable, and free from bias.[10] Failure to measure and use appraisal results effectively in human resource decision-making and career development negates the primary purpose of performance evaluations. Effective performance management thus begins with defining the job and its performance standards, which will now be discussed.

FIGURE 10.1 Performance Management Process

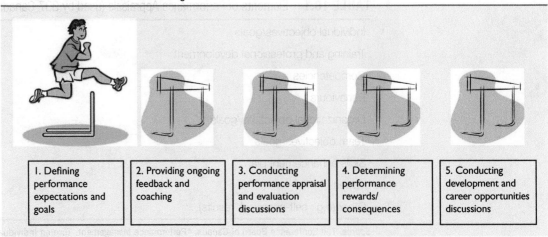

| 1. Defining performance expectations and goals | 2. Providing ongoing feedback and coaching | 3. Conducting performance appraisal and evaluation discussions | 4. Determining performance rewards/ consequences | 5. Conducting development and career opportunities discussions |

STEP 1: DEFINING PERFORMANCE EXPECTATIONS

HR Competency

20100

task performance An individual's direct contribution to their job-related processes.

Defining performance expectations and goals is a critical step in employees' understanding of how their work makes a contribution to achieving business results. Over the last 30 years there has been more recognition that job performance is a multidimensional construct which can be split into what has become widely acknowledged as *task* versus *contextual* performance.[11]

Task performance reflects an individual's direct contribution to their job-related processes. Focusing on tasks means that performance expectations are grounded in realistic job demands and align with the organization's strategic objectives and implementation plans. They may also be partially based on previous performance evaluations.

However, as part of the movement toward more corporate social responsibility, expectations are beginning to extend beyond job skills and skills required for promotion to addressing the concept of whole person development (aligned with the direction, attitudes, motivation, and advancement opportunities of the employee). In addition to task performance, contextual performance is often evaluated as a second factor contributing to an employee's overall work-related performance. **Contextual performance** reflects an individual's indirect contribution to the organization by improving the organizational, social, and psychological behaviours that contribute to organizational effectiveness beyond those specified for the job. This includes extra-role behaviours and contextual factors like "demonstrates a positive attitude" and "pitches in to help others when needed," which have surfaced as contextual performance expectations.[12] These goals may be informally known, but not formally defined, which can become problematic in performance management. Employees also need to be aware of which behaviours are expected and which are discretionary to maintain the legitimacy of the performance management system.

contextual performance An individual's indirect contribution to the organization by improving the organizational, social, and psychological behaviours that contribute to organizational effectiveness beyond those specified for the job.

Ultimately, the performance management process cannot be separated from performance measurement. Performance expectations need to be developed in a legally defensible (correlated with job activities), clear, and measurable way. In addition, they must be communicated and supported as such by the organization. Aligned with the sales associate example, a "personal selling" activity can be measured in terms of how many dollars of sales the associate is to generate personally. "Keeping customers away from executives" can be measured with a standard of no more than 10 customer complaints per year being the sales associate's target. In general, employees should always know ahead of time how and on what basis they will be appraised. It is important to note that expectations cannot discriminate directly or indirectly against anyone on protected grounds (gender, age, disability, and so on).

HR Competency

30100

Hints TO ENSURE LEGAL COMPLIANCE

In global companies, performance appraisal criteria may need to be modified to be consistent with cultural norms and values. In the West, where individuals have an inalienable right to choose their own lifestyles and moralities, performance criteria cannot be based on personal character, but instead need to focus on more objective criteria, such as job competence, abilities, and achievements. However, global values change perceptions of performance management, as highlighted in the Expert Opinion box.

Confucian values (used in parts of Asia including China) lead to an emphasis on appraisals that are based upon personal attitudes and moral characteristics that appear to reflect traditional values, such as hard work, and loyalty and respect toward senior staff. Some specific examples are accepting overtime

"I'm done all my paper work. Need help with yours."

cartoonresource/Fotolia

expert opinion
academic viewpoint

Dr. Mila Lazarova

Identification: Dr. Mila Lazarova (PhD), Canada Research Chair in Global Workforce Management

Affiliation: Beedie School of Business, Simon Fraser University

1. What are some of the significant challenges when managing people globally that HR managers should be aware of?

The key challenges have changed over the years. Currently, availability of talent is critical. Companies are reporting that it is difficult to recruit people to undertake assignments. Also, the demographics of those who do go abroad is changing. We now see more women, younger people, and people without families who are more willing and interested in international mobility.

What hasn't changed is that families that accompany expatriates are still struggling to adjust to foreign locations. It becomes a catch-22 situation, given that it's hard for employees to adjust without their families (they are a great source of social support), but family adjustment can also be a source of concern or stress for the employee when family members themselves struggle to adjust. On that note, the traditional pattern of international employee mobility was focused around three to five year assignments. Now, multiple alternatives such as short-term assignments or commuter assignments (Monday–Friday) are being introduced, partly with the intent of enabling employees to overcome personal or family challenges that come along with global mobility.

2. What performance management challenges are associated with international assignments?

This is highly dependent on the role. Higher-level employees usually report to head office, but mid-level employees might have a lack of clarity regarding what performance criteria apply to them (home or host country). In terms of higher-level expatriates evaluated by headquarters, research shows that local or context-dependent issues might not be considered fully in their performance review. For example, communication style or perceptions of leadership can all be culturally or regionally dependent, or their jobs may involve unique challenges such as delay in decision-making due to the need to consult with local constituents such as unions that may not be well understood by their superiors. The criteria and perceptions regarding performance evaluation may vary based on who is conducting the performance evaluation.

Research identifies that in the slight majority of situations, a local or subsidiary company representative is engaged in performance evaluations of those on international assignment and in a smaller fraction of the cases, the head office manager alone conducts the evaluation.

3. Are there options for employees who are unable to work abroad, but want global experience?

Generally, given that many of us work in a global environment, an employee would want to have some access to global experience. However, one can get such experience without changing offices. Rather than physical mobility, employees can gain some global experience through working on teams that are global or highly diverse, or through interacting with global customers or suppliers. Even if the employee cannot travel abroad, some exposure to international human resource management can be highly beneficial. This is very much the case in Canada where we have a large immigrant population and working across cultural borders is quite common.

Source: Reprinted by permission from Dr. Mila Lazarova.

EVIDENCE-BASED HR

work; being punctual, careful, helpful, loyal, and respectful toward senior staff; as well as being persistent, adaptable, dedicated, and hard working.

Research found three performance appraisal factors that were very acceptable to Chinese employees: work dedication, work efficiency, and teamwork. Work dedication behaviours, such as punctuality, loyalty, working hard, and dedication toward one's work, exist in both Eastern and Western cultures.[13] Employee efficiency has long been considered important to good job performance, as it is considered to be a means to achieve organizational goals. Chinese employees appear to recognize this managerial objective since they were willing to be evaluated on criteria that assess the efficiency of their work. Teamwork is a behavioural manifestation of the group orientation in Eastern cultures.

STEP 2: PROVIDING ONGOING COACHING AND FEEDBACK

HR Competency

40400

Some companies only engage in performance reviews annually, often tying the outcomes of the performance review with compensation, promotion, and lateral movement decisions. In recent years, there has been growing dialogue about moving away from annual performance reviews to more ongoing forms of feedback and performance appraisal discussions, as highlighted in the HR in the News box.

Throughout the performance management process, managers and their reports should continue to discuss progress. A performance improvement plan (often referred to as a PIP) can be used to focus such discussions and facilitate ongoing performance improvement. A PIP highlights in writing the expectations of the employer and employee, complete with the timeline (often 30 to 90 days) required to bring performance to acceptable levels. It lists objectives, in clear and actionable terms that are considered to be reasonable, aimed at improving performance, complete with a date of follow-up and the names of parties who engaged in the conversation. It is important to have open, two-way communication, and both the employee and the manager need to check in frequently throughout the performance management process to talk about progression toward goals.

In some organizations, strategies and objectives change quickly. In such cases, managers and employees may need to change their goals to be consistent. Employees are responsible for monitoring their own performance and asking for help. This promotes employee ownership and control over the process.

HR IN THE NEWS

Frequency of Performance Evaluations

The traditional model of annual performance reviews, with employees graded on relatively static, long-term goals is in decline. Instead, there has been some movement toward more meaningful, ongoing and frequent (monthly or quarterly) performance feedback to employees, supported by new evaluation software that provides real-time metrics to managers.

The process of setting objectives, aligning work, evaluating performance, and getting feedback more regularly is a movement that is not limited to HR, but is part of the broader level management system and leadership imperatives. Some of the newer performance management systems allow gamification to track employee performance, offering incentives like gift cards, points, or tokens to employees who populate the required information in a timely manner.[14]

STEP 3: CONDUCT PERFORMANCE APPRAISAL AND EVALUATION DISCUSSION

The appraisal itself is generally conducted with the aid of a predetermined and formal method, like one or more of those described in this section.

Formal Appraisal Methods

Graphic Rating Scale

graphic rating scale A scale that lists a number of traits and a range of performance for each. The employee is then rated by identifying the score that best describes his or her level of performance for each trait.

The **graphic rating scale** is the simplest and most popular technique for appraising performance. **Figure 10.2** shows a typical rating scale. It lists traits (such as reliability) and a range of performance values (from unsatisfactory to outstanding) for each one. The supervisor rates each employee by circling or checking the score that best describes his or her performance for each trait. The assigned values are then totalled.

Instead of appraising generic traits or factors, many firms specify the duties to be appraised. For a payroll coordinator, these might include being the liaison with accounting and benefits staff, continually updating knowledge regarding relevant legislation, maintenance of payroll records, data entry and payroll calculations, and ongoing responses to employee inquiries regarding payroll issues.

Alternation Ranking Method

Ranking employees from best to worst on a trait or traits is another method for evaluating employees. Because it is usually easier to distinguish between the worst and best

FIGURE 10.2 Alternation Ranking Scale

ALTERNATION RANKING SCALE

For the Trait: _____

For the trait you are measuring, list all the employees you want to rank. Put the highest-ranking employee's name on line 1. Put the lowest-ranking employee's name on line 20. Then list the next highest ranking on line 2, the next lowest ranking on line 19, and so on. Continue until all names are on the scale.

Highest-ranking employee

1. _____	11. _____
2. _____	12. _____
3. _____	13. _____
4. _____	14. _____
5. _____	15. _____
6. _____	16. _____
7. _____	17. _____
8. _____	18. _____
9. _____	19. _____
10. _____	20. _____

Lowest-ranking employee

alternation ranking method
Ranking employees from best to worst on a particular trait.

employees than to rank them, an **alternation ranking method** is popular. First, list all employees to be rated, and then cross out the names of any not known well enough to rank. Then, on a form such as that shown in Figure 10.2, indicate the employee who is the highest on the characteristic being measured and also the one who is the lowest. Then choose the next highest and the next lowest, alternating between highest and lowest until all the employees to be rated have been ranked.

Paired Comparison Method

paired comparison method
Ranking employees by making a chart of all possible pairs of employees for each trait and indicating the better employee of the pair.

The **paired comparison method** helps to make the ranking method more precise. For every trait (quantity of work, quality of work, and so on), every employee is paired with and compared with every other employee.

Suppose that five employees are to be rated. In the paired comparison method, a chart is prepared, as in **Figure 10.3**, of all possible pairs of employees for each trait. Then, for each trait, indicate (with a + or −) who is the better employee of the pair. Next, the number of times that an employee is rated as better is added up. In Figure 10.3, employee Maria was ranked highest (she has the most + marks) for quality of work, while Art was ranked highest for creativity.

Forced Distribution Method

forced distribution method
Predetermined percentages of ratees are placed in various performance categories.

Jack Welch, retired chief executive officer of General Electric (GE), is most often associated with the **forced distribution method**, which places predetermined percentages of ratees in performance categories. At GE, the bell curve was used to identify the top 10–20 percent of the workforce (which are then identified as those exceeding expectations, with a focus on receiving the highest compensation increases and advancement opportunities), the bottom 10 percent (which are identified as those not meeting expectations, with a focus on coaching for improvement or possible termination). The remaining employees, by default, are considered the backbone of the workforce and receive moderate compensation increases and development opportunities. While the method allows for a concentration of effort and resources on those deemed to be top performers, this method has been criticized as being demotivating because the majority of the workforce are classified as at or below average.[15]

FIGURE 10.3 Ranking Employees by the Paired Comparison Method

FOR THE TRAIT "QUALITY OF WORK"						FOR THE TRAIT "CREATIVITY"					
	Employee Rated:						Employee Rated:				
As Compared with:	A Art	B Maria	C Chuck	D Diane	E José	As Compared with:	A Art	B Maria	C Chuck	D Diane	E José
A Art		+	+	−	−	A Art		−	−	−	−
B Maria	−		−	−	−	B Maria	+		−	+	+
C Chuck	−	+		+	−	C Chuck	+	+		−	+
D Diane	+	+	−		+	D Diane	+	−	+		−
E José	+	+	+	−		E José	+	−	−	+	

↑ Maria Ranks Highest Here   ↑ Art Ranks Highest Here

Note: "+" means "better than" and "−" means "worse than." For each chart, add up the number of + signs in each column to get the highest-ranked employee.

In 2012, 3 percent of organizations polled by the Conference Board of Canada use forced distribution, while 44 percent of organizations did not use it explicitly, but had guidelines to force a normal distribution of performance evaluations. While the method allows for a concentration of effort and resources on those deemed to be top performers, this method has been criticized as being demotivating, since half of the workforce is classified as at or below average.[16]

Critical Incident Method

critical incident method Keeping a record of uncommonly good or undesirable examples of an employee's work-related behaviour and reviewing the list with the employee at predetermined times.

With the **critical incident method**, the supervisor keeps a log of desirable or undesirable examples or incidents of each employee's work-related behaviour. Then, every six months or so, the supervisor and employee meet to discuss the latter's performance by using the specific incidents as examples.

This method has several advantages. It provides specific hard facts for explaining the appraisal. It also ensures that a manager thinks about the employee's appraisal throughout the year, because the incidents must be accumulated; therefore, the rating does not just reflect the employee's most recent performance. Keeping a running list of critical incidents should also provide concrete examples of what an employee can do to eliminate any performance deficiencies.

The critical incident method can be adapted to the specific job expectations laid out for the employee at the beginning of the year. Thus, in the example presented in Table 10.2, one of the assistant plant manager's continuing duties is to supervise procurement and to minimize inventory costs. The critical incident shows that the assistant plant manager let inventory storage costs rise 15 percent; this provides a specific example of what performance must be improved in the future.

The critical incident method is often used to supplement another appraisal technique, like a ranking system. It is useful for identifying specific examples of good and poor performance and for planning how deficiencies can be corrected. It is not as useful by itself for comparing employees nor, therefore, for making salary decisions.

Narrative Forms

Some employers use narrative forms to evaluate employees. For example, the form in Figure 10.1 presented a suggested format for identifying a performance issue and presenting a *performance improvement plan* (PIP). The performance problem is described in specific detail, and its organizational impact is specified. The improvement plan identifies measurable improvement goals, provides directions regarding training and any other suggested activities to address the performance issue, and encourages the employee to add ideas about steps to be taken to improve performance. Therefore, a PIP essentially

TABLE 10.2 Examples of Critical Incidents for an Assistant Plant Manager

Continuing Duties	Targets	Critical Incidents
Schedule production for plant	Full utilization of employees and machinery in plant; orders delivered on time	Instituted new production scheduling system; decreased late orders by 10 percent last month; increased machine utilization in plant by 20 percent last month
Supervise procurement of raw materials and inventory control	Minimize inventory costs while keeping adequate supplies on hand	Let inventory storage costs rise 15 percent last month; over-ordered parts "A" and "B" by 20 percent; under-ordered part "C" by 30 percent
Supervise machinery maintenance	No shutdowns because of faulty machinery	Instituted new preventative maintenance system for plant; prevented a machine breakdown by discovering faulty part

facilitates a constructive discussion between an employee and his or her manager, and provides clarity as to how to improve work performance. Finally, the outcomes and consequences, both positive and negative, are explicitly stated. A summary performance appraisal discussion then focuses on problem solving.[17]

Behaviourally Anchored Rating Scales

A **behaviourally anchored rating scale (BARS)** combines the benefits of narratives, critical incidents, and quantified ratings by anchoring a series of quantified scales, one for each performance dimension, with specific behavioural examples of good or poor performance. The guiding principle to BARS is that by elaboration of the dimension and rating scale, it gives raters a uniform interpretation as to the types of behaviour being measured.[18] BARS usually involves a scale of nine anchors, although seven and five anchors have also been used.[19]

The midpoint scales are more difficult to develop in a standardized format than the scale extremes. Recent efforts have focused on addressing midpoint scale development to influence inter-rater reliability and inter-rater agreement.[20] The research suggests that all levels of the scale be anchored with statements reflecting how users are to interpret them to increase uniform use of the scale. As well, developers of the scales should be involved in the training of users to increase the consistency in how the scale is used, which increases the effectiveness and legal defensibility of the performance appraisal. **Figure** 10.4 provides an example of a BARS for one performance dimension: "sales skills."

Developing a BARS can be more time-consuming than developing other appraisal tools, like graphic rating scales. But BARS may also have important advantages:[21]

behaviourally anchored rating scale (BARS) An appraisal method that aims to combine the benefits of narratives, critical incidents, and quantified ratings by anchoring a quantified scale with specific narrative examples of good and poor performance.

EVIDENCE-BASED HR

HR Competency
10600

FIGURE 10.4   Behaviourally Anchored Rating Scale

SALES SKILLS

Skilfully persuading customers to purchase products; using product benefits and opportunities effectively; closing skills; adapting sales techniques appropriately to different customers; effectively overcoming objections to purchasing products.

5 — If a customer insists on a particular brand name, the salesperson perseveres. Although products with this particular brand name are not available, the salesperson does not give up; instead, the salesperson persuades the customer that his or her needs could be better met with another product.

4 — The salesperson treats objections to purchasing the product seriously; works hard to counter the objections with relevant positive arguments regarding the benefits of the product.

3 — When a customer is deciding on which product to purchase, the salesperson tries to sell the product with the highest profit magin.

2 — The salesperson insists on describing more features of the product even though the customer wants to purchase it right now.

1 — When a customer states an objection to purchasing a product, the salesperson ends the conversation, assuming that the prospect must not be interested.

1. *A more accurate measure.* People who know the job and its requirements better than anyone else does develop BARS. The result should therefore be a good measure of performance on that job.

2. *Clearer standards.* The critical incidents along the scale help to clarify what is meant by extremely good performance, average performance, and so forth.

3. *Feedback.* The critical incidents may be more useful in providing feedback to appraisees than simply informing them of their performance rating without providing specific behavioural examples.

4. *Independent dimensions.* Systematically clustering the critical incidents into five or six performance dimensions (such as "knowledge and judgment") should help to make the dimensions more independent of one another. For example, a rater should be less likely to rate an employee high on all dimensions simply because he or she was rated high in "conscientiousness."

5. *Consistency.* BARS evaluations also seem to be relatively consistent and reliable in that different raters' appraisals of the same person tend to be similar.[22]

Management by Objectives (MBO)

management by objectives (MBO) Involves setting specific measurable goals with each employee and then periodically reviewing the progress made.

Stripped to its essentials, **management by objectives (MBO)** requires the manager and employee to jointly set specific measurable goals and periodically discuss progress toward these goals, aligned with a comprehensive, *organization-wide goal-setting and appraisal program.* When managers and employees set goals collaboratively, employees become more engaged and committed to the goal, leading to a higher rate of success.[23] While there is a notion that difficult goals (also referred to as "stretch goals") can increase personal growth and professional development, and improve organizational effectiveness,[24] it is important to set objectives that match the job description and the person's abilities. Goals that push an employee too far beyond his or her abilities may lead to burnout.[25] To motivate performance, the objectives must be fair and attainable.

HR Competency

30100

1. *Set the organization's goals.* Establish an organization-wide plan for the next year and set goals.

2. *Set departmental goals.* Department heads and their superiors jointly set goals for their departments.

3. *Discuss departmental goals.* Department heads discuss the department's goals with all employees in the department (often at a department-wide meeting) and ask them to develop their own individual goals; in other words, how can each employee contribute to the department's attainment of its goals?

4. *Define expected results (set individual goals).* Here, department heads and employees set short-term performance targets.

5. *Performance reviews: Measure the results.* Department heads compare the actual performance of each employee with the expected results.

6. *Provide feedback.* Department heads hold periodic performance review meetings with employees to discuss and evaluate progress in achieving expected results.

Using MBO has three potential problems. *Setting unclear, unmeasurable objectives* is the main one. Such an objective as "will do a better job of training" is useless. Conversely, "will have four employees promoted during the year" is a measurable objective. Second, MBO is *time-consuming.* Taking the time to set objectives, measure progress, and provide feedback can take several hours per employee per year, over and above the time already spent doing each person's appraisal. Third, setting objectives with an employee sometimes turns into a *tug of war*; managers push for higher goals and employees push for lower ones. It is thus important to know the job and the person's ability. To motivate performance, the objectives must be fair and attainable.

Mixing the Methods

Most firms combine several appraisal techniques. The graphic rating scale with behavioural incidents defines values for the traits being measured. The quantifiable ranking method permits comparisons of employees and is therefore useful for making salary, transfer, and promotion decisions. The critical incidents provide specific examples of performance relative to expectations and can be used to develop the high and low anchors for the BARS technique.[26] Ultimately, no one single solution is best for all performance management systems. Instead, resource constraints (time, money, people) and organizational factors (budget, turnover, strategy) will help determine which of the options is best for each organization.

The Use of Technology in Performance Appraisals

Over the past few years, web-based performance management has moved from being a leading-edge approach adopted by only large companies to a mainstream practice that is quickly becoming an industry standard among medium and small organizations.[27] It enables managers to keep computerized notes on employees, combine these with ratings on several performance traits, and then generate written text to support each part of the appraisal.

But the true value in web-based performance management goes beyond simply automating time-consuming, tedious tasks like tracking down paper-based appraisal forms. They ultimately improve the overall performance management process, starting with higher completion rates, which can dramatically increase the value of performance management within organizations of all sizes. Performance management systems provide employees with a clear development path and a better understanding of how their goals are aligned with those of the organization, which in turn increases their support of the process. Managers have the information they need to ensure development plans are relevant and executed. Executives have a clear picture of the organization's talent strategy and how it ties into the bottom line.

Most web-based performance management systems provide advanced reporting capabilities, which allow managers to track the status of performance management initiatives easily. Goal management functions enable organizations to link individual goals to strategic corporate goals, meaning that executives have insight into the progress being made on corporate objectives. Succession planning tools provide executives with a clear plan to build a talent pool to meet the organization's business needs and address potential attrition.

In a relatively short time, employee performance management has undergone a rapid evolution with the development of powerful, web-based tools. HR professionals are no longer mired in paperwork and other mundane administrative tasks. They have more time to focus on meeting strategic objectives, better tools to implement best practices programs, and access to critical workforce metrics they can share with their executive team.

electronic performance monitoring (EPM) Having supervisors electronically monitor the amount of computerized data an employee is processing per day and thereby his or her performance.

Electronic performance monitoring (EPM) is in some respects the ultimate in computerized appraising. Electronic performance monitoring means having supervisors electronically observe the employee's output or whereabouts. This typically involves using computer networks and wireless audio or video links to monitor and record employees' work activities. It includes, for instance, monitoring a data clerk's hourly keystrokes, tracking via GPS the whereabouts of delivery drivers, and monitoring the calls of customer service clerks.

Performance Appraisal Problems and Solutions

Few of the things a manager does are fraught with more peril than appraising employees' performance. Employees in general tend to be overly optimistic about what their ratings will be, and they also know that their raises, career progress, and peace of mind may well hinge on how they are rated. Thus, an honest appraisal inevitably involves an emotional component, which is particularly difficult when managers are not trained on formal appraisal discussion skills. The result is often dishonest appraisals or avoidance of appraisals.[28]

Even more problematic, however, are the numerous structural problems that can cast serious doubt on just how fair the whole process is. Fortunately, research shows that action by management to implement a more acceptable performance appraisal system can increase employee trust in management.[29] According to several studies, the majority of organizations view their performance management systems as ineffective. More focus on the execution of performance appraisal is required instead of searching for new techniques and methods.[30] Some of the main appraisal problems and how to solve them, as well as several other pertinent appraisal issues, will now be reviewed.

Validity and Reliability

Appraisal systems must be based on performance criteria that are valid for the position being rated and must be reliable, in that their application must produce consistent ratings for the same performance. Employee concerns about appraisal fairness are influenced by these characteristics of the performance appraisal system.

Criteria used in performance appraisal must be accurate, or valid, to produce useful results. Criteria must be (1) relevant to the job being appraised, (2) broad enough to cover all aspects of the job requirements, and (3) specific. For example, including a broad criterion, such as "leadership," may not be relevant to non-management jobs and may be so vague that it can be interpreted in many different ways.

Effective appraisal criteria are precise enough to result in consistent measures of performance when applied across many employees by many different raters. This is difficult to achieve without quantifiable and measurable criteria.

Rating Scale Problems

Seven main problems can undermine such appraisal tools as graphic rating scales: unclear standards, the halo effect, central tendency, leniency or strictness, appraisal bias, the recency effect, and the similar-to-me bias.

Unclear Performance Standards   The problem of **unclear performance standards** is illustrated in **Table 10.3**. Although the graphic rating scale seems objective, it would probably result in unfair appraisals because the traits and degrees of merit are open to interpretation. For example, different supervisors would probably differently define "good" performance, "fair" performance, and so on. The same is true of traits, such as "quality of work" or "creativity." There are several ways in which to rectify this problem. The best way is to develop and include descriptive phrases that define each trait. For example, the form provided in as Table 10.3 fails to specify what was meant by "outstanding," "very good," and "good" quality of work. More specificity or definitions differentiating the categories will result in appraisals that are more consistent and more easily explained.

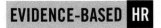

TABLE 10.3   Example of a Graphic Rating Scale with Unclear Standards

Please evaluate your employee using the following table.

	Excellent	Good	Fair	Poor
Quality of work				
Quantity of work				
Creativity				
Integrity				

Note: For example, what exactly is meant by "good," "quantity of work," and so forth?

halo effect In performance appraisal, the problem that occurs when a supervisor's rating of an employee on one trait biases the rating of that person on other traits.

Halo Effect   The **halo effect** means that the rating of an employee on one trait (such as "gets along with others") biases the way that person is rated on other traits (such as "reliability"). This problem often occurs with employees who are especially friendly (or unfriendly) toward the supervisor. For example, an unfriendly employee will often be rated unsatisfactory for all traits rather than just for the trait "gets along well with others." Being aware of this problem is a major step toward avoiding it. Supervisory training can also alleviate the problem.[31]

central tendency A tendency to rate all employees in the middle of the scale.

Central Tendency   Many supervisors have a **central tendency** when filling in rating scales. For example, if the rating scale ranges from one to seven, they tend to avoid the highs (six and seven) and lows (one and two) and rate most of their employees between three and five. If a graphic rating scale is used, this central tendency could mean that all employees are simply rated "average." Such a restriction can distort the evaluations, making them less useful for promotion, salary, or counselling purposes. Ranking employees instead of using a graphic rating scale can avoid this central tendency problem, because all employees must be ranked and thus cannot all be rated average.

strictness/leniency The problem that occurs when a supervisor has a tendency to rate all employees either low or high.

Strictness/Leniency   Some supervisors tend to rate all of their employees consistently high (or low), just as some instructors are notoriously high graders and others are not. Fear of interpersonal conflict is often the reason for leniency.[32] Conversely, evaluators tend to give more weight to negative attributes than to positive ones.[33] This **strictness/leniency** problem is especially serious with graphic rating scales, since supervisors are not necessarily required to avoid giving all of their employees low (or high) ratings. However, when ranking employees, a manager is forced to distinguish between high and low performers. Thus, strictness/leniency is not a problem with the ranking or forced distribution approaches.

Day of the Zombie Performance Reviews

Appraisal Bias   Individual differences among ratees in terms of a wide variety of characteristics, such as age, race, and sex, can affect their ratings, often quite apart from their actual performance.[34] In fact, research shows that less than half of performance evaluation ratings are actually related to employee performance and that most of the rating is based on idiosyncratic factors.[35] This is known as **appraisal bias**. Not only does this bias result in inaccurate feedback, but it is also illegal under human rights legislation. Although age-related bias is typically thought of as affecting older workers, one study found a negative relationship between age and performance evaluation for entry-level jobs in public accounting firms.[36]

appraisal bias The tendency to allow individual differences, such as age, race, and sex, to affect the appraisal ratings that these employees receive.

Interestingly, the friendliness and likeability of an employee have been found to have little effect on that person's performance ratings.[37] However, an employee's previous performance can affect the evaluation of his or her current performance.[38] The actual error can take several forms. Sometimes the rater may systematically overestimate improvement by a poor worker or decline by a good worker, for instance. In some situations—especially when the change in behaviour is more gradual—the rater may simply be insensitive to improvement or decline. In any case, it is important to rate performance objectively. Such factors as previous performance, age, or race should not be allowed to influence results.

The **recency effect** occurs when ratings are based on the employee's most recent performance, whether good or bad. To the extent that this recent performance does not exemplify the employee's average performance over the appraisal period, the appraisal is biased.

If a supervisor tends to give higher ratings to employees with whom he or she has something in common, the **similar-to-me bias** is occurring. This bias can be discriminatory if it is based on similarity in race, gender, or other prohibited grounds.

How to Avoid Appraisal Problems

There are at least four ways in which managers can minimize the impact of appraisal problems, such as bias and central tendency. First, raters must be familiar with the problems just discussed. Understanding the problem can help to prevent it.

Second, training supervisors on how to eliminate rating errors, such as the halo effect, leniency, and central tendency, can help them avoid these problems.[39] In a typical training program, raters are shown videos of jobs being performed and are asked to rate the worker. Ratings made by each participant are then placed on a flip chart and the various errors (such as leniency and halo) are explained. For example, if a trainee rated all criteria (such as quality, quantity, and so on) about the same, the trainer might explain that a halo error had occurred. Typically, the trainer gives the correct rating and then illustrates the rating errors made by the participants.[40] According to one study, computer-assisted appraisal training improved managers' ability to conduct performance appraisal discussions with their employees.[41]

Rater training will not eliminate all rating errors or ensure absolute accuracy. In practice, several factors—including the extent to which pay is tied to performance ratings, union pressure, employee turnover, time constraints, and the need to justify ratings—may be more important than training. This means that improving appraisal accuracy calls not only for training but also for reducing outside factors, such as union pressure and time constraints.[42] It has also been found that employee reaction to current performance reviews is affected by past appraisal feedback, which is beyond the control of the current manager.[43]

Third, raters must choose the right appraisal tool. Each tool, such as the graphic rating scale or critical incident method, has its own advantages and disadvantages. For example, the ranking method avoids central tendency but can cause ill feelings when employees' performances are, in fact, all "high" (see **Table 10.4)**.

Fourth, errors in performance appraisals can be reduced by using multiple raters in the evaluation. Multiple raters increase the validity and accuracy of the rating by controlling for individual biases or idiosyncrasies. Also, responsibility for poor appraisals is diffused; therefore, raters are more comfortable giving a poor rating. When raters are accountable for their rating, reliability also increases.[44] As an additional benefit, multiple ratings may be more legally defensible.

EVIDENCE-BASED HR

recency effect The rating error that occurs when ratings are based on the employee's most recent performance rather than on performance throughout the appraisal period.

similar-to-me bias The tendency to give higher performance ratings to employees who are perceived to be similar to the rater in some way.

HR Competency

40300

TABLE 10.4   Important Advantages and Disadvantages of Appraisal Tools

	Advantages	Disadvantages
Graphic rating scale	Simple to use; provides a quantitative rating for each employee.	Standards may be unclear; halo effect, central tendency, leniency, and bias can also be problems.
Alternation ranking	Simple to use (but not as simple as graphic rating scale); avoids central tendency and other problems of rating scales.	Can cause disagreements among employees and may be unfair if all employees are, in fact, excellent.
Paired comparison method	A more precise ranking method that involves multiple traits.	Difficult to use as employee numbers increase; differences may not be noticeable enough to rank.
Forced distribution method	End up with a predetermined number of people in each group.	Appraisal results depend on the adequacy of the original choice of cut-off points.
Critical incident method	Helps specify what is "right" and "wrong" about the employee's perform-ance; forces the supervisor to evaluate employees on an ongoing basis.	Difficult to rate or rank employees relative to one another; cannot be used to defend salary decisions.
Narrative form	Explicitly states improvement goals and associated outcomes or consequences.	Employees may take these too personally.
Behaviourally anchored rating scale (BARS)	Provides behavioural "anchors"; very accurate; high inter-rater reliability.	Difficult to develop.
Management by objectives	Tied to jointly agreed-upon performance objectives.	Risk of unclear performance measures, time-consuming, and inflated/deflated goals due to tug of war.

Who Should Do the Appraising?

Who should actually rate an employee's performance? Several options exist as to who can be involved in the performance management appraisal process.

Supervisors

Supervisors' ratings are still the heart of most appraisal systems. Getting a supervisor's appraisal is relatively easy and also makes a great deal of sense. The supervisor should be—and usually is—in the best position to observe and evaluate the performance of employees reporting to him or her and is responsible for their performance.

Self

Employees' self-ratings of performance are sometimes used, generally in conjunction with supervisors' ratings. Employees value the opportunity to participate in performance appraisal more for the opportunity to be heard than for the opportunity to influence the end result.[45] Nevertheless, the basic problem with self-ratings is that employees usually rate themselves higher than they are rated by supervisors or peers.[46] In one study, for example, it was found that when asked to rate their own job performance, 40 percent of the employees in jobs of all types placed themselves in the top 10 percent ("one of the best"), while virtually all remaining employees rated themselves

The best performance appraisal systems are those in which the supervisor or manager makes an ongoing effort to coach and monitor employees instead of leaving evaluation to the last minute.

either in the top 25 percent ("well above average") or at least in the top 50 percent ("above average"). Usually no more than 1 percent or 2 percent will place themselves in a below-average category, and then almost invariably in the top below-average category. However, self-ratings have been found to correlate more highly with performance measures if employees know that this comparison will be made and if they are instructed to compare themselves with others.[47]

Supervisors requesting self-appraisals should know that their appraisals and their employees' self-appraisals may accentuate appraiser–appraisee differences and rigidify positions.[48] Furthermore, even if self-appraisals are not formally requested, each employee will enter the performance review meeting with his or her own self-appraisal in mind, and this will usually be higher than the supervisor's rating.

Peers

The appraisal of an employee by his or her peers can be effective in predicting future management success. Peers may have more opportunity to observe ratees and to observe them at more revealing times than supervisors do. One potential problem is *logrolling*; here, all the peers simply get together to rate each other highly.

With more firms using self-managing teams, peer or team appraisals are becoming more popular. One study found that peer ratings had an immediate positive impact on perceptions of open communication, motivation, group cohesion, and satisfaction, and these were not dependent on the ratio of positive to negative feedback.[49] Thus, peer appraisals would appear to have great potential for work teams.

Committees

Many employers use rating committees to evaluate employees. These committees usually comprise the employee's immediate supervisor and three or four other supervisors. Using multiple raters can be advantageous. Although there may be a discrepancy in the ratings made by individual supervisors, the composite ratings tend to be more reliable, fair, and valid.[50] Using several raters can help cancel out problems like bias and the halo effect on the part of individual raters. Furthermore, when there are variations in raters' ratings, they usually stem from the fact that raters often observe different facets of an employee's performance and the appraisal ought to reflect these differences.[51] Even when a committee is not used, it is common to have the appraisal reviewed by the manager immediately above the one who makes the appraisal.

Subordinates

Traditionally, supervisors feared that being appraised by their employees would undermine their management authority. However, with today's flatter organizations and empowered workers, much managerial authority is a thing of the past, and employees are in a good position to observe managerial performance.[52] Thus, more firms today are letting employees anonymously evaluate their supervisors' performance, a process many call *upward feedback*.[53] When conducted throughout the firm, the process helps top managers diagnose management styles, identify potential "people" problems, and take corrective action with individual managers as required. Such employee ratings are especially valuable when used for developmental rather than evaluative purposes.[54] Managers who receive feedback from employees who identify themselves view the upward appraisal process more positively than do managers who receive anonymous feedback; however, employees (not surprisingly) are more comfortable giving anonymous responses, and those who have to identify themselves tend to provide inflated ratings.[55] Research comparing employee and peer ratings of managers found them to be comparable.[56]

EVIDENCE-BASED **HR**

Upward feedback from reporting employees is quite effective in terms of improving the supervisor's behaviour, according to the research evidence. One study examined data for 92 managers who were rated by one or more reporting employees in each of four administrations of an upward feedback survey over two and a half years. The reporting employees were asked to rate themselves and their managers in surveys that consisted of 33 behavioural statements. The feedback to the managers also contained results from previous administrations of the survey so that they could track their performance over time.

According to the researchers, managers whose initial performance level was lower than the average employee performance level improved performance by the next performance assessment and sustained this improvement two years later. Interestingly, the results also suggest that it is not necessarily the specific feedback that caused the performance improvement, because low-performing managers seemed to improve over time even if they did not receive any feedback. Instead, learning what the critical supervisory behaviours were (as a result of themselves filling out the appraisal surveys) and knowing that they might be appraised may have been enough to result in the improved supervisory behaviours. In a sense, therefore, it is the existence of the formal upward feedback program rather than the actual feedback itself that may signal and motivate supervisors to get their behaviours in line with what they should be.[57]

360-Degree Appraisal

Many Canadian firms are now using what is called **360-degree appraisal**, or "multi-source feedback." Here, as shown in **Figure 10.5**, performance information is collected "all around" an employee—from his or her supervisors, subordinates, peers, and internal or external customers.[58] This feedback was originally used only for training and development purposes, but it has rapidly spread to the management of performance and pay.[59] The 360-degree approach supports the activities of performance feedback, coaching, leadership development, succession planning, and rewards and recognition.[60] The Expert Opinion box highlights the use of multiple sources for performance appraisals.

There are a number of reasons for the rapid growth of 360-degree appraisal, despite the significant investment of time required for it to function successfully. Today's

FIGURE 10.5 360-Degree Performance Appraisals

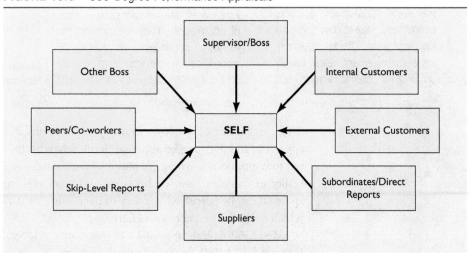

Source: Alma M. McCarthy, Thomas N. Garavan, "360° Feedback Process: Performance, Improvement and Employee Career Development," *Journal of European Industrial Training*, 25, no. 1 (2001), pp. 5–32. Reprinted by permission from Emerald Group Publishing Limited.

expert opinion
industry expert

Marnie Armstrong

Identification: Mrs. Marnie Armstrong, Human Resource and Organizational Development Professional and former Adjunct Professor of HR Strategic Planning

Specialization: Progressive experience in roles of HR Management and Leadership in Canada, with an expertise in Negotiation, Leadership and Organizational Development

1. What do you think are the biggest obstacles to successfully completing performance evaluations accurately in an organization?

I. *Timeliness:* We tend to look at performance management as an annual event, but performance management involves a more connected, day-to-day, on the job approach. Effective performance management relies heavily on ongoing communication and relationship building between the employee and the leader, as well as quarterly achievement statements to ensure that the ultimate annual review will show no surprises.

II. *Motivation:* Individual motivators vary. Hence, an added layer of complexity when managing performance is understanding how reward and recognition vary, and ensuring that they are effective at incentivizing and motivating the desired behaviour.

III. *Fairness:* Employees and leaders are concerned with fairness, which is reflected in the level of equity in performance ratings and related compensation. Employees are more likely to accept and correct poor performance if they believe that their review was fair and unbiased.

IV. *Accuracy:* Organizations still view these much like report card writing in elementary schools, with standard paragraphs or rankings that place many as "average." While the employer is attempting to cost-save, the employees who get rated this way decide that their extra efforts are mediocre and become further disengaged.

2. How can these obstacles be overcome?

It's time to re-think the why, what, and how of performance management. Employees are an amazing source of information. They will provide the realities, contingent on a healthy workplace culture free from reprisal and unhealthy competition. The best performance evaluation system I ever worked with was jointly developed with employees. It became a dialogue tool about performance where the employee initiated and completed it. Employees took responsibility for scheduling their performance reviews, sharing the accomplishments they were particularly proud of for each quarter, and these were bundled into the annual review. The effort and limitations of time were decreased and employees felt empowered and accountable for navigating their performance and career track. To ensure this was managed appropriately, leaders were also evaluated on "performance management."

3. What do you think the future of performance appraisals will looks like?

I. These may be online, real-time, employee-driven and allow for collective influence from several appropriate sources, allowing for both a community-mindedness to sharing reward and recognition and a positive approach to development.

II. We may even toss the formalities out and allow for conceptual review to determine the value of the respective contribution to the organization. This implies we reward excellence in performance everyday as a normal approach to compensation, including reconsidering re-earnable bonuses and less-limited potential to achieve great results.

Source: Reprinted by permission from Marnie Armstrong.

flatter organizations employ a more open communicative climate conducive to such an approach, and 360-degree appraisal fits closely with the goals of organizations committed to continuous learning. A multiple-rater system is also more meaningful in today's reality of complex jobs, with matrix and team reporting relationships. A 360-degree appraisal can be perceived as a jury of peers, rather than the supervisor as a single judge, which enhances perceptions of fairness.[61]

Most 360-degree appraisal systems contain several common features (including Internet-based 360-degree feedback systems, as described in Chapter 3). They are usually applied in a confidential and anonymous manner. Appropriate parties—peers, superiors, employees, and customers, for instance—complete survey questionnaires about an individual. The questionnaires must be custom-designed and linked to the organization's strategic direction, vision, and values.[62] All this information is then compiled into individualized reports. When the information is being used for self-development purposes only, the report is presented to the person being rated, who then meets with his or her own supervisor and information pertinent for the purpose of developing a self-improvement plan is shared. When the information is being used for management of performance or pay, the information is also provided to the ratee's supervisor, and a supportive and facilitative process to follow up is required to ensure that the behavioural change required for performance improvement is made.[63]

EVIDENCE-BASED **HR**

There is a limited amount of research data on the effectiveness of 360-degree feedback. Some organizations have abandoned it for appraisal purposes because of negative attitudes from employees and inflated ratings.[64] Some studies have found that the different raters often disagree on performance ratings.[65] A recent study by researchers at Concordia University in Montreal found that 360-degree feedback is popular among Canadian employers, despite such problems as the amount of time and effort involved, lack of trust in the system by employees, and lack of fit with strategic goals and other HR practices. The results showed that organizations that successfully implemented 360-degree feedback were those that had the most clarity on what their initial objectives were. Organizations that rely exclusively on external consultants to establish 360-degree appraisal have less success than organizations that are more sensitive to contextual factors, such as the readiness of employees and the culture of the organization.[66]

HR Competency

20600

Some experts suggest that 360-degree feedback be used for developmental purposes only.[67] In general, it is advisable to use 360-degree feedback for developmental/career-planning purposes initially, and then to determine whether the organization is ready to use it for evaluative appraisal purposes. A pilot test in one department is often recommended. Once a decision to use 360-degree appraisal has been made, organizations should consider the following advice:[68]

An Ethical Dilemma

Is it fair to factor in employee self-ratings in 360-degree performance appraisal, when we know that these appraisals tend to be inflated?

- Have the performance criteria developed by a representative group that is familiar with each job.
- Be clear about who will have access to reports.
- Provide training for all supervisors, raters, and ratees.
- Assure all raters that their comments will be kept anonymous.
- Plan to evaluate the 360-degree feedback system for fine-tuning.

Formal Appraisal Discussions

formal appraisal discussion An interview in which the supervisor and employee review the appraisal and make plans to remedy deficiencies and reinforce strengths.

The essence of a performance appraisal is the feedback provided in a one-on-one conversation called the **formal appraisal discussion**. This is an interview in which the supervisor and employee review the appraisal and make plans to remedy deficiencies and reinforce strengths. Unfortunately, surveys show that less than half of companies describe their performance appraisal systems as effective or very effective because of weak execution due to managers abdicating their responsibility for screening out poor performers.[69] This discussion is often avoided by supervisors and managers who have not been trained to provide constructive feedback and to deal with defensive employees. Ultimately, feedback should be ongoing, making the formal appraisal discussion one of many performance discussions. The HR by the Numbers box highlights key metrics regarding employee performance feedback.

HR | by the Numbers

Performance Interview Feedback

57% of 899 employees surveyed by the Harvard Business Review (HBR) prefer corrective feedback over praise or recognition[70]

92% of respondents in the HBR study agreed that "negative (redirecting) feedback, if delivered appropriate, is effective at improving performance"[71]

14.9% lower turnover rates of employees who received performance review feedback, when compared with those who received no feedback[72]

50% of high-performing employees expect at least one monthly performance meeting (formal or informal) with their boss[73]

53% of high performers believe that managers meet their (the high-performing employees) performance feedback expectations[74]

PERSONAL INVENTORY ASSESSMENT

Learn About Yourself
Diagnosing Poor Performance and Enhancing Motivation

Types of Appraisal Outcomes

There are three basic types of formal appraisal discussions, each with its own objectives:[75]

Satisfactory—Promotable

Here, the person's performance is satisfactory and there is a promotion ahead. This is the easiest of the three formal appraisal discussions. The objective is to discuss the person's career plans and to develop a specific action plan for the educational and professional development that the person needs to move to the next job.

Satisfactory—Not Promotable

This interview is for employees whose performance is satisfactory but for whom promotion is not possible. Perhaps there is no more room in the company; some employees are happy where they are and do not want a promotion.[76] The objective here is not to improve or develop the person but to maintain satisfactory performance.

This situation is not easy. The best option is usually to find incentives that are important to the person and are enough to maintain satisfactory performance. These might include extra time off, a small bonus, additional authority to handle a slightly enlarged job, and verbal reinforcement in the form of "Well done!"

Unsatisfactory—Correctable vs. Uncorrectable

When the person's performance is unsatisfactory but correctable, the interview objective is to lay out an *action plan* (such as a PIP) for correcting the unsatisfactory performance. If the employee's performance is unsatisfactory and the situation uncorrectable, there is usually no need for any formal appraisal discussion because the person's performance is not correctable anyway. Either the person's poor performance is tolerated for now, or he or she is dismissed.

Preparing for the Formal Appraisal Discussion

An important component of the performance management process is the effective use of feedback. This often happens in a formal appraisal discussion after the performance has been evaluated. There are three things to do in preparation for the interview.[77] First, assemble the data. Study the person's job description, compare the employee's performance to the standards, and review the files of the employee's previous appraisals. Next, prepare the employee. Give the employee at least a week's notice to review his or her own work, read over his or her job description, analyze problems he or she may be dealing with, and gather questions and comments for the interview. Finally, find a mutually agreeable time and place and allow plenty of time for the interview. Interviews with non-supervisory staff should take no more than an hour. Appraising management employees often takes two or three hours. Be sure that the interview is conducted in a private place where there will be no interruptions. It is important to keep in mind what is said and how it is said.

The Strategic HR box provides an example of how management teams in a global company were guided on managing the formal appraisal discussion.

How to Conduct the Interview

EVIDENCE-BASED HR

Constructive feedback is considered a positive and motivating experience.[78] There are four things to keep in mind when conducting a formal appraisal discussion to ensure the feedback is constructive.[79]

1. *Be direct and specific.* Talk in terms of objective work data. Use examples, such as absences, tardiness, quality records, inspection reports, scrap or waste, orders processed, productivity records, material used or consumed, timeliness of tasks or projects, control or reduction of costs, numbers of errors, costs compared with budgets, customers' comments, product returns, order processing time, inventory level and accuracy, accident reports, and so on.

2. *Do not get personal.* Do not say, "You are too slow in producing those reports." Instead, try to compare the person's performance with a standard ("These reports should normally be done within 10 days"). Similarly, do not compare the person's performance with that of other people ("He is quicker than you are").

3. *Encourage the person to talk.* Stop and listen to what the person is saying; ask open-ended questions, such as, "What do you think we can do to improve the situation?" Use phrases such as, "Go on," or "Tell me more." Restate the person's last point as a question, such as, "You do not think that you can get the job done?"

4. *Develop an action plan.* Do not get personal, but do make sure that by the end of the interview you have (a) provided specific examples of performance that does and does not need attention or improvement, (b) made sure the person understands how he or she should improve his or her performance, (c) obtained an agreement from the person that he or she understands the reasons for the appraisal, and (d) developed an action plan that shows steps to achieving specified goals and the results expected. Be sure that a timeline is included in the plan.

STRATEGIC HR

Jaguar Land Rover Formal Appraisal Discussion Training

In 2008, an Indian conglomerate (Tata) took over the Jaguar Land Rover car maker. This triggered a new set of management behaviours, including the redesign of the performance management process. Management was coached on techniques for managing behaviour during the formal appraisal discussion, including the following suggestions:

- Verbally acknowledge your observations—providing verbal feedback based on observations allows the individual receiving feedback to reflect on cause and effect
- Be empathetic—demonstrating sincere concern and ability to put yourself in the other's position
- Listen actively—accurately and clearly listen to the comments being made and reflect on the main content of the issues

- Questioning—elicit information using a variety of probing questions (open-ended and close-ended)
- Communicate non-verbally—demonstrate body language that suggests and elicits open and honest information sharing
- Speak rationally, clearly, and calmly—consider the conversation a mutual exchange of information, perspectives, and challenges without being irrationally or emotionally overwhelmed or skewed

The training program is viewed as a success by management and participants alike. Jaguar Land Rover believes that managers are now equipped with the skills to implement the performance management system successfully.

Source: Based on J. Hicks, "Jaguar Land Rover Bosses Get to Grips with Performance Management: Program Teaches Practical Skills for the Workplace," *Human Resource Management International Digest* (2011), volume 19, issue 4, pp. 10–12.

How to Handle Criticism and Defensive Employees

EVIDENCE-BASED HR

When a supervisor tells someone his or her performance is poor, the first reaction is often denial. Denial is a defence mechanism. By denying the fault, the person avoids having to question his or her own competence.

Understanding and dealing with defensiveness is an important appraisal skill that requires the following:[80]

1. Recognize that defensive behaviour is normal.

2. Never attack a person's defences. Do not try to "explain someone" to himself or herself by saying things like, "You know the real reason you are using that excuse is that you cannot bear to be blamed for anything." Instead, try to concentrate on the act itself ("sales are down") rather than on the person ("you are not selling enough").

3. Postpone action. Sometimes it is best to do nothing at all. People frequently react to sudden threats by instinctively hiding behind their "masks." Given sufficient time, however, a more rational reaction usually takes over.

4. Recognize human limitations. Do not expect to be able to solve every problem that comes up, especially the human ones. More importantly, remember that a supervisor should not try to be a psychologist. Offering employees understanding is one thing; trying to deal with deep psychological problems is another matter entirely.

Ensuring that the Formal Appraisal Discussion Leads to Improved Performance

It is important to clear up performance problems by setting goals and a schedule for achieving them. However, even if you have obtained agreement from your employees about the areas for performance improvement, they may or may not be satisfied with their appraisals. In one study, researchers found that whether or not employees expressed satisfaction with their formal appraisal discussions depended mostly on three factors: (1) not feeling threatened during the interview, (2) having an opportunity to present their ideas and feelings and to influence the course of the interview, and (3) having a helpful and constructive supervisor conduct the interview.[81]

Ultimately, the main objective of performance appraisals is to improve employee performance, keeping performance expectations clear and targeted on activities that build value for the organization. In dealing with employee performance issues, legal experts suggest that management follow seven steps to ensure that performance appraisals have the desired effect and are legally defensible:

1. Let the employee know that his or her performance is unacceptable and explain your minimum expectations.

2. Ensure that your expectations are reasonable.

3. Let employees know that warnings play a significant role in the process of establishing just cause; employees must be warned and told that discharge will result if they continue to fail to meet minimum standards.

4. Ensure that you take prompt corrective measures when required; failure to do so could lead to a finding that you condoned your employee's conduct.

5. Avoid sending mixed messages, such as a warning letter together with a "satisfactory" performance review.

6. Provide the employee with a reasonable amount of time to improve performance.

7. Be prepared to provide your employees with the necessary support to facilitate improvement.[82]

Hints : **TO ENSURE LEGAL COMPLIANCE**

How to Handle a Formal Written Warning

There will be times when an employee's performance is so poor that a formal written warning is required. Such written warnings serve two purposes: (1) They may serve to shake the employee out of his or her bad habits, and (2) they can help the manager defend his or her rating of the employee, both to his or her boss and (if needed) to a court or human rights commission.

Written warnings should identify the standards under which the employee is judged, make it clear that the employee was aware of the standard, specify any violation of the standard, indicate that the employee has had an opportunity to correct his or her behaviour, and specify what the employee must now do to correct his or her behaviour.

STEP 4: DETERMINE PERFORMANCE REWARDS/ CONSEQUENCES

Sometime after the performance review has taken place, the manager should use the salary planning guidelines to determine the appropriate rewards or consequences, comparing actual performance against the defined levels. Performance rewards are given through merit pay or extra payment such as a cash bonus. The two most important aspects used to determine the appropriate reward/consequence are achievement of goals and how the employee meets the defined standards. Further detail on compensation and rewards is provided in Chapters 11 and 12.

STEP 5: CAREER DEVELOPMENT DISCUSSION

During this discussion, the manager and employee discuss opportunities for development to strengthen or improve the employee's knowledge, skills, and abilities. Business needs must be balanced with the employee's preferences. These opportunities may focus on actions to boost performance in the area of current goals or to develop new knowledge aimed at a future career plan. Further detail on career planning and development is provided in Chapter 9.

LEGAL AND ETHICAL ISSUES IN PERFORMANCE MANAGEMENT

Ethics should be the bedrock of performance management. Accurate, well-documented performance records and performance appraisal feedback are necessary to avoid legal penalties and to defend against charges of bias based on grounds prohibited under human rights legislation, such as age, sex, and so on. As one commentator puts it,

> The overall objective of high-ethics performance reviews should be to provide an honest assessment of performance and to mutually develop a plan to improve the individual's effectiveness. That requires that we tell people where they stand and that we be straight with them.[83]

Ashland Canada Ltd., an automotive products marketing company in British Columbia, was fined $20 000 for dismissing a sales employee based on an "unacceptable" performance rating even though the employee had exceeded his sales goals. The British Columbia Supreme Court found that the performance rating was unwarranted and undeserved, and criticized Ashland's human resources department for a "reprehensible and substantial departure" from good faith dealings with the employee.[84] In another case, a worker in a government mental health facility was terminated for unsatisfactory performance after 10 years of work, with no performance evaluations and no disciplinary record. An adjudicator determined that the employer had failed to establish that the worker's job performance was unsatisfactory, that she had not been given a chance to improve, and that the employer did not have just cause for termination. The employer was required to pay compensation in lieu of reinstatement.[85]

Hints : **TO ENSURE LEGAL COMPLIANCE**

Guidelines for developing an effective appraisal process include the following:[86]

1. Conduct a job analysis to ascertain characteristics (such as "timely project completion") required for successful job performance. Use this information to create job performance standards.

2. Incorporate these characteristics into a rating instrument. (The professional literature recommends rating instruments that are tied to specific job behaviours, that is, BARS.)

3. Make sure that definitive performance standards are provided to all raters and ratees.

4. Use clearly defined individual dimensions of job performance (like "quantity" or "quality") rather than undefined, global measures of job performance (like "overall performance").

5. When using a graphic rating scale, avoid abstract trait names (such as "loyalty," "honesty") unless they can be defined in terms of observable behaviours.

6. Employ subjective supervisory ratings (essays, for instance) as only one component of the overall appraisal process.

7. Train supervisors to use the rating instrument properly. Give instructions on how to apply performance appraisal standards ("outstanding," "satisfactory," and so on) when making judgments. Ensure that subjective standards are not subject to bias.

8. Allow appraisers regular contact with the employee being evaluated.

9. Whenever possible, have more than one appraiser conduct the appraisal, and conduct all such appraisals independently. This process can help to cancel out individual errors and biases.

10. Use formal appeal mechanisms and a review of ratings by upper-level managers.

11. Document evaluations and reasons for any termination decision.

12. Where appropriate, provide corrective guidance to assist poor performers in improving their performance.

CHAPTER SUMMARY

1. The five steps in the performance management process are (1) defining performance expectations and goals, (2) providing ongoing feedback and coaching, (3) conducting performance appraisal and evaluation discussions, (4) determining performance rewards/consequences, and (5) conducting development and career opportunities discussions.

2. The performance management process cannot be separated from performance measurement.

Performance expectations must be legally defensible (correlated with job activities), clear, and measurable, including task-based and contextual performance elements. Although appraisals can be a difficult interpersonal task for managers, they cannot be eliminated. The key success factor is the quality of the performance appraisal dialogue between managers and employees. More training on how to effectively conduct these discussions is required.

3. There are a number of performance appraisal methods. Graphic rating scales are simple to use and facilitate comparison of employees, but the performance standards are often unclear and bias can be a problem. Alternation ranking is a simple method that avoids central tendency, but it can be unfair if most employees are doing well. Paired comparison ensures that all employees are compared with each other, but it can also be unfair if most employees are performing similarly. Narrative forms provide concrete information to the employee but are time-consuming and can be subjective. The forced distribution method ensures differentiation of performance ratings but can be demotivating for employees classified as less than average. The critical incident method is very specific about the employee's strengths and weaknesses and forces the supervisor to evaluate employees on an ongoing basis, but it makes it difficult to compare employees. BARS is very accurate, but is difficult and time-consuming to develop. MBO ties performance ratings to jointly agreed-upon performance objectives, but it is time-consuming to administer.

4. Appraisal problems to be aware of include unclear standards, the halo effect, central tendency, leniency or strictness, appraisal bias, the recency effect, and the similar-to-me bias.

5. The use of 360-degree feedback has grown rapidly. Performance information is collected from the individual being appraised, his or her supervisor, other employees reporting to the person being appraised, and customers. This approach supports the activities of performance appraisal, coaching, leadership development, succession planning, and employee rewards and recognition.

6. There are multiple types of formal appraisal discussion. When performance is unsatisfactory but correctable, the objective of the interview is to set out an action plan for correcting performance. For employees whose performance is satisfactory but for whom promotion is not possible, the objective of the interview is to maintain satisfactory performance. Finally, the satisfactory-and-promotable interview has the main objective of discussing the person's career plans and developing a specific action plan for the educational and professional development that the person needs to move on to the next job.

MyManagementLab

Study, practise, and explore real business situations with these helpful resources:

- **Interactive Lesson Presentations:** Work through interactive presentations and assessments to test your knowledge of management concepts.
- **PIA (Personal Inventory Assessments):** Enhance your ability to connect with key concepts through these engaging self-reflection assessments.
- **Study Plan:** Check your understanding of chapter concepts with self-study quizzes.
- **Videos:** Learn more about the management practices and strategies of real companies.
- **Simulations:** Practise decision-making in simulated management environments.

KEY TERMS

360-degree appraisal *(p. 239)*
alternation ranking method *(p. 229)*
appraisal bias *(p. 235)*
behaviourally anchored rating scale (BARS) *(p. 231)*
central tendency *(p. 235)*
contextual performance *(p. 225)*
critical incident method *(p. 230)*
electronic performance monitoring (EPM) *(p. 233)*
forced distribution method *(p. 229)*
formal appraisal discussion *(p. 241)*

graphic rating scale *(p. 228)*
halo effect *(p. 235)*
management by objectives (MBO) *(p. 232)*
paired comparison method *(p. 229)*
performance management *(p. 223)*
recency effect *(p. 236)*
similar-to-me bias *(p. 236)*
strictness/leniency *(p. 235)*
task performance *(p. 225)*
unclear performance standards *(p. 234)*

REVIEW AND DISCUSSION QUESTIONS

1. Describe the five steps in the performance appraisal process.

2. Explain how to ensure that the performance appraisal process is carried out ethically and without violating human rights laws.

3. Discuss the pros and cons of using different potential raters to appraise a person's performance.

4. What are the four key actions in conducting a formal appraisal discussion?

5. Explain how to handle a defensive employee in a formal appraisal discussion.

CRITICAL THINKING QUESTIONS

1. Assume you are presenting to an upper-year group of business students and one student asks the question, "Which performance appraisal system is the best?" How would you respond to that question?

2. How can the problem of inconsistency between managers who are rating workers be solved or at least diminished? Make two or more suggestions.

3. Given the difficulty with providing traditional performance standards for jobs that are quite flexible, what sort of "standards" could be developed for these flexible jobs?

4. Some HR professionals avoid using BARS given that it is so time-consuming to develop. How could the development steps be streamlined?

5. Do you agree with the use of forced distribution methods to rate employees? Why or why not?

6. How might a supervisor handle a situation in which negative appraisals in the past have caused an employee to undervalue his or her performance?

7. Discuss how employees might respond to the proposed implementation of electronic performance management systems, such as call monitoring, and so on. How might an organization deal with employees' reactions?

8. How might a supervisor deal with an extremely defensive yet productive member of his or her team in the event of having to deliver the "improvement portion" of the employee's performance appraisal? What techniques would the supervisor need to use to maximize the efficacy of the appraisal and reduce the defensibility of the employee?

EXPERIENTIAL EXERCISES

1. Just about every week, Donald Trump tells another "apprentice," "You're fired!" Review recent (or archived) episodes of Donald Trump's *Apprentice* show and answer this: What performance appraisal system did Mr. Trump use, and do you think it resulted in valid appraisals? What techniques discussed in this chapter did he seem to apply? How would you suggest he change his appraisal system to make it more effective?

2. Working individually or in groups, develop, over a week, a set of critical incidents covering the classroom performance of one of your instructors. Categorize the critical incidents to identify themes within activities that are viewed positively and negatively.

Expand on this identification by assessing how the one-week period may be affecting the results and what differences you would have expected had you selected a different week within the year to conduct the assessment.

3. Working in groups, using the NOC job description for cafeteria staff at a local university or college, develop a graphic rating scale with behavioural incidents for a job of a chef within the cafeteria. You may also want to consider your own experience when constructing your form.

Once you have drafted your form, exchange forms with another student or group. Critique and suggest possible improvements to the forms. Then with your revised form in hand, develop statements of behavioural incidents for two of your rating scale items to address the following circumstances:

- The employee has achieved outstanding results.
- The employee meets acceptable standards.

- The employee has performed very poorly in this aspect of the job.

Be prepared to share and critique statements developed by other students. Debrief the exercise as directed.

RUNNING CASE

Running Case: LearnInMotion.com

The Performance Appraisal

Jennifer and Pierre disagree over the importance of having performance appraisals. Pierre says it's quite clear whether any particular LearnInMotion.com employee is doing his or her job. It's obvious, for instance, if the salespeople are selling, if the web designer is designing, if the web surfer is surfing, and if the content management people are managing to get the customers' content up on the website in a timely fashion. Pierre's position, like that of many small-business managers, is that "we have 1000 higher-priority things to attend to," such as boosting sales and creating the calendar. And in any case, he says, the employees already get plenty of day-to-day feedback from him or Jennifer regarding what they're doing right and what they're doing wrong.

This informal feedback notwithstanding, Jennifer believes that a more formal appraisal approach is required.

For one thing, they're approaching the end of the 90-day "introductory" period for many of these employees, and the owners need to make decisions about whether they should go or stay. And from a practical point of view, Jennifer simply believes that sitting down and providing formal, written feedback is more likely to reinforce what employees are doing right and get them to modify things they may be doing wrong. "Maybe this is one reason we're not getting enough sales," she says. They've been debating this for about an hour. Now, they want you, their management consultant, to advise them on what to do.

QUESTIONS

1 What performance appraisal problems will LearnInMotion.com encounter if they continue on the course of not using formalized performance appraisals?
2 What guidelines would you recommend to Pierre and Jennifer for developing an effective appraisal system?

CASE INCIDENT

A Performance Dilemma

Brenda Jackson, a newly hired human resources manager, has been on the job for approximately six months and is in the process of trying to create a new performance appraisal system for her employer, Starbrite Manufacturing Systems. Brenda has reviewed the company's current employee files and has noted that no formal performance appraisals exist in the files. This situation is of great concern to Brenda.

In response, Brenda schedules a meeting with the CEO to discuss her concerns and to gain his support to ultimately recommend the designing of a new performance appraisal system. After the meeting, Brenda is happy at gaining the CEO's approval but starts to feel overwhelmed

at the large task she has in pulling the new performance management system together. This is where you come in to help Brenda by answering the following questions.

QUESTIONS

1 Discuss the performance management process highlighted in the chapter and how it will aid Brenda in creating this new performance appraisal system for her employer.
2 Discuss and suggest the type of appraisal methods that Brenda should recommend the company use.
3 Discuss the rating errors that Brenda must be aware of and how these can be avoided.

CHAPTER
11

graja/Shutterstock

Strategic Pay Plans

LEARNING OUTCOMES

AFTER STUDYING THIS CHAPTER, YOU SHOULD BE ABLE TO

EXPLAIN the strategic importance of total rewards.

DESCRIBE four basic considerations an organization needs to make when determining compensation decisions.

EXPLAIN in detail each of the three stages in establishing pay rates.

DISCUSS competency-based pay.

DESCRIBE the elements of compensation for special positions: executives, managers, and professionals.

DEFINE pay equity and **EXPLAIN** its importance today.

REQUIRED HR COMPETENCIES

10200: Develop an understanding of the application of governance principles and methods by keeping current with the leading practices to contribute to and implement approved strategy.

20300: Adhere to legal requirements as they pertain to human resources policies and practices to promote organizational values and manage risk.

20600: Promote an evidence-based approach to the development of human resources policies and practices using current professional resources to provide a sound basis for human resources decision-making.

60100: Create a total rewards structure that encompasses compensation, pensions, benefits, and perquisites to maintain consistency, fairness, and organizational competitiveness, comply with legal requirements, and encourage desired behaviour.

60200: Implement the total rewards structure using appropriate job evaluation systems and market comparisons to ensure consistency, fairness, and organizational competitiveness, compliance with legal requirements, performance, and desired behaviour.

90100: Make informed business decisions using financial and operating information to align human resources with business strategy.

THE STRATEGIC IMPORTANCE OF TOTAL EMPLOYMENT REWARDS

HR Competency

60100

employee compensation All forms of pay or rewards going to employees and arising from their employment.

direct financial payments Pay in the form of wages, salaries, incentives, commissions, and bonuses.

indirect financial payments Pay in the form of financial benefits such as insurance.

HR Competency

90100

HR Competency

10200

EVIDENCE-BASED HR

Employee compensation includes all forms of pay going to employees and arising from their employment. It has two main components, **direct financial payments** (wages, salaries, incentives, commissions, and bonuses) and **indirect financial payments** (financial benefits like employer-paid insurance and vacations).

In turn, employers can make direct financial payments to employees based on increments of time or based on performance. Time-based pay still predominates. Blue-collar and clerical workers receive hourly or daily wages, for instance. Others, like managers or web designers, tend to be salaried and paid weekly, monthly, or yearly.

The second direct payment option is to pay for performance. For example, piecework ties compensation to the amount of production (or number of "pieces") the worker turns out. Sales commissions tie pay to sales. Many employers' pay plans combine time-based pay and incentives.

In this chapter, we explain how to formulate plans for paying employees a time-based wage or salary. Subsequent chapters cover performance-based financial incentives and bonuses (Chapter 12) and employee benefits (Chapter 13).

Several factors should influence any pay plan's design. These include strategic policy considerations, as well as equity, legal, and union considerations.

Aligning Total Rewards with Strategy

The compensation plan should first advance the firm's strategic aims—management should produce an *aligned reward strategy*. This means creating a compensation package (including wages, incentives, and benefits) that produces the employee behaviours the firm needs to achieve its competitive strategy.[1]

We will see that many employers formulate a total rewards strategy to support their broader strategic aims. *Total rewards* encompass the traditional pay, incentives, and benefits, but also things such as more challenging jobs (job design), career development, and recognition programs.

Table 11.1 lists illustrative questions to ask when crafting a strategy-oriented pay policy.

The world's most admired companies excel at taking a total rewards approach.

Impact of Rewards

The purposes of rewards are to attract, retain, motivate, and engage employees. *Engagement* refers to a positive emotional connection to the employer and a clear understanding of the strategic significance of the job, which results in discretionary effort on the part of the employee. A recent study by Towers Watson found that, for Canadians, competitive base pay was the number one factor in attracting employees to

TABLE 11.1 Do Our Compensation Policies Support Our Strategic Aims?

- What are our strategic aims?
- What employee behaviours and skills do we need to achieve our strategic aims?
- What compensation policies and practices—salary, incentive plans, and benefits—will help to produce the employee behaviours we need to achieve our strategic aims?

an organization, having excellent career opportunities was the most important factor in retaining employees, and senior management's interest in employee well-being was the top factor influencing employee engagement.[2] Similarly, a study of 446 organizations across Canada by Western Compensation and Benefits Consultants found that the most effective attraction strategy was offering competitive base salaries, and the top reason for turnover among employees was dissatisfaction with cash compensation. Opportunities for advancement, work–life balance programs, and competitive benefits programs are also used by over 70 percent of Canadian companies to attract talent.[3]

HR Competency

60100

BASIC CONSIDERATIONS IN DETERMINING PAY RATES

Henry was suspicious of the job offer right from the beginning.

cartoonresource/Fotolia

HR Competency

20300

Hints | TO ENSURE LEGAL
COMPLIANCE

pay equity Providing equal pay to male-dominated job classes and female-dominated job classes of equal value to the employer.

Four basic considerations influence the formulation of any pay plan: legal requirements, union issues, compensation policy, and equity.

Legal Considerations in Compensation

All of the 14 jurisdictions regulating employment in Canada (ten provinces, three territories, and the federal jurisdiction) have laws regulating compensation. Thus, HR managers must pay careful attention to which legislation affects their employees. Further, these laws are constantly changing and require continual monitoring to ensure compliance. Legislation affecting compensation administration is discussed below.

Employment/Labour Standards Acts (Canada Labour Code)

Employment/labour laws set minimum standards regarding pay, including minimum wage, maximum hours of work, overtime pay, paid vacation, paid statutory holidays, termination pay, record keeping of pay information, and more. There are variations in some of the minimum standards for students, trainees, domestics, nannies, seasonal agricultural workers, and others. Executive, administrative, and professional employees are generally exempt from the overtime pay requirements.

Pay Equity Acts

The purpose of **pay equity** legislation is to redress systemic gender discrimination in compensation for work performed by employees in female-dominated job classes. Pay equity requires that equal wages be paid for jobs of equal value or "worth" to the employer, as determined by gender-neutral (i.e., free of any bias based on gender) job evaluation techniques. Although such factors as differences in hours worked, experience levels, education levels, and level of unionization contribute to the wage gap, systemic discrimination is also present.[4] More information about pay equity is provided later in the chapter. The HR by the Numbers box highlights the impact of using different perspectives to identify how meaningful differences in pay can be overall.

HR by the Numbers

Have We Achieved Pay Equity Yet?[5]

$0.7–2 m estimated per-woman lifetime-difference financial loss (depending on education) due to pay inequities

Sept. 17 71 percent of the way through the calendar year, marking the day women in Canada start working for free, according to the Equal Pay Coalition

16% amount young women earn less than males (among university graduates)

71 cents women earn for each dollar a man earns in Ontario

27% amount young women earn less than males (among high school graduates)

HR Competency
20300

HR Competency
20300

Frank Gunn/The Canadian Press

Work stoppages may reflect employee dissatisfaction with pay plans and other forms of compensation, such as pensions.

EVIDENCE-BASED HR

Workers Compensation Laws

In addition, each jurisdiction has its own *workers' compensation laws*. The objective of these laws is to provide a prompt, sure, and reasonable income to victims of work-related accidents and illnesses. The Employment Insurance Act is aimed at protecting Canadian workers from total economic destitution in the event of employment termination that is beyond their control. Employers and employees both contribute to the benefits provided by this act. This act also provides up to 45 weeks of compensation for workers unemployed through no fault of their own (depending on the unemployment rate in the claimant's region and other factors). Maternity leave, parental leave, and compassionate care leave benefits are also provided under the Employment Insurance Act.[6]

Human Rights Acts

All jurisdictions have enacted human rights laws to protect Canadians from discrimination on a number of grounds in employment and other areas. These grounds differ somewhat among jurisdictions, but most prohibit discrimination in employment (such as in compensation and promotion) on the basis of age, sex, colour, race/ancestry/place of origin, religion/creed, marital/family status, and physical or mental disability.

Canada/Quebec Pension Plan

All employees and their employers must contribute to the Canada/Quebec Pension Plan throughout the employee's working life. Pension benefits based on the employee's average earnings are paid during retirement. Details of these and other benefits are provided in Chapter 13.

Union Influences on Compensation Decisions

Unions and labour relations laws also influence how pay plans are designed. Historically, wage rates have been the main issue in collective bargaining. However, other issues—including time off with pay, income security (for those in industries with periodic layoffs), cost-of-living adjustments, and pensions—are also important.[7]

The Canada Industrial Relations Board and similar bodies in each province and territory oversee employer practices and ensure that employees are treated in accordance with their legal rights. Their decisions underscore the need to involve union officials in developing the compensation package.

Union Attitudes toward Compensation Decisions

Several classic studies shed light on union attitudes toward compensation plans and on commonly held union fears.[8]

Many union leaders fear that any system used to evaluate the worth of a job can become a tool for management malpractice. They tend to believe that no one can judge the relative value of jobs better than the workers themselves. In addition, they believe that management's usual method of using several compensable factors (like "degree of responsibility") to evaluate and rank the worth of jobs can be a manipulative device for restricting or lowering the pay of workers. One implication is that the best way in which to gain the co-operation of union members in evaluating the worth of jobs is to get their active involvement in this process and in assigning fair rates of pay to these jobs. However, management has to ensure that its prerogatives—such as the right to use the appropriate job evaluation technique to assess the relative worth of jobs—are not surrendered.

HR Competency

20600

Compensation Policies

An employer's compensation policies provide important guidelines regarding the wages and benefits that it pays. A number of factors are taken into account when developing a compensation policy, including whether the organization wants to be a leader or a follower regarding pay, business strategy, and the cost of different types of compensation. Important policies include the basis for salary increases, promotion and demotion policies, overtime pay policy, and policies regarding probationary pay and leaves for military service, jury duty, and holidays. Compensation policies are usually written by the HR or compensation manager in conjunction with senior management.[9]

Equity and Its Impact on Pay Rates

In studies at Emory University, researchers investigated how capuchin monkeys reacted to inequitable pay. Some monkeys got sweet grapes in return for trading pebbles; others got cucumber slices. If a monkey receiving a cucumber slice saw a neighbour get grapes, it slammed down the pebble or refused to eat.[10] The moral may be that even lower primates demand fair treatment in pay.

Equity Theory of Motivation

equity theory a theory suggesting that people are motivated to maintain a balance between what they perceive as their contributions and their rewards.

Among humans too, *the* **equity theory** *of motivation* postulates that people are motivated to maintain a balance between what they perceive as their contributions and their rewards. Equity theory states that if a person perceives an inequity, a tension or drive will develop that motivates him or her to reduce the tension and perceived inequity. Research tends to support equity theory, particularly as it applies to those underpaid.[11] For example, in one study, turnover of retail buyers was significantly lower when the buyers perceived fair treatment in rewards and in how employers allocated rewards.[12] Over-paying can sometimes backfire too, perhaps "due to feelings of guilt or discomfort."[13]

In compensation, one can address *external, internal, individual,* and *procedural* equity.[14]

HR Competency

60200

external equity An employee perception of pay as fair given the pay rates in other organizations.

internal equity An employee perception of pay as fair given the pay rates of others in the organization.

- *External equity* refers to how a job's pay rate in one company compares to the job's pay rate in other companies.

- *Internal equity* refers to how fair the job's pay rate is when compared to other jobs within the same company (for instance, is the sales manager's pay fair, when compared to what the production manager earns?).

- *Individual equity* refers to the fairness of an individual's pay as compared with what his or her co-workers are earning for the same or very similar jobs within the company, based on each person's performance.

- *Procedural equity* refers to the "perceived fairness of the processes and procedures used to make decisions regarding the allocation of pay."[15]

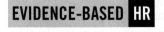

HR IN THE NEWS

Whole Foods Adds Transparency via Salary Disclosure

Employees are often curious regarding how much they get paid relative to co-workers, but it's often considered taboo to ask a colleague about their compensation levels. Curious employees at Whole Foods can now access a Wage Disclosure Report (onsite access only) providing information as to how much colleagues are paid.

There is a potential that this level of disclosure could lead to tension in the workplace, but Whole Foods has found that the disclosure helps promote conversations between employees and management regarding what contributions the individual is making, motivating employees to perform better or commit to a career plan in the organization.[16]

Addressing Equity Issues

Managers use various means to address such equity issues. For example, they use salary surveys (surveys of what other employers are paying) to monitor and maintain external equity. They use job analysis and comparisons of each job ("job evaluation") to maintain internal equity. They use performance appraisal and incentive pay to maintain individual equity. And they use communications, grievance mechanisms, and employees' participation to help ensure that employees view the pay process as procedurally fair. Some firms administer surveys to monitor employees' pay satisfaction. Questions typically include, "How satisfied are you with your pay?" and "What factors do you believe are used when your pay is determined?"[17]

To head off discussions that might prompt feelings of internal inequity, some firms maintain strict secrecy over pay rates, with mixed results.[18] However, "open pay" policies can backfire. In one firm, employees vigorously opposed paying a high salary to a great candidate unless everyone else's pay went up too, for instance.[19] And for external equity, online pay sites like Salary.com make it easy to see what one could earn elsewhere. Whole Foods has taken a unique approach to managing perceptions of equity, as highlighted in the HR in the News box.

ESTABLISHING PAY RATES

There are a number of steps required to establish pay rates. First, conduct a job evaluation to determine what factors will be compensated. This often includes the classification/grading method or the point method. Next, the company should conduct the wage/salary survey. There are multiple methods to conduct this, as outlined below. Last, job evaluation and salary information is combined to determine pay rates for each job.

Stage 1: Preparing for Job Evaluation

job evaluation A systematic comparison to determine the relative worth of jobs within a firm.

benchmark job A job that is critical to the firm's operations or that is commonly found in other organizations.

Job evaluation is aimed at determining a job's relative worth. It is a formal and systematic comparison of jobs within a firm to determine the worth of one job relative to another, and it eventually results in a job hierarchy. The basic procedure is to compare the content of jobs in relation to one another, for example, in terms of their effort, responsibility, skills, and working conditions. Job evaluation usually focuses on **benchmark jobs** that are critical to the firm's operations or that are commonly found in other organizations. Rohm and Haas, a multinational chemical company, ensures that its benchmark jobs represent all the various business units and departments in the organization, are drawn from all levels of the organization, have large numbers of incumbents, are clear and well known in the industry, are stable and easily understood in terms of purpose and work content, and are visible and well understood by all employees.[20] The resulting evaluations of benchmark jobs are used as reference points around which other jobs are arranged in order of relative worth.

Compensable Factors

compensable factor A fundamental, compensable element of a job, such as skill, effort, responsibility, and working conditions.

Jobs can be compared intuitively by deciding that one job is "more important" or "of greater value or worth" than another without digging any deeper into why in terms of specific job-related factors. This approach, called the *ranking method*, is hard to defend to employees or others who may not agree with the resulting job hierarchy. As an alternative, jobs can be compared by focusing on certain basic factors that they have in common. In compensation management, these basic factors are called **compensable factors**. They are the factors that determine the definition of job content, establish how the jobs compare with one another, and set the compensation paid for each job.

Some employers develop their own compensable factors. However, most use factors that have been popularized by packaged job evaluation systems or by legislation. For example, most of the pay equity acts in Canada focus on four compensable factors: *skill, effort, responsibility*, and *working conditions*. As another example, the job evaluation method popularized by the Hay Group consulting firm focuses on four compensable factors: *know-how, problem solving, accountability*, and *working conditions*. Often, different job evaluation systems are used for different departments, employee groups, or business units. Identifying compensable factors plays a pivotal role in job evaluation. All jobs in each employee group, department, or business unit are evaluated *using the same compensable factors*. An employer thus evaluates the same elemental components for each job within the work group and is then better able to compare jobs—for example, in terms of the degree of skill, effort, responsibility, and working conditions present in each.[21]

Job Evaluation Committee

Job evaluation is largely a judgmental process and one that demands close co-operation among supervisors, compensation specialists, and the employees and their union representatives. The main steps involved include

The job evaluation committee typically includes several employees and has the important task of evaluating the worth of each job using compensable factors.

Pressmaster/Shutterstock

identifying the need for the program, getting cooperation, and choosing an evaluation committee; the committee then carries out the actual job evaluation.[22]

A **job evaluation committee** is established to ensure the representation of the points of view of various people who are familiar with the jobs in question, each of whom may have a different perspective regarding the nature of the jobs. The committee may include employees, HR staff, managers, and union representatives.

The evaluation committee first identifies 10 or 15 key benchmark jobs. These will be the first jobs to be evaluated and will serve as the anchors or benchmarks against which the relative importance or value of all other jobs can be compared. Then the committee turns to its most important function—actually evaluating the worth of each job. For this, the committee will probably use either the job classification method or the point method.

Job Evaluation Methods

There are a number of job evaluation methods that can be applied to compensation decisions. The most popular are classification methods and the point method, both of which are discussed below.

Classification Method

The **classification/grading method** involves categorizing jobs into groups. The groups are called **classes** if they contain similar jobs, or **grades** if they contain jobs that are similar in difficulty but otherwise different.

This method is widely used in the public sector. The federal government's UT (University Teaching) job group is an example of a job class because it contains similar jobs involving teaching, research, and consulting. Conversely, the AV (Audit, Commerce, and Purchasing) job group is an example of a job grade because it contains dissimilar jobs, involving auditing, economic development consulting, and purchasing.

There are several ways in which to categorize jobs. One is to draw up class descriptions (similar to job descriptions) and place jobs into classes based on their correspondence to these descriptions. Another is to draw up a set of classifying rules for each class (for instance, the amount of independent judgment, skill, physical effort, and so on that the class of jobs requires). Then the jobs are categorized according to these rules.

The usual procedure is to choose compensable factors and then develop class or grade descriptions that describe each class in terms of the amount or level of compensable factor(s) in jobs. The federal government's classification system, for example, employs different compensable factors for various job groups. Based on these compensable factors, a **grade/group description** is written. Then, the evaluation committee reviews all job descriptions and slots each job into its appropriate class or grade.

The job classification method has several advantages. The main one is that most employers usually end up classifying jobs anyway, regardless of the job evaluation method that they use. They do this to avoid having to work with and develop pay rates for an unmanageable number of jobs; with the job classification method, all jobs are already grouped into several classes. The disadvantages are that it is difficult to write the class or grade descriptions and that considerable judgment is required in applying them. Yet many employers use this method with success.

Point Method

The **point method** is widely used in the private sector and requires identifying several compensable factors. The extent or degree to which each factor is present in the job is evaluated, a corresponding number of points is assigned for each factor, and the number of points for each factor is summed to arrive at an overall point value for the job.

job evaluation committee
A diverse group (including employees, HR staff, managers, and union representatives) established to ensure the fair and comprehensive representation of the nature and requirements of the jobs in question.

classification/grading method A method for categorizing jobs into groups.

classes Groups of jobs based on a set of rules for each class, such as amount of independent judgment, skill, physical effort, and so forth. Classes usually contain similar jobs—such as all secretaries.

grades Groups of jobs based on a set of rules for each grade, where jobs are similar in difficulty but otherwise different. Grades often contain dissimilar jobs, such as secretaries, mechanics, and firefighters.

EVIDENCE-BASED HR

HR Competency
20600

grade/group description A written description of the level of compensable factors required by jobs in each grade; used to combine similar jobs into grades or classes.

point method A job evaluation method in which a number of compensable factors are identified, the degree to which each of these factors is present in the job is determined, and an overall point value is calculated.

FIGURE 11.1 Commonly Used Factors and Sub-Factors in the Point System

Factor	Sub-Factors
Skill	Education and Experience
	Interpersonal Skill
Effort	Physical Effort
	Mental Effort
Responsibility	Supervision of Others
	Planning
Working Conditions	Physical Environment
	Travel

To use the point method, it is necessary to have current job descriptions and job specifications based on a thorough job analysis. The foundation of the job evaluation plan is a number of compensable factors that must be agreed upon. In Canada, four compensable factors are commonly used: skill, effort, responsibility, and working conditions. These factors are general and can mean different things in different workplaces. Therefore sub-factors of each one may also be determined to clarify the specific meaning of each factor, as shown below.

Each sub-factor must be carefully defined to ensure that the evaluation committee members will apply them consistently. An example of a sub-factor definition is presented in **Figure 11.1**.

Point systems involve a quantitative technique that is easily explained to and used by employees. However, it can be difficult and time-consuming to develop a point plan and to effectively train the job evaluation user group. This is one reason why many organizations adopt a point plan developed and marketed by a consulting firm. In fact, the availability of a number of ready-made plans probably accounts in part for the wide use of point plans in job evaluation.

If the committee assigned pay rates to each individual job, it would be difficult to administer since there might be different pay rates for hundreds or even thousands of jobs. Even in smaller organizations there is a tendency to try to simplify wage and salary structures as much as possible. Therefore, the committee will probably want to group similar jobs (in terms of their number of points, for instance) into grades for pay purposes. Then, instead of having to deal with pay rates for hundreds of jobs, it might only have to focus on pay rates for 10 or 12 groupings of jobs.

pay grade Comprises jobs of approximately equal value.

A **pay grade** comprises jobs of approximately equal value or importance, as determined by job evaluation. If the point method was used, the pay grade consists of jobs falling within a range of points. If the classification system was used, then the jobs are already categorized into classes or grades. The next stage is to obtain information on market pay rates by conducting a wage/salary survey.

Stage 2: Conduct a Wage/Salary Survey

wage/salary survey A survey aimed at determining prevailing wage rates.

Compensation or **wage/salary surveys** play a central role in determining pay rates for jobs.[23] An employer may use wage/salary surveys in three ways. First, survey data are used to determine pay rates for benchmark jobs that serve as reference points or anchors for the employer's pay scale, meaning that other jobs are then paid based on their relative worth compared to the benchmark jobs. Second, an increasing number of positions are paid solely based on the marketplace (rather than relative to the firm's benchmark jobs).[24]

As a result of the current shift away from long-term employment, compensation is increasingly shaped by market wages and less by how it fits into the hierarchy of jobs in one organization. Finally, surveys also collect data on employee benefits, work–life programs, pay-for-performance plans, recognition plans, and so on to provide a basis on which to make decisions regarding other types of rewards.

Formal and Informal Surveys by the Employer

Most employers rely heavily on formal or informal surveys of what other employers are paying.[25] Informal telephone surveys are good for collecting data on a relatively small number of easily identified and quickly recognized jobs, such as when a bank's HR director wants to determine the salary at which a newly opened customer service representative's job should be advertised. Informal discussions among human resources specialists at regular professional association meetings are other occasions for informal salary surveys. Some employers use formal questionnaire surveys to collect compensation information from other employers, including things like number of employees, overtime policies, starting salaries, and paid vacations.

Commercial, Professional, and Government Salary Surveys

Many employers also rely on surveys published by various commercial firms, professional associations, or government agencies. For example, Statistics Canada provides monthly data on earnings by geographic area, by industry, and by occupation.

Table 11.2 provides an example of earnings data by industry and occupation, which can be used to establish pay, determine average changes, benchmark compensation, and so on. Statistics Canada also makes more detailed data regarding industry-specific benchmarks readily available.

The Toronto Board of Trade conducts five compensation surveys annually, covering executive; management; professional, supervisory, and sales; information technology; and administrative and support positions. The surveys include information from small, medium, and large employers in the Greater Toronto Area. A separate survey of employee benefits and employment practices is also conducted.

Private consulting or executive recruiting companies, such as Towers Watson, Mercer, and Hewitt Associates, annually publish data covering the compensation of senior and middle managers and members of boards of directors. Professional organizations, such as the Certified General

"According to these advanced formulas ... we are way underpaid."

cartoonresource/Fotolia

TABLE 11.2 Average Weekly Earnings by Industry 2012–2013 in Canada (including overtime)

	April 2012	April 2013	April 2012 to April 2013
Industry	$	$	% change
Industrial aggregate excluding unclassified businesses	890.51	910.25	+2.2
Goods-producing industries	1,140.42	1,156.75	+1.4
Service-producing industries	833.32	855.28	+2.6

Source: Statistics Canada, *Earnings, average weekly, by industry, monthly*, CANSIM table 281-0028.

Accountants and Professional Engineers Ontario, conduct surveys of compensation practices among members of their associations.

For some jobs, salaries are determined directly based on formal or informal salary surveys like those available from Monster.ca. In most cases, though, surveys are used to price benchmark jobs around which other jobs are then slotted based on their relative worth as determined through job evaluation.

Salary Survey Interpretation and Use

Data from the Hay Group consulting firm indicate that large organizations participate in an average of 11 compensation surveys and use information from seven of them to administer their own compensation practices.[26]

Upward bias can be a problem regardless of the type of compensation survey used. At least one compensation expert argues that the way in which most surveys are constructed, interpreted, and used leads almost invariably to a situation in which firms set higher wages than they otherwise might. For example, "companies like to compare themselves against well-regarded, high-paying, and high-performing companies," so baseline salaries tend to be biased upward. Similarly, "companies that sponsor surveys often do so with an implicit (albeit unstated) objective: to show the company [is] paying either competitively or somewhat below the market, so as to justify positive corrective action." For these and similar reasons, it is probably wise to review survey results with a skeptical eye and to acknowledge that upward bias may exist and should perhaps be considered when making decisions.[27]

Whatever the source of the survey, the data must be carefully assessed for accuracy before they are used to make compensation decisions. Problems can arise when the organization's job descriptions only partially match the descriptions contained in the survey, the survey data were collected several months before the time of use, the participants in the survey do not represent the appropriate labour market for the jobs being matched, and so on.[28]

Now all the information necessary to move to the next stage—determining pay for jobs—has been obtained.

Stage 3: Combine the Job Evaluation and Salary Survey Information to Determine Pay for Jobs

The final stage is to assign pay rates to each pay grade. (Of course, if jobs were not grouped into pay grades, individual pay rates would have to be assigned to each job.) Assigning pay rates to each pay grade (or to each job) is usually accomplished with a **wage curve**.

wage curve A graphic description of the relationship between the value of the job and the average wage paid for this job.

The wage curve graphically depicts the market pay rates currently being paid for jobs in each pay grade, relative to the job evaluation points for each job or grade. An example of a wage curve is presented in **Figure 11.2**. Note that pay rates are shown on the vertical axis, while the points for pay grades are shown along the horizontal axis.

The purpose of the wage curve is to show the relationship between the value of the job as determined by one of the job evaluation methods and the current average pay rates for each job or grade.

There are several steps in determining pay for pay grades using a wage curve. First, find the average pay for each pay grade, since each of the pay grades consists of several jobs. Next, plot the pay rates for each pay grade, as was done in

An Ethical Dilemma

What should employers do when there is a shortage of a certain type of skill and they cannot attract any workers unless they pay a market rate above the maximum of their salary range for that job? How should other jobs (without a skills shortage) in the same company in the same salary range be paid?

FIGURE 11.2 Plotting a Wage Curve

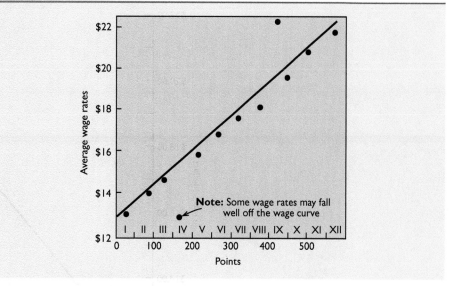

Note: The average market pay rate for jobs in each grade (Grade I, Grade II, Grade III, etc.) is plotted, and the wage curve is fitted to the resulting points.

Figure 11.2. Then fit a line (called a "wage line") through the points just plotted. This can be done either freehand or by using a statistical method known as regression analysis. Finally, determine pay for jobs. Wages along the wage line are the target wages or salary rates for the jobs in each pay grade.

Developing Rate Ranges

pay ranges A series of steps or levels within a pay grade, usually based on years of service.

Most employers do not just pay one rate for all jobs in a particular pay grade. Instead, they develop **pay ranges** for each grade so that there might, for instance, be 10 levels or "steps" and 10 corresponding pay rates within each pay grade. One way to depict the rate ranges for each grade is with a wage structure, as in **Figure 11.3**. The wage structure graphically depicts the range of pay rates (in this case, per hour) to be paid for each grade.

The use of pay ranges for each pay grade has several benefits. First, the employer can take a more flexible stance with respect to the labour market; for example, some flexibility makes it easier to attract experienced, higher-paid employees into a pay grade where the starting salary for the lowest step may be too low to attract such experienced people. Pay ranges also allow employers to provide for performance differences between employees within the same grade or between those with differing seniority. As in Figure 11.3, most employers structure their pay ranges to overlap a bit so that an employee with greater experience or seniority may earn more than an entry-level person in the next higher pay grade. Pay rates generally vary based on compensable factors, as highlighted in the Expert Opinion box. The expert opinion extends beyond income disparity to also include a discussion on the challenges associated with young workers.

Broadbanding

broadbanding Reducing the number of salary grades and ranges into just a few wide levels or "bands," each of which then contains a relatively wide range of jobs and salary levels.

The trend today is for employers to reduce their salary grades and ranges from 10 or more down to three to five, a process that is called **broadbanding**. Broadbanding means combining salary grades and ranges into just a few wide levels or "bands," each of which then contains a relatively wide range of jobs and salary levels (see **Figure 11.4**).

FIGURE 11.3   Wage Structure

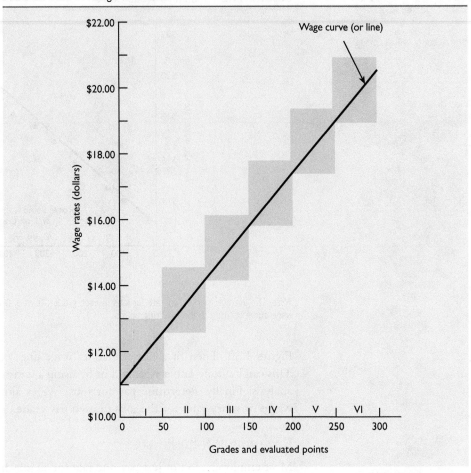

FIGURE 11.4   Broadbanding

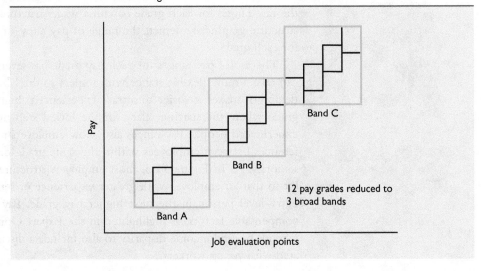

Broadbanding a pay system involves several steps. First, the number of bands is decided on and each is assigned a salary range. The bands usually have wide salary ranges and also overlap substantially. As a result, there is much more flexibility to move employees from job to job within bands and less need to "promote" them to new grades just to give them higher salaries.

academic **viewpoint**

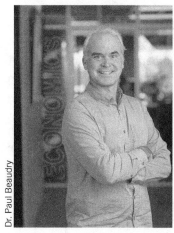

Dr. Paul Beaudry

Identification: Dr. Paul Beaudry (PhD), Canada Research Chair in Macroeconomics, Fellow at Bank of Canada and the Royal Society of Canada, Research Associate at the National Bureau of Economics Research

Affiliation: School of Economics, University of British Columbia

Focus: Macroeconomic effects (inflation, business cycles, financial markets, technology change, globalization), as well as determinants of aggregate employment and wages

1. **Over the last two decades, how has labour income distribution changed in Canada?**

There is a marked change in labour income distribution over the last two decades. Generally, skill level is rewarded with associated income levels; jobs requiring low skill levels offer low pay, while jobs requiring high skill levels offer high pay. The spread between high and low earners has increased, with a decrease in income levels of low wage earners as a major catalyst to this spread. This is a critical issue in eastern Canada. In comparison, with the recent boom in Alberta, less educated workers are still doing well, so concerns regarding income disparity and returns associated with education are less prominent in some parts of central and western Canada.

Key drivers for low income are jobs that have high repetition, routine tasks, and some level of mechanization. Due to globalization, some low-skill, low-income jobs are replaced by machine, while others are outsourced to emerging countries. Comparatively, high-skilled (therefore high-earning) jobs are somewhat more protected from outsourcing and automation.

2. **Your recent research finds that the wage difference between men and women shrunk in the 1980s and 1990s. What is the explanation for this?**

Aligned with my response to question 1, typically jobs that were at risk since 2000 were blue-collar, manufacturing jobs; traditionally jobs with low female representation. Technology has been an equalizing factor. With automation, cognitive abilities and technological skill levels are the primary considerations in employment, rather than physical ability. In recent years, women have been doing better than men on acquiring numeracy skills and analytical skills in post-secondary education.

3. **Evidence shows that young workers often have a low level of personal savings. How can this information be used to drive management decisions about employee compensation?**

The costs of education, lifestyle decisions, and income levels all play a role in the financial pressures that young people feel.

Pensions are a big issue. Young workers need to reduce debt levels, but also want to save. An employer can share the responsibility of educated young workers on the benefits and potentials associated with pension benefits and other longer term investments. These employees need information regarding investments and taxation.

Universities are trying to build joint equity schemes to help new professors buy homes. For example, the cost of housing in Vancouver rose 12 percent from 2012 to 2013, with the average detached home selling for $929 500 in Jan 2014.[29] Employers in high-cost cities might consider a similar agreement to help young workers secure homes.

Source: Reprinted by permission from Dr. Paul Beaudry.

Broadbanding's basic advantage is that it injects greater flexibility into employee compensation.[30] The new, broad salary bands can include both supervisors and those reporting to them. Broadbanding also facilitates less specialized, boundaryless jobs and organizations. Less specialization and more participation in cross-departmental processes generally mean enlarged duties or capabilities and more possibilities for alternative career tracks.

Correcting Out-of-Line Rates

The actual wage rate for a job may fall well off the wage line or well outside the rate range for its grade. This means that the average pay for that job is currently too high or too low relative to other jobs in the firm. If a point falls well below the line, a pay raise for the job may be required. If the plot falls well above the wage line, pay cuts or a pay freeze may be required.

Underpaid employees should have their wages raised to the minimum of the rate range for their pay grade, assuming that the organization wants to retain the employees and has the funds. This can be done either immediately or in one or two steps.

red circle pay rate A rate of pay that is above the pay range maximum.

Pay rates of overpaid employees are often called **red circle pay rates**, and there are several ways to cope with this problem. One is to freeze the rate paid to employees in this grade until general salary increases bring the other jobs into line with it. A second alternative is to transfer or promote some or all of the employees involved to jobs for which they can legitimately be paid their current pay rates. The third alternative is to freeze the rate for six months, during which time attempts are made to transfer or promote the overpaid employees. If this is not possible, then the rate at which these employees are paid is cut to the maximum in the pay range for their grade. The Centre for Addiction and Mental Health engages in regular salary surveys, as detailed in the Expert Opinion box.

expert opinion
industry viewpoint

Adam Hewitt

Identification: Mr. Adam Hewitt, Manager, Total Rewards and HRIS at Centre for Addiction and Mental Health (CAMH)

Focus: Managing a team of Compensation, Pension, Benefits, Attendance Support and HRIS Specialists, ensuring that customer service and accurate recommendations and advice is provided to all CAMH

1. **CAMH conducts surveys regularly to determine the competitiveness of the pay and benefits package offered. Why is this a priority for the company?**

   The aging population is driving both increasing labour demand (due to an increased demand for services) and decreasing labour supply (due to projected retirements). Health care is a tight knit community of employers and employees, so we have to maintain compensation at a competitive level in order to attract and retain talent. For some positions, our competitors are outside of the industry (e.g., financial or IT positions).

   We have a three-pronged approach to benchmarking. We use the Ontario Hospital Association (OHA) survey of 90–95 Ontario hospitals, with information for compensation ranging from management positions to front-line worker comparators, by region. In addition, we use an independent consulting company to do our own market review of both public and private companies. Lastly, given that we are specialized, we also focus in on four core competitors who are reviewed as well. Overall, our target is to meet the market in compensation.

2. **Two main challenges in benchmarking are determining who the competitors are for talent and securing accurate metrics for the exercise. How does CAMH overcome these challenges?**

   OHA has developed an intelligent survey, including definitions, which standardizes interpretation of questions to a great extent. In the past, we've used sub-committees with other hospitals to determine standardized collection and reporting of metrics (e.g., benefit utilization rates) so we can compare them fairly.

3. **An overlooked consideration is what to do when a compensation benchmarking exercise demonstrates that the company significantly exceeds market-based compensation. What are some practical solutions to this?**

   I.   For union positions, with proper notice, a reclassification of a position into a lower classification could occur at any point throughout the year. Should the union disagree with the reclassification, they would then go through the grievance process. Alternatively, the reclassification could also be discussed and negotiated during Collective Agreement bargaining.

   II. For non-unionized positions, we investigate this to determine if compensation exceeding the market is fair or required. We have market sensitive bands for specific positions outside of the norm (e.g., international scientists).

   III. We can wait until turnover or internal mobility to make a correction.

   IV. We also check to see if the positions need the premium based on market competitiveness.

Source: Reprinted by permission from Mr. Adam Hewitt.

PAY FOR KNOWLEDGE

Pay-for-knowledge systems are known as *competency-based pay* (for management and professional employees) and *skill-based pay* (for manufacturing employees). These plans pay employees for the range, depth, and types of knowledge that they are capable of using, rather than for the job that they currently hold. Competencies are individual knowledge, skills, and behaviours that are critical to successful individual or corporate performance based on their relation to the organization's visions, values, and business strategy.[31]

Core competencies describe knowledge and behaviours that employees throughout the organization must exhibit for the organization to succeed, such as "customer service orientation" for all hotel employees. *Functional competencies* are associated with a particular organizational function, such as "negotiation skills" for salespeople, or "safety orientation" for pilots. *Behavioural competencies* are expected behaviours, such as "always walking a customer to the product they are looking for rather than pointing."[32] A pay-for-knowledge program should include the following:

- Competencies and skills—directly important to job performance—that can be defined in measurable and objective terms. Skills tend to be easier to define and measure than competencies.

- New and different competencies that replace obsolete competencies or competencies that are no longer important to job performance. If additional competencies are needed, the obsolete competency should be removed from the program.

- On-the-job training, not "in the classroom" training. Those who possess the competencies or skills should teach them. Also include on-the-job assessment, which can be supplemented by paper-and-pencil exams administered on the job.[33]

As an example, in a manufacturing plant setting, workers would be paid based on their attained skill levels. In a three-level plan:

1. Level 1 would indicate limited ability, such as knowledge of basic facts and ability to perform simple tasks without direction.
2. Level 2 would mean that the employee has attained partial proficiency and could, for instance, apply technical principles on the job.
3. Level 3 would mean that the employee is fully competent in the area and could, for example, analyze and solve production problems.

Construction workers today are often compensated for their work through the method of skill-based pay.

Although only about 15 to 20 percent of workplaces use pay for knowledge at present, experts predict that the viewpoint that people, rather than jobs, provide advantages to organizations will continue to grow in popularity. They foresee the emergence of new pay systems combining competencies and market values.[34] The greatest challenge is measurement of competencies. As time goes on, employees often become dissatisfied if these measurements are not valid or if the people responsible for assessing competencies are considered incompetent or biased.[35] Another major employee concern is that pay be linked sufficiently to performance as well as competencies. Some compensation consultants suggest that firms should not pay for competencies at the exclusion of rewards for high performance results. For example, competencies could be linked to the determination of base salary combined with bonuses that are based on performance.[36] One final issue for many Canadian companies is that pay-for-knowledge systems do not meet pay equity requirements.[37]

PAY FOR EXECUTIVE, MANAGERIAL, AND PROFESSIONAL JOBS

Developing a compensation plan to pay executive, managerial, and professional employees is similar in many respects to developing a plan for other employees.[38] The basic aims of the plan are the same in that the goal is to attract good employees and maintain their commitment. Yet for executive, managerial, and professional jobs, job evaluation provides only a partial answer to the question of how to pay these employees. Executives, managers, and professionals are almost always paid based on their performance as well as on the basis of static job demands, like working conditions.

Compensating Executives and Managers

There are five elements in an executive/managerial compensation package: salary, benefits, short-term incentives, long-term incentives, and perquisites.[39] The amount of salary paid usually depends on the value of the person's work to the organization and how well the person is honouring his or her responsibilities. Salary is the cornerstone of executive compensation, because it is the element on which the others are layered, with benefits, incentives, and perquisites often awarded in some proportion to base pay.

An Ethical Dilemma

Is it right that CEOs earn enormous amounts of money when most employees are getting small increases each year (sometimes even less than inflation)?

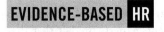

Executive compensation tends to emphasize performance incentives more than other employee pay plans do, since organizational results are likely to reflect the contributions of executives more directly than those of other employees. The heavy incentive component of executive compensation can be illustrated by using some of Canada's best-paid executives as an example.[40] The highest paid executive in Canada in 2013 was Gerald W. Schwartz, who earned a total compensation of $87 916 026, of which only $1 399 611 was base salary.[41] A study on CEO pay determined that firm size accounts for 40 percent of the variance of total CEO pay, while firm performance accounts for less than 5 percent of the variance.[42]

There has been considerable debate regarding whether top executives are worth what they are paid. Some argue that the job of an executive is increasingly difficult. The stakes are high, and job tenure is often short. Expectations are getting higher, the questions from shareholders are more direct, and the challenge of navigating an organization through difficult economic times has never been so great. However, shareholder activism regarding executive pay has attempted to tighten the restrictions on what firms pay their top executives.

Some believe that pay for performance is taking hold, with companies now making stronger links between company performance and CEO total compensation. Others believe that linking pay to performance is still inadequate in the majority of companies. Most agree that better disclosure of executive pay is required, and groups such as the Canadian Securities Administrators and the Canadian Coalition for Good Governance are pressing for dramatic changes in executive compensation disclosure.[43]

Compensating Professional Employees

Compensating non-supervisory professional employees, like engineers and scientists, presents unique problems. Analytical jobs require creativity and problem solving, compensable factors not easily compared or measured. Furthermore, the professional's economic impact on the firm is often related only indirectly to the person's actual efforts; for example, the success of an engineer's invention depends on many factors, like how well it is produced and marketed.

In theory, the job evaluation methods explained previously can be used for evaluating professional jobs.[44] The compensable factors here tend to focus on problem solving, creativity, job scope, and technical knowledge and expertise. The job classification method is commonly used—a series of grade descriptions are written, and each position is slotted into the grade having the most appropriate definition.

In practice, traditional methods of job evaluation are rarely used for professional jobs because it is so difficult to identify compensable factors and degrees of factors that meaningfully capture the value of professional work. "Knowledge and the skill of applying it," as one expert notes, "are extremely difficult to quantify and measure."[45]

market-pricing approach An approach usually limited to determining compensation for professional jobs based on values established for similar benchmark jobs in the market.

As a result, most employers use a **market-pricing approach** in evaluating professional jobs. They price professional jobs in the marketplace to the best of their ability to establish the values for benchmark jobs. These benchmark jobs and the employer's other professional jobs are then slotted into a salary structure. Specifically, each professional discipline (like mechanical engineering or electrical engineering) usually ends up having four to six grade levels, each of which requires a fairly broad salary range. This approach helps ensure that the employer remains competitive when bidding for professionals whose attainments vary widely and whose potential employers are found literally worldwide.[46]

PAY EQUITY

Historically, the average pay for Canadian women has been considerably lower than that for men. In 1967, women's average wages were 46.1 percent of men's average wages. **Table 11.3** shows the most recent wage gap statistics. Some of this gap is due to the fact that women do more part-time work than men, but even when full-year, full-time workers are compared, the gap has stalled at approximately 30 percent since

TABLE 11.3 Male–Female Average Earnings Ratio* for Full-Year, Full-Time Workers in Canada

Year	Average earnings, females (dollars)	Average earnings, males (dollars)	Female-to-male average earnings ratio (percent)
1990	37 800	56 700	66.7
1995	40 200	55 100	73.0
2000	42 000	59 800	70.6
2005	44 000	62 400	70.5
2010	48 700	66 100	73.6

*Earnings stated in constant year 2011 dollars.
Source: Statistics Canada, CANSIM Table 202-0102.

HR IN THE NEWS

Cost of Systemic Pay Inequities

Instances of pay inequity continue to occur, even in large, structured organizations. Several internal assessments of pay equity at the University of British Columbia established that on average, compensation of full-time female professors was $14 000 less than that of their male counterparts.

After adjusting for confounding factors (such as specialization, tenure, etc.), a $3000 gap in pay still existed. As a result, in 2013, the university gave all 880 tenure-tracked and tenured female faculty members a 2 percent increase in base salary in order to achieve pay equity. The increase was made retroactive to January 1, 2010, at a cost of $2 million to the university.

A similar situation occurred at Western University in 2006, resulting in individual adjustments to female faculty members' salaries to compensate for the $2200 post-confounding factor difference in pay between men and women. These cases highlight how the struggle for income parity between genders is far from over, and a challenge in even the most structured organizations. [49]

1998. The wage gap is narrower for single women over those who are married, and for younger women when compared to those who are older.[47] The HR in the News box highlights how pay equity issues can exist in large organizations as well.

Six provinces (Ontario, Quebec, Manitoba, Nova Scotia, New Brunswick, and Prince Edward Island) have created separate proactive legislation that specifically requires that pay equity be achieved. Ontario and Quebec require pay equity in both the public and the private sectors, whereas the legislation in the other four provinces applies only to the public sector. In the federal jurisdiction and the Yukon (public sector only), human rights legislation requires equal pay for work of equal value.

The wage gap has narrowed since the introduction of pay equity legislation, but there is still no explanation other than systemic discrimination for much of the 30 percent gap that still persists.[48] In the long term, the best way to remove the portion of the wage gap resulting from systemic discrimination is to eliminate male- and female-dominated jobs by ensuring that women have equal access to and are equally represented in all jobs.

CHAPTER SUMMARY

1. A total rewards approach considers individual reward components as part of an integrated whole to determine the best mix of rewards that are aligned with business strategy and provide employee value, all within the cost constraints of the organization.

Alignment is the extent to which rewards support outcomes that are important to achieving the organization's strategic objectives. Employee value is created when rewards are meaningful to employees and influence their affiliation with the organization.

2. Establishing pay rates involves three stages: job evaluation (to ensure internal equity), conducting wage/salary surveys (to ensure external equity), and combining job evaluation and salary survey results to determine pay rates. Job evaluation is aimed at determining the relative worth of jobs within a firm. It compares jobs with one another based on their content, which is usually defined in terms of compensable factors, such as skill, effort, responsibility, and working conditions. Jobs of approximately equal value are combined into pay grades for pay purposes. Salary surveys collect data from other employers in the marketplace who are competing for employees in similar kinds of positions. The wage curve shows the average market wage for each pay grade (or job). It illustrates what the average wage for each grade should be and whether any present wages or salaries are out of line.

3. Competency-based pay plans (also known as "pay for knowledge") provide employee compensation based on the skills and knowledge that they are capable of using, rather than the job that they currently hold.

4. The five basic elements of compensation for managers are salary, benefits, short-term incentives, long-term incentives, and perquisites.

5. Pay equity is intended to redress systemic gender discrimination as measured by the wage gap, which indicates that full-time working women in Canada make about 70 cents for every dollar made by full-time working men. Pay equity requires equal pay for female-dominated jobs of equal value to male-dominated jobs (where value is determined through job evaluation).

MyManagementLab

Study, practise, and explore real business situations with these helpful resources:

- **Interactive Lesson Presentations:** Work through interactive presentations and assessments to test your knowledge of management concepts.
- **PIA (Personal Inventory Assessments):** Enhance your ability to connect with key concepts through these engaging self-reflection assessments.
- **Study Plan:** Check your understanding of chapter concepts with self-study quizzes.
- **Videos:** Learn more about the management practices and strategies of real companies.
- **Simulations:** Practise decision-making in simulated management environments.

KEY TERMS

benchmark job *(p. 256)*
broadbanding *(p. 261)*
classes *(p. 257)*
classification/grading method *(p. 257)*
compensable factor *(p. 256)*
direct financial payments *(p. 251)*
employee compensation *(p. 251)*
external equity *(p. 254)*
equity theory *(p. 254)*
grade/group description *(p. 257)*
grades *(p. 257)*
indirect financial payments *(p. 251)*

internal equity *(p. 254)*
job evaluation *(p. 256)*
job evaluation committee *(p. 257)*
market-pricing approach *(p. 267)*
pay equity *(p. 252)*
pay grade *(p. 258)*
pay ranges *(p. 261)*
point method *(p. 257)*
red circle pay rate *(p. 264)*
wage curve *(p. 260)*
wage/salary survey *(p. 258)*

REVIEW AND DISCUSSION QUESTIONS

1. What are the five components of total rewards?
2. Describe what is meant by the term "benchmark job."
3. What is the relationship between compensable factors and job specifications?
4. What are the pros and cons of the following methods of job evaluation: ranking, classification, factor comparison, point method?
5. Explain the term "competencies" and explain the differences among core, functional, and behavioural competencies.
6. Explain what is meant by the market-pricing approach in evaluating professional jobs.
7. Explain what pay equity legislation is intended to accomplish, what action is required by the legislation to accomplish it, and how effective the legislation has been in accomplishing its objectives.

CRITICAL THINKING QUESTIONS

1. Do you think that transactional or relational rewards have more impact on overall organizational performance?
2. Why do companies pay for compensation surveys where job matching may be difficult rather than conducting their own surveys?
3. It was recently reported in the news that the base pay for Canadian bank CEOs range in the millions of dollars, and the pay for the governor of the Bank of Canada is less than half of that of the lowest paid bank CEO. How do you account for this difference? Should anything be done about this? Why or why not?
4. Do you agree with paying people for competencies and skills that they are rarely required to use on the job?
5. What are some of the potential reasons that gender-based pay discrimination is so hard to eradicate?
6. Why do you think there is such a discrepancy between the pay rates of executives and employees? Is this fair? Why or why not?

EXPERIENTIAL EXERCISES

1. Working individually or in groups, conduct salary surveys for the positions of entry-level accountant and entry-level chemical engineer. What sources did you use, and what conclusions did you reach? If you were the HR manager for a local engineering firm, what would you recommend that each job be paid?
2. Obtain information on the pay grades and rate ranges for each pay grade at your college or university. Do they appear to be broadbands? If not, propose specific broadbands that could be implemented.
3. You have been asked by the owner of your medium-sized import and export company (200+ people) to develop a way to standardize pay ranges for different jobs in the company. He says he is tired of employees complaining about the pay they get compared to others and is concerned that if he does nothing someone will complain about inequitable pay practices. Outline the steps you will follow to do this. Make sure to give a rationale for the type of job evaluation system you propose as well as for the method you

suggest to obtain comparable salary data. The jobs he is most concerned about are

- sales representative
- shipping and receiving manager
- multilingual contract negotiator
- accounts receivable clerk
- shipping clerk.

4. You are the HR manager at a large construction firm headquartered in Edmonton. Most of the company's administrative staff are also in Edmonton. You have regional and local site offices across the country. Draft a memo to employees about your company's new pay-for-knowledge and skills policy. Make sure to document at least one fully complete section on how this policy will be administered. Your professor may give you some ideas on what might be considered or you may create your own circumstances under which pay for knowledge and skills will be applied.

RUNNING CASE

Running Case: LearnInMotion.com

The New Pay Plan

LearnInMotion.com does not have a formal wage structure, nor does it have rate ranges or use compensable factors. Jennifer and Pierre base wage rates almost exclusively on those prevailing in the surrounding community, and they temper these by trying to maintain some semblance of equity among what workers with different responsibilities are paid. As Jennifer says, "Deciding what to pay dot-com employees is an adventure: Wages for jobs like web designer and online salesperson are always climbing dramatically, and there's not an awful lot of loyalty involved when someone else offers you 30 percent or 40 percent more than you're currently making." Jennifer and Pierre are therefore continually scanning various sources to see what others are paying for positions like theirs. They peruse the want ads almost every day and conduct informal surveys among their friends at other dot-coms. Once or twice a week, they also check compensation websites like Monster.ca.

Although the company has taken a somewhat unstructured, informal approach to establishing its compensation plan, the firm's actual salary schedule is guided by several basic pay policies. For one thing, the difficulty they had recruiting and hiring employees caused them to pay salaries 10 to 20 percent above what the market would seem to indicate. Jennifer and Pierre write this off to the need to get and keep good employees. As Jennifer says, "If you've got 10 web designers working for you, you can afford to go a few extra weeks without hiring another one, but when you need one designer and you have none, you've got to do whatever you can to get that one designer hired." Their somewhat informal approach has also led to some potential inequities. For example, the two salespeople—one a man, the other a woman—are earning different salaries, and the man is making about 30 percent more. If everything was going fine—for instance, if sales were up and the calendar was functional—perhaps they wouldn't be worried. However, the fact is that the two owners are wondering if a more structured pay plan would be a good idea. Now they want you, their management consultant, to help them decide what to do.

QUESTIONS

1. Describe the total rewards model and its five components and whether it would benefit LearnInMotion.com.
2. What are some basic considerations in determining pay rates that LearnInMotion.com must be aware of?
3. Using the three stages of establishing pay rates, provide recommendations to LearnInMotion.com in regard to job evaluation, wage/salary surveys, and how to combine the first two steps to determine pay rates for LearnInMotion.com's jobs.

Kadmy/Fotolia

Pay-for-Performance and Financial Incentives

LEARNING OUTCOMES

AFTER STUDYING THIS CHAPTER, YOU SHOULD BE ABLE TO

DISCUSS the impact of money as a means to incentivize employee motivation and **COMPARE** fixed and variable pay plans and the appropriate use of each.

COMPARE the four types of organization-wide incentive plans available to all employees.

EXPLAIN how to use short-term and long-term incentives for managers and executives.

ANALYZE the main advantages and disadvantages of salary plans and commission plans for salespeople.

EXPLAIN under what conditions it is best to use an incentive plan.

ANALYZE the emerging emphasis on employee recognition.

REQUIRED HR COMPETENCIES

20600: Promote an evidence-based approach to the development of human resources policies and practices using current professional resources to provide a sound basis for human resources decision-making.

60100: Create a total rewards structure that encompasses compensation, pensions, benefits, and perquisites to maintain consistency, fairness, and organizational competitiveness, comply with legal requirements, and encourage desired behaviour.

60400: Provide information about the total value of and changes to total rewards using appropriate media to achieve understanding and encourage performance and desired behaviour.

90100: Make informed business decisions using financial and operating information to align human resources with business strategy.

MONEY AND MOTIVATION

fixed pay Compensation that is independent of the performance level of the individual, group, or organization.

variable pay Any plan that ties pay to productivity or profitability.

◀●┤Simulate on MyManagementLab

Motivation

Today's efforts to achieve the organization's strategy through motivated employees include fixed and variable compensation plans. **Fixed pay** represents compensation that is independent of the performance level of the individual, group, or organization. Fixed compensation includes base pay and other forms of relatively consistent compensation (for example, allowances) that satisfy the need for income stability. In contrast, **variable pay** represents any plan that links pay with productivity, profitability, or some other measure of organizational performance. Employers continue to increase their use of variable pay plans while holding salary increases or fixed compensation at modest levels. On average, organizations spend roughly 11 percent of total pay-related spending on variable pay-related expenses. More than 84 percent of Canadian employers have one or more types of variable pay plans in place. Cash bonuses or incentives are the most common form of short-term incentives, used in 83 percent of organizations that have short-term incentive plans in place.[1]

Variable pay facilitates management of total compensation by keeping base pay inflation controlled. The fundamental premise of variable pay plans is that top performers must get top pay to secure their commitment to the organization. Thus, accurate performance appraisal or measurable outcomes is a precondition of effective pay-for-performance plans. Another important prerequisite for effective variable pay plans is "line of sight," or the extent to which an employee can relate his or her daily work to the achievement of overall corporate goals. Employees need to understand corporate strategy and how their work as individual employees is important to the achievement of strategic objectives.[2]

The entire thrust of such programs is to treat workers like partners and get them to think of the business and its goals as their own. It is thus reasonable to pay them more like partners, too, by linking their pay more directly to performance. For example, the owners of a Surrey, British Columbia–based trucking company handed out bonus cheques totalling more than $400 000 to more than 400 employees in August 2005. Over the preceding five years, the owners had grown Coastal Pacific Xpress (CPX) by 500 percent and decided to reward their employees for their hard work.[3]

Motivation and Incentives

Several motivation theories have particular relevance to designing incentive plans.

Motivators and Frederick Herzberg

Frederick Herzberg said the best way to motivate someone is to organize the job so that doing it provides the challenge and recognition we all need to help satisfy "higher-level" needs for things like accomplishment and recognition. These needs are relatively insatiable, says Herzberg, so challenging work provides a sort of built-in motivation generator. Doing things to satisfy a worker's "lower-level" needs for things like better pay and working conditions just keeps the person from becoming dissatisfied.

Herzberg says the factors ("hygienes") that satisfy lower-level needs are different from those ("motivators") that satisfy or partially satisfy higher-level needs. If *hygiene* factors (factors outside the job itself, such as working conditions, salary, and incentive pay) are inadequate, employees become dissatisfied. However, adding more of these hygienes (like incentives) to the job (supplying what Herzberg calls "extrinsic motivation") is an inferior way to try to motivate someone, because lower-level needs are quickly satisfied. Inevitably the person says, in effect, "I want another raise."

Instead of relying on hygienes, says Herzberg, managers interested in creating a self-motivated workforce should emphasize "job content" or *motivator* factors. Managers do this by enriching workers' jobs so that the jobs are more challenging, and by providing feedback and recognition—they make doing the job intrinsically motivating, in other words. In organizational psychology, **intrinsic motivation** is motivation that derives from the pleasure someone gets from doing the job or task. It comes from "within" the person, rather than from externally, such as a financial incentive plan. Intrinsic motivation means that just doing the task provides the motivation. Herzberg makes the point that relying exclusively on financial incentives is risky. The employer should also provide the recognition and challenging work that most people desire.

Demotivators and Edward Deci

Psychologist Edward Deci's work highlights another potential downside to relying too heavily on extrinsic rewards: They may backfire. Deci found that extrinsic rewards could at times actually detract from the person's intrinsic motivation.[4] The point may be stated thusly: Be cautious in devising incentive pay for highly motivated employees, lest you inadvertently demean and detract from the desire they have to do the job out of a sense of responsibility.

Expectancy Theory and Victor Vroom

In general, people won't pursue rewards they find unattractive, or where the odds of success are very low. Psychologist Victor Vroom's expectancy motivation theory echoes these commonsense observations. He says a person's motivation to exert some level of effort depends on three things: the person's **expectancy** (in terms of probability) that his or her effort will lead to performance;[5] **instrumentality**, or the perceived connection (if any) between successful performance and actually obtaining the rewards; and **valence**, which represents the perceived value the person attaches to the reward.[6] In Vroom's theory:

$$\text{Motivation} = (E \times I \times V)$$

where E represents expectancy, I instrumentality, and V valence. If E or I or V is zero or inconsequential, there will be no motivation.

Vroom's theory has three implications for how managers design incentive plans.

- First, if employees don't *expect* that effort will produce performance, no motivation will occur. So, managers must ensure that their employees have the skills to do the job, and believe they can do the job. Thus training, job descriptions, and confidence building and support are important in using incentives.

- Second, Vroom's theory suggests that employees must see the *instrumentality* of their efforts—they must believe that successful performance will in fact lead to getting the reward. Managers can accomplish this, for instance, by creating easy to understand incentive plans.

- Third, the reward itself must be of *value* to the employee. Ideally, the manager should take into account individual employee preferences.

Types of Incentive Plans

There are several types of incentive plans. Individual incentive programs give income over and above base salary to individual employees who meet a specific individual performance standard. Informal incentives may be awarded, generally to individual

intrinsic motivation Motivation that derives from the pleasure someone gets from doing the job or task.

expectancy A person's expectation that his or her effort will lead to performance.

instrumentality The perceived relationship between successful performance and obtaining the reward.

valence The perceived value a person attaches to the reward.

EVIDENCE-BASED HR

employees, for accomplishments that are not readily measured by a standard, such as "to recognize the long hours that this employee put in last month," or "to recognize exemplary customer service this week." Group incentive programs are like individual incentive plans, but they provide payments over and above base salary to all team members when the group or team collectively meets a specified standard for performance, productivity, or other work-related behaviour. Organization-wide incentive plans provide monetary incentives to all employees of the organization. Examples are profit-sharing plans that provide employees with a share of the organization's profits in a specified period, and gainsharing programs designed to reward employees for improvements in organizational productivity. Finally, non-monetary recognition programs motivate employees through praise and expressions of appreciation for their work.

For simplicity, these plans will be discussed as follows: incentives for all employees, incentives for operations employees, team or group incentives, incentives for senior managers and executives, incentives for salespeople, and organization-wide incentives.

HR Competency

20600

INCENTIVES FOR ALL EMPLOYEES

Many employers have incentive plans in which virtually all employees can participate. These include merit pay, profit-sharing, employee stock ownership, and gainsharing plans.

Merit Pay

merit pay (merit raise) Any salary increase awarded to an employee based on his or her individual performance.

Merit pay or a **merit raise** is any salary increase that is awarded to an employee based on his or her individual performance. It is different from a bonus in that it usually represents a continuing increment, whereas the bonus represents a one-time payment. Although the term "merit pay" can apply to the incentive raises given to any employees—office or factory, management or non-management—the term is more often used with respect to white-collar employees, and particularly professional, office, and clerical employees.

Merit pay has both advocates and detractors and is the subject of much debate.[7] Advocates argue that only pay or other rewards tied directly to performance can motivate improved performance. They contend that the effect of awarding identical pay raises to all employees (without regard to individual performance) may actually detract from performance by showing employees that they will be rewarded the same regardless of how they perform.

Conversely, merit pay detractors present good reasons why merit pay can backfire. One is that the usefulness of the merit pay plan depends on the validity of the performance appraisal system, because if performance appraisals are viewed as unfair, so too will the merit pay that is based on them. Second, supervisors often tend to minimize differences in employee performance when computing merit raises. They give most employees about the same raise, either because of a reluctance to alienate some employees or a desire to give everyone a raise that will at least help them to stay even with the cost of living. A third problem is that almost every employee thinks that he or she is an above-average performer; being paid a below-average merit increase can thus be demoralizing. Finally, some believe that merit pay pits employees against each other and harms team spirit.[8]

However, although problems like these can undermine a merit pay plan, the consensus of opinion is that merit pay can and does improve performance. It is critical, however, that performance appraisals be carried out effectively.[9]

Traditional merit pay plans have two basic characteristics: (1) merit increases are usually granted to employees at a designated time of the year in the form of a higher base salary (or *raise*); and (2) the merit raise is usually based exclusively on individual performance, although the overall level of company profits may affect the total sum available for merit raises.[10] In some cases, merit raises are awarded in a single lump sum once a year, without changing base salary. Occasionally, awards are tied to both individual and organizational performance.

Employee Share Purchase/Stock Ownership Plan

employee share purchase/ stock ownership plan (ESOP)
A plan whereby a trust is established to hold shares of company stock purchased for or issued to employees. The trust distributes the stock to employees on retirement, separation from service, or as otherwise prescribed by the plan.

Employee share purchase/stock ownership plans (ESOPs) are in place at approximately 60 percent of Canadian organizations with publicly traded stock.[11] A trust is established to purchase shares of the firm's stock for employees by using cash from employee (and sometimes employer) contributions. Employers may also issue treasury shares to the trust instead of paying cash for a purchase on the open market. The trust holds the stock in individual employee accounts and distributes it to employees, often on retirement or other separation from service. Some plans distribute the stock to employees once a year.

The corporation receives a tax deduction equal to the fair market value of the shares that are purchased by the trustee by using employer contributions, but not for any treasury shares issued. The value of the shares purchased with employer contributions, and of any treasury shares issued, is a taxable benefit to the employees in the year of purchase of the shares. This tax treatment can create two problems. First, if the plan requires employees to complete a certain period of service before taking ownership of the shares and the employee leaves before being eligible for ownership, the employee has paid tax on the value of shares that he or she never owns. Therefore, most plans have immediate vesting.[12] Second, if the value of the shares drops, employees may have paid tax on a greater amount than they will receive when they eventually sell the shares.

Hints : **TO ENSURE LEGAL COMPLIANCE**

ESOPs can encourage employees to develop a sense of ownership in and commitment to the firm, particularly when combined with good communication, employee involvement in decision-making, and employee understanding of the business and the economic environment.[13] For example, one employee at Creo, a digital products company in Burnaby, British Columbia, that offers an ESOP said, "It's not just the shares. It's the way of thinking. I'm extremely happy here."[14]

Profit-Sharing Plans

profit-sharing plan A plan whereby most or all employees share in the company's profits.

In a **profit-sharing plan**, most or all employees receive a share of the company's profits. Fewer than 15 percent of Canadian organizations offer profit-sharing plans.[15] These plans are easy to administer and have a broad appeal to employees and other company stakeholders. In addition to helping attract, retain, and motivate workers, profit-sharing plans have tax advantages for employees, including tax deferrals and income splitting. The main weakness of profit-sharing plans is "line of sight." It is unlikely that most employees perceive that they personally have the ability to influence overall company profit. It has been found that these plans produce a one-time productivity improvement but no change thereafter. Another weakness of these plans is that they typically provide an annual payout, which is not as effective as more frequent payouts.[16]

EVIDENCE-BASED HR

National Center for Employee Ownership
www.nceo.org

There are several types of profit-sharing plans. In *cash plans*, the most popular, a percentage of profits (usually 15 to 20 percent) is distributed as profit shares at regular intervals. Profit-sharing plans can also be added to collective bargaining agreements, as highlighted in the HR in the News box.

HR IN THE NEWS

Air Canada Pilots Secure Financial Incentives in Collective Bargaining Agreement

Pilots working for Air Canada secured a 10-year collective bargaining agreement (legally binding union–employer contract) that provided them with a 2 percent annual wage increase, and an improved profit-sharing formula. Pilots hired after the contract comes into effect will secure higher starting wages and a $10 000 signing bonus. All pilots will also receive a 2 percent cash bonus in both 2016 and 2017.

The deal is considered a landmark deal, providing evidence of a culture shift at Air Canada. The agreement, which expires in 2024, offers stability and long-term cost-certainty, and also frames the relationship between management and pilots as more of a partnership.[17]

Gainsharing Plans

gainsharing plan An incentive plan that engages employees in a common effort to achieve productivity objectives and share the gains.

A **gainsharing plan** is an incentive plan that engages many or all employees in a common effort to achieve a company's productivity objectives; any resulting incremental cost-saving gains are shared among employees and the company.[18] Popular types of gainsharing plans include the Rucker and improshare plans.

The basic difference between these plans is in the formula used to determine employee bonuses.[19] The Rucker formula uses sales value minus materials and supplies, all divided into payroll expenses. It includes participative management systems that use committees. The improshare plan creates production standards for each department. It does not include a participative management component but instead considers participation an outcome of the bonus plan.

The financial aspects of a gainsharing program can be quite straightforward. Assume that a supplier wants to boost quality. Doing so would translate into fewer customer returns, less scrap and rework, and therefore higher profits. Historically, $1 million in output results in $20 000 (2 percent) scrap, returns, and rework. The company tells its employees that if next month's production results in only 1 percent scrap, returns, and rework, the 1 percent saved would be a gain to be split 50/50 with the workforce, less a small amount reserved for months in which scrap exceeds 2 percent.

INCENTIVES FOR OPERATIONS EMPLOYEES

Piecework Plans

piecework A system of pay based on the number of items processed by each individual worker in a unit of time, such as items per hour or items per day.

Several incentive plans are particularly well suited for use with operations employees, such as those doing production work.[20] **Piecework** is the oldest incentive plan and still the most commonly used. Earnings are tied directly to the worker's production levels—the person is paid a piece rate for each unit that he or she produces or processes. Thus, if Tom Smith gets paid a piecework rate of $2.50 per customer phone query completed via phone in his customer service position, then he would make $75 for completing 30 calls a day and $100 for 40 calls a day.

Developing a workable piece-rate plan requires both job evaluation and (usually) industrial engineering. The crucial issue in piece-rate planning is the production standard, however, and this standard is usually developed by industrial engineers. With a **straight piecework plan**, Tom Smith would be paid on the basis of the customer service calls he completes; there would be no guaranteed minimum wage. However, after passage of employment/labour standards legislation, it became necessary for most employers to guarantee their workers a minimum wage. With a **guaranteed piecework plan**, Tom Smith would be paid the minimum wage whether or not he completed enough customer calls a day required to make minimum wage—for example, four calls per hour if minimum wage is $10.00 per hour. As an incentive to increase production he would, however, also be paid the piece rate of $0.50 for each call he completed over the number required to make minimum wage.

"Piecework" generally implies straight piecework, a strict proportionality between results and rewards regardless of the level of output. Thus, in Smith's case, he continues to get $0.50 apiece for managing customer calls, even if he completes many more than planned (say, 100 per day). Other types of piecework incentive plans call for a sharing of productivity gains between worker and employer such that the worker does not receive full credit for all production above normal.[21]

The **differential piece-rate plan** is like the standard piece-rate plan with one major difference: With a piece-rate plan, the worker is paid a particular rate for each piece that he or she produces; with the differential piece-rate plan, the worker is rewarded by a *premium that equals the percentage by which his or her performance exceeds the standard*. The plan assumes the worker has a guaranteed base rate. The base rate may, but need not, equal the hourly rate determined by the job evaluation; however, it must meet or exceed the minimums established in the applicable Employment Standards Act.

straight piecework plan A set payment for each piece produced or processed.

guaranteed piecework plan The minimum hourly wage plus an incentive for each unit produced above a set number of units per hour.

differential piece-rate plan A plan by which a worker is paid a basic hourly rate plus an extra percentage of his or her base rate for production exceeding the standard per hour or per day. It is similar to piecework payment but is based on a percentage premium.

Advantages and Disadvantages

Piecework incentive plans have several advantages. They are simple to calculate and easily understood by employees. Piece-rate plans appear equitable in principle, and their incentive value can be powerful since rewards are directly tied to performance.

Piecework also has some disadvantages. A main one is its somewhat unsavoury reputation among many employees, based on some employers' habits of arbitrarily raising production standards whenever they find their workers earning "excessive" wages. Since the piece rate is quoted on a per-piece basis, in workers' minds production standards become tied inseparably to the amount of money earned. When an attempt is made to revise production standards, it is met with considerable worker resistance, even if the revision is fully justified.[22]

The differential piece-rate plan has most of the advantages of the piecework plan and is fairly simple to compute and easy to understand. The incentive is expressed in units of time instead of in monetary terms (as it is with the standard piece-rate system). Therefore, there is less of a tendency on the part of workers to link their production standard with their pay. Furthermore, the clerical job of recomputing piece rates whenever hourly wage rates are re-evaluated is avoided.

Such problems as these have led some firms to drop their piecework plans and to substitute team-based incentive plans or programs, such as gainsharing.

Team or Group Incentives

team or group incentive plan
A plan in which a production standard is set for a specific work group and its members are paid incentives if the group exceeds the production standard.

There are several ways in which to implement **team or group incentive plans**.[23] One is to set work standards for each member of the group and maintain a count of the output of each member. Members are then paid based on one of three formulas: (1) all members receive the pay earned by the highest producer; (2) all members receive the pay earned by the lowest producer; or (3) all members receive payment equal to the average pay earned by the group.

The second approach is to set a production standard based on the final output of the group as a whole; all members then receive the same pay, based on the piece rate that exists for the group's job. The group incentive can be based on either the piece rate or standard hour plan, but the latter is somewhat more prevalent.

A third option is to choose a measurable definition of group performance or productivity that the group can control. For instance, broad criteria, such as total labour hours per final product, could be used; piecework's engineered standards are thus not necessarily required here.[24]

There are several reasons to use team incentive plans. Sometimes, several jobs are interrelated, as they are on project teams. Here, one worker's performance reflects not only his or her own effort but that of co-workers as well; thus, team incentives make sense. Team plans also reinforce group planning and problem solving and help to ensure that collaboration takes place. In Japan, employees are rewarded as a group to reduce jealousy, make group members indebted to one another (as they would be to the group), and encourage a sense of co-operation. There tends to be less bickering among group members over who has "tight" production standards and who has "loose" ones. Group incentive plans also facilitate on-the-job training, since each member of the group has an interest in getting new members trained as quickly as possible.[25]

A group incentive plan's chief disadvantage is that each worker's rewards are no longer based solely on his or her own effort. To the extent that the person does not see his or her effort leading to the desired reward, a group plan may be less effective at motivating employees than an individual plan is.

EVIDENCE-BASED **HR**

Group incentive plans have been found to be more effective when there are high levels of communication with employees about the specifics of the plan, when there is strong worker involvement in the plan's design and implementation, and when group members perceive the plan as fair.[26]

INCENTIVES FOR SENIOR MANAGERS AND EXECUTIVES

There are five elements in an executive/managerial compensation package: salary, benefits, short-term incentives, long-term incentives, and perquisites.[27] Salary is the cornerstone of executive compensation because it is the element on which the others are layered, with benefits, incentives, and perquisites often awarded in some proportion to base pay. There has been considerable debate regarding whether top executives are worth what they are paid. Some argue that the job of an executive is increasingly difficult. The stakes are high, and job tenure is often short. Expectations are getting higher, the questions from shareholders are more direct, and the challenge of navigating an organization through difficult economic times has never been so great. However, shareholder activism regarding executive

An Ethical Dilemma

Is it right that CEOs earn enormous amounts of money when most employees are getting small increases each year (sometimes even less than inflation)?

HR Competency

20600

pay has attempted to tighten the restrictions on what firms pay their top executives. The Expert Opinion box discusses how short-term and long-term incentives can be organized or considered within the HR framework.

Short-Term Incentives

More than 90 percent of firms in Canada with variable pay plans provide an *annual bonus*.[28] Unlike salaries, which rarely decline with reduced performance, short-term incentive bonuses can easily result in an increase or decrease of up to 70 percent or

expert opinion
academic viewpoint

Dr. Anne Wilson

Identification: Dr. Anne Wilson (PhD), Canada Research Chair in Social Psychology

Affiliation: Department of Psychology, Wilfred Laurier

Focus: Examining what contributes to people's motivation to work toward long-term goals; understanding how people think about temporally near and distant incentives to help promote successful goal-pursuit

1. **How do people interpret short-term versus long-term incentives differently?**

   Generally, people are very good at mobilizing to respond to immediate consequences or incentives, but struggle more with pursuing long-term goals. People have a natural tendency to value immediate rewards more than distant future incentives: the field of behavioural economics has well-documented this phenomenon of temporal discounting. Because imminent rewards loom larger than distant ones, it can be hard to stay motivated by long-term goals or incentives when their benefits won't be enjoyed for quite some time. Doing so usually involves incurring costs in the present to benefit some imagined future self.

   One reason people have trouble sacrificing now to achieve future benefits is that the future self they are working for can often feel almost like a stranger. One way to address this problem is to find ways to promote a closer psychological connection to one's future self. In my lab, we increase this connection by framing future outcomes to seem closer in time: if the future seems temporally close, people feel more identified with their future self. Similarly, research lead by Dr. Hal E. Hershfield (UCLA) has increased people's felt connection to future selves using some ingenious technology: they ask people to make financial decisions (spend now or invest for the future) while viewing a photo of their "virtually aged" future self. People were more likely to make investment decisions to benefit their older self when their older self was looking back at them! In sum, increasing the closeness people feel to future goals can help them make decisions that balance short-term and long-term goals.

2. **How can long-term goals or rewards or incentives be developed to make them more appealing?**

   My research demonstrates that people's perception of time is subjective and it can be very malleable.

The same future point in time could feel impossibly remote to one person and seem just around the corner to another. Future goals can also be framed to seem closer. For example, discussing a 2-year goal in light of a 10-year timeframe is perceived as more short term than a 2-year goal in light of a 2-year timeframe. Even very subtle manipulations of how time is visualized (e.g., putting goals on an extended time line) or verbally described (e.g., it's "coming up soon") can be effective at reframing time perceptions, helping people perceive the goals as more short term.

3. **In an organizational or workplace setting, how can managers use this research to determine organizational or individual short-term or long-term incentives?**

   It can help for managers to recognize that long-term incentives might not always motivate. Visioning exercises, for instance, imagining what the company will look like in two or five years, may help people vividly imagine and connect with future goals or rewards. Managers can also split up longer-term incentives into shorter-term rewards. For example, rather than offering three weeks of vacation at the distant end of a major project, employees might be more enticed if some rewards are more immediate: for instance, offering one week of vacation after a milestone in the middle of the project, followed by more downtime at the end.

Source: Reprinted by permission from Anne Wilson.

more in total pay relative to the previous year. Three basic issues should be considered when awarding short-term incentives: eligibility, fund-size determination, and individual awards.

Eligibility

Eligibility is usually decided in one of three ways. The first criterion is *key position*. Here, a job-by-job review is conducted to identify the key jobs (typically only line jobs) that have a measurable impact on profitability. The second approach to determining eligibility is to set a *salary-level* cut-off point; all employees earning over that threshold amount are automatically eligible for consideration for short-term incentives. Finally, eligibility can be determined by *salary grade*. This is a refinement of the salary cut-off approach and assumes that all employees at a certain grade or above should be eligible for the short-term incentive program. The simplest approach is just to use salary level as a cut-off.[29]

How Much to Pay Out (Fund Size)

Next, a decision must be made regarding the fund size—the total amount of bonus money that will be available—and there are several formulas to do this. Some companies use a *non-deductible formula*. Here a straight percentage (usually of the company's net income) is used to create the short-term incentive fund. Others use a *deductible formula* on the assumption that the short-term incentive fund should begin to accumulate only after the firm has met a specified level of earnings.

In practice, what proportion of profits is usually paid out as bonuses? In fact, there are no hard-and-fast rules about what an ideal payout size would be, and some firms do not even have a formula for developing the bonus fund. One alternative is to reserve a minimum amount of the profits, say 10 percent, for safeguarding shareholders' investments, and then to establish a fund for bonuses equal to 20 percent of the corporate operating profit before taxes in excess of this base amount. Thus, if the operating profits were $100 000, then the management bonus fund might be 20 percent of $90 000, or $18 000.

Determining Individual Awards

The third issue is determining the *individual awards* to be paid. In some cases, the amount is determined on a discretionary basis (usually by the employee's boss), but typically a target bonus is set for each eligible position and adjustments are then made for greater or less than targeted performance. A maximum amount, perhaps double the target bonus, may be set. Performance ratings are obtained for each manager, and preliminary bonus estimates are computed. Estimates for the total amount of money to be spent on short-term incentives are thereby made and compared with the bonus fund available. If necessary, the individual estimates are then adjusted.

An Ethical Dilemma

Is it ethical to provide potentially large bonuses to managers and executives on a purely discretionary basis, not necessarily related to performance?

Many experts argue that, in most organizations, managerial and executive-level bonuses should be tied to both organizational and individual performance, and there are several ways to do this.[30] Perhaps the simplest is the *split-award method*, which breaks the bonus into two parts. Here, the manager actually gets two separate bonuses, one based on his or her individual effort and one based on the organization's overall performance. Thus, a manager might be eligible for an individual performance bonus of up to $10 000 but receive an individual performance bonus of only $8000 at the end of the year, based on his or her individual performance evaluation. In addition, though, the person might also receive a second bonus of $8000 based on the company's profits for the year. Thus, even if there were no company profits, the high-performing manager would still get an individual performance bonus.

One drawback to this approach is that it pays too much to the marginal performer, who, even if his or her own performance is mediocre, at least gets that second, company-based bonus. One way to get around this problem is to use the *multiplier method*. For example, a manager whose individual performance was "poor" might not even receive a company-performance-based bonus, on the assumption that the bonus should be a *product* of individual *and* corporate performance. When either is very poor, the product is zero.

Whichever approach is used, outstanding performers should get substantially larger awards than do other managers. They are people that the company cannot afford to lose, and their performance should always be adequately rewarded by the organization's incentive system. Conversely, marginal or below-average performers should never receive awards that are normal or average, and poor performers should be awarded nothing. The money saved on those people should be given to above-average performers.[31]

Long-Term Incentives

The Conference Board of Canada
www.conferenceboard.ca

HR Competency

60100

capital accumulation programs
Long-term incentives most often reserved for senior executives.

Long-term incentives are intended to motivate and reward top management for the firm's long-term growth and prosperity and to inject a long-term perspective into executive decisions. If only short-term criteria are used, a manager could, for instance, increase profitability in one year by reducing plant maintenance; this tactic might, however, reduce profits over the next two or three years. This issue of long- versus short-term perspective has received considerable attention in the past several years as shareholders have become increasingly critical of management focus on short-term returns at the expense of long-term increase in share price. The deep economic recession that began in late 2008 following the sub-prime mortgage lending crisis in the United States resulted in increasing regulatory focus on this type of compensation.

Long-term incentives are also intended to encourage executives to stay with the company by giving them the opportunity to accumulate capital (in the form of company shares) based on the firm's long-term success. Long-term incentives, or **capital accumulation programs**, are most often reserved for senior executives but have more recently begun to be extended to employees at lower organizational levels.[32] Approximately 60 percent of Canadian private sector organizations provide long-term incentives. They are rarely provided to public sector employees.[33]

Some of the most common long-term incentive plans (for capital accumulation) in Canada are stock options, performance share unit plans, restricted share unit plans, and deferred share unit plans.[34] The popularity of these plans changes over time because of economic conditions and trends, internal company financial pressures, changing attitudes toward long-term incentives, and changes in tax law, as well as other factors.

HR Competency

90100

Stock Options

stock option The right to purchase a stated number of shares of a company stock at today's price at some time in the future.

The **stock option** is the most popular long-term incentive in Canada, but its use is decreasing. Forty-six percent of organizations using long-term incentives provided stock options in 2011, compared with 57 percent in 2005 and 72 percent in 2002.[35] A stock option is the right to purchase a specific number of shares of company stock at a specific price at some point in the future.

Often a vesting (waiting) period is required to ensure that the employee has contributed to any increase in stock price, which also aligns the stock option with the goal of long-term retention of talent. The executive thus hopes to profit by exercising his or her option to buy the shares in the future, but at today's price. The assumption is that the price of the stock will go up rather than going down or staying the same. For example, if shares provided at an option price of $20 per share are exercised (bought) later for $20 when the market price is $60 per share and sold on the stock market when the market price is $80 per share, a cash gain of $60 per share results. The difference between fair market value of the stock at the time the option is sold and the amount paid by the employee to acquire it is treated as a taxable benefit. Often, the employee benefits since they are only required to pay capital gains tax on 50 percent of the gain. In comparison, from the employer's perspective, capital gains from cash incentive plans and stock purchase plans are taxed at full income inclusion levels. Thus, stock option plans are often seen as a cash windfall with no downside risk but unlimited upside potential.[36]

Proposals have been made to require that stock options be shown as an expense on company financial statements because the excessive issuing of options dilutes share values for shareholders and creates a distorted impression of the true value of a company.

Plans Providing Share "Units"

Although the use of stock options persists, a new approach based on providing "units" instead of stock has become increasingly common.[37] Executives are granted a specified number of units whose value is equal to (and fluctuates with) a company's share price, subject to certain conditions. A *performance share unit plan* provides units subject to the achievement of predetermined financial targets, such as profit or growth in earnings per share (often over a multiyear period). If the performance goals are met, then the value of the units is paid to the executive in cash or stock. The units have no value if the pre-established performance criteria are not met. In a *restricted share unit plan*, units are promised to the executive but will be forfeited if an executive leaves the company before a vesting period (typically three years). If the executive is still employed at the company after the vesting period, the full value of the units based on the current stock price is payable in cash or stock. In a *deferred share unit plan*, units are promised to the executive but are only payable when the executive leaves the company.

INCENTIVES FOR SALESPEOPLE

Sales compensation plans have typically relied heavily on incentives (sales commissions), although this varies by industry. In the real estate industry, for instance, salespeople are paid entirely via commissions, while in the pharmaceutical industry, salespeople tend to be paid a salary. However, the most prevalent approach is to use a combination of salary and commissions to compensate salespeople.[38]

The widespread use of incentives for salespeople is due to three factors: tradition, the unsupervised nature of most sales work, and the assumption that incentives are needed to motivate salespeople. The pros and cons of salary, commission, and combination plans follow.

Salary Plan

In a salary plan, salespeople are paid a fixed salary, although there may be occasional incentives in the form of bonuses, sales contest prizes, and the like. There are several reasons to use straight salary. It works well when the main sales objective is prospecting (finding new clients) or when the salesperson is mostly involved in account servicing, such as developing and executing product training programs for a distributor's sales force or participating in national and local trade shows.[39] Jobs like these are often found in industries that sell technical products. This is one reason why the aerospace and transportation equipment industries have a relatively heavy emphasis on salary plans for their salespeople.

There are advantages to paying salespeople on a straight salary basis. Salespeople know in advance what their income will be, and the employer also has fixed, predictable sales force expenses. Straight salary makes it simple to switch territories or quotas or to reassign salespeople, and it can develop a high degree of loyalty among the sales staff. Commissions tend to shift the salesperson's emphasis to making the sale rather than to prospecting and cultivating long-term customers. A long-term perspective is encouraged by straight salary compensation.

The main disadvantage is that salary plans do not depend on results.[40] In fact, salaries are often tied to seniority rather than to performance, which can be demotivating to potentially high-performing salespeople who see seniority—not performance—being rewarded.

Commission Plan

Commission plans pay salespeople in direct proportion to their sales—they pay for results and only for results. The commission plan has several advantages. Salespeople have the greatest possible incentive, and there is a tendency to attract high-performing salespeople who see that effort will clearly lead to rewards. Sales costs are proportional to sales rather than fixed, and the company's selling investment is reduced. The commission basis is also easy to understand and compute.

The commission plan also has drawbacks, however. Salespeople focus on making a sale and on high-volume items; cultivating dedicated customers and working to push hard-to-sell items may be neglected. Wide variances in income between salespeople may occur and this can lead to a feeling that the plan is inequitable. More serious is the fact that salespeople are encouraged to neglect other duties, like servicing small accounts. In addition, pay is often excessive in boom times and very low in recessions. The use of commission-based compensation plans in the real estate industry is discussed in the Expert Opinion box.

Recent research evidence presents further insights into the impact of sales commissions. One study addressed whether paying salespeople on commission "without a financial net" might induce more salespeople to leave. The participants in this study were 225 field sales representatives from a telecommunications company. Results showed that paying salespeople a commission accounting for 100 percent of pay was the situation that resulted in the highest turnover of salespersons by far. Turnover was much lower in the situation in which salespeople are paid a combination of a base salary plus commissions.[41] These findings suggest that although 100 percent commissions can drive higher sales by focusing the attention of strong-willed salespeople on maximizing sales, without a financial safety net it can also undermine the desire of salespeople to stay.

EVIDENCE-BASED HR

expert ▲ opinion
industry viewpoint

Gurinder Sandhu

Identification: Mr. Gurinder Sandhu,
Executive Vice President and Regional Director at RE/MAX Ontario–Atlantic Canada

1. The real estate industry is an example of an industry built on the commission model. What is the basic compensation structure in the industry?

It differs by province, but in Ontario commission for the real estate transaction associated with home sales is traditionally 5 percent, although there are some lower commission models based on the range of service offered and the brand (which often determines level of expertise, marketing, and support provided to home owners). Realtors must be affiliated with a brokerage. Brokers assume a commission split with realtors. The commission split may or may not include administrative fees, as determined by each brokerage.

The traditional commission model was a flat percent-based model, however there has been a recent movement to a progressive commission-based model. For example, for the first $50 000 in commission earned, the broker may get a predetermined percent of the realtor's commission, with that value reducing at predetermined intervals. Higher performing realtor's thrive using the new model.

2. In your experience, what do you find to be the motivation for people to work in this environment?

I. This is a relationship-based business. Realtors who do well are excellent at relationship building and last for decades.

II. Salespeople are inherently driven by performance-based pay. There is a relatively clear correlation between performance and pay. Total compensation varies by brand and location. While data is not readily available, based on average cost of homes and the number of homes sold, it is estimated that the average realtor in Toronto earns $60 000. The average realtor in RE/MAX (for which we do have data) earns about $110 000.

III. There is a perception of a more flexible lifestyle. We have found that the best performers allocate time for personal and professional activity. As entrepreneurs, realtors need to commit to their profession, develop expertise, and network, which can occur at various times throughout the day (rather than a traditional 9–5 schedule).

3. Based on your expertise, what are some of the risk considerations real estate agents and others working in similar commission-based compensation models need to consider?

I. Some people underestimate the amount of work that is required to be an effective or successful realtor. This leads to a high failure rate in the first year of work. The tenure aspect builds repeat clientele, geographical and process expertise, and community recognition required to succeed.

II. The industry requires the ability to handle rejection. Realtors develop thick skin, especially in the early part of their career as they build their contacts and base of recurring revenue.

III. Technology has created a market for international networking as realtors and information exchange for clients. Traditionally, consumers had access to limited information, but with the release of listing information, the role of the realtor has morphed from that of a purveyor of information to one of decipherer of information, trusted advisor, and negotiator. Realtors need to transform data to knowledge about competitive homes in the area as well as community concerns (e.g., schools, crime rates) and get the best value for their buyers and sellers.

IV. There are some low-costs models out there, which may be perceived to add insecurity to the compensation model of the industry, but Canadian home buyers/sellers have become discerning over the years; they recognize the value associated with dealing with experienced realtors and their ability to mitigate risks.

Source: Reprinted by permission from Gurinder Sandhu.

The effects on the salesperson of a commission pay plan could also depend on that person's personality. A second study investigated 154 sales representatives who were responsible for contacting and renewing existing members and for identifying and adding new members. A number of the sales reps in this study were more extroverted than were the others—they were more sociable, outgoing, talkative, aggressive, energetic, and enthusiastic.[42] It might be expected that extroverted salespeople would usually generate higher sales than less extroverted ones, but in this study extroversion was positively associated with higher performance (in terms of percentage of existing members renewing their memberships and the count of new members paying membership fees) *only when the salespeople were explicitly rewarded for accomplishing these tasks*. Thus, being extroverted did not always lead to higher sales; extroverts only sold more than those less extroverted when their rewards were contingent on their performance.

Combination Plan

There has been a definite movement away from the extremes of straight commission or fixed salary to combination plans for salespeople. Combination plans provide some of the advantages of both straight salary and straight commission plans and also some of their disadvantages. Salespeople have a floor to their earnings. Furthermore, the company can direct its salespeople's activities by detailing what services the salary component is being paid for, while the commission component provides a built-in incentive for superior performance.

However, the salary component is not tied to performance, and the employer is therefore trading away some incentive value. Combination plans also tend to become complicated, and misunderstandings can result. This might not be a problem with a simple "salary plus commission" plan, but most plans are not so simple. For example, there is a "commission plus drawing account" plan, whereby a salesperson is paid basically on commissions but can draw on future earnings to get through low sales periods. Similarly, in the "commission plus bonus" plan, salespeople are again paid primarily on the basis of commissions, but they are also given a small bonus for directed activities, like selling slow-moving items.

DEVELOPING EFFECTIVE INCENTIVE PLANS

There are two major practical considerations in developing an effective incentive plan: when to use it and how to implement it.

When to Use Incentives

Before deciding to implement an incentive plan, it is important to remember several points:

1. *Performance pay cannot replace good management.* Performance pay is supposed to motivate workers, but lack of motivation is not always the culprit. Ambiguous instructions, lack of clear goals, inadequate employee selection and training, unavailability of tools, and a hostile workforce (or management) are just a few of the factors that impede performance.

2. *Firms get what they pay for.* Psychologists know that people often put their effort where they know they will be rewarded. However, this can backfire. An incentive plan that rewards a group based on how many pieces are produced could lead to rushed production and lower quality. Awarding a plant-wide incentive for reducing accidents may simply reduce the number of reported accidents.

3. *"Pay is not a motivator."* [43] Psychologist Frederick Herzberg makes the point that money only buys temporary compliance; as soon as the incentive is removed, the "motivation" disappears too. Instead, Herzberg says, employers should provide adequate financial rewards and then build other motivators, like opportunities for achievement and psychological success, into their jobs.

4. *Rewards rupture relationships.* Incentive plans have the potential for reducing teamwork by encouraging individuals (or individual groups) to blindly pursue financial rewards for themselves.

5. *Rewards may undermine responsiveness.* Since the employees' primary focus is on achieving some specific goal, like cutting costs, any changes or extraneous distractions mean that achieving that goal will be harder. Incentive plans can, therefore, mediate against change and responsiveness.

HR Competency

60100

EVIDENCE-BASED HR

Research by two professors at the University of Alberta focused on resolving a long-standing debate about whether extrinsic rewards can backfire by reducing intrinsic motivation, or whether extrinsic rewards boost performance and enhance intrinsic motivation. The authors concluded that *careful* management of rewards does enhance performance. Common problem areas to be avoided include not tying rewards to performance, not delivering on all rewards initially promised, and delivering rewards in an authoritarian style or manner.[44]

Potential pitfalls like these do not mean that financial incentive plans cannot be useful or should not be used. They do suggest, however, that goals need to be reasonable and achievable, but not so easily attained that employees view incentives as entitlements.[45] In general, any incentive plan is more apt to succeed if implemented with management support, employee acceptance, and a supportive culture characterized by teamwork, trust, and involvement at all levels.[46] This probably helps to explain why some of the longest-lasting incentive plans, like the improshare and Rucker plans, depend heavily on two-way communication and employee involvement in addition to incentive pay.

Therefore, in general, it makes more sense to use an incentive plan when units of output can be measured, the job is standardized, the workflow is regular, and delays are few or consistent. It is also important that there be a clear relationship between employee effort and quantity of output and that quality is less important than quantity, or, if quality is important, that it is easily measured and controlled.

How to Implement Incentive Plans

There are several specific commonsense considerations in establishing any incentive plan. Of primary importance is "line of sight." The employee or group must be able to see their own impact on the goals or objectives for which incentives are being provided.[47]

Research indicates that there are seven principles that support effective implementation of incentive plans that lead to superior business results:

1. Pay for performance—and make sure that performance is tied to the successful achievement of critical business goals.

2. Link incentives to other activities that engage employees in the business, such as career development and challenging opportunities.

3. Link incentives to measurable competencies that are valued by the organization.

4. Match incentives to the culture of the organization—its vision, mission, and operation principles.

5. Keep group incentives clear and simple—employee understanding is the most important factor differentiating effective from ineffective group incentive plans.

6. Overcommunicate—employees become engaged when they hear the message that they are neither faceless nor expendable.

7. Remember that the greatest incentive is the work itself. For example, highly skilled engineers at MacDonald Dettwiler and Associates Ltd. in Richmond, British Columbia, feel valued and appreciated when they are chosen by their peers to work on project teams, to work on the Canada space arm, or to work on a project to save the rainforest, and they don't require large financial incentives to work hard.

EMPLOYEE RECOGNITION PROGRAMS

In today's fast-changing environment, recognition is emerging as a critical component of the total rewards mix.[48] Why? Because lack of recognition and praise is the number one reason that employees leave an organization. The traditional role of recognition plans has been to reward employees for long service, but today's employees value being appreciated by an employer throughout their career. In fact, recent Japanese research has shown that people get as excited about receiving a compliment as they do about receiving a cash reward because both activate the same reward centre in the brain (the striatum).[49]

An employee's introduction to a corporate recognition culture needs to start on the day he or she is hired. For example, the employee could receive a welcome note, a nameplate, and a personalized gift pack that includes a company T-shirt and coffee mug. These things are all very easy to do, and they send a clear message to a new employee.[50] Recognition and other simple incentives are particularly effective in smaller entrepreneurial companies, as explained in the Entrepreneurs and HR box.

ENTREPRENEURS and HR

Recognition and Incentives for Entrepreneurs

Entrepreneurs may not have the time or money to provide many formal incentive programs. But there are many other approaches they can use to motivate employees toward achieving the strategic objectives of the organization. There are three guides to follow.[51]

First, the best option for motivating employees is also the simplest—make sure the employee has a doable goal and that he or she agrees with it. It makes little sense to try to motivate employees in other ways (such as with financial incentives) if they don't know their goals or don't agree with them. Psychologist Edwin Locke and his colleagues have consistently found that specific, challenging goals lead to higher task performance than specific, unchallenging goals or vague goals or no goals. The best goals are SMART goals—specific, measurable, attainable, relevant, and timely.

Second, recognizing an employee's contribution is a simple and powerful motivational tool. Studies show that recognition has a positive impact on performance, either alone or in combination with financial rewards. For example, in one study, combining financial rewards with recognition produced a 30 percent performance increase in service firms, almost twice the effect of using each reward alone.

Third, there are numerous positive reinforcement rewards that can be used on a day-to-day basis, independent of formal incentive plans. A short list would include the following: challenging work assignments, freedom to choose own work activity, having fun built into work, more of a preferred task, role as boss' stand-in when he or she is away, role in presentations to top management, job rotation, encouragement of learning and continuous improvement, being provided with ample encouragement, being allowed to set own goals, and expression of appreciation in front of others.

Employees consistently say that they receive little recognition. One study found that only 50 percent of managers give recognition for high performance, and that up to 40 percent of workers feel that they never get recognized for outstanding performance. Nurses are one group of employees that has long suffered from lack of respect. They feel ignored and undervalued as subservient assistants to doctors. The shortage of nurses in Canada has forced employers to consider treating nurses with the respect and recognition they deserve as invaluable contributors of knowledge and skills to the healthcare system.[52]

Some believe that this lack of recognition occurs because expressing generous appreciation means talking about feelings in public, which may make managers feel vulnerable. However, when lack of recognition and praise is resulting in the loss of valued employees, managers need to confront such apprehension and start recognizing their employees for their achievements. Why? Because employees favour recognition from supervisors and managers by a margin of two-to-one over recognition from other sources.[53] Thus, line managers are critical to the success of recognition programs.

Recognition is also cost-effective. It takes 5 to 15 percent of pay to have an impact on behaviour when a cash reward is provided, but only 3 to 5 percent when a non-cash form of reward is used (such as recognition and modest gifts).[54] Company DNA, an incentives provider, offers an online points system where recognition points can be spent on merchandise with merchant partners, such as Eddie Bauer, La Senza, Canadian Tire, and Future Shop.[55] There appears to be a growing interest by employees in having recognition awards linked to "green" or charitable causes, such as time off for volunteering.[56] Some key metrics on the use of recognition is provided in the HR by the Numbers box.

Effective recognition is specific, immediate, personal, and spontaneous. Making time to recognize the individual in front of his or her colleagues is critical to the success of the program. Personal attention and public celebration create recognition that is personal in nature and that addresses the deep needs that we all have for belonging and contributing to something worthwhile. By making it memorable, the recognition experience will continue to evoke emotion and make the employee feel that his or her individual effort made a difference.

Recognition programs are more effective than cash in achieving improved employee attitudes, increased workloads and hours of work, and improved productivity (speed of work/intensity of work). They can build confidence, create a positive and supportive environment, build a sense of pride in accomplishments, inspire people to increase their efforts, and help people feel valued. Recognition can act as a strategic change effort if recognition criteria are aligned with business strategy, employee input is solicited regarding program design and implementation, and a recognition culture is created.[65] The Strategic HR box highlights rewards that matter by generational categorizations.

Finally, recognition is also important for high performers, who focus on what needs to be done to exceed expectations. These employees are driven by internal motivation and look to reward programs to add fuel to their achievements. Recognition satisfies "wants" rather than "needs" (where cash bonuses often go); such programs eliminate guilt about owning luxury items, provide bragging rights, and create a lasting impression in the employee's memory.[66]

HR by the Numbers

Providing Meaningful Rewards to Employees in Canada

97% of organizations surveyed have an employee reward and recognition program in place[57]

45% of all organization recognition budgets are spent on long-service recognition programs[58]

$123 average annual spending on recognition programs per employee in public sector organizations[59]

$208 average annual spending on recognition programs per employee in private sector organizations[60]

71% of organizations maintain recognition programs in an attempt to increase employee engagement[61]

$111 average value of recognition provided to employees achieving their five-year tenure milestone[62]

92% of organizations have programs in place allowing managers to recognize employees with outstanding individual achievement[63]

70% of organizations have programs in place allowing managers to provide group rewards (team performance)[64]

STRATEGIC HR

Rewards That Work

Traditionalists (born 1922–1945)

- Flexible schedules that allow them to work seasonally
- Health and fitness rewards
- Entertainment rewards that they would not purchase for themselves

Boomers (born 1946–1964)

- Recognition and being appreciated for their work
- Travel rewards
- Luxury and health-related rewards

Gen X-ers (born 1965–1980)

- Gadgets and high-tech rewards that are state-of-the-art technology
- Work–life balance rewards
- Flexibility to allow time for family, friends, and meaningful life experiences

Gen Y-ers (born 1981–2000)

- Relationship enhancers, such as electronic communications equipment
- Personalized rewards where they can choose colours and accessories
- Charitable rewards, like time off to volunteer

Source: Based on Rewards That Work. Adapted from R. Stotz, "Targeting Employee Incentives for Maximum Performance," *Workspan* (June 2006), pp. 46–48.

CHAPTER SUMMARY

1. When designing effective financial incentive plans, it's important to understand the relationship between money and motivation. A job needs to satisfy a person's higher-level needs, as well as intrinsic and extrinsic needs. Rewards can be used as a behaviour-modification–based approach to help change behaviour through rewards and recognition contingent on performance.

2. Merit pay, profit-sharing plans, employee share purchase/stock ownership plans, and gainsharing plans are examples of organization-wide incentive plans, usually made available to all employees. Merit pay is an increase in base pay (fixed) which is tied directly to individual performance. Profit-sharing plans provide a share of company profits to all employees in the organization. The problem with such plans is that sometimes the link between a person's efforts and rewards is unclear. Stock purchase plans provide a vehicle for employees to purchase company stock with their own and sometimes employer contributions. Gainsharing plans engage employees in a common effort to achieve a company's productivity objectives in which incremental cost savings are

shared among employees and the company. All these plans are intended to increase employee commitment toward the organization and are ultimately designed to motivate workers.

3. Piecework is the oldest type of incentive plan. Here, a worker is paid a piece rate for each unit that he or she produces. The differential piece-rate plan rewards workers by a premium that equals the percentage by which their performance is above standard. Group incentive plans are useful when the workers' jobs are highly interrelated.

4. Most management employees receive a short-term incentive, usually in the form of an annual bonus linked to company or divisional profits. Long-term incentives are intended to motivate and reward top management for the firm's long-term growth and prosperity and to inject a long-term perspective into executive decisions.

5. Salary plans for salespeople are effective when the main sales objective is finding new clients or servicing accounts. The main disadvantage of salary plans is that pay is not tied to performance. Commission plans

attract high-performing salespeople who see that performance will clearly lead to rewards. The problem with straight commission plans is that there is a tendency to focus on "big-ticket" or "quick-sell" items and to disregard long-term customer relationships.

6. Incentive plans are particularly appropriate when units of output are easily measured, employees can control output, the effort–reward relationship is clear, work delays are under employees' control, and quality is not paramount.

7. Employee recognition plans are growing in popularity as a cost-effective method of retaining employees by praising their achievements. Recognition has the most impact when it is sincerely and meaningfully provided by the supervisor in a public presentation format.

MyManagementLab

Study, practise, and explore real business situations with these helpful resources:

- **Interactive Lesson Presentations:** Work through interactive presentations and assessments to test your knowledge of management concepts.
- **PIA (Personal Inventory Assessments):** Enhance your ability to connect with key concepts through these engaging self-reflection assessments.
- **Study Plan:** Check your understanding of chapter concepts with self-study quizzes.
- **Videos:** Learn more about the management practices and strategies of real companies.
- **Simulations:** Practise decision-making in simulated management environments.

KEY TERMS

capital accumulation programs *(p. 282)*
differential piece-rate plan *(p. 278)*
employee share purchase/stock ownership
  plan (ESOP) *(p. 276)*
expectancy *(p. 274)*
fixed pay *(p. 273)*
gainsharing plan *(p. 277)*
guaranteed piecework plan *(p. 278)*
instrumentality *(p. 274)*

intrinsic motivation *(p. 274)*
merit pay (merit raise) *(p. 275)*
piecework *(p. 277)*
profit-sharing plan *(p. 276)*
stock option *(p. 282)*
straight piecework plan *(p. 278)*
team or group incentive plan *(p. 279)*
valence *(p. 274)*
variable pay *(p. 273)*

REVIEW AND DISCUSSION QUESTIONS

1. Compare and contrast six types of incentive plans.

2. What is merit pay? Do you think it's a good idea to award employees merit pay? Why or why not?

3. Describe the three basic issues to be considered when awarding short-term management bonuses.

4. Explain how stock options work. What are some of the reasons that stock options have been criticized in recent years?

5. When and why should a salesperson be paid a salary? A commission? Salary and commission combined?

6. Explain five reasons why incentive plans fail.

7. Why are recognition plans useful for motivating high performers?

CRITICAL THINKING QUESTIONS

1. A major consulting firm recently launched a new "project managers' incentive" plan. Basically, senior managers in the company were told to award $5000 raises (not bonuses) to about 40 percent of the project managers in their team based on how good of a job they did in managing people on their projects, meeting deadlines, and the number of projects each project manager was responsible for that year. There were no additional criteria provided, given the wide variance in projects and teams that the consulting firm secures in a given year. What are the potential advantages and pitfalls of such an incentive program? What areas of support or concern do you think project managers might have with the incentives? What areas of support or concern do you think senior managers might have with the incentives?

2. Is it ethical for companies to offer incentive bonuses only to top managers? Why or why not? What are the pros and cons of making such bonuses available to all employees who meet performance criteria?

3. Give four examples of when you would suggest using rewards for all employees rather than individual incentive programs.

4. In this chapter, we listed a number of reasons that experts give for not instituting a pay-for-performance plan in a vacuum (such as "rewards rupture relationships"). Do you think that these points (or any others) are valid? Why or why not?

5. Recognition can take many forms. Prepare a list of some forms of recognition that would be particularly motivational for Generation Y employees and explain why you have chosen them.

6. Think of organizations that have been in the news in the last few years because of scandals. Which of these involved incentives? What were the problems and how could they have been avoided?

EXPERIENTIAL EXERCISES

1. Working individually or in groups, develop an incentive plan for each of the following positions: web designer, hotel manager, and used-car salesperson. What factors had to be taken into consideration?

2. Employee recognition plans are growing in popularity. There has been some debate in research literature suggesting that once incentives are provided, they are viewed as entitlements by employees and therefore become non-removable. Assume that you are working for your local university or college in the HR department. Due to financial restraints, it has been suggested that the university eliminate a $5000 gift certificate award offered to professors who publish in specific top-tier journals (which cost the university $225 000 last year alone). Interview two professors in your university or college to understand their position on the incentive. Based on the information provided in this chapter and your interviews, draft a memo targeted to faculty assuming you were forced to adopt the cut and effectively communicate the change.

3. Express Automotive, an automobile mega-dealership with more than 600 employees that represents 22 brands, has just received a very discouraging set of survey results. It seems its customer satisfaction scores have fallen for the ninth straight quarter. Customer complaints included the following:

- It was hard to get prompt feedback from mechanics by phone.

- Salespeople often did not return phone calls.

- The finance people seemed "pushy."

- New cars were often not properly cleaned or had minor items that needed immediate repair or adjustment.

- Cars often had to be returned to have repair work redone.

The table on the following page describes Express Automotive's current compensation system.

The class is to be divided into five groups. Each group is assigned to one of the five teams in column one. Each group should analyze the compensation package for its team. Each group should be able to identify the ways in which the current compensation plan (1) helps company performance or (2) impedes company performance. Once the groups have

Team	Responsibility	Current Compensation Method
Sales force	Persuade buyers to purchase a car.	Very small salary (minimum wage) with commissions; commission rate increases with every 20 cars sold per month.
Finance office	Help close the sale; persuade customer to use company finance plan.	Salary, plus bonus for each $10 000 financed with the company.
Detailing	Inspect cars delivered from factory, clean them, and make minor adjustments.	Piecework paid on the number of cars detailed per day.
Mechanics	Provide factory warranty service, maintenance, and repair.	Small hourly wage, plus bonus based on (1) number of cars completed per day and (2) finishing each car faster than the standard estimated time to repair.
Receptionists/phone service personnel	Act as primary liaison between customer and sales force, finance, and mechanics.	Minimum wage.

completed their analyses, the following questions are to be discussed as a class:

a. In what ways might your group's compensation plan contribute to the customer service problems?
b. Do the rewards provided by your department impede the work of other departments?
c. What recommendations would you make to improve the compensation system in a way that would likely improve customer satisfaction?

4. Working in groups, brainstorm ways in which a company that previously provided generous incentive pay and bonuses might provide less costly incentives to encourage employee commitment and productivity in recessionary times when company revenues are falling. Create a communications plan to announce the changes to employees who may have come to expect and rely on these incentives. Critique your plan from the employee perspective.

RUNNING CASE

Running Case: LearnInMotion.com

The Incentive Plan

Of all its HR programs, those relating to pay for performance and incentives are LearnInMotion.com's most fully developed. For one thing, the venture capital firm that funded it was very explicit about reserving at least 10 percent of the company's stock for employee incentives. The agreement with the venture capital firm also included very explicit terms and conditions regarding LearnInMotion.com's stock option plan. The venture fund agreement included among its 500 or so pages the specific written agreement that LearnInMotion.com would have to send to each of its employees, laying out the details of the company's stock option plan.

Although there was some flexibility, the stock option plan details came down to this:

1. Employees would get stock options (the right to buy shares of LearnInMotion.com stock) at a price equal to 15 percent less than the venture capital fund paid for those shares when it funded LearnInMotion.com.

2. The shares will have a vesting schedule of 36 months, with one-third of the shares vesting once the employee has completed 12 full months of employment with the company, and one-third vesting on successful completion of each of the following two full 12-month periods of employment.

3. If an employee leaves the company for any reason before his or her first full 12 months with the firm, the person is not eligible for stock options.

4. If the person has stock options and leaves the firm for any reason, he or she must exercise the options within 90 days of the date of leaving the firm or lose the right to exercise them.

5. The actual number of options an employee gets depends on the person's bargaining power and on how much Jennifer and Pierre think the person brings to the company. The options granted generally ranged from options to buy 10 000 shares for some employees up to 50 000 shares for others, but this has not raised any questions to date. When a new employee signs on, he or she receives a letter of offer. This provides minimal details regarding the option plan; after the person has completed the 90-day introductory period, he or she receives the five-page document describing the stock option plan, which Jennifer or Pierre, as well as the employee, sign.

Beyond that, the only incentive plan is the one for the two salespeople. In addition to their respective salaries, both salespeople receive about 20 percent of any sales they bring in, whether those sales are from advertising banners or course listing fees. It's not clear to Jennifer and Pierre whether this incentive is effective. Each salesperson gets a base salary regardless of what he or she sells (one gets about $50 000, the other about $35 000). However, sales have simply not come up to the levels anticipated.

Jennifer and Pierre are not sure why. It could be that Internet advertising has dried up. It could be that their own business model is no good or there's not enough demand for their company's services. They may be charging too much or too little. It could be that the salespeople can't do the job because of inadequate skills or inadequate training. Or, of course, it could be the incentive plan. ("Or it could be all of the above," as Pierre somewhat dejectedly said late one Friday evening.) They want to try to figure out what the problem is. They want you, their management consultant, to help them figure out what to do.

QUESTIONS

1 Is LearnInMotion.com's current compensation program motivating their staff? Or is it hindering employee performance?

2 Should LearnInMotion.com use a mix of individual, team, and organizational incentives? If so, recommend specific incentives that the company should use and discuss why you recommended each.

3 Do you think changing the compensation strategy will positively affect this firm? If so, how specifically?

CASE INCIDENT

A New Compensation Program to Motivate Performance

Marilyn Brown started her chain of 10 wedding boutiques approximately five years ago. She presently operates within southwestern Ontario and has been enjoying record profits. Marilyn's wedding boutiques provide full-service amenities to future brides, including wedding planning services, custom fittings, and locating hard-to-find wedding dresses.

Marilyn's customer service philosophy is that customers are number one and must be satisfied with their purchases. However, recently, there has been a rise in complaints regarding the lack of friendly service being provided, and three long-standing employees have threatened to leave unless their compensation is adjusted in response to servicing Marilyn's very demanding clients. Currently, Marilyn pays all of her staff the same base salary of $14 per hour without any benefits. Marilyn feels that this approach promotes equity and eliminates any perceptions of favouritism between employees regarding compensation.

Since receiving the negative complaints and the threats of some of her staff leaving, Marilyn has decided she needs to rethink her compensation philosophy and needs your help.

QUESTIONS

1 What are the specific problems with Marilyn's current compensation program?

2 Discuss the types of compensation programs and plans available to Marilyn to motivate and retain her existing staff.

3 Should Marilyn use only one type of compensation plan, or a combination plan for her employees? Discuss your recommendation in detail.

CHAPTER
13

Employee Benefits and Services

LEARNING OUTCOMES

AFTER STUDYING THIS CHAPTER, YOU SHOULD BE ABLE TO

EXPLAIN the strategic role of employee benefits.

DESCRIBE six government-sponsored benefits.

EXPLAIN why the cost of health insurance benefits is increasing and how employers can reduce these costs.

DESCRIBE the two categories of pension plans and the shift that is occurring in their relative popularity.

DISCUSS three types of personal employee services and seven types of job-related services offered to employees.

EXPLAIN how to set up a flexible benefits program.

REQUIRED HR COMPETENCIES

20600: Promote an evidence-based approach to the development of human resources policies and practices using current professional resources to provide a sound basis for human resources decision-making.

30100: Promote engagement, commitment, and motivation of employees by developing, implementing, and evaluating innovative strategies to enhance productivity, morale, and culture.

60100: Create a total rewards structure that encompasses compensation, pensions, benefits, and perquisites to maintain consistency, fairness, and organizational competitiveness, comply with legal requirements, and encourage desired behaviour.

60300: Evaluate the total rewards structure using appropriate metrics, monitoring trends, and innovations to ensure consistency, fairness, organizational competitiveness, compliance with legal requirements, performance, and desired behaviour and to identify recommendations for the organization's leadership.

60400: Provide information about the total value of and changes to total rewards using appropriate media to achieve understanding and encourage performance and desired behaviour.

90100: Make informed business decisions using financial and operating information to align human resources with business strategy.

THE STRATEGIC ROLE OF EMPLOYEE BENEFITS

employee benefits Indirect financial payments given to employees. They may include supplementary health and life insurance, vacation, pension plans, education plans, and discounts on company products.

HR Competency

60100

Employee benefits and services can be defined as all the indirect financial payments that an employee receives during his or her employment with an employer.[1] Benefits are generally provided to all of a firm's employees and include such things as time off with pay, supplementary health and life insurance, and employee assistance plans. Employee services, traditionally a minor aspect of compensation, are becoming more sought after by today's employees in the post-job-security era. Research indicates that benefits do matter to employees and that, if they are aligned with business strategy, they can help to attract and retain the right people to achieve business objectives.[2]

Employee benefits are an important part of most employees' compensation, particularly given today's reality of modest salary increases.[3] For the aging workforce, health-care benefits are becoming increasingly important. Employee benefits are in the midst of an evolution based on the aging population, the looming labour shortage in Canada, and advances in healthcare. Each of these factors is expected to increase the cost of benefits, which is already at an all-time high.[4]

Administering benefits today represents an increasingly specialized task, because workers are more financially sophisticated and demanding, and because benefit plans must comply with a wide variety of laws. Providing and administering benefits is also an increasingly expensive task. Benefits as a percentage of payroll (for public and private sectors combined) are approximately 37 percent today (compared with about 15 percent in 1953). Most employees do not realize the market value and high cost to the employer of their benefits.

Certain benefits are mandated by law, and most Canadian companies voluntarily provide additional employee benefits such as group life insurance, health and dental care insurance, and retirement benefits. In the remainder of this chapter, government-sponsored benefits, voluntary employer-sponsored benefits, employee services, flexible benefits, and benefits administration will be discussed. Table 13.1 provides a summary of mandated and voluntary benefits.

GOVERNMENT-MANDATED BENEFITS

Canada has one of the world's finest collections of social programs to protect its citizens when they cannot earn income. Employers and employees provide funding for these plans, along with general tax revenues.

TABLE 13.1 Objectives of a Benefits Strategy

Objectives of benefits strategy	Percent of organizations that rated the objective as "very important"
Complying with accounting, regulatory, and company standards	51
Containing benefits costs	50
Increasing job satisfaction/employee engagement	35
Reducing absenteeism	29
Addressing the diverse needs of employees	22

Source: Thorpe, Karla; Martin, Heidi; Lamontagne, Elyse (2012). The Conference Board of Canada. "Benefits Benchmarking 2012," p. 3. Reprinted by permission.

Employment Insurance (EI)

Employment insurance (EI) is a federal program intended to provide temporary financial assistance to eligible persons who experience interruption to their work through no fault of their own. EI benefits are not payable when an employee is terminated for just cause—for example, for theft of company property—or when an employee quits for no good reason. EI is perceived to be a benefit, since it provides employees who are laid off, terminated without just cause, or who quit their job for a justifiable reason (such as harassment) with an alternative form of government income until they secure employment.

In addition to loss of employment through no fault of the employee, eligibility is also restricted to persons who have paid into the account (for example, a contractor who does not contribute to the EI account is ineligible for the benefit), have worked a minimum number of hours in a specified time, and are willing and able to work.

The EI benefit is generally 55 percent of average earnings during the last 14 to 45 weeks of the qualifying period or a maximum weekly rate (for example, as of January 1, 2014, in Ontario the maximum weekly rate was $514), depending on the regional unemployment rate. The benefit is payable for up to 45 weeks, depending on factors like the regional unemployment rate. To continue receiving EI benefits, individuals must demonstrate that they are actively seeking work. Claimants are encouraged to work part time, as they can earn up to 25 percent of their EI benefit amount before these earnings will be deducted from the benefit.[5]

To receive benefits, an employee must first have worked a minimum number of hours during a minimum number of weeks called a *qualifying period* (the number of hours and weeks varies among regions of the country). Then there is a waiting period from the last day of work until benefits begin. The waiting period varies but is often two weeks. If the employee was provided with severance pay or holiday pay at the time of losing the job, these payments must run out before the waiting period begins.

The EI program is funded by contributions from eligible employees and their employers. Employee contributions are collected by payroll deduction, and employers pay 1.4 times the employee contribution. Employer contributions can be reduced if the employer provides a wage loss replacement plan for employee sick leave.

Hints TO ENSURE LEGAL COMPLIANCE

A supplemental unemployment benefit (SUB) plan is an agreement between an employer and the employees (often the result of collective bargaining) for a plan that enables employees who are eligible for EI benefits to receive additional benefits from a SUB fund created by the employer. SUB plans help employees maintain their standard of living during periods of unemployment (most often maternity leave) by receiving a combined benefit closer to their actual working wage. Most SUBs provide benefits of 90 percent of the working wage or greater.[6] Work-sharing programs are a related arrangement in which employees work a reduced workweek and receive EI benefits for the remainder of the week. The Canada Employment Insurance Commission must approve SUB plans and work-sharing programs.

Pay on Termination of Employment

Employment/labour standards legislation requires that employees whose employment is being terminated by the employer be provided with termination pay when they leave. The amount to be paid varies among jurisdictions and with the circumstances, as follows. Specifically, it should be noted that employees often confuse severance pay with reasonable advanced notice pay.

Reasonable Advance Notice Periods

advance/reasonable notice
Advance written notice required if the employer is going to terminate employment of a worker without cause.

An employee must be provided with advance written notice if the employer is going to terminate his or her employment, unless the employee is working on a short-term contract or is being fired for just cause (such as continued poor performance, theft, or if the employee initiated the termination of employment). The amount of **advance notice (also known as reasonable notice)** that is required applies only to employees whose employment relationship is terminated through no cause of their own, increases with the length of employment of the employee (e.g., one week per year of employment to a specified maximum), and varies among jurisdictions. In practice, many employers do not provide advance written notice. Instead, they ask the employee to cease working immediately and provide the employee with a lump sum equal to their pay for the notice period. This amount is called **pay in lieu of reasonable notice**.

pay in lieu of reasonable notice   A lump-sum equal to an employee's pay for the notice period provided to employees who cease working immediately.

Advanced Notice for Mass Layoffs

The provinces of British Columbia, Manitoba, Ontario, New Brunswick, and Newfoundland and Labrador require that additional pay be provided when a layoff of 50 or more employees occurs. The rationale behind this regulation is that larger layoffs result in longer time to re-employment, so in cases of larger layoffs the employees are given longer reasonable notice periods. In Nova Scotia and Saskatchewan, additional pay is required if 10 or more employees are being laid off. The amount of additional pay ranges from six weeks to 18 weeks, depending on the province and the number of employees being laid off.

Severance Pay

severance pay   An additional payout on top of the minimum notice period requirements and only applies if the specific conditions in the applicable jurisdiction are met.

Severance pay is an additional payout on top of the minimum notice period requirements and only applies if the specific conditions in the applicable jurisdiction are met. Employees only in Ontario and the federal jurisdiction may be eligible for severance pay in addition to pay in lieu of notice in certain termination situations (no other jurisdictions mandate severance pay). For example, in Ontario, employees with five or more years of service may be eligible for severance pay if (1) the employer's annual Ontario payroll is $2.5 million or more, or (2) the employer is closing down the business and 50 or more employees will be losing their jobs within a six-month period. The amount of the severance pay is one week's pay for each year of employment (maximum 26 weeks). In the federal jurisdiction system, employees who have been employed for 12 months or more receive the greater of either two days' worth of wages for every year employed with the company or a total of five days' wages (for example, an employee who has been with the company for one year would be entitled to five days' worth of severance, which is the greater of the two options above). Severance pay is an additional payout on top of the minimum notice period requirements and only applies if the specific conditions in the applicable jurisdiction are met.

Leave of Absence

All provinces and territories and the federal jurisdiction require unpaid leaves of absence to be provided to employees in certain circumstances. Maternity/parental leave is provided in every jurisdiction (usually after one year of service). The amount of maternity leave is 17 or 18 weeks in each jurisdiction (15 weeks in Alberta), but parental and adoption leaves range from 34 to 52 weeks. Employees who take these leaves of absence are guaranteed their old job or a similar job when they return to work. Parental leave benefits can be taken by one parent or split between both parents.

Bereavement leave on the death of a family member is provided for employees in some but not all jurisdictions. The amount of time off varies by jurisdiction and depends on the closeness of the relationship between the employee and the deceased. Bereavement leave is usually unpaid, but in some cases it can be partially or fully paid. All jurisdictions except Alberta provide compassionate care leave for employees who are caring for a critically or terminally ill relative (six weeks of EI is payable during these leaves).[7] Quebec has extended compassionate leave to cover situations where close family members are victims of criminal acts, commit suicide, or where a child disappears.[8]

Some employers provide full or partial pay for all or part of legally required unpaid leaves by "topping up" what employees receive from EI, such that the total amount they receive more closely matches their regular salary. For example, in some cases bereavement leave may be partially or fully paid by the employer.

Having a clear procedure for any leave of absence is essential. An application form should be the centrepiece of any such procedure. In general, no employee should be given a leave until it is clear what the leave is for. If the leave is for medical or family reasons, medical certification should be obtained from the attending physician or medical practitioner. A form like this creates a record of the employee's expected return date and the fact that, without an authorized extension, his or her employment may be terminated.

Although these leaves are unpaid, it is incorrect to assume that the leave is costless to the employer. For example, one study concluded that the costs associated with recruiting new temporary workers, training replacement workers, and compensating for the lower level of productivity of these workers could represent a substantial expense over and above what employers would normally pay their full-time employees.[9]

Canada/Quebec Pension Plan (C/QPP)

Canada/Quebec Pension Plans (C/QPP) Programs that provide three types of benefits: retirement income, survivor or death benefits payable to the employee's dependants regardless of age at time of death, and disability benefits payable to employees with disabilities and their dependants. Benefits are payable only to those individuals who make contributions to the plans or to their family members.

The **Canada/Quebec Pension Plans (C/QPP)** were introduced in 1966 to provide working Canadians with a basic level of financial security on retirement or disability. Four decades later, these benefits do indeed provide a significant part of most Canadians' retirement income. Almost all employed Canadians between the ages of 18 and 65 are covered, including self-employed individuals. Casual and migrant workers are excluded, as are people who are not earning any employment income, such as homemakers or volunteers. The benefits are portable, meaning that pension rights are not affected by changes in job or residence within Canada. Both contributions and benefits are based only on earnings up to the "year's maximum pensionable earnings" (intended to approximate the average industrial wage), as defined in the legislation. Benefits are adjusted based on inflation each year in line with the consumer price index. Contributions made by employees (4.95 percent of pensionable earnings as of January 2014) are matched by employers.[10]

Three types of benefits are provided: retirement pensions, disability pensions, and survivor benefits. The *retirement pension* is calculated as 25 percent of the average earnings (adjusted for inflation up to the average inflation level during the last five years before retirement) over the years during which contributions were made. Plan members can choose to begin receiving benefits at any time between the ages of 60 and 70. Benefits are reduced on early retirement before a predetermined age (usually 65) and are increased in the case of late retirement. *Disability benefits* are only paid for severe disabilities that are expected to be permanent or to last for an extended period. The disability benefit is 75 percent of the pension benefit earned at the date of disability, plus a flat-rate amount per child. *Survivor benefits* are paid on the death of a plan member. A lump-sum payment is made to the plan member's estate, and a monthly pension is also payable to the surviving spouse and each dependent child.

Workers' Compensation

Workers' compensation laws are aimed at providing sure, prompt income and medical benefits to victims of work-related accidents or illnesses or their dependants, regardless of fault. Every province and territory and the federal jurisdiction has its own workers' compensation law. These laws impose compulsory collective liability for workplace accidents and work-related illnesses. This means that employees and employers cannot sue each other regarding the costs of workplace accidents or illnesses. Workers' compensation is, in effect, a "no fault" insurance plan designed to help injured or ill workers get well and return to work. For an injury or illness to be covered by workers' compensation, one must only prove that it arose while the employee was on the job. It does not matter that the employee may have been at fault; if he or she was on the job when the injury or illness occurred, he or she is entitled to workers' compensation. For example, suppose all employees are instructed to wear safety goggles when working at their machines, and one does not and is injured. Workers' compensation benefits will still be provided. The fact that the worker was at fault in no way waives his or her claim to benefits.

Employers collectively pay the full cost of the workers' compensation system, which can be an onerous financial burden for small businesses. The cost varies by industry and with actual employer costs; employer premiums are tax deductible. Workers' compensation boards (or equivalent bodies) exist in each jurisdiction to determine and collect payments from employers, determine rights to compensation, and pay workers the amount of benefit to which they are entitled under the legislation in their jurisdiction. Employers and employees have some representation on these boards, but usually both parties believe they should have more control.

Workers' compensation benefits include payment of expenses for medical treatment and rehabilitation, and income benefits during the time in which the worker is unable to work (temporarily or permanently) because of his or her disability (partial or total). Survivor benefits are payable if a work-related death occurs. All benefits are non-taxable.

HR Competency

90100

Association of Workers' Compensation Boards of Canada **www.awcbc.org**

Controlling Workers' Compensation Costs

All parties agree that a renewed focus on accident prevention is the best way to manage workers' compensation costs over the long term. Minimizing the number of workers' compensation claims is an important goal for all employers. Although workers' compensation boards pay the claims, the premiums for most employers depend on the number and amount of claims that are paid. Minimizing such claims is thus important. The Expert Opinion box highlights how proactive management of musculoskeletal pain can help control costs associated with disabilities. In practice, there are two basic approaches to reducing workers' compensation claims. First, firms try to reduce accident- or illness-causing conditions in facilities by instituting effective *safety and health programs* and complying with government safety standards. Second, since workers' compensation costs increase the longer an employee is unable to return to work, employers have become involved in instituting *rehabilitation programs* for injured or ill employees. These include physical therapy programs and career counselling to guide such employees into new, less strenuous or stressful positions. Workers are required to co-operate with return-to-work initiatives, such as modified work.[11] When Purolator's workers' compensation costs came to $13 million, it decided to use both of these approaches to reduce costs. The company hired occupational nurses, conducted physical demands analyses of many of its jobs, strengthened its return-to-work program, tied injury reduction to managers' bonuses, and increased its interaction with doctors.[12]

HR Competency

60200

Dr. Pierre Côté

Identification: Dr. Pierre Côté (PhD), Associate Professor and Canada Research Chair in Disability Prevention and Rehabilitation

Affiliation: Faculty of Health Sciences, University of Ontario Institute of Technology (UOIT) and Director, UOIT-CMCC Centre for the Study of Disability Prevention and Rehabilitation

1. **What causes musculoskeletal pain?**

A musculoskeletal condition, such as back, neck, or knee pain at work, is actually multi-causal in nature. This is often precipitated by injury (acute trauma, i.e., falling or sprain, or non-traumatic, i.e., repetitive strain). The broader psychosocial environment in the workplace is critical for triggering and resolving musculoskeletal pain. Research demonstrates that people who are dissatisfied with work report high stress levels, or indicate low decision-making autonomy of the workforce are generally higher at risk for musculoskeletal pain. There are personal factors, such as general health or individual psychological characteristics (e.g., depression) that increase risk. In addition, the healthcare system is another point of influence.

The timeliness and nature of the feedback or treatment is critical to ensure successful return to work. For example, if treatment is only clinical in nature, rather than integrative, that individual may be more likely to experience a longer disability or time to recovery.

2. **How can musculoskeletal pain that leads to disabilities impact the workplace?**

The job design should consider the physical and psychosocial aspects which trigger musculoskeletal pain. In addition, using evidence-based approaches to pain management can help reduce the likelihood that musculoskeletal pain will result in a disability. Most workers with musculoskeletal pain get better in a few weeks. Others require an integrated solution involving the union, the worker, and clinical stakeholders in the mix to find a solution. Research shows that when individuals return to work with multistakeholder intervention, they can succeed return to work. Critical to this multistakeholder intervention is a negotiated stakeholder decision, rather than a unilateral decision in which the employee and other stakeholders do not have an opportunity to express their voice or help find a middle ground.

3. **What can organizations do to ensure musculoskeletal pain is proactively managed?**

In the health sciences, we use the concept of primary prevention. The list is not exhaustive, but highlights some of the key points to consider. First, the psychosocial environment should be healthy, including good working relationships with managers and co-workers. Second, the organization should ensure that a culture of health and well-being is prioritized. This includes legitimizing injury. For example, if a worker is hurt they don't get labelled as a whiner. This also includes fully addressing a culture of presenteeism, which can have long-term detrimental effects on the individual and the organization.

In addition, organizational leadership is required to champion initiatives associated with management of health risks. The physical makeup of work is critical as well. Poorly configured work sections are associated with neck and upper extremity injuries. The influence of stress, demands, and work conditions need to be managed for both onsite and remote workers.

Source: Reprinted by permission from Pierre Cote.

Paid Time Off

Firms should address several holiday- and vacation-related policy issues, such as how many vacation days employees get, and which days (if any) are paid holidays. In addition, provincial or jurisdictional legislation determines minimum breaks to be given in a work day, which is a consideration for HR and managers.

Vacations

More firms are taking a more flexible vacation leave approach. For example, IBM gives each employee at least three weeks' vacation, but doesn't track how much vacation each takes. Employees just make informal arrangements with supervisors.[13] Vacation policy decisions include:

- Are employees paid for accrued vacation time if they quit before taking their vacations?

- Are employees paid for a holiday if they don't come to work the day before and the day after the holiday?

- And, should employers pay some premium—such as time and a half—when employees must work on holidays?

In contrast, some employers emphasize centralized absence oversight (called "integrated absence management"). This starts with collecting data. For instance, how many people are on leave; how many days of work is the employer losing; how much is the employer spending to replace absent workers; and what units have the attendance problems?[14] These employers then closely monitor all aspects of their employees' leaves and absences.

Legislated Holidays

The number of paid holidays similarly varies considerably from one jurisdiction to another, from a minimum of five to a maximum of nine. The most common paid holidays include New Year's Day, Good Friday, Canada Day, Labour Day, and Christmas and Boxing Day. Other common holidays include Victoria Day, Thanksgiving Day, and Remembrance Day. Additional holidays may be observed in each province, such as Saint-Jean-Baptiste Day in Quebec.

HR Competency

20600

Paid Breaks

While vacation requirements mandate paid time off, in terms of full days of work off, there are also mandated paid and unpaid time off requirements within a work day at the provincial, territorial, or federal level. For example, in Nova Scotia, an employee shift of over five hours requires a minimum 30-minute uninterrupted break. If the employee is under direct control of the employer and expected to be available for work during this time, then the break must be paid. If not, then it can be unpaid. Similar conditions apply in each jurisdiction. Contrary to popular belief, coffee or other rest breaks in addition to the eating period are often not government mandated. If the employee is free to leave the workplace, then the employer does not have to pay for the time.

VOLUNTARY EMPLOYER-SPONSORED BENEFITS

Although they are not required to do so, employers often provide many other employee benefits. There are some benefits that appear to be more valued by Canadian employees, based on a 2012 Mercer survey (as highlighted in **Figure 13.1**), however offering a mix of benefits appears to be the norm in most organizations. Several of the most common types of employee benefits will now be described.

HR Competency

60200

Life Insurance

group life insurance Life insurance provided at lower rates for all employees, including new employees, regardless of health or physical condition.

Virtually all employers provide **group life insurance** plans for their employees. As a group, employees can obtain lower rates than if they bought such insurance as individuals. In addition, group plans usually contain a provision for coverage of all employees—including new ones—regardless of health or physical condition.

FIGURE 13.1 Top Benefits Choices among Canadians

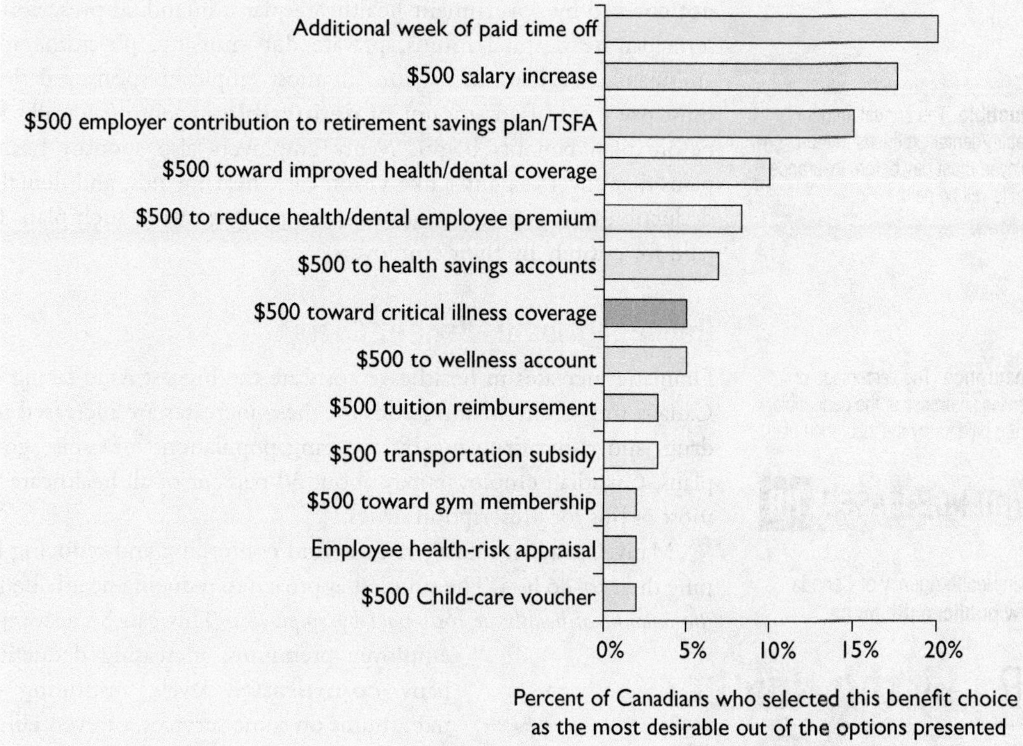

Additional week of paid time off
$500 salary increase
$500 employer contribution to retirement savings plan/TSFA
$500 toward improved health/dental coverage
$500 to reduce health/dental employee premium
$500 to health savings accounts
$500 toward critical illness coverage
$500 to wellness account
$500 tuition reimbursement
$500 transportation subsidy
$500 toward gym membership
Employee health-risk appraisal
$500 Child-care voucher

0%   5%   10%   15%   20%

Percent of Canadians who selected this benefit choice as the most desirable out of the options presented

Source: Reprinted by permission of Canadian HR Reporter. © Copyright Thomson Reuters Canada Ltd., 2013, Toronto, Ontario.

In most cases, the employer pays 100 percent of the base premium, which usually provides life insurance equal to about two years' salary. Additional life insurance coverage is sometimes made available to employees on an optional, employee-paid basis. **Accidental death and dismemberment coverage** provides a fixed lump-sum benefit in addition to life insurance benefits when death is accidental. It also provides a range of benefits in case of accidental loss of limbs or sight and is often paid for by the employer.

Critical illness insurance provides a lump-sum benefit to an employee who is diagnosed with and survives a life-threatening illness. This benefit bridges the gap between life insurance and disability insurance by providing immediate funds to relieve some the financial burden associated with the illness (such as paying for out-of-country treatment or experimental treatment) or enabling employees to enjoy their remaining time by pursuing activities that would normally be beyond their financial means.[15]

accidental death and dismemberment coverage Employer-paid benefit that provides a fixed lump-sum benefit in addition to life insurance benefits when death is accidental or a range of benefits in case of accidental loss of limbs or sight.

critical illness insurance The benefit that provides a lump-sum benefit to an employee who is diagnosed with and survives a life-threatening illness.

Supplementary Healthcare/Medical Insurance

Most employers provide their employees with supplementary healthcare/medical insurance (over and above that provided by provincial healthcare plans). Along with life insurance and long-term disability, these benefits form the cornerstone of almost all benefits programs.[16] Supplementary healthcare insurance is aimed at providing protection against medical costs arising from off-the-job accidents or illness.

Most supplementary health insurance plans provide insurance at group rates, which are usually lower than individual rates and are generally available to all employees—including new ones—regardless of health or physical condition. Supplementary healthcare plans provide major medical coverage to meet medical expenses not covered by government healthcare plans, including prescription drugs, private or semi-private hospital rooms, private duty nursing, physiotherapy, medical supplies, ambulance services, and so on. In most employer-sponsored drug plans, employees must pay a specified amount of **deductible** expense (typically $25 or $50) per year before plan benefits begin. Many employers also sponsor health-related insurance plans that cover expenses like vision care, hearing aids, and dental services, often with deductibles. In a majority of cases, the participants in such plans have their premiums paid for entirely by their employers.[17]

deductible The annual amount of health/dental expenses that an employee must pay before insurance benefits will be paid.

coinsurance The percentage of expenses (in excess of the deductible) that are paid for by the insurance plan.

Reducing Health-Benefit Costs

Dramatic increases in healthcare costs are the biggest issue facing benefits managers in Canada today. The main reasons for these increases are increased use of expensive new drugs and rising drug use by an aging population.[18] Despite government healthcare plans, Canadian employers pay about 30 percent of all healthcare expenses in Canada, most of this for prescription drugs.[19]

Many Canadian managers now find controlling and reducing healthcare costs topping their to-do lists. The simplest approach to reducing health-benefit costs is to *increase the amount of healthcare costs paid by employees.* This can be accomplished by increasing employee premiums, increasing deductibles, reducing company **coinsurance** levels, instituting or lowering annual maximums on some services, or even eliminating coverage for spouses, private hospital rooms, and other benefits. An Angus Reid poll of 1500 Canadians found that three-quarters of the respondents were willing to pay higher premiums to cover the high cost of prescription drugs.[20]

Another cost-reduction strategy is to publish a *restricted list of drugs* that will be paid for under the plan to encourage the use of generic rather than more expensive brand-name drugs. New drugs may not be covered if equally effective, cheaper alternatives are available. This approach should be combined with employee education to effectively manage the demand for drugs.[21]

A third approach is *health promotion.* In-house newsletters can caution workers to take medication properly and advertise programs on weight management, smoking cessation, exercise classes, on-site massage therapy, nutrition counselling, and other wellness programs. After 10 years of providing an on-site exercise program for employees, Canada Life Assurance Company found that absenteeism dropped 24 percent for employees who exercised two to three times per week.[23] Employee assistance programs can help to combat alcohol and drug addiction and provide stress-management counselling. The HR by the Numbers box provides key metrics associated with smoking cessation programs in the workplace.

A fourth approach is to implement *risk-assessment* programs. Such programs are being used by CIBC and other companies. A third party conducts a confidential survey of the health history and lifestyle choices of employees to identify common

EVIDENCE-BASED HR

Public Health Agency of Canada
www.publichealth.gc.ca

HR | by the Numbers

Smoking and the Workplace[22]

$3,396 estimated annual per-employee cost to organization associated with smoking

73% of employer health/benefit plans cover prescription smoking cessation medicines

2.7 the number of additional days per year that employees who smoke are absent from work, when compared to non-smokers

40% of employer health/benefits plans cover nicotine replacement therapies like gums, lozenges, and patches

12% the average percentage of smokers employed in an organization

19% of Canadian organizations completely ban smoking on their property

Success with Workplace Smoking Cessation Programs

4–7% typical smoking quit rate without medication or counselling

27% of participants in the Alberta and Northwest Territories Lung Association workplace smoking cessation program were smoke-free one year after the end of the program

40% of participants in the Windsor-Essex County Health Units pharmacist-led smoking cessation program were smoke-free six months after the program ended

health risk factors, such as those associated with heart disease or mental health, so that problem-specific programs can be implemented.[24]

Finally, *healthcare spending accounts* (HCSA) are offered by more than 90 percent of Canadian employers, either alone or in combination with a standard healthcare plan.[25] The employer establishes an annual account for each employee containing a certain amount of money (determined by the employer to control costs). The employee can spend the money on healthcare costs as he or she wants. This provides flexibility for the employee. These accounts are governed by the Income Tax Act, which allows expenses not normally covered under employer-sponsored healthcare plans (such as laser eye surgery) and defines dependants more broadly than most employer plans.[26]

Retiree Health Benefits

Another concern is the cost of health benefits provided to retirees. These benefits typically include life insurance, drugs, and private/semi-private hospital coverage. Some continue coverage to a surviving spouse. Retiree benefit costs are already exceeding the costs for active employees in some organizations, in part because many early retirees between the ages of 50 and 65 are not yet eligible for government health benefits that start at age 65. Employers are required to disclose liabilities for retiree benefits in their financial statements. These liabilities are not required to be pre-funded and thus are at risk in the case of business failure.[27]

Employers can cut costs by increasing retiree contributions, increasing deductibles, tightening eligibility requirements, and reducing maximum payouts.[28] The last few years have seen a trend away from employer-provided retiree health benefits. This trend is expected to continue as a result of rising healthcare costs, growing retiree populations, uncertain business profitability, and federal regulations that provide only limited opportunities for funding retiree medical benefits.[29]

An on-site employee fitness centre

Photographee.eu/Fotolia

An Ethical Dilemma

Should it be the employer's responsibility to cover healthcare costs for early retirees until they become eligible for government healthcare benefits at age 65?

short-term disability plans Plans that provide pay to an employee when he or she is unable to work because of a non-work-related illness or injury.

sick leave Provides pay to an employee when he or she is out of work because of illness.

Short-Term Disability Plans and Sick Leave Plans

Short-term disability plans (also known as salary continuation plans) provide a continuation of all or part of an employee's earnings when the employee is absent from work because of non-work-related illness or injury. Usually a medical certificate is required if the absence extends beyond two or three days. These plans typically provide full pay for some period (often two or three weeks) and then gradually reduce the percentage of earnings paid as the period of absence lengthens. The benefits cease when the employee returns to work or when the employee qualifies for long-term disability. These plans are sometimes provided through an insurance company.

Sick leave provides pay to employees when they're out of work due to illness. Most policies grant full pay for a specified number of sick days—perhaps 12 per year, usually accumulating at the rate of, say, one day per month of service.

Sick leave often gets out of control because employers don't measure it. In one survey, only 57 percent of employers formally tracked sick days for their exempt employees.[30] Three-fourths of the employers couldn't provide an estimate of what sick pay was costing them. Therefore, the employer should first have a system in place for monitoring sick leaves and for measuring their financial impact.[31]

A 2013 study of 1513 Canadians provides evidence as to the abuse of sick time, identifying that 54 percent of Canadians admit to calling in sick when they were not sick.[32] The reasons include: feeling stressed or burned out (65 percent), needing to care for a sick child (35 percent), having too heavy a workload (13 percent), and having insufficient paid vacation days (12 percent). Limiting sick days is equally problematic in that seriously ill or injured employees get no pay once their sick days are used up; thus, the policy can encourage legitimately sick employees to come to work despite their illness.

HR Competency

20600

EVIDENCE-BASED HR

"I'm a struggling actor hired by your insurance company. Your policy doesn't cover a real doctor."

© andrewgenn / Fotolia

Cost-Reduction Tactics

Employers use several tactics to reduce excessive sick leave absence. Some repurchase unused sick leave at the end of the year by paying their employees a sum for each unused sick day. The problem is that legitimately sick employees may come to work. Others hold monthly lotteries in which only employees with perfect monthly attendance are eligible for a cash prize. At Marriott, employees can trade the value of some sick days for other benefits. Others aggressively investigate all absences, calling absent employees at home.[33]

Many employers use *pooled paid leave plans* (or *"banks"*).[34] These plans lump together sick leave, vacation, and personal days into a single leave pool. For example, one hospital previously granted new employees 25 days off per year (10 vacation days, three personal days, and 12 sick days). Employees used, on average, 5 of those 12 sick days (as well as all vacations and personal days).[35] The pooled paid leave plan allowed new employees to accrue 18 days to use as they saw fit (special absences like serious short-term illnesses and bereavement leave were handled separately). The pooled plan reduced absences. Most firms don't include legislated holidays in their paid time off "banks."[36]

Long-Term Disability Plans

Long-term disability insurance is aimed at providing income protection or compensation for loss of income because of long-term illness or injury that is not work related. The disability payments usually begin when normal short-term disability or sick leave is used up and may continue to provide income to age 65 or beyond. The disability benefits usually range from 50 to 75 percent of the employee's base pay.

The number of long-term disability claims in Canada is rising sharply. This trend is expected to accelerate as the average age of the workforce continues to increase because

National Institute of Disability Management and Research
www.nidmar.ca

Canadian Council on Rehabilitation and Work
www.ccrw.org

the likelihood of chronic illness, such as arthritis, heart disease, and diabetes, increases with age. Therefore, disability management programs with a goal of returning workers safely back to work are becoming a priority in many organizations.[37] For example, employers are beginning to put more effort into managing employees with episodic disabilities, which are chronic illnesses such as HIV, lupus, multiple sclerosis, arthritis, and some cancers and mental illnesses that are unpredictable. These employees may have long periods of good health followed by unpredicted episodes of poor health.[38]

Disability management is a proactive, employer-centred process that coordinates the activities of the employer, the insurance company, and healthcare providers in an effort to minimize the impact of injury, disability, or disease on a worker's capacity to successfully perform his or her job. Maintaining contact with a worker who is ill or injured is imperative in disability management so that the worker can be involved in the return-to-work process from the beginning. Ongoing contact also allows the employer to monitor the employee's emotional well-being, which is always affected by illness or injury.[39]

Effective disability management programs include prevention, early assessment and intervention regarding employee health problems, monitoring and management of employee absences, and early and safe return-to-work policies.[40] The three most common approaches to returning a worker with a disability to work are reduced work hours, reduced work duties, and workstation modification.[41] Evaluating the physical capabilities of the worker is an important step in designing work modifications to safely reintegrate injured workers. In many cases, the cost of accommodating an employee's disability can be quite modest.

disability management A proactive, employer-centred process that coordinates the activities of the employer, the insurance company, and healthcare providers in an effort to minimize the impact of injury, disability, or disease on a worker's capacity to successfully perform his or her job.

HR Competency

60300

World Federation for Mental Health
www.wfmh.org

Mental Health Benefits

Mental health issues continue to be the leading cause of short- and long-term disability claims in Canada. Psychiatric disabilities are the fastest growing of all occupational disabilities, with depression being the most common (even though only 32 percent of those afflicted seek treatment, as they do not want to admit it to their employer).[42]

For Canadian employers, the cost of mental health benefits is about $51 billion annually.[43] Despite the staggering costs, depression is not being addressed in a systematic way, and employers are unprepared to deal with stress, depression, and anxiety in the workplace. Some of the challenges involved in improving this situation are shown in **Figure 13.2**. Only one-third of employers have implemented return-to-work programs

FIGURE 13.2   The Top Challenges in Improving How Mental Health Issues Are Addressed in the Workplace[44]

Challenge identified by management	% of companies identifying this as a challenge
1. Employee perceptions and stigma related to mental health issues	60%
2. Lack of front-line manager awareness	54%
3. Inability to identify suitable modified work	40%
4. Inability to introduce significant flexibility options	39%
5. Lack of tools and support	29%
6. Lack of funds/budget for program enhancements	23%
7. Lack of senior management buy-in	20%
8. Don't know where to start	14%
9. Other	8%

specific to mental health. Companies such as Bell Canada, Alcan, and Superior Propane are trying to help reduce costs with prevention and early intervention programs, including psychiatric counselling and peer-support groups.[45]

Sabbaticals

A few employers provide sabbatical leaves for employees who want time off to rejuvenate or to pursue a personal goal. Sabbatical leaves are usually unpaid, but some employers provide partial or full pay. Sabbaticals can help to retain employees and to avoid employee burnout, without the employee losing job security or seniority.

Retirement Benefits

pension plans Plans that provide income when employees reach a pre-determined retirement age.

Employer-sponsored **pension plans** are intended to supplement an employee's government-sponsored retirement benefits, which, on average, make up 50 percent of the average Canadian's retirement income.[46] Unlike government-provided retirement benefits, employer-sponsored pension plans are pre-funded. Money is set aside in a pension fund to accumulate with investment income until it is needed to pay benefits at retirement. Pension fund assets have grown rapidly over the past 40 years. Much of this money is invested in Canadian stocks and bonds because of laws restricting the investment of these assets in foreign securities.

Two Categories of Pension Plans

defined benefit pension plan A plan that contains a formula for determining retirement benefits.

Pension plans fall into two categories—defined benefit pension plans and defined contribution pension plans. A **defined benefit pension plan** contains a formula for determining retirement benefits so that the actual benefits to be received are defined ahead of time. For example, the plan might include a formula, such as 2 percent of final year's earnings for each year of service, which would provide a pension of 70 percent of final year's earnings to an employee with 35 years of service.

defined contribution pension plan A plan in which the employer's contribution to the employees' retirement fund is specified.

A **defined contribution pension plan** specifies what contribution the employer will make to a retirement fund set up for the employee. The defined contribution plan does not define the eventual benefit amount, only the periodic contribution to the plan. In a defined benefit plan, the employee knows ahead of time what his or her retirement benefits will be on retirement. With a defined contribution plan, the employee cannot be sure of his or her retirement benefits until retirement, when his or her share of the money in the pension fund is used to buy an annuity. Thus, benefits depend on both the amounts contributed to the fund and the retirement fund's investment earnings.

Canadian Association for Retired Persons
www.carp.ca

Benefits and Pensions Monitor
www.bpmmagazine.com

Association of Canadian Pension Management
www.acpm.com

There are two other types of defined contribution arrangements. Under a *group registered retirement savings plan (group RRSP)*, employees can have a portion of their compensation (which would otherwise be paid in cash) put into an RRSP by the employer. The employee is not taxed on those set-aside dollars until after he or she retires (or removes the money from the plan). Most employers do not match all or a portion of what the employee contributes to the group RRSP because employer contributions are considered taxable income to employees. Instead, the employer often establishes a **deferred profit-sharing plan (DPSP)** and contributes a portion of company profits into the DPSP fund, where an account is set up for each employee. No employee contributions to a DPSP are allowed under Canadian tax law. Group RRSP/DPSP combinations are popular in Canada because no tax is

deferred profit-sharing plan (DPSP) A plan in which a certain amount of company profits is credited to each employee's account, payable at retirement, termination, or death.

TABLE 13.2   Registered Pension Plans by Type

Plan type	
Defined benefit plans	61.53%
Defined contribution plans	35.04%
Composite or combination plans*	0.70%
Defined benefit and contribution plans	2.60%
Other types of plans**	0.15%
Gender	
Male	50.07%
Female	49.93%

*In composite or combination plans, the pension has both defined benefit and defined contribution characteristics.

**These plans may be for different classes of employees, or one benefit type may be for current employees and the other for new employees, or these plans may be hybrid plans in which the pension benefit is the better of that provided by defined benefit or defined contribution provisions.

Source: Adapted from Statistics Canada, CANSIM, table 280-0016, "Registered pension plans (RPPs) and members, by type of plan and sector," www.statcan.gc.ca/tables-tableaux/sum-som/l01/cst01/famil120a-eng.htm.

paid until money is received from the plans at the time of the employee's death or termination of employment (at retirement or otherwise). As shown in Table 13.2, both plans are quite popular, and a few companies use combination or other forms of pension plans.

The entire area of pension planning is complicated, a result of the laws governing pensions. For example, companies want to ensure that their pension contributions are tax deductible and must therefore adhere to the Income Tax Act. The provincial and federal jurisdictions also have laws governing employer-sponsored pension plans. In some cases, the complicated and overlapping federal and provincial legislation can make employers question whether or not to sponsor a pension plan.[47] Legislation regarding pension plans varies around the world, and Canada's regulators can learn important lessons from other countries' successes and failures, as described in the Global HRM box.

Employers must pay careful attention to their obligation to educate and inform (but not advise) plan members about pension investments. There have been cases where plan members who were unhappy with the information provided by the employer and surprised by small benefits have sued their employers and won. The severe economic recession that began in late 2008 resulted in major shrinkage in the value of pension funds and highlighted issues with both types of plans. For defined benefit plans, the recession necessitated major increases in contributions to pension funds in order to maintain their required funding levels.[48] Although some jurisdictions eased the funding rules temporarily to allow more time to repay funding shortfalls, defined benefit plans began to be called an "endangered species."[49] For defined contribution plans, many plan members nearing retirement saw no other option but to defer retirement and continue working until the markets recovered and their pension fund account balance recovered to an amount that would provide them with the retirement income they needed. These issues created considerable debate about the adequacy of retirement savings for future generations.

Hints : **TO ENSURE LEGAL COMPLIANCE**

GLOBAL HRM

Defined Benefit Pension Problems and Solutions Around the World

Many countries designed generous defined benefit social security programs between 1950 and 1970 based on fertility rates that created a stable population. The actual experience of declining populations in many countries, particularly Japan, created serious intergenerational inequity as younger employees were subsidizing older ones. Solutions included increasing contribution rates (Belgium, Canada), raising the normal retirement age to 67 (European Union), both of these (Germany), moving to defined contribution plans (Australia, France, Switzerland, United Kingdom), and even more complex protective legislation (Netherlands). Japan first permitted defined contribution plans in 2001, and they have slowly become more prevalent.

Unfortunately, none of these national actions seem to be the optimal solution to the global defined benefits plan issue. The numerous retirement savings plans known as "provident funds" in Asia and defined contribution plans in Australia seem to be doing fairly well. The European Union encourages the creation of pan-European pension plans where an employer can create a plan in one location and cover all European employees under that single plan.

This encourages employee mobility and reduces administrative costs. The plans must comply with the rules from the plan's home country while still respecting some of the pension laws of other countries where employees reside or have retired. Countries such as Luxembourg, Ireland, and Belgium have tried to create the best tax and legal environment to attract these plans, but it is too early to tell if a leader will emerge.

The European Union situation is very similar to our Canadian system with its patchwork of legislation. Given Canada's population of 33 million, versus 700 million in Europe, it is clear that our pension landscape should have been more straightforward from the outset and desperately needs to be simplified. But until we find better ways to enhance and preserve defined benefit plans, employers will have to make some difficult decisions. Country by country, they must choose between assuming the risks and higher administrative costs of sponsoring defined benefit plans or moving to defined contribution plans, which typically do not produce the same retirement value to each dollar spent and are less flexible as an HR tool.

Source: "Around the World in Six Pages," BenefitsCanada (August 2008), pp. 14–19. Used by permission from Rogers Media, Inc.

When designing a pension plan, there are several legal and policy issues to consider:[50]

- *Membership requirements.* For example, at what minimum number of years of service do employees become eligible to join the plan?

- *Benefit formula (defined benefit plans only).* This usually ties the pension to the employee's final earnings, or an average of his or her last three to five years' earnings.

- *Retirement age.* Traditionally, the normal retirement age in Canada has been 65. However, since mandatory retirement is now prohibited by human rights laws across the country, employees cannot be required to retire at age 65. Some plans call for "30 and out." This permits an employee to retire after 30 years of continuous service, regardless of the person's age.

- *Funding.* The question of how the plan is to be funded is another key issue. One aspect is whether the plan will be contributory or non-contributory. In the former, contributions to the pension fund are made by both employees and the employer. In a non-contributory fund, only the employer contributes.

vesting A provision that employer money placed in a pension fund cannot be forfeited for any reason.

- *Vesting.* Employee **vesting** rights is another critical issue in pension planning. Vesting refers to the money that the employer has placed in the pension fund that cannot be forfeited for any reason; the employees' contributions can never be forfeited. An employee is vested when he or she has met the requirements set out in the plan, whereby, on termination of employment, he or she will receive future benefits based on the contributions made to the plan by the *employer* on behalf of the

cartoonresource/Fotolia

"I need someone in SuperHuman Resources."

employee. In most provinces, pension legislation requires that employer contributions be vested once the employee has completed two years of service. Plans may vest more quickly than required by law. If the employee terminates employment before being vested, he or she is only entitled to a refund of his or her own contributions plus interest (unless the employer has decided to be more generous). Once an employee is vested, all contributions are "locked in" and cannot be withdrawn by the employee on termination of employment; that is, employees must wait until retirement to receive a pension from the plan. Most plans permit the employee to transfer the amount into a locked-in RRSP (see the discussion on portability below), but the money cannot be accessed until retirement.

portability A provision that employees who change jobs can transfer the lump-sum value of the pension they have earned to a locked-in RRSP or their new employer's pension plan.

- *Portability.* Canadian employers today are required by pension legislation to make their pensions more "portable" for employees on termination of employment. **Portability** means that employees in defined contribution plans can take the money in their company pension account to a new employer's plan or roll it over into a locked-in RRSP. For defined benefit plans, the lump-sum value of the benefit earned can be transferred.

Phased Retirement

phased retirement An arrangement whereby employees gradually ease into retirement by using reduced workdays or shortened workweeks.

The labour shortage is resulting in employers seeking to retain older employees. At the same time, many Canadians wishing to retire early are finding that they are not in a financial position to do so and that they need to continue working to age 60, 65, or even later.[51] The idea of **phased retirement**, whereby employees gradually ease into retirement using reduced workdays or shortened workweeks, has been increasing in Canada. Constraints under the Income Tax Act and pension legislation in some jurisdictions are slowly being loosened, and it is now possible for older workers to receive some benefits from their pension plan while they are being paid to continue to work.[52]

Supplemental Employee Retirement Plans (SERPs)

supplemental employee retirement plans (SERPs) Plans that provide the additional pension benefit required for employees to receive their full pension benefit in cases where their full pension benefit exceeds the maximum allowable benefit under the Income Tax Act.

The Income Tax Act has not changed the maximum pension benefit permissible under the act (for tax deductibility of plan contributions) since 1976. Thus, many Canadians have their pension benefits capped at less than what their defined benefit plan formula would otherwise provide. Originally this situation only created problems for highly paid executives, but in recent years more and more employees have been affected. **Supplemental employee retirement plans (SERPs)** are intended to provide the difference in pension benefit and thus restore pension adequacy for high earners.

A Towers Perrin survey found that nearly three-quarters of employers provide SERPs (including about two-thirds of small employers with fewer than 500 employees). The survey also found that 53 percent of SERP sponsors cover employees below the executive level in "broad-based" plans. Most SERPs are "pay-as-you-go" plans; that is, they do not have a fund established to accumulate money to pay the benefits (because contributions are not tax deductible). However, the security of SERP benefits has been improving, as 41 percent of plans are now secured in some manner.[53]

EMPLOYEE SERVICES

Although an employee's time off and insurance and retirement benefits account for the largest portion of an organization's benefits costs, many employers also provide a range of services, including personal services (such as counselling), job-related services (such as childcare facilities), and executive perquisites (such as company cars and planes for executives). The HR by the Numbers box highlights the importance of these types of employee services (including those discussed in Chapter 12) on retaining employees.

HR | by the Numbers

Incentives that Matter

32% of employers reported that they experienced exit of top performers in the previous year[54]

88% of 3900 employees surveyed by CareerBuilder identify that salary matters more than job title[55]

59% of surveyed employees think having a flexible schedule is important to workers[56]

40% of employees surveyed identified that having half-day Fridays would be the one perk that would make their workplace more satisfying[57]

50% of workers feel that increasing employee recognition via awards, cash prizes, and company trips would reduce voluntary turnover[58]

flextime A work schedule in which employees' workdays are built around a core of midday hours, and employees determine, within limits, what other hours they will work.

compressed workweek Schedule in which employee works fewer but longer days each week.

Flexible Work Schedules

Flexible work schedules are popular.[59] Single parents use them for balancing work and family responsibilities. And for many millennial employees, flexible work schedules provide a way to pursue their careers without surrendering the quality of life they desire. There are several flexible work schedule options.

Flextime

Flextime is a plan whereby employees' workdays are built around a core of midday hours, such as 11:00 A.M to 2:00 P.M. Thus, workers may opt to work from 7:00 A.M to 3:00 P.M or from 11:00 A.M to 7:00 P.M. The number of employees in formal flextime programs—from 4 percent of operators to 17 percent of executive employees—doesn't tell the whole story. Many more employees take advantage of informal flexible work schedules.[60] The effect of flextime for most employees is about one hour of leeway before 9:00 A.M or after 5:00 P.M.[61]

Telecommuting

Telecommuting—using technology to work away from the office—is popular. About 48 percent of employers offer ad hoc telecommuting options, while 17 percent offer them on a full-time basis.[62] Some jobs have much higher rates. For example, almost 45 percent of medical transcription is reportedly work from home.[63] On the other hand, Yahoo famously said it needed its employees "working side by side" and brought them back to the office from telecommuting.[64]

Compressed Workweeks

Many employees, like airline pilots, do not work conventional 5-day, 40-hour workweeks. Workers like these typically have **compressed workweek** schedules—they work fewer days each week, but each day they work longer hours. Some firms have four 10-hour day workweeks. Some workers—in hospitals, for instance—work three 12-hour shifts, and then take off for four days.[65]

Effectiveness of Flexible Work Schedule Arrangements

Studies show that flexible work schedules have positive effects on employee productivity, job satisfaction, and employee absenteeism; the effect on absenteeism is generally greater than on productivity. Highly flexible programs were less effective than less flexible ones.[66]

HR IN THE NEWS

NES Rentals

Seeking to cut costs while maintaining its reputation for great products and service, NES Rentals sent their employees home. Today, three-fourths of their customer support, collections, finance, and other back-office workers at their Chicago office work from home at least part of the week.[67] They no longer have dedicated desks, but share space in the office. The CEO says productivity has increased 20 percent. Employee turnover dropped from 7 percent in 2009 to "virtually non-existent" in 2010. NES is leasing 40 percent less office space, saving $100 000 in real estate expenses. He estimates NES's total savings from instituting this new telecommuting benefit at about $350 000 annually.[68]

Some experts argue that 12-hour shifts increase fatigue and accidents. To reduce potential side effects, some employers install treadmills and exercise bikes, and special lights that mimic daylight.

Other Flexible Work Arrangements

job sharing Allows two or more people to share a single full-time job.

Job sharing allows two or more people to share a single full-time job. For example, two people may share a 40-hour-per-week job, with one working mornings and the other working afternoons. About 22 percent of the firms questioned in one survey indicated that they allow job sharing.[69] Job sharing can be particularly useful for retirement-aged employees. It allows them to reduce their hours while the company retains their expertise.[70] **Work sharing** refers to a temporary reduction in work hours by a group of employees during economic downturns as a way to prevent layoffs. Thus, 400 employees may all agree to work (and be paid for) only 35 hours per week, rather than 40, to avoid a layoff of 50 workers.

work sharing A temporary reduction in work hours by a group of employees during economic downturns as a way to prevent layoffs.

Personal Services

First, many companies provide personal services that most employees need at one time or another. These include credit unions, counselling, employee assistance plans, and social and recreational opportunities. The intent of these services is to help employees balance work–life issues, aid them in dealing with non-work issues that may affect work-related issues, and provide employees with a sense of overall well-being.

Credit Unions

Credit unions are usually separate businesses established with the assistance of the employer. Employees usually become members of a credit union by purchasing a share of the credit union's stock for $5 or $10. Members can then deposit savings that accrue interest at a rate determined by the credit union's board of directors. Perhaps more important to most employees, loan eligibility and the rate of interest paid on the loan are usually more favourable than those found in banks and finance companies.

Counselling Services

Employers are also providing a wider range of counselling services to employees. These include *financial counselling* (for example, how to overcome existing debt problems), *family counselling* (for marital problems and so on), *career counselling* (for example, analyzing one's aptitudes and deciding on a career), *job placement counselling* (for helping terminated or disenchanted employees find new jobs), and *pre-retirement counselling* (aimed at preparing retiring employees for what many find is the trauma of retiring). Many employers also make available to employees a full range of *legal counselling* services through legal insurance plans.[71]

Employee Assistance Plans (EAPs)

employee assistance plan (EAP)
A company-sponsored program to help employees cope with personal problems that are interfering with or have the potential to interfere with their job performance, as well as issues affecting their well-being or the well-being of their families.

An **employee assistance plan (EAP)** is a formal employer program that provides employees (and often their family members) with confidential counselling or treatment programs for problems such as mental health issues, marital/family problems, work–life balance issues, stress, legal problems, substance abuse, and other addictions such as gambling. They are particularly important for helping employees who suffer workplace trauma—ranging from harassment to physical assault. There was a significant increase in EAP usage during the economic recession that began in late 2008, particularly in the areas of financial problems and stress.[72]

The number of EAPs in Canada is growing because they are a proactive way for organizations to reduce absenteeism and disability costs. A general estimate is that 10 percent of employees use EAP services. With supervisory training in how to identify employees who may need an EAP referral, usage can be expanded to more employees who need help.[73]

EAP counsellors can be employed in-house, or the company can contract with an external EAP firm.[74] It is important to assess the services provided by external EAP providers before using them, as quality levels vary. Whatever the model, an EAP provider should be confidential, accessible to employees in all company locations, and timely in providing service, and should offer highly educated counsellors and provide communication material to publicize the plan to employees. They should also provide utilization reports on the number of employees using the service and the types of services being provided, without compromising confidentiality.[75]

Other Personal Services

Finally, some employers also provide various social and recreational opportunities for their employees, including company-sponsored athletic events, dances, annual summer picnics, craft activities, and parties. In practice, the benefits offered are limited only by creativity in thinking up new benefits. For example, pharmaceutical giant Pfizer Inc. provides employees with free drugs made by the company, including Viagra.[76]

Voluntary Job-Related Services

Job-related services aimed directly at helping employees perform their jobs, such as educational subsidies and childcare centres, constitute a second group of services. Top employers often provide a range of voluntary employee services, often based on the requirements of their unique workforce, as highlighted in the HR in the News box.

HR IN THE NEWS

Various Incentives Offered by Canada's Top Employers

The Globe and Mail, in conjunction with Media Corp, publishes an annual list of the top 100 employers in Canada. These companies often use a wide range of employee incentives. For example, in the 2014 list:

- Aboriginal Peoples Television Network Inc (APTN) provided its 140 employees subsidies for tuition and professional accreditation.
- Agrium Inc made profit sharing available to all of its 3774 employees.
- The Bank of Canada offered free on-site fitness facilities for its 1454 employees.
- The Centre for Addiction and Mental Health offered a top-up of up to 87 percent of an employee's salary for maternity/paternity leave.
- The Department of Finance Canada provided pre-retirement transition options to any of its 791 employees who are within two years of retirement.
- Ericsson Canada Inc arranged for an on-site daycare facility.
- ISM Canada provided monthly "coffee break massages" in addition to the tension relieving messages employees can receive at their desk.
- At George Brown College, employees started with four weeks of vacation.[77]

Jörg Lantelme/Fotolia

Subsidizing childcare facilities for children of employees has many benefits for the employer, including lower employee absenteeism.

Subsidized Childcare

Eighty percent of Canadian families with young children have both parents working.[78] Subsidized childcare is offered to assist in balancing these work and life responsibilities. Many employers simply investigate the childcare facilities in their communities and recommend certain ones to interested employees, but more employers are setting up company-sponsored childcare facilities themselves, both to attract young parents to the payroll and to reduce absenteeism. In this case, the centre is a separate, privately run venture, paid for by the firm. IKEA, Husky Injection Molding Systems, IBM, and the Kanata Research Park have all chosen this option. Where successful, the hours of operation are structured around parents' schedules, the childcare facility is close to the workplace (often in the same building), and the employer provides 50 to 75 percent of the operating costs. Two emerging benefits are childcare for mildly ill children and emergency backup childcare.[79]

To date, the evidence regarding the actual effects of employer-sponsored childcare on employee absenteeism, turnover, productivity, recruitment, and job satisfaction is positive, particularly with respect to reducing obstacles to coming to work and improving workers' attitudes.[80]

Eldercare

With the average age of the Canadian population rising, eldercare is increasingly a concern for many employers and individuals. It is a complex, unpredictable, and exhausting process that creates stress for the caregiver, the family, and co-workers. Eldercare is expected to become a more common workplace issue than childcare as the twenty-first century progresses.[81]

Company eldercare programs are designed to assist employees who must help elderly parents or relatives who are not fully able to care for themselves, up to and including palliative care of the dying. Eldercare benefits include flexible hours, support groups, counselling, free pagers, and adult daycare programs. Referral services to help employees connect with the wide variety of services for the elderly are particularly helpful for employees with eldercare responsibilities.[82] For example, BMO Financial Group's EAP can be used to find nursing homes by entering a postal code and using the list of questions provided to assist in selecting the best one.

Subsidized Employee Transportation

Some employers also provide subsidized employee transportation. An employer can negotiate with a transit system to provide free year-round transportation to its employees. Other employers facilitate employee carpooling, perhaps by acting as the central clearinghouse to identify employees from the same geographic areas who work the same hours.

Food Services

Food services are provided in some form by many employers; they allow employees to purchase meals, snacks, or coffee on-site, usually at relatively low prices. Even employers that do not provide full dining facilities generally make available food services, such as coffee wagons or vending machines, for the convenience of employees.

Educational Subsidies

Educational subsidies, such as tuition refunds, have long been a popular benefit for employees seeking to continue or complete their education. Payments range from all tuition and expenses to some percentage of expenses to a flat fee per year of, say, $500 to $600. Most companies pay for courses directly related to an employee's present job. Many also reimburse tuition for courses that are not job related (such as a secretary taking an accounting class) that pertain to the company business, and those that are part of a degree or diploma program. In-house educational programs include remedial work in basic literacy and training for improved supervisory skills. The Expert Opinion box highlights how some organizations have a wide variety of options available to employees for education or training, often aligning the scope of educational subsidies with the organizations approach to training and development.

Family-Friendly Benefits

One of the top drivers of workforce commitment in Canada is management's recognition of personal and family life. Ninety percent of responding employees in one survey said work–life benefits were "important" or "very important" to them.[83] Recognition of the pressures

© Ed Kashi/VII/Corbis

Boomers are the "Sandwich Generation," caring for both children and elderly parents.

expert opinion
industry viewpoint

Agostino DeGasperis

Identification: Mr. Agostino DeGasperis,
VP People, Labatt Breweries of Canada

1. What is Labatt Brewery of Canada's approach to developing and rewarding employees?

Our approach is embedded throughout the organization and can be found in multiple areas within our 10 guiding principles. For example, our first principle is about the organization's dream: "Our shared dream energizes everyone to work in the same direction: to be the best beer company in a better world." The next two focus on our people: "Great people, allowed to grow at the pace of their talent and compensated accordingly, are the most valuable assets of our company" and "We must select people who,

with the right development, challenges and encouragement, can be better than ourselves. We will be judged by the quality of our teams." These principles develop accountability and responsibility for actions, and demonstrate a larger organizational commitment to talent management.

2. Who is responsible for talent management in the organization?

We don't believe that talent management is a function limited to HR. Potential managers are involved in selecting and coaching the talent and our evaluation includes not only individual performance and development metrics, but also how well the team is working together. We use performance evaluation to explore opportunities for coaching, alternative solutions, training or other alternatives to help employees overcome issues, to achieve optimal job performance.

3. What kinds of support are offered to employees looking to develop their skills or competencies?

Employees experience a relatively steep learning curve once they join the organization and we subscribe to the 70-20-10 model in terms of development. The organization is open to giving opportunity to people in ways that benefit both the individual and the organization. Our programs reward our employees based on their

specific talent or performance (rather than tenure). There are a number of options available to employees (as highlighted below), and employees often conduct training and development on the job at no additional expense to them:

- Under our parent company Anheuser-Busch InBev (ABI), there is an established ABI University. Employees can engage in thousands of online training modules, or go through progressive curriculum that varies in focus from broad to narrow.

- At the management level, we have specific schools, for example, the district sales manager school, the brewing school, etc. These involve the rotation of online and face-to-face components.

- We partner with St. Louis University to deliver an internal MBA program targeted to top talent.

- We often bring in speakers as subject matter experts (from Harvard University, Kellogg School of Management at Northwestern University, etc.).

- We send people to specific universities to acquire specific knowledge (e.g., MIT for logistics, University of Chicago Illinois for big data management).[84]

Source: Reprinted by permission from Agostino DeGasperis.

HR Competency

30100

EVIDENCE-BASED HR

of balancing work and family life has led many employers to bolster what they call their "family-friendly" benefits. Examples include flexible work hours, on-site childcare, and eldercare benefits.

Family-friendly benefits are intended to reduce the extent to which work–family conflicts spill over into the employee's job and undermine the person's job satisfaction and performance. Research has found that "the relationship between job satisfaction and various [work–family] conflict measures is strong and negative across all samples; people with high levels of [work–family] conflict tend to be less satisfied with their jobs."[85] Similarly, there was a strong negative correlation between work–family conflict and the extent to which the employees were satisfied with their lives in general. Managers should therefore understand that providing their employees with family-friendly benefits can have very positive effects on the employees, one of which is making them more satisfied with their work and their jobs.

Executive Perquisites

Perquisites (perks, for short) are usually given to only a few top executives. Perks can range from the substantial to the almost insignificant. A bank chairperson may have a chauffeur-driven limousine and use of a bank-owned property in the Caribbean. Executives of large companies often use a corporate jet for business travel. At the other extreme, perks may entail little more than the right to use a company car.[86]

A multitude of popular perks fall between these extremes. These include management loans (which typically enable senior officers to use their stock options); salary guarantees (also known as *golden parachutes*) to protect executives if their firms are the targets of acquisitions or mergers; financial counselling (to handle top executives' investment programs); and relocation benefits, often including subsidized mortgages, purchase of the executive's current house, and payment for the actual move. A potpourri of other executive perks include outplacement assistance, company cars, chauffeured limousines, security systems, company planes and yachts, executive dining rooms, legal services, tax assistance, liberal expense accounts, club memberships, season tickets, credit cards, and subsidized education for their children. Perks related to wellness and quality of life (such as physical fitness programs) are highly valued in today's stressful environment. An increasingly popular new perk offered at KPMG, TELUS, and Ernst & Young is concierge service, intended to carry out errands, such as grocery shopping or organizing a vacation, for busy executives.[87]

HR Competency

90100

An Ethical Dilemma

Is it ethical for executive perquisites to continue if the company is facing financial problems?

FLEXIBLE BENEFITS PROGRAMS

flexible benefits programs
Individualized benefit plans to accommodate employee needs and preferences.

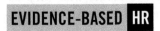

Research conducted more than 30 years ago found that an employee's age, marital status, and sex influenced his or her choice of benefits.[88] For example, preference for pensions increased significantly with employee age, and preference for the family dental plan increased sharply as the number of dependants increased. Thus, benefits that one worker finds attractive may be unattractive to another. In the last 25 years in Canada, there has been a significant increase in **flexible benefits programs** that permit employees to develop individualized benefits packages for themselves by choosing the benefits options they prefer. In 1980, there were no flex plans in Canada, but by 2005, 41 percent of employers offered flex benefits plans. Benefit consultants Hewitt Associates report that 85 percent of Canadian employers either have a flex plan in place or expect to implement one at some point. Fifty-three percent either have a full flex plan now or are in the process of creating one.[89]

Employers derive several advantages from offering flexible benefit plans: the two most important being cost containment and the ability to meet the needs of an increasingly diverse workforce. Hewitt Associates' surveys have found that, over the years, the most important advantage of implementing flexible benefits has been meeting diverse employee needs. However, in 2005, for the first time in survey history, the concern about containing benefit cost increases surpassed meeting diverse employee needs as the most significant reason to implement flexible plans. In more recent surveys, 100 percent of respondents reported that their flex plans were meeting or exceeding their expectations regarding meeting employee needs, and the level of satisfaction with flex plans as a cost containment measure was 78 percent.[90]

Flexible benefits plans empower the employee to put together his or her own benefit package, subject to two constraints. First, the employer must carefully limit total cost for each total benefits package. Second, each benefit plan must include certain items that are not optional. These include, for example, Canada/Quebec Pension Plan, workers' compensation, and employment insurance. Subject to these two constraints, employees can pick and choose from the available options. Thus, a young parent might opt for the company's life and dental insurance plans, while an older employee opts for an improved pension plan. The list of possible options that the employer might offer can include many of the benefits discussed in this chapter—vacations, insurance benefits, pension plans, educational services, and so on. The flexibility is, of course, the main advantage of this type of plan. Although most employees favour flexible benefits, some do not like to spend time choosing among available options, and some choose inappropriate benefits. Communication regarding the choices available in a flexible plan is considered the biggest challenge for employers. A majority of flex plan sponsors provide a plan website. However, even with new technology employers still find face-to-face communication is the preferred method for providing initial information about a new flex plan.[91] The recent rapid increase in the number of flexible plans in Canada indicates that the pros outweigh the cons.

BENEFITS ADMINISTRATION

HR Competency

60400

Whether it is a flexible benefits plan or a more traditional one, benefits administration is a challenge. Even in a relatively small company with 40 to 50 employees, the administrative problems of keeping track of the benefits status of each employee can be a time-consuming task as employees are hired and separated and as they use or want to change their benefits. However, software is available to assist with this challenge. Many companies make use of some sort of benefits spreadsheet software to facilitate tracking benefits and updating information. Another approach is outsourcing benefits administration to a third-party expert. The major advantages are greater efficiency and consistency, and enhanced service.[92]

Keeping Employees Informed

Benefits communication, particularly regarding pension plans and flexible benefits, is increasingly important as a large number of people are approaching retirement. Correct information must be provided in a timely, clear manner. Pension legislation across Canada specifies what information must be disclosed to plan members and their spouses. Court challenges concerning information on benefits plans are on the rise as people's awareness of their right to information grows.[93]

Increasingly, organizations are using new technology, such as intranets, to ensure that up-to-date information is provided in a consistent manner. Some companies are now using real-time e-statements. At Hewlett Packard (Canada), an electronic pension booklet is available on the company's intranet, and a pension-modelling tool can be accessed through the web. The modelling software allows employees to fill in their personal information to calculate various "what if" scenarios.[94]

CHAPTER SUMMARY

1. The strategic importance of employee benefits is increasing in the post–job-security era. When benefits are aligned with business strategy, they can help to attract and retain the right people to achieve business objectives.

2. Six major government-mandated benefits are employment insurance, pay on termination of employment, leaves of absence, Canada/Quebec Pension Plan, workers' compensation, and paid time off.

3. Health insurance costs are rising because of expensive new drugs, rising drug use by an aging population, and reductions in coverage under provincial healthcare plans. These costs can be reduced by increasing the amount of healthcare costs paid by employees, publishing a restricted list of the drugs that will be paid for under the plan, implementing health and wellness promotion plans, using risk-assessment programs, and offering health services spending accounts.

4. The two categories of pension plans are defined benefit plans and defined contribution plans. Defined benefit plans provide a benefit based on a formula related to years of service, and the employer assumes the investment risk associated with the pension fund assets. Defined contribution plans provide for specified contributions to a pension fund by the employer,

and the benefit will vary depending on the rate of return on the pension fund assets (employees assume the investment risk).

5. Three types of personal employee services offered by many organizations include credit unions, counselling services, and employee assistance plans. Seven types of job-related services offered by many employers include subsidized childcare, eldercare, subsidized employee transportation, food services, educational subsidies, family-friendly benefits, and executive perks.

6. The flexible benefits approach allows the employee to put together his or her own benefit plan, subject to total cost limits and the inclusion of certain compulsory items. The employer first determines the total cost for the benefits package. Then a decision is made as to which benefits will be compulsory (such as Canada/Quebec Pension Plan, workers' compensation, and employment insurance). Then other benefits are selected for inclusion in the plan, such as life insurance, health and dental coverage, short- and long-term disability insurance, and retirement plans. Sometimes vacations and employee services are included as well. Then employees select the optional benefits they prefer with the money they have available to them under the total plan.

MyManagementLab

Study, practise, and explore real business situations with these helpful resources:

- **Interactive Lesson Presentations:** Work through interactive presentations and assessments to test your knowledge of management concepts.
- **PIA (Personal Inventory Assessments):** Enhance your ability to connect with key concepts through these engaging self-reflection assessments.
- **Study Plan:** Check your understanding of chapter concepts with self-study quizzes.
- **Videos:** Learn more about the management practices and strategies of real companies.
- **Simulations:** Practise decision-making in simulated management environments.

(P)(I)(A) PERSONAL INVENTORY ASSESSMENT

KEY TERMS

accidental death and dismemberment coverage *(p. 303)*

advance/reasonable notice *(p. 298)*

Canada/Quebec Pension Plans (C/QPP) *(p. 299)*

coinsurance *(p. 304)*

compressed workweek *(p. 312)*

critical illness insurance *(p. 303)*

deductible *(p. 304)*

deferred profit-sharing plan (DPSP) *(p. 308)*

defined benefit pension plan *(p. 308)*

defined contribution pension plan *(p. 308)*

disability management *(p. 307)*

employee assistance plan (EAP) *(p. 314)*

employee benefits *(p. 296)*

employment insurance (EI) *(p. 297)*

flexible benefits programs *(p. 318)*

flextime *(p. 312)*

group life insurance *(p. 302)*

job sharing *(p. 313)*

pay in lieu of reasonable notice *(p. 298)*

pension plans *(p. 308)*

phased retirement *(p. 311)*

portability *(p. 311)*

severance pay *(p. 298)*

short-term disability plans *(p. 305)*

sick leave *(p. 305)*

supplemental employee retirement
    plans (SERPs) *(p. 311)*

vesting *(p. 310)*

workers' compensation *(p. 300)*

work sharing *(p. 313)*

REVIEW AND DISCUSSION QUESTIONS

1. Explain two main approaches to reducing workers' compensation claims.

2. Explain what companies are doing to reduce health-benefit costs.

3. Explain the difference between sick leave plans and short-term disability plans.

4. Explain the difference between a defined benefit pension plan and a defined contribution pension plan.

5. Why are long-term disability claims increasing so rapidly in Canada?

6. Outline the kinds of services provided by EAPs.

7. Explain the pros and cons of flexible benefits from both an employer and employee perspective.

CRITICAL THINKING QUESTIONS

1. You are applying for a job as a manager and are at the point of negotiating salary and benefits. What questions would you ask your prospective employer concerning benefits? Describe the benefits package that you would try to negotiate for yourself.

2. What are pension "vesting" and "portability"? Why do you think these are (or are not) important to a recent university or college graduate?

3. You are the HR consultant to a small business with about 40 employees. Currently, the business offers only the legal minimum number of days for vacation and paid holidays and the legally mandated benefits. Develop a list of other benefits that you believe should be offered, along with your reasons for suggesting them.

4. If you were designing a retirement benefit for a mid-sized organization that had not previously offered one, what type of plan would you recommend to them and why?

5. What questions might an employee who currently has no benefits or a minimal coverage standard benefits plan have about flexible benefits? How can an organization address these questions and concerns? List suggested topics for a new flexible benefits plan communication plan and include at least two suggestions about the appropriate media to be used.

6. Should an employer with a pension plan that covers employees in several provinces give each group the minimum vesting and portability benefits for their province, or take the most generous of these and provide it to all employees? Why or why not?

EXPERIENTIAL EXERCISES

1. Working individually or in groups, compile a list of the perks available to the following individuals: the head of your local public utilities commission, the president of your college or university, and the president of a large company in your area. Do they all have certain perks in common? What do you think accounts for any differences?

2. Working individually or in groups, contact your provincial workers' compensation board (or equivalent regulatory body in your province/territory) and compile a list of its suggestions for reducing workers' compensation costs. What seem to be the main recommendations?

RUNNING CASE

Running Case: LearnInMotion.com

The New Benefits Plan

LearnInMotion.com provides only legislatively required benefits for all its employees. These include participation in employment insurance, Canada Pension Plan, and workers' compensation. No employee services are provided.

Jennifer can see several things wrong with the company's policies regarding benefits and services. First, she wants to determine whether similar companies' experiences with providing health and life insurance benefits make hiring easier or reduces employee turnover. Jennifer is also concerned that the company has no policy regarding vacations or sick leave. Informally, at least, it is understood that employees get a one-week vacation after one year's work. However, the policy regarding pay for such days as New Year's and Thanksgiving has been inconsistent. Sometimes new employees, on the job only two or three weeks, are paid fully for one of these holidays; sometimes employees who have been with the firm for six months or more get paid for only half a day. No one really knows what the company's chosen "paid" holidays are. Jennifer knows these policies must be more consistent.

She also wonders about the wisdom of establishing some type of retirement plan for the firm. Although everyone working for the firm is still in their 20s, she believes a defined contribution plan in which employees contribute a portion of their pre-tax salary, to be matched up to some limit by a contribution from LearnInMotion.com, would contribute to the sense of commitment she and Pierre would like to create among their employees. However, Pierre isn't so sure. His position is that if they don't get sales up pretty soon, they're going to burn through their cash. Now they want you, their management consultant, to help them decide what to do.

QUESTIONS

1 Which benefit and services policy would you recommend LearnInMotion.com change first and why?
2 What changes would you recommend to Jennifer regarding their lack of a vacation policy?
3 As most of LearnInMotion.com's staff are in their 20s, what type of pension plan would appeal to this employee demographic? Why?

CASE INCIDENT

Technology Plus's Benefit Dilemma

To stay competitive, many organizations today are choosing to restructure their benefit programs. Technology Plus is an example of such a company. Technology Plus has 150 employees, including upper management, skilled tradespersons, sales representatives, and customer service representatives. Five years ago this company was enjoying huge profits and could afford their current benefits program; however, times have changed and now they need to find cost savings without laying off any of the staff.

Up to this point, Technology Plus has offered all of their staff a premium benefits program, including much more than government-required benefits of employment insurance, Canada Pension Plan, worker's compensation, standard vacation of two weeks per year, and access to legislated leaves of absence. They offer group life insurance of three times salary, accidental death and dismemberment

insurance of three times salary, extended healthcare benefits (with vision care, dental care, hearing aids, and more), long-term disability of 75 percent of salary (employer paid), and a defined benefit pension plan. They also provide a wellness program, an employee assistance plan, and many other services such as subsidized childcare and assistance with eldercare. However, now they need your help in deciding how to restructure their benefit plan to find significant cost savings but still provide meaningful benefit coverage for their employees.

QUESTIONS

1 What voluntary employer-sponsored benefits should this company maintain and which ones should they not maintain in your opinion? Why?
2 Would a flexible benefit program save this organization money if administered properly?

zulufoto/Fotolia

CHAPTER

14

Occupational Health and Safety

LEARNING OUTCOMES

**AFTER STUDYING THIS CHAPTER, YOU
SHOULD BE ABLE TO**

ANALYZE the responsibilities and
rights of employees and employers under
occupational health and safety legislation.

EXPLAIN WHMIS legislation.

ANALYZE in detail three basic causes
of accidents.

DESCRIBE how accidents at work can
be prevented.

EXPLAIN why employee wellness
programs are becoming increasingly
popular.

DISCUSS six major employee health
issues at work and **RECOMMEND** how
they should be handled.

REQUIRED HR COMPETENCIES

20300: Adhere to legal requirements as they pertain to human resources policies and
practices to promote organizational values and manage risk.

20600: Promote an evidence-based approach to the development of human resources
policies and practices using current professional resources to provide a sound basis for
human resources decision-making.

50100: Promote a collaborative work environment between the employer, the union
(where it exists), employees, and other representative groups through clear and open
communication to achieve a respectful, productive, and engaged workforce.

50200: Interpret legislation, collective agreements (where applicable), and policies
consistent with legal requirements and organizational values to treat employees in a
fair and consistent manner and manage the risk of litigation and conflict.

80100: Promote the health and safety of employees through an understanding of
legislation, regulations, and standards to increase organizational awareness, ensure
compliance, and manage risk.

80200: Develop health, safety, and wellness policies, procedures, roles, and responsibilities for leaders and employees, to ensure compliance through training, monitoring, and
providing appropriate safeguards and disability management.

80300: Encourage employee wellness by endorsing healthy lifestyles, educating employees,
and providing opportunities for enhancement of wellness to sustain overall employee and
organizational health.

80400: Establish a proactive approach to mental health and psychological well-being
in the workplace by enhancing awareness at all levels of the organization to improve
performance.

STRATEGIC IMPORTANCE OF OCCUPATIONAL HEALTH AND SAFETY

tiverylucky/Fotolia

On April 28 each year, a day of mourning is observed for Canadian workers killed or injured on the job.

lost-time injury rate Measures any occupational injury or illness resulting in an employee being unable to fulfill full work assignments, not including any fatalities.

EVIDENCE-BASED HR

Health and safety initiatives are part of a strategic approach to human resources management. Service provided to clients and customers is a function of how employees are treated, and employee health, safety, and wellness management are important determinants of employee perceptions regarding fair treatment by the organization. Further, investment in disability management and proactive wellness programs create measurable bottom-line returns.[1]

Another reason that safety and accident prevention concerns managers is that the work-related accident figures are staggering. **Lost-time injury rate** measures any occupational injury or illness resulting in an employee being unable to fulfill full work assignments, not including any fatalities. According to the Association of Workers' Compensation Boards of Canada, in 2013 there were 902 deaths and 241 934 lost-time injuries resulting from accidents at work.[2] On average, 17 Canadian workers died at work each week.[3] These figures do not include minor injuries that do not involve time lost from work beyond the day of the accident. Moreover, these figures do not tell the full story. They do not reflect the human suffering incurred by injured or ill workers and their families.

Workplace health concerns are also widespread. Surveys have shown that 61 percent of Canadians believe that workplace accidents are inevitable.[4] According to the Canadian Centre for Justice Statistics, 17 percent of all self-reported incidents of violent victimization, including sexual assault, robbery, and physical assault, occur at the respondents' place of work, representing over 356 000 violent workplace incidents in Canada in one year alone.[5] This statistic is particularly disturbing because workplace accidents are largely preventable.

BASIC FACTS ABOUT OCCUPATIONAL HEALTH AND SAFETY LEGISLATION

occupational health and safety legislation Laws intended to protect the health and safety of workers by minimizing work-related accidents and illnesses.

principle of joint responsibility An implicit and explicit expectation that both workers and employers must maintain a hazard-free work environment and enhance the health and safety in the workplace.

All provinces, territories, and the federal jurisdiction have **occupational health and safety legislation** based on the **principle of joint responsibility**. The concept of joint responsibility is based on an implicit and explicit expectation that both workers and employers must maintain a hazard-free work environment and enhance the health and safety in the workplace.[6]

Purpose

These laws fall into three categories: general health and safety rules, rules for specific industries (for example, mining), and rules related to specific hazards (for example, asbestos). As discussed in detail in Chapter 2, a piece of legislation is a law (called an Act), and thus has mandatory compliance requirements. In addition to Acts, employers may also be following guidelines as established by regional, provincial, industry-specific, national or international sources. Guidelines are recommended standards or statements, often derived from legislation, but do not have the force of law or regulation.

In some jurisdictions, occupational health and safety Acts are combined into one overall law with regulations for specific industries and hazards, while in others they remain separate. The regulations are very complex and cover almost every conceivable hazard in great detail, as shown in **Figure 14.1**. Some legislation is workplace

FIGURE 14.1   Limited Examples of Occupational Health and Safety Legislation[7]

Federal Standards	
Canada Labour Code	An act regulating the health and safety of federal or inter-provincial workplaces such as: Canada Accident Investigation and Reporting Regulations, Canada Building Safety Regulations, Canada Dangerous Substances Regulations, Canada Electrical Safety Regulations, Canada Machine Guarding Regulations, Canada Materials Handling Regulations, Canada Safe Illumination Regulations, Employment Safety Order for Railway Aerodroms and Air-Stations
Canadian Centre for Occupational Health and Safety Act	An act promoting health and safety in the workplace in Canada with a focus on physical and mental health
Criminal Code of Canada	An act identifying criminal offences, and prescribing procedures regarding conduct of criminal law proceedings
Hazardous Products Act	An act defining hazardous products and use, including disclosure of product concentration and risks (WHMIS)
Human Pathogens and Toxins Act	An act promoting safety and security with respect to human pathogens and toxins
Transportation of Dangerous Goods Act	An act focusing on public safety specific to the transportation of dangerous goods
Provincial Standards	
Occupational Health and Safety Acts	The name of the primary workplace OH&S legislation in the following jurisdictions: Alberta, New Brunswick, Newfoundland and Labrador, Nova Scotia, Ontario, Prince Edward Island, Saskatchewan, Yukon
Workplace Safety and Health Act	The name of the primary workplace OH&S legislation in Manitoba
Workers Compensation Board Act	The name of the primary workplace OH&S legislation in British Columbia
Northwest Safety Act	The name of the primary workplace OH&S legislation in the Northwest Territories and Nunavut
Act Respecting Occupational Health and Safety	The name of the primary workplace OH&S legislation in Quebec

specific, but a number of applicable laws or Acts are not (e.g., the Criminal Code of Canada is not limited to the workplace alone). Provisions of occupational health and safety legislation differ significantly across Canada (as do their names), but most have certain basic features in common.

Responsibilities and Rights of Employers and Employees

In all jurisdictions, employers are responsible for taking every reasonable precaution to ensure the health and safety of their workers. This is called the **due diligence** requirement. Specific duties of the employer include filing government accident reports, maintaining records, ensuring that safety rules are enforced, and posting safety notices and legislative information.[8] Court decisions suggest that employers must enforce safe work procedures through a progressive discipline process to establish a defence of due diligence when workers do not follow safety rules and are injured on the job.[9]

due diligence Employers' responsibility regarding taking every reasonable precaution to ensure the health and safety of their workers.

Employees are responsible for taking reasonable care to protect their own health and safety and, in most cases, that of their co-workers. Specific requirements include wearing protective clothing and equipment and reporting any contravention of the law or regulations.

Employees have three basic rights under the joint responsibility model:

1. the right to know about workplace safety hazards
2. the right to participate in the occupational health and safety process
3. the right to refuse unsafe work if they have "reasonable cause" to believe that the work is dangerous

reasonable cause A complaint about a workplace hazard has not been satisfactorily resolved, or a safety problem places employees in immediate danger.

Reasonable cause usually means that a complaint about a workplace hazard has not been satisfactorily resolved, or a safety problem places employees in immediate danger. If performance of a task would adversely affect health and safety, a worker cannot be disciplined for refusing to do the job.

Joint Health and Safety Committees

The function of joint health and safety committees is to provide a non-adversarial atmosphere where management and labour can work together to ensure a safe and healthy workplace. Most jurisdictions *require* a joint health and safety committee to be established in each workplace with a minimum number of workers (usually 10 or 20). In the other jurisdictions, the power to require a committee to be formed lies with the government (Alberta), Chief Safety Officer (Northwest Territories and Nunavut), or union (Quebec: can request, not require). Committees are usually required to consist of between 2 and 12 members, at least half of whom must represent workers. In small workplaces, one health and safety representative may be required.

The committee is generally responsible for making regular inspections of the workplace to identify potential health and safety hazards, evaluate the hazards, and implement solutions. Hazard control can be achieved by addressing safety issues before an accident or injury happens, identifying ways in which a hazardous situation can be prevented from harming workers, and establishing procedures to ensure that a potential hazard will not recur. Health and safety committees are also responsible for investigating employee complaints, accident investigation, development and promotion of measures to protect health and safety, and dissemination of information about health and safety laws and regulations. In Ontario, at least one management and one labour representative must be certified in occupational health and safety through a provincial training program. Committees are often more effective if the company's health and safety manager acts as an independent expert rather than as a management representative.[10]

The Supervisor's Role in Safety

Most jurisdictions impose a personal duty on supervisors to ensure that workers comply with occupational health and safety regulations. They place a specific obligation on supervisors to advise and instruct workers about safety, to ensure that all reasonable precautions have been taken to provide for the safety of all employees, and to minimize risk of injuries or illness.

Safety-minded managers must aim to instill in their workers the desire to work safely. Minimizing hazards (by ensuring that spills are wiped up, machine guards are adequate, and so forth) is important, but no matter how safe the workplace is, there will be accidents unless workers want to and do act safely. Of course, supervisors try to watch each employee closely, but most managers know that this will not work. In the final analysis, the best (and perhaps only) alternative is to get workers to want to work safely. Then, when needed, safety rules should be enforced.[11]

Enforcement of Occupational Health and Safety Laws

In all Canadian jurisdictions, occupational health and safety law provides for government inspectors to periodically carry out safety inspections of workplaces. Health and safety inspectors have wide powers to conduct inspections in any workplace at any time without a warrant or prior notification and may engage in any examination and inquiry that they believe necessary to ascertain whether the workplace is in compliance with the law. Safety inspectors may order a variety of actions on the part of employers and employees, including orders to stop work or stop using tools, install first aid equipment, and stop emission of contaminants. Governments have been criticized for weak enforcement of health and safety laws, and several provinces have recently strengthened their inspection services.[12]

Penalties consist of fines and/or jail terms. Governments across Canada are increasingly turning to prosecutions as a means of enforcing health and safety standards. In 2008, Alberta imposed a record $5 million in penalties against companies for health and safety violations.[13] Other provinces are increasing the number of charges laid against both individual managers and organizations.[14]

Canadian corporate executives and directors may be held directly responsible for workplace injuries, and in some cases corporate officers have been convicted and received prison sentences for health and safety violations.[15] The Criminal Code includes a criminal offence (known as Bill C-45 amendments, and commonly referred to as "corporate killing") that imposes criminal liability on "all persons" who direct the work of other employees and fail to ensure an appropriate level of safety in the workplace. Criminal Code convictions can be penalized by incarceration up to life in prison, and financial fines can be imposed on guilty parties, as highlighted in the HR in the News box.

Control of Toxic Substances

Most occupational health and safety laws require basic precautions with respect to toxic substances, including chemicals, biohazards (such as HIV/AIDS and SARS), and physical agents (such as radiation, heat, and noise). An accurate inventory of these

HR IN THE NEWS

Criminal Negligence at Work

The first company to be charged with and plead guilty to criminal negligence causing death of a worker was Transpavé, a concrete block manufacturer in Quebec. The incident involved a young employee who was crushed by heavy machinery when he tried to remove debris jamming a stacking machine. The machine did have a safety guard device, but the device had been disabled almost two years prior to the accident. In addition, the court found that the company had inadequate programs to ensure safe operations of the machine, and there was a lack of training regarding safety and hazards in the workplace. As a result, the company was found to be negligent in its responsibility of safety in the workplace and the company was fined $110 000.[16]

Workplace Hazardous Materials Information System (WHMIS)
A legally mandated system designed to protect workers by providing information about hazardous materials in the workplace.

HR Competency

20300

WHMIS Training
www.whmis.net

substances must be maintained, maximum exposure limits for airborne concentrations of these agents adhered to, the substances tested, and their use carefully controlled.

The **Workplace Hazardous Materials Information System (WHMIS)** is a Canada-wide, legally mandated system designed to protect workers by providing crucial information about hazardous materials or substances in the workplace. WHMIS was the outcome of a cooperative effort among the federal, provincial, and territorial governments together with industry and organized labour. The WHMIS legislation has three components:[17]

1. Labelling of hazardous material containers to alert workers that there is a potentially hazardous product inside (see **Figure 14.2** for examples of hazard symbols).

2. Material safety data sheets (MSDS) to outline a product's potentially hazardous ingredients and the procedures for safe handling of the product

3. Employee training to ensure that employees can identify WHMIS hazard symbols, read WHMIS supplier and workplace labels, and read and apply the information on an MSDS.

Occupational Health and Safety and Other Legislation

Health and safety, human rights, labour relations, and employment standards laws are in force in every jurisdiction in Canada in an interlaced web of legislation. For example, Bill 168 came into effect in June 2010 as an amendment to the Ontario Occupational Health and Safety Act. The amendment has specific legislation requiring the employer to develop violence and harassment policies/programs, report and investigate violence and harassment situations, develop violence-related emergency response procedures,

FIGURE 14.2   WHMIS Symbols

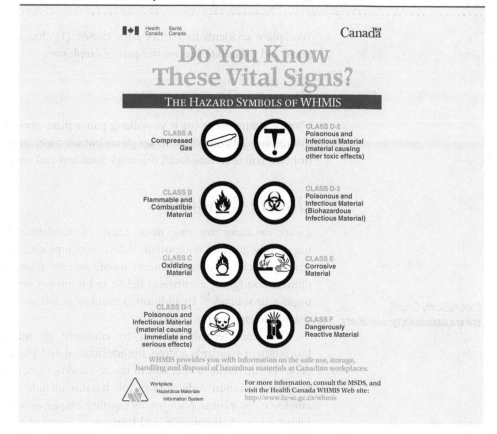

and deal with complaints, incidents, and threats of violence through a formalized process. Such changes to legislation may be specific or vague, local or national, and short or long term, but the role of HR in addressing and responding to changing occupational health and safety legislation will remain critical.

In addition, situations arise in which it is difficult to know which law is applicable, or which one takes precedence over another. For example, are the human rights of one employee to wear a ceremonial knife related to his or her religion more important than the safety of other employees? How much discipline is acceptable to labour arbitrators for health and safety violations? Should fights in the workplace be considered a safety hazard? Is sexual harassment a safety hazard? And how long does an employer have to tolerate poor performance from an alcoholic employee whose attempts at treatment fail? In Saskatchewan, human rights and occupational health and safety legislation overlap because sexual harassment is considered to be a workplace hazard.[18]

Similarly, to promote inclusion of persons with disabilities, the Ontario government developed the Accessibility for Ontarians with Disabilities Act, with a schedule for full accessibility by 2025. While this is not employment specific, the mandatory regulations aimed at inclusion have a workplace impact. For example, organizations with 20 or more employees are required to file a compliance report, outlining the types of policies, processes, efforts, and assistive devices offered to people with disabilities in the workplace. The Ministry of Economic Development, Trade and Employment has the power to conduct workplace audits and enforce compliance. Fines for failure to comply are of up to $100 000 for each day that a company is non-compliant.

WHAT CAUSES ACCIDENTS?

Workplace accidents have three basic causes: (1) chance occurrences, (2) unsafe conditions, and (3) unsafe acts on the part of employees.

Chance Occurrences

Chance occurrences (such as walking past a plate-glass window just as someone hits a ball through it) contribute to accidents but are more or less beyond management's control. We will therefore focus on *unsafe conditions* and *unsafe acts.*

Unsafe Conditions

Unsafe conditions are one main cause of accidents. They include such factors as improperly guarded equipment; defective equipment; hazardous procedures in, on, or around machines or equipment; unsafe storage (congestion, overloading); improper illumination (glare, insufficient light); and improper ventilation (insufficient air change, impure air source).[19] In addition, a number of factors have been found to increase the risk of violence in the workplace.

Canada Safety Council
www.canadasafetycouncil.org

The basic remedy here is to eliminate or minimize the unsafe conditions. Government standards address the mechanical and physical conditions that cause accidents. Furthermore, a checklist of unsafe conditions can be used to conduct a job hazard analysis. Common indicators of job hazards include increased numbers of accidents, employee complaints, poor product quality, employee modifications to workstations, and higher levels of absenteeism and turnover.[20] Some of these outcomes such as absenteeism can be managed through HR programs or policies, as highlighted in the HR in the News box, but elimination of minimization of unsafe conditions can address some of the causes of these outcomes.

In addition to unsafe conditions, three other work-related factors contribute to accidents: the *job itself,* the *work schedule,* and the *psychological climate* of the workplace. Certain jobs are inherently more dangerous than others. According to one study, for example, the job of crane operator results in about three times more accident-related hospital visits than does the job of supervisor. Similarly, the work of some departments is inherently safer than that of others. An accounting department usually has fewer accidents than a shipping department.

Work schedules and fatigue also affect accident rates. Accident rates usually do not increase too noticeably during the first five or six hours of the workday. Beyond that, however, the accident rate increases quickly as the number of hours worked increases. This is due partly to fatigue. It has also been found that accidents occur more often during night shifts. The HR by the Numbers box indicates metrics associated with non-standard work scheduling.

Finally, many experts believe that the psychological climate of the workplace affects the accident rate. For example, accidents occur more frequently in plants with a high seasonal layoff rate and those where there is hostility among employees, many garnished wages, and blighted living conditions. Temporary stress factors, such as high workplace temperature, poor illumination,

HR | by the Numbers

Balancing Scheduling of Employees and Health Concerns[21]

33% of Canadian employees work some form of shift work (e.g., rotating shifts, evenings or weekend shifts, on-call shifts, 24-hour shifts)

23% increased risk of heart attack for shift workers over non-shift workers

17.4% increased risk of coronary events for shift workers over non-shift workers

5% increased risk of stroke for shift workers over non-shift workers

20–30 average additional weight gain (in lbs.) of shift workers after 10–15 years of working shifts when compared to non-shift workers

HR IN THE NEWS

Managing High Absenteeism

Transat Tours Canada has almost 300 call centres responding to 1.3 million calls per year. However, they were troubled by an average monthly absenteeism rate of 13%. To combat this challenge, they instituted a 4-step solution. Post-implementation, absenteeism rates have dropped to 3%–4%.

First, managers initiate a verbal conversation with employees who show certain trends in absenteeism (e.g., calling in sick on Mondays regularly, taking two to three days off at a time, and so on). If there was no improvement after the conversation, another conversation with an accompanying email debrief was executed.

In the next stage, the same discussion occurred, however the director and HR were informed. In stage three, the director attended the meeting, and by stage four, written notification with a possible suspension is administered.[22]

EVIDENCE-BASED HR

and a congested workplace, are also related to accident rates. It appears that workers who work under stress or who consider their jobs to be threatened or insecure have more accidents than those who do not work under these conditions.[23]

Unsafe Acts

Most safety experts and managers know that it is impossible to eliminate accidents just by improving unsafe conditions. People cause accidents, and no one has found a surefire way to eliminate *unsafe acts* by employees, such as:

- throwing materials
- operating or working at unsafe speeds (either too fast or too slow)
- making safety devices inoperative by removing, adjusting, or disconnecting them
- using unsafe equipment or using equipment unsafely
- using unsafe procedures in loading, placing, mixing, and combining
- taking unsafe positions under suspended loads
- lifting improperly
- distracting, teasing, abusing, startling, quarrelling, and instigating horseplay

Such unsafe acts as these can undermine even the best attempts to minimize unsafe conditions, and the progressive discipline system should be used in such situations.

Personal Characteristics

A model summarizing how personal characteristics are linked to accidents is presented in **Figure 14.3**. Personal characteristics (personality, motivation, and so on) can serve as the basis for certain undesirable attitudes and behaviour tendencies, such as the tendency to take risks. These behaviour tendencies can, in turn, result in unsafe acts, such as inattention and failure to follow procedures. It follows that such unsafe acts increase the probability of someone having an accident.[24]

Years of research have failed to unearth any set of traits that accident repeaters seem to have in common. Instead, the consensus is that the person who is accident-prone on one job may not be that way on a different job—that accident proneness is *situational*. For example, *personality traits* (such as emotional stability) may distinguish accident-prone workers on jobs involving risk; *lack of motor skills* may distinguish accident-prone workers on jobs involving coordination. In fact, many human traits have been found to be related to accident repetition in specific situations, as the following discussion illustrates.[25]

EVIDENCE-BASED **HR**

Vision

Vision is related to accident frequency for many jobs. For example, passenger car drivers, intercity bus drivers, and machine operators who have high visual skills have fewer injuries than those who do not.[26]

Literacy

The risk of accidents is higher for employees who cannot read and understand machinery operating instructions, safety precautions, equipment and repair manuals, first aid

FIGURE 14.3 How Personal Factors May Influence Employee Accident Behaviour

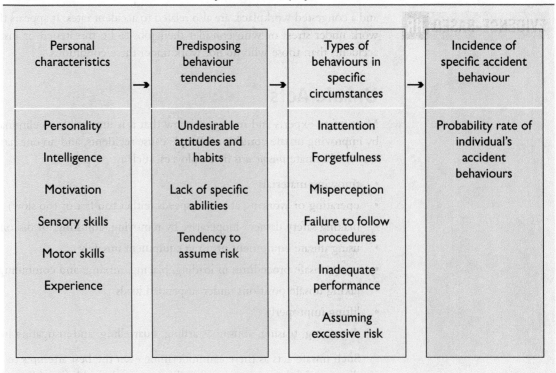

Personal characteristics	Predisposing behaviour tendencies	Types of behaviours in specific circumstances	Incidence of specific accident behaviour
Personality	Undesirable attitudes and habits	Inattention	Probability rate of individual's accident behaviours
Intelligence		Forgetfulness	
Motivation	Lack of specific abilities	Misperception	
Sensory skills		Failure to follow procedures	
Motor skills	Tendency to assume risk		
Experience		Inadequate performance	
		Assuming excessive risk	

instructions, or organizational policies on workplace health and safety. Low literacy skills potentially put workers and their co-workers in harm's way and increase the likelihood of work stoppages due to accidents or errors.[27] This situation is complicated by the fact that most workers with low literacy skills believe that their skills are good or excellent.[28]

A report by the Conference Board of Canada concluded that employers can reduce accidents by improving employees' literacy skills. They found an inverse relationship between industries requiring a high level of health and safety and investment in literacy skills.[29] This finding, together with the reality that people with lower levels of literacy often end up in more dangerous occupations like trucking, manufacturing, or construction, where literacy requirements are low compared to more intellectual jobs, clearly indicates the need for action to heighten literacy skills of workers.

Age

Accidents are generally most frequent among people between the ages of 17 and 28, declining thereafter to reach a low in the late 50s and 60s. Although different patterns might be found with different jobs, this age factor repeats year after year. Across Canada, young workers between the ages of 15 and 24 (often students in low-paying summer jobs) are over five times more likely to be injured during their first four weeks on the job than others, which raises questions about the supervision and training of young workers.[30] Suggestions regarding training of young workers are provided in the Workforce Diversity box.

Perceptual versus Motor Skills

HR Competency

80200

If a worker's perceptual skill is greater than or equal to his or her motor skill, the employee is more likely to be a safe worker than another worker whose perceptual skill is lower than his or her motor skill.[31] In other words, a worker who reacts more quickly than he or she can perceive is more likely to have accidents.

In summary, these findings provide a partial list of the human traits that have been found to be related to higher accident rates, and they suggest that, for specific jobs, it seems to be possible to identify accident-prone individuals and to screen them out. Overall, it seems that accidents can have multiple causes. With that in mind, accident prevention will be discussed.

WORKFORCE DIVERSITY

Guiding Young Workers in Health and Safety

The Canadian Centre for Occupational Health and Safety suggests that to reduce the likelihood of accidents and injuries to young workers, the following basic steps should be observed:

1. *Assign suitable work.* Limit jobs to those with moderate to low long training times, limited responsibility, low-risk tasks, or those that do not require isolated working conditions.
2. *Understand young workers.* Young workers may be risk adverse, reluctant to ask questions or change work processes without understanding the risk associated with that.

3. *Provide training.* Prevent young workers from performing any task until they have been properly trained and from leaving the work area unless required, as other worksites may have special hazards. Encourage them to ask questions, and enforce proper use of hazardous equipment and/or protective equipment. Provide emergency or disaster plan training.
4. *Supervise.* Ensure supervisors are qualified to organize and direct work; aware of applicable laws and regulations, as well as actual and potential workplace hazards.

Source: Based on Canadian Centre for Occupational Health and Safety (CCOHS), "Employers: Guiding Young Workers in Health and Safety," www.ccohs.ca/youngworkers/employers.html.

HOW TO PREVENT ACCIDENTS

In practice, accident prevention involves reducing both unsafe conditions and unsafe acts.

Reducing Unsafe Conditions

Reducing unsafe conditions is an employer's first line of defence. Safety engineers can design jobs to remove or reduce physical hazards. In addition, supervisors and managers play a role in reducing unsafe conditions by ensuring that employees wear personal protective equipment, an often difficult chore. However, only 4 percent of accidents stem from unsafe working conditions, and therefore more attention will be paid to accident prevention methods that focus on changing employee behaviours.

Reducing Unsafe Acts

Reducing unsafe acts is the second basic approach, and there are four specific actions that can help to reduce unsafe acts: selection testing, top-management commitment, training and education, and positive reinforcement.

Selection Testing

Certain selection tests can help screen out accident-prone individuals before they are hired. For example, measures of muscular coordination can be useful because coordination is a predictor of safety for certain jobs. Tests of visual skills can be important because good vision plays a part in preventing accidents in many occupations, including operating machines and driving. A test called the Employee Reliability Inventory (ERI), which measures reliability dimensions such as emotional maturity, conscientiousness, safe job performance, and courteous job performance, can also be helpful in selecting employees who are less likely to have accidents.

Employee Reliability Inventory
www.eri.com

A Canadian study conducted in a major industrial plant compared injury costs for a group of employees that were subjected to post-offer screening to assess their physical capability to perform job duties, and another group that did not receive post-offer screening. Injury costs over five years for the screened group were $6500 and for the non-screened group were $2 073 000—a highly significant difference.[32]

Many employers would like to inquire about applicants' workers' compensation history before hiring, in part to avoid habitual workers' compensation claimants and accident-prone individuals. However, inquiring about an applicant's workers' compensation injuries and claims can lead to allegations of discrimination based on disability. Similarly, applicants cannot be asked whether they have a disability, nor can they be asked to take tests that tend to screen out those with disabilities.

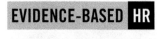

Employers can ask each applicant whether he or she has the ability to perform the essential duties of the job and ask, "Do you know of any reason why you would not be able to perform the various functions of the job in question?" Candidates can also be asked to demonstrate job-related skills, provided that every applicant is required to do so. Any selection test that duplicates the physical requirements of the job at realistic levels and the type of work expected does not violate human rights law, as long as it is developed and imposed honestly and in good faith to test whether or not the applicant can meet production requirements.[33]

Leadership Commitment

Studies consistently find that successful health and safety programs require a strong leadership and management commitment. This commitment manifests itself in in the values, resource allocation and culture established by leaders, and when senior managers are personally involved in safety activities on a routine basis. The Expert Opinion box summarizes the role of leaders in safety management.

Leaders and managers work together ensuring safety matters can be given high priority in company meetings and production scheduling, involving safety officer(s) with relatively high rank and status, and including safety training in new workers' training. For example, linking managers' bonuses to safety improvements can reinforce a firm's commitment to safety and encourage managers to emphasize safety. HR managers have an important role to play in communicating the importance of health and safety to senior management by demonstrating how it affects the bottom line.

HR Competency

80300

Training and Education

Safety training is another technique for reducing accidents. The Canadian Centre for Occupational Health and Safety and several safety associations, such as the Industrial Accident Prevention Association (IAPA), are available to partner in training efforts. The Canadian Federation of Independent Business offers online training leading to a Small Business Health and Safety (SBHS) certificate.

All employees should be required to participate in occupational health and safety training programs, and opportunities for employee input into the content and design of such programs is advisable. The training should include a practical evaluation process to ensure that workers are applying the acquired knowledge and following recommended safety procedures. Such training is especially appropriate for new employees.

Industrial Accident Prevention Association
www.iapa.ca

Safety posters can also help reduce unsafe acts. However, posters are no substitute for a comprehensive safety program; instead, they should be combined with other techniques, like screening and training, to reduce unsafe conditions and acts. Posters with pictures may be particularly valuable for immigrant workers if their first language is not the language of the workplace.

Positive Reinforcement

Safety programs based on positive reinforcement can improve safety behaviour at work. Employees often receive little or no positive reinforcement for performing safely. One approach is to establish and communicate a reasonable goal (in terms of observed incidents performed safely) so that workers know what is expected of them in terms of good performance. Employees are encouraged to increase their performance to the new safety goal for their own protection and to decrease costs for the company. Various observers (such as safety coordinators and senior managers) walk through the plant regularly, collecting safety data. The results are then posted on a graph charting the percentage of incidents performed safely by the group as a whole, thus providing workers with feedback on their safety performance. Workers can compare their current safety performance with their assigned goal. In addition, supervisors should praise workers when they perform selected activities safely.[34]

Controlling Workers' Compensation Costs

Workers' compensation costs are often the most expensive benefit provided by an employer. For example, the average workplace injury in Ontario costs more than $59 000 in workers' compensation benefits. Indirect costs are estimated to be about four times the direct costs.[35] Each firm's workers' compensation premiums are proportional to its workers' compensation experience rate. Thus, the more claims a firm has, the more the firm

Dr. Catherine Loughlin

academic **viewpoint**

Identification: Dr. Catherine Loughlin (PhD), Canada Research Chair in Management and on the Board of Directors at the CN Centre for Occupational Health and Safety

Affiliation: Social Sciences and Humanities, Saint Mary's University

Focus: Linking health and productivity for the workforce of the future, specifically focused on management responsibility and perspective on decision-making in the workplace.

1. Your research is really focused on putting occupational health from the leadership perspective. Why did you assume this focus?

Some people discriminate between leadership and management. Management is a formal role assigned by the organization. Managers may be leaders or may not. My research is focused on leadership. Leaders have accountability, responsibility, and influence. They need to actively construct systems to help the organization maximize its outputs.

Coming from an industrial/organizational psychology background, I realized early in my career that the conversation of employee well-being wasn't as prevalent in the business realm or in business schools. The issue of employee well-being and structures to support this are critical to organizational success and longevity. Additionally, there is a real interest in the topic from both students and leaders.

2. What is the relationship between employees' perceptions of their managers' leadership styles and the employees' psychological well-being?

Leaders control the allocation of resources, the systems and policies that shape the organization's culture. Thus, leaders create an environment for employees that affect both their productivity and well-being. Research shows that employees who trust that their leaders will act in their best interest experience lower perceptions of workplace-related risks and lower resource depletion, which ultimately reduces their stress levels while increasing productivity. These workers don't consume cognitive and emotional energy trying to protect themselves.

We typically look at intrinsic and extrinsic rewards or conditions as starting points of predicting employee outcomes, but the system is constructed by leaders.

3. What are the implications of your work in regards to provision of leadership training as a means of minimizing workplace risks for employees?

Training of leaders is very customized, but there are a few common experiences.

I. First, generally, leaders lack feedback. The leaders' perception of what the situation is (perceptions of priorities, culture, system, employee well-being, etc.) can be very different than what the employees perceive. While some organizations use employee surveys to collect feedback, the survey rarely provides a mechanism for individualized leader feedback. The gap analysis is required to determine required training and development initiatives for leaders.

II. Leaders need to model behaviour through the choices that they make about resource allocation, as well as what they do (which at times can be more important than what they say). Leaders can reflect on the impact of the actions and choices they make, and how these impact employees.

III. Leaders need to recognize that policies on paper cannot be translated into practice unless the culture is aware/aligned. For example, individual behaviour as well as group level behaviour (e.g., counterproductive behaviour, helping others) should be evaluated in performance appraisals to align with a focus on employee well-being

Source: Reprinted by permission from Catherine Loughlin.

will pay in premiums. A new online tool is available for small businesses in Ontario to calculate the true costs of a workplace injury, as explained in the Entrepreneurs and HR box.

Before the Accident

Association of Workers' Compensation Boards of Canada **www.awcbc.org**

Canadian Injured Workers Alliance **www.ciwa.ca**

The appropriate time to begin "controlling" workers' compensation claims is before the accident happens, not after. This involves taking all the steps previously summarized. For example, firms should remove unsafe conditions, screen out employees who might be accident-prone for the job in question (without violating human rights legislation), and establish a safety policy and loss control goals.

ENTREPRENEURS and HR

Small Business Safety Calculator

The Industrial Accident Prevention Association (IAPA)'s free small business safety calculator helps businesses identify and quantify time-related and direct costs associated with workplace injuries. The calculator is available online at www.iapa.ca/sbc. The categories and identification of time-related and direct costs in the chart below identify some of the key considerations in the IAPA calculator.

Category	Time-related costs	Direct costs
Incident Costs	Time required to: provide first aid, transport individuals to hospital/clinic/home, return area to previous safety levels	First aid supplies and equipment used, including ambulance or taxi fees
Investigation Costs	Time required to: investigate the accident, complete related paperwork, report the incident to the WSIB and meet with WSIB officers, meeting associated with the accident	Transmittal and administrative fees
Replacement Costs	Time required to: hire or relocate and train replacement worker	Trainer costs and associated recruitment and selection costs
Damage Costs	Time required to: assess, repair, replace, clean the damage	Outside contractors and materials, disposal, replacement parts, equipment
Productivity Costs	Lost productivity due to disruption of all affected workers, reduced productivity of injured worker after return to work	

After the Accident—Facilitating the Employee's Return to Work

Employers should provide first aid, make sure that the worker gets quick medical attention, make it clear that they are interested in the injured worker and his or her fears and questions, document the accident, file any required accident reports, and encourage a speedy return to work. Perhaps the most important and effective thing an employer can do to reduce costs is to develop an aggressive return-to-work program.

The National Institute of Disability Management and Research (NIDMAR) in Victoria, British Columbia, recommends following the three Cs:

1. *commitment* to keeping in touch with the worker and ensuring his or her return to work

2. *collaboration* among the parties involved, including medical, family, and workers' compensation

3. *creativity* in focusing on how to use the worker's remaining abilities on the job[36]

Specific actions to encourage early return to work can be internal or external to the organization. Internally, an employer can set up rehabilitation committees to identify modified work, including relevant stakeholders, such as the employee and his or her colleagues, HR professionals, union representatives, and managers.

Functional abilities evaluations (FAEs) are an important step in facilitating the return to work. The FAE is conducted by a healthcare professional with an aim to

- improve the chances that the injured worker will be safe on the job

- help the worker's performance by identifying problem areas of work that can be addressed by physical therapy or accommodated through job modification

HR Competency

50100

- determine the level of disability so that the worker can either go back to his or her original job or be accommodated[37]

Externally, the employer can work with the employee's family to ensure that they are supportive, mobilize the resources of the EAP to help the employee, ensure that physical and occupational therapists are available, and make the family physician aware of workplace accommodation possibilities.

OCCUPATIONAL HEALTH AND SAFETY CHALLENGES IN CANADA

A number of health-related issues and challenges can undermine employee performance at work. These include alcoholism and substance abuse, stress and burnout, repetitive strain injuries, workplace toxins, workplace smoking, influenza pandemics, and workplace violence.

Substance Abuse

HR Competency

20300

Hints TO ENSURE LEGAL COMPLIANCE

The effects of substance abuse on the employee and his or her work are severe. Both the quality and quantity of work decline sharply, and safety may be compromised. When dealing with alcohol and substance abuse on the job, employers must balance conflicting legal obligations. On the one hand, under human rights laws, alcoholism and drug addiction are considered to be disabilities. On the other hand, under occupational health and safety legislation, employers are responsible for maintaining due diligence. As a result, employers worry that when they accommodate an employee with an addiction, they may not be ensuring a safe work environment for other employees.[38]

Further, drug and alcohol testing in Canada is only legal in situations where three conditions determined by the Supreme Court are met:

1. The test is rationally connected to the performance of the job.
2. The test is adopted in an honest and good-faith belief that it is necessary for the fulfillment of a legitimate work-related purpose.
3. The test is reasonably necessary to the accomplishment of the work-related purpose. [39]

Random drug tests do not measure actual impairment and are therefore unjustifiable. Arbitrary alcohol testing of one or more employees but not others is not usually justifiable, but for employees in safety-sensitive positions, such as airline pilots, it may be justifiable. "For cause" and "post-incident" testing for either alcohol or drugs may be acceptable in specific circumstances. Positive test results should generally result in accommodation of the employee. Immediate dismissal is not generally justifiable.[40]

Recognizing the substance abuser on the job can pose a problem. The early symptoms can be similar to those of other problems and thus hard to classify. Problems range from tardiness to prolonged, unpredictable absences in later stages of addiction. Supervisors should be the company's first line of defence in combating substance abuse in the workplace, but they should not try to be company detectives or medical diagnosticians. Guidelines for supervisors should include the following:[41]

- If an employee appears to be under the influence of drugs or alcohol, ask how the employee feels and look for signs of impairment, such as slurred speech. An employee judged to be unfit for duty may be sent home but not fired on the spot.

- Make a written record of observed behaviour and follow up each incident. In addition to issuing a written reprimand, managers should inform workers of the number of warnings that the company will tolerate before requiring termination. Regardless of any suspicion of substance abuse, concerns should be focused on work performance, expected changes, and available options for help.

- Troubled employees should be referred to the company's employee assistance program.

The four traditional techniques for dealing with substance abuse are discipline, discharge, in-house counselling, and referral to an outside agency. Discharge is used to deal with alcoholism and drug problems only after repeated attempts at rehabilitation have failed. In-house counselling can be offered by the employer's medical staff or the employee assistance plan. External agencies such as Alcoholics Anonymous can also be used.

In Grande Prairie, Alberta, a clinic was established by the Alberta Alcohol and Drug Abuse Commission as a result of requests from the business community for a treatment centre that could deal with workplace-specific issues. It offers quick enrollment in its 30-day alcohol treatment program or the 50-day cocaine treatment program for $175 per day, plus months of follow-up, helping 180 clients a year return to work as soon as possible.[42]

Job-Related Stress

Workplace stress is a pervasive problem that is getting worse. Job stress has serious consequences for both the employee and the organization. The human consequences of job stress include anxiety, depression, anger, and various physical consequences, such as cardiovascular disease, headaches, and accidents. In Canada, the total cost of mental health problems approximates 17 percent of payroll, and the overall economic impact of work-related mental health problems is estimated to be $51 billion annually.[43] Stress also has serious consequences for the organization, including reductions in productivity and increased absenteeism and turnover.[44] Lost productivity at work due to health-related issues can cost the average Canadian organization up to $10 million each year.[45] Mental health issues are the leading cause of both short- and long-term disability claims.[46] Many organizations make physical safety a priority, but too often work environments that clearly have the potential for serious consequences from stress are simply tolerated.[47] Perhaps this reflects the fact that two-thirds of companies underestimate the prevalence of mental illness in the workplace, and only 13 percent of senior executives have a strong awareness of the impact of mental health on their workplaces.[48]

Organizations begin to suffer when too many employees feel that the relentless pace of work life is neither sustainable nor healthy. Why is this happening? Job stress has two main sources: environmental factors and personal factors. First, a variety of external, *environmental factors* can lead to job stress. Two factors are particularly stress-inducing. The first is a high-demand job, such as one with constant deadlines coupled with low employee control. The second is high levels of mental and physical effort combined with low rewards in terms of compensation or acknowledgement.[49] Healthcare workers, whose jobs typically include these factors, are more stressed than any other group.[50] However, no two people react to the same job in an identical way, since *personal factors* also influence stress. For example, Type A personalities—people who are workaholics and who feel driven to always be on time and meet deadlines—normally place themselves under greater stress than do others. Similarly, one's patience, tolerance for ambiguity, self-esteem, health and exercise, and work and sleep patterns can also affect how one reacts to stress. Add to job stress the stress caused by non–job-related issues like divorce, postpartum depression, seasonal affective disorder, and work–family conflict, and many workers are problems waiting to happen.

Employees are being asked to do more with less, creating work overload, increased time pressures, and tighter deadlines (almost one-third of Canadian workers consider themselves workaholics).[51] More people are working in "precarious" employment, such as temporary or part-time work with no benefits.[52] The sheer volume of email imposes terrific amounts of pressure and distraction on employees, taking a toll on their emotional equilibrium. The result is a corporate climate characterized by fatigue, depression, and anxiety.[53]

Reducing Job Stress

Stress is not necessarily dysfunctional. Too little stress creates boredom and apathy. Performance is optimal at a level of stress that energizes but does not wear someone out.[54] Studies find that stress may result in a search that leads to a better job or to a career that makes more sense given the person's aptitudes. A modest level of stress may even lead to more creativity if a competitive situation results in new ideas being generated.

There are things that a person can do to alleviate stress, ranging from commonsense remedies, such as getting more sleep, eating better, and taking vacation time, to more exotic remedies, such as biofeedback and meditation. Finding a more suitable job, getting counselling through an EAP or elsewhere, and planning and organizing each day's activities are other sensible responses.[55]

"I've been feeling a lot of work related stress."

cartoonresource/Fotolia

HR Competency

80400

The organization and its HR specialists and supervisors can also play a role in identifying and reducing job stress. Offering an EAP is a major step toward alleviating the pressure on managers to try to help employees cope with stress. About 40 percent of EAP usage is related to stress at work. For the supervisor, important activities include monitoring each employee's performance to identify symptoms of stress and then informing the person of the organizational remedies that may be available, such as EAPs, job transfers, or other counselling. Also important are fair treatment and permitting the employee to have more control over his or her job.[56]

The importance of control over a job was illustrated by the results of a study in which the psychological strain caused by job stress was reduced by the amount of control that employees had over their job. The less stressful jobs did have high demands in terms of quantitative workload, the amount of attention that the employees had to pay to their work, and work pressure; however, they also ranked high in task clarity, job control, supervisory support, and employee skill utilization. The researchers conclude that "to achieve a balanced system, that is, to reduce psychological strain, [job] demands and [ambiguity regarding the future of the job] need to be lowered, while skill utilization, task clarity, job control, and supervisor support need to be increased."[57]

Burnout

burnout The total depletion of physical and mental resources caused by excessive striving to reach an unrealistic work-related goal.

Many people fall victim to **burnout**—the total depletion of physical and mental resources—because of excessive striving to reach an unrealistic work-related goal. Burnout begins with cynical and pessimistic thoughts and leads to apathy, exhaustion, withdrawal into isolation, and eventually depression.[58] Burnout victims often do not lead well-balanced lives; virtually all of their energies are focused on achieving their work-related goals to the exclusion of other activities, leading to physical and sometimes mental collapse.

Post-Traumatic Stress Disorder (PTSD)

Post-traumatic stress disorder (PTSD) refers to a series of symptoms that can develop after exposure to an actual or perceived threated death or serious injury, or after a threat of injury (including physical and emotional) to self or others.[59] According to the Diagnostic and Statistical Manual of Mental Disorders, there are three main clusters of symptoms that must be experienced for longer than a month to meet the full criteria for diagnosing PTSD: re-experiencing the event (e.g., nightmares); avoidance of emotions, persons, physical space associated with the event; and increased arousal (e.g., insomnia, hypervigilance).

PTSD can be triggered by an event or series of events (workplace related or not), and is prevalent in specific professions. Emergency services (e.g., firefighters, police officers, paramedics), healthcare practitioners (e.g., doctors, nurses, 911 call attendants), and high stress jobs (e.g., air traffic controller, pilot, social support workers, bank agents, train/subway drivers) experience high levels of PTSD, but the issue of experience with traumatic events is not just limited to these professions. In the workplace, violence associated with clients (e.g., robbery), other employees (e.g., threats or actual harm caused), organization events (e.g., industrial accidents), or occurrences outside of the organization (e.g. 9/11, mass flooding etc.) can trigger PTSD. The effect of PTSD is not limited to the person suffering from it, but can take an emotional toll on the those who have strong relationships with the victim, as highlighted in the HR in the News box.

"Alright, I'll okay a personal day."

cartoonresource/Fotolia

Workers' Compensation and Stress-Related Disability Claims

All Canadian jurisdictions provide benefits for post-traumatic stress caused by a specific and sudden workplace incident. However, when it comes to chronic stress, there is very limited or no coverage, depending on the jurisdiction.[63] The rationale is that stress has multiple causes, including family situations and personal disposition. Research suggests, however, that a significant portion of chronic stress is often work related. In particular, high-demand/low-control jobs (such as an administrative assistant with several demanding bosses) are known to be "psychotoxic." Consequently, employees who are denied workers' compensation benefits for chronic stress that they believe to be work related are suing their employers. The courts are recognizing these claims and holding employers responsible for actions of supervisors who create "poisoned work environments" through harassment and psychological abuse. Courts are finding that a fundamental implied term of any employment relationship is that the employer will treat the employee fairly and with respect and dignity and that the due diligence requirement includes protection of employees from psychological damage as well as physical harm.[64]

Repetitive Strain Injuries

repetitive strain injuries (RSIs)
Activity-related soft-tissue injuries of the neck, shoulders, arms, wrists, hands, back, and legs.

Repetitive strain injuries (RSIs) are rapidly becoming the most prevalent work-related injury because of the increasing number of "knowledge" workers who use computers. RSI is an umbrella term for a number of "overuse" injuries affecting muscles, tendons, and nerves of the neck, back, chest, shoulders, arms, and hands. Typically arising as aches and pains, these injuries can progress to become crippling disorders that prevent sufferers from working and from leading normal lives. Warning signs of RSI include tightness or stiffness in the hands, elbow, wrists, shoulders, and neck; numbness and tingling in the fingertips; hands falling asleep; and frequent dropping of tools.[65]

A variety of workplace factors can play a role in the development of RSIs, including repetition, work pace, awkward or fixed positions, forceful movements, vibration, cold temperatures, and insufficient recovery time. RSIs are costly for employers in terms of compensation claims, overtime, equipment modification, retraining, and lost productivity. As with any other workplace safety issue, employers are required under occupational health and safety law to put controls in place to prevent RSIs. British Columbia has the most rigorous requirements regarding protection of workers against RSIs, and unions are calling for other provinces to follow suit. Employers must advise and train workers about the risk of RSIs from workplace activity, identify and assess job-related RSI risk factors, encourage workers to report RSI symptoms early, and use ergonomic interventions.[66]

HR Competency

80300

Ergonomics

ergonomics An interdisciplinary approach that seeks to integrate and accommodate the physical needs of workers into the design of jobs. It aims to adapt the entire job system—the work, environment, machines, equipment, and processes—to match human characteristics.

Poorly designed workstations, bad posture, and long periods of time working on computers are common conditions leading to RSIs, and these are easily preventable. **Ergonomics** is the art of fitting the workstation and work tools to the individual, which is necessary because there is no such thing as an average body. **Figure 14.4** illustrates ergonomic factors at a computer workstation. The most important preventive measure is to have employees take short breaks every half-hour or hour to do simple stretches at their workstations.[67]

Ergonomically designed workstations have been found to increase productivity and efficiency, as well as reduce injuries. The Institute for Work and Health studied 200 tax collectors who were in sedentary, computer-intensive jobs. Workers who were given a highly adjustable chair combined with a 90-minute ergonomics training session

FIGURE 14.4   Computer Ergonomics

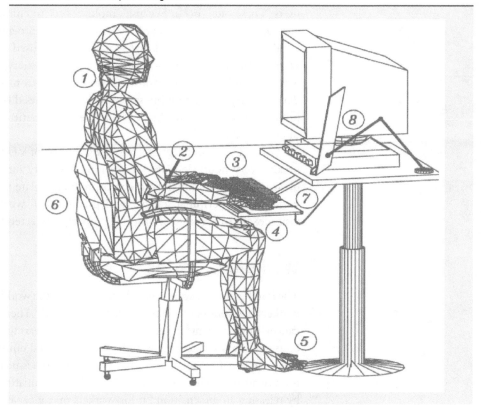

Note: This diagram is just an example. Workstation set-ups will vary according to the particular desk style, monitor, tray mount, or other accessories used.

1. The monitor should be set at a height so that your neck will be straight.
2. Your elbow joints should be at about 90 degrees, with the arms hanging naturally at the sides.
3. Keep your hands in line with the forearms, so the wrists are straight, not bending up, down, or to either side.
4. Thighs should be roughly parallel to the floor, with your feet flat on the floor or footrest if necessary.
5. Your chair should be fully adjustable (i.e., for seat height, backrest height and seat pan tilt, and, preferably, armrests). It should have a well-formed lumbar (lower back) support to help maintain the lumbar curve.
6. There should be enough space to use the mouse. Use a wrist rest or armrest so that your wrist is straight and your arm muscles are not overworked.
7. Use an adjustable document holder to hold source documents at the same height, angle, and distance as the monitor.

Source: © Queen's Printer for Ontario, 2000. Reproduced with permission.

reported less musculoskeletal pain over their workday, compared with workers who received just the training or nothing at all. Productivity increased nearly 18 percent because of the reduction in pain and more effective use of workspaces.[68]

Ergonomics will become more and more important as the workforce ages, and the physical demands of work will need to be adapted to accommodate some of the many physical changes typically associated with aging, including changes in muscular strength, hand function, cardiovascular capacity, vision, and hearing.

Video Display Terminals

The physical demands of new technologies have brought a new set of RSIs. The fact that many workers today must spend hours each day working with video display terminals (VDTs) is creating new health problems at work. Short-term eye problems, like burning, itching, and tearing, as well as eyestrain and eye soreness, are common complaints among

EVIDENCE-BASED HR

HR Competency
20600

video display operators. Backaches and neck aches are also widespread among display users. These often occur because employees try to compensate for display problems like glare and immovable keyboards by manoeuvring into awkward body positions.

Researchers also found that employees who used VDTs and had heavy workloads were prone to psychological distress, such as anxiety, irritability, and fatigue. There is also a tendency for computer users to suffer from RSIs, such as *carpal tunnel syndrome* (a tingling or numbness in the fingers caused by the narrowing of a tunnel of bones and ligaments in the wrist) caused by repetitive use of the hands and arms at uncomfortable angles.[69]

General recommendations regarding the use of VDTs include giving employees rest breaks every hour, designing maximum flexibility into the workstation so that it can be adapted to the individual operator, reducing glare with devices, such as shades over windows and terminal screens, and giving VDT workers a complete pre-placement vision exam to ensure that vision is properly corrected to reduce visual strain.[70]

Workplace Toxins

The leading cause of work-related deaths around the world is cancer. Hundreds of Canadian workers die from occupational cancer each year.[71] There is an erroneous perception that cancer-causing agents in the workplace are disappearing. Employers often face significant costs to eliminate carcinogens in the workplace, and unions are often so preoccupied with wage and benefit increases that they don't bring the issue to the bargaining table (although the Canadian Labour Congress has launched an initiative to reduce work-related cancers by releasing an information kit for workers on cancer-causing materials on the job).[72] In addition to known carcinogens, such as asbestos and benzene, new chemicals and substances are constantly being introduced into the workplace without adequate testing.[73] Workers' compensation laws in several provinces have been amended to provide benefits to firefighters who develop specific job-related cancers.[74]

Workplace Smoking

Smoking is a serious problem for employees and employers. Employers face higher costs for healthcare and disability insurance, as smoking is associated with numerous health problems. Employees who smoke have reduced productivity and a significantly greater risk of occupational accidents than do non-smokers. Employees who smoke also expose non-smoking co-workers to toxic second-hand smoke.

Smokers who are also exposed to other carcinogens in the workplace, such as asbestos, have dramatically higher rates of lung cancer. The effects of on-the-job exposure to radon on lung cancer rates were found to last up to 14 years, and the cancer rates were greatly increased for smokers.[75]

Most Canadian jurisdictions have banned smoking in workplaces. Health Canada is urging employers to implement smoking cessation programs for employees to achieve better health for employees, better business results, legislative compliance, increased employee satisfaction (especially for the 80 percent of Canadians who do not smoke), and avoidance of litigation.[76]

Viral Pandemic

Recent major outbreaks of viral diseases like influenza have alarmed people around the world and reminded everyone that a major viral pandemic is inevitable at some time in the future. A study by the Conference Board of Canada found that although almost

80 percent of executives are concerned about the impact of a pandemic on their organization, only 4 percent of their organizations had developed a pandemic preparedness plan.[77]

HR will be a key player in responding to a pandemic as most employers are planning to continue their business operations using the existing workforce—in other words, with substantially fewer employees. Immediate decisions will be required regarding telecommuting and working at remote worksites, compensation for absent employees, and maintenance of occupational health for employees who are working on company premises.[78] Even in the plans that do exist, there is little detail on the status of quarantined employees, compensating employees who cover for absent co-workers, responding to employee refusals to work in an unsafe environment, and business shutdown if health and safety officers declare the entire workplace to be unsafe.[79]

A pandemic preparedness plan should address prevention, containment, response to employee work refusals, creation of a pandemic preparation and response team, viability of continuing company operations, security of company premises, sickness/disability coverage, leaves to care for sick family members or children at home if schools are closed, and visitors to company premises.[80] Communication will be a critical component of pandemic management (likely using email, intranet, and hotlines), particularly if travel bans are imposed.[81] Unionized organizations will also need to consult their collective agreements and may wish to consult with the union when making pandemic preparedness plans.[82]

HR Competency

50200

Violence at Work

Workplace violence is defined by the International Labour Organization (ILO) as incidents in which an employee is abused, threatened, or assaulted in circumstances relating to work, and it includes harassment, bullying, intimidation, physical threats, assaults, and robberies. Most workplace violence arises from members of the public—customers or strangers—rather than co-workers. Canada is the fourth-worst country in the world for workplace violence (the United States is seventh) according to ILO data.[83]

The first-ever Statistics Canada report on criminal victimization in the workplace, released in 2007, indicated that one in every five violent incidents in Canada (such as physical and sexual assault, or armed robbery) occurred in the workplace. Physical assault was the most common violent incident, representing 71 percent of all incidents of workplace violence.[84] Violence against employees at work is particularly prevalent for women in healthcare professions. More than one-third of nurses are physically assaulted and almost half suffer emotional abuse.[85] Reports of abuse of nurses by clinical area of practice are shown in **Figure 14.5**.

Workplace Violence and the Law

Canadian Initiative on
Workplace Violence
www.workplaceviolence.ca

Most Canadian jurisdictions now have workplace violence legislation in place covering physical violence, and some include psychological/emotional violence as well. Human rights laws across the country prohibit various forms of harassment and bullying. Employers may be found vicariously liable for the violent acts of their employees on the basis that the employer negligently hired or negligently retained someone whom they should reasonably have known could cause the violent act; employers may also be found liable when they are aware of violent incidents and fail to respond.[86]

Prevention and Control of Workplace Violence

There are several concrete steps that employers can take to reduce the incidence of workplace violence, as outlined earlier in the chapter to reduce unsafe acts (selection testing, top-management commitment, training and education, and positive reinforcement). Specific to violence in the workplace, a company can also identify

FIGURE 14.5 Reports of Abuse by Clinical Area of Practice

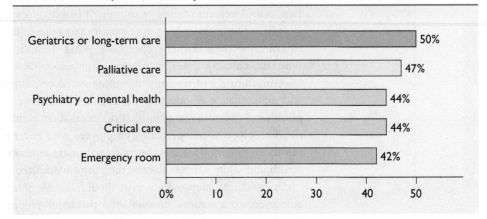

Source: From Factors Related to On-the-Job Abuse of Nurses by Patients, Health Reports, 20, no. 2 (2009), pp. 1–13.

EVIDENCE-BASED **HR**

jobs with high risk of violence, instituting a workplace violence policy, and, heightening security measures.

Identify Jobs with High Risk of Violence   Reliable predictors of workplace violence fall into three basic categories:

1. The instigator of the violence specifically enters the work environment with the intent to engage in criminal behaviour (theft, for instance) and generally has no other legitimate reason to be in the workplace. Jobs such as those of taxi drivers or gas station attendants have the highest risk for this type of violence.

2. The instigator is the recipient of a service or object offered at the targeted workplace. Jobs such as those of nurses or social workers are at risk for this type of violence.

3. The instigator is a potential or former employee (or, for example, a disgruntled employee).

Identifying and redressing these hazards and risk factors, such as installing safety shields for taxi drivers and bus drivers, can help to reduce victimization.[87]

Institute a Workplace Violence Policy   Firms should develop, support, and communicate a workplace violence policy that clearly communicates management's commitment to preventing violent incidents. The policy should state that no degree or type of violence is acceptable in the workplace, provide definitions of prohibited conduct, specify consequences of violating the policy, encourage reporting of violent incidents, include prohibitions and sanctions for retaliation or reprisal, and specify that all physical assaults will be reported to police.[88]

HR Competency

80300

Heighten Security Measures   Security precautions to reduce the risk of workplace violence include improving external lighting, using drop safes to minimize cash on hand and posting signs noting that only a limited amount of cash is on hand, installing silent alarms and surveillance cameras, increasing the number of staff members on duty, and closing establishments during high-risk hours late at night and early in the morning. In workplaces serving members of the public, some important precautions for employee safety include providing staff training in conflict resolution and defusing anger; having security staff to refuse admittance to anyone who appears intoxicated, visibly angry, or threatening; and instituting a recognizable "help" signal to alert other staff members that assistance is required.[89]

EMPLOYEE WELLNESS PROGRAMS

employee wellness program
A program that takes a proactive approach to employee health and well-being.

PERSONAL INVENTORY ASSESSMENT

Learn About Yourself
Flourishing Scale

There are three elements in a healthy workplace: the physical environment, the social environment, and health practices. **Employee wellness programs** take a proactive approach to all these areas of employee well-being (as opposed to EAPs, which provide reactive management of employee health problems). Wellness initiatives often include stress management, nutrition and weight management, smoking cessation programs, tai chi, heart health (such as screening cholesterol and blood pressure levels), physical fitness programs, and workstation wellness through ergonomics. Even simple things like providing safe bicycle lockup and change rooms or making fresh fruit and water available can make a difference.[90]

Glenn Riseley

Identification: Mr. Glenn Riseley

Affiliation: Founder and President, Global Corporate Challenge

1. **Your company assumes a shared responsibility approach to employee wellness. What is the role of the manager or organizational leader in this approach?**

Our business has a very simple end goal, and that is to make people healthy. We realize that regardless of how much conversation is happening at societal and governmental levels, people are often not taking personal responsibility for their health. We believe that the organization or workplace can provide a supportive environment to institutionalize healthy practices.

Our program establishes teams within an organization that compete in a race around the world, in which individuals volunteer to wear a device measuring their physical activity. The teams attempt to take the number of steps required to "walk around the world." In this 100-day challenge, employees start to change the way they look at their work environment: they start taking stairs rather than elevators, or park further away, or go for a walk during breaks.

There is a good business case around developing healthy workplaces and employees, especially given that labour force trends in Canada suggest future labour shortages. By sharing a commitment to employee wellness, both the organization and the individual employee can benefit.

2. **What is the role and responsibility of the employee in this approach?**

Employee participation in wellness programs is largely voluntary. While the employer provides the location and the funding, the employee's commitment is critical to the program success. Through establishing teams, a certain level of accountability to others can be embedded in an approach to wellness, which increases likelihood of the employee continuing or completing the wellness initiative. Often through tracking biometrics, stress levels, job performance, and other metrics, employees realize their individual and collective benefits associated with wellness in a meaningful way.

Misguided approaches focus on doing wellness to the employee, rather than the employee taking responsibility for these initiatives. We see this in the form of incentives for filling in health forms, or penalties for noncompliance.

Wellness programs have to be practical enough to empower the employee to succeed, and long-term enough to help change patterns. In addition to any technology used to help employees get more active, organizations should provide support through nutritional awareness and education to help employees make better choices about the overall health.

3. **Based on your experience, what are the major benefits of adopting an approach to healthier employees?**

In Canada, the average worker took 3000 steps a day before joining the program. By the end of the program, the average worker is taking 13 000 steps a day. The employees are surprised to realize how inactive their lives have become and that awareness is often a catalyst for change. Through simply empowering employees to move, eat better, and sleep better, the individual and the organization benefit. Our research confirms that employees who move, eat better, and sleep better have 41 percent fewer sick days; 52 percent felt more engaged at work, 54 percent expressed higher job satisfaction, and 33 percent increase productivity through a 100-day commitment to the challenge. Two out of every three participants also report a decrease in stress levels at work or home, demonstrating the impact of wellness initiatives on multiple aspects of the employee's life.

Source: Reprinted by permission from Mr. Glenn Riseley.

Wellness and prevention efforts need to be understood and undertaken as a process—a long-term commitment to a holistic focus on the total person and viewed as a management strategy to achieve measurable outcomes related to productivity, cost reduction, recruitment/retention, and profit. A focus on wellness will also be driven by the shrinking workforce, an increase in postponed retirement, increased awareness of mental health, and medical and technological advances.[91] The Expert Opinion box highlights how workplace wellness initiatives work well when there is top-management support.

Experience has shown that wellness programs are very effective; there is overwhelming evidence that money invested in a wellness program is returned many times over.[92] For example, Seven Oaks General Hospital in Winnipeg, which has a 10-year-old Wellness Institute, reports a turnover rate of 4.5 percent, well under half of the industry average in Winnipeg of 11.9 percent.[93] A study of heart health wellness initiatives reported a return on investment of 415 percent.[94] NCR Canada saved $600 000 in direct and indirect costs during the first year of its wellness program; absenteeism was cut by more than half after 12 months and was still one-third lower after 36 months.[95]

HR Competency

80400

HR Competency

20600

CHAPTER SUMMARY

1. Employers and employees are held jointly responsible for maintaining the health and safety of workers, including participation on joint health and safety committees. Employers are responsible for "due diligence"—taking every reasonable precaution to ensure the health and safety of their workers. Supervisors are responsible for ensuring workplace policies are well communicated and adhered to by employees, and that employees concerns are dealt with in a safe and systematic manner. Employees are responsible for protecting their own health and safety and that of their co-workers. Employees have the right to know about workplace safety hazards, the right to participate in the occupational health and safety process, and the right to refuse unsafe work.

2. The Workplace Hazardous Materials Information System (WHMIS) is a Canada-wide, legally mandated system designed to protect workers by providing crucial information about hazardous materials and substances in the workplace. WHMIS requires labelling of hazardous material containers, material safety data sheets, and employee training.

3. There are three basic causes of accidents—chance occurrences, unsafe conditions, and unsafe acts on the part of employees. In addition, three other work-related factors—the job itself, the work schedule, and the psychological climate—also contribute to accidents.

4. One approach to preventing accidents is to reduce unsafe conditions by identifying and removing potential hazards. Another approach to improving safety is to reduce unsafe acts—for example, through selection and placement, education and training, positive reinforcement, top-management commitment, and monitoring work overload and stress.

5. Substance abuse is an important and growing health problem among employees. Techniques to deal with this challenge include disciplining, discharge, in-house counselling, and referrals to an outside agency. Stress, depression, burnout and PTSD are other potential health problems at work. Job stress can be reduced by ensuring that employees take breaks each day, providing access to counselling, and giving employees more control over their jobs. Repetitive strain injuries occur as a result of repetitive movements, awkward postures, and forceful exertion. Ergonomics is very effective at reducing RSIs.

6. Workplace toxins can be carcinogenic, and some governments are providing workers' compensation benefits to workers with job-related cancer. Employees who smoke have reduced productivity and greater health costs. Governments across Canada have increasingly banned workplace smoking. Violence against employees is a serious problem at work. Steps that can reduce workplace violence include improved security arrangements, better employee screening, and workplace violence training.

7. Employee wellness programs aim to improve employees' health and reduce costs for sickness and disability claims, workers' compensation, and absenteeism. Wellness initiatives include physical fitness programs, smoking cessation programs, relaxation classes, and heart health monitoring.

MyManagementLab

Study, practise, and explore real business situations with these helpful resources:

- **Interactive Lesson Presentations:** Work through interactive presentations and assessments to test your knowledge of management concepts.
- **PIA (Personal Inventory Assessments):** Enhance your ability to connect with key concepts through these engaging self-reflection assessments.
- **Study Plan:** Check your understanding of chapter concepts with self-study quizzes.
- **Videos:** Learn more about the management practices and strategies of real companies.
- **Simulations:** Practise decision-making in simulated management environments.

KEY TERMS

burnout *(p. 340)*
due diligence *(p. 326)*
employee wellness program *(p. 347)*
ergonomics *(p. 342)*
lost-time injury rate *(p. 324)*
occupational health and safety legislation *(p. 324)*

principle of joint responsibility *(p. 324)*
reasonable cause *(p. 326)*
repetitive strain injuries (RSIs) *(p. 342)*
Workplace Hazardous Materials Information System (WHMIS) *(p. 328)*

REVIEW AND DISCUSSION QUESTIONS

1. Discuss the purpose of occupational health and safety legislation and who the agents responsible for enforcing it are.

2. Explain the differences and similarities in the employer, supervisor, and employee roles and responsibilities in maintaining safe workplace conditions.

3. Explain factors that contribute to unsafe acts, and identify how these factors can be controlled to reduce unsafe working conditions.

4. Describe how to reduce workers' compensation costs, both before and after an accident.

5. Explain the four traditional techniques for dealing with substance abuse.

6. Analyze the legal and safety issues concerning workplace toxins.

7. Identify factors contributing to violence at work and explain how to reduce these factors.

CRITICAL THINKING QUESTIONS

1. What is your opinion on the following question: "Is there such a thing as an accident-prone person?" What is the impact of your answer to this question on how organizations can manage occupational health and safety in an organization?

2. Young people have a disproportionately high number of workplace accidents. In your opinion, what factors have impacted this statistic? Why do you think that is? What role does the organization play in reducing workplace accidents among younger employees? What role do younger employees play in reducing workplace accidents?

3. Develop guidelines for determining the point at which to terminate an employee who shows tendencies of violence in the workplace. Assess a situation from the position of kitchen staff at a large restaurant. Reminder: Your guidelines must stay within legal limits and should also be realistic.

4. You notice that one of your employees consistently comes in to work on Monday morning nursing a hangover. For most of the morning, she appears distant and reclusive. Do you approach her to discuss the situation, or do you feel that is an invasion of privacy?

5. Given the disappointing progress in reducing workplace injuries and deaths, do you think that the "corporate killing" law should be used more aggressively?

6. Assume that you have an employee working in your company who has been treated several times already for substance abuse through the company counselling program. Today, the manager found him "stoned" again, trying to operate a piece of equipment in an unsafe manner. The manager just came to you and said "Fire him! I've had enough! He's not only endangering himself, but other workers." The company has a no substance use while at work and zero tolerance for arriving at work in an impaired state policy that all employees are aware of and have signed off on as part of the code of conduct. What steps can/should your company take in this circumstance?

EXPERIENTIAL EXERCISES

1. In a group of four to six students, spend about 30 to 45 minutes in and around one of the buildings on your campus identifying health and safety hazards. Research whether or not these unsafe conditions violate the applicable health and safety legislation. Develop recommendations to enhance building safety for each location and debrief your colleagues on these recommendations.

2. Review a workplace-violence consulting website and contact a workplace-violence consultant. Gather information on what advice is provided to clients on preventing workplace violence, and ask for a sample workplace-violence policy. Prepare a brief presentation to the class on your findings.

3. On your own, identify the workplace hazards that might be present in the following workplaces:
   - car repair and auto body shop
   - home renovations supplies and equipment storage area
   - live concert venue
   - health clinic dealing with homeless people
   - office with many employees working on computers and paper files
   - chemical plant finished product storage area

Think about what these companies can and should do to ensure that their employees are safe at work. Once you have completed your own list of answers, work with a group of four or five other students to compare your lists. Brainstorm other hazards and solutions.

4. Depression has been described as a "clear and present danger" to business, as it manifests itself in alcoholism, absenteeism, injury, physical illness, and lost productivity. Estimates suggest that an employee with depression who goes untreated costs the company twice what treatment costs per year. A Harvard University study projects that, by 2020, depression will become the biggest source of lost workdays in developed countries; the World Health Organization predicts that depression will rank second as a cause of disability on a global basis by the same year. Young workers (aged 15 to 24) are most at risk.

   Assuming the role of a career counsellor to newly hired graduates in a large retail company (The Bay, Costco, Walmart, and so on), explain the employee and employer outcomes of stress and depression in an informed and actionable way.

RUNNING CASE

Running Case: LearnInMotion.com

The New Health and Safety Program

At first glance, a dot-com is one of the last places you would expect to find potential health and safety hazards—or so Jennifer and Pierre thought. There is no danger of moving machinery, no high-pressure lines, no cutting or heavy lifting, and certainly no forklift trucks. However, there are health and safety problems.

In terms of unsafe conditions, for instance, two things dot-com companies have lots of are cables and wires. There are cables connecting the computers to each other and to the servers, and in many cases separate cables running from some computers to separate printers. There are 10 telephones in the office, all on five-metre phone lines that always seem to be snaking around chairs and tables. There is, in fact, an astonishing amount of cable considering that this is an office with fewer than 10 employees. When the installation specialists wired the office (for electricity, high-speed DSL, phone lines, security system, and computers), they estimated that they used more than five kilometres of cable of one sort or another. Most of the cables are hidden in the walls or ceilings, but many of them snake their way from desk to desk and under and over doorways.

Several employees have tried to reduce the nuisance of having to trip over wires whenever they get up by putting their plastic chair pads over the wires closest to them. However, that still leaves many wires unprotected. In other cases, they brought in their own packing tape and tried to tape down the wires in those spaces where they are particularly troublesome, such as across doorways.

The cables and wires are one of the more obvious potential accident-causing conditions. The firm's programmer, before he left the firm, had tried to repair the main server while the unit was still electrically alive. To this day, they are not exactly sure where he stuck the screwdriver, but the result was that he was "blown across the room," as Pierre puts it. He was all right, but it was still a scare.

And although the company has not received any claims yet, every employee spends hours at his or her computer, so carpal tunnel syndrome is a risk, as are eyestrain and strained backs. One recent incident particularly scared them. The firm uses independent contractors to deliver the firm's book and online courses in Toronto and two other cities. A delivery person was riding his bike at the corner of King and Bay Streets in Toronto, where he was struck by a car. Luckily he was not hurt, but the bike's front wheel was wrecked, and the close call got Pierre and Jennifer thinking about their lack of a safety program.

It's not just the physical conditions that concern the company's two owners. They also have some concerns about potential health problems, such as job stress and burnout. Although the business may be (relatively) safe with respect to physical conditions, it is also relatively stressful in terms of the demands it makes in terms of hours and deadlines. It is not at all uncommon for employees to get to work by 7:30 or 8 A.M. and to work through until 11 P.M. or midnight, at least five and sometimes six or seven days per week. Getting the company's new calendar fine-tuned and operational requires 70-hour workweeks for three weeks from five of LearnInMotion.com's employees.

The bottom line is that both Jennifer and Pierre feel quite strongly that they need to do something about implementing a health and safety plan. Now they want you, their management consultant, to help them actually do it.

QUESTIONS

1 If LearnInMotion.com happened to receive a visit from the Ministry of Labour, what specific areas do you feel they would be ordered to change and why?

2 As owners of LearnInMotion.com, do Jennifer and Pierre have specific responsibilities for ensuring their employees' health and safety is maintained and for having a health and safety policy in place which is subsequently enforced?

3 What unsafe conditions and acts were described in this case?

CASE INCIDENT

Ramona's Health and Safety Nightmare

Ramona McKenzie was on her way to work on a cloudy Monday morning when she got the call on her cellphone that no human resources manager wants to receive: An employee had just been injured at her workplace.

While turning into the company driveway, Ramona sees an ambulance, the injured worker, and a number of other employees surrounding the injured worker. Ramona parks her car, rushes over to where the employee is lying, and inquires about what happened.

The injured employee informs Ramona that she fell on the way into the building because no salt had been laid earlier in the morning to melt the ice on the parking lot. At this point, the ambulance takes the injured employee to the hospital and Ramona asks to speak to the plant manager in his office.

Shaken by everything that had occurred, Ramona asks the plant manager to find out why no salt had been put on the parking lot, as this was the norm after a significant snowfall. The plant manager informs Ramona that he would do this but also notes that the injured worker was wearing high-heeled shoes while on her way into the building. He also says that the employee arrived to work unusually early, before any other workers, since she felt she had a few tasks she wanted to complete for a meeting scheduled at noon and wanted more time to prepare. She claimed that she informed her supervisor very casually at the end of the day yesterday that she may be arriving to work early to finish the project by the deadline.

Now that you know the facts of this scenario, please assist Ramona by answering the following questions.

QUESTIONS

1   Could this accident have been prevented? If yes, how? If no, why not?

2   Who is responsible for this accident?

3   What does Ramona have to do to ensure a smooth return to work for the injured worker after the accident?

Managing Employee Separations

Turnover, Communication, and Employee Engagement

LEARNING OUTCOMES

AFTER STUDYING THIS CHAPTER, YOU SHOULD BE ABLE TO

DEFINE voluntary and involuntary turnover and explain the impact of each.

DISCUSS the drivers and outcomes of each turnover method.

ANALYZE important HR considerations in ensuring fairness in dismissals, layoffs, and terminations.

DISCUSS the three foundations of a fair and just disciplinary process.

DEFINE wrongful dismissal and constructive dismissal.

EXPLAIN the six steps in the termination interview.

EXPLAIN various techniques for ensuring effective employee communication in organizations to help manage turnover.

REQUIRED HR COMPETENCIES

10700: Consult in the development of a change management strategy considering the goals, resources required, and forces of resistance to achieve the organization's plan.

20100: Conduct human resources responsibilities and build productive relationships consistent with standards of practice with due diligence and integrity to balance the interests of all parties.

20200: Adhere to ethical standards for human resources professionals by modelling appropriate behaviour to balance the interests of all stakeholders.

20300: Adhere to legal requirements as they pertain to human resources policies and practices to promote organizational values and manage risk.

20400: Recommend ethical solutions to the organization's leadership by analyzing the variety of issues and options to ensure responsible corporate governance and manage risk.

20600: Promote an evidence-based approach to the development of human resources policies and practices using current professional resources to provide a sound basis for human resources decision-making.

30200: Develop initiatives through which leaders align culture, values, and work groups to increase the productivity and engagement of employees.

30300: Demonstrate the value of employee engagement using appropriate measures to encourage productivity, continuous improvement and innovation, and to enhance attraction and retention.

30400: Partner with appropriate leadership to communicate with employees, the union, and organizational stakeholders on organizational challenges and developments to create understanding and enhance affiliation with the organization.

THE IMPORTANCE OF MANAGING EMPLOYEE SEPARATIONS

Issues of recruitment and selection focus on growing the human resource talent within an organization. Who leaves, how they are treated during the exit, what the cause or nature of the exit is, and how remaining employees perceive this all impacts the long-term

academic viewpoint

Dr. Christian Vandenberghe

Expert: Dr. Christian Vandenberghe (PhD), Canada Research Chair in Management of Employee Engagement and Performance

Affiliation: Department of Management, HEC Montreal

Focus: Expertise in industrial and organizational psychology, organizational commitment, performance management, employee retention, and change management

1. **Some of your past research has focused on the causes of turnover. Based on this research, what can managers do to improve employee retention?**

Job characteristics are important drivers of retention, and often reflected in the job scope (diversity of skills and tasks, autonomy, feedback, significance of job, etc.). These characteristics improve or enhance commitments to the organization, increasing employee retention. Managers have power and control over these characteristics. Transformational leadership has been found to improve employees' perspectives toward work, and both leaders and managers have a role in stimulating the employee. Accordingly, they can strengthen the relationship with supportive behaviour to help employees face job demands. This increases retention.

Management also act as a link to the global organization or team members. They transmit support, and justice practices to their teams, which can emphasize and strengthen retention. Research has found that managers who have more networks, are more central in the organization, have values that match the organization, and are more politically astute are perceived to legitimately represent the organization. These types of managers transmit a sense of the organization to the employee, thereby strengthening the employee to organization relationship.

2. **What is the profile of employee engagement that is the most beneficial to employee health?**

Research profiling employees' commitment on different dimensions includes affective commitment, normative commitment, and continuous commitment. We know that these types of commitment have an impact on employee health, especially affective commitment. Once employees develop an emotional/affective link to the organization, the values of the organization become part of their identity. This congruence makes work more meaningful and ensures psychologically healthy employees. There is a negative aspect to continuance commitment. When an employee stays with the organization because of limited external employment opportunities, the result is employee perceptions of alienation, frustration, anxiety, etc. The best profile is one with high levels of affective and normative commitment and a low level of continuance commitment.

3. **Your research considers the emotional, moral, and instrumental nature of employee engagement. Are these equally important to employee performance?**

Job performance (in-role aspects or more discretionary aspects) is influenced by organizational commitment. Research has shown that affective commitment is a strong predictor of performance. Research also consistently demonstrates that continuous commitment has very little correlation to job performance. This is partially attributable to the fact that once an employee has an instrumental link to the organization, they will meet minimal requirements of doing the job, and don't invest more in doing the job better.

My research identifies that high levels of normative commitment, combined with high levels of continuous commitment, impede job performance. The negative influence may stem from a forced obligation to the company. The commitment in these situations is externally driven, and the employee experience is based on limited choices or alternative options. This is not a good motivator for driving strong performance.

Source: Reprinted by permission from Dr. Christian Vandenberghe.

sustainability of the organization. The role of HRM is often overlooked in managing employee engagement and communication during a time of employee separations.

This chapter first reviews employee separations by categorizing the possible causes and consequences of employee separations. Methods of reducing turnover and the negative implications of turnover on remaining employees (including legal compliance, two-way communication, and fair treatment programs) are explored later in the chapter. The Expert Opinion box shares research insight to help identify and understand the relationship between turnover and employee engagement.

MANAGING TURNOVER

Employee exits can become a huge challenge for organizations. The time, money, and resources invested in recruiting, training, and maintaining employees is lost when employees exit a firm. Additionally, employee exits disrupt the organization's ability to produce and maintain the right quantity and quality of talent and derail the organization's focus on larger strategic issues. For example, the retail sector often has high turnover levels, with very few long-tenured employees. Similarly, in the hospitality industry, one in every five employees leaves the company in any given year.[1]

turnover The termination of an individual's employment with an organization.

An organization's labour force is in constant fluctuation as employees continuously enter and exit the workforce. **Turnover** refers to the termination of an individual's employment with an organization. Turnover can be either permanent or temporary and can be a result of action taken by either the employee or employer. There are many possible reasons for an employee to separate from a firm. An online study of over 1000 Canadians asked people why they left their last employer. Results are highlighted in **Table 15.1**. The most common reason given by those interviewed was downsizing or restructuring activity, followed by a desire to find new challenges, then ineffective leadership.

HR Competency

20100

A study of over 34 000 workers in the Canadian labour force found that as an employee gains tenure in a company, his or her likelihood of quitting or being dismissed or laid off is significantly reduced. Additionally, individuals who hold occupations in management and administration-related positions are less likely to be laid off than individuals in other occupations. However, on average, the personal characteristics

TABLE 15.1 Reasons for Turnover

Reasons for Turnover (in order of reported reason)[2]	
Voluntary Reasons	**Involuntary Reasons**
Employee sought new challenges = 30 percent	Downsizing or restructuring = 54 percent
Ineffective leadership = 25 percent	Company financially unstable = 13 percent
Poor relationship with managers = 22 percent	Company/job relocated = 12 percent
Employee desired work–life balance = 21 percent	
Employee felt contributions weren't valued = 21 percent	
Employee seeking better compensation or benefits = 18 percent	
Employee seeking better personal values = 17 percent	
Employee seeking better fit for skills = 16 percent	

of employees who get laid off in relation to those who quit are opposite. For example, higher education reduces the likelihood that an employee will be laid off, but increases the probability that they will quit. Employees in the goods industry are more likely to experience a layoff, whereas employees in the service industry are more likely to voluntarily leave their job via quitting.[3]

Turnover rates vary by industry (for example, the construction industry and consumer services industries typically have the highest turnover levels in Canada, while public services has the lowest turnover levels), by the size of the company (smaller organizations typically have higher turnover rates), and by age (older workers are less likely to experience turnover than younger workers).[4] High turnover is problematic given that the cost of turnover ranges from 150 percent of salary to 250 percent of salary.[5] Ultimately, the combination of having a company incur the cost of turnover as well as the cost of day-to-day operations can be economically damaging.

HR Competency
20600

Cost of Turnover

Direct costs associated with turnover are often easier to estimate given that they are more visible (for example, cost of advertising and interviewing, cost of moving expenses offered to the new candidate), while indirect costs associated with turnover are often overlooked, but are still considerable (for example, lost productivity during the employment gap, training curve productivity losses). There are four main components associated with the cost of the turnover: separation costs, vacancy costs, replacement costs, and training costs.

HR Competency
10700

voluntary turnover Employee-initiated termination of employment, such as quits, retirement, or resignation.

involuntary turnover Employer-initiated termination of employment, such as dismissal or layoff.

- Separation costs—the cost of exit interviews, administrative functions associated with the turnover, and separation or severance pay
- Vacancy costs—the net savings or cost incurred of increased overtime, the use of temporary workers, and the loss of sales associated with the vacancy
- Replacement costs—the cost of recruiting and hiring a replacement to fill the vacant position (including the cost of interviews, testing, administrative expenses, travel/moving expenses, and so on)
- Training costs—formal and informal training (including the performance differential between employees exiting the organization and their replacements)[6]

Overall, the reasons for turnover can be classified into two subgroups: voluntary and involuntary. **Voluntary turnover** is employee initiated, usually in the form of quits or retirement. The decision to discontinue employment with the firm is made by the employee, without management enticement. **Involuntary turnover** is employer initiated and is usually in the form of dismissals or layoffs. Regardless, the employee has little or no personal say in this turnover decision. Employee exits from a firm are usually a mix of voluntary and involuntary turnover.

"There isn't enough blame to go around, there's only enough for you."

cartoonresource/Fotolia

Voluntary Turnover

Voluntary turnover includes quitting, resignations, and retirements, presenting a specific and immediate challenge to organizational success. In voluntary turnover, the employee initiates the termination of employment. Often, departing employees migrate to competing firms and create situations where their knowledge, skills, and abilities developed within the firm can be used to disadvantage the firm. As a result, voluntary turnover presents unanticipated HR challenges of replacing and retraining employees.

One of the biggest strategic challenges of voluntary turnover is the lack of managerial control. Voluntary turnover can be functional (where bad performers leave and good performers stay), which can help reduce suboptimal organizational performance, or dysfunctional (where good performers leave and bad performers stay), which can be detrimental to a firm's success.[7]

A review of turnover research identifies predictors of voluntary turnover. Individual-level variables found to have a statistically significant relationship with voluntary job loss are (1) low organizational commitment, (2) low role clarity, (3) low tenure, (4) high role conflict, and (5) low overall job satisfaction. Additionally, age and marital status were negatively correlated with voluntary turnover, while education was positively correlated with voluntary turnover.[8]

While an employer cannot always predict the reasoning behind voluntary turnover, it is important to try to understand which types of employees are likely to leave and why. This helps manage and prevent dysfunctional or excessive turnover. **Table 15.2** provides information highlighting the difference between why employees say they engage in voluntary turnover and why employers think employees engage in voluntary turnover. Rather than making incorrect assumptions regarding the triggers of turnover, information about the reason can be collected in exit interviews, staff surveys, and annual HR reviews.[9] Collecting this type of information can lead to trends that companies can use to screen certain types of individuals in the selection process. Additionally, these trends may lead organizations to develop methods of reducing turnover among current employees. In doing so, organizations obtain the information required to reduce turnover, retain effective employees, and decrease direct costs associated with turnover.

Quits or Resignations

Quitting is legally recognized as a voluntary resignation in which the employee terminates the employment relationship, often in the form of a resignation letter. Employees often elect to leave a company based on work-related factors (for example, the employee dislikes the boss or feels that there is too much pressure or stress), or non-work-related factors (return to school, moving).[10] Either way, employee quits are most often caused by low job satisfaction.[11]

Competitive factors often play a significant role in a person's desire to resign from a company, including opportunities for employment in other organizations. Consequently, perceived job alternatives and high labour demands influence an employee's perception

---

EVIDENCE-BASED HR

HR Competency

20600

quitting Voluntary, employee-initiated resignation.

TABLE 15.2 Why Do Employees Engage in Voluntary Turnover? (In Priority Order)

According to Managers	According to Employees
insufficient pay or unfair pay practices	insufficient pay or unfair pay practices
a desire to pursue personal goals	a lack of honesty, integrity, ethics
an excessive workload	a lack of trust in senior leaders
a job opportunity	a lack of work–life balance
a lack of feedback or recognition	an unhealthy or undesirable culture

Source: Reprinted by permission of Canadian HR Reporter. © Copyright Thomson Reuters Canada Ltd., 2013, Toronto, Ontario.

of ease of employment in other organizations, and are often carefully considered by the employee prior to resignation. Globalization, technological advancements, and market pressures have also created an increasingly turbulent economy, and over the last few decades large-scale labour mobility has become the norm. The result has been a decline in employee job tenure and job stability.

In Canada, employment-related legislation clearly identifies employer responsibilities at the time of involuntary turnover (such as minimum notice periods and severance pay), but there also exists equivalent employer-oriented protections in the case of employee-initiated turnover. The jurisdiction's specific Employment Standards Act (ESA) may provide information regarding notice of voluntary turnover (e.g., under the Ontario ESA employees with less than two years of employment with the same employer are required to provide at least one week of notice when quitting; while those with more than two years of employment with the same employer must provide at least two weeks' notice when quitting).

Lawsuits are rare and often limited to fiduciary employees (those employed in positions of implicit trust). The HR in the News box provides an example. A key outcome of recent cases in which the employer was awarded damages from an employee who failed to provide adequate notice, the courts suggested that termination of employment was a decision that carried a mutual obligation, and that employees should give a reasonable amount of notice to allow the employer to find a suitable replacement.[12]

Retirement

At a time when the skilled workforce was being replaced by an unskilled, assembly and task-oriented workforce, employers were forcing employees to take retirement at age 65 so they could replace older and often more expensive workers with younger

HR IN THE NEWS

Employees Failed to Provide Notice for Resignations

Recently, the Supreme Court of Canada found Don Delamont, a former branch manager at RBC Dominion Securities, personally liable for almost $1.5 million in lost profit. In 2000, he had organized a mass exodus of employees from RBC (none of whom gave reasonable notice) to Merrill Lynch. The Supreme Court also found that all of the employees were liable for failure to give reasonable notice of termination, resulting in an additional $40 000 in damages.[13]

More recently, the Ontario Court of Appeal upheld an award for $20 million in damages against four key employees of GapTOPS Ltd, who quit their jobs with only two weeks of notice, immediately began working for a competitor (Forsyth), and quickly solicited clients from the previous employer.[14]

An employee contemplating different retirement options

and less costly labour. Governments responded by introducing a series of acts aimed at providing financial support for people reaching "retirement age" to prevent poverty among the oldest generation. When launched, mandatory retirement at the age of 65 was not a reality for a significant portion of the workforce. In the early 1900s, average male life expectancy was 47 years and female life expectancy was 50 years.[15] Medical discoveries, eradication of infectious diseases, and implementation of public health measures (like water chlorination) have resulted in a significant increase in average lifespan on an international scale. According to Statistics Canada, average life expectancy for men in 2011 was 78.3 years, while average life expectancy for women was 83 years.

However, a combination of legal advancements on anti-discriminatory employment policies (such as age-based discrimination claims), labour scarcity, and peoples' desires to choose their own lifestyle, circumstances, or priorities has resulted in the abolishment of mandatory retirement in Canada. Now, retirement is viewed as voluntary turnover rather than involuntary turnover. The average age of retirement for public sector employees is 60 years, and for private sector employees it is 62. However, there is a large range of possible retirement ages, with some 40-year-olds eligible to retire from their organizations while 87-year-olds continue to be employed.[16]

One of the challenges associated with the retirement of employees, from an organizational standpoint, is the difficulty in predicting when employees will retire. Developing succession or replacement plans around potential retires and finding ways to their transfer of tacit and social knowledge becomes paramount to how an organization deals with retirement. Some companies are managing the labour shortage created by retiring employees by offering "**retirees on call**" programs, where retirees can come back on a part-time or as-needed basis, or by offering "**phased retirement**," where employees gradually reduce the number of hours that they work.[17]

Court decisions have confirmed that employers do have some legal responsibility to help employees prepare for retirement.[18] Most employers provide some type of formal **pre-retirement counselling** aimed at easing the passage of their employees into retirement.[19] Retirement education and planning firms provide services to assist upcoming retirees with such issues as lifestyle goals (including part-time or volunteer work, or moving to another country), financial planning, relationship issues, and health issues. Both individual and group transition counselling are offered in seminars and workshops featuring workbooks, questionnaires, discussions, group exercises, and software products.[20]

Involuntary Turnover

There are many reasons why an organization might engage in involuntary turnover. Job performance may be below acceptable standards and the organization decides to dismiss an employee. Economic or financial pressures may result in a decision to downsize through mass layoffs. The organization may be engaging in a new strategic direction and has chosen to close down or outsource one or more business units. In any of these cases, the decision to terminate employment is made by the organization and its agents, not by the individual employee.

Employee dismissal and downsizing are two of the most common situations in which employees perceive that they are treated unfairly. This reaction is not surprising given the negative ramifications to the employee in each case (job loss). Thus, it

Helder Almeida/Fotolia

HR Competency

20300

retirees on call A program where retirees can continue to work on a part-time or as-needed basis post-retirement.

phased retirement Potential retirees gradually reduce the number of hours worked per week over time.

pre-retirement counselling Counselling provided to employees some months (or even years) before retirement, which covers such matters as benefits advice, second careers, and so on.

The Retirement Education Centre
www.iretire.org

The Financial Education Institute of Canada
www.financialknowledgeinc.com

is important for all managers and HR professionals to be aware of how to conduct involuntary turnover fairly and legally.

Specifically, employer-initiated termination should be fair and occur after all reasonable steps to rehabilitate or salvage the employment relationship through employee discipline have failed. The legal system in Canada has repeatedly articulated the rights of employees to fair treatment, not only during the term of employment but also during the discipline and dismissal process. A fair and just disciplinary process is based on three foundations: rules and regulations, progressive discipline, and an appeals process.

Dismissal for Just Cause

Dismissal is the most drastic disciplinary step that can be taken toward an employee and one that must be handled with deliberate care. While dismissals damage the goodwill of a company as well as sever the employment relationship, there are undoubtedly times when dismissal is required, and in these instances it should be carried out forthrightly.[21] Some examples are provided in the HR in the News box. In cases where an employee was **dismissed for just cause**, it is considered an employer-initiated termination based on an employee's poor behaviours, therefore no severance, reasonable notice periods, or additional payments beyond what the employee has already earned are owed (for example, earned vacation time that is unused must be paid out). In cases of dismissal for just cause, the onus of proof lies on management to prove that performance in the past was below acceptable levels and that the organization provided feedback and allowed for opportunities to correct behaviours that led to poor performance (as discussed in detail in Chapter 10). In Canada, research finds that the group of employees who lose their jobs due to dismissal are no different in terms of age, gender, education, occupation, and industry than those who remain employed (no turnover). [22]

HR Competency

20300

Hints TO ENSURE LEGAL COMPLIANCE

dismissal Involuntary termination of an employee's employment.

dismissal for just cause An employer-initiated termination based on an employee's poor behaviours; in these situations, no severance, reasonable notice periods, or additional payments beyond what the employee has already earned are owed.

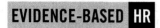
EVIDENCE-BASED HR

HR IN THE NEWS

Digital Presence Matters

Executives can forget that their digital presence is a big concern for their employers, especially when their tweets can impact the organizational image or reputation.

In May 2013, Rakesh Agarwal (PayPal's director of global strategy) tweeted a number of inappropriate tweets discussing fellow employees (e.g., "Duck you Smedley you useless middle manager."). The following day he took to Twitter to apologize to his colleagues and claimed that the series of tweets were part of his test experience on android that were only meant for a colleague. Within days, a new tweet from PayPal surfaced that read "Rakesh Agarwal is no longer with the company. Treat everyone with respect. No excuses. PayPal has zero tolerance."[23]

There is no clear definition of what behaviour constitutes "just cause" for dismissal.[24] Any allegation of just cause must be considered using a contextual approach, looking at not only the alleged behaviour, but the entirety of the employment relationship.[25] If an employer is considering making an allegation of just cause, it is crucial to investigate fully and fairly before any decision is made. The fundamental question is whether or not the employee has irreparably harmed the relationship to the point that it would be unreasonable to expect the employer to continue the employment relationship.[26]

Just cause can often be demonstrated in cases of disobedience, incompetence, dishonesty, insubordination, fighting, and persistent absence or lateness.[27] However, just cause cannot be assessed in isolation and may vary depending on the possible consequences of the misconduct, the status of the employee, and the circumstances of the case. The burden of proof rests with the employer in cases of dismissal or layoff. In Canada, courts often do not accept the assertion of just cause by the employer, and unions almost never do—one union alleged that a death threat made by an employee to his supervisor was "mild insubordination."[28]

Employee misconduct (including theft, expense account fraud, abuse of sick leave, and so on) is a fundamental violation of the employment relationship and can constitute just cause.[29] Unfortunately, the prevalence of theft behaviour is alarming, as highlighted in the HR by the Numbers box.

Insubordination is a form of misconduct that often provides grounds for just cause dismissal, although it may be relatively difficult to describe and to prove. To that end, it is important to communicate to employees that some acts are considered insubordinate whenever and wherever they occur. These generally include the following:[36]

1. Direct disregard of the boss' authority; refusal to obey the boss' reasonable instructions—particularly in front of others.

2. Deliberate defiance of clearly stated company policies, rules, regulations, and procedures.

3. Public criticism of the boss; contradicting or arguing with him or her.

4. Contemptuous display of disrespect—making insolent comments and portraying these feelings in terms of the employee's attitude on the job.

5. Disregard for the chain of command, shown by going around the immediate supervisor or manager with a complaint, suggestion, or political manoeuvre.

6. Participation in (or leadership of) an effort to undermine and remove the boss from power.

PERSONAL INVENTORY ASSESSMENT

Learn About Yourself
Managing Interpersonal Conflict

insubordination Wilful disregard or disobedience of the boss' authority or legitimate orders; criticizing the boss in public.

HR by the Numbers

Prevalence of Theft Behaviour

47% of retail "inventory shrinkage" is attributable to employees[30]

$4 bil estimated annual costs of employee theft to Canadian retailers[31]

9 percentage of cabin stock Air Canada estimates it loses per year to employee theft and the estimated dollars lost per day per employee to employee theft at Air Canada[32]

$60K the amount one employee confessed to stealing over two years from a small retailer after a month of video monitoring by a private investigation firm[33]

10% of small-to-medium businesses claim that employee theft played a critical role in the eventual bankruptcy of their organizations[34]

26% of Canadian small and medium businesses report experiencing at least one workplace fraud incident in 2010, including misappropriation of inventory, assets and cash.[35]

334 the section in the Criminal Code in Canada that outlines punishment for theft

Rules and Regulations

A set of clear expectations informs employees ahead of time as to what is and is not considered acceptable behaviour in the workplace. Employees must be informed, preferably in writing, of what behaviours or actions are not permitted. This is usually done during the employee's orientation (and included in the employee orientation handbook), or when rules or regulations in the workplace change. Examples of such rules include:

- Poor work performance is not acceptable. Each employee is expected to perform his or her work properly and efficiently, and to meet established standards of quality.

- Liquor and drug use is not permitted on work premises. The use of either during working hours or working under the influence of drugs or alcohol is strictly prohibited.

- Safety rules must be followed at all times.

An Ethical : Dilemma

Is it ethical to apply disciplinary action in cases of ongoing absenteeism and tardiness because of family responsibilities? What other approach could be used?

HR Competency

20200

downsizing Refers to an intentional decision made by executives within the organization that involves a reduction of the workforce to improve efficiency or effectiveness of the organization by affecting the work process. Often the term layoff is used to define downsizing in research and organizations.

layoff The temporary withdrawal of employment to workers for economic or business reasons.

HR Competency

30400

"Cut, cut, cut ... I feel like I'm working in a butcher shop."

cartoonresource/Fotolia

Progressive Discipline

A system of progressive penalties is the second foundation of effective discipline. Penalties may range from verbal warnings, to written warnings, to suspension (paid or unpaid) from the job, and finally to dismissal. The severity of the penalty is usually a function of the type of offence and the number of times the offence has occurred. For example, most companies issue warnings for the first instance of unexcused lateness. However, for chronic lateness, dismissal is the more usual disciplinary action. Finally, there should be an appeals process as part of the disciplinary process; this helps to ensure procedural fairness.

Downsizing via Layoff

As organizations adapt to ever-changing demands, markets, technologies, and competitors, downsizing via layoffs have become an accepted and familiar organizational activity. Alternative names for downsizing include layoffs, job cuts, rightsizing, reduction in workforce, and mass terminations, to list just a few. While downsizing and layoffs technically have different definitions, the two terms are largely used interchangeably in research and in the business world. Technically, "**downsizing**" refers to an intentional decision made by executives within the organization that involves a reduction of the workforce to improve efficiency or effectiveness of the organization by affecting the work process.[37] In a **layoff**, workers are sent home for a period of time (often undefined), in a situation where three conditions are present: (1) there is no work available for the employees, (2) management expects the no-work situation to be temporary and probably short term, and (3) management intends to recall the employees when work is again available.[38]

Layoffs that involve unionized employees are almost always based on seniority or conditions outlined in the collective bargaining agreement. However, layoffs that occur in non-unionized environments or affect non-unionized employees occur regularly and are not significantly standardized or influenced by third-party limitations.

Many employers today recognize the enormous investments that organizations have in recruiting, screening, and training their employees. As a result, they may be hesitant to lay off employees at the first signs of business decline. Instead, they are using new approaches to either limit the effects of a layoff or eliminate the layoffs entirely.

There are several alternatives to layoffs. One such alternative is a voluntary reduction in pay, where all employees agree to reductions in their pay to keep everyone working. Other employers arrange to have all or most of their employees accumulate their vacation time and to concentrate their vacations during slow periods. Other employees agree to take voluntary time off, which again has the effect of reducing the employer's payroll and avoiding the need for a layoff.

Another way to avoid layoffs is the use of contingent employees hired with the understanding that their work is temporary and they may be laid off at any time.[39] Finally, the work-sharing program, available through Service Canada, allows employers to reduce the workweek by one to three days, and employees can claim employment insurance for the time not worked.

CONSIDERATIONS DURING INVOLUNTARY TURNOVER

PERSONAL INVENTORY ASSESSMENT

Learn About Yourself
Strategies for Handling Conflict

A study of 996 recently fired or laid off workers found that wrongful dismissal claims were strongly correlated with the way workers felt they had been treated at the time of termination. They also found a "vendetta effect," where the instances of wrongful dismissal claims became stronger as negative treatment became more extreme. The researchers concluded that many wrongful dismissal lawsuits could be avoided if effective human resource practices, specifically treating employees fairly, were employed. Providing clear, honest explanations of termination decisions, and handling the termination in a way that treats people with dignity and respect, can be especially favourable to the company's reputation, as well as reduce the employee's negative feelings toward themselves and the company.[40]

Providing Reasonable Notice

In Canada, the employer–employee relationship is governed by an employment contract—a formal agreement (in writing or based on mutual understanding) made between the two parties. If the contract is for a specific length of time, the contract ends at the expiration date and the employee cannot be prematurely dismissed without just cause.

> **HR Competency**
>
> 20400

More commonly, employees are hired under an implied contract where the understanding is that employment is for an indefinite period of time and may be terminated by either party only when reasonable notice is given.[41] Employers cannot hire and fire employees at will, as is the case in the United States. Canadian employers can only terminate an employee's employment without reasonable notice when just cause exists. If there is no employment contract and just cause is not present, then a termination without reasonable notice is considered unfair and is known as **wrongful dismissal**.

wrongful dismissal An employee dismissal that does not comply with the law or does not comply with a written or implied contractual arrangement.

Reasonable notice legislation has requirements for employers who are terminating employees via a layoff. In smaller layoff situations, employees are provided with a minimum reasonable working notice (meaning that they will continue to work while knowing what their official end date of employment will be). When a large group of employees are terminated via a mass layoff, the length of reasonable notice is based on the number of employees laid off, rather than the length of time that the employee has been with the organization. The amount of notice varies by jurisdiction and with the number of employees being terminated, but it generally ranges from 6 to 18 weeks.

reasonable notice legislation
Laws that require an employer to notify employees in the event that they decide to terminate employees through layoffs (i.e., no just cause). Minimum notice varies on size of the layoffs, with smaller layoffs determining minimum notice based on employee tenure and mass layoffs determining minimum notice based on total layoff size.

In some jurisdictions, employers are allowed to provide payment in lieu of reasonable notice (working time), allowing them to terminate employees without cause relatively quickly. Payments are often conditional on the employee signing a general release of all legal claims against the employer. The laws do not prevent the employer from closing down, nor do they require saving jobs; they simply give employees time to seek other work or retraining by giving them advance notice of their termination.

> **HR Competency**
>
> 20300

Often, the amount of notice considered reasonable when an employer decides to terminate the employment relationship is beyond the minimum notice requirements of employment/labour standards legislation. A rule of thumb some organizations follow for reasonable notice is about three to four weeks per year of service. The employee can accept the notice given (and sign any required release form) or can sue for wrongful dismissal if the notice is considered unacceptable. The court will review the circumstances of the dismissal and make a final decision on the amount of notice to be provided. The courts generally award a period of notice based on their assessment of how long it will take the employee to find alternative employment, taking into account the employee's age, salary, length of service, the level of the job, and other factors. Rarely have notice periods exceeded 24 months.[42]

bad-faith damages Reserved for extreme circumstances in which the employers was untruthful, misleading, or unduly insensitive to the employee in the course of a dismissal.

Bad-Faith Damages

In 1997, "bad-faith conduct" on the part of the employer in dismissing an employee was added as another factor considered by the courts in determining the period of reasonable notice.[43] At a minimum, employers are required to be candid, reasonable, honest, and forthright with their employees in the course of dismissal and should refrain from engaging in conduct that is unfair or in bad faith, such as being untruthful, misleading, or unduly insensitive. The resulting additional periods of notice are unpredictable, often around three to four months, but sometimes considerably higher.[44] A significant change to the assessment of bad-faith damages was established by a 2008 decision by the Supreme Court of Canada, which ruled that bad-faith damages apply to only the most extreme conduct and that damages should not be provided by extending the notice period but by compensation for actual damages suffered by the employee.[45] Nevertheless, it is still clear that employers must treat employees with dignity and respect at all times, especially at the time of dismissal.[46]

punitive damages Reserved for malicious or outrageous cases in which an employer engages in harsh and vindictive treatment of an employee, or if the employee suffered undue distress from not being given adequate notice of termination.

constructive dismissal When the employer makes unilateral changes in the employment contract that are unacceptable to the employee, even though the employee has not been formally terminated.

Punitive Damages

In extreme cases, employers may also be ordered to pay **punitive damages** for harsh and vindictive treatment of an employee, or damages for aggravated or mental distress if the employee suffered undue distress from not being given adequate notice of termination.[47] In 2005, the largest punitive damage award in Canadian history was handed down when Honda Canada was ordered to pay $500 000 to a terminated employee for its mistreatment of the employee, who was disabled due to chronic fatigue syndrome.[48] The amount was later reduced to $100 000 by an appeal court and eliminated entirely by the Supreme Court of Canada, who ruled in 2008 that punitive damages should only apply in exceptional cases with wrongful acts by the employer that are truly malicious and outrageous.[49]

Constructive Dismissal

Constructive dismissal is considered to occur when the employer makes unilateral changes in the employment contract that are recognized as unacceptable according to the employee, even though the employee has not been formally terminated.[50] The most common changes in employment status that are considered to constitute constructive dismissal are demotion, reduction in pay and benefits, forced resignation, forced early retirement, forced transfer, and

"Now that we've hired you we would like to restructure the position."

cartoonresource/Fotolia

changes in job duties and responsibilities. An employee who believes that he or she has been constructively dismissed can sue the employer for wrongful dismissal. If the judge agrees that constructive dismissal occurred, then a period of notice to be provided to the employee can be determined.

For example, a long-term employee of Ontario Power Generation was affected by a shift in the company's focus that largely eliminated his responsibilities for business development. He was told that he would be "underutilized for the foreseeable future" and that if he didn't like the changes, he could resign or retire. He resigned shortly thereafter and sued for constructive dismissal. The court found that the essential terms of his employment had been substantially changed. The court also discovered that the company had no plan to provide him with work and that he had been constructively dismissed. He was awarded 24 months' pay.[51]

Avoiding Wrongful Dismissal Suits

Dismissals for cause may result in the employee filing a wrongful dismissal lawsuit. A wrongful dismissal accusation is one in which the terminated employee contends that the employer terminated the employment relationship in violation of relevant law (based on age, gender, or other protected grounds), the contract of employment (implied or explicit), or the employer's own dismissal procedures. More recent accusations have stemmed from how the dismissal was carried out (perceptions of fairness) or employee perception that the reason for the termination did not qualify as "just cause."

There are several steps that can be taken to avoid wrongful dismissal suits.[52] Employers should have clear termination clauses written in the employment contracts. They should also document all disciplinary actions, which should be based on a progressive discipline policy that is articulated clearly to all employees and consistently applied. The use of a formal resignation letter is another mandatory, but often overlooked, consideration when terminating employees. In addition to the letter, the termination meeting should be private, have two members of management present, and include a procedure for allowing the employee to collect his or her belongings in the least disruptive manner.

If a wrongful dismissal suit is made against the company, the firm should:[53]

- Review the claim carefully before retaining an employment lawyer, and investigate for other improper conduct; ask for a legal opinion on the merits of the case; work with the lawyer and provide all relevant facts and documentation; and discuss any possible letter of reference with the lawyer.

- Never allege cause if none exists, and avoid defamatory statements.

- Consider mediation as an option, or offer to settle to save time and money.

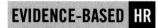

EMPLOYEE ENGAGEMENT AND FAIRNESS IN EMPLOYEE SEPARATIONS

Employee Engagement

employee engagement The emotional and intellectual involvement of employees in their work, such as intensity, focus, and involvement in his or her job and organization.

Employee engagement is a positive, fulfilling, work-related state of mind characterized by vigour, dedication, and absorption.[54] It is a heightened emotional and intellectual connection that an employee has for his or her job, organization, manager, or co-workers, that in turn influences the employee to apply additional discretionary

expert opinion
industry viewpoint

Mark Bania

Identification: Mr. Mark Bania, Managing Director, CareerBuilder of Canada

Focus: Management and development of sales groups (both inside and outside), creating and deploying a nationwide sales and brand development strategy, and partnering with multiple business units to ensure that solutions are tailored to Canadian market needs

1. How does CareerBuilder of Canada foster employee engagement within their three-pillar approach?

I. It is important for us that everyone from the top to the bottom of the organization understands what the definition of employee engagement means. We try to identify what the ideal work environment is and give performance-based flexibility (e.g., travel, work from home, etc.) with clear expectations. These expectations are then embedded in the Key Performance Indicators (KPI) we measure and assess.

II. We feel we are hiring not just the individual, but also their support system and community. With the blurred lines between workspace and home, we try to recognize the employee as a whole. For example, in the summer months we offer half-day Fridays, but full compensation, to help balance work–life priorities of employees. Interestingly, we experience a productivity boost during the summer months, which identifies for us that we have incentivized the right behaviours.

III. As part of a global initiative, we offer tuition reimbursement which has wildly successful. Rather than focusing on exclusively job-related training, we encourage and support employees who develop a broad and highly transferable skill set. We experience a higher retention rate for employees who take advantage of these types of programs over those who don't.

2. How do you ensure that employee expectations are communicated effectively and clearly?

Aligned with our perspective on employee engagement, we believe that fairness and communication should be embedded throughout the employee lifecycle, including recruitment, selection, training, development, and separations. For example, we have weekly one-to-one meetings between employees and their managers identifying performance metrics and KPI concerns. We also have monthly director one-to-one meetings and broader quarterly business meetings at the global level. Through this, we can help individuals overcome any obstacles to success, and identify resources in the organization available to the employee to help offload challenges or provide organizational support, including identifying areas for development.

3. As a part of a large multinational organization, what are some of the challenges you face in regards to employees expressing their voice to management?

Some employees may have fears associated with uncertainty or concerns because of the speed of change, global information, or communication challenges that typically occur in large organizations. Through these multiple levels of regular and structured meetings, employees have an opportunity for communication with higher-level executives, which includes two-way communication. The meetings provide an opportunity to share any broader level changes or new perspectives that should be considered and learn best practices from others as well.

Source: Reprinted by permission from Mark Bania.

distributive justice Fairness of a decision outcome.

procedural justice Fairness of the process used to make a decision.

effort.[55] The Expert Opinion box provides a current and clear awareness of how to manage employee engagement to reduce turnover. Engaged employees feel a vested interest in the company's success and are both willing and motivated to perform to levels that exceed the stated job requirements (see **Figure 15.1**).[56]

Over 30 years of organizational research clearly indicates that employees are sensitive to the treatment they receive, and that they have strong perceptions regarding the fairness of their experiences at work.[57] In respect to employee relations, experts generally define organizational justice in terms of three components: distributive justice, procedural justice, and interactional justice. **Distributive justice** refers to the fairness and justice of the outcome of a decision (Would a comparable employee have the same outcome related to the employee separation?). **Procedural justice** refers to the

FIGURE 15.1 Top Drivers of Attraction, Retention, and Sustainable Engagement in Canada

TOP DRIVERS OF ATTRACTION, RETENTION, AND SUSTAINABLE ENGAGEMENT IN CANADA

Driver	Attraction	Retention	Sustainable Engagement
1	Base pay/salary	Base pay/salary	Leadership
2	Job security	Opportunities to advance in my career	Stress, Balance & Workload
3	Opportunities to advance in my career	Trust/confidence in senior leadership	Career Development
4	Challenging work	Relationship with supervisor/manager	Supervision
5	Opportunities to learn new skills	Ability to manage or limit work-related stress	Goals & Objectives

Source: Closing the Engagement Gap: A Road Map for Driving Superior Business Performance. Towers Perrin Workforce Study 2007–2008, p. 21. Used by permission from Towers Watson.

interactional justice Fairness in interpersonal interactions, treating others with dignity and respect.

fairness of the process (Is the process my company uses to make decisions about terminations or employee separations fair?). **Interactional justice** refers to the manner in which managers conduct their interpersonal dealings with employees and, in particular, the degree to which they treat employees with dignity and respect as opposed to abuse or disrespect (Does my supervisor treat me with respect when assessing factors related to the separation?). There are a number of examples in which an employer engaged in questionable tactics during employee separations, and had to suffer a loss in employment branding and reputation as a result, as outlined in the HR in the News box.

HR IN THE NEWS

Mass Layoffs Gone Wrong

HMV in the UK gathered employees together for a mass layoff, including the employee responsible for the company's Twitter account. During the layoff announcement tweets sent out included, "We're live tweeting from the HR firing session, this is so exciting!" and "We've all been fired, in a group, of 50+ people! And those who ruined the business are safe ... hooray!"[58]

Similarly, Burnaby, BC–based Best Buy and Future Shop shuttered up 15 locations across Canada, without giving workers any notice or warning. Employees showed up for work on January 31, 2013, to find doors locked and signs on the doors saying that the location was closed effective immediately. These closures affected around 900 employees, representing 5 percent of the organization's workforce.[59]

Suggestion Programs

Employees can often offer well-informed, thoughtful, and creative suggestions regarding issues ranging from malfunctioning vending machines to unlit parking lots to a manager spending too much of the department's money on travel. Dofasco Inc.'s suggestion program has been a success story for decades. Employees can receive cash awards of up to $50 000, depending on the savings realized by implementing the suggestion. Suggestion programs like these have several benefits. They let management continually monitor employees' feelings and concerns while making it clear that employees have several channels through which to communicate concerns and get responses. The net effect is less likelihood that minor employee issues will manifest themselves into organizational concerns.

Employee Opinion Surveys

employee opinion surveys
Communication devices that use questionnaires to ask for employees' opinions about the company, management, and work life.

Many firms also administer periodic anonymous **employee opinion surveys**. For maximum benefit, surveys should be conducted regularly and the results must be provided to participants.[60] An employee satisfaction survey, called the Employee Feedback System (EFS), has been developed by the National Quality Institute and the Workplace Health Research Unit at Brock University.[61] The EFS examines 16 areas ranging from job satisfaction and co-worker cohesion to quality focus and employee commitment.

Recently, employees began to use blogs to express opinions about their employers, and employer concerns arose about damage to their reputation and possible disclosure of confidential company information. Some corporations, such as IBM, Cisco, and Sun Microsystems, have chosen to trust their employees and have suggested guidelines and specific tactics so that employees can blog without causing themselves or their employers any grief.[62] However, there are also cases where employees have been terminated for posting negative opinions about their employer, and arbitration boards have upheld the terminations, finding that postings about managers, co-workers, and the work environment are sufficient grounds for discharge.[63] A blogging policy is recommended by legal experts and should include directions to refrain from disclosing any confidential company information or embarrassing or demeaning information about the company and its employees.[64]

Communication from Management

PERSONAL INVENTORY ASSESSMENT

Learn About Yourself
Communicating Supportively

To increase employee engagement, many firms give employees extensive data on the performance of and prospects for their operations. Traditionally, newsletters and verbal presentations were the most effective methods used to disseminate information from the company to employees. More recently, organizations have used videos, email, and intranets.[65] Blogs can also be used by senior managers to connect with employees. When Jim Estill sold his company and became CEO of the larger combined operation, he found employees of the acquiring company "treated me like I was some sort of Martian." He started a blog (80 percent company-related content and 20 percent personal) and soon overcame the problem—staff even sent him pictures from their kids' birthday parties! In addition, staff sent the blog to vendors and customers, which elevated him in their eyes as well.[66]

HR Competency
30300

The Termination Interview

Dismissing an employee is one of the most difficult tasks that a manager will face at work.[67] The dismissed employee, even if warned many times in the past, will often still

termination interview The interview in which an employee is informed of the fact that he or she has been dismissed.

react with total disbelief or even violence. Guidelines for the **termination interview** itself follow.

1. *Plan the interview.* Carefully schedule the meeting on a day early in the week, and try to avoid Fridays, pre-holidays, and vacation times. Have the employee agreement, human resources file, and release announcement (internal and external) prepared in advance. Be available at a time after the interview in case questions or problems arise, and have phone numbers ready for medical or security emergencies.

2. *Get to the point.* As soon as the employee arrives, give the person a moment to get comfortable and then inform him or her of the decision.

3. *Describe the situation briefly.* In three or four sentences, explain why the person is being let go. For instance, "Production in your area is down 4 percent, and we are continuing to have quality problems. We have talked about these problems several times in the past three months, and the solutions are not being followed through. We have to make a change."[68] Remember to describe the situation rather than attacking the employee personally.

4. *Listen.* It is important to continue the interview until the person appears to be talking freely and seems reasonably calm about the reasons for his or her termination and the severance package that he or she is to receive. Behavioural indications can be used to help gauge the person's reaction and to decide how best to proceed. Five major reactions often occur:

Termination interviews are among the most difficult tasks that managers face, but there are guidelines for making them less painful for both parties.

- First, some employees will be *hostile and angry,* expressing hurt and disappointment. In such cases, remain objective while providing information on any outplacement or career counselling to be provided, being careful to avoid being defensive or confronting the person's anger.

- Second, some employees may react in a *defensive, bargaining* manner, based on their feelings of fear and disbelief. In this case, it is important to acknowledge that this is a difficult time for the employee and then provide information regarding outplacement counselling without getting involved in any bargaining discussions.

- Third, the employee may proceed in a *formal, controlled* manner, indicative of a suppressed, vengeful reaction and the potential for legal action. In this case, allow the employee to ask any questions pertaining to his or her case (avoiding side issues) in a formal tone while leading into information about the outplacement counselling to be provided.

- Fourth, some employees will maintain a *stoic* façade, masking their shock, disbelief, and numbness. In this case, communicate to the employee that his or her shock is recognized and that the details can be handled later if the employee prefers. Answer any questions arising at that point and provide information on outplacement counselling.

- A fifth reaction is an *emotional* one involving tears and sadness, indicating grief and worry on the part of the employee. Allow the person to cry and provide tissues. When the person regains his or her composure, explain the outplacement counselling process.

An Ethical Dilemma

Is it ethical to "buy out" an undesirable employee with severance pay and a good letter of reference in order to avoid prolonged wrongful dismissal litigation, even if you know the letter is misleading to potential future employers?

HR Competency

20200

5. *Review all elements of the severance package.* Describe severance payments, benefits, and the way in which references will be handled. However, under no conditions should any promises or benefits beyond those already in the severance package be implied. The termination should be complete when the person leaves.

6. *Identify the next step.* The terminated employee may be disoriented, so explain where he or she should go on leaving the interview. Remind the person whom to contact at the company regarding questions about the severance package or references.

CHAPTER SUMMARY

1. Turnover can be voluntary (employee initiated) or involuntary (employer initiated). HR considerations in managing turnover include making sure that there is enough talent to complete production demands as well as minimizing turnover costs to the organization.

2. A fair and just disciplinary process is based on three prerequisites: rules and regulations, a system of progressive penalties, and an appeals process.

3. Employees who are dismissed without just cause must be provided with reasonable notice. This means paying them for several weeks or months in addition to the legally required notice period on termination. If the employee does not believe that the period of notice is reasonable, he or she may file a wrongful dismissal lawsuit. Constructive dismissal occurs when the employer makes unilateral changes in the employment contract that are unacceptable to the employee, even though the employee has not been formally terminated.

4. Employee engagement is a positive, fulfilling, work-related state of mind characterized by vigour, dedication, and absorption. Organizational factors such as senior leadership, opportunities for learning and development, and company image and reputation are the primary influencers of engagement. Outcomes of employee engagement include improvements in recruiting, retention, turnover, individual productivity, customer service, and customer loyalty, as well as growth in operating margins and increased profit margins and revenue growth rates.

5. Techniques for ensuring effective employee communication include suggestion programs, employee opinion surveys, and communication from management.

6. The six steps in the termination interview are to plan the interview carefully, get to the point, describe the situation, listen until the person has expressed his or her feelings, discuss the severance package, and identify the next step.

MyManagementLab

Study, practise, and explore real business situations with these helpful resources:

- **Interactive Lesson Presentations:** Work through interactive presentations and assessments to test your knowledge of management concepts.
- **PIA (Personal Inventory Assessments):** Enhance your ability to connect with key concepts through these engaging self-reflection assessments.
- **Study Plan:** Check your understanding of chapter concepts with self-study quizzes.
- **Videos:** Learn more about the management practices and strategies of real companies.
- **Simulations:** Practise decision-making in simulated management environments.

P I A PERSONAL INVENTORY ASSESSMENT

KEY TERMS

bad-faith damages *(p. 364)*
constructive dismissal *(p. 364)*
dismissal *(p. 360)*
dismissal for just cause *(p. 360)*
distributive justice *(p. 366)*
downsizing *(p. 362)*
employee engagement *(p. 365)*
employee opinion surveys *(p. 368)*
insubordination *(p. 361)*
interactional justice *(p. 367)*
involuntary turnover *(p. 356)*
layoff *(p. 362)*

phased retirement *(p. 359)*
pre-retirement counselling *(p. 359)*
procedural justice *(p. 366)*
punitive damages *(p. 364)*
quitting *(p. 357)*
reasonable notice legislation *(p. 363)*
retirees on call *(p. 359)*
termination interview *(p. 369)*
turnover *(p. 355)*
voluntary turnover *(p. 356)*
wrongful dismissal *(p. 363)*

REVIEW AND DISCUSSION QUESTIONS

1. Explain why organizations today are concerned with voluntary turnover.

2. Describe the issues of reasonable notice in layoffs and how it relates to employee perspectives of fairness or intent to file wrongful dismissal lawsuits.

3. Explain how fairness in employee termination can be ensured, particularly the prerequisites to progressive discipline guidelines.

4. What are the various steps in the termination interview?

5. Define employee engagement and discuss at least three methods for managing it.

CRITICAL THINKING QUESTIONS

1. Should a company consider providing termination packages to employees who have ongoing disciplinary problems rather than taking the time and effort to go through the progressive discipline process?

2. Assume that in one department of your organization the voluntary turnover rate is double the rate that other departments have. What factors might

contribute to this? What issues would you investigate? Is voluntary turnover necessarily bad and in need of correction?

3. Discuss the options presented as alternatives to layoffs. Which of these would appeal to you, your family members, and friends? Why? What challenges do these alternatives pose to organizations?

EXPERIENTIAL EXERCISES

1. Working individually or in groups, obtain copies of the student handbook for your college or university and determine to what extent there is a formal process through which students can air grievances.

Would you expect the process to be effective? Why or why not? Based on contact with students who have used the grievance process, has it been effective?

2. Working individually or in groups, determine the nature of the academic discipline process in your college or university. Does it appear to be an effective one? Based on this chapter, should any modification be made to the student discipline process?

3. A computer department employee made an entry error that ruined an entire run of computer reports. Efforts to rectify the situation produced a second batch of improperly run reports. As a result of the series of errors, the employer incurred extra costs of $2400, plus a weekend of overtime work by other computer department staffers. Management suspended the employee for three days for negligence and also revoked a promotion for which the employee had previously been approved.

   Protesting the discipline, the employee stressed that she had attempted to correct her error in the early stages of the run by notifying the manager of computer operations of her mistake. Maintaining that the resulting string of errors could have been avoided if the manager had followed up on her report and stopped the initial run, the employee argued that she had been treated unfairly; she was being severely punished but the manager had not been disciplined at all, even though he had compounded the problem. Moreover, citing her "impeccable" work record and management's acknowledgement that she had always been a "model employee," the employee insisted that the denial of her previously approved promotion was "unconscionable."

   a. In groups, determine what your decision would be if you were the arbitrator. Why? (Your instructor will inform you of the actual arbitrator's decision when you discuss this exercise in class.)

   b. Do you think that the employer handled the disciplinary situation correctly? Why? What would you have done differently?

3. Working with a partner, review the following scenario and discuss your responses.
   Maggie sat there stunned. Her boss had just told her that, as a result of the merger with the ABC Company, she would be reporting to the vice-president of customer service and that her title would be associate vice-president of customer service. "This can't be. My job is the VP of customer service. How can I report to another VP?"

   Has Maggie been demoted? Constructively dismissed? Discuss the rationale for your answer.

4. While branding a company as a desirable employer is important, sometimes the actions of one employee can have a major impact on the employer brand. For example, in July 2011, a disgruntled Whole Foods employee anonymously released his resignation letter online…and the letter went viral. The former employee accused the company of adopting practices that violated their stated core philosophy (e.g., throwing away food rather than donating it), including items that the former employee saw as HR failures (e.g., providing "poorly made, ugly" T-shirts as incentives, requesting employees call in when they will be late even though their lateness would still be documented, "discriminating against employees" by offering healthier employees discounts, etc.).[70]

   a. Can employers prevent former employees from publicly shaming the organization?

   a. In your opinion, were the HR concerns highlighted here indicative of a HR failure?

   b. How can a company respond to these types of individual efforts that go viral?

RUNNING CASE

Running Case: LearnInMotion.com

Fair Treatment in Disciplinary Action

Because the employees at LearnInMotion.com use high-cost computer equipment to do their jobs, Jennifer and Pierre have always felt strongly about not allowing employees to eat or drink at their desks. Jennifer was

therefore surprised to walk into the office one day to find two employees eating lunch at their desks. There was a large pizza in a box, and the two of them were sipping soft drinks and eating slices of pizza and submarine sandwiches from paper plates. She could see that there were grease and soft drink spills on their desks, and the office smelled of onions and pepperoni. In addition to looking unprofessional, the mess on the desks increased the possibility that the computers could be damaged. One of the employees continued to use his computer with greasy fingers between bites.

Although this was a serious matter, neither Jennifer nor Pierre believes that what the employees were doing is grounds for immediate dismissal, partly because there is no written policy on eating at the workstations. They just assumed that people would use their common sense. The problem is that they do not know what to do. It seems to them that the matter calls for more than just a warning but less than dismissal. As their management consultant, how would you answer the following questions?

QUESTIONS

1 What is a progressive discipline policy, and should LearnInMotion.com put one in place, formally and in writing within their human resources policy manual?
2 If LearnInMotion.com puts a progressive disciplinary policy in place and these two employees choose to eat at their desks again, would this constitute "just cause" termination?
3 If LearnInMotion.com chooses to terminate these two employees right now, would they face any legal ramifications?

CASE INCIDENT

An Inappropriate Email

Roger Miller, the director of human resources for Virtual Reality Media, was returning to his office after a half-day training session on how to retain and engage today's top talent when he received a disturbing phone call. Randy, the manager of the multimedia lab, called to let Roger know about an email he had just been copied on.

One of Randy's salespeople, John, had sent all of his fellow staff within the multimedia lab department a very derogatory email about Randy; the email said that Randy was a useless supervisor who should not be in a management position because he does not know what he is doing and should be fired.

Randy is very upset and wants Roger to terminate John. This is where you come in to help Roger.

QUESTIONS

1 Assume you are Roger. Specifically, what should you do now?
2 How should you do it?
3 Is this a just cause termination?

Sean Kilpatrick/The Canadian Press

CHAPTER

16

Labour Relations

LEARNING OUTCOMES

AFTER STUDYING THIS CHAPTER, YOU SHOULD BE ABLE TO

DISCUSS the key elements of Canada's labour laws.

OUTLINE the five steps in the labour relations process.

DESCRIBE the five steps in a union organizing campaign.

OUTLINE the three ways to obtain union recognition.

DESCRIBE the three steps in the collective bargaining process.

EXPLAIN the typical steps in a grievance procedure.

REQUIRED HR COMPETENCIES

10300: Provide effective leadership for human resources, with due recognition of the roles and responsibilities of the governing body and the organization's leadership and their relationships with other stakeholders, to implement the business plan and manage risk.

20600: Promote an evidence-based approach to the development of human resources policies and practices using current professional resources to provide a sound basis for human resources decision-making.

50100: Promote a collaborative work environment between the employer, the union (where it exists), employees, and other representative groups through clear and open communication to achieve a respectful, productive, and engaged workforce.

50200: Interpret legislation, collective agreements (where applicable), and policies consistent with legal requirements and organizational values to treat employees in a fair and consistent manner and manage the risk of litigation and conflict.

50300: Recommend labour and employee relations strategies based on risks, costs, and opportunities in order to achieve business objectives.

50400: Negotiate as a means to resolve labour issues consistent with the law, economic and societal trends, and established objectives and strategies to achieve agreement.

INTRODUCTION TO LABOUR RELATIONS

labour union (union) An officially recognized association of employees practising a similar trade or employed in the same company or industry who have joined together to present a united front and collective voice in dealing with management.

labour–management relations The ongoing interactions between labour unions and management in organizations.

collective bargaining agreement (union contract) A formal agreement between an employer and the union representing a group of employees regarding terms and conditions of employment.

collective bargaining Negotiations between a union and an employer to arrive at a mutually acceptable collective agreement.

bargaining unit The group of employees in a firm, a plant, or an industry that has been recognized by an employer or certified by a labour relations board (LRB) as appropriate for collective bargaining purposes.

HR Competency

| 50100

labour relations strategy A component of an organization's HR strategy specific to the overall plan for dealing with unions, which sets the tone for its union–management relationship.

HR Competency

| 50100

Canadian Labour and Business Centre
www.clbc.ca

Canadian LabourWatch Association
www.labourwatch.com

A **labour union (or union)** is an officially recognized body representing a group of employees who have joined together to present a collective voice in dealing with management. The purposes of unionization are to influence HR policies and practices that affect bargaining unit members, such as pay and benefits; to achieve greater control over the jobs being performed, greater job security, and improved working conditions; and to increase job satisfaction and meet employees' affiliation needs. The term **labour–management relations** refers to the ongoing interactions between labour unions and management in organizations.

The presence of a labour union alters the relationship between employees and the firm and has implications for planning and implementing a business strategy. Managerial discretion and flexibility in dealing with employees and in implementing and administering HR policies and procedures are reduced. For example, union seniority provisions in the **collective bargaining agreement (union contract)** also known as a CBA, negotiated through **collective bargaining**, govern the selection of employees for transfers, promotions, and training programs and specify the order in which employees can be laid off and recalled. Many other terms and conditions of employment for **bargaining unit** members are determined and standardized through collective bargaining, rather than being left to management's discretion.

An organization's *labour relations (LR) strategy*, one component of its HR strategy, is its overall plan for dealing with unions, which sets the tone for its union–management relationship. The decision to accept or avoid unions is the basis of an organization's LR strategy.[1]

Managers in firms choosing a *union acceptance strategy* view the union as the legitimate representative of the firm's employees. Such a relationship can lead to innovative initiatives and win–win outcomes. Managers select a *union avoidance strategy* when they believe that it is preferable to operate in a non-unionized environment. Walmart is well known for its preference to remain non-union (and has even closed stores that have attempted to unionize).[2] To avoid unions, companies can either adopt a *union substitution approach,* in which they become so responsive to employee needs that there is no incentive for them to unionize (as is the case at Dofasco), or adopt a *union suppression approach* when there is a desire to avoid a union at all costs (for example, Walmart challenged the constitutionality of Saskatchewan's labour laws all the way to the Supreme Court of Canada, but lost).[3]

Canada's Labour Laws

Canadian labour laws have two general purposes:

1. To provide a common set of rules for fair negotiations
2. To protect the public interest by preventing the impact of labour disputes from inconveniencing the public

As with other employment-related legislation, there are 13 provincial/territorial jurisdictions, as well as federal labour relations legislation for employees subject to federal jurisdiction. There are a number of common characteristics in the LR legislation across Canada, which can be summarized as follows:

- Procedures for the certification of a union
- The requirement that a collective agreement be in force for a minimum of one year

Air Canada workers on strike in 2011

- Procedures that must be followed by one or both parties before a strike or lockout is legal
- The prohibition of strikes or lockouts during the life of a collective agreement
- The requirement that disputes over matters arising from interpretation of the collective agreement be settled by final and binding arbitration
- Prohibition of certain specified "unfair practices" on the part of labour and management
- Establishment of a labour relations board or the equivalent; labour relations boards are tripartite—made up of representatives of union and management, as well as a neutral chair or a vice-chair, typically a government representative.

Labour relations legislation attempts to balance employees' rights to engage in union activities with employers' rights to manage. For example, managers are prohibited from interfering with and discriminating against employees who are exercising their rights under the LR legislation. One restriction on unions is that they are prohibited from calling or authorizing an unlawful strike.

The Labour Movement in Canada Today

business unionism The activities of labour unions focusing on economic and welfare issues, including pay and benefits, job security, and working conditions.

The primary goal of labour unions active in Canada today is to obtain economic benefits and improved treatment for their members. It may involve lobbying for legislative changes pertaining to these issues. This union philosophy, with its emphasis on economic and welfare goals, has become known as **business unionism**. Unions strive

HR IN THE NEWS

Collective Agreement Puts Aboriginals First

The collective bargaining agreement at Voisey's Bay Nickel Company in Labrador includes a clause outlining order of preference for vacant positions, training opportunities, or promotions. Innu and Inuit people are on top of this order of preference, starting with those in the bargaining unit, followed by those already employed by Voisey's Bay and then by Innu and Inuit outside candidates. Among non-Aboriginals, priority goes to Labrador residents. Those with union membership rank first, followed by Voisey's Bay employees, and then those in the community. Aboriginals make up more than half of the bargaining unit. To reflect the employee population, the CBA includes a clause categorizing National Aboriginal Day on June 21 as a paid holiday.[4]

to ensure *job security* for their members and to attain *improved economic conditions* and *better working conditions* for their members. Most unions today also become involved in broader political and social issues affecting their members. Activities aimed at influencing government economic and social policies are known as **social (reform) unionism**. For example, unions have recognized the special circumstances of Aboriginal workers, as outlined in the HR in the News box.

Types of Unions

The labour unions in Canada can be classified according to the following characteristics:

1. *Type of worker eligible for membership.* All the early trade unions in Canada were **craft unions**—associations of persons performing a certain type of skill or trade (for example, carpenters or bricklayers). Examples in today's workforce include the British Columbia Teachers' Federation and the Ontario Nurses' Association. An **industrial union** is a labour organization comprising all the workers eligible for union membership in a particular company or industry, irrespective of the type of work performed.

2. *Geographical scope.* Labour unions with head offices in other countries (most often the United States) that charter branches in both Canada and one or more countries are known as *international unions.* Labour unions that charter branches in Canada only and have their head office in this country are known as *national unions.* A small number of employees belong to labour unions that are purely *local* in geographical scope.

3. *Labour congress affiliation.* A third way of distinguishing among labour unions is according to affiliation with one or another central labour organization. These central organizations include the following:

   - *Canadian Labour Congress (CLC).* The CLC is the major central labour organization in Canada and has over 3 million affiliated union members. Most international and national unions belong to the CLC, as well as all directly chartered local unions, local/district labour councils, and provincial/territorial federations of labour.

   - *Confédération des syndicats nationaux (CSN)*—in English, Confederation of National Trade Unions (CNTU). This organization is the Quebec counterpart of the CLC and has more than 300 000 members.

   - *American Federation of Labor and Congress of Industrial Organizations (AFL–CIO).* The American counterpart of the CLC is the AFL–CIO. The two organizations operate independently, but since most international unions in the CLC are also members of the AFL–CIO, a certain degree of common interest exists.

The basic unit of the labour union movement in Canada is the **local**, formed in a particular location. For HR managers and front-line supervisors, the union locals are generally the most important part of the union structure. Key players within the local are the elected officials known as **union stewards**, who are responsible for representing the interests and protecting the rights of bargaining unit employees in their department or area. The Strategic HR box discusses the formation and focus of Unifor, Canada's largest private sector union.

Membership Trends

The membership in unions as a percentage of the labour force had been steadily decreasing a few decades ago. It has stabilized at slightly under 30 percent of the Canadian workforce, however rates vary by industry, as highlighted in **Table 16.1**. Various factors

---

social (reform) unionism
Activities of unions directed at furthering the interests of their members by influencing the social and economic policies of governments at all levels, such as speaking out on proposed legislative reforms.

craft union Traditionally, a labour organization representing workers practising the same craft or trade, such as carpentry or plumbing.

industrial union A labour organization representing all workers eligible for union membership in a particular company or industry, including skilled trades people.

American Federation of Labor and Congress of Industrial Organizations (AFL–CIO)
www.aflcio.org

local A group of unionized employees in a particular location.

union steward A union member elected by workers in a particular department or area of a firm to act as their union representative.

STRATEGIC HR

Forming Unifor

On Labour Day in 2013, Unifor became the largest private sector union in Canada. Created through the merger of Canadian Auto Workers (CAW) and the Communication, Energy and Paperworkers, Unifor has a combined membership of more than 300 000 employees in a wide range of blue- and white-collar occupations, with 750 local unions operating under the Unifor banner.

Given the size and mandate of Unifor, it aims to engage members for political action, in an attempt to extend benefits of unions to all interested Canadians and the Canadian economy at large. Unifor also has experts in labour relations, economics, communication, total compensation, and employment law, whose expertise can be used by constituents.

TABLE 16.1   Total Employment, Union Density, and Total Unionized Workers, 2012

Industry	Total employment (000s)	Union density (percent)	Total unionized workers (000s)
Health care and social assistance	1,830	52.7	964
Education	1,210	67.6	818
Retail trade	2,370	12.2	289
Construction	840	30.3	254
Transportation and warehousing	690	41.1	284
Utilities	140	63.8	92

Source: The Conference Board of Canada, "Industrial Relations Outlook 2013: Embracing the 'New Normal'," December 2012, p. 3. Reprinted with permission.

HR Competency

50100

were responsible for membership decline, including a dramatic increase in service sector and white-collar jobs, combined with a decrease in employment opportunities in industries that had traditionally been highly unionized, such as manufacturing. More effective HR practices in non-unionized firms are another contributing factor.[5]

Traditionally, unions have targeted full-time, manufacturing workers (which used to be almost exclusively older males) for membership. Canadian unions are unique in that they have managed to refocus their target on membership to better align with workforce realities, as highlighted in the Expert Opinion box. As a result, the rate of decline in union membership is not nearly as significant in Canada as it is elsewhere (for example, the United States). This can be attributed to three significant issues: global competition, demographics, and unionization of white-collar workers in Canada.

Global Competition

Globalization is transforming the dynamics of labour relations in Canada such that employers are being forced to become more militant, and unions are struggling to maintain their influence at the bargaining table.[6] Some unions face the difficult choice of negotiating concessions or watching jobs go to lower-cost countries.

Demographics

The focus of union collective bargaining efforts must align with the workplace demographics. The aging of the workforce and pending labour shortage affects unions as

industry viewpoint

Jerry Dias

Identification: Mr. Jerry Dias, President, Unifor

1. **Given the volume and forecast for contingent workers in Canada, how can these groups be organized and gain a collective voice?**

Statistically, more than half of the jobs created in the last five years in Canada have been contingent work oriented. We've had success in organizing these contingent workers because we are focused on helping find real opportunities and solutions that are specific to the type of work. For example, we recently unionized at Casino Rama in Orillia, Ontario, where a significant portion of the 1800 jobs unionized were part time in nature.

We find that a union is instrumental in securing decent pay and benefits for people who are in non-traditional jobs, but these employees also want and need protection from unfair labour practices (such as changing scheduled work hours with minimal notice, unfair terminations, etc.), as well as assistance increasing the number of hours employees work. Through this, we can prevent situations in which an individual is required to work two to three part-time jobs with low pay and minimal benefit, in order to work the number of hours required to earn a basic level of income.

2. **The new generation of workers (Gen-Y) has unique needs and perspectives when compared to previous generations. How can unions address these differences?**

Young people are looking at jobs differently than what may be portrayed in the media. They graduate from school and try transitioning into their careers, but often cannot find well-paying, meaningful, progressive jobs in their field. The concept of this generation being loyal to themselves over their employer might be more indicative of the employment opportunities that are presented, rather than their true desire for a career and job stability. Organized labour helps to address these concerns.

Young people today are also the first generation to have less opportunity than their parents. They are also very technically savvy, so any forms of organized labour, such as ours, need to communicate using a multimedia approach (Twitter, social media, LinkedIn, websites, blogs, etc.). This generation generally values information, and appreciates both timely and accurate information.

3. **What are the challenges that Unifor faces today and in the near future?**

We were established in August 2013, and the recognition of the Unifor brand has been great. A big focus of the organization is to not only serve our members, needs well, but also spend time on issues of interest to the greater community. The labour movement cannot survive in isolation, and community and labour relations experience a reciprocated relationship. For example, in a recent settlement we were able to get the organization to commit funds for women's issues regarding employment in the local and regional communities, with a special focus on Aboriginal women. It is critical that we continue to gain broad-based support for the changing perception of the labour movement, and stay linked and connected with the communities we serve (members and beyond).

Source: Reprinted by permission from Jerry Dias.

well as HR managers.[7] It has been suggested that unions and management may need to work together to attract and retain workers. Retention concerns may make employers more willing to offer job security in exchange for promises of productivity and flexibility from unions. Pensions and benefits for older workers and retirees has also become more of a union priority.

Unionization of White-Collar Employees

Difficulties in attempting to resolve grievances and lack of job security have led to increased interest in unionization among white-collar workers. Service sector workers, such as those in retail stores, fast-food chains, and government agencies, as well as managers and professionals (including university/college faculty), have been targeted for organizing campaigns. Since these jobs tend to have more women and young people than manufacturing jobs, unions are now focusing more on work–family issues as well as the health and safety risks associated with white-collar jobs, such as the potential for repetitive strain injuries from working at video display terminals (computers or laptops).[8]

THE LABOUR RELATIONS PROCESS

As illustrated in **Figure 16.1**, the labour relations process consists of five steps. Each of these five steps is reviewed in detail below.

Step 1: Desire for Collective Representation

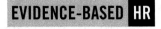

Based on a review of 36 research studies internationally, three classifications were developed to explain why individuals join unions:[9]

- *Dissonance-based reasons.* When expectations of work (work should be enjoyable and rewarding, for example) and the experience of work (the work environment is unpleasant and pay is low) are in conflict, the desire to join a union is triggered. However if dissonance is the reason why employees want to unionize, then they

FIGURE 16.1 An Overview of the Labour Relations Process

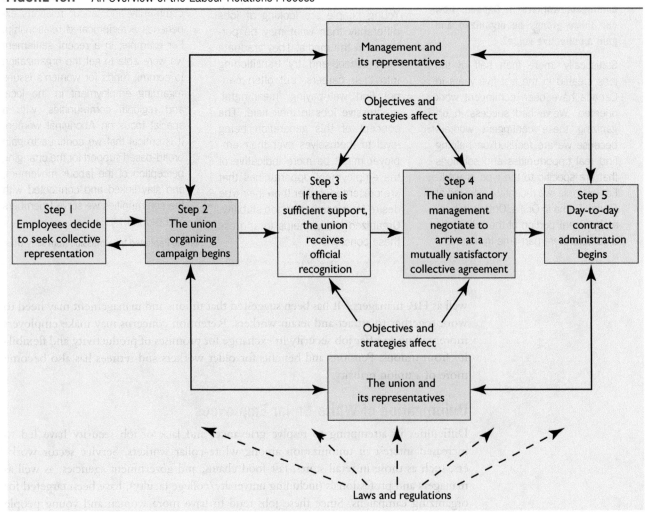

will only do so if they think the union will be effective in remedying the associated discontent or frustration with the work expectations versus experiences dissonance.

- *Utility-based reasons.* An individual's decision to join a union can also be attributed to a rational calculation of the costs and benefits of unionization, where individuals compare the costs and benefits of remaining non-unionized versus becoming unionized. The selection of which decision to make is largely based on the calculation of the cost/benefit analysis.[10]

- *Political/ideological reasons.* An individual's political or ideological beliefs may influence their understanding of and desire for collective versus individual negotiation of employment terms.[11]

However, research studies have made it clear that dissatisfaction alone will not lead to unionization. More important seems to be the employees' belief that it is only through unity that they can protect themselves from the arbitrary whims of management. *In other words, it is only when workers are dissatisfied and believe that they are without the ability to change the factors causing dissatisfaction, except through collective action, that they become interested in unionizing.*[12]

Numerous studies suggest that age, gender, education levels, and other demographic factors are highly correlated with the desire to join a union. However, there is little consistency with the findings of the studies, with the exception of two groups: People over the age of 60 and black workers are consistently likely to have a desire to join a union.[13]

It has been theorized that this is largely due to perceptions of employment-related discrimination. In Canada, there is a difference in unionization rates among private and public sector employees, as highlighted in the HR by the Numbers box. It has also been suggested that each workplace is unique, so the demographic characteristics of one workforce may impact the desire to join a union in a way that isn't highly generalizable or applicable to a larger population.

Union membership also has an positive impact on compensation, hours worked, and pay equity in Canada. In June 2013, the average wage rate for unionized employees was significantly higher than for non-unionized employees (average hourly rate unionized = \$27.02, non-unionized = \$21.89[20]), and in 2010 average hours worked per week was higher for unionized employees in Canada (unionized = 35.6 hours, non-unionized = 34.9[21]). On average, full-time female unionized workers earned 94 percent of the hourly wages of their male counterparts, and part-time female unionized workers earned 14 percent more than their male counterparts.[22]

HR by the Numbers

Unionization Trends in Canada

75% of public sector employees are unionized[14]

17% of private sector employees are unionized[15]

60% of employers in a unionized environment identify wages as a current negotiation issue (wages were the most commonly identified management issue)[16]

45% of employers in a unionized environment identify productivity as a current negotiation issue[17]

84% of union representatives identify wages as a current negotiation issue (wages were the most commonly identified union issue)[18]

47% of union representatives identify employment security as a current negotiation issue[19]

Step 2: Union Organizing Campaign

Once interest in joining a union has been aroused, the union organizing process begins. There are five steps typically involved in this process:

1. *Employee/union contact.* A formal organizing campaign may be initiated by a union organizer or by employees acting on their own behalf. Most organizing campaigns are begun by employees who get in touch with an existing union.[23] However, large unions have a number of *union organizers* on staff who are responsible for identifying organizing opportunities and launching organizing campaigns. During these initial discussions, employees investigate the advantages of union representation,

and the union officials start to gather information about the employees' sources of dissatisfaction.

2. *Initial organizational meeting.* The union organizer then schedules an initial meeting with the individuals who first expressed an interest in unionization and co-workers who subsequently express their support. The aim is to identify employees who would be willing to help the organizer direct the campaign.

3. *Formation of an in-house organizing committee.* This committee comprises a group of employees who are dedicated to the goal of unionization and who are willing to assist the union organizer.

4. *The organizing campaign.* Members of the in-house committee then contact employees, present the case for unionization, and encourage as many employees as possible to sign an **authorization card**, indicating their willingness to be represented by the union in collective bargaining with the employer.

authorization card A card signed by an employee that indicates his or her willingness to have the union act as his or her representative for purposes of collective bargaining.

5. *The outcome.* There are a number of possible outcomes to a unionization campaign, including rejection by the majority of eligible employees. For a union to become the bargaining unit for a group of employees, it must be certified by a labour relations board (LRB) or receive official recognition from the employer.

An Ethical Dilemma

Knowing that the head office plans to close your facility if a unionization bid is successful, how should you, as a manager, respond to inquiries from employees about the impact of a union?

Employer Response to an Organizing Campaign

There may be cases when an employer feels that the employees are considering organizing a union (some common signs of this are highlighted in **Table 16.2**). If the employer prefers that the group seeking unionization retain its non-union status, a careful campaign is usually mounted to counteract the union drive. Normally, HR department staff members head up the campaign, although they may be assisted by a consultant or labour lawyer. Absolutely critical to the success of a company's counter-campaign is supervisory training. Supervisors need to be informed about what they can and cannot do or say during the organizing campaign to ensure that they avoid actions that might directly or inadvertently provide fuel for the union's campaign, while at the same time refraining from violating LR legislation.

TABLE 16.2 Signs of Organizing Activity

- disappearance of employee lists or directories
- more inquiries than usual about benefits, wages, promotions, and other HR policies and procedures
- questions about management's opinion of unions
- an increase in the number or nature of employee complaints or grievances
- a change in the number, composition, and size of informal groups at lunch and coffee breaks
- the sudden popularity of certain employees (especially if they are the informal leaders)
- the sudden cessation of employee conversation when a member of management approaches, or an obvious change in employees' behaviour toward members of management, expressed either formally or informally
- the appearance of strangers in the parking lot
- the distribution of cards, flyers, or pro-union buttons

Source: Based on part on L. Field, "Early Signs," *Canadian HR Reporter* (November 29, 1999), p. 14.

As much information about the union as possible should be obtained pertaining to dues, strike record, salaries of officers, and any other relevant facts that might cause employees to question the benefits of unionization. Communication strategies can be planned, with the aim of reminding employees about the company's good points, pointing out disadvantages of unionization, and refuting any misleading union claims. The employer's case for remaining non-union should be presented in a factual, honest, and straightforward manner.

Under the law, employers are granted the right to do the following:

- Express their views and opinions regarding unions

- State their position regarding the desirability of remaining non-union

- Prohibit distribution of union literature on company property on company time

- Increase wages, make promotions, and take other HR actions, as long as they would do so *in the normal course of business*; in most jurisdictions, however, once an application for certification is received by the LRB, wages, benefits, and working conditions are frozen until the application is dealt with

- Assemble employees during working hours to state the company's position, as long as employees are advised of the purpose of the meeting in advance, attendance is optional, and threats and promises are avoided (employers have no obligation to give the union the same opportunity)

Step 3: Union Recognition

A union can obtain recognition as a bargaining unit for a group of workers in three basic ways: (1) voluntary recognition, (2) the regular certification process, and (3) a pre-hearing vote. Bargaining rights can also be terminated in various ways.

Voluntary Recognition

An employer in every Canadian jurisdiction except Quebec can voluntarily recognize a union as the bargaining agent for a group of its employees. Although fairly rare, this may occur if an employer has adopted a union acceptance strategy and believes that employees want to be represented by that union.

Regular Certification

The normal union certification procedure is for the union to present evidence of at least a minimum level of membership support for a bargaining unit that they have defined, in the form of signed authorization cards, to the appropriate LRB, along with an application for **certification**. The minimum level of support required to apply for certification varies by jurisdiction, from 25 percent of the bargaining unit in Saskatchewan to 65 percent in Manitoba.[24] The LRB then determines whether the bargaining unit defined by the union is appropriate for collective bargaining purposes.

In most jurisdictions LRBs can grant *automatic certification* without a vote if the applicant union can demonstrate a high enough level of support for the proposed bargaining unit (generally 50 or 55 percent). Automatic certification may also be granted in some jurisdictions if the employer has engaged in unfair practices. If the level of support is not sufficient for automatic certification, but is above a specified minimum level (between 25 and 45 percent, depending on jurisdiction), the LRB will order and supervise a **representation vote**.[25] Eligible employees have the opportunity to cast a secret ballot, indicating whether or not they want the union to be certified. In some jurisdictions, to gain certification the voting results must indicate that *more than*

HR Competency

50200

Hints **TO ENSURE LEGAL COMPLIANCE**

certification The procedure whereby a labour union obtains a certificate from the relevant LRB declaring that the union is the exclusive bargaining agent for a defined group of employees in a bargaining unit that the LRB considers appropriate for collective bargaining purposes.

representation vote A vote conducted by the LRB in which employees in the bargaining unit indicate, by secret ballot, whether or not they want to be represented, or continue to be represented, by a labour union.

50 percent of the potential bargaining unit members are in support of the union. In other jurisdictions, the standard is the support of *more than 50 percent of those voting*.[26] If the union loses, another election cannot be held among the same employees for at least one year. Only about 20 percent of certifications are the result of a vote—roughly four out of five certifications are the result of authorization cards alone.[27]

Pre-Hearing Votes

pre-hearing vote An alternative mechanism for certification, used in situations in which there is evidence of violations of fair labour practices early in the organizing campaign.

In most jurisdictions, a **pre-hearing vote** may be conducted where there is evidence of violations of fair labour practices early in an organizing campaign. In such a case, the LRB may order a vote before holding a hearing to determine the composition of the bargaining unit. The intent is to determine the level of support for the union as quickly as possible, before the effect of any irregularities can taint the outcome. The ballot box is then sealed until the LRB determines whether the bargaining unit is appropriate and, if so, which employees are eligible for membership. If the bargaining unit is deemed appropriate by the LRB, only the votes of potential bargaining unit members are counted, and if the majority of the ballots cast support the union, it is certified.

Termination of Bargaining Rights

decertification The process whereby a union is legally deprived of its official recognition as the exclusive bargaining agent for a group of employees.

All labour relations acts provide procedures for workers to apply for the **decertification** of their unions. Generally, members may apply for decertification if the union has failed to negotiate a collective agreement within one year of certification, or if they are dissatisfied with the performance of the union. The LRB holds a secret-ballot vote, and if more than 50 percent of the ballots cast (or bargaining unit members, depending on jurisdiction) are in opposition to the union, the union will be decertified. A labour union also has the right to notify the LRB that it no longer wants to continue to represent the employees in a particular bargaining unit. This is known as "termination on abandonment." Once the LRB has declared that the union no longer represents the bargaining unit employees, any collective agreement negotiated between the parties is void.

Step 4: Collective Bargaining

Collective bargaining is the process by which a formal collective agreement is established between labour and management. The collective agreement is the cornerstone of the Canadian LR system. Both union and management representatives are required to bargain in good faith. This means that they must communicate and negotiate, that proposals must be matched with counterproposals, and that both parties must make every reasonable effort to arrive at an agreement.

Steps typically involved in the collective bargaining process include (1) preparation for bargaining, (2) face-to-face negotiations, and (3) obtaining approval for the proposed contract. There are two possible additional steps. First, when talks break down, third-party assistance is required by law in every jurisdiction except Saskatchewan.[28] The second additional step is a strike/lockout or interest arbitration if the parties arrive at a bargaining impasse. Each of these steps will be described next.

Preparation for Negotiations

Good preparation leads to a greater likelihood that desired goals will be achieved. Preparation for negotiations involves planning the bargaining strategy and process and assembling data to support bargaining proposals. Both union and management will gather data on general economic trends, analyze other collective agreements and trends in collective bargaining, conduct an analysis of grievances, review the existing contract or the union's organizing campaign promises, conduct wage and salary surveys at competitor organizations, prepare cost estimates of monetary proposals, and make plans for a possible strike or lockout. In addition, management negotiators will obtain input from supervisors. Union negotiators will obtain input from union stewards, obtain the company's financial information (if it is a public company), gather demographic information on their membership, and obtain input from members. The list of items a team can negotiate for is relatively endless, but shortlisting and prioritizing issues is critical to successful negotiations.

Once these steps are completed, each side forms a negotiating team and an initial bargaining plan/strategy is prepared. Initial proposals are then finalized and presented for approval by either senior management or the union membership.

Face-to-Face Negotiations

Under LR legislation, representatives of either union or management can give written notice to the other party of their desire to negotiate a first collective agreement or renew an existing one. Early in the negotiating process, demands are exchanged—often before the first bargaining session. Then both negotiating teams can make a private assessment of the other team's demands. Usually, each team finds some items with which they can agree quite readily and others on which compromise seems likely. Tentative conclusions are also made regarding which items, if any, are potential strike or lockout issues.

Location, Frequency, and Duration of Meetings   Negotiations are generally held at a neutral, offsite location, such as a hotel meeting room, so that there is no psychological advantage for either team and so that interruptions and work distractions can be kept to a minimum. Each side generally has another room in which intra-team meetings, known as **caucus sessions**, are held.

Generally, meetings are held as often as either or both parties consider desirable, and they last as long as progress is being made. Marathon bargaining sessions, such as those lasting all night, are not typical until conciliation has been exhausted and the clock is ticking rapidly toward the strike/lockout deadline. As per the Expert Opinion box, negotiations are strategic, interactive, and can be quite methodological in nature.

Initial Bargaining Session   The initial meeting of the bargaining teams is extremely important in establishing the climate that will prevail during the negotiating sessions that follow. A cordial attitude can help to relax tension and ensure that negotiations proceed smoothly. Generally, the first meeting is devoted to an exchange of demands (if this has not taken place previously) and the establishment of rules and procedures that will be used during negotiations.

Subsequent Bargaining Sessions   In traditional approaches to bargaining, each party argues for its demands and resists those of the other at each negotiating session. At the same time, both are looking for compromise alternatives that will enable an agreement to be reached. Every proposal submitted must be either withdrawn temporarily or permanently, accepted by the other side in its entirety, or accepted in a modified form. Ideally, both sides should come away from negotiations feeling that they have attained many of their basic bargaining goals and confident that the tentative agreement reached will be acceptable to senior management and the members of the bargaining unit.

For each issue on the table to be resolved satisfactorily, the point at which agreement is reached must be within limits that the union and employer are willing to

International Labour Organization
www.ilo.org

HR Competency

50200

caucus session A session in which only the members of one's own bargaining team are present.

Francisco Cruz/Francisco Cruz/SuperStock

Negotiating a collective agreement

Dr. Rene Kirkegaard

Identification: Dr. Rene Kirkegaard (PhD), Canada Research Chair in Risk Management and Regulations

Focus: Impact of regulations to even the playing field for contests, competitions, or negotiations

1. **What is game theory?**

Game theory is a methodology. It is a toolbox to put ideas into an algebraic analysis in order to evaluate strategic interaction. Put another way, it's the study of strategic decision-making between two or more individuals, teams, or entities. Game theory formalizes a sequence of events or decisions that lead to a specific outcomes; the mathematical analysis of the sequence of events can help predict the outcome.

It is important to keep in mind that in some situations there may be conflict between the two entities and in others there may be no conflict. Sometimes a simple miscoordination of parties with similar desired outcomes can lead to an undesired outcome. Stated differently, not all games are zero-sum games. There can be win–win outcomes, win–lose outcomes, and lose–lose outcomes.

2. **In your research, you describe contests as very complicated games. Can you describe some of the factors that lead to the complexity, of contests, competitions, or negotiations?**

One side has private information regarding what's important to them. In the context of labour relations, management may have information regarding firm profitability or future strategic direction. The employee representative can have a better sense of the labour value in the industry, employment opportunities with competitors, and how good or bad the working environment actually is. This information becomes a bargaining chip. For example, the employee representatives might highlight poor work conditions to entice management to offer more. Concessions are textbook applications of game theory, as they are strategically manipulated as part of the game or negotiation.

3. **How can one improve their negotiation skills based on game theory?**

Experience improves ability to apply game theory. Experienced negotiators know not to take the first offer at its face value. They recognize the first offer as an opening gambit. Game theory normally assumes players are rational. While emotions may take over, trained and experienced negotiators are presumably better able to manage their emotions. Experience matters.

For instance, a study done on highly experienced Wimbledon tennis players confirmed that their behaviour on the court largely conform to game theory. They do so by attempting to make serves unpredictable, as game theory would suggest. In other words, experience makes it more likely that a player applies game theory, knowingly or not. However, if one wants to deliberately use game theory to improve one's negotiation skills, a good place to start is by asking simple questions like: "What is my opponent's most preferred outcome? What would he be willing to give up for a concession? What can I learn about his preferences from his initial offer?" Thus, game theory teaches us to think about the problem from the point of view of the person on the other side of the table.

Source: Reprinted by permission from Rene Kirkegaard.

bargaining zone The area defined by the bargaining limits (resistance points) of each side, in which compromise is possible, as is the attainment of a settlement satisfactory to both parties.

distributive bargaining A win–lose negotiating strategy where one party gains at the expense of the other.

HR Competency

50400

accept, often referred to as the **bargaining zone**. As illustrated in **Figure 16.2**, if the solution desired by one party exceeds the limits of the other party, then it is outside of the bargaining zone. Unless that party modifies its demands sufficiently to bring them within the bargaining zone, or the other party extends its limits to accommodate such demands, a bargaining deadlock is the inevitable result.

Distributive bargaining is an approach often typified as "win–lose" bargaining because the gains of one party are normally achieved at the expense of the other.[29] It is appropriately involved when the issues being discussed pertain to the distribution of things that are available in fixed amounts, such as wage increases and benefits improvements. However, it may also be used when there is a history of distrust and adversarial relations, even when dealing with issues on which a more constructive approach is possible.

As indicated in Figure 16.2, distributive bargaining is characterized by three distinct components: the initial point, the target point, and the resistance point. The initial point for the union is usually higher than what the union expects to receive from

FIGURE 16.2 The Bargaining Zone and Characteristics of Distributive Bargaining

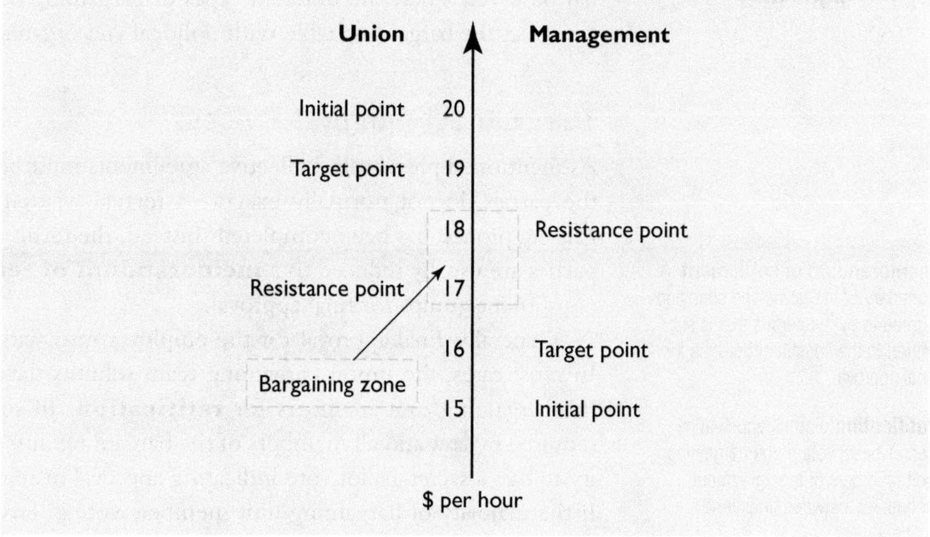

management. The union target point is next, and represents the negotiating team's assessment of what is realistically achievable from management. The union's bargaining zone limit is its resistance point, which represents its minimally acceptable level.

These points are essentially reversed for management. The management team's initial point is its lowest level, which is used at the beginning of negotiations. Next is its target point, the desired agreement level. Management's resistance point forms the other boundary of the bargaining zone.

Integrative bargaining is an approach that assumes that a win–win solution can be found but also acknowledges that one or both sides can be losers if the bargaining is not handled effectively.[30] Integrative bargaining strategies require that both management and union negotiators adopt a genuine interest in the joint exploration of creative solutions to common problems.

Issues pertaining to work rules, job descriptions, and contract language can often be handled effectively by using an integrative approach; these are situations in which management negotiators are not intent on retaining management rights and both sides are committed to seeking a win–win solution. Wage rates and vacation entitlements are more likely to be fixed-sum issues that are handled by a distributive approach.

The objective of integrative bargaining is to establish a creative negotiating relationship that benefits labour and management. Becoming increasingly popular these days is a relatively new integrative approach known as **mutual gains (interest-based) bargaining**, which is another win–win approach to LR issues. All key union and management negotiators are trained in the fundamentals of effective problem solving and conflict resolution. Such training is often extended to other employees to ensure that the principles of mutual gains (interest-based) bargaining are incorporated into the organization's value system and that co-operation becomes a year-round corporate objective.[31]

Solutions must take the interests of each party into account. A joint sense of accountability is fostered and ongoing joint union–management initiatives can result from the negotiating process. In addition, the tools that are used at the bargaining table can be applied to the resolution of all workplace issues. Although mutual gains (interest-based) bargaining has been put into practice in about 40 percent of Canadian negotiations, experts warn that implementation is difficult, as it requires a grassroots culture change.[32]

integrative bargaining A negotiating strategy in which the possibility of win–win, lose–win, win–lose, and lose–lose outcomes is recognized, and there is acknowledgement that achieving a win–win outcome will depend on mutual trust and problem solving.

mutual gains (interest-based) bargaining A win–win negotiating approach based on training in the fundamentals of effective problem solving and conflict resolution, in which the interests of all stakeholders are taken into account.

HR Competency

50300

HR Competency

10300

Thus, the negotiating process is far more complex than it may appear to a casual observer. There are different types of bargaining strategies involved, and each side arrives at the bargaining table with political and organizational interests at stake.

The Contract Approval Process

As mentioned previously, collective agreements must be written documents. However, the parties do not normally execute a formal written document until after the bargaining process has been completed. Instead, the terms and conditions agreed to by the parties are usually reduced to a **memorandum of settlement** and submitted to the constituent groups for final approval.

memorandum of settlement A summary of the terms and conditions agreed to by the parties that is submitted to the constituent groups for final approval.

ratification Formal approval by secret-ballot vote of the bargaining unit members of the agreement negotiated between union and management.

Generally, final approval for the employer rests with the senior management team. In most cases, the union bargaining team submits the memorandum of settlement to the bargaining unit members for **ratification**. In some jurisdictions, ratification is required by law, and all members of the bargaining unit must be given ample opportunity to cast a secret-ballot vote indicating approval or rejection of the proposed contract. If the majority of bargaining unit members vote in favour of the proposal, it goes into effect. If the proposed collective agreement is rejected, union and management negotiators must return to the bargaining table and seek a more acceptable compromise. In such instances, third-party assistance is often sought.

A challenge lies in the fact that the collective bargaining agreement (CBA) is a legally binding document outlining employer and employee terms and conditions of work. However, if there is no CBA in place (e.g., it has not yet been established or it is expired), the terms and conditions of the CBA are not explicitly or directly legally binding. Some companies that adopt the union avoidance strategy may engage in questionable behaviour when unionized employees are not covered by a CBA, as per the example provided in the HR in the News box.

HR IN THE NEWS

Walmart's Approach to Unions Proves Costly

In late 2004, the Walmart location in Saguenay, Quebec unionized. The location was financially strong, and objectives were being met, with discussion of upcoming bonuses. In February 2005, before a collective bargaining agreement could be secured, Walmart shut the location down. Management argued that the firm was not profitable, letting all of the employees go. The closing of the store has been the subject of a long judicial saga of decisions and appeals.[33]

In 2014, the Supreme Court of Canada ruled that the location closure was problematic, and ordered that workers should be compensated for lost wages with interest. The court stated that the decision to close the location violated Section 59 of the Quebec Labour Code, which states that working conditions must not be altered during the unionization process.[34]

Once approval has been received from the constituent groups, the bargaining team members sign the memorandum of settlement. Once signed, this memorandum serves as the collective agreement until the formal document is prepared and contract administration begins.

Third-Party Assistance and Bargaining Impasses

Legislation in all Canadian jurisdictions provides for conciliation and mediation services. Although the terms *conciliation* and *mediation* are often used interchangeably, they have quite distinct and different meanings.

Conciliation is the intervention of a neutral third party whose primary purpose is to bring the parties together and keep them talking so they can reach a mutually satisfactory collective agreement. The only means available to a conciliator to bring the parties to agreement is persuasion—he or she is not permitted to have any direct input into the negotiation process or to impose a settlement. Conciliation is typically requested after the parties have been negotiating for some time and are starting to reach a deadlock, or after talks have broken down. The aim of conciliation is to try to help the parties avoid the hardship of a strike or lockout.

In all jurisdictions except Saskatchewan, strikes and lockouts are prohibited until third-party assistance has been undertaken (conciliation is required in all but two jurisdictions). In most jurisdictions in which third-party assistance is mandatory, strikes/lockouts are prohibited until conciliation efforts have failed and a specified time period has elapsed.[35]

Mediation is the intervention of a neutral third party whose primary purpose is to help the parties fashion a mutually satisfactory agreement. Mediation is usually a voluntary process, typically occurring during the countdown period prior to a strike or lockout or during the strike or lockout itself. The mediator's role is an active one. It often involves meeting with each side separately and then bringing them together in an attempt to assist them in bridging the existing gaps. He or she is allowed to have direct input into the negotiation process but cannot impose a settlement.

When the union and management negotiating teams are unable to reach an agreement, and once the conciliation process has been undertaken (where required), the union may exercise its right to strike or request interest arbitration, and the employer may exercise its right to lock out the bargaining unit members. Alternatively, bargaining unit members may continue to work without a collective agreement once the old one has expired until talks resume and an agreement is reached.

Strikes A **strike** can be defined as a temporary refusal by bargaining unit members to continue working for the employer. When talks are reaching an impasse, unions will often hold a **strike vote**. Legally required in some jurisdictions, such a vote seeks authorization from bargaining unit members to strike if necessary. A favourable vote does not mean that a strike is inevitable. In fact, a highly favourable strike vote is often used as a bargaining ploy to gain concessions that will make a strike unnecessary. The results of a strike vote also help the union negotiating team members determine their relative bargaining strength. Unless strike action is supported by a substantial majority of bargaining unit members, union leaders are rarely prepared to risk a strike and must therefore be more willing to compromise, if necessary, to avoid a work stoppage.

conciliation The often mandatory use of a neutral third party who has no direct input on the negotiation process to help an organization and the union representing a group of its employees communicate more effectively with the aim of coming to a mutually satisfactory collective agreement.

mediation The often voluntary use of a neutral third party who has direct input on the negotiation process to help an organization and the union representing its employees to reach a mutually satisfactory collective agreement.

strike The temporary refusal by bargaining unit members to continue working for the employer.

strike vote Legally required in some jurisdictions, it is a vote seeking authorization from bargaining unit members to strike if necessary. A favourable vote does not mean that a strike is inevitable.

"The servers are on strike."

cartoonresource/Fotolia

Since a strike can have serious economic consequences for bargaining unit members, the union negotiating team must carefully analyze the prospects for its success. Striking union members receive no wages and often have no benefits coverage until they return to work, although they may draw some money from the union's strike fund. Work stoppages are also costly for employers, customers, and suppliers.

When a union goes on strike, bargaining unit members often **picket** the employer. To ensure as many picketers as possible, the union may make strike pay contingent on picket duty. Picketers stand at business entrances, carrying signs advertising the issues in dispute, and attempt to discourage people from entering or leaving the premises.

Boycott Another economic weapon available to unions is a **boycott**, which is a refusal to patronize the employer. A boycott occurs when a union asks its members, other union members, the employer's customers/clients, and supporters in the general public not to patronize the business involved in the labour dispute. Such action can harm the employer if the union is successful in gaining a large number of supporters. As with a strike, a boycott can have long-term consequences if former customers/clients develop a bias against the employer's products or services or make a change in buying habits or service provider that is not easily reversed.

The duration and ultimate success of a strike depends on the relative strength of the parties. Once a strike is settled, striking workers return to their jobs. During a labour dispute many people are put under remarkable pressure, and relationships essential to effective post-settlement work dynamics can be tarnished—especially in firms that rely heavily on teamwork. Post-settlement work environments are often riddled with tension, derogatory remarks, and hostility.

Lockout Although not a widely used strategy in Canada, a **lockout** is legally permissible. This involves the employer prohibiting the bargaining unit employees from entering the company premises as a means of putting pressure on the union to agree to the terms and conditions being offered by management. Sometimes the employer chooses to close operations entirely, which means that non-striking employees are also affected. Most employers try to avoid this option, since doing so means that the well-being of innocent parties is threatened, and a lockout may damage the firm's public image. A brief description of the timeline and outcomes of the 2012–2013 NHL lockout are provided in the Strategic HR box.

Unlawful Strikes and Lockouts A **wildcat strike** is a spontaneous walkout, not officially sanctioned by the union leaders, that is illegal if it occurs during the term of a collective agreement. An unlawful strike is one that contravenes the relevant LR legislation and lays the union and its members open to charges and possible fines or periods of imprisonment if found guilty. For example, it is illegal for a union to call a strike involving employees who do not have the right to strike because of the essential nature of their services, such as nurses or police officers. In all jurisdictions, it is illegal to call a strike during the term of an existing collective agreement.

Arbitration involves the use of an outside third party to investigate a dispute between an employer and union and impose a settlement. A sole arbitrator or three-person arbitration board may be involved. Arbitrators listen to evidence, weigh it impartially and objectively, and make a decision based on the law or the contract language. An arbitrator is not a judge, however. First, arbitration hearings tend to be much more informal than courtroom proceedings. Second, the arbitrator is not bound by precedents to the extent that a judge is usually held.[38] Third, both the law and court decisions have given the

picket Stationing groups of striking employees, usually carrying signs, at the entrances and exits of the struck operation to publicize the issues in dispute and discourage people from entering or leaving the premises.

boycott An organized refusal of bargaining unit members and supporters to buy the products or use the services of the organization whose employees are on strike in an effort to exert economic pressure on the employer.

lockout The temporary refusal of a company to continue providing work for bargaining unit employees involved in a labour dispute, which may result in closure of the establishment for a time.

An Ethical Dilemma

Is it ethical for a firm to close the establishment during a labour dispute if that results in non-striking employees being laid off?

wildcat strike A spontaneous walkout, not officially sanctioned by the union leadership, which may be legal or illegal, depending on its timing.

arbitration The use of an outside third party to investigate a dispute between an employer and union and impose a settlement.

STRATEGIC HR

NHL Lockout Timeline (2012–2013 season)

June 29, 2012	Initial meeting in Toronto between the NHLPA (representing NHL players for all 30 teams) and NHL management.
July 13, 2012	NHL management team put its initial offer on the table, asking for a reduction in players' share of hockey-related revenue from 57 percent to 43 percent, and suggested changes in contract rules.
August 19, 2012	NHLPA put its initial offer on the table: salary caps of $69 million and more revenue sharing between teams.
September 13, 2012	No agreement reached. NHL Board of Governors approves potential for lockout when collective bargaining agreement (CBA) expires.
September 15, 2012	CBA expired, NHL management triggered lockouts.
January 6, 2013	Commissioner Gary Bettman and the NHLPA Executive Director Donald Fehr jointly announced tentative deal.
January 12, 2013	NHLPA approved new CBA. Lockout officially ended. [36]

Impact of Lockout?

Of over 2000 Canadians surveyed	41 percent	felt more negative about the sport after the most recent lockout.
	37 percent	planned to spend less on merchandise.
	35 percent	planned to watch fewer games.[37]

arbitration function considerable power and freedom. Arbitration decisions are final and binding and cannot be changed or revised.

interest arbitration The imposition of the final terms of a collective agreement.

interest dispute A dispute between an organization and the union representing its employees over the terms of a collective agreement.

Interest arbitration may be used to settle an **interest dispute** regarding the terms of a collective agreement by imposing the terms of the collective agreement. The right to interest arbitration is legally mandated for workers who are not permitted to strike, such as hospital and nursing home employees, police officers and firefighters in most jurisdictions, and some public servants.[39] Interest arbitration is also involved when special legislation is passed ordering striking or locked-out parties back to work because of public hardship.

The Collective Agreement: Typical Provisions

The eventual outcome of collective bargaining, whether negotiated by the parties or imposed by an arbitrator, is a formal, written collective agreement.

union recognition clause Clarifies the scope of the bargaining unit by specifying the employee classifications.

Union Recognition Clause A *union recognition clause* clarifies the scope of the bargaining unit by specifying the employee classifications included therein or listing those excluded.

union security clause The contract provisions protecting the interests of the labour union, dealing with the issue of membership requirements and, often, the payment of union dues.

Union Security/Checkoff Clause All Canadian jurisdictions permit the inclusion of a **union security clause** in the collective agreement to protect the interests of the labour union. This clause deals with the issue of membership requirements and, often, the payment of union dues. There are various forms of union security clauses:[40]

closed shop Only union members in good standing may be hired by the employer to perform bargaining unit work.

- A **closed shop** is the most restrictive form of union security. Only union members in good standing may be hired by the employer to perform bargaining unit work. This type of security clause is common in the construction industry.

union shop Membership and dues payment are mandatory conditions of employment.

- In a **union shop**, membership and dues payment are mandatory conditions of employment. Although individuals do not have to be union members at the time that they are hired, they are required to join the union on the day on which they commence work or on completion of probation.

- In a *modified union shop,* the individuals who were bargaining unit members at the time of certification or when the collective agreement was signed are not obliged to join the union, although they must pay dues, but all subsequently hired employees must do both.

maintenance-of-membership arrangement Individuals voluntarily joining the union must remain members during the term of the contract.

- Under a **maintenance-of-membership arrangement**, individuals voluntarily joining the union must remain members during the term of the contract. Membership withdrawal is typically permitted during a designated period around the time of contract expiration. Dues payment is generally mandatory for all bargaining unit members.

Rand formula All members of the bargaining unit pay union dues, but employees have the choice to join the union or not.

- The **Rand formula** is the most popular union security arrangement. It does not require union membership, but it does require that all members of the bargaining unit pay union dues. It is a compromise arrangement that recognizes the fact that the union must represent all employees in the bargaining unit and should therefore be entitled to their financial support, but also provides the choice to join or not join the union.

open shop Union membership is voluntary and non-members are not required to pay dues.

- An **open shop** is a type of security arrangement whereby union membership is voluntary and non-members are not required to pay dues.

An Ethical Dilemma

Given the fact that some workers have religious or other objections to unions, is the Rand formula ethical?

No-Strike-or-Lockout Provision   There must be a clause in every contract in Canada forbidding strikes or lockouts while the collective agreement is in effect. The intent is to guarantee some degree of stability in the employment relationship during the life of the collective agreement, which must be at least one year. Saskatchewan and Quebec are the only jurisdictions that impose a maximum duration of three years.[41] In general, the duration of collective agreements in Canada is increasing.[42]

Management Rights Clause   The management rights clause clarifies the areas in which management may exercise its exclusive rights without agreement from the union, and the issues that are not subject to collective bargaining. It typically refers to the rights of management to operate the organization, subject to the terms of the collective agreement. Any rights not limited by the clause are reserved to management.

Arbitration Clause   All Canadian jurisdictions require that collective agreements contain a clause providing for the final and binding settlement, by arbitration, of all disputes arising during the term of a collective agreement. Such disputes may relate to the application, interpretation, or administration of the agreement, as well as alleged contraventions by either party.

Step 5: Contract Administration

After a collective agreement has been negotiated and signed, the contract administration process begins. Both union and management are required to abide by the contract provisions. It is also in day-to-day contract administration that the bulk of labour–management relations occurs. Regardless of the amount of time and effort put into the wording of the contract, it is almost inevitable that differences of opinion will arise regarding the application and interpretation of the agreement. Seniority and discipline issues tend to be the major sources of disagreement between union and management.

cartoonresource/Fotolia

"Ultimately my decisions are based on logic."

Seniority

Unions typically prefer to have employee-related decisions determined by **seniority**, which refers to length of service in the bargaining unit. In many collective agreements, seniority is the governing factor in layoffs and recalls (the most senior employees are the last to be laid off and the first to be recalled) and a determining factor in transfers and promotions. In some collective agreements, seniority is also the determining factor in decisions pertaining to work assignments, shift preferences, allocation of days off, and vacation time.

Unions prefer the principle of seniority as an equitable and objective decision-making criterion, ensuring that there is no favouritism. Managers often prefer to place greater weight on ability or merit.

seniority Length of service in the bargaining unit.

PERSONAL INVENTORY ASSESSMENT

Learn About Yourself
Workplace Discipline Assessment

Discipline

Almost all collective agreements give the employer the right to make reasonable rules and regulations governing employees' behaviour and to take disciplinary action if the rules are broken. In every collective agreement, bargaining unit members are given the right to file a grievance if they feel that any disciplinary action taken was too harsh or without just cause.

Most collective agreements restrict an employer's right to discipline employees by requiring proof of just cause for the disciplinary action imposed. Since just cause is open to different interpretations, disciplinary action is a major source of grievances. Thus, disciplinary issues must be handled in accordance with the terms of the collective agreement and backed by carefully documented evidence. Even when disciplinary action is handled carefully, the union may argue that there were extenuating circumstances that should be taken into consideration. Supervisors have to strike a delicate balance between fairness and consistency.

When discipline cases end up at arbitration, two independent decisions are made. The first is whether the employee actually engaged in some form of misconduct. Then, if that question is answered in the affirmative, an assessment must be made of whether such misconduct warrants the particular discipline imposed, as well as whether such disciplinary action violated the collective agreement.

HR Competency

20600

Grievance Resolution and Rights Arbitration

A **grievance** is a written allegation of a contract violation relating to a disagreement about its application or interpretation. When such alleged violations or disagreements arise, they are settled through the grievance procedure. A multistep grievance procedure, the last step of which is final and binding arbitration, is found in virtually all collective agreements. Such procedures have been very effective in resolving day-to-day problems arising during the life of the collective agreement.

The primary purpose of the grievance procedure is to ensure the application of the contract with a degree of justice for both parties. Secondary purposes include providing the opportunity for the interpretation of contract language, such as the meaning of "sufficient ability", serving as a communications device through which managers can become aware of employee concerns and areas of dissatisfaction, and bringing to the attention of both union and management those areas of the contract requiring clarification or modification in subsequent negotiations.

grievance A written allegation of a contract violation, filed by an individual bargaining unit member, the union, or management.

Steps in the Grievance Procedure The grievance procedure involves systematic deliberation of a complaint at progressively higher levels of authority in the company and union, and most provide for arbitration as a final step. Grievances are usually filed by individual bargaining unit members. If the issue in contention is one that may affect a number of union members, either at that time or in the future, the union may file a *policy grievance.* Management also has the right to use the grievance procedure to process a complaint about the union, although such use is rare. Although the number of steps and people involved at each grievance procedure vary, **Figure 16.3** illustrates a typical sequence.

As illustrated in Figure 16.3, the typical first step of the grievance procedure is the filing of a written complaint with the employee's immediate supervisor. If the problem is not resolved to the satisfaction of the employee at the first step, he or she may then take the problem to the next higher managerial level designated in the contract, and so on through all the steps available. Time limits are typically provided for resolution at each step. Failure to respond within the specified time limit may result in the grievance being automatically processed at the next step or being deemed to have been withdrawn or resolved. Ninety percent or more of all grievances are settled, abandoned, or withdrawn before arbitration.

Rights Arbitration Grievances relating to the interpretation or administration of the collective agreement are known as **rights disputes**. If these cannot be resolved internally, they must be referred to arbitration for a final and binding decision. The process involved in resolving such issues is known as **rights arbitration**.

A written arbitration award is issued at the conclusion of most rights arbitration cases, indicating that the grievance has been upheld or overturned. In disciplinary cases, it is also possible for an arbitration award to substitute a penalty that is more or less severe than the one proposed by union or management.

THE IMPACT OF UNIONIZATION ON HRM

Unionization results in a number of changes relating to HRM, all relating back to the requirements of the collective agreement. A union does have an impact on the way in which managers perform their HR responsibilities; when union leaders are treated as partners, they can provide a great deal of assistance with HR functions.

Once an organization is unionized, the HR department is typically expanded by the addition of an LR specialist or section. In a large firm with a number of bargaining units, human resources and labour relations may form two divisions within a broader department, often called industrial relations or employee relations.

In a unionized setting, management has less freedom to make unilateral decisions. This change may lead managers and supervisors to feel that they have lost some of their authority, which can cause resentment, especially since they inevitably find that unionization results in an increase in their responsibilities. Supervisors are often required to produce more written records than ever before, since documentation is critical at grievance and arbitration hearings.

All HR policies must be consistent with the terms of the collective agreement. Union representatives are often involved in the formulation of any policies that affect bargaining unit members—such as those pertaining to disciplinary rules and regulations—or are at least consulted as such policies are being drafted. Unionization also generally results in greater centralization of employee record keeping, which helps to ensure consistency and uniformity.

HR Competency
| 50400

rights dispute A disagreement between an organization and the union representing its employees regarding the interpretation or application of one or more clauses in the current collective agreement.

rights arbitration The process involved in the settlement of a rights dispute.

HR Competency
| 50300

HR Competency
| 20600

FIGURE 16.3 A Typical Grievance Procedure

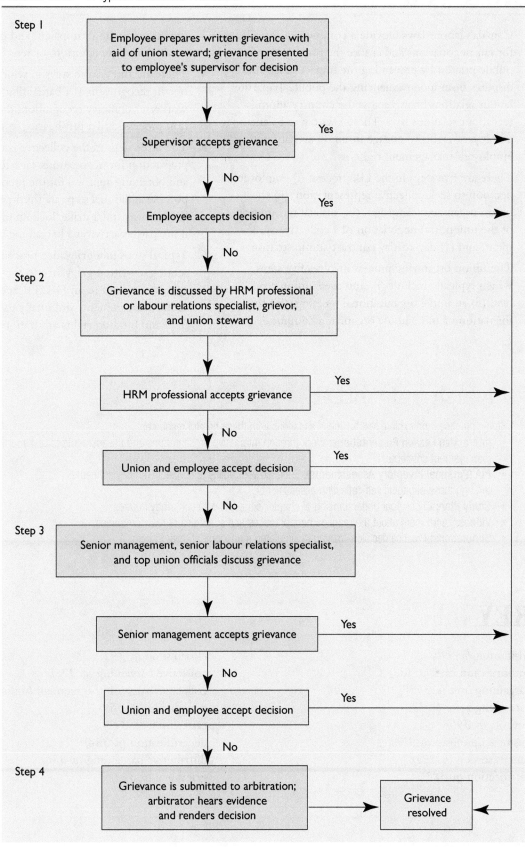

CHAPTER SUMMARY

1. Canada's labour laws provide a common set of rules for fair negotiations and ensure the protection of public interest by preventing the impact of labour disputes from inconveniencing the public. Tripartite labour relations boards across the country administer labour relations laws. These laws try to balance employees' rights to engage in union activity with employers' management rights.

2. There are five steps in the LR process: (i) employees' decision to seek collective representation, (ii) the union organizing campaign, (iii) official recognition of the union, (iv) negotiation of a collective agreement, and (v) day-to-day contract administration.

3. The union organizing process involves five steps, which typically include (i) employee/union contact, (ii) an initial organizational meeting, (iii) the formation of an in-house organizing committee,

(iv) an organizing campaign, and (v) the outcome—certification, recognition, or rejection.

4. There are three basic ways in which a union can obtain recognition as a bargaining unit for a group of workers: voluntary recognition, the regular certification process, and a pre-hearing vote.

5. The three steps in the collective bargaining process are preparation for negotiations, face-to-face negotiations, and obtaining approval for the proposed contract. Two possible additional steps are third-party assistance if talks break down and a strike/lockout or interest arbitration if the parties arrive at a bargaining impasse.

6. Typical steps in a grievance procedure involve presenting a written grievance to the worker's immediate supervisor, then to an HR/LR specialist, then to senior management, and finally to an arbitrator for final and binding rights arbitration.

MyManagementLab

Study, practise, and explore real business situations with these helpful resources:
- **Interactive Lesson Presentations:** Work through interactive presentations and assessments to test your knowledge of management concepts.
- **PIA (Personal Inventory Assessments):** Enhance your ability to connect with key concepts through these engaging self-reflection assessments.
- **Study Plan:** Check your understanding of chapter concepts with self-study quizzes.
- **Videos:** Learn more about the management practices and strategies of real companies.
- **Simulations:** Practise decision-making in simulated management environments.

KEY TERMS

arbitration *(p. 390)*
authorization card *(p. 382)*
bargaining unit *(p. 375)*
bargaining zone *(p. 386)*
boycott *(p. 390)*
business unionism *(p. 376)*
caucus session *(p. 385)*
certification *(p. 383)*

closed shop *(p. 391)*
collective bargaining *(p. 375)*
collective bargaining agreement (union contract) *(p. 375)*
conciliation *(p. 389)*
craft union *(p. 377)*
decertification *(p. 384)*
distributive bargaining *(p. 386)*
grievance *(p. 393)*

industrial union *(p. 377)*
integrative bargaining *(p. 387)*
interest arbitration *(p. 391)*
interest dispute *(p. 391)*
labour–management relations *(p. 375)*
labour union (union) *(p. 375)*
labour relations strategy *(p. 375)*
local *(p. 377)*
lockout *(p. 390)*
maintenance-of-membership arrangement *(p. 392)*
mediation *(p. 389)*
memorandum of settlement *(p. 388)*
mutual gains (interest-based) bargaining *(p. 387)*
open shop *(p. 392)*
picket *(p. 390)*

pre-hearing vote *(p. 384)*
Rand formula *(p. 392)*
ratification *(p. 388)*
representation vote *(p. 383)*
rights arbitration *(p. 394)*
rights dispute *(p. 394)*
seniority *(p. 393)*
social (reform) unionism *(p. 377)*
strike *(p. 389)*
strike vote *(p. 389)*
union recognition clause *(p. 391)*
union security clause *(p. 391)*
union shop *(p. 392)*
union steward *(p. 377)*
wildcat strike *(p. 390)*

REVIEW AND DISCUSSION QUESTIONS

1. Cite three examples of unfair labour practices on the part of management and three on the part of unions.

2. Explain three of the challenges facing the union movement in Canada today.

3. Describe five signs to which managers should be alert to detect an organizing campaign.

4. Explain the bargaining zone and draw a diagram to illustrate this concept.

5. Explain the six common forms of union security clause.

6. Explain how arbitration differs from conciliation and mediation and differentiate between interest arbitration and rights arbitration.

CRITICAL THINKING QUESTIONS

1. Discuss why Dofasco, a company that has remained union-free for many years, allowed the United Steelworkers access to its workers in Hamilton to try to sign them up as union members. In your opinion, why was this attempt by the union unsuccessful?

2. "If supervisors communicate effectively with employees, deal with their concerns, and treat them fairly, employees are far less likely to be interested in forming or joining a union." Do you agree or disagree with this statement? Why?

3. Two possible approaches to labour relations are union acceptance and union avoidance. Determine which

of these strategies seems to have been adopted in a firm in which you have been employed or with which you are familiar. Provide evidence to back up your answer.

4. As the LR specialist, what steps would you take to prepare the firm and management team if you believed that a strike was a possible outcome of the upcoming negotiations?

5. As the HR manager, how would you handle a situation in which a supervisor has knowingly violated the collective agreement when scheduling overtime?

EXPERIENTIAL EXERCISES

1. Assume that you are the vice-president of HR at a relatively new non-union firm that has been experiencing rapid growth. In view of the management team's desire to remain non-union, you have been asked to prepare a report to the other senior management team members, making specific recommendations regarding strategies that the firm should adopt to help ensure that the employees will have no desire to unionize.

2. Working with two or three classmates, devise a management counter-campaign to a unionization attempt, ensuring that all recommended courses of action are legal.

3. Obtain a copy of two collective agreements. Compare and contrast the following provisions: union recognition, management rights, union security, grievance procedures, and arbitration clauses. What do you think led to the differences? Which contract do you think in its entirety is better for employees? Why?

4. Read the following scenario and then, based on the role your team has been assigned by your instructor and the preparation time allowed, develop a negotiating strategy, including your bargaining zone, that you think will enable you to reach a fair and reasonable outcome for all parties. Before coming to the bargaining table, pick a chief negotiator for your team. Negotiate a settlement.

Scenario

ABC manufacturing is a large multinational machinery and heavy equipment manufacturer. The last two years have been very difficult, with more competition coming from offshore companies whose labour costs are much lower than those in Canada. The company is losing money and is considering whether to lay off workers in one or more of its Canadian plants, perhaps opening a new plant in Mexico or somewhere else in Central America. The union contract is up and negotiations will begin soon.

5. Research past issues of Canadian HR publications and find at least two labour arbitration awards, one that finds in favour of the organization and the other that finds in favour of the union. Prepare a brief presentation on what you find fair/unfair in these settlements. Be prepared to discuss why you think this.

RUNNING CASE

Running Case: LearnInMotion.com

The Grievance

When coming in to work one day, Pierre was surprised to be taken aside by Jason, one of their original employees, who met him as he was parking his car. "Jennifer told me I was suspended for two days without pay because I came in late last Thursday," said Jason. "I'm really upset, but around here Jennifer's word seems to be law, and it sometimes seems like the only way anyone can file a grievance is by meeting you like this in the parking lot."

Pierre was very disturbed by this revelation and promised the employee that he would discuss the situation with Jennifer. He began mulling over possible alternatives.

QUESTIONS

1   Does LearnInMotion.com run the potential risk of becoming unionized through its reactive managerial policy by one instead of both owners?
2   What are the primary reasons why people unionize?
3   Should a union wish to organize LearnInMotion.com employees, what are the five steps in the labour relations process a union must go through?

London Tokyo New Delhi New York Berlin

Corepics VOF/Shutterstock

CHAPTER

17

Managing Human Resources in a Global Business

LEARNING OUTCOMES

AFTER STUDYING THIS CHAPTER, YOU SHOULD BE ABLE TO

EXPLAIN how global movement of labour has an impact on HRM in Canada.

DESCRIBE the influence of intercountry differences on the workplace.

EXPLAIN how to improve global assignments through employee selection.

DISCUSS the major considerations in formulating a compensation plan for international employees.

DESCRIBE the main considerations in repatriating employees from abroad.

EXPLAIN the role and influence of international talent on Canadian organizations.

DISCUSS challenges immigrants to Canada face and **IDENTIFY** the role of multiple stakeholders in ensuring successful integration of talent in Canada.

REQUIRED HR COMPETENCIES

10100: Impact the organization and human resources practices by bringing to bear a strategic perspective that is informed by economic, societal, technological, political, and demographic trends to enhance the value of human resources.

10200: Develop an understanding of the application of governance principles and methods by keeping current with leading practices to contribute to and implement approves strategy.

20600: Promote an evidence-based approach to the development of human resources policies and practices using current professional resources to provide a sound basis for human resources decision-making.

30100: Promote engagement, commitment, and motivation of employees by developing, implementing, and evaluating innovative strategies to enhance productivity, morale, and culture.

40100: Create a workforce plan by identifying current and future talent needs to support the organization's goals and objectives.

40200: Increase the attractiveness of the employer to desirable potential employees by identifying and shaping the organization's employee value proposition to build a high quality workforce.

40300: Execute a workforce plan by sourcing, selecting, hiring, onboarding, and developing people to address competency needs and retain qualified talent aligned with the organization's strategic objectives.

THE GLOBALIZATION OF BUSINESS AND STRATEGIC HR

expatriates Employees who are citizens of the country where the parent company is based who are sent to work in another country.

workforce mobility The focus on managing the recruitment, relocation, and retention of employees who complete work-related tasks and activities outside of the core or primary head office or region of the company.

HR Competency
40200

immigrant A person residing in Canada who was born outside of Canada (excluding temporary foreign workers, Canadian citizens born outside of Canada, and those with student or work visas).

HR Competency
40200

The globalization of business is now the norm. European market unification is ongoing and the economies of Brazil, Russia, India, and China are burgeoning. Huge Canadian companies like Noranda, Alcan, and Molson have long had extensive overseas operations, but today the vast majority of companies are finding that their success depends on their ability to market and manage overseas operations. Thousands of Canadian corporations with international operations are now relocating employees overseas on a regular basis. These employees, called **expatriates**, are citizens of the country where the parent company is based who are sent to work in another country.

Workforce mobility programs focus on managing the recruitment, relocation, and retention of employees who complete work-related tasks and activities outside of the core or primary head office or region of the company. These programs are enabled by technological advancements, globalization, tight labour markets, and customer demands and have a direct impact on company profits. Research by Runzheimer International shows that organizations can improve profitability by 1 to 4 percent simply by making workforce mobility management a strategic priority and by managing mobility programs in a more integrated way. This is because disjointed management of mobility programs often results in employee confusion, aggravation, frustration, and disengagement.[1]

Canada is also increasingly influenced by globalization within our borders. According to Statistics Canada, an **immigrant** is a person residing in Canada who was born outside of Canada (excluding temporary foreign workers, Canadian citizens born outside of Canada, and those with student or working visas).[2] Roughly one in every five persons residing in Canada is foreign born. In addition, most of the labour force growth over the last decade has been attributable to immigration, and immigrants continue to be a critical component of Canada's workforce.

Thus, the impact of globalization on the human resource management landscape of Canada includes both Canadians working internationally and international members (mainly immigrants) working in Canada. This chapter reviews both elements of global HRM.

HOW INTERCOUNTRY DIFFERENCES AFFECT HRM

To a large extent, companies operating only within Canada's borders have the luxury of dealing with a relatively limited set of economic, cultural, and legal variables. However, a company that is operating multiple units abroad does not operate in an environment of such relative homogeneity with respect to HRM. For example, minimum legally mandated holidays may range from none in the United States to five weeks per year in Luxembourg. In addition, there are country-specific regulations that affect employees; as an example, there are no formal requirements for employee participation in Italy, but in Denmark, employee representatives on boards of directors are required in companies with more than 30 employees.

Another troubling issue is the need for tight security and terrorism awareness training for employees sent to countries with an increased risk of kidnapping of foreign executives.[3] The point is that managing the HR functions in multinational companies is complicated enormously by the need to adapt HR policies and procedures to the differences among countries in which each subsidiary is based.[4]

Intercountry variations in culture, economic systems, labour costs, and legal and industrial relations systems complicate the task of selecting, training, and managing employees abroad. These variations result in corresponding differences that make the job of expatriate managers much more complex and difficult than when at home. International assignments thus run a relatively high risk of failing unless these differences are taken into account when selecting, training, and compensating international assignees.

Fotolia

"Can't we visit the branches without it being a vision quest?"

Cultural Factors

Wide-ranging cultural differences from country to country demand corresponding differences in HR practices among a company's foreign subsidiaries. The first step is understanding the differences in underlying cultural values in different societies. Major studies have clarified some basic dimensions of international cultural differences. For example, societies differ in power distance—the extent to which the less powerful members of institutions accept and expect that power will be distributed unequally.[5] The institutionalization of such an inequality is higher in some countries (such as Mexico and Japan) than in others (such as Sweden and the Netherlands).

Societies also differ when it comes to individualism versus collectivism—the degree to which ties between individuals are normally loose rather than close. In more individualistic countries, such as Canada and the United States, individuals look out for themselves and their immediate families. However, in more collectivist countries, such as China and Pakistan, an individual's identity is strongly linked to their extended family group, and sometimes even to their work group. Interestingly, the one-child policy in China has resulted in a younger generation that is much more individualistic, known for job-hopping and lack of company loyalty.[6]

Such intercountry cultural differences have several HR implications. First, they suggest the need for adapting HR practices, such as training and pay plans, to local cultural norms. They also suggest that HR staff members in a foreign subsidiary should include host-country citizens. A high degree of sensitivity and empathy for the cultural and attitudinal demands of co-workers is always important when selecting expatriate employees to staff overseas operations.

Economic Systems

Differences in economic systems among countries also translate into intercountry differences in HR practices. In free enterprise systems, for instance, the need for efficiency tends to favour HR policies that value productivity, efficient workers, and staff cutting where market forces dictate. Moving along the scale toward more socialist systems, HR practices tend to shift toward preventing unemployment, even at the

Sunday Alamba/AP/The Canadian Press

A worker walks past a broken electricity transformer in Lagos, Nigeria. Despite having one of the world's great energy reserves, corruption and mismanagement have left Africa's oil giant chronically short of electricity.

expense of sacrificing efficiency. For example, in communist Vietnam, workplace culture involves a siesta after lunch for workers, and managers spend a lot time out of the office enhancing personal and social relationships.[7]

Legal Systems

Labour laws vary considerably around the world. China, for instance, continues to update its labour laws, which now include many similarities to those in the West. Discrimination is prohibited on most of the grounds commonly found in western countries, with the exception of age. However, enforcement of labour laws is haphazard.[8]

When it comes to employee termination, the amount of notice with pay to be provided, continuation of benefits, notification of unions, and minimum length of service to qualify for severance payments vary significantly and can in some cases have a major impact on labour costs.[9]

Health and safety laws vary from non-existent in many African states to Britain's Corporate Manslaughter and Corporate Homicide Act, which tightens liability of senior management for health and safety offences.[10] In other countries like China, worker health and safety laws exist but are largely unenforced.[11]

Labour Cost Factors

Differences in labour costs require clear HR interpretation and associated practices. A more informed review of labour productivity indicates that the cost of doing business abroad should not be viewed as a wage issue alone. In some countries, despite significantly lower wages, there may be higher unit labour costs. HR considerations such as benefits, training expenses, and turnover must be considered when evaluating labour costs.

Industrial Relations Factors

Industrial relations, and specifically the relationship among the workers, the union, and the employer, vary dramatically from country to country and have an enormous impact on HRM practices. For example, in Germany co-determination is the rule: that is, employees have the legal right to a voice in setting company policies. In this and several other countries, workers elect their own representatives to the supervisory board of the employer, and there is also a Vice-President for labour at the top management level.[12] Conversely, in many other countries, the state has minimal interference in the relations between employers and unions. In China, company unions fall under the administration of the local Communist Party committee, which often shares long-term goals with the company. Thus, unions seldom play an effective role in labour disputes.[13]

International Labour Organization
www.ilo.org

GLOBAL RELOCATION

global nomads employees who
continuously more from country to
country on multiple assignments.

The number of expatriates working abroad is continuing to increase. Since 2009, there was a 2.7 percent annual increase in the number of expats globally.[14] The number of **"global nomads"** (employees who continuously move from country to country on multiple assignments) has also increased.[15] In addition, there has been a gradual increase in the number of female expatriates, who have long been underrepresented in the expatriate ranks.[16]

EVIDENCE-BASED HR

Family issues rank as the number one concern when it comes to employee relocations, and many employees are reluctant to accept expatriate assignments for this reason.[17] Employees who are considering an international assignment will also want to know how working and living in another country will affect their compensation, benefits, and taxes, and what kind of relocation assistance they will receive. From a practical perspective, some of the most pressing challenges are techniques used to recruit, select, train, compensate, and provide family support for employees who are based abroad, such as the following:

1. *Candidate identification, assessment, and selection.* In addition to the required technical and business skills, key traits to consider for global assignments include cultural sensitivity, interpersonal skills, and flexibility.

2. *Cost projections.* The average cost of sending an employee and his or her family on an overseas assignment is reportedly between three and five times the employee's pre-departure salary; as a result, quantifying total costs for a global assignment and deciding whether to use an expatriate or a local employee are essential in the budgeting process.

3. *Assignment letters.* The assignee's specific job requirements and remuneration, vacation, home leave, and repatriation arrangements will have to be documented and formally communicated in an assignment letter.[18]

4. *Compensation, benefits, and tax programs.* There are many ways in which to compensate employees who are transferred abroad, given the vast differences in living expenses around the world. Some common approaches to international pay include home-based pay plus a supplement and destination-based pay.

5. *Relocation assistance.* The assignee will probably have to be assisted with such matters as maintenance of a home and automobiles, shipment and storage of household goods, and so forth. The average cost of a permanent international relocation for a Canadian employee is between $50 000 and $100 000.[19]

6. *Family support.* Cultural orientation, educational assistance, and emergency provisions are just some of the matters to be addressed before the family is moved abroad.

The last two issues relate to the heightened focus on the spouse and family, who are vitally important in today's climate of relocation refusals because of concerns about a mother-in-law's homecare, the children's education, a spouse's career, and the difficulty of adjusting to new surroundings while juggling family responsibilities at the same time as focusing on the new job. Although the typical expatriate has traditionally been a male with a non-working spouse, dual career families are now the norm. Major work–life balance relocation challenges thus include career assistance for the spouse and education and school selection assistance for the children.[20] Cross-cultural and language training programs will also probably be required. Policies for repatriating the expatriate when he or she returns home are another matter that must be addressed.

Sending employees abroad and managing HR globally is complicated by the nature of the countries into which many firms are expanding. Today's expatriates are heading to China (now the most likely destination for a foreign assignment) and other emerging economies.[21] Strategic HR involvement in the design and implementation of a global expansion strategy is required right from the start. Extensive research may be required with regard to local hiring practices, the availability of skilled labour, and employment regulations. Research in Canada identifies hassle factors associated with expat assignments by country, as highlighted in the Expert Opinion box.

academic **viewpoint**

Dr. Paul Beamish

Identification: **Dr. Paul Beamish (PhD)**, Canada Research Chair in International Management, Executive Director of Ivey Publishing

Affiliation: Ivey Business School, Western University

Focus: International strategic management, specifically: joint ventures and alliances

1. Success or failure of managers in foreign investment locations is critical to success or failure of the project. Based on your research, what influences a manager's willingness to work in foreign locations?

A lot of analysis in business schools tends to take a rational, analytical perspective based on sound economic logic. Yet some of it forgets the role of the manager. The manager responsible for a foreign location needs to feel safe (personal safety, quality of water/food, transportation, etc.). This experience will be beneficial to his or her career in the organization.

One of our studies found that the longer it takes to travel between the head office and the subsidiary, the less likely it is that the subsidiary will be profitable. Executives found that the time added in transit resulted in fatigue, which led to poorer oversight of people, and reduced opportunities to develop relationship. Subsidiaries that were more than 16 hours in travel time from headquarters experienced 23 percent higher turnover than others.

2. What is the "hassle" factor and how can it be used by organizations?

The hassle factor is an 11-factor composite measure of travel inconveniences by country. Travel inconveniences have a negative effect on the relationship between foreign investment potential of the company and realized investment.

The hassle factor brings the manager back into the equation when organizing international expansion. Research found that difficulty travelling to and residing in certain places impacts managerial preferences of and willingness to partake in expatriate assignments. We have currently released the hassle factor online as an interactive world map (www.hasslefactor.org), enabling organizations and individuals to explore countries of interest. This information will be updated annually.

3. As the economy continues to globalize, do you predict convergence or divergence of hassle factor scores over time?

As long as there are huge disparities in economic development, the hassle factors will persist, so I don't imagine that they will converge anytime soon. In part, this is a story of economic development; things are improving around the world, however, the change is slow and sporadic.

As a complement of this project, I established the "39 Country Initiative," in which universities in the world's 39 poorest countries are able to use Ivey's case collection at no cost. In addition, we collect and ship container loads of teaching material (mostly textbooks) to these locales. This is an example of how we can give back and help equalize access to education, which is a critical component of global progress. It helps business students in the poorest countries deal with one of the ultimate hassles: poverty.

Source: Reprinted by permission from Dr. Paul Beamish.

EVIDENCE-BASED

Why Expatriate Assignments Fail

expatriate assignment failure
Early return of an expatriate from a global assignment.

Global mobility management is important because the cost of **expatriate assignment failure**—early return from an expatriate assignment—can reach a million dollars.[22] There is some evidence that the rate of early departures, at least, is declining. This appears to be because more employers are taking steps to reduce expatriates' problems abroad. For example, they are selecting expatriates more carefully, helping spouses to get jobs abroad, and providing more ongoing support to the expatriate and his or her family.[23] As another example, some companies have formal "global buddy" programs. Here, local managers assist new expatriates with advice on things such as office politics, norms of behaviour, and where to receive emergency medical assistance.[24]

Discovering why expatriate assignments fail is an important research task, and experts have made considerable progress. According to a 2014 survey by Cartus,

63 percent of respondents identify changing business conditions as a reason for expatriate failure, followed by the inability of the family to adjust (61 percent). In addition, 76 percent rate family or personal circumstances as the reason why employees turn down opportunities for expatriate assignments.[25] Some factors can help with adjustment once an employee is sent abroad. In a study of 143 expatriate employees, extroverted, agreeable, and emotionally stable individuals were less likely to want to leave early.[26] Furthermore, the person's intentions are important. Specifically, people who want expatriate careers try harder to adjust to such a life.[27]

cartoonresource/Fotolia

"I am concerned you might bail."

Non-work factors like family pressures usually loom large in expatriate failures. In one study, managers listed, in descending order of importance for leaving early, inability of spouse to adjust, manager's inability to adjust, other family problems, manager's personal or emotional immaturity, and inability to cope with larger overseas responsibility.[28] Managers of European firms emphasized only the inability of the manager's spouse to adjust as an explanation for the expatriate's failed assignment. Similarly, other studies emphasize the effects of a dissatisfied spouse on the international assignment.[29]

Canadian companies have reported low failure rates for expatriates relative to other countries, particularly the United States, which has a failure rate of 40 to 50 percent.[30] Canadians may be more culturally adaptable than their American counterparts because they are already familiar with bilingualism and multiculturalism. In fact, Canadian executives are in demand across the globe. The country's diverse ethnic makeup has produced a generation of business leaders who mix easily with different cultures.[31]

Many employers have tried to eliminate issues that lead to expatriate assignment failures by shortening the assignment length and having the family remain at home. Expatriate assignments have traditionally been for terms of three to five years, but recently there has been a trend toward short-term global assignments instead of permanent relocations.[32] A survey by global consulting firm KPMG found that short-term assignments of less than 12 months are almost as prevalent as long-term assignments (more than five years).[33]

Short-term assignment alternatives include frequent extended business trips with corresponding time spent back at home, short-term assignments of between three months and a year with frequent home leave (once every 12 weeks on average), and the dual household arrangement, where the employee's family remains at home and the employee sets up a small household for himself or herself in the foreign country. Often, firms neglect to prepare employees for short-term assignments in the same way they do for the long-term variety, which leads to problems such as lack of cross-cultural awareness, extreme loneliness, and feeling undervalued on returning to the home office.[34] Companies that provide strong support to expatriate employees stand a higher chance of success.[35]

CONSIDERATIONS IN GLOBAL HRM

HR Competency

10100

Careful screening is just the first step in ensuring that a foreign assignee is successful. The employee may then require special training and, additionally, international HR policies must be formulated for compensating the firm's overseas managers and maintaining healthy labour relations.

Global Staffing Policy

ethnocentric staffing policy
Policies that align with the attitude that home-country managers are superior to those in the host country.

Canadian Employee Relocation Council
www.cerc.ca

The Expatriate Group
www.expat.ca

HR Competency

20600

polycentric staffing policy Policies that align with the belief that only host-country managers can understand the culture and behaviour of the host-country market.

geocentric staffing policy
Policies that align with the belief that the best manager for any specific position anywhere on the globe may be found in any of the countries in which the firm operates.

 Simulate on MyManagementLab

Managing in a Global Environment

There are three international staffing policies. An **ethnocentric staffing policy** is based on the attitude that home-country managers are superior to those in the host country, and all key management positions are filled by parent-country nationals. At Royal Dutch Shell, for instance, virtually all financial controllers around the world are Dutch nationals. Reasons given for ethnocentric staffing policies include lack of qualified host-country senior management talent, a desire to maintain a unified corporate culture and tighter control, and the desire to transfer the parent firm's core competencies (for example, a specialized manufacturing skill) to a foreign subsidiary more expeditiously.

A **polycentric staffing policy** is based on the belief that only host-country managers can understand the culture and behaviour of the host-country market, and therefore foreign subsidiaries should be staffed with host-country nationals and its home office headquarters with parent-country nationals. This may reduce the local cultural misunderstandings that expatriate managers may exhibit. It will also almost undoubtedly be less expensive. One expert estimates that an expatriate executive can cost a firm up to three times as much as a domestic executive because of transfer expenses and other expenses such as schooling for children, annual home leave, and the need to pay income taxes in two countries.

A **geocentric staffing policy** assumes that management candidates must be searched for globally, on the assumption that the best manager for any specific position anywhere on the globe may be found in any of the countries in which the firm operates. This allows the global firm to use its human resources more efficiently by transferring the best person to the open job, wherever he or she may be. It can also help to build a stronger and more consistent culture and set of values among the entire global management team. Team members here are continually interacting and networking with one another as they move from assignment to assignment around the globe and participate in global development activities.

Selection for Global Assignments

An Ethical Dilemma

How ethical is it for a multinational organization to recruit expatriate staff for managerial positions when similarly qualified staff can be identified in the host country?

HR Competency

40100

International managers can be expatriates, locals (citizens of the countries where they are working), or third-country nationals (citizens of a country other than the parent or the host country), such as a British executive working in a Tokyo subsidiary of a Canadian multinational bank.[36] Expatriates represent a minority of managers; most managerial positions are filled by locals rather than expatriates in both headquarters and foreign subsidiary operations.

There are several reasons to rely on local, host-country management talent for filling the foreign subsidiary's management ranks. Many people simply prefer not to work in a foreign country, and in general the cost of using expatriates is far greater than the cost of using local management talent. The multinational corporation may be viewed locally as a "better citizen" if it uses local management talent, and indeed some governments actually press for the localization of management. There may also be a fear that expatriates, knowing that they are posted to the foreign subsidiary for only a few years, may overemphasize short-term projects rather than focus on perhaps more necessary long-term tasks.

There are also several reasons for using expatriates—either parent-country or third-country nationals—for staffing subsidiaries. The major reason is technical competence. In other words, employers may be unable to find local candidates with the required technical qualifications. Multinationals also increasingly view a successful stint abroad as a required step in leadership development. Control is another important reason. Multinationals sometimes assign expatriates from their headquarters staff abroad on the assumption that these managers are more steeped in the firm's policies and culture and more likely to unquestioningly implement headquarters' instructions.

Orienting and Training Employees for Global Assignments

Cross-cultural training is very important for creating realistic expectations, which in turn are strongly related to cross-cultural adjustment.[37] A four-step approach to cross-cultural training is often used as discussed in **Figure 17.1**.

In addition to cross-cultural training, leadership development opportunities are often an important learning component of expatriate assignment.[38] At IBM, for instance, such development includes the use of a series of rotating assignments that permits overseas managers to grow professionally. At the same time, IBM and other major firms have established management development centres around the world where executives can go to hone their skills. Beyond that, classroom programs (such as those at the London Business School, or at INSEAD in France) provide overseas executives with the opportunities that they need to hone their functional and leadership skills.

International Compensation

The concept of international compensation management can present some unexpected and complicated problems. Compensation programs throughout a global firm must be both integrated (to maximize overall effectiveness) and differentiated (to effectively motivate and meet the specific needs of the various categories and locations of employees). On the one hand, there is logic in maintaining company-wide pay scales and policies so that,

FIGURE 17.1   Levels of Cross-Cultural Training

Level 1
Focuses on the impact of cultural differences and on raising trainee awareness of such differences.
Level 2
Focuses on attitudes and aims at getting participants to understand how attitudes (both negative and positive) are formed and how they influence behaviour.
Level 3
Provides factual knowledge about the target country.
Level 4
Provides skill building in areas like language and adjustment and adaptation skills.

FIGURE 17.2 Approaches to Compensation for Global Assignment, 2013[43]

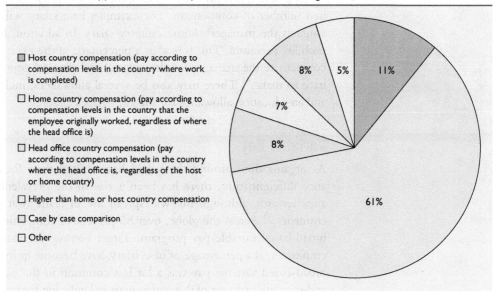

☐ Host country compensation (pay according to compensation levels in the country where work is completed)

☐ Home country compensation (pay according to compensation levels in the country that the employee originally worked, regardless of where the head office is)

☐ Head office country compensation (pay according to compensation levels in the country where the head office is, regardless of the host or home country)

☐ Higher than home or host country compensation

☐ Case by case comparison

☐ Other

for instance, divisional marketing directors throughout the world are all paid within the same narrow range. This reduces the risk of perceived inequities and dramatically simplifies the job of keeping track of disparate country-by-country wage rates. However, most multinational companies have recognized the need to make executive pay decisions on a global level, and executive pay plans are gradually becoming more uniform.[39] As shown in **Figure 17.2**, the majority of global assignment compensation (61 percent) is aligned to pay expatriates according to compensation levels in their home country.

On the other hand, the practice of not adapting pay scales to local markets can present an HR manager with more problems than it solves. The fact is that living in Tokyo is many times more expensive than living in Calgary, while the cost of living in Bangalore, India, is considerably lower than living in Toronto.[40] If these cost-of-living differences are not considered, it may be almost impossible to get managers to accept assignments in high-cost locations. One way to handle the problem is to pay a similar base salary company-wide and then add on various allowances according to individual market conditions.[41]

Compensation professionals also face the challenge of designing programs that motivate local employees in each country as well as internationally mobile employees of all nationalities. Some multinational companies deal with this problem by conducting their own annual compensation surveys. Others use a global career progression framework that includes the flexibility to accommodate local practices and still maintain organization-wide consistency.[42]

The Balance Sheet Approach

balance sheet approach A method of formulating expatriate pay based on equalizing purchasing power across countries.

An Ethical Dilemma

Is it ethical to pay expatriates using the balance sheet approach when local staff at the same level receive far less compensation?

The most common approach to formulating expatriate pay is to equalize purchasing power across countries, a technique known as the **balance sheet approach**. The basic idea is that each expatriate should enjoy the same standard of living that he or she would have had at home. The employer estimates what the cost of major expenses like housing would be in the expatriate's home country and the equivalent cost of each in the host country. Any differences—such as higher housing expenses—are then paid by the employer.

In practice, this involves building the expatriate's total compensation around a limited number of components. For example, base salary will normally be in the same range as the manager's home-country salary. In addition, however, there might be a mobility premium. This is paid as a percentage of the executive's base salary, in part to compensate the manager for the cultural and physical adjustments that he or she will have to make.[44] There may also be several allowances, including a housing allowance and an education allowance for the expatriate's children.

Variable Pay

As organizations around the world have shifted their focus to individual performance differentiation, there has been a rise in the prevalence of individual performance rewards, although the widespread use of team awards remains in a few Asian countries.[45] Across the globe, over 85 percent of companies offer at least one type of broad-based variable pay program. Target bonuses for management and professional employees, as a percentage of base salary, have become quite similar globally. Although broad-based variable pay was a lot less common in the past, it has now gone global and is an integral part of the compensation landscape for management and professional employees in every region.

International EAPs

Employee assistance programs (EAPs) are also going global, helping expatriates take care of their mental health, which is often affected by the stressful relocation process. A worldwide survey found that more than half of expatriates are weighed down by added stress caused by longer hours, extended workdays/workweeks, and cultural differences, among other factors. Two-thirds feel the strain of managing the demands of work and the well-being of family.[46] The proactive approach is to contact employees before departure to explain the program's services; then, about three months after arrival, families are contacted again. By this time, they have usually run into some challenges from culture shock and will welcome some assistance. The expatriates and their families have then established a connection with the EAP to use for ongoing support.[47]

Problems such as homesickness, boredom, withdrawal, depression, compulsive eating and drinking, irritability, marital stress, family tension, and conflict are all common reactions to culture shock. Employees on short-term assignment without their families can experience extreme loneliness. Treatment for psychiatric illnesses varies widely around the world, as do the conditions in government-run mental health institutions, and consultation with an EAP professional having extensive cross-cultural training may be critical in ensuring that appropriate medical treatment is obtained.[48]

Performance Appraisal of Global Managers

Several issues complicate the task of appraising an expatriate's performance. The question of who actually appraises the expatriate is crucial. Local management must have some input, but the appraisal may then be distorted by cultural differences. Thus, an expatriate manager in India may be evaluated somewhat negatively by his host-country bosses, who find the use of participative decision-making or other behaviours on the part of the expatriate to be inappropriate in their culture. However, home-office managers may be so geographically distanced from the expatriate that they cannot provide valid appraisals because they are not fully aware of the situation that the manager actually faces. Therefore, problems can arise if the expatriate is measured by objective criteria, such as profits and market share, but local events, such as political instability, undermine the manager's performance while remaining "invisible" to home-office staff.

REPATRIATION

repatriation The process of moving the expatriate and his or her family back home from the foreign assignment.

Repatriation is the process of moving the expatriate and his or her family back home from the foreign assignment. Sometimes, repatriation can be more difficult than going abroad.[49] Up to half of expatriates leave their organization following a repatriation, usually because they are not able to use their newly developed skills and capabilities in their roles on their return.[50] Their expert knowledge and international expertise often ends up with the competition.

Several repatriation problems are very common. One is the expatriate's fear that he or she has been "out of sight, out of mind" during an extended foreign stay and has thus lost touch with the parent firm's culture, top executives, and those responsible for the firm's management selection processes. Indeed, such fears can be well founded: Many repatriates are temporarily placed in mediocre or makeshift jobs. Ironically, the company often undervalues the cross-cultural skills acquired abroad, and the international posting becomes a career-limiting, rather than career-enhancing, move. Many are shocked to find that the executive trappings of the overseas job (private schools for the children and a company car and driver, for instance) are lost on return, and that the executive is again just a small fish in a big pond. Perhaps more exasperating is the discovery that some of the expatriate's former colleagues have been more rapidly promoted while he or she was overseas. Even the expatriate's family may undergo a sort of reverse culture shock, as the spouse and children face the often daunting task of picking up old friendships and habits or starting schools anew on their return.[51]

Progressive multinationals anticipate and avoid these problems by taking a number of sensible steps:[52]

1. *Writing repatriation agreements.* Many firms use repatriation agreements, which guarantee in writing that the international assignee will not be kept abroad longer than some period (such as five years) and that on return he or she will be given a mutually acceptable job.

2. *Assigning a sponsor.* The employee should be assigned a sponsor/mentor (such as a senior manager at the parent firm's home office). This person's role is to look after the expatriate while he or she is away. This includes keeping the person apprised of significant company events and changes back home, monitoring his or her career interests, and nominating the person to be considered for key openings when the expatriate is ready to come home.

3. *Providing career counselling.* Provide formal career counselling sessions to ensure that the repatriate's job assignments on return will meet his or her needs.

4. *Keeping communication open.* Keep the expatriate "plugged in" to home-office business affairs through management meetings around the world and frequent home leave combined with meetings at headquarters. Only 18 percent of companies in a Watson Wyatt global survey had a global communication plan in place to keep employees around the world informed about what the company was doing.

5. *Offering financial support.* Many firms pay real estate and legal fees and help the expatriate to rent or in some other way to maintain his or her residence so that the repatriate and his or her family can actually return "home."

6. *Developing reorientation programs.* Provide the repatriate and his or her family with a reorientation program to facilitate the adjustment back into the home culture.

7. *Building in return trips.* Expatriates can benefit from more frequent trips to the home country to ensure that they keep in touch with home-country norms and changes during their international assignment.

MANAGING GLOBAL WORKERS WITHIN CANADA

The successful integration of immigrants and foreign workers into the Canadian labour market is increasingly becoming of interest to organizations, Canadian public policy makers, and HR professionals alike. The issues of underemployment of immigrants and foreign workers is especially critical today, given the aging workforce, the rate of immigration to Canada (almost one in every five persons residing in Canada is foreign born), and our dependence on immigrants to maintain our labour force size. Additionally, the labour and talent scarcity further fuels the need for successful integration and utilization of immigrants in the Canadian labour force. In 2013, the top six source countries of immigrants to Canada were China, India, Philippines, Pakistan, Iran, and the United States.[53]

HR Competency

10100

HR IN THE NEWS

Changes to the Temporary Foreign Workers Programs

In June 2014, the Minister of Employment and Social Development and the Minister of Citizenship and Immigration announced a comprehensive overhaul of the Temporary Foreign Worker Program (TFWP) and the creation of an International Mobility Program (IMP). Employers who want to bring in workers under the TFWP will need to request employees through an approval process, using a new Labour Market Impact Assessment (LMIA). The LMIA fee also increased from $275 for every foreign worker to $1000.

The main catalyst for the reforms was to ensure Canadians are given priority for available jobs. The reforms will limit access to the TFWP, tighten the labour market assessment needed for the program (LMA), and enforce stronger penalties for employers who violate the rules. In addition, Canadian businesses will have to make more effort to recruit and train Canadians for vacancies.[54]

The ability to employ temporary foreign workers and the issue of integrating immigrants are critical to the country's economic success. The HR in the News box highlights recent changes to the foreign workers program and briefly provides considerations that employers who want to bring in foreign workers should consider.

Canadian employers note that hiring immigrants increases the employer's language skills, generation of new ideas, and enhances the company's reputation.[55] Research has found that diverse groups make higher-quality decisions, generate more creative ideas, use more creative problem-solving techniques, and have the potential for higher rates of productivity.[56] A survey of human resources professionals found that 91 percent of respondents felt that diversity initiatives help the organization maintain a competitive advantage, largely through enhanced corporate culture, employee morale, retention, and recruitment.[57] An example of a company with a well-recognized diversity initiative is highlighted in the Expert Opinion box.

HR Competency

40300

---

expert opinion
industry viewpoint

Yvonne Farquharson

Identification: Ms. Yvonne Farquharson, Sr. HR Generalist, Medtronics of Canada Limited

1.   What is Medtronic of Canada's approach to diversity management?

We look at diversity management from the perspective of both being an opportunity and an advantage. Our business and customers are diverse, so we like a labour pool that reflects that. Therefore our diversity and inclusion program is seen as a strategic goal for our organization. Our program includes building competencies to increase awareness regarding diversity and inclusion.

We focus on highlighting diverse celebrations, aided by a diversity calendar showcasing employees at work and play in different events. In addition, we utilized a consultant to train a number of employees on intercultural interventions, including members of our management team, HR, Communications, and ground-level employees who are part of our Diversity and Inclusion Coalition. This involved measuring individual cultural competency, identifying gaps, and building training to address identified development needs. We also promote and host a multicultural fair within the organization showcasing diversity, which acts as an educational tool for cultural awareness for our employees. Two years ago, we established a mentorship program, with a longer career focus on assimilation and career development.

2.   Why is diversity management important at the organizational level?

Through management of diversity, the organization benefits from an opportunity to tap in to various cultures, lifestyles, and different points of view that help the organization achieve its mission. The benefits include a highly engaged workforce, high levels of employee motivation, and we have been branded as an employer of choice.

3.   What challenges do managers often overlook when implementing diversity management programs?

For any diversity initiative to succeed, there must be champions in the organization. We need to educate our employees and leadership about what diversity and inclusion means. It has been said that diversity is the mix and inclusion is making the mix work. Champions help us move the agenda forward. So, organizations should be clear to secure senior executive level commitment for such programs.

Metrics associated with diversity or inclusion programs are challenging. It's hard to pin down the actual organizational value impact to the bottom line of these initiatives, as well as associated reliable statistics. Internal and external surveys can help demonstrate how the workforce feels included, respected, and think that their opinions are taken into consideration.

The last challenge to highlight is overcoming "diversity fatigue." I would recommend not just looking at designated groups, but all groups within the organization that may be over or under represented. There is a requirement to manage perceptions of adverse impact, and inclusion should not marginalize any group.

Source: Reprinted by permission from Ms. Yvonne Farquharson.

FIGURE 17.3 Immigrant Engagement and Employment Continuum

Stage 1 Immigrant-Friendly Attraction and Recruitment Practices	Stage 2 Immigrant-Friendly Integration and Development Practices	Stage 3 Immigrant-Friendly Retention Practices
• Expand recruitment methods beyond standard practices. • Implement culturally sensitive screening practices. • Provide information and pre-employment training to immigrant/international job seekers through community organizations. • Offer bridging and mentoring programs to immigrant/international job seekers. • Help obtain recognition of foreign qualifications through credential service agencies or in-house competency tests. • Provide assistance for immigrants/ international job seekers to acquire credential papers/documents.	• Offer workplace mentoring programs. • Provide professional language and communication skills training programs. • Support and encourage the achievement of their professional goals and objectives.	• Promote cultural awareness. • Supports affinity groups. • Provide cultural diversity training. • Engage executive support for diversity.

Source: "Immigrant-Friendly Businesses: Effective Practices for Attracting, Integrating, and Retaining Immigrants in Canadian Workplaces," November 2009, p. 15. Reprinted by permission.

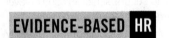

The Conference Board of Canada suggests that the effective integration and utilization of immigrants in the workforce requires a commitment to recruiting and attracting talent, development and retention, identifying that efforts to create an inclusive organization require multiple HR and management interventions. The summary in **Figure 17.3** suggests that the approach to managing immigrants in the Canadian workforce should be strategic, proactive, and planned.

The unemployment level and challenges of employment represent only part of the obstacles of immigrant and foreign workforce integration in Canada. Another significant challenge is the underutilization of immigrant skills because they are being hired for positions that they are overqualified to perform. Statistics Canada has reported that the percentage of long-term immigrants who had successfully completed a university degree and who only found jobs with low educational requirements (such as clerks, truck drivers, salespeople, cashiers, and taxi drivers) has risen steadily over the last two decades. The resulting skills mismatch puts pressure on HR departments to find the right talent needed for a position, on the organization to provide more extensive training and development programs, and on society as a whole because of the lost value of experience and knowledge acquired by its members.[58]

A survey by Statistics Canada found that 70 percent of newcomers said they had encountered problems or barriers in the job-finding process. The results can be broadly categorized into a lack of Canadian work experience, poor transferability of foreign credentials, and a lack of literacy skills in either of the official languages.

HR Competency

30100

Barrier 1: Lack of Canadian Experience

Work experience helps individuals develop skills in communication, work patterns, and team work that are recognized and valued by organizations. It can help people identify career paths and requirements of desired positions. It can shape perceptions of the world of work and set expectations of the employer. It can also provide an opportunity for individuals to network with others, which can assist their future job search efforts.

Understandably, most employers look for familiar references when assessing candidates, such as experiences and companies that they recognize on résumés or during interviews. Often immigrants feel like they are in a Catch-22 situation where they cannot secure a job without the proven Canadian experience, and they cannot acquire the Canadian experience without securing a job.

This situation is deepened because of a lack of recognition for foreign work, which is consistently discounted in the Canadian labour market.[59] As immigrants enter the Canadian workforce, research on earnings shows low, or even zero, returns (monetary recognition) for their foreign work experience.[60] When only their Canadian work experience is taken into account, immigrants' earnings are similar to those of the Canadian-born with the same years of Canadian experience, regardless of how many years of international experience the immigrant had prior to joining the Canadian workforce. The HR by the Numbers box provides summary statistics regarding immigrant experiences in Canada. These results suggest a significant inability to transfer and recognize skills and experiences immigrants acquired in their country of origin to the Canadian labour market, representing a lost value to the immigrant.

Almost two in every three new immigrants fail to find employment in the same field in which they were employed in their native country. For example, before arriving in Canada, only 10.2 percent of men and 12.1 percent of women were employed in sales and service-related occupations. Six months after arrival in Canada, 24.9 percent of men and 37.3 percent of women were employed in these occupations.[62]

Options to help overcome challenges associated with lack of Canadian experience and devaluation of foreign experience include the following:[63]

HR : by the Numbers

Immigrant Experiences in Canada, in 2011[61]

8.4% the unemployment rate of all immigrants aged 25 to 54

13.6% the unemployment rate of landed immigrants with five years or less in Canada

4.3% the unemployment rate in Alberta of landed immigrants with five years or less in Canada

28.1% of very recent landed immigrants reside in Quebec, making Quebec the recipient of most of Canada's landed immigrants

22.1% of very recent landed immigrants reside in Alberta

79% of weekly wages earned by Canadian-born workers with a university degree are earned by recent immigrants with a university degree

HR Competency

40300

1. Educate employers, recruiters, and hiring managers to develop skills needed to recognize and effectively interpret skills from different countries.

2. Provide clear statements in job descriptions as to the extent and nature of work experience required to complete job requirements. Offer candidates an opportunity to demonstrate the skills in a simulated or field setting.

3. Use apprenticeships effectively. Some trades mandate apprenticeships (for example, in Ontario there are 20 trades with a mandatory apprenticeship component), whereas others are voluntary. This creates an option where apprenticeships can be used to develop and evaluate the skills of foreign-trained workers. Alternatively, some provinces (like Alberta) allow immigrants with significant foreign experience in a trade the opportunity to write an exam to receive certification.

4. Partner with industry-based assessment centres (for example, Workplace Integration of Skilled Newcomers in the Trades, Internationally Educated Engineer Qualification Bridging Program) to develop bridging programs to integrate foreign experience of immigrants.

At the same time, immigrants to Canada have a responsibility toward learning about Canadian workplace norms and customs and presenting their experiences or qualifications to Canadian recruiters in a clear and effective way. There must also be an

GLOBAL HRM

Successful Integration of Immigrants in Canada

There are many examples of innovative, forward-thinking companies that have developed initiatives to aid in the successful integration of immigrants into their workforce. The result is a competitive advantage and ability to recognize and recruit strong talent.

- RBC requires recruiters and managers to be trained in cross-cultural awareness to help interpret and understand past experiences related to the job. This represents a two-way mutual understanding approach to recruitment.

- Assiniboine Credit Union assumes an organic approach by training managers and employees on diversity and

cultural awareness, offering a mentorship or buddy program, and regularly soliciting and communicating feedback from the programs, which then aids in modifying the programs.

- Manulife offers paid internships (of 4 to 12 months) and formalizes the process by having clear indications of who is eligible for the programs offered (must be in Canada less than three years, have at least three years of foreign experience, and so on).

Source: Based on G. Larose and G. Tillman, "Valorizing Immigrants' Non-Canadian Work Experience" (Ottawa, ON: Work and Learning Knowledge Centre, 2009).

awareness of Canadian laws and regulations. There are many ways organizations can help with this, as discussed in the Global HRM box.

Barrier 2: Poor Transferability of Foreign Education or Training

While finding a job can be difficult for many, the employment prospects for new immigrants are often diminished due to poor recognition of foreign qualifications. Licensing bodies of certain trades and professions may not accept foreign-obtained certification, and employers have difficulty assessing foreign education in a meaningful way.[64] In 2008, over 42 percent of new immigrants were working in occupations that required lower levels of education than what they had attained. Of Canadian-born workers, the rate was 28 percent.[65]

The result is the underutilization of foreign workers in Canada. A study of over 7700 new immigrants found that within four years after landing in Canada, only 28 percent with foreign credentials had received recognition for these credentials (meaning that the employer/institution recognizes the credential as being legitimate within determined standards).[66] Women and older immigrants are less likely to have foreign education recognized in Canada. Also, immigrants from South Korea, the Philippines, and France have the lowest rates of full foreign credentials recognition, while immigrants from the United States and United Kingdom have the highest rates.[67]

Canadian literature on the assessment of foreign training, using prior learning assessment and recognition (PLAR) methods, is extensive. PLAR is a system meant to aide in the recognition of the learning adults acquire outside of formal Canadian education; it attempts to standardize recognition of skills and abilities in a meaningful way. Many colleges and universities in Canada rely on PLAR to evaluate foreign credentials.

Barrier 3: Lack of Literacy Skills

Literacy is the ability to identify, understand, interpret, create, communicate, compute, and use printed and written materials associated with varying contexts. In a global economy, it is critical that employees have the ability to express themselves in the official language(s) of the country they are employed in. The education levels of new immigrants have been steadily rising over recent years due to changes in immigration criteria.

Literacy and adult education falls mainly under the jurisdiction of provincial and territorial governments. The federal government plays a role in developing policy and delivering some funding for literacy initiatives. In May 2007, Citizenship and Immigration Canada established the Foreign Credential Referral Office (FCRO) to guide, monitor, and facilitate the assessment of foreign credentials. In October 2010, the FCRO took over responsibility from HRSDC for the Canadian Immigrant Integration Program. That year, the FCRO aided in online and over the phone inquiries from over 25 000 immigrants.[68]

Six months after arrival in Canada, only three in every five immigrants report that they are able to speak English well or very well, and only one in every ten immigrants report the same about French.[69] Language training increases an immigrant's likelihood of gaining employment or advancing within an organization. Roughly 45 percent of new immigrants partake in language training in English once employed in Canada, and 10 percent are trained in French.[70]

Language ability has also been shown to improve labour-market outcomes among educated immigrants.[71] The earnings differential between immigrants and Canadian-born individuals would narrow by about 20 percent if immigrants had the same average literacy scores as the native born. Consequently, this would eliminate more than half of the immigrant earnings disadvantage among university educated workers alone. The variance and in some cases lack of literacy skills in Canada's official languages is viewed as a significant barrier to the successful integration of immigrants in the labour market.

Thus, while literacy deficiencies among immigrants have an important impact on earnings differentials, the impact is decidedly smaller than the effect of low returns associated with foreign experience among the highly educated. Controlling for literacy does not affect the relative patterns of returns to foreign- and Canadian-acquired experience. Immigration is vital to Canada's population growth and economic prosperity. Yet, while demand for their skills grows, many highly competent newcomers to Canada remain underemployed.

CHAPTER SUMMARY

1. Globalization affects HRM in two significant ways. First, workforce mobility forces companies to focus on international recruitment, retention, and relations strategies to take advantage of the skills offered by workers who were not born in Canada. Second, immigrants into Canada present a significant source of labour force growth, and successful integration of these immigrants can yield significant benefits for the organization.

2. Intercountry differences include cultural factors (such as power distance, individualism versus collectivism, and gender egalitarianism), economic systems, labour cost factors, and industrial relations factors. These affect HRM in a variety of ways.

3. Global relocation strategies must consider effective selection, training, compensation, labour relations,

and performance appraisals for expatriates and global managers. For example, in reference to compensation, the balance sheet approach allows the employer to estimate expenses for income taxes, housing, and goods and services and pay supplements to the expatriate in such a way as to maintain the same standard of living that he or she would have had at home.

4. Repatriation problems are common but can be minimized. They include the often well-founded fear that the expatriate is "out of sight, out of mind" and difficulties in reassimilating the expatriate's family back into home-country culture. Suggestions for avoiding these problems include using repatriation agreements, assigning a home-country sponsor/mentor, offering career counselling, keeping the expatriate plugged in to home-office business,

building in return trips, providing financial support to maintain the expatriate's home-country residence, and offering reorientation programs to the expatriate and his or her family.

5. Newcomers to Canada face a variety of challenges associated with securing full employment. Specifically, a lack of Canadian work experience, poor transferability of foreign credentials, and a lack of language skills in English or French are seen as the greatest barriers to employment for newcomers, according to both immigrants and employers.

6. These barriers result in significant underemployment of immigrants, or a skills mismatch, which further exasperates the skills shortage that employers experience.

7. Newcomers to Canada and employers can benefit from modifying recruitment and selection procedures to offer opportunities to assess the skills of immigrants as part of the selection process, using apprenticeships effectively, partnering with assessment centres to recognize skills, and educating employers, recruiters, and managers about how to recognize and interpret skills from another country.

MyManagementLab

Study, practise, and explore real business situations with these helpful resources:

- **Interactive Lesson Presentations:** Work through interactive presentations and assessments to test your knowledge of management concepts.
- **PIA (Personal Inventory Assessments):** Enhance your ability to connect with key concepts through these engaging self-reflection assessments.
- **Study Plan:** Check your understanding of chapter concepts with self-study quizzes.
- **Videos:** Learn more about the management practices and strategies of real companies.
- **Simulations:** Practise decision-making in simulated management environments.

P I A PERSONAL INVENTORY ASSESSMENT

KEY TERMS

balance sheet approach *(p. 409)*
ethnocentric staffing policy *(p. 407)*
expatriate assignment failure *(p. 405)*
expatriates *(p. 401)*
geocentric staffing policy *(p. 407)*

global nomad *(p. 403)*
immigrant *(p. 401)*
polycentric staffing policy *(p. 407)*
repatriation *(p. 411)*
workforce mobility *(p. 401)*

REVIEW AND DISCUSSION QUESTIONS

1. Specifically, what are some of the uniquely international activities that an international HR manager typically engages in?

2. Explain three broad global HR challenges.

3. Discuss the reasons why expatriate assignments fail and what is being done to reduce the failure rate.

4. How does compensation of an expatriate differ from that of a home-office manager? How can some of the unique problems of compensating the expatriate be avoided?

5. Describe five actions that can be taken by expatriate managers in other countries to increase their personal safety.

6. What are the three biggest obstacles to securing full employment of immigrants and foreign workers in Canada? How can these be managed?

7. Why is the issue of underemployment of foreign-trained persons important to Canadian employers?

CRITICAL THINKING QUESTIONS

1. You are the president of a small business. In what ways do you expect that being involved in international business activity will affect HRM in your business?

2. A firm is about to send its first employees overseas to staff a new subsidiary. The president asks why such assignments fail and what can be done to avoid such failures. Write a memo in response to these questions.

3. What can an organization do to ensure that the skills acquired on an international assignment are used when the employee returns to his or her home country?

4. How would you assess the credentials of foreign-trained persons? What agencies are available for you to contact?

5. What obstacles to successful integration of global talent do you think exist in your company? What solutions can you recommend to overcome these obstacles?

EXPERIENTIAL EXERCISES

1. Choose three traits that are useful for selecting international assignees, and create a straightforward test (not one that uses pencil and paper) to screen candidates for these traits.

2. Describe the most common approach to formulating expatriate pay. Use a library source to determine the relative cost of living in five countries this year, and explain the implications of such differences for drafting a pay plan for managers being sent to each country.

3. Either in pairs or groups of four or five, develop an outline for an initial four-hour cross-cultural training program. What training resources, tools, and processes might you use? Be prepared to give a rationale for your program.

4. Check online and find at least two websites that deal with or otherwise discuss the expatriate experience, and note the concerns and suggestions expressed. Compare these to the text discussion. How do the actual expatriate experiences you found influence your current attitude toward working overseas? What are your major concerns? What excites you?

RUNNING CASE

Running Case: LearnInMotion.com

Going Abroad

According to its business plan and in practice, LearnInMotion.com "acquires content globally but delivers it locally." In other words, all the content and courses and other material that it lists on its site come from content providers all over the world. However, the "hard copy" (book and CD-ROM) courses are delivered, with the help of independent contracting delivery firms, locally in Ontario and Quebec.

Now the company is considering an expansion. Although the most logical strategic expansion would probably entail adding cities in Canada, one of LearnInMotion.com's major content providers—a big training company in England—believes there is a significant market for LearnInMotion.com services in England, particularly in London, Oxford, and Manchester (all of which are bustling business centres, and all of which have well-known universities). The training company has offered to finance and co-own a branch of LearnInMotion.com in London. They want it housed in the training firm's new offices in Mayfair, near Shepherd Market, in London. This is an easily accessible (if somewhat expensive) area, within easy walking distance of Hyde Park and not far from the London Underground Piccadilly line, which runs directly through the city to Heathrow airport.

Everyone concerned wants to make sure the new operation can "hit the ground running." This means either Jennifer or Pierre will have to move to London almost at once and take one salesperson and one of the content management people along. Once there, this small team could hire additional employees locally, and then, once the new operation is running successfully, return to Ottawa, probably within three or four months.

Jennifer and Pierre have decided to go ahead and open the London office, but this is not a decision they've taken lightly, since there are many drawbacks to doing so. The original, Ottawa-based site is not generating anywhere near the sales revenue it was supposed to at this point, and being short three key employees is not going to help. Neither the board of directors nor the representatives of the venture capital fund were enthusiastic about the idea of expanding abroad. However, they went along with it, and the deciding factor was probably the cash infusion that the London-based training firm was willing to make. It basically provided enough cash to run not just the London

operation but the one in Ottawa as well for an additional six months.

Having made the decision to set up operations abroad, Jennifer and Pierre now need to turn to the multitude of matters involved in the expansion—for instance, obtaining the necessary licenses to open the business in England and arranging for phone lines (all carried out with the assistance of the London-based training firm). However, it's also obvious to Jennifer and Pierre that there are considerable human resources management implications involved in moving LearnInMotion.com employees abroad and in staffing the operation once they're there. Now they want you, their management consultant, to help them actually do it.

QUESTIONS

1 What intercountry differences will affect the human resources management practices of LearnInMotion. com?

2 Should LearnInMotion.com use a global selection policy to source talent for their London operation?

3 How should LearnInMotion.com implement a global HR system?

CASE INCIDENT

"Boss, I Think We Have a Problem"

Central Steel Door Corporation has been in business for about 20 years, successfully selling a line of steel industrial-grade doors as well as the hardware and fittings required for them. Focusing mostly on the United States and Canada, the company had gradually increased its presence from the New York City area, first into New England and then down the Atlantic coast, then through the Midwest and west, and finally into Canada. The company's basic expansion strategy was always the same: Choose an area, open a distribution centre, hire a regional sales manager, and then let that regional sales manager help staff the distribution centre and hire local sales reps.

Unfortunately, the company's traditional success in finding sales help for its North American locations has not extended to its overseas operations. With the introduction of the new European currency in 2002, Mel Fisher, president of Central Steel Door, decided to expand his

company abroad into Europe. However, the expansion has not gone smoothly at all. He tried for three weeks to find a sales manager by advertising in the *International Herald Tribune,* which is read by businesspeople in Europe and by American expatriates living and working in Europe. Although the ads placed in the *Tribune* also run for about a month on the *Tribune's* website, Fisher has so far received only five applications. One came from a possibly viable candidate, whereas four came from candidates whom Fisher refers to as "lost souls"—people who seem to have spent most of their time travelling aimlessly from country to country sipping espresso in sidewalk cafés. When asked what he had done for the last three years, one told Fisher he'd been on a "walkabout."

Other aspects of his international HR activities have been equally problematic. Fisher alienated two of his US sales managers by sending them to Europe to temporarily run the European operations, but neglecting to work out a compensation package that would cover their relatively high living expenses in Germany and Belgium. One ended up staying the better part of the year, and Fisher was rudely surprised to be informed by the Belgian government that his sales manager owed thousands of dollars in local taxes. The managers had hired about 10 local people to staff each of the two distribution centres. However, without full-time local European sales managers, the level of sales was disappointing, so Fisher decided to fire about half of the distribution centre employees. That's when he got an emergency phone call from his temporary sales manager in Germany: "I've just been told that all these employees should have had written employment agreements and that

we can't fire anyone without at least one year's notice, and the local authorities here are really up in arms. Boss, I think we have a problem."

QUESTIONS

1 Based on this chapter and the case incident, compile a list of 10 international HR mistakes Fisher has made so far.

2 How would you have gone about hiring a European sales manager? Why?

3 What would you do now if you were Fisher?

Notes

Chapter 1

1. O. Parker, *The Strategic Value of People: Human Resource Trends and Metrics* (Ottawa, ON: The Conference Board of Canada, July 2006); E. Andrew, "Most Canadian Companies Are Still Not Treating Human Resources as a Serious Strategic Issue," *Workspan Focus Canada* (February 2006), pp. 14–16; S. Prashad, "All Aligned: How to Get HR on Board with Business," *HR Professional* (February/March 2005), pp. 19–29.

2. O. Parker, *It's the Journey That Matters: 2005 Strategic HR Transformation Study Tour.* (Ottawa, ON: The Conference Board of Canada, March 2006).

3. N. Bontis, "Made to Measure: Linking Human Capital Metrics with Organizational Performance," *HR Professional* (August/September 2007), pp. 16–20; B. Becker, M. Huselid, P.S. Pickus, and M.F. Spratt, "HR as a Source of Shareholder Value: Research and Recommendations," *Human Resource Management* 36, no. 1 (Spring 1997), pp. 39–47; B. Becker and B. Gerhart, "The Impact of Human Resource Management on Organizational Performance: Progress and Prospects," *Academy of Management Journal*, 39, no. 4 (August 1996), pp. 779–801; M. Huselid, "The Impact of Human Resources Management Practices on Turnover, Productivity, and Corporate Performance," *Academy of Management Journal*, 38 (1995), pp. 635–672; P. Wright, G. McMahan, B. McCormick, and S. Sherman, "Strategy, Core Competence, and HR Involvement as Determinants of HR Effectiveness and Refinery," *Human Resource Management*, 37, no. 37 (1998), pp. 17–31.

4. C. Clegg, M. Patterson, A. Robinson, C. Stride, T.D. Wall, and S.J. Wood, "The Impact of Human Resource and Operational Management Practices on Company Productivity: A Longitudinal Study," *Personnel Psychology*, 61 (Autumn 2008), pp. 467–501.

5. A. Lado and M.C. Wilson, "Human Resource Systems and Sustained Competitive Advantage: A Competency-Based Perspective," *Academy of Management Review*, 19 (1994), pp. 699–727.

6. J.E. Delery and D.H. Doty, "Modes of Theorizing in Strategic Human Resource Management: Tests of Universalistic, Contingency, and Configurational Performance Predictions," *Academy of Management Journal*, 39, no. 4 (1996), pp. 802–835.

7. M. Huselid, "The Impact of Human Resources Management Practices on Turnover, Productivity, and Corporate Performance," *Academy of Management Journal*, 38 (1995), pp. 635–672.

8. Adrienne Fox, "Do Assignments Outside HR Pay Off?" *HR Magazine*, November 2011, p. 32. See also Lorna Collier, "More CFOs Landing in HR Territory," *Workforce Management*, October 2011, p. 8.

9. Steve Bates, "No Experience Necessary? Many Companies Are Putting Non-HR Executives in Charge of HR with Mixed Results," *HR Magazine* 46, no. 11 (November 2001), pp. 34–41. See also Fay Hansen, "Top of the Class," *Workforce Management*, June 23, 2008, pp. 1, 25–30.

10. This data comes from "Small Business: A Report of the President" (1998), www.SBA.gov/ADV/stats, accessed March 9, 2006. See also "Statistics of U.S. Businesses and Non-Employer Status," www.SBA.gov/ADV_oh/research/data.html, accessed March 9, 2006; and James Rosen, "Economists Credit Small Business 'Gazelles' with Job Creation," www.foxnews.com/us/2011/04/25/economistscredit-small-business-gazelles-job-creation/, accessed October 5, 2012

11. F.W. Taylor, "The Principles of Scientific Management," in J.M. Sharfritz and J.S. Ott (eds.), *Classics of Organization Theory*, 2nd ed. (Chicago, IL: The Dorsey Press, 1987), pp. 66–81.

12. D.G. Nickels, J.M. McHugh, S.M. McHugh, and P.D Berman, *Understanding Canadian Business*, 2nd ed. (Toronto, ON: Irwin, 1997), p. 220.

13. This discussion is based on E.E. Lawler III, "Human Resources Management," *Personnel* (January 1988), pp. 24–25.

14. J. Miller, "HR Outsourcing and the Bottom Line," *Workspan* (October 2008), pp. 76–81; J. Berkow, "People Skills Required," *National Post* (October 19, 2005).

15. R.J. Cattaneo and A.J. Templer, "Determining the Effectiveness of Human Resources Management," in T.H. Stone (ed.), *ASAC: Personnel and Human Resources Division Proceedings* (Halifax, NS: St. Mary's University, June 1988), p. 73.

16. T. Belford, "HR Focusing on How It Can Add Value," *Globe and Mail* (March 25, 2002), p. B11.

17. S. Dobson, "Business Acumen Critical for HR: Survey," *Canadian HR Reporter* (May 9, 2011).

18. S. Modi, "Is the CEO the New Chief Talent Officer in Global Recruitment and HR?" Monster Thinking, (July 6, 2011), www.monsterthinking.com/2011/07/06/is-the-ceo-the-new-chief-talent-officer-in-global-recruitmentand-hr/ (accessed September 26, 2011).

19. Meehan, A., and Leung, K. "Canada's Top 100 Employers 2015." Edited by Richard Yerema and Kristina Leung. *Canada's Top 100 Employers Magazine*, 2014. Retrieved from http://issuu.com/ct100./docs/ct100-magazine-2015?e=14200235/9961408

20. R. Wright, *Measuring Human Resources Effectiveness Toolkit* (Ottawa, ON: The Conference Board of Canada, 2004); U. Vu, "The HR Leader's Contribution in an Engaged Organization," *Canadian HR Reporter* (May 22, 2006); D. Brown, "Measuring Human Capital Crucial, ROI Isn't, Says New Think-Tank Paper," *Canadian HR Reporter* (October 25, 2004), pp. 1, 4; J. Douglas and T. Emond, "Time to Pop the Question: Are Your Employees Engaged?" *WorldatWork Canadian News* (Third Quarter, 2003), pp. 12–14.

21. R. Baumruk, "The Missing Link: The Role of Employee Engagement in Business Success," *Workspan* (November 2004), pp. 48–52; N. Winter, "Tuned In and Turned On," *Workspan* (April 2003), pp. 48–52.

22. D.S. Cohen, "Behaviour-Based Interviewing," *Human Resources Professional* (April/May 1997), p. 29.

23. *CCHRA Awareness Study* (Toronto, ON: CCHRA and Ekos Research Associates, 2008).

24. B.E. Becker, M.A. Huselid, and D. Ulrich, *The HR Scorecard: Linking People, Strategy and Performance* (Boston, MA: Harvard Business School Press, 2001); D. Brown, "Measuring the Value of HR," *Canadian HR Reporter* (September 24, 2001), pp. 1, 5. See also E. Beaudan, "The Failure of Strategy: It's All in the Execution, *Ivey Business Journal* (January/February 2001).

25. A. Aijala, B. Walsh, and J. Schwartz, *Aligned at the Top: How Business and HR Executives View Today's Most Significant People Challenges—And What They're Doing About It.* Deloitte Development LLC, 2007.

26. *Canada's Demographic Revolution: Adjusting to an Aging Population* (Ottawa, ON: The Conference Board of Canada, March 2006).

27. Robert Grossman, "IBM's HR Takes a Risk," *HR Management*, April 2007, pp. 54–59.

28. See Dave Ulrich, "The New HR Organization," *Workforce Management*, December 10, 2007, pp. 40–44; and Dave Ulrich, "The 21st-Century HR Organization," *Human Resource Management* 47, no. 4 (Winter 2008), pp. 829–850. Some writers distinguish among three basic human resource management subfields: *micro HRM* (which covers the HR subfunctions such as recruitment and selection), *strategic HRM*, and *international HRM*. Mark Lengnick Hall et al., "Strategic Human Resource Management: The Evolution of the Field," *Human Resource Management Review* 19 (2009), pp. 64–85.

29. See, for example, www.personneltoday.com/blogs/hcglobal-human-capital-management/2009/02/theres-no-such-thing-as-eviden.html, accessed April 18, 2009.

30. The evidence-based movement began in medicine. In 1996, in an editorial published by the *British Medical Journal,* David Sackett, MD, defined *evidence-based medicine* as "use of the best-available evidence in making decisions about patient care" and urged his colleagues to adopt its tenets. "Evidence-Based Training™: Turning Research into Results for Pharmaceutical Sales Training," An AXIOM White Paper © 2006 AXIOM Professional Health Learning LLC. All rights reserved.

31. O. Parker, *The Strategic Value of People: Human Resource Trends and Metrics* (Ottawa, ON: The Conference Board of Canada, July 2006).

32. R. Kaplan and D. Norton, *The Strategy-Focused Organization: How Balanced Scorecard Companies Thrive in the New Business Environment* (Boston, MA: Harvard Business School Press, 1996); S. Mooraj, D. Oyon, and D. Hostettler, "The Balanced Scorecard: A Necessary Good or an Unnecessary Evil?" *European Management Journal* 17, no. 5 (October 1999), pp. 481–491; B. Becker, M. Huselid, and D. Ulrich, *The HR Scorecard: Linking People, Strategy and Performance* (Boston, MA: Harvard Business School Press, 2001); M. Huselid, B. Becker, and R. Beatty, *The Workforce Scorecard: Managing Human Capital to Execute Strategy* (Boston, MA: Harvard Business School Press, 2006).

33. This section is based on www.cchra.ca.

34. S. Klie, "Senior HR Designation Unveiled," *Canadian HR Reporter* (July 7, 2009).

35. D. McDougall, "Employees Want an Ethical Work Environment," *Canadian HR Reporter* (April 10, 2000), p. 4

36. S. Klie, "Most HR Professionals Have Been Coerced," *Canadian HR Reporter* (June 16, 2008).

37. "KPMG's Ethics Survey 2000—Managing for Ethical Practice," cited in L. Young, "Companies Not Doing Right," *Canadian HR Reporter* (April 10, 2000), p. 17.

38. Based on Walker Information Canada Inc. study, cited in J. Martin, "Studies Suggest a Link between Employees' Perception of a Firm's Ethics—and Loyalty," *Recruitment & Staffing*, Supplement to *Canadian HR Reporter* (September 20, 1999), p. G7; D. McDougall, "Employees Want an Ethical Work Environment," *Canadian HR Reporter* (April 10, 2000), p. 4

39. Mountain Equipment Coop. www.mec.ca (July 29, 2009).

40. G. Ferris, D. Frink, and M.C. Galang, "Diversity in the Workplace: The Human Resources Management Challenge," *Human Resource Planning* 16, no. 1 (1993), p. 42.

41. Statistics Canada, *Immigration and Ethnocultural Diversity in Canada*, Catalogue no. 99-010-X2011001, p. 4.

42. Ibid.

43. K. Milligan, "What the Data Shows about Female Breadwinners in Canada," *Maclean's*, June 10, 2013.

44. Statistics Canada, *2011 Census of Population*, Statistics Canada Catalogue no. 98-311-XCB2011018.

45. Statistics Canada, *Aboriginal Peoples in Canada: First Nations People, Métis and Inuit,* Catalogue no. 99-011-X2011001, p. 5.

46. Statistics Canada, *Aboriginal Peoples in Canada: First Nations People, Métis and Inuit,* Catalogue no. 99-011-X2011001, p. 4.

47. C. Williams, "Disability in the Workplace," *Perspectives on Labour and Income* 18, no.1 (February 2006), pp. 16–24.

48. Ibid.

49. Statistics Canada, *Labour Force Historical Review*, Catalogue No.71F0004XCB, 2007.

50. A. Campbell and N. Gagnon, *Literacy, Life and Employment: An Analysis of Canadian International Adult Literacy Survey (IALS) Microdata* (Ottawa, ON: Conference Board of Canada, January 2006).

51. J. Bernier, *The Scope of Federal Labour Standards and Nontraditional Work Situations* (Submission to the Federal Labour Standards Review, October 2005), pp. 5–13.

52. A. Silliker, "More Firms Hiring Contract Workers," *Canadian HR Reporter*, May 7, 2011, Vol. 25(9), p. 1.

53. M. Vartiainen, M. Hakonen, S. Koivisto, P. Mannonen, M. P. Nieminen, V. Ruohomaki, and A. Vartola, *Distributed and Mobile: Places, People and Technology* (Helsinki Finland: Oy Yliopistokustannus University Press, 2007), p. 75.

54. C. Clark, "The World Is Flat: Work-Life Trends to Watch," *Workspan* (January 2009), pp. 17–19.

55. K. Williams, "Privacy in a Climate of Electronic Surveillance," *Workplace News* (April 2005), p. 10.

56. P. Benimadhu, "Startling Business Shifts Causing a Rethink of Work," *InsideEdge* (Summer 2008), p. 10.

57. "Multinational Corporation," http://en.wikipedia.org/wiki/Multinational_corporation (accessed August 17, 2006).

58. S. Nolen, "Step 1: Keep Workers Alive," *Globe and Mail* (August 5, 2006), pp. B4–B5.

59. U. Vu, "Climate Change Sparks Attitude Shift," *Canadian HR Reporter* (March 26, 2007), p. 11.

60. S. Dobson, "Fairmont Finds It's Easy Being Green," *Canadian HR Reporter* (March 26, 2007).

61. R. Stringer, *Leadership and Organizational Climate* (Upper Saddle River, NJ: Prentice-Hall, 2002).

Chapter 2

1. S. Dobson, "Business Acumen Critical for HR: Survey," *Canadian HR Reporter* (May 9, 2011).

2. P. Verge and G. Vallee, "Un droit du travail? Essai sur la spicifite du droit du travail," Editions Yvon Blais, Cowansville, (1997).

3. Canadian Charter of Rights and Freedoms, as part of the Constitution Act of 1982.

4. Canadian Charter of Rights and Freedoms, Section 15(1).

5. *Annual Report of the Canadian Human Rights Commission* (Ottawa, ON: Government of Canada, 1991), p. 65.

6. A.P. Aggarwal, *Sex Discrimination: Employment Law and Practices* (Toronto, ON: Butterworths Canada, 1994).

7. H.J. Jain, "Human Rights: Issues in Employment," *Human Resources Management in Canada* (Toronto, ON: Prentice-Hall Canada, 1995), p. 50.

8. Ontario Human Rights Commission, *Human Rights at Work* (Toronto, ON: Government of Ontario, 1999), pp. 63–64.

9. S. Rudner, "Just Cause—Back from the Dead?" *Canadian HR Reporter* (September 22, 2008); M. Bélanger and R. Ravary, "Supreme Court of Canada Sets Limits on Employer's Duty to Accommodate," *McCarthy Tétrault e-Alert* (July 24, 2008); D. Elenbaas, "Undue Hardship: Supreme Court of Canada Clarifies the Standard—or Does it?" *Ultimate HR Manual*, 39 (August 2008), pp. 1–3.

10. "Policy and Guidelines on Disability and the Duty to Accommodate," Ontario Human Rights Commission (December, 2009), www.ohrc.on.ca/en/resources/Policies/PolicyDisAccom2/pdf (accessed September 26, 2011).

11. British Columbia (Public Service Employee Relations Commission) v. BCGSEU, [1999] 3 S.C.R. 3 at para. 68.

12. According to the US National Library of Medicine, www.ncbi.nlm.nih.gov/pubmedhealth/PMH0001295.

13. "Disability and the Duty to Accommodate: Your Rights and Responsibilities," Ontario Human Rights Commission, www.ohrc.on.ca/en/issues/disability (accessed November 23, 2011).

14. J.R. Smith, "Bipolar Employee Awarded $80,000" *Canadian HR Reporter* (April 7, 2008); C. Hall, "Just Because You Can't See Them Doesn't Mean They're Not There: 'Invisible Disabilities,'" *Ultimate HR Manual*, 34 (March 2008), pp. 1–3; "Duty to Accommodate Mental Health Disability Upheld in Landmark Ontario Human Rights Decision," *Ultimate HR Manual*, 33 (February 2008), p. 6.

15. According to the Supreme Court Ruling by Brian Dickson Chief Justice of Canadia, Janzen v. Platy Enterprises Ltd., 1989.

16. S. Klie, "Harassment Twice as Bad for Minority Women," *Canadian HR Reporter* (April 10, 2006).

17. S. Dobson, "Tackling the Bullies," *Canadian HR Reporter* (March 9, 2009).

18. B. Kuretzky, "When Push Comes to Shove," *Workplace News* (November/December 2005), p. 22; U. Vu, "Employers Waiting for Courts to Define Bullying," *Canadian HR Reporter* (September 12, 2005), pp. 1, 13.

19. "Saskatchewan's Anti-Bullying Law Now in Effect," *Canadian HR Reporter* (October 4, 2007); S. Rudner, "Psychological Harassment Hurts Employees, Productivity," *Canadian HR Reporter* (October 21, 2007).

20. J.R. Smith, "Employers: Don't Let Workplace Harassment Catch You Off Guard," *Canadian HR Reporter* (October 22, 2007); *Anti-Harassment Policies for the Workplace: An Employer's Guide* (Canadian Human Rights Commission, March 2006), p. 3.

21. J.R. Smith, "Employer's Damage Control Leads to Big-Time Damages," *Canadian HR Reporter* (June 1, 2009); "Employer Vicariously Liable for Supervisor's Abusive Conduct," *Ultimate HR Manual*, 49 (June 2009), p. 7.

22. A.P. Aggarwal, *Sexual Harassment in the Workplace*, 2nd ed. (Toronto, ON: Butterworths Canada, 1992), pp. 10–11.

23. N.C. MacDonald, "Keeping the Bedroom out of the Boardroom," *Canadian HR Reporter* (October 22, 2007).

24. *Anti-Harassment Policies for the Workplace: An Employer's Guide* (Canadian Human Rights Commission, March 2006), pp. 16–25.

25. "Construction Firms Fight B.C. Human Rights Ruling," *HR Professional* (April/May 2009), p. 13.

26. S. Klie, "Muslims Face Discrimination in Workplace," *Canadian HR Reporter* (February 27, 2006).

27. "Key Provisions of Ottawa's Same-Sex Legislation," *Canadian HR Reporter* (March 27, 2000), p. 11.

28. Canadian Human Rights Commission, www.chrc-ccdp.ca/adr/settlements/archives2/page5-en.asp (accessed August 13, 2006).

29. Canadian Human Rights Commission, www.chrc-ccdp.ca/discrimination/age-en.asp (accessed August 13, 2006).

30. Ontario Human Rights Commission, www.ohrc.on.ca/english/publicatoins/age-policy_5.shtml (accessed June 2, 2006).

31. A.B. Bakan and A. Kobyashi, *Employment Equity Policy in Canada: An Interprovincial Comparison* (Ottawa, ON: Status of Women Canada, March 2000), pp. 9–10.

32. Statistics Canada. Table 282-0008 - Labour force survey estimates (LFS), by North American Industry Classification System (NAICS), sex and age group, annual.

33. *Women in Canada: Work Chapter Updates*, Statistics Canada, Catalogue No. 89F0133XIE, 2006.

34. S. Klie, "Feds Discriminated Against Nurses," *Canadian HR Reporter* (February 25, 2008).

35. K.A. Zavitz, "Intolerance Costly Problem for Employers," *Canadian HR Reporter* (December 15, 2008).

36. C. Williams, "Disability in the Workplace," *Perspectives on Labour and Income* 7, no. 2 (February 2006), pp. 16–23.

37. S. Klie, "Senior HR Designation Unveiled," *Canadian HR Reporter* (July 7, 2009).

38. "2006 Census: Ethnic Origin, Visible Minorities, Place of Work and Mode of Transportation," Statistics Canada (April 2, 2008), www.statcan.gc.ca/daily-quotidien/080402/dq080402a-eng.htm (accessed September 26, 2011).

39. Barbage, Maria, "Ottawa-based Company Fined $8,000 for Telling Job Applicants It 'only Hires White Men'" *Legal Post*, September 9, 2014.

40. W. Cukier and M. Yap, *DiverseCity Counts: A Snapshot of Diversity in the Greater Toronto Area*. (Toronto, ON: The Diversity Institute, Ryerson University, May 2009).

41. Galarneau, D., and Fecteau, E. Statistics Canada. 2014. *The ups and downs of minimum wage*, Catalogue no. 75-006-X.

42. Statistics Canada, *Study: Enterprises with employees in many provinces or territories, 2001 to 2011*, http://www.statcan.gc.ca/daily-quotidien/140905/dq140905d-eng.htm (accessed September 12, 2014).

43. P. Israel, "Employee Misconduct … Employer Responsibility?" *Canadian HR Reporter* (May 20, 2002), p. 5.

44. P. Israel, "Spying on Employees … and It's Perfectly Legal," *Canadian HR Reporter* (April 21, 2003), p. 5.

45. M. Draaisma, "Computer Use Policy in Workplace Is a Must, Says Toronto Lawyer," *Ultimate HR Manual* (May 2009), pp. 1–4.

46. A.P. Cleek, "Six Steps to an Effective Workplace Blogging Policy," *Ultimate HR Manual* (August 2007), pp. 6–7.

47. E. Kuzz, "More Rules for Employee Information Protection," *Canadian HR Reporter* (September 9, 2002), p. 16; D. Brown, "10 Months to Get Ready," *Canadian HR Reporter* (February 24, 2003), pp. 1, 11.

48. D. Fallows, "Technology Paves the Way for Big Brother," *Canadian HR Reporter* (April 9, 2007).

49. K. Williams, "Privacy in a Climate of Electronic Surveillance," *Workplace News* (April 2005), p. 10; S. Hood, "What's Private, What's Not?" *HR Professional* (February/March 2006), pp. 20–28; P. Strazynski, "Falsely Accused Employee Gets $2.1 Million," *Canadian HR Reporter* (July 14, 2008).

Chapter 3

1. Timothy Appel, "Better Off a Blue-Collar," *The Wall Street Journal*, July 1, 2003, p. B-1.

2. Statistics Canada. *Table 281-0023 - Employment (SEPH), unadjusted for seasonal variation, by type of employee for selected industries classified using the North American Industry Classification System (NAICS), monthly (persons)*, CANSIM (database).

3. Canada. Department of Finance. "The State of the Canadian Labour Market" (2014). Cat No.: F1-23/3-2014E.

4. See "Charting the Projections: 2010–2020," *Occupational Outlook Quarterly* (Winter 2011). www.bls.gov/ooq/2011/winter/winter2011ooq.pdf, www.bls.gov/emp/optd/optd003.pdf, accessed July 29, 2012.

5. Moshiri, S., & Simpson, W. (2011). Information technology and the changing workplace in canada: Firm-level evidence. Industrial and Corporate Change, 20(6), 1601. Retrieved from http://search.proquest.com/docview/910801457?accountid=11233

6. Gouveia, Aaron. "2013 Wasting Time at Work Survey." Salary.com. Retrieved from http://www.salary.com/2013-wasting-time-at-work-survey/slide/6/.

7. Canada. Health Canada. "Reducing Work-Life Conflict: What Works? What Doesn't?" January 2008. Retrieved from http://hc-sc.gc.ca/ewh-semt/pubs/occup-travail/balancing-equilibre/index-eng.php#a13.

8. See, for example, "Engine of Change," *Workforce Management*, July 17, 2006, pp. 20–30.

9. Moncarz and Reaser, "The 2010 Job Outlook in Brief."

10. Richard Crawford, *In the Era of Human Capital* (New York: Harper Business, 1991), p. 26; Russell Crook et al., "Does Human Capital Matter? A Meta-Analysis of the Relationship Between Human Capital and Firm Performance," *Journal of Applied Psychology* 96, no. 3 (2011), pp. 443–456.

11. Peter Drucker, "The Coming of the New Organization," *Harvard Business Review*, January–February 1998, p. 45. See also James Guthrie et al., "Correlates and Consequences of High Involvement Work Practices: The Role of Competitive Strategy," *International Journal of Human Resource Management*, February 2002, pp. 183–197.

12. Society for Human Resource Management, "Workforce Readiness and the New Essential Skills," *Workplace Visions*, no. 2 (2008), p. 5.

13. "Companies Continue to Invest in HR Technology to Manage Workforce, Towers Perrin Reports." www.hrtools.com/training_performance/companies_continue_to_invest_in_hr_technology_to_manage_workforce_towers_perrin_reports.aspx (accessed August 26, 2008); Towers Perrin, www.towersperrin.com (accessed August 20, 2008).

14. Lejeune, Tristan. "Technology: Technology Pushing HR Delivery Changes." Employee Benefit News 27.13 (2013): 26. ProQuest. Web. 9 Dec. 2014."; O'Grady, John. "Outlook for Human Resources in the ICT Labour Market, 2011-2016." Information and Communications Technology Council. March 2011. From http://www.ictc-ctic.ca/wp-content/uploads/2012/06/ICTC_Outlook2011_EN_11-11.pdf.

15. S. Shrivastava and J.B. Shaw, "Liberating HR through Technology," *Human Resource Management* (Fall 2003), p. 201.

16. W.J. Jones and R.C. Hoell, "Human Resource Information System Courses: An Examination of Instructional Methods," *Journal of Information Systems Education* (Fall 2005), p. 321.

17. A.S. Targowski and S.P. Deshpande, "The Utility and Selection of an HRIS," *Advances in Competitiveness Research* (Autumn 2001), p. 42.

18. S. Shrivastava and J.B. Shaw, "Liberating HR through Technology," *Human Resource Management* (Fall 2003), p. 201.

19. R. Zampetti and L. Adamson, "Web-Based Employee Self-Service: A Win–Win Proposition for Organizations and Employees," in A.J. Walker (ed.), *Web-Based Human Resources* (New York, NY: McGraw-Hill, 2001), p. 15.

20. P. Vernon, "Delivering on the Promise of HR Transformation" (November 29, 2004), www.humanresourcesmagazine.com.au/articles/CB/0C0293CB.asp?Type=61&Category=872 (accessed August 20, 2009).

21. Ibid.

22. J. Schramm, "HR Technology Competencies: New Roles for HR Professionals," *2006 SHRM Research Quarterly*, p. 2.

23. P. Vernon, "Delivering on the Promise of HR Transformation" (November 29, 2004), www.humanresourcesmagazine.com.au/articles/CB/0C0293CB.asp?Type=61&Category=872 (accessed August 20, 2009).

24. J. Collison, "2005 HR Technology Survey Report," SHRM Research, p. vii.

25. "HRIS for the HRIS Professional: What You Need to Know," *HR Focus* (June 2005), pp. 10–11.

26. S. Shrivastava and J.B. Shaw, "Liberating HR through Technology," *Human Resource Management* (Fall 2003), p. 201.

27. J. Johnston, "What Does It Take to Put in an HRMS?" *Canadian HR Reporter* (October 22, 2001), p. G3.

28. A. Doran, "HRMS in the New Millennium: What Will the Next 10 years Bring Us and What Is the International Perspective?" in *21 Tomorrows New Formula: Concept-Driven Innovation through Strategic HR* (2000), pp. 29–35.

29. W.J. Jones and R.C. Hoell, "Human Resource Information System Courses: An Examination of Instructional Methods," *Journal of Information Systems Education* (Fall 2005), pp. 321–329

30. A.R. Hendrickson, "Human Resource Information Systems: Backbone Technology of Contemporary Human Resources," *Journal of Labor Research* (Summer 2003), p. 381.

31. M.J. Kavanaugh and M. Thite, *Human Resource Information Systems* (Thousand Oaks, CA: Sage Publications, 2009).

32. Ibid.

33. E.W.T. Ngai and F.K.T. Wat, "Human Resource Information Systems: A Review and Empirical Analysis," Department of Management and Marketing, The Hong Kong Polytechnic University (July 7, 2004), p. 297.

34. R. Zampetti and L. Adamson, "Web-Based Employee Self-Service: A Win–Win Proposition for Organizations and Employees," in A.J. Walker (ed.), *Web-Based Human Resources* (New York, NY: McGraw-Hill, 2001), p. 15.

35. M. Mayfield, "Human Resource Information Systems: A Review and Model Development," *Advances in Competitiveness Research* (January 1, 2003), pp. 139–152.

36. A.R. Hendrickson, "Human Resource Information Systems: Backbone Technology of Contemporary Human Resources," *Journal of Labor Research* (Summer 2003), p. 381.

37. J. Sullivan, "The Six Levels of HRIS Technology," in R.H. Stambaugh (ed.), *21 Tomorrows: HR Systems in the Emerging Workplace of the 21st Century* (Dallas, TX: Rector Duncan & Associates, 2000), pp. 79–86.

38. J.W. Boudreau, "Talentship and HR Measurement and Analysis: From ROI to Strategic Organizational Change," *Human Resource Planning* (2006), p. 30.

39. G. Safran, "Getting the I out of your HRIS," *Canadian HR Reporter* (February 26, 2001), p. 21.

40. J. Schramm, "HR Technology Competencies: New Roles for HR Professionals," *2006 SHRM Research Quarterly*, (2006) p. 2.

41. See Brian Becker and Mark Huselid, "Measuring HR? Benchmarking Is Not the Answer!" *HR Magazine* 8, no. 12 (December 2003), www.charmed.org, accessed February 2, 2008.

42. Ibid.

43. George Marakas, *Decision Support Systems* (Upper Saddle River, NJ: Prentice Hall, 2003), p. 326.

44. A.S. Targowski and S.P. Deshpande, "The Utility and Selection of an HRIS," *Advances in Competitiveness Research* (Autumn 2001), p. 42.

45. "HR Execs Trade Notes on Human Resource Information Systems," *BNA Bulletin to Management* (December 3, 1998), p. 1. See also Brian Walter, "But They Said Their Payroll Program Complied with the FLSA," *Public Personnel Management* 31, no. 1 (Spring 2002), pp. 79–94.

46. "HR Execs Trade Notes on Human Resource Information Systems," *BNA Bulletin to Management* (December 3, 1998), p. 2. See also Ali Velshi, "Human Resources Information," *The Americas Intelligence Wire* (February 11, 2004).

47. Connie Winkler, "Quality Check: Better Metrics Improve HR's Ability to Measure— and Manage—the Quality of Hires," *HR Magazine* 52, no. 5 (May 2007), pp. 93–94, 96, 98.

48. Ibid.

49. John Zonneveld, "GM Dealer Training Goes Global," *Training & Development*, December 2006, pp. 47–51. See also "What's Next for the LMS?" *Training & Development*, September 2011, p. 16.

50. "The Next Generation of Corporate Learning," *Training & Development*, June 2003, p. 47.

51. Ibid.

52. For a list of guidelines for using e-learning, see, for example, Mark Simon, "E-Learning No How," *Training & Development*, January 2009, pp. 34–39.

53. Human Resources and Social Development Canada, "Employment Equity Computerized Reporting System (EECRS) Software," www.hrsdc.gc.ca/asp/gateway.asp?hr=en/lp/lo/lswe/we/ee_tools/software/eecrs/index-we.shtml&hs=wzp (accessed August 17, 2006).

54. However, one study concludes that Web-based performance management systems don't seem to improve performance management system effectiveness. Edward Lawler III et al., "What Makes Performance Appraisals Effective?" *Compensation & Benefits Review* 44, no. 4 (2012), p. 196.

55. www.employeeappraiser.com/index.php, accessed January 10, 2008.

56. "Companies Aim to Transform HR Delivery Strategy to Meet New Employee Needs, Watson Wyatt Study Finds," www.watsonwyatt.com/news/press.asp?ID=17525 (accessed August 20, 2009).

57. Lisa Cullen, "Safety Committees: A Smart Business Decision," *Occupational Hazards*, May 1999, pp. 99–104. See also www.osha.gov/Publications/osha2098.pdf, accessed May 26, 2007; and D. Kolman, "Effective Safety Committees," *Beverage Industry* 100, no. 3 (March 2009), pp. 63–65.

58. www.aihaaps.ca/palm/occhazards.html, accessed April 26, 2009.

59. Jagger, Stephen, April 11, 2014, Krisply Kreme Philippenes Chooses Payrollhero.ph http://blog.payrollhero.com/2014/04/11/krispy-kreme-philippines-chooses-payrollhero/last accessed Dec 18, 2014.

60. Michael Blotzer, "PDA Software Offers Auditing Advances," *Occupational Hazards*, December 2001, p. 11.

61. John Garber, "Introduction to the Human Resource Discipline of Safety and Security," www.shrm.org/templates_tools/toolkits, accessed May 27, 2012.

62. Mike Powell, "Sustaining Your Safety Sweep Audit Process," *EHS Today*, December 2012, pp. 35–36.

63. Lin Grensing-Pophal, "HR Audits: Know the Market, Land Assignments," SHRM Consultants Forum, December 2004, www.shrm .org/-hrdisciplines/consultants/Articles/Pages/CMS_010705.aspx, accessed July 7, 2010.

64. Grensing-Pophal, "HR Audits: Know the Market"; and Bill Coy, "Introduction to the Human Resources Audit," La Piana Associates, Inc., www.lapiana.org/consulting, accessed May 1, 2008.

65. Dana R. Scott, "Conducting a Human Resources Audit," *New Hampshire Business Review*, August 2007. See also Eric Krell, "Auditing Your HR Department," *HR Magazine*, September 2011, pp. 101–103.

66. Ed Frauenheim, "Keeping Score with Analytics Software," *Workforce Management* 86, no. 10 (May 21, 2007), pp. 25–33. See also Andrew McAfee and Eric Brynjolfsson, "Big Data: The Management Revolution," *Harvard Business Review*, October 2012, pp. 61–68.

67. Steven Baker, "Data Mining Moves to Human Resources," *Bloomberg Businessweek*, March 12, 2009, www.BusinessWeek.com/magazine/, accessed April 13, 2011.

68. Baker, op cit. See also "HR Analytics," *Workforce Management*, August 2012, p. 24.

69. Ed Frauenheim, "Numbers Game," *Workforce Management* 90, no. 3 (March 2011), p. 21.

70. Thomas Davenport, Jeanne Harris, and Jeremy Shapiro, "Competing on Talent Analytics," *Harvard Business Review*, October 2010, pp. 52–58.

71. Cliff Stevenson, "Five Ways High Performance Organizations Use HR Analytics," www.i4cp.com/print/trendwatchers/2012/12/12/fiveways-high-performance-organizations-use-hranalytics, accessed July 14, 2013.

72. Ibid., p. 54.

73. S. Shrivastava and J.B. Shaw, "Liberating HR through Technology," *Human Resource Management* (Fall 2003), pp. 201–215.

74. A.R. Hendrickson, "Human Resource Information Systems: Backbone Technology of Contemporary Human Resources," *Journal of Labor Research* (Summer 2003), p. 381.

75. "Bridgefield Group ERP/Supply Chain Glossary," http://bridgefieldgroup.com/bridgefieldgroup/glos2.htm (accessed June 29, 2006).

76. Halogen Software, www.halogensoftware.com (accessed June 29, 2006).

77. S. Shrivastava and J.B. Shaw, "Liberating HR through Technology," *Human Resource Management* (Fall 2003), pp. 201–215; J.G. Meade, *The Human Resources Software Handbook* (San Francisco, CA: Jossey-Bass/Pfeiffer, 2003), p. 85.

78. J.G. Meade, *The Human Resources Software Handbook* (San Francisco, CA: Jossey-Bass/Pfeiffer, 2003), p. 85.

79. J.C. Hubbard, K.A. Forcht, and D.S. Thomas, "Human Resource Information Systems: An Overview of Current Ethical and Legal Issues," *Journal of Business Ethics* (September 1998), pp. 1320–1321.

80. K.A. Kovach, A.A. Hughes, P. Fagan, and P.G. Maggitti, "Administrative and Strategic Advantages of HRIS," *Employment Relations Today* (Summer 2002), p. 46.

81. J. Caplan, "eHR in Greater China: The Future of HR Takes Flight," *China Staff* (March 2004), p. 3.

82. B. Jorgensen, "eHR Is Playing a Larger Role in Corporate Communications, but Companies Must Make a Business for Additional Spending," *Electronic Business* (August 2002), p. 36.

83. R. Zampetti and L. Adamson, "Web-Based Employee Self-Service: A Win–Win Proposition for Organizations and Employees," in A.J. Walker (ed.), *Web-Based Human Resources*. (New York, NY: McGraw-Hill, 2001), p. 15; H.C. Gueutal and D.L. Stone, *The Brave New World of eHR* (San Francisco, CA: Jossey-Bass, 2005), p. 192.

84. R. Zampetti and L. Adamson, "Web-Based Employee Self-Service: A Win–Win Proposition for Organizations and Employees," in A.J. Walker (ed.), *Web-Based Human Resources* (New York, NY: McGraw-Hill, 2001), p. 15.

85. "Do More to Get More from HR Systems," *HR Focus* (June 2006), p. 3.

86. Ibid.

87. T.J. Keebler and D.W. Rhodes, "E-HR Becoming the 'Path of Least Resistance,'" *Employment Relations Today* (Summer 2002), pp. 57–58.

88. D. Brown, "eHR—Victim of Unrealistic Expectations," *Canadian HR Reporter* (March 11, 2002), p. 2.

89. J. Collison, "2005 HR Technology Survey Report," *SHRM Research*, pp. 3–4.

90. S. Shrivastava and J.B. Shaw, "Liberating HR through Technology," *Human Resource Management* (Fall 2003), p. 205.

Chapter 4

1. "Three-fourths of HR pros use job analysis data for recruitment" reterived from http://www.staffingindustry.com/Research-Publications/Daily-News/Three-fourths-of-HR-pros-use-job-analysis-data-for-recruitment-32515.

2. Ibid.

3. Ibid.

4. Ibid.

5. Ibid.

6. Ibid.

7. R. I. Henderson (ed.), *Compensation Management in a Knowledge-Based World* (Upper Saddle River, NJ: Prentice-Hall, 2003), pp. 135–138.; See also P.W. Wright and K. Wesley, "How to Choose the Kind of Job Analysis You Really Need," *Personnel*, 62 (May 1985), pp. 51–55; C.J. Cranny and M.E. Doherty, "Importance Ratings in Job Analysis: Note on the Misinterpretation of Factor Analyses," *Journal of Applied Psychology* (May 1988), pp. 320–322.

8. J. Heerwagen, K. Kelly, and K. Kampschroer, "The Changing Nature of Organizations, Work, and Workplace," *Whole Building Design Group (WBDG), National Institute of Building Sciences* (February 2006).

9. C. Babbage, *On the Economy of Machinery and Manufacturers* (London: Charles Knight, 1832), pp. 169–176; reprinted in Joseph Litterer, *Organizations* (New York: John Wiley and Sons, 1969), pp. 73–75.

10. F. Herzberg, "One More Time, How Do You Motivate Employees?" *Harvard Business Review*, 46 (January–February 1968), pp. 53–62.

11. Next two sections based on Jeffrey Shippmann et al., "The Practice of Competency Modeling," *Personnel Psychology*, 53, no. 3 (2000), p. 703; P. Singh, "Job Analysis for a Changing Workplace," *Human Resource Management Review*, 18 (2008), pp. 87–99.

12. Adapted from Richard Mirabile, "Everything You Wanted to Know About Competency Modeling," *Training and Development,* 51, no. 8 (August 1997), pp. 73–78.

13. Dennis Kravetz, "Building a Job Competency Database: What the Leaders Do," Kravetz Associates (Bartlett, Illinois, 1997).

14. G.M. Parker, *Cross-Functional Teams: Working with Allies, Enemies and Other Strangers* (San Francisco: Jossey-Bass, 2003), p. 68.

15. "Collaboration for Virtual Teams," *HR Professional* (December 2002/January 2003), p. 44.

16. Note that the PAQ (and other quantitative techniques) can also be used for job evaluation.

17. E. Cornelius III, F. Schmidt, and T. Carron, "Job Classification Approaches and the Implementation of Validity Generalization Results," *Personnel Psychology*, 37 (Summer 1984), pp. 247–260; E. Cornelius III, A. DeNisi, and A. Blencoe, "Expert and Naïve Raters Using the PAQ: Does It Matter?"

Personnel Psychology, 37 (Autumn 1984), pp. 453–464; L. Friedman and R. Harvey, "Can Raters with Reduced Job Description Information Provide Accurate Position Analysis Questionnaire (PAQ) Ratings?" *Personnel Psychology,* 34 (Winter 1986), pp. 779–789; R. J. Harvey et al., "Dimensionality of the Job Element Inventory: A Simplified Worker-Oriented Job Analysis Questionnaire," *Journal of Applied Psychology* (November 1988), pp. 639–646; S. Butler and R. Harvey, "A Comparison of Holistic versus Decomposed Rating of Position Analysis Questionnaire Work Dimensions," *Personnel Psychology* (Winter 1988), pp. 761–772.

18. This discussion is based on H. Olson et al., "The Use of Functional Job Analysis in Establishing Performance Standards for Heavy Equipment Operators," *Personnel Psychology,* 34 (Summer 1981), pp. 351–364.

19. Human Resources Development Canada, *National Occupation Classification Career Handbook,* (2006).

20. Grant, Adam M., Berg, Justin M., Cable, Daniel M. "Job Titles As Identity Badges: How Self-Reflective Titles Can Reduce Emotional Exhaustion." *Academy of Management Journal* 2014, Vol. 57, No. 4, 1201–1225.

21. R. J. Plachy, "Writing Job Descriptions That Get Results," *Personnel* (October 1987), pp. 56–58. See also M. Mariani, "Replace with a Database," *Occupational Outlook Quarterly,* 43 (Spring 1999), pp. 2–9.

22. J. Evered, "How to Write a Good Job Description," *Supervisory Management* (April 1981), p. 16.

23. Ibid, p. 18.

24. P.H. Raymark, M.J. Schmidt, and R.M. Guion, "Identifying Potentially Useful Personality Constructs for Employee Selection," *Personnel Psychology* 50 (1997), pp. 723–726.

Chapter 5

1. *Performance and Potential 2000–2001: Seeking Made in Canada Solutions* (Ottawa, ON: Conference Board of Canada, 2000), p. 51.

2. HRSDC, Looking Ahead: A 10-Year Outlook for the Canadian Labour Market (2006–2015), Statistics Canada, January 29, 2007, www.hrsdc.gc.ca/eng/publications_resources/research/categories/labour_market_e/sp_615_10_06/supply.shtml (accessed September 26, 2011).

3. S. Klie, "Guesses Just Don't Cut It Anymore," *Canadian HR Reporter* (March 24, 2008).

4. Martin, Heidi, and Richard Brisbois. *HR Trends and Metrics, Third Edition: The Canadian Context for Strategic Workforce Planning.* Ottawa: The Conference Board of Canada, 2014.

5. Ibid.

6. Ibid.

7. Ibid.

8. Ibid.

9. Ibid.

10. Ibid.

11. Ibid.

12. Ibid.

13. This is a modification of a definition found in P. Wallum, "A Broader View of Succession Planning," *Personnel Management* (September 1993), pp. 43–44.

14. "Succession Planning for Family Business," BDO Canada (September 12, 2010), www.bdo.ca/library/publications/familybusiness/succession/planning1.cfm (accessed September 26, 2011).

15. HRSDC, Looking Ahead: A 10-Year Outlook for the Canadian Labour Market (2006–2015), Statistics Canada, (January 29, 2007), www.hrsdc.gc.ca/eng/publications_resources/research/categories/labour_market_e/sp_615_10_06/supply.shtml (accessed September 26, 2011).

16. Berthiaume, Lee. "Canadian Air Force Bending on Medical Requirements to Deal with Experienced Pilot Shortage." *National Post,* January 3, 2013.; Campion-Smith, Bruce. "Air Force Hiring Foreign Pilots to Fly Front-line Jets." *The Toronto Star,* June 23, 2014.

17. A. Coughlin, *Alberta's Labour Shortage Just the Tip of the Iceberg* (Conference Board of Canada Executive Action, 2006); G. Hodgson and G. McGowan, "Taking Sides: Is Alberta's Labour Shortage a Doomsday Scenario?" *Canadian HR Reporter* (July 17, 2006); P. Brethour, "Oil Patch Labour Crisis Seen Spreading to Rest of Country; "Husky Head Raises Alarm Over Rising Costs, Saying Projects at Risk," *Globe and Mail* (April 20, 2006), http://www.theglobeandmail.com/report-on-business/oil-patchlabour-crisis-seen-spreading-to-rest-of-country/article707140/ (accessed September 9, 2012).

18. "Mining Industry Needs 80,000 Workers," *Canadian HR Reporter* (March 26, 2007), p. 2; S. Klie, "Construction Demand Outpaces Labour Growth," *Canadian HR Reporter* (September 10, 2007); "Non-profits Facing Labour Shortage," *Canadian HR Reporter* (July 9, 2007); U. Vu, "Mounties Prepare For Recruiting Spree," *Canadian HR Reporter* (October 23, 2006); "Manufacturing Sector Labours to Address Human Resources Issues," Conference Board of Canada, *InsideEdge* (Spring 2008), p. 18; S. Klie, "Short Circuiting Labour Supply," *Canadian HR Reporter* (December 15, 2008).

19. *Canadian Perspectives on ICT Outsourcing and Offshoring* (Toronto ON: IDC, 2007); S. Klie, "IT Offshoring Growing," *Canadian HR Reporter* (October 22, 2007); L. Young, "IT University Enrolment Plunges," *Canadian HR Reporter* (December 3, 2007); S; Klie, "Price Tag of IT Shortage: $10 Billion Per Year," *Canadian HR Reporter* (February 11, 2008); S. Klie, "Women Could Solve IT Worker Shortage," *Canadian HR Reporter* (October 20, 2008).

20. H. Sokoloff, "Legal Exodus," *National Post* (March 17, 2005), p. FP3; "Baby Boomers an HR Problem for Funeral Services," *Canadian HR Reporter* (January 16, 2006), p. 2; "Today's Forecast: Meteorologist Shortage," *Canadian HR Reporter* (December 5, 2005), p. 2; "Engineers in Short Supply," *Canadian HR Reporter* (November 21, 2005), p. 2; S. Klie, "Fewer Accountants Is a Bad Thing—Really," *Canadian HR Reporter* (February 13, 2006), p. 3; "Alberta Labour Shortage Draining Civil Service," *Canadian HR Reporter* (January 30, 2006), p. 2.

21. A.L. Delbecq, A.H. Van DelVen, and D.H. Gustafson, *Group Techniques for Program Planning: A Guide to Nominal and Delphi Processes* (Glenview, IL: Scott Foresman, 1975).

22. G. Milkovich, A.J. Annoni, and T.A. Mahoney, "The Use of Delphi Procedures in Manpower Forecasting," *Management Science* (1972), pp. 381–388.

23. "Feds Help Employers Avoid Layoffs," *HR Professional* (June/July 2009), p. 12.

24. W.F. Cascio and C.E. Young, "Financial Consequences of Employment Change Decisions in Major U.S. Corporations: 1982–2000," in K.P. DeMeuse and M.L. Marks (eds.), *Resizing the Organization,* pp. 131–156 (San Francisco, CA: Jossey-Bass, 2003).

25. M. MacKillop, "Ballpark Justice," *Human Resources Professional* (September 1994), pp. 10–11.

Chapter 6

1. "Effective Recruiting Tied to Stronger Financial Performance," *WorldatWork Canadian News* (Fourth Quarter, 2005), pp. 18–19.

2. K. Peters, "Public Image Ltd," *HR Professional* (December 2007/January 2008), pp. 24–30; S. Klie, "Getting Employees to Come to You," *Canadian HR Reporter* (November 19, 2007), pp. 9–10; S. Klie, "Tuning into TV's Recruitment Reach," *Canadian HR Reporter* (September 25, 2006).

3. G. Bouchard, "Strong Employer Brand Can Tap Scarce Resource: Talent," *Canadian HR Reporter* (November 19, 2007), p. 10.

4. K. Peters, "Public Image Ltd," *HR Professional* (December 2007/January 2008), pp. 24–30; G. Bouchard, "Strong Employer Brand Can Tap Scarce Resource: Talent," *Canadian HR Reporter* (November 19, 2007), p. 10; M. Morra, "Best in Show," *Workplace News* (September/October 2006), pp. 17–21; M. Shuster, "Employment Branding: The Law of Attraction!" *Workplace* (January/February 2008), pp. 14–15.

5. K. Peters, "Public Image Ltd," *HR Professional* (December 2007/January 2008), pp. 24–30; S. Klie, "Getting Employees to Come to You," *Canadian HR Reporter* (November 19, 2007), pp. 9–10.

6. S. Klie, "Getting Employees to Come to You," *Canadian HR Reporter* (November 19, 2007), pp. 9–10; M. Shuster, "Employment Branding: The Law of Attraction!" *Workplace* (January/February 2008), pp. 14–15.

7. A. Watanabe, "From Brown to Green, What Colour Is Your Employment Brand?" *HR Professional* (February/March 2008), pp. 47–49.

8. M. Morra, "Best in Show," *Workplace News* (September/October 2006), pp. 17–21.

9. R. Milgram, "Getting the Most Out of Online Job Ads," *Canadian HR Reporter* (January 28, 2008).

10. "Recruitment Tops HR Areas Expecting 'Enormous Change,'" *Canadian HR Reporter* (December 6, 2004), p. G3; *Hewitt Associates Timely Topic Survey* (February 2004).

11. L. Petrecca, "With 3000 Job Applications a Day, Google Can Be Picky," *USA Today* (May 18, 2010), (accessed September 9, 2012). www.usatoday.com/money/workplace/2010-05-19-jobs19_VA_N.htm

12. D. Dahl and P. Pinto, "Job Posting, an Industry Survey," *Personnel Journal* (January 1977), pp. 40–41.

13. J. Daum, "Internal Promotion—Psychological Asset or Debit? A Study of the Effects of Leader Origin," *Organizational Behavior and Human Performance*, 13 (1975), pp. 404–413.

14. See, for example, A. Harris, "Hiring Middle Management: External Recruitment or Internal Promotion?" *Canadian HR Reporter* (April 10, 2000), pp. 8–10.

15. A. Doran, "Technology Brings HR to Those Who Need It," *Canadian HR Reporter* (October 6, 1997), p. 8.

16. M. Sharma, "Welcome Back!" *HR Professional* (February/March 2006), pp. 38–40; E. Simon, "You're Leaving the Company? Well, Don't Be a Stranger," *Globe and Mail* (December 22, 2006), p. B16.

17. Retrieved from "Our Story." Career Edge Organization. https://careeredge.ca/en/about/history.

18. Career Edge, www.careeredge.ca (accessed May 31, 2009).

19. N. Laurie and M. Laurie, "No Holds Barred in Fight for Students to Fill Internship Programs," *Canadian HR Reporter* (January 17, 2000), pp. 15–16.

20. Dobson, Sarah. "Human Resources Professionals Sour on Unpaid Internships: Survey." *Canadian Reporter*, April 7, 2014.

21. Ibid.

22. Ibid.

23. Sagan, Aleksandra. "Unpaid Internships Exploit 'vulnerable Generation'" CBC News. July 2, 2013. From http://www.cbc.ca/news/canada/unpaid-internships-exploit-vulnerable-generation-1.1332839.

24. Tomlinson, Kathy. "Intern's Death after Overnight Shift Sparks Outcry." CBC News. September 10, 2013. From http://www.cbc.ca/news/canada/british-columbia/intern-s-death-after-overnight-shift-sparks-outcry-1.1704532.

25. Kennedy, Maev. "Bank Intern Moritz Erhardt Died from Epileptic Seizure, Inquest Told." The Guardian. November 22, 2013. From http://www.theguardian.com/business/2013/nov/22/moritz-erhardt-merrill-lynch-intern-dead-inquest.

26. Halifax Career Fair. Retrieved from http://www.halifaxcareerfair.ca/.

27. Human Resources Professionals Association of Ontario, www.hrpao.org (accessed June 25, 2003).

28. D. Hurl, "Letting the Armed Forces Train Your Managers," *Canadian HR Reporter* (December 3, 2001), pp. 8–9.

29. L. Blake, "Ready-Trained, Untapped Source of Skilled Talent—Courtesy Canadian Forces," *Workplace*, www.workplace-mag.com (accessed December 2, 2008).

30. U. Vu, "Security Failures Expose Résumés," *Canadian HR Reporter* (May 24, 2003); P. Lima, "Talent Shortage? That Was Yesterday. Online Recruiters Can Deliver More Candidates for Your Job Openings and Help You Find Keepers," *Profit: The Magazine for Canadian Entrepreneurs* (February/

March 2002), pp. 65–66; "Online Job Boards," *Canadian HR Reporter* (February 11, 2002), pp. G11–G15.

31. U. Vu, "Security Failures Expose Résumés," *Canadian HR Reporter* (May 24, 2003).

32. S. Bury, "Face-Based Recruiting," *Workplace* (September/October 2008), pp. 19–21.

33. G. Stanton, "Recruiting Portals Take Centre Stage in Play for Talent," *Canadian HR Reporter* (September 25, 2000), pp. G1–G2.

34. A. da Luz, "Video Enhances Online Job Ads," *Canadian HR Reporter* (February 11, 2008).

35. D. Brown, "Canadian Government Job Boards Lag on Best Practices," *Canadian HR Reporter* (January 13, 2003), p. 2.

36. T. Martell, "Résumé Volumes Push Firms to Web," *ComputerWorld Canada* (April 7, 2000), p. 45.

37. A. Altass, "E-Cruiting: A Gen X Trend or Wave of the Future?" *HR Professional* (June–July 2000), p. 33.

38. "Corporate Spending Millions on Ineffective Web Recruiting Strategies," *Canadian HR Reporter* (September 25, 2000), p. G5.

39. A. Snell, "Best Practices for Web Site Recruiting," *Canadian HR Reporter* (February 26, 2001), pp. G7, G10.

40. S. Bury, "Face-Based Recruiting," *Workplace* (September/October 2008), pp. 19–21.

41. D. Harder, "Recruiting in Age of Social Networking," *Canadian HR Reporter* (April 21, 2008).

42. Service Canada, Job Bank, http://jb-ge.hrdc-drhc.gc.ca (accessed May 31, 2009).

43. W.H. Wiesner and R.J. Oppenheimer, "Note-Taking in the Selection Interview: Its Effect upon Predictive Validity and Information Recall," *Proceedings of the Annual Conference Meeting. Administrative Sciences Association of Canada* (Personnel and Human Resources Division, 1991), pp. 97–106.

44. J.A. Parr, "7 Reasons Why Executive Searches Fail," *Canadian HR Reporter* (March 12, 2001), pp. 20, 23.

45. Association of Canadian Search, Employment and Staffing Services (ACSESS), www.acsess.org (accessed August 8, 2006).

46. Statistics Canada, *The Daily* (April 8, 2005); Association of Canadian Search, Employment and Staffing Services (ACSESS), "Media Kit: Media Fact Sheet," www.acsess.org/NEWS/factsheet.asp (accessed May 31, 2009).

47. T. Lende, "Workplaces Looking to Hire Part-Timers," *Canadian HR Reporter* (April 22, 2002), pp. 9, 11.

48. K. LeMessurier, "Temp Staffing Leaves a Permanent Mark," *Canadian HR Reporter* (February 10, 2003), pp. 3, 8.

49. A. Ryckman, "The 5 Keys to Getting Top Value from Contractors," *Canadian HR Reporter* (December 2, 2002), p. 25; S. Purba, "Contracting Works for Job Hunters," *Globe and Mail* (April 24, 2002).

50. "Flexible Staffing in the Aerospace Industry," *Airfinance Journal I Aircraft Economic Yearbook* (2001), pp. 14–17.

51. M. Potter, "A Golden Opportunity for Older Workers to Energize Firms," *Canadian HR Reporter* (April 25, 2005), p. 13.

52. L. Cassiani, "Looming Retirement Surge Takes on New Urgency," *Canadian HR Reporter* (May 21, 2001), pp. 1, 10.

53. K. Thorpe, *Harnessing the Power: Recruiting, Engaging, and Retaining Mature Workers* . (Ottawa, ON: Conference Board of Canada, 2008).

54. Inclusion Network, www.inclusionnetwork.ca (accessed May 31, 2009); Aboriginal Human Resource Council, http://aboriginalhr.ca (accessed May 31, 2009).

55. Society for Canadian Women in Science and Technology, www.harbour.sfu.ca/scwist/index_files/Page1897.htm (accessed May 31, 2009); C. Emerson, H. Matsui, and L. Michael, "Progress Slow for Women in Trades, Tech, Science," *Canadian HR Reporter* (February 14, 2005), p. 11.

56. WORKInk, www.workink.com (accessed May 31, 2009).

Chapter 7

1. C. Kapel, "Giant Steps," *Human Resources Professional* (April 1993), pp. 13–16.

2. P. Lowry, "The Structured Interview: An Alternative to the Assessment Center?" *Public Personnel Management,* 23, no. 2 (Summer 1994), pp. 201–215.

3. Steps two and three are based on the Kepner-Tregoe Decision-Making Model.

4. S.A. Way and J.W. Thacker, "Selection Practices: Where Are Canadian Organizations?" *HR Professional* (October/November 1999), p. 34.

5. L.J. Katunich, "How to Avoid the Pitfalls of Psych Tests," *Workplace News Online* (July 2005), p. 5; *Testing and Assessment—FAQ/Finding Information About Psychological Tests,* APA Online, www.apa.org/science/faq-findtests. html (accessed August 1, 2006).

6. M. McDaniel et al., "The Validity of Employment Interviews: A Comprehensive Review and Meta-analysis," *Journal of Applied Psychology,* 79, no. 4 (1994).

7. C. Kapel, "Giant Steps," *Human Resources Professional* (April 1993), pp. 13–16.

8. P. Lowry, "The Structured Interview: An Alternative to the Assessment Center?" *Public Personnel Management,* 23, no. 2 (Summer 1994), pp. 201–215.

9. Steps two and three are based on the Kepner-Tregoe Decision-Making Model.

10. Wright, "At Google, It Takes a Village to Hire an Employee."

11. Kevin Delaney, "Google Adjusts Hiring Process as Needs Grow," *The Wall Street Journal,* October 23, 2006, pp. B1, B8; http://googleblog.blogspot. com/2009/01/changesto-recruiting.html, accessed March 25, 2009.

12. S.A. Way and J.W. Thacker, "Selection Practices: Where Are Canadian Organizations?" *HR Professional* (October/November 1999), p. 34.

13. L.J. Katunich, "How to Avoid the Pitfalls of Psych Tests," *Workplace News Online* (July 2005), p. 5; *Testing and Assessment—FAQ/Finding Information About Psychological Tests,* APA Online, www.apa.org/science/faq-findtests. html (accessed August 1, 2006).

14. M. McDaniel et al., "The Validity of Employment Interviews: A Comprehensive Review and Meta-analysis," *Journal of Applied Psychology,* 79, no. 4 (1994).

15. "Hiring: Psychology and Employee Potential," *HR Professional* (August/ September 2008), p. 16.

16. Ibid.

17. S. Bakker, "Psychometric Selection Assessments," *HR Professional* (April/ May 2009), p. 21.

18. Canadian Psychological Association, *Guidelines for Educational and Psychological Testing,* www.cpa.ca/documents/PsyTest.html (accessed May 31, 2009).

19. R.M. Yerkes, "Psychological Examining in the U.S. Army: Memoirs of the National Academy of Sciences," Washington DC: U.S. Government Printing Office, Vol. 15 (1921).

20. F.L. Schmidt and J. Hunter, "General Mental Ability in the World of Work: Occupational Attainment and Job Performance," *Journal of Personality and Social Psychology,* 86, no. 1 (2004), 162–173.

21. M. Zeidner, I. G. Matthews, and R.D. Roberts, "Emotional Intelligence in the Workplace: A Critical Review" *Applied Psychology: An International Review,* 53, no. 3 (2004), pp. 371–399.

22. "Emotional Intelligence Testing," *HR Focus* (October 2001), pp. 8–9.

23. Results of meta-analyses in one recent study indicated that isometric strength tests were valid predictors of both supervisory ratings of physical performance and performance on work simulations. See B.R. Blakley, M. Quinones, M.S. Crawford, and I.A. Jago, "The Validity of Isometric Strength Tests," *Personnel Psychology,* 47 (1994), pp. 247–274.

24. C. Colacci, "Testing Helps You Decrease Disability Costs," *Canadian HR Reporter* (June 14, 1999), p. G4.

25. K. Gillin, "Reduce Employee Exposure to Injury with Pre-Employment Screening Tests," *Canadian HR Reporter* (February 28, 2000), p. 10.

26. This approach calls for construct validation, which, as was pointed out, is extremely difficult to demonstrate.

27. Myers-Briggs Type Indicator (MBTI) Assessment, www.cpp.com/products/ mbti/index.asp (accessed May 31, 2009).

28. See, for example, D. Cellar et al., "Comparison of Factor Structures and Criterion Related Validity Coefficients for Two Measures of Personality Based on the Five-Factor Model," *Journal of Applied Psychology,* 81, no. 6 (1996), pp. 694–704; J. Salgado, "The Five Factor Model of Personality and Job Performance in the European Community," *Journal of Applied Psychology,* 82, no. 1 (1997), pp. 30–43.

29. M.R. Barrick and M.K. Mount, "The Big Five Personality Dimensions and Job Performance: A Meta-Analysis," *Personnel Psychology,* 44 (Spring 1991), pp. 1–26.

30. C. Robie, K. Tuzinski, and P. Bly, "A Survey of Assessor Beliefs and Practices Related to Faking," *Journal of Managerial Psychology* (October 2006), pp. 669–681.

31. C. Robie, "Effects of Perceived Selection Ratio on Personality Test Faking," *Social Behavior and Personality,* 34, no. 10 (2006), 1233–1244.

32. E. Silver and C. Bennett, "Modification of the Minnesota Clerical Test to Predict Performance on Video Display Terminals," *Journal of Applied Psychology,* 72, no. 1 (February 1987), pp. 153–155.

33. L. Siegel and I. Lane, *Personnel and Organizational Psychology* (Homewood, IL: Irwin, 1982), pp. 182–183.

34. J. Weekley and C. Jones, "Video-Based Situational Testing," *Personnel Psychology,* 50 (1997), p. 25.

35. Ibid, pp. 26–30.

36. D. Chan and N. Schmitt, "Situational Judgment and Job Performance," *Human Performance,* 15, no. 3 (2002), pp. 233–254.

37. S. Klie, "Screening Gets More Secure," *Canadian HR Reporter* (June 19, 2006).

38. Canadian Human Rights Commission, *Canadian Human Rights Commission Policy on Alcohol and Drug Testing* (June 2002).

39. Based on Joseph Walker, "Meet the New Boss: Big Data," *The Wall Street Journal,* September 20, 2012, p. B1.

40. Bill Roberts, "Hire Intelligence," *HR Magazine,* May 2011, p. 64.

41. See, for example, Meg Breslin, "Can You Handle Rejection?" *Workforce Management,* October 2012, pp. 32–36

42. M. McDaniel et al., "The Validity of Employment Interviews: A Comprehensive Review and Meta-Analysis," *Journal of Applied Psychology,* 79, no. 4 (1994), p. 599.

43. J.G. Goodale, *The Fine Art of Interviewing* (Englewood Cliffs, NJ: Prentice Hall Inc., 1982), p. 22; see also R.L. Decker, "The Employment Interview," *Personnel Administrator,* 26 (November 1981), pp. 71–73.

44. M. Campion, E. Pursell, and B. Brown, "Structured Interviewing: Raising the Psychometric Properties of the Employment Interview," *Personnel Psychology,* 41 (1988), pp. 25–42.

45. M. McDaniel et al., "The Validity of Employment Interviews: A Comprehensive Review and Meta-Analysis," *Journal of Applied Psychology,* 79, no. 4 (1994).

46. Data from D. S. Chapman, & P. M. Rowe. 2001. "The impact of videoconference technology, interview structure," Journal of Occupational and Organizational Psychology, Vol. 74, p. 279–298. and interviewer gender on interviewer evaluations in the employment interview: A Field experiment. of Occupational and Organizational Psychology, Vol. 74, p. 279–298.

47. D.S. Chapman and P.M. Rowe, "The Impact of Video Conferencing Technology, Interview Structure, and Interviewer Gender on Interviewer Evaluations in the Employment Interview: A Field Experiment," *Journal*

of Occupational and Organizational Psychology, 74 (September 2001), pp. 279–298.

48. M. McDaniel et al., "The Validity of Employment Interviews: A Comprehensive Review and Meta-Analysis," *Journal of Applied Psychology,* 79, no. 4 (1994), p. 601.

49. Ibid.

50. "Lights, Camera…Can I Have a Job?" *Globe and Mail* (March 2, 2007), p. C1; A. Pell, *Recruiting and Selecting Personnel* (New York, NY: Regents, 1969), p. 119.

51. Amy Levin-Epste, "Job Interview Horror Stories". Retrieved from http://www.cbsnews.com/news/job-interview-horror-stories/.

52. Ibid.

53. Ibid.

54. Ibid.

55. J.G. Goodale, *The Fine Art of Interviewing* (Englewood Cliffs, NJ: Prentice Hall Inc., 1982), p. 26.

56. A. Pell, "Nine Interviewing Pitfalls," *Managers* (January 1994), p. 29; T. Dougherty, D. Turban, and J. Callender, "Confirming First Impressions In the Employment Interview: A Field Study of Interviewer Behavior," *Journal of Applied Psychology,* 79, no. 5 (1994), p. 663.

57. See A. Pell, "Nine Interviewing Pitfalls," *Managers* (January 1994), p. 29; P. Sarathi, "Making Selection Interviews Effective," *Management and Labor Studies,* 18, no. 1 (1993), pp. 5–7; J. Shetcliffe, "Who, and How, to Employ," *Insurance Brokers' Monthly* (December 2002), pp. 14–16.

58. G.J. Sears and P.M. Rowe, "A Personality-Based Similar-to-Me Effect in the Employment Interview: Conscientious, Affect-versus-Competence Mediated Interpretations, and the Role of Job Relevance," *Canadian Journal of Behavioural Sciences,* 35 (January 2003), p. 13.

59. This section is based on E.D. Pursell, M.A. Campion, and S.R. Gaylord, "Structured Interviewing: Avoiding Selection Problems," *Personnel Journal,* 59 (1980), pp. 907–912; G.P. Latham, L.M. Saari, E.D. Pursell, and M.A. Campion, "The Situational Interview," *Journal of Applied Psychology,* 65 (1980), pp. 422–427; see also M. Campion, E. Pursell, and B. Brown, "Structured Interviewing: Raising the Psychometric Properties of the Employment Interview," *Personnel Psychology,* 41 (1988), pp. 25–42; J.A. Weekley and J.A. Gier, "Reliability and Validity of the Situational Interview for a Sales Position," *Journal of Applied Psychology,* 72 (1987), pp. 484–487.

60. A. Pell, *Recruiting and Selecting Personnel* (New York, NY: Regents, 1969), pp. 103–115.

61. W.H. Wiesner and R.J. Oppenheimer, "Note-Taking in the Selection Interview: Its Effect upon Predictive Validity and Information Recall," *Proceedings of the Annual Conference Meeting. Administrative Sciences Association of Canada* (Personnel and Human Resources Division, 1991), pp. 97–106.

62. V. Tsang, "No More Excuses," *Canadian HR Reporter* (May 23, 2005); L.T. Cullen, "Getting Wise to Lies," *TIME* (May 1, 2006), p. 27.

63. Ibid.

64. Rachel Abrams, Walmart Vice President Forced Out for Lying About Degree. Retrieved from http://www.nytimes.com/2014/09/17/business/17tovar.html?_r=1

65. Chad Brooks, BusinessNewsDaily Senior Writer, Yahoo CEO Not Alone: 7 Execs Busted for Resume Lies. Retrieved from http://www.businessnews-daily.com/2523-yahoo-ceo-resume.html

66. Ibid.

67. L. Fischer, "Gatekeeper," *Workplace News* (August 2005), pp. 10–11.

68. "Background Checks," *HR Professional* (June/July 2008), p. 16.

69. T. Humber, "Recruitment Isn't Getting Any Easier," *Canadian HR Reporter* (May 23, 2005).

70. C. Hall and A. Miedema, "But I Thought You Checked?" *Canadian HR Reporter* (May 21, 2007).

71. R. Zupek, "Is Your Future Boss Researching You Online?" CareerBuilder.ca, www.careerbuilder.ca/blog/2008/10/09/cb-is-your-future-boss-researchingyou-online (accessed May 24, 2009).

72. J.R. Smith, "Damaging Reference Survives Alberta Privacy Challenge," *Canadian HR Reporter* (January 28, 2008).

73. A.C. Elmslie, "Writing a Reference Letter—Right or Wrong?" *Ultimate HR Manual,* 44 (January 2009), pp. 1–3.

74. A. Moffat, "The Danger of Digging too Deep," *Canadian HR Reporter* (August 11, 2008); see also P. Israel, "Providing References to Employees: Should You or Shouldn't You?" *Canadian HR Reporter* (March 24, 2003), pp. 5–6; T. Humber, "Name, Rank and Serial Number," *Canadian HR Reporter* (May 19, 2003), pp. G1, G7.

75. J.A. Breaugh, "Realistic Job Previews: A Critical Appraisal and Future Research Directions," *Academy of Management Review,* 8, no. 4 (1983), pp. 612–619.

76. P. Buhler, "Managing in the '90s: Hiring the Right Person for the Job," *Supervision* (July 1992), pp. 21–23; S. Jackson, "Realistic Job Previews Help Screen Applicants and Reduce Turnover," *Canadian HR Reporter* (August 9, 1999), p. 10.

77. S. Jackson, "Realistic Job Previews Help Screen Applicants and Reduce Turnover," *Canadian HR Reporter* (August 9, 1999), p. 10.

78. B. Kleinmutz, "Why We Still Use Our Heads Instead of Formulas: Toward an Integrative Approach," *Psychological Bulletin,* 107 (1990), pp. 296–310.

Chapter 8

1. Conference Board of Canada, Learning and Development Outlook, 12th edition, Feb 2014

2. M. Akdere and S. Schmidt, "Measuring the Effects of Employee Orientation Training on Employee Perception," *The Business Review* (Summer 2007), pp. 322–327.

3. B.W. Pascal, "The Orientation Wars," *Workplace Today* (October 2001), p. 4.

4. B. Pomfret, "Sound Employee Orientation Program Boosts Productivity and Safety," *Canadian HR Reporter* (January 25, 1999), pp. 17–19.

5. L. Shelat, "First Impressions Matter—A Lot," *Canadian HR Reporter* (May 3, 2004), pp. 11, 13.

6. For a recent discussion of socialization, see, for example, G. Chao et al., "Organizational Socialization: Its Content and Consequences," *Journal of Applied Psychology,* 79, no. 5 (1994), pp. 730–743.

7. S. Jackson, "After All That Work in Hiring, Don't Let New Employees Dangle," *Canadian HR Reporter* (May 19, 1997), p. 13.

8. A. Macaulay, "The Long and Winding Road," *Canadian HR Reporter* (November 16, 1998), pp. G1–G10.

9. R. Biswas, "Employee Orientation: Your Best Weapon in the Fight for Skilled Talent," *Human Resources Professional* (August/September 1998), pp. 41–42.

10. "Employee Onboarding Guides New Hires," *Workspan* (January 2009), p. 119.

11. D. Chhabra, "What Web-Based Onboarding Can Do for Your Company," *Workspan* (May 2008), pp. 111–114.

12. R. Harrison, "Onboarding: The First Step in Motivation and Retention," *Workspan* (September 2007), pp. 43–45.

13. D. Brown, "Execs Need Help Learning the Ropes Too," *Canadian HR Reporter* (April 22, 2002), p. 2.

14. Ibid.

15. "The Critical Importance of Executive Integration," *Drake Business Review* (December 2002), pp. 6–8.

16. S. Mingail, "Employers Need a Lesson in Training," *Canadian HR Reporter* (February 11, 2002), pp. 22–23.

17. U. Vu, "Trainers Mature into Business Partners," *Canadian HR Reporter* (July 12, 2004), pp. 1–2.

18. V. Galt, "Training Falls Short: Study," *Globe and Mail* (July 9, 2001), p. M1.

19. A. Tomlinson, "More Training Critical in Manufacturing," *Canadian HR Reporter* (November 4, 2002), p. 2.

20. Munro, Daniel. "Employers Must Start Investing in Skills Training or Risk Having Public Policy Nudge Them Along." The Conference Board of Canada. May 12, 2014. From http://www.conferenceboard.ca/press/speech_oped/14-05-12/employers_must_start_investing_in_skills_training_or_risk_having_public_policy_nudge_them_along.aspx

21. D. Brown, "PM Calls for Business to Spend More on Training," *Canadian HR Reporter* (December 16, 2002), pp. 1, 11; D. Brown, "Budget Should Include More for Training: Critics," *Canadian HR Reporter* (March 10, 2003), pp. 1–2; D. Brown, "Legislated Training, Questionable Results," *Canadian HR Reporter* (May 6, 2002), pp. 1, 12.

22. N.L. Trainor, "Employee Development the Key to Talent Attraction and Retention," *Canadian HR Reporter* (November 1, 1999), p. 8.

23. Bank of Montreal, www.bmo.com (accessed May 31, 2009).

24. L. Johnston, "Employees Put High Price on Learning, Development," *Canadian HR Reporter* (November 3, 2008); S. Klie, "Higher Education Leads to Higher Productivity," *Canadian HR Reporter* (December 3, 2007).

25. D. LaMarche-Bisson, "There's More than One Way to Learn," *Canadian HR Reporter* (November 18, 2003), p. 7.

26. M. Belcourt, P.C. Wright, and A.M. Saks, *Managing Performance through Training and Development*, 2nd ed. (Toronto, ON: Nelson Thomson Learning, 2000); see also A.M. Saks and R.R. Haccoun, "Easing the Transfer of Training," *Human Resources Professional* (July–August 1996), pp. 8–11.

27. J.A. Colquitt, J.A. LePine, and R.A. Noe, "Toward an Integrative Theory of Training Motivation: A Meta-Analytic Path Analysis of 20 Years of Research," *Journal of Applied Psychology,* 85 (2000), pp. 678–707.

28. M. Georghiou, "Games, Simulations Open World of Learning," *Canadian HR Reporter* (May 5, 2008).

29. K.A. Smith-Jentsch et al., "Can Pre-Training Experiences Explain Individual Differences in Learning?" *Journal of Applied Psychology,* 81, no. 1 (1986), pp. 100–116.

30. J.A. Cannon-Bowers et al., "A Framework for Understanding Pre-Practice Conditions and Their Impact on Learning," *Personnel Psychology,* 51 (1988), pp. 291–320.

31. Based on K. Wexley and G. Latham, *Developing and Training Human Resources in Organizations* (Glenview, IL: Scott, Foresman, 1981), pp. 22–27.

32. G. Na, "An Employer's Right to Train," *Canadian HR Reporter* (October 6, 2008).

33. J.C. Georges, "The Hard Realities of Soft Skills Training," *Personnel Journal,* 68, no. 4 (April 1989), pp. 40–45; R.H. Buckham, "Applying Role Analysis in the Workplace," *Personnel,* 64, no. 2 (February 1987), pp. 63–65; J.K. Ford and R. Noe, "Self-Assessed Training Needs: The Effects of Attitudes towards Training, Management Level, and Function," *Personnel Psychology,* 40, no. 1 (Spring 1987), pp. 39–54.

34. G.N. Nash, J.P. Muczyk, and F.L. Vettori, "The Role and Practical Effectiveness of Programmed Instruction," *Personnel Psychology,* 24 (1971), pp. 397–418.

35. N. Day, "Informal Learning Gets Results," *Workforce* (June 1998), p. 31.

36. S. Williams, "'Classroom' Training Alive and Changing," *Canadian HR Reporter* (October 6, 2008).

37. *The Economic Impact of Post-Secondary Education in Canada.* Ottawa: The Conference Board of Canada, 2014.

38. Ibid.

39. Ibid.

40. Stenberg, A., Luna, X., & Westerlund, O. (2014). Does formal education for older workers increase earnings? – evidence based on rich data and long-term follow-up. Labour, 28(2), 163-189. doi:http://dx.doi.org/10.1111/labr.12030

41. Ibid.

42. K. Wexley and G. Latham, *Developing and Training Human Resources in Organizations* (Glenview, IL: Scott, Foresman, 1981), p. 107.

43. "Apprenticeship Grant Gets Going," *Canadian HR Reporter* (January 25, 2007); "New Funding for Apprenticeships," *Canadian HR Reporter* (May 3, 2004), p. 2; "Ontario Boosts Apprenticeship Program with $37 Million Investment," *Canadian HR Reporter* (April 7, 2000); ThinkTrades (Alberta Aboriginal Apprenticeship Project), www.thinktrades.com/candidates.htm (accessed June 13, 2006).

44. "German Training Model Imported," *BNA Bulletin to Management* (December 19, 1996), p. 408; L. Burton, "Apprenticeship: The Learn While You Earn Option," *Human Resources Professional* (February/March 1998), p. 25; H. Frazis, D.E. Herz, and M.W. Harrigan, "Employer-Provided Training: Results from a New Survey," *Monthly Labor Review*, 118 (1995), pp. 3–17.

45. O. Diss, "Deploying a New E-Learning Program?" *HR Professional* (October– November 2005), p. 16.

46. P. Weaver, "Preventing E-Learning Failure," *Training & Development* (August 2002), pp. 45–50; K. Oakes, "E-Learning," *Training & Development* (March 2002), pp. 73–75; see also P. Harris, "E-Learning: A Consolidation Update," *Training & Development* (April 2002), pp. 27–33; C.R. Taylor, "The Second Wave," *Training & Development* (October 2002), pp. 24–31; E. Wareham, "The Educated Buyer," *Computing Canada* (February 18, 2000), p. 33; A. Tomlinson, "E-Learning Won't Solve All Problems," *Canadian HR Reporter* (April 8, 2002), pp. 1, 6.

47. M. Emery and M. Schubert, "A Trainer's Guide to Videoconferencing," *Training* (June 1993), p. 60.

48. K. Wexley and G. Latham, *Developing and Training Human Resources in Organizations* (Glenview, IL: Scott, Foresman, 1981), p. 141; see also R. Wlozkowski, "Simulation," *Training and Development Journal,* 39, no. 6 (June 1985), pp. 38–43.

49. W. Powell, "Like Life?" *Training & Development* (February 2002), pp. 32–38; see also A. Macaulay, "Reality-Based Computer Simulations Allow Staff to Grow through Failure," *Canadian HR Reporter* (October 23, 2000), pp. 11–12.

50. M. Belcourt, P.C. Wright, and A.M. Saks, *Managing Performance through Training and Development*, 2nd ed. (Toronto, ON: Nelson Thomson Learning, 2002), pp. 188–202.

51. P. Weaver, "Preventing E-Learning Failure," *Training & Development* (August 2002), pp. 45–50.

52. M. Belcourt, P.C. Wright, and A.M. Saks, *Managing Performance through Training and Development*, 2nd ed. (Toronto, ON: Nelson Thomson Learning, 2002), pp. 188–202.

53. Ibid, p. 9.

54. D. Kirkpatrick, "Effective Supervisory Training and Development," Part 3, "Outside Programs," *Personnel,* 62, no. 2 (February 1985), pp. 39–42. Among the reasons training might not pay off on the job are a mismatching of courses and trainees' needs, supervisory slip-ups (with supervisors signing up trainees and then forgetting to have them attend the sessions when the training session is actually given), and lack of help in applying skills on the job.

55. N.L. Trainor, "Evaluating Training's Four Levels," *Canadian HR Reporter* (January 13, 1997), p. 10.

56. C. Knight, "Awards for Literacy Announced," *Canadian HR Reporter* (December 29, 1997), p. 10.

57. *Reading the Future: Planning to Meet Canada's Future Literacy Needs* (Ottawa, ON: Canadian Council on Learning, 2008).

58. "New Report Reveals the Future of Literacy in Canada's Largest Cities," Canadian Council on Learning, www.ccl-cca.ca/CCL/Newsroom/Releases/20100908literacy2031.html (accessed July 7, 2011).

59. S. Coulombe, J-F. Tremblay, and S. Marchand, *International Adult Literacy Study: Literacy Scores, Human Capital and Growth Across 14 OECD Countries*, Statistics Canada, Catalogue No. 89-552-MIE, 2004; S. Mingal,

"Tackling Workplace Literacy a No-Brainer," *Canadian HR Reporter* (November 22, 2004), pp. G3, G10; D. Brown, "Poor Reading, Math Skills a Drag on Productivity, Performance," *Canadian HR Reporter* (February 28, 2005), pp. 1, 10.

60. U. Vu, "Workplace Language Training Gets Cash Boost," *Canadian HR Reporter* (May 19, 2008); K. Wolfe, "Language Training for the Workplace," *Canadian HR Reporter* (June 6, 2005), pp. 1, 13.

61. R. Rosen and P. Digh, "Developing Globally Literate Leaders," *Training & Development* (May 2001), pp. 70–81.

62. B. Siu, "Cross-Cultural Training and Customer Relations: What Every Manager Should Know," *Canadian HR Reporter* (November 15, 1999), pp. G3, G15.

63. D. Roberts and B. Tsang, "Diversity Management Training Helps Firms Hone Competitive Edge," *Canadian HR Reporter* (June 19, 1995), pp. 17–18.

64. L. Young, "Retail Sector Seeks to Upgrade Education, Training to Solve Human Resource Woes," *Canadian HR Reporter* (February 8, 1999), p. 11; see also B. Nagle, "Superior Retail Training Blends Customer Service, Product Knowledge," *Canadian HR Reporter* (July 15, 2002), pp. 7–8; D. Brown, "Is Retail Ready to Buy Training?" *Canadian HR Reporter* (July 15, 2002), pp. 7–8.

65. Canadian Retail Institute, www.retaileducation.ca/cms/sitem.cfm/ certification_&_training (accessed May 31, 2009).

66. Based on J. Laabs, "Team Training Goes Outdoors," *Personnel Journal* (June 1991), pp. 56–63; see also S. Caudron, "Teamwork Takes Work," *Personnel Journal,* 73, no. 2 (February 1994), pp. 41–49.

67. B. Donais, "Training Managers in Handling Conflict," *Canadian HR Reporter* (March 12, 2007); A. Tomlinson, "A Dose of Training for Ailing First-Time Managers," *Canadian HR Reporter* (December 3, 2001), pp. 7, 10.

68. L.C. McDermott, "Developing the New Young Managers," *Training & Development* (October 2001), pp. 42–48; A. Tomlinson, "A Dose of Training for Ailing First-Time Managers," *Canadian HR Reporter* (December 3, 2001), pp. 7, 10.

Chapter 9

1. Barbara Greene and Liana Knudsen, "Competitive Employers Make Career Development Programs a Priority," San Antonio Business Journal 15, no. 26 (July 20, 2001), p. 27.

2. M. Duarte, "O indivíduo e a organização: Perspectivas de desenvolvimento" (The Individual and the Organization: Perspectives of Development)," *Psychologica (Extra-Série)* (2004), pp. 549–557.

3. M. Savickas, L. Nota, J. Rossier, J. Dauwalder, M. Duarte, J. Guichard, S. Soresi, R. Van Esbroeck, and A. Van Vianen, "Life Designing: A Paradigm for Career Construction in the 21st Century," *Journal of Vocational Behavior* (May 2009), pp. 239–250.

4. M. Duarte, "O indivíduo e a organização: Perspectivas de desenvolvimento" (The Individual and the Organization: Perspectives of Development)," *Psychologica (Extra-Série)* (2004), pp. 549–557.

5. W. Enelow, *100 Ways to Recession-Proof Your Career* (Toronto, ON: McGraw-Hill, 2002), p. 1.

6. P. Linkow, "Winning the Competition for Talent: The Role of the New Career Paradigm in Total Rewards," *Workspan* (October 2006), pp. 28–32.

7. M. Watters and L. O'Connor, *It's Your Move: A Personal and Practical Guide to Career Transition and Job Search for Canadian Managers, Professionals and Executives* (Toronto, ON: HarperCollins, 2001).

8. For example, one survey of Baby Boomers concluded that "allowed to excel" was the most frequently mentioned factor in overall job satisfaction in an extensive attitude survey of Canadian supervisors and middle managers between 30 and 45 years of age; J. Rogers, "Baby Boomers and Their Career Expectations," *Canadian Business Review* (Spring 1993), pp. 13–18.

9. See, for example, R. Chanick, "Career Growth for Baby Boomers," *Personnel Journal,* 71, no. 1 (January 1992), pp. 40–46.

10. R. Sheppard, "Spousal Programs and Communication Curb Relocation Rejections," *Canadian HR Reporter* (November 1, 1999), p. 17.

11. D. Quinn Mills, *Labor–Management Relations* (New York, NY: McGraw-Hill, 1986), pp. 387–396.

12. G. Dessler, *Winning Commitment* (New York, NY: McGraw-Hill, 1993), pp. 144–149.

13. See J. Famularo, *Handbook of Modern Personnel Administration* (New York, NY: McGraw-Hill, 1972), p. 17.

14. J. Swain, "Dispelling Myths about Leadership Development," *Canadian HR Reporter* (June 3, 2002), p. 27.

15. J. Cooper, "Succession Planning: It's Not Just for Executives Anymore," *Workspan* (February 2006), pp. 44–47.

16. Ibid.

17. Hall, Colin. *Learning and Development Outlook—12th Edition: Strong Learning Organizations, Strong Leadership.* Ottawa: The Conference Board of Canada, 2014.

18. O'Brien, Katie. *Succession Management: A Better Approach to Succession Planning.* Ottawa: The Conference Board of Canada, 2014.

19. P. Cantor, "Succession Planning: Often Requested, Rarely Delivered," *Ivey Business Journal* (January/February 2005), pp. 1–11.

20. R. Cheloha and J. Swain, "Talent Management System Key to Effective Succession Planning," *Canadian HR Reporter* (October 10, 2005), pp. 5, 8.

21. U. Vu, "Beware the Plan That's Led Too Much by HR," *Canadian HR Reporter* (October 10, 2005), pp. 6–7.

22. "Half of Companies Fail to Update Succession Plans," *Workplace e-Newsletter,* www.workplace-mag.com/Half-of-companies-fail-to-updatesuccession-plans.html (accessed May 31, 2009).

23. For discussions of the steps in succession planning, see, for example, K. Nowack, "The Secrets of Succession," *Training and Development* (November 1994), pp. 49–55; D. Brookes, "In Management Succession, Who Moves Up?" *Human Resources* (January/February 1995), pp. 11–13.

24. K. Spence, "The Employee's Role in Succession Planning," *Canadian HR Reporter* (February 14, 2000), p. 13.

25. Torres, Rosalinde. "The Rise of the Not-So-Experienced CEO - HBR." Harvard Business Review. December 26, 2014. https://hbr.org/2014/12/ the-rise-of-the-not-so-experienced-ceo.

26. J. Orr, "Job Rotations Give Future Leaders the Depth They Need," *Canadian HR Reporter* (January 30, 2006), pp. 17, 20.

27. D. Yoder, H.G. Heneman, J. Turnbull, and C.H. Stone, *Handbook of Personnel Management and Labor Relations* (New York, NY: McGraw Hill, 1958); see also J. Phillips, "Training Supervisors Outside the Classroom," *Training and Development Journal,* 40, no. 2 (February 1986), pp. 46–49.

28. K. Wexley and G. Latham, *Developing and Training Human Resources in Organizations* (Glenview, IL: Scott, Foresman, 1981), p. 207.

29. D. Brown, "Action Learning Popular in Europe, Not Yet Caught on in Canada," *Canadian HR Reporter* (April 25, 2005), pp. 1–17.

30. IPM Management Training and Development, "Workplace.ca," www. workplace.ca (accessed March 31, 2003).

31. L. Cassiani, "Taking Team Building to New Heights," *Canadian HR Reporter* (February 26, 2001), pp. 8, 17.

32. J. Famularo, *Handbook of Modern Personnel Administration* (New York, NY: McGraw-Hill, 1972), pp. 21.7–21.8.

33. L. Morin and S. Renaud, "Corporate University Basics," *Workplace Gazette,* 7, no. 4, pp. 61–71.

34. E. Lazarus, "Corporate University," *HR Professional* (June/July 2006), pp. 28–29; "City of Richmond Wins International Award," www.richmond. ca/__shared/printpages/page4754.htm (accessed May 8, 2009).

35. Based on A. Kraut, "Developing Managerial Skill via Modeling Techniques: Some Positive Research Findings—A Symposium," *Personnel Psychology,* 29, no. 3 (Autumn 1976), pp. 325–361.

36. K. Wexley and G. Latham, *Developing and Training Human Resources in Organizations* (Glenview, IL: Scott, Foresman, 1981), p. 193.

37. J. Hinrichs, "Personnel Testing," in M. Dunnette (ed.), *Handbook of Industrial and Organizational Psychology* (Chicago, IL: Rand McNally, 1976), p. 855.

38. J. Kay, "At Harvard on the Case," *National Post Business* (March 2003), pp. 68–78.

39. A.M. Young and P.L. Perrewé, "What Did You Expect? An Examination of Career-Related Support and Social Support Among Mentors and Protégés," *Journal of Management,* 20 (2000), pp. 611–632; "Mentoring Makes Better Employees," *Workplace Today* (June 2001), p. 12; S. Butyn, "Mentoring Your Way to Improved Retention," *Canadian HR Reporter* (January 27, 2003), pp. 13, 15.

40. S. Klie, "Mentoring Accelerates Leadership Development," *Canadian HR Reporter* (March 23, 2009).

41. A.K. Buahene and G. Kovary, "Reversing the Roles: Why Gen Ys Can Make Great Mentors," *Canadian HR Reporter* (May 4, 2009).

42. D. Crisp, "Leadership Values Evolving," *Canadian HR Reporter* (September 8, 2008); S. Klie, "Holistic Approach to Developing Leaders Best," *Canadian HR Reporter* (October 27, 2008).

43. D. Brown, "Banking on Leadership Development," *Canadian HR Reporter* (January 17, 2005), pp. 7, 9.

44. Maple Leaf Foods, "Developing Leaders," www.mapleleaf.com/Working/YourDevelopment.aspx (accessed June 13, 2006).

45. R.J. Kramer, "Growing the New Business Leader," *The Conference Board Executive Action Series*, no. 208 (September 2006).

46. E. Chadnick, "Is HR Prepared to Keep the Keepers?" *Canadian HR Reporter* (January 29, 2007).

47. L. Finkelstein, "Coaching SaskEnergy to Higher Performance," *Canadian HR Reporter* (December 1, 2008).

48. Banff Centre, www.banffcentre.ca/departments/leadership/programs/framework.asp#model (accessed May 31, 2009).

Chapter 10

1. J.T. Rich, "The Solutions for Employee Performance Management," *Workspan* (February 2002), pp. 32–37.

2. J.A. Rubino, "Aligning Performance Management and Compensation Rewards Successfully," *WorldatWork Canadian News* (Fourth Quarter, 2004), pp. 12–16.

3. P. Nel, O. Van Dyk, G. Haasbroek, H. Schultz, T. Sono, and A. Werner, *Human Resource Management,* (Cape Town, South Africa: Oxford University Press, 2004).

4. J. Kochnarski and A. Sorenson, "Managing Performance Management," *Workspan* (September 2005), pp. 20–37.

5. E.E. Lawler and M. McDermott, "Current Performance Management Practices," *WorldatWork Journal*, 12, no. 2, pp. 49–60.

6. D. Bell, J. Blanchet, and N. Gore, "Performance Management: Making It Work Is Worth the Effort," *WorldatWork Canadian News,* 12, no. 11 (Fourth Quarter, 2004), pp. 1, 27–28.

7. D. Brown, "HR Improving at Performance Management," *Canadian HR Reporter* (December 2, 2002), pp. 1, 14.

8. "The Performance-Management Process," *Workspan* (October 2006), p. 96.

9. A. Silliker, "Performance Appraisals Mandatory at Most Firms," *Canadian HR Reporter* (October 8, 2012), Vol. 25(17), p. 1.

10. R. Thorndike, "Concepts of Culture-Fairness," *Journal of Educational Measurement* (Summer, 1971), pp. 63–70.

11. S. Motowidlo and J. Van Scotter, "Evidence That Task Performance Should Be Distinguished from Contextual Performance," *Journal of Applied Psychology* (November 1993), pp. 475–480.

12. R. Tett, K. Fox, and P. Palmer, "Task and Contextual Performance as Formal and Expected Work Behaviors," Paper presented at the 18th annual Society of Industrial Organizational Psychologists conference (Orlando, FL, April, 2002).

13. Robert J. Taormina and Jennifer H. Gao (2009). Identifying Acceptable Performance Appraisal Criteria: An International Perspective. Asia Pacific Journal of Human Resources 47(1), pp. 102–125. Copyright © 2009, Australian Human Resources Institute.

14. Brandon, John. "Beyond Meritocracy: 6 Ways IT Employee Performance Evaluations Are Changing." PC Advisor News RSS. March 31, 2014. http://www.pcadvisor.co.uk/news/enterprise/3509383/beyond-meritocracy-6-ways-it-employee-performance-evaluations-are-changing/.

15. C.L. Hughes, "The Bell-Shaped Curve That Inspires Guerrilla Warfare," *Personnel Administrator* (May 1987), pp. 40–41.

16. The Conference Board of Canada, "Performance Management: Turning Individual Stress to Oganizational Strategy," June 2012.

17. R. Girard, "Are Performance Appraisals Passé?" *Personnel Journal,* 67, no. 8 (August 1988), pp. 89–90.

18. D. Bernardin and P. Smith, "A Clarification of Some Issues Regarding the Development and Use of Behaviorally Anchored Ratings Scales (BARS)," *Journal of Applied Psychology* (August 1981), pp. 458–463.

19. D. Bownas and H. Bernardin, "Critical Incident Technique," in S. Gael (Ed.), *The Job Analysis Handbook for Business, Industry, and Government* (New York, NY: Wiley, 1988), pp. 1120–1137.

20. N. Hauenstein, R. Brown, and A. Sinclair, "BARS and Those Mysterious, Missing Middle Anchors," *Journal of Business and Psychology* (May 2010), pp. 663–672.

21. J. Goodale and R. Burke, "Behaviorally Based Rating Scales Need Not Be Job Specific," *Journal of Applied Psychology,* 60 (June 1975).

22. K.R. Murphy and J. Constans, "Behavioral Anchors as a Source of Bias in Rating," *Journal of Applied Psychology,* 72, no. 4 (November 1987), pp. 573–577.

23. E. Mone and M. London, *Employee Engagement through Effective Performance Management: A Manager's Guide* (New York, NY: Routledge, 2009).

24. S. Kerr and S. Landouer, "Using Stretch Goals to Promote Organizational Effectiveness and Personal Growth: General Electric and Goldman Sachs," *Academy of Management Executive* (November 2004), pp. 134–138.

25. C. Maslach and M. Leiter, "Early Predictors of Job Burnout and Engagement," *Journal of Applied Psychology* (May 2008), pp. 498–512.

26. M. Levy, "Almost-Perfect Performance Appraisals," *Personnel Journal,* 68, no. 4 (April 1989), pp. 76–83.

27. P. Loucks, "Plugging into Performance Management," *Canadian HR Reporter* (February 26, 2007).

28. C. Howard, "Appraise This!" *Canadian Business* (May 23, 1998), p. 96.

29. E. Farndale, V. Hope-Hailey, and C. Kelliher, "High Commitment Performance Management: The Roles of Justice and Trust," *Personnel Review* (2011), pp. 5–23.

30. E. Mone, C. Eisinger, K. Guggenheim, B. Price, and C. Stine, "Performance Management at the Wheel: Driving Employee Engagement in Organizations," *Journal of Business and Psychology* (May 2011), pp. 205–212.

31. K.S. Teel, "Performance Appraisal: Current Trends, Persistent Progress," *Personnel Journal,* 59, no. 4 (April 1980), pp. 296–316.

32. D. Brown, "Performance Management Systems Need Fixing: Survey," *Canadian HR Reporter* (April 11, 2005), pp. 1, 10; M. Waung and S. Highhouse, "Fear of Conflict and Empathic Buffering: Two Explanations for the Inflation of Performance Feedback," *Organizational Behavior and Human Decision Processes,* 71 (1997), pp. 37–54.

33. Y. Ganzach, "Negativity (and Positivity) in Performance Evaluation: Three Field Studies," *Journal of Applied Psychology,* 80 (1995), pp. 491–499.

34. T.J. Maurer and M.A. Taylor, "Is Sex by Itself Enough? An Exploration of Gender Bias Issues in Performance Appraisal," *Organizational Behavior and Human Decision Processes,* 60 (1994), pp. 231–251; see also C.E.

Lance, "Test for Latent Structure of Performance Ratings Derived from Wherry's (1952) *Theory of Ratings,*" *Journal of Management,* 20 (1994), pp. 757–771.

35. S.E. Scullen, M.K. Mount, and M. Goff, "Understanding the Latent Structure of Job Performance Ratings," *Journal of Applied Psychology,* 85 (2001), pp. 956–970.

36. A.M. Saks and D.A. Waldman, "The Relationship between Age and Job Performance Evaluations for Entry-Level Professionals," *Journal of Organizational Behavior,* 19 (1998), pp. 409–419.

37. W.C. Borman, L.A. White, and D.W. Dorsey, "Effects of Ratee Task Performance and Interpersonal Factors in Supervisor and Peer Performance Ratings," *Journal of Applied Psychology,* 80 (1995), pp. 168–177.

38. K. Murphy, W. Balzer, M. Lockhart, and E. Eisenman, "Effects of Previous Performance on Evaluations of Present Performance," *Journal of Applied Psychology,* 70, no. 1 (1985), pp. 72–84; see also K. Williams, A. DeNisi, B. Meglino, and T. Cafferty, "Initial Decisions and Subsequent Performance Ratings," *Journal of Applied Psychology,* 71, no. 2 (May 1986), pp. 189–195.

39. S. Appelbaum, M. Roy, and T. Gillilan, "Globalization of Performance Appraisals: Theory and Applications," *Management Decision* (2011), pp. 570–585.

40. J. Hedge and M. Cavanagh, "Improving the Accuracy of Performance Evaluations: Comparison of Three Methods of Performance Appraiser Training," *Journal of Applied Psychology,* 73, no. 1 (February 1988), pp. 68–73.

41. B. Davis and M. Mount, "Effectiveness of Performance Appraisal Training Using Computer Assistance Instruction and Behavior Modeling," *Personnel Psychology,* 37 (Fall 1984), pp. 439–452.

42. T. Athey and R. McIntyre, "Effect of Rater Training on Rater Accuracy: Levels of Processing Theory and Social Facilitation Theory Perspectives," *Journal of Applied Psychology,* 72, no. 4 (November 1987), pp. 567–572.

43. M.M. Greller, "Participation in the Performance Appraisal Review: Inflexible Manager Behavior and Variable Worker Needs," *Human Relations,* 51 (1998), pp. 1061–1083.

44. R. Arvey, and J. Campion, (1982). "The Employment Interview: A Summary and Review of Recent Research," *Personnel Psychology* (June 1982), pp. 281–322; W. Wiesner and S. Cronshaw, "A Meta-Analytic Investigation of the Impact of Interview Format and Degree of Structure on the Validity of the Employment Interview," *Journal of Occupational Psychology* (1988), pp. 275–290; K. Murphy, and J. Cleveland, *Understanding Performance Appraisal: Social, Organizational, and Goal-Based Perspectives* (Thousand Oaks, CA: Sage, 1995).

45. B.D. Cawley, L.M. Keeping, and P.E Levy, "Participation in the Performance Appraisal Process and Employee Reactions: A Meta-Analytic Review of Field Investigations," *Journal of Applied Psychology,* 83 (1998), pp. 615–633.

46. J.W. Lawrie, "Your Performance: Appraise It Yourself!" *Personnel,* 66, no. 1 (January 1989), pp. 21–33; includes a good explanation of how selfappraisals can be used at work; see also A. Furnham and P. Stringfield, "Congruence in Job-Performance Ratings: A Study of 360° Feedback Examining Self, Manager, Peers, and Consultant Ratings," *Human Relations,* 51 (1998), pp. 517–530.

47. P.A. Mabe III and S.G. West, "Validity of Self-Evaluation of Ability: A Review and Meta-Analysis," *Journal of Applied Psychology,* 67, no. 3 (1982), pp. 280–296.

48. J. Russell and D. Goode, "An Analysis of Managers' Reactions to Their Own Performance Appraisal Feedback," *Journal of Applied Psychology,* 73, no. 1 (February 1988), pp. 63–67; M.M. Harris and J. Schaubroeck, "A Meta-Analysis of Self–Supervisor, Self–Peer, and Peer–Supervisor Ratings," *Personnel Psychology,* 41 (1988), pp. 43–62.

49. V.V. Druskat and S.B. Wolff, "Effects and Timing of Developmental Peer Appraisals in Self-Managing Work Groups," *Journal of Applied Psychology,* 84 (1999), pp. 58–74.

50. M.M. Harris and J. Schaubroeck, "A Meta-Analysis of Self–Supervisor, Self–Peer, and Peer–Supervisor Ratings," *Personnel Psychology,* 41 (1988), pp. 43–62.

51. W.C. Borman, "The Rating of Individuals in Organizations: An Alternate Approach," *Organizational Behavior and Human Performance,* 12 (1974), pp. 105–124.

52. H.J. Bernardin and R.W. Beatty, "Can Subordinate Appraisals Enhance Managerial Productivity?" *Sloan Management Review* (Summer 1987), pp. 63–73.

53. M. London and A. Wohlers, "Agreement between Subordinate and Self-Ratings in Upward Feedback," *Personnel Psychology,* 44 (1991), pp. 375–390.

54. Ibid, p. 376.

55. D. Antonioni, "The Effects of Feedback Accountability on Upward Appraisal Ratings," *Personnel Psychology,* 47 (1994), pp. 349–355.

56. T.J. Maurer, N.S. Raju, and W.C. Collins, "Peer and Subordinate Performance Appraisal Measurement Equivalence," *Journal of Applied Psychology,* 83 (1998), pp. 693–702.

57. R. Reilly, J. Smither, and N. Vasilopoulos, "A Longitudinal Study of Upward Feedback," *Personnel Psychology,* 49 (1996), pp. 599–612.

58. K. Nowack, "360-Degree Feedback: The Whole Story," *Training and Development* (January 1993), p. 69; for a description of some of the problems involved in implementing 360-degree feedback, see M. Budman, "The Rating Game," *Across the Board,* 31, no. 2 (February 1994), pp. 35–38.

59. C. Romano, "Fear of Feedback," *Management Review* (December 1993), p. 39; see also M.R. Edwards and A.J. Ewen, "How to Manage Performance and Pay with 360-Degree Feedback," *Compensation and Benefits Review,* 28, no. 3 (May/June 1996), pp. 41–46.

60. G.P. Latham, J. Almost, S. Mann, and C. Moore, "New Developments in Performance Management," *Organizational Dynamics,* 34, no. 1 (2005), pp. 77–87; R. Brillinger, "The Many Faces of 360-Degree Feedback," *Canadian HR Reporter* (December 16, 1996), p. 21.

61. J.F. Milliman, R.A. Zawacki, C. Norman, L. Powell, and J. Kirksey, "Companies Evaluate Employees from All Perspectives," *Personnel Journal,* 73, no. 11 (November 1994), pp. 99–103.

62. R. Brillinger, "The Many Faces of 360-Degree Feedback," *Canadian HR Reporter* (December 16, 1996), p. 20.

63. Ibid.

64. D.A. Waldman, L.A. Atwater, and D. Antonioni, "Has 360-Degree Feedback Gone Amok?" *Academy of Management Executive,* 12 (1998), pp. 86–94.

65. P.E. Levy, B.D. Cawley, and R.J. Foti, "Reactions to Appraisal Discrepancies: Performance Ratings and Attributions," *Journal of Business and Psychology,* 12 (1998), pp. 437–455.

66. M. Derayeh and S. Brutus, "Learning from Others' 360-Degree Experiences," *Canadian HR Reporter* (February 10, 2003), pp. 18, 23.

67. A.S. DeNisi and A.N. Kluger, "Feedback Effectiveness: Can 360-Degree Appraisal Be Improved?" *Academy of Management Executive,* 14 (2000), pp. 129–139.

68. T. Bentley, "Internet Addresses 360-Degree Feedback Concerns," *Canadian HR Reporter* (May 8, 2000), pp. G3, G15.

69. D. Brown, "Performance Management Systems Need Fixing: Survey," *Canadian HR Reporter* (April 1, 2005), pp. 1, 10.

70. Zenger, Jack, and Joseph Folkman. "Your Employees Want the Negative Feedback You Hate to Give - HBR." Harvard Business Review. January 15, 2014. https://hbr.org/2014/01/your-employees-want-the-negative-feedback-you-hate-to-give.

71. Ibid.

72. Haralalka, Aniruddh, and Chee Tung Leong. "Why Strengths Matter in Training." Why Strengths Matter in Training. http://www.gallup.com/businessjournal/153341/why-strengths-matter-training.aspx

73. Willyerd, Karie. "What High Performers Want at Work - HBR." Harvard Business Review. November 18, 2014. https://hbr.org/2014/11/what-high-performers-want-at-work.

74. Ibid.

75. See also J. Greenberg, "Using Explanations to Manage Impressions of Performance Appraisal Fairness," *Employee Responsibilities and Rights Journal,* 4, no. 1 (March 1991), pp. 51–60.

76. R.G. Johnson, *The Appraisal Interview Guide,* Chapter 9 (New York, NY: AMACOM, 1979).

77. J. Block, *Performance Appraisal on the Job: Making It Work* (New York, NY: Executive Enterprises Publications, 1981), pp. 58–62; see also T. Lowe, "Eight Ways to Ruin a Performance Review," *Personnel Journal,* 65, no. 1 (January 1986).

78. J.W. Smither and M. London, "Best Practices in Performance Management," in J.W. Smither & M. London (Eds.), *Performance Management: Putting Research into Action* (San Francisco, CA: Jossey-Bass, 2009).

79. J. Block, *Performance Appraisal on the Job: Making It Work* (New York, NY: Executive Enterprises Publications, 1981), pp. 58–62.

80. M. Feinberg, *Effective Psychology for Managers* (New York, NY: Simon & Schuster, 1976).

81. J. Pearce and L. Porter, "Employee Response to Formal Performance Appraisal Feedback," *Journal of Applied Psychology,* 71, no. 2 (May 1986), pp. 211–218.

82. D.B. Jarvis and R.E. McGilvery, "Poor Performers," *HR Professional* (June/July 2005), p. 32.

83. L. Axline, "Ethical Considerations of Performance Appraisals," *Management Review* (March 1994), p. 62.

84. M. McDougall and L. Cassiani, "HR Cited in Unfair Performance Review," *Canadian HR Reporter* (September 10, 2001), pp. 1, 6.

85. "Health Worker's Performance Review Unfair," *Workplace Today* (June 2001), p. 23.

86. G. Barrett and M. Kernan, "Performance Appraisal and Terminations: A Review of Court Decisions Since Brito v. Zia with Implications for Personnel Practices," *Personnel Psychology,* 40, no. 3 (Autumn 1987), pp. 489–504.

Chapter 11

1. Richard Henderson, *Compensation Management* (Reston, VA: Reston Publishing, 1980), pp. 101–127; and Stacey L. Kaplan, "Total Rewards in Action: Developing a Total Rewards Strategy," *Benefits & Compensation Digest* 42, no. 8 (August 2005), pp. 32–37.

2. *Towers Perrin 2007 – 2008 Global Workforce Study* (Stamford CT: Towers Perrin, 2008), www.towersperrin.com/tp/getwebcachedoc?webc=HRS/USA/2008/200802/GWS_handout_web.pdf (accessed September 26, 2011).

3. "Employee Attraction and Retention," Western Compensation and Benefits Consultants, www.wcbc.ca/news/attractionretention (accessed September 26, 2011).

4. D. Brown, "StatsCan Unable to Explain Gender Wage Gap," *Canadian HR Reporter* (January 31, 2000), p. 3.

5. Based on "Women Work for Free as of Sept. 17," Canadian HR Reporter (September 18, 2008); and M. Cornish, "Much Work to Be Done on Pay Equity," Canadian HR Reporter (February 28, 2008).

6. J. Dawe, "Compassionate Care Benefit: A New Alternative for Family Caregivers," *Workplace Gazette* (Summer 2004); S. Klie, "Feds Expand Eligibility for Compassionate Care," *Canadian HR Reporter* (July 17, 2006).

7. "GM, Daimler-Chrysler Workers Ratify Agreements," *Workplace Today* (December 1999), p. 11.

8. Harold Jones, "Union Views on Job Evaluations: 1971 vs. 1978," *Personnel Journal,* 58 (February 1979), pp. 80–85.

9. R. Sahl, "Job Content Salary Surveys: Survey Design and Selection Features," *Compensation and Benefits Review* (May–June 1991), pp. 14–21.

10. Nicholas Wade, "Play Fair: Your Life May Depend on It," *The New York Times,* September 12, 2003, p. 12.

11. Robert Bretz and Stephen Thomas, "Perceived Inequity, Motivation, and Final Offer Arbitration in Major League Baseball," *Journal of Applied Psychology,* June 1992, pp. 280–282; Reginald Ell, "Addressing Employees' Feelings of Inequity: Capitalizing on Equity Theory in Modern Management," *Supervision* 72, no. 5 (May 2011), pp. 3–6.

12. James DeConinck and Duane Bachmann, "An Analysis of Turnover Among Retail Buyers," *Journal of Business Research* 58, no. 7 (July 2005), pp. 874–882.

13. Michael Harris et al., "Keeping Up with the Joneses: A Field Study of the Relationships Among Upward, Lateral, and Downward Comparisons and Pay Level Satisfaction," *Journal of Applied Psychology* 93, no. 3 (2008), pp. 665–673.

14. David Terpstra and Andre Honoree, "The Relative Importance of External, Internal, Individual, and Procedural Equity to Pay Satisfaction," *Compensation & Benefits Review,* November/December 2003, pp. 67–74.

15. Ibid., p. 68.

16. Dobson, Sarahh. " 'You Make How Much?' " *HR Reporter,* April 7, 2014.

17. Millicent Nelson et al., "Pay Me More: What Companies Need to Know About Employee Pay Satisfaction," *Compensation & Benefits Review,* March/April 2008, pp. 35–42.

18. Pay inequities manifest in unexpected ways. In one study, the researchers studied the impact of keeping pay rates secret, rather than publicizing them on individual employees' test performance. They found that individuals with lower levels of tolerance for inequity reacted particularly harshly to pay secrecy in terms of weaker individual test performance. Peter Bamberger and Elena Belogolovsky, "The Impact of Pay Secrecy on Individual Test Performance," *Personnel Psychology* 60, no. 3 (2010), pp. 965–996.

19. Rachel Emma Silverman, "Psst . . . . This Is What Your Coworker Is Paid," *The Wall Street Journal,* January 30, 2013, p. B6.

20. E. Sibray and J.B. Cavallaro, "Case Study: Market Data and Job Evaluation Equals the Best of Both Worlds," *Workspan,* (July 2007), pp. 27–30.

21. Job analysis can be a useful source of information on compensable factors, as well as on job descriptions and job specifications. For example, a quantitative job analysis technique like the position analysis questionnaire generates quantitative information on the degree to which the following five basic factors are present in each job: having decision making/communication/social responsibilities, performing skilled activities, being physically active, operating vehicles or equipment, and processing information. As a result, a job analysis technique like the PAQ is actually also appropriate as a job evaluation technique (or, some say, more appropriate), in that jobs can be quantitatively compared with one another on those five dimensions, and their relative worth thus ascertained.

22. H. Risher, "Job Evaluation: Validity and Reliability," *Compensation and Benefits Review,* 21 (January–February 1989), pp. 22–36.

23. S. Werner, R. Konopaske, and C. Touhey, "Ten Questions to Ask Yourself about Compensation Surveys," *Compensation and Benefits Review,* 31 (May/June 1999), pp. 54–59.

24. P. Cappelli, *The New Deal at Work: Managing the Market-Driven Workforce* (Boston, MA: Harvard Business School Press, 1999).

25. S. Werner, R. Konopaske, and C. Touhey, "Ten Questions to Ask Yourself about Compensation Surveys," *Compensation and Benefits Review,* 31 (May/June 1999), pp. 54–59.

26. "Compensation Surveys on the Internet," *Canadian HR Reporter* (February 10, 1997), p. 6.

27. F.W. Cook, "Compensation Surveys Are Biased," *Compensation and Benefits Review* (September–October 1994), pp. 19–22.

28. K.R. Cardinal, "The Art and Science of the Match, or Why Job Matching Keeps Me Up at Night," *Workspan* (February 2004), pp. 53–56; S. Werner, R. Konopaske, and C. Touhey, "Ten Questions to Ask Yourself about Compensation Surveys," *Compensation and Benefits Review*, 31 (May/June 1999), pp. 1–6; see also U. Vu, "Know-How Pays in Comp Surveys," *Canadian HR Reporter* (April 7, 2003), p. 13.

29. News, CBC. "House Prices Still Rising in Toronto, Vancouver." CBCnews. February 5, 2014. Retrieved from http://www.cbc.ca/news/business/house-prices-still-rising-in-toronto-vancouver-1.2524167.

30. D. Hofrichter, "Broadbanding: A 'Second Generation' Approach," *Compensation and Benefits Review* (September–October 1993), pp. 53–58; see also G. Bergel, "Choosing the Right Pay Delivery System to Fit Banding," *Compensation and Benefits Review*, 26 (July–August 1994), pp. 34–38.

31. C. Bacca and G. Starzmann, "Clarifying Competencies: Powerful Tools for Driving Business Success," *Workspan* (March 2006), pp. 44–46.

32. Ibid.

33. P.K. Zingheim and J.R. Schuster, "Reassessing the Value of Skill-Based Pay," *WorldatWork Journal* (Third Quarter, 2002).

34. P.K. Zingheim, J.R. Schuster, and M.G. Dertien, "Measuring the Value of Work: The 'People-Based' Pay Solution," *WorldatWork Journal* (Third Quarter, 2005), pp. 42–49.

35. S. St.-Onge, "Competency-Based Pay Plans Revisited," *Human Resources Professional* (August/September 1998), pp. 29–34; J. Kochanski and P. Leblanc, "Should Firms Pay for Competencies: Competencies Have to Help the Bottom Line," *Canadian HR Reporter* (February 22, 1999), p. 10.

36. F. Giancola, "Skill-Based Pay—Issues for Consideration," *Benefits & Compensation Digest*, 44, no. 5 (May 2007), pp. 10–15.

37. D. Tyson, *Canadian Compensation Handbook* (Toronto, ON: Aurora Professional Press, 2002).

38. D. Yoder, *Personnel Management and Industrial Relations* (Englewood Cliffs, NJ: Prentice Hall, 1970), pp. 643–645.

39. B.R. Ellig, "Executive Pay: A Primer," *Compensation & Benefits Review* (January–February 2003), pp. 44–50.

40. "The Top 1000: Top 50 Highest Paid Executives, 2007," www. reporton-business. com/v5/content/tp1000-2007/index.php?view-top_50_execs (accessed November 26, 2008).

41. McFarland, Janet. "Executive Compensation: Canada's 100 Top-paid CEOs." The Globe and Mail. June 1, 2014. http://www.theglobeandmail.com/report-on-business/careers/management/executive-compensation/executive-compensation-2014/article18721871/.

42. H.L. Tosi, S. Werner, J.P. Katz, and L.R. Gomez-Mejia, "How Much Does Performance Matter? A Meta-Analysis of CEO Pay Studies," *Journal of Management*, 26 (2000), pp. 301–339.

43. M.A. Thompson, "Investors Call for Better Disclosure of Executive Compensation in Canada," *Workspan Focus Canada* (2006), pp. 5–6.

44. P. Moran, "Equitable Salary Administration in High-Tech Companies," *Compensation and Benefits Review*, 18 (September–October 1986), pp. 31–40.

45. R. Sibson, *Compensation* (New York, NY: AMACOM, 1981), p. 194.

46. B. Bridges, "The Role of Rewards in Motivating Scientific and Technical Personnel: Experience at Elgin AFB," *National Productivity Review* (Summer 1993), pp. 337–348.

47. M. Drolet, "The Male–Female Wage Gap," *Perspectives,* Statistics Canada (Spring 2002), pp. 29–37; E. Carey, "Gender Gap in Earnings Staying Stubbornly High," *Toronto Star* (March 12, 2003), p. A9.

48. D. Brown, "StatsCan Unable to Explain Gender Wage Gap," *Canadian HR Reporter* (January 31, 2000), p. 3.

49. A. Silliker, "UBC Giving 2 Percent Raise to All Tenure-Stream Female Faculty," *Canadian HR Reporter* (March 11, 2013), Vol. 26(5), p. 3.

Chapter 12

1. A. Cowan, *Compensation Planning Outlook 2011* (Ottawa, ON: Conference Board of Canada, 2011).

2. P.K. Zingheim and J.R. Schuster, *Pay People Right! Breakthrough Reward Strategies to Create Great Companies* (San Francisco, CA: Jossey-Bass, 2000); D. Brown, "Top Performers Must Get Top Pay," *Canadian HR Reporter* (May 8, 2000), pp. 7, 10; V. Dell'Agnese, "Performance-Based Rewards, Line-of-Sight Foster Ownership Behaviour in Staff," *Canadian HR Reporter* (October 8, 2001), p. 10.

3. S. Klie, "'Employees First' at CPX," *Canadian HR Reporter* (September 26, 2005), pp. 1, 3.

4. See, for example, Edward Deci, *Intrinsic Motivation* (New York: Plenum, 1975).

5. Ruth Kanfer, "Motivation Theory," in Harry C. Triandis, Marvin D. Dunnette, and Leaetta M. Hough, *Handbook of Industrial and Organizational Psychology* (Palo Alto, CA: Consulting Psychologists Press, 1994), p. 113. For a recent discussion about applying Vroom's principles, see B. Schaffer, "Leadership and Motivation." *Supervision* 69, no. 2 (February 2008), pp. 6–9.

6. For a discussion, see John P. Campbell and Robert Prichard, "Motivation Theory in Industrial and Organizational Psychology," in Marvin Dunnette (ed.), *Industrial and Organizational Psychology* (Chicago: Rand McNally, 1976), pp. 74–75; Kanfer, "Motivation Theory," pp. 115–116; and B. Schaffer, "Leadership and Motivation," op cit.

7. See, for example, W. Kearney, "Pay for Performance? Not Always," *MSU Business Topics* (Spring 1979), pp. 5–16; see also H. Doyel and J. Johnson, "Pay Increase Guidelines with Merit," *Personnel Journal,* 64 (June 1985), pp. 46–50.

8. J. Pfeffer and R.I. Sutton, *Hard Facts, Dangerous Half-Truths, and Total Nonsense* (Boston MA: Harvard Business School Press, 2006).

9. W. Seithel and J. Emans, "Calculating Merit Increases: A Structured Approach," *Personnel,* 60, no. 5 (June 1985), pp. 56–68; D. Gilbert and G. Bassett, "Merit Pay Increases Are a Mistake," *Compensation and Benefits Review,* 26, no. 2 (March–April 1994), pp. 20–25.

10. S. Minken, "Does Lump Sum Pay Merit Attention?" *Personnel Journal* (June 1988), pp. 77–83; J. Newman and D. Fisher, "Strategic Impact Merit Pay," *Compensation and Benefits Review* (July–August 1992), pp. 38–45.

11. C. Baarda, *Compensation Planning Outlook 2006* (Ottawa, ON: Conference Board of Canada, 2006).

12. R. Murrill, "Executive Share Ownership," *Watson Wyatt Memorandum,* 11, no. 1 (March 1997), p. 11.

13. P. Robertson, "Increasing Productivity through an Employee Share Purchase Plan," *Canadian HR Reporter* (September 20, 1999), pp. 7, 9.

14. C. Beatty, "Our Company: Employee Ownership May Sound Drastic, but It Can Work," *HR Professional* (June/July 2004), p. 20.

15. A. Cowan, *Compensation Planning Outlook 2009* (Ottawa, ON: Conference Board of Canada, 2009).

16. B. Duke, "Are Profit-Sharing Plans Making the Grade?" *Canadian HR Reporter* (January 11, 1999), pp. 8–9.

17. Marowits, Ross. "Air Canada Pilots Ratify 10-year Contract with 20% Wage Increase." The Globe and Mail. October 31, 2014. http://www.theglobeand-mail.com/report-on-business/air-canada-pilots-ratify-10-year-contract/article21401537/.

18. B.W. Thomas and M.H. Olson, "Gainsharing: The Design Guarantees Success," *Personnel Journal* (May 1988), pp. 73–79; see also "Aligning Compensation with Quality," *Bulletin to Management, BNA Policy and Practice Series* (April 1, 1993), p. 97.

19. See T.A. Welbourne and L. Gomez Mejia, "Gainsharing Revisited," *Compensation and Benefits Review* (July–August 1988), pp. 19–28.

20. R. Henderson, *Compensation Management* (Reston, VA: Reston, 1979), p. 363. For a discussion of the increasing use of incentives for blue-collar

employees, see, for example, R. Henderson, "Contract Concessions: Is the Past Prologue?" *Compensation and Benefits Review,* 18, no. 5 (September–October 1986), pp. 17–30; see also A.J. Vogl, "Carrots, Sticks and Self-Deception," *Across-the-Board,* 3, no. 1 (January 1994), pp. 39–44.

21. D. Belcher, *Compensation Administration* (Englewood Cliffs, NJ: Prentice Hall, 1973), p. 314.

22. For a discussion of these, see T. Wilson, "Is It Time to Eliminate the Piece Rate Incentive System?" *Compensation and Benefits Review* (March–April 1992), pp. 43–49.

23. A. Saunier and E. Hawk, "Realizing the Potential of Teams through Team-Based Rewards," *Compensation and Benefits Review* (July–August 1994), pp. 24–33; S. Caudron, "Tie Individual Pay to Team Success," *Personnel Journal,* 73, no. 10 (October 1994), pp. 40–46.

24. Some other suggestions are equal payments to all members on the team; differential payments to team members based on their contributions to the team's performance; differential payments determined by a ratio of each group member's base pay to the total base pay of the group. See K. Bartol and L. Hagmann, "Team-Based Pay Plans: A Key to Effective Teamwork," *Compensation and Benefits Review* (November–December 1992), pp. 24–29.

25. J. Nickel and S. O'Neal, "Small Group Incentives: Gainsharing in the Microcosm," *Compensation and Benefits Review* (March–April 1990), p. 24; see also J. Pickard, "How Incentives Can Drive Teamworking," *Personnel Management* (September 1993), pp. 26–32; S. Caudron, "Tie Individual Pay to Team Success," *Personnel Journal* (October 1994), pp. 40–46; For an explanation of how to develop a successful group incentive program, see K.D. Scott and T. Cotter, "The Team That Works Together Earns Together," *Personnel Journal,* 63 (March 1984), pp. 59–67.

26. L.N. McClurg, "Team Rewards: How Far Have We Come?" *Human Resource Management,* 40 (Spring 2001), pp. 73–86; see also A. Gostick, "Team Recognition," *Canadian HR Reporter* (May 21, 2001), p. 15.

27. B.R. Ellig, "Executive Pay: A Primer," *Compensation & Benefits Review* (January–February 2003), pp. 44–50.

28. A. Cowan, *Compensation Planning Outlook 2009* (Ottawa, ON: Conference Board of Canada, 2009).

29. B.R. Ellig, "Incentive Plans: Short-Term Design Issues," *Compensation Review,* 16, no. 3 (Third Quarter, 1984), pp. 26–36; B. Ellig, *Executive Compensation—A Total Pay Perspective* (New York, NY: McGraw-Hill, 1982), p. 187.

30. F.D. Hildebrand Jr., "Individual Performance Incentives," *Compensation Review,* 10 (Third Quarter, 1978), p. 32.

31. Ibid., pp. 28–33.

32. P. Brieger, "Shareholders Target CEO Compensation," *Financial Post* (April 7, 2003), p. FP5; see also S.M. Van Putten and E.D. Graskamp, "End of an Era? The Future of Stock Options," *Compensation and Benefits Review* (September–October 2002), pp. 29–35; N. Winter, "The Current Crisis in Executive Compensation," *WorldatWork Canadian News* (Fourth Quarter, 2002), pp. 1–3; R.M. Kanungo and M. Mendonca, *Compensation: Effective Reward Management* (1997), p. 237.

33. A. Cowan, *Compensation Planning Outlook 2011* (Ottawa, ON: Conference Board of Canada, 2011).

34. R. Levasseur and D. D'Alessandro, "Preparing for Changes in Executive Compensation," *Workspan Canada: Workspan Focus* (January 2009), pp. 101–104.

35. A. Cowan, *Compensation Planning Outlook 2011* (Ottawa, ON: Conference Board of Canada, 2011).

36. R. Murrill, "Executive Share Ownership," *Watson Wyatt Memorandum,* 11, no. 1 (March 1997), p. 11.

37. R. Levasseur and D. D'Alessandro, "Preparing for Changes in Executive Compensation," *Workspan Canada: Workspan Focus* (January 2009), pp. 101–104.

38. J. Tallitsch and J. Moynahan, "Fine-Tuning Sales Compensation Programs," *Compensation and Benefits Review,* 26, no. 2 (March–April 1994), pp. 34–37.

39. Straight salary by itself is not, of course, an incentive compensation plan as we use the term in this chapter; J. Steinbrink, "How to Pay Your Sales Force," *Harvard Business Review,* 57 (July–August 1978), pp. 111–122.

40. T.H. Patten, "Trends in Pay Practices for Salesmen," *Personnel,* 43 (January–February 1968), pp. 54–63; see also C. Romano, "Death of a Salesman," *Management Review,* 83, no. 9 (September 1994), pp. 10–16.

41. D. Harrison, M. Virick, and S. William, "Working Without a Net: Time, Performance, and Turnover Under Maximally Contingent Rewards," *Journal of Applied Psychology,* 81 (1996), pp. 331–345.

42. G. Stewart, "Reward Structure as Moderator of the Relationship between Extroversion and Sales Performance," *Journal of Applied Psychology,* 81 (1996), pp. 619–627.

43. R.J. Long, "Ensuring Your Executive Compensation Plan Is an Asset Rather Than a Liability," *Canadian HR Reporter* (October 19, 1998), pp. 15–16; see also D. Brown, "Bringing Stock Options Back to the Surface," *Canadian HR Reporter* (May 7, 2001), p. 2.

44. J. Cameron and W.D. Pierce, *Rewards and Intrinsic Motivation: Resolving the Controversy* (Westport, CT: Bergin & Garvey, 2002); see also G. Bouchard, "When Rewards Don't Work," *Globe and Mail* (September 25, 2002), p. C3.

45. P.K. Zingheim and J.R. Schuster, *Pay People Right! Breakthrough Reward Strategies to Create Great Companies* (San Francisco, CA: Jossey-Bass, 2000).

46. S. Gross and J. Bacher, "The New Variable Pay Programs: How Some Succeed, Why Some Don't," *Compensation and Benefits Review* (January–February 1993), pp. 55–56; see also G. Milkovich and C. Milkovich, "Strengthening the Pay–Performance Relationship: The Research," *Compensation and Benefits Review* (November–December 1992), pp. 53–62; J. Schuster and P. Zingheim, "The New Variable Pay: Key Design Issues," *Compensation and Benefits Review* (March–April 1993), pp. 27–34.

47. D. Belcher, *Compensation Administration* (Englewood Cliffs, NJ: Prentice Hall, 1973), pp. 309–310.

48. A. Avalos, "Recognition: A Critical Component of the Total Rewards Mix," *Workspan* (July 2007), pp. 32–35.

49. K. Izuma, D.N. Saito, and N. Sadato, "Processing of Social and Monetary Rewards in the Human Striatum," *Neuron,* 58, no. 2 (April 24, 2008), pp. 284–294.

50. J. Mills, "Gratitude à la carte," *Workplace News* (January 2005), p. 12; L. McKibbon-Brown, "Beyond the Gold Watch: Employee Recognition Today," *Workspan* (April 2003), pp. 44–46.

51. E.A. Locke & G.P. Latham, *A Theory of Goal Setting and Task Performance* (Englewood Cliffs NJ: Prentice Hall, 1990); R. Nelson, *1001 Ways to Reward Employees* (New York, NY: Workmen Publishing, 1994), p. 19; S.J. Peterson & F. Luthans, "The Impact of Financial and Nonfinancial Incentives on Business Unit Outcomes Over Time," *Journal of Applied Psychology,* 91, no. 1 (2006) pp. 156–165.

52. A. Welsh, "The Give and Take of Recognition Programs," *Canadian HR Reporter* (September 22, 1997), pp. 16–17, 22; J.M. Kouzas and B.Z. Posner, *Encouraging the Heart: A Leader's Guide to Rewarding and Recognizing Others* (San Francisco, CA: Wiley, 2003); D. Brown, "Canada Wants Nurses Again, but Will Anyone Answer the Call?" *Canadian HR Reporter* (January 15, 2001), pp. 1, 14, 15.

53. J.M. Kouzas and B.Z. Posner, *Encouraging the Heart: A Leader's Guide to Rewarding and Recognizing Others* (San Francisco, CA: Wiley, 2003); see also B. Nelson, "Why Managers Don't Recognize Employees," *Canadian HR Reporter* (March 11, 2002), p. 9; L. Cassiani, "Lasting Impressions through Recognition," *Canadian HR Reporter* (March 12, 2001), p. 7; J. Mills, "A Matter of Pride: Rewarding Team Success," *Canadian HR Reporter* (March 8, 1999), p. 16; L. Young, "How Can I Ever Thank You?" *Canadian HR Reporter* (January 31, 2000), pp. 7, 9.

54. E. Wright and K. Ryan, "Thanks a Million (More or Less)," *Canadian HR Reporter* (March 9, 1998), pp. 19, 21, 23; see also "How to Sell Recognition to Top Management," *Canadian HR Reporter* (June 1, 1998), p. 21; B. Nelson, "Cheap and Meaningful Better than Expensive and Forgettable," *Canadian HR Reporter* (August 13, 2001), p. 22.

55. L. Davidson, "The Power of Personal Recognition," *Workforce* (July 1999), pp. 44–49; see also A. Gostick and C. Elton, "Show Me the Rewards," *Canadian HR Reporter* (March 12, 2001), pp. 7, 10; V. Scott and B. Phillips, "Recognition Program Links Achievement to Corporate Goals," *Canadian HR Reporter* (December 14, 1998), pp. 22–23; R. Clarke, "Building a Recognition Program: Alternatives and Considerations," *Canadian HR Reporter* (November 2, 1998), pp. 17, 19; E. Wright and K. Ryan, "Thanks a Million (More or Less)," *Canadian HR Reporter* (March 9, 1998), pp. 19, 21, 23; L. Davidson, "The Power of Personal Recognition," *Workforce* (July 1999), pp. 44–49; D. Brown, "Recognition an Integral Part of Total Rewards," *Canadian HR Reporter* (August 12, 2002), pp. 25, 27.

56. U. Vu, "Green Recognition a Mere Whisper," *Canadian HR Reporter* (August 11, 2008); U. Vu, "What Green Recognition Looks Like," *Canadian HR Reporter* (August 11, 2008).

57. Stewart, Nicole. "Making It Meaningful: Recognizing and Rewarding Employees in Canadian Organizations." *The Conference Board of Canada*, 2011.

58. Ibid.

59. Ibid.

60. Ibid.

61. Ibid.

62. Ibid.

63. Ibid.

64. Ibid.

65. J. Jackson, "The Art of Recognition," *Canadian HR Reporter* (January 15, 2001), p. 22; see also B.P. Keegan, "Incentive Programs Boost Employee Morale," *Workspan* (March 2002), pp. 30–33; S. Nador, "Beyond Trinkets and Trash," *Canadian HR Reporter* (May 20, 2002), pp. 15, 19.

66. H. Hilliard, "How to Reward Top Performers When Money Is No Object," *Canadian HR Reporter* (August 13, 2001), pp. 21, 23.

Chapter 13

1. Based on F. Hills, T. Bergmann, and V. Scarpello, *Compensation Decision Making* (Fort Worth, TX: The Dryden Press, 1994), p. 424; see also L.K. Beatty, "Pay and Benefits Break Away from Tradition," *HR Magazine,* 39 (November 1994), pp. 63–68.

2. R.K. Platt, "A Strategic Approach to Benefits," *Workspan* (July 2002), pp. 23–24.

3. S. Beech and J. Tompkins, "Do Benefits Plans Attract and Retain Talent?" *Benefits Canada* (October 2002), pp. 49–53.

4. F. Holmes, "Talking about an Evolution," *Benefits Canada* (September 2001), pp. 30–32; J. Thomas and M. Chilco, "Coming of Age," *Benefits Canada* (March 2001), pp. 36–38.

5. http://www.servicecanada.gc.ca/eng/sc/ei/sew/weekly_benefits.shtml.

6. "EI Top-Ups Common—Survey," *Canadian HR Reporter* (February 23, 1998), p. 15.

7. S. Klie, "Feds Expand Eligibility for Compassionate Care," *Canadian HR Reporter* (July 17, 2006).

8. "Tragedy Leaves of Absence," *HR Professional* (October/November 2008), p. 16.

9. D. Gunch, "The Family Leave Act: A Financial Burden?" *Personnel Journal* (September 1993), p. 49.

10. http://www.tax-services.ca/cpp-ei-maximum-2014-rates-contributions-deductions/

11. H. Amolins, "Workers Must Cooperate in Return to Work," *Canadian HR Reporter* (November 3, 1997), p. 8; C. Knight, "Ontario Businesses Ready for New WCB," *Canadian HR Reporter* (November 17, 1997), p. 9.

12. U. Vu, "How Purolator Dealt with Skyrocketing Costs," *Canadian HR Reporter* (March 13, 2006).

13. Ken Belson, "At IBM, a Vacation Anytime, or Maybe No Vacation at All," *The New York Times*, August 31, 2007, pp. A1–A18.

14. Robert Grossman, "Gone But Not Forgotten," *HR Magazine*, September 2011, p. 44; then put in place solutions such as rigorous absenteeism claims reviews.

15. S. Pellegrini, "Considering Critical," *Benefits Canada* (April 2002), pp. 71–73.

16. "Employee Benefits in Small Firms," *BNA Bulletin to Management* (June 27, 1991), pp. 196–197.

17. "Employee Benefits," *Commerce Clearing House Ideas and Trends in Personnel* (January 23, 1991), pp. 9–11.

18. S. Dobson, "Health-Care Costs Maintain Dramatic Rise," *Canadian HR Reporter* (July 13, 2009).

19. *Canadian Health Care Trend Survey Results 2009* (Toronto, ON: Buck Consultants).

20. C. Kapel, "Unitel Asks Employees to Share Costs," *Canadian HR Reporter* (June 17, 1996), p. 17; see also J. Sloane and J. Taggart, "Runaway Drug Costs," *Canadian HR Reporter* (September 10, 2001), pp. 17–18; "Deductibles Could Be Making a Comeback," *Canadian HR Reporter* (February 26, 2001), pp. 2, 16.

21. J. Norton, "The New Drug Invasion," *Benefits Canada* (June 1999), pp. 29–32.

22. The Conference Board of Canada, "Smoking Cessation and the Workplace: Briefing 2—Smoking Cessation Programs in Canadian Workplaces," June 2013; American Cancer Society, "A Word About Quitting Success Rates," January 17, 2013, www.cancer.org/healthy/stayawayfromtobacco/guideto-quittingsmoking/guide-to-quitting-smoking-success-rates. Accessed June 21, 2013.

23. S. Felix, "Healthy Alternative," *Benefits Canada* (February 1997), p. 47; A. Dimon, "Money Well Spent," *Benefits Canada* (April 1997), p. 15.

24. A. Dimon, "Money Well Spent," *Benefits Canada* (April 1997), p. 15.

25. D. Jones, "Accounting for Health: The Present and Future of HCSAs and Other Consumer-Driven Health Care Products in Canada," *Benefits Canada* (January 2009), pp. 21–23.

26. J. Taggart, "Health Spending Accounts: A Prescription for Cost Control," *Canadian HR Reporter* (October 22, 2001), pp. 16, 18; see also "How Spending Accounts Work," *Canadian HR Reporter* (February 24, 2003), p. 16.

27. K. Gay, "Post-Retirement Benefits Costing Firms a Fortune," *Financial Post* (June 2, 1995), p. 18; S. Lebrun, "Turning a Blind Eye to Benefits," *Canadian HR Reporter* (February 24, 1997), p. 2; S. Pellegrini, "Keep Benefits Costs Low by Assessing Retiree Health," *Canadian HR Reporter* (June 14, 1999), pp. 9–10; M. Warren, "Uncovering the Costs," *Benefits Canada* (November 1996), p. 41; G. Dufresne, "Financing Benefits for Tomorrow's Retirees," *Canadian HR Reporter* (April 6, 1998), p. 11.

28. A. Khemani, "Post-Retirement Benefits Liability Grows," *Canadian HR Reporter* (November 4, 1996), p. 17; see also M. Warren, "Retiree Benefits Come of Age," *Benefits Canada* (May 2000), pp. 73–77.

29. *2008 Post-Retirement Trends* (Toronto, ON: Mercer Human Resources Consulting).

30. "Creating Holistic Time Off Programs Can Significantly Reduce Expenses," *Compensation & Benefits Review*, July/August 2007, pp. 18–19.

31. See, for example, Rita Zeidner, "Strategies for Saving in a Down Economy," *HR Magazine*, February 2009, p. 28.

32. I. Ray-Ghosal & L. Shafee, "New Survey Finds 54 Percent of Canadians Admitting to Playing Hookey From Work: Feeling Burned or Stressed Out Cited as Key Reason," Kronos Press Release, May 15, 2013.

33. "Making Up for Lost Time: How Employers Can Curb Excessive Unscheduled Absences," *BNA Human Resources Report*, October 20, 2003, p. 1097. See also W. H. J. Hassink et al., "Do Financial Bonuses Reduce Employee Absenteeism? Evidence from a Lottery," *Industrial and Labor Relations Review* 62, no. 3 (April 2009), pp. 327–342.

34. "SHRM Benefits Survey Finds Growth in Employer Use of Paid Leave Pools," *BNA Bulletin to Management*, March 21, 2002, p. 89.

35. See M. Michael Markowich and Steve Eckberg, "Get Control of the Absentee-Minded," *Personnel Journal*, March 1996, pp. 115–120; "Exploring the Pluses, Minuses, and Myths of Switching to Paid Time Off Banks," *BNA Bulletin to Management* 55, no. 25 (June 17, 2004), pp. 193–194.

36. Society for Human Resource Management 2009 Employee Benefits Survey, quoted in Martha Frase, "Taking Time Off to the Bank," *HR Magazine*, March 2010, p. 42.

37. W. Pyper, "Aging, Health and Work," *Perspectives on Labour and Income* (Spring 2006), p. 48; S. Klie, "Private Health Coverage Enters Benefits Realm," *Canadian HR Reporter* (September 12, 2005), pp. 1, 22.

38. "Managing Episodic Disabilities Course," *HR Professional* (February–March 2009), p. 18.

39. A. Blake, "A New Approach to Disability Management," *Benefits Canada* (March 2000), pp. 58–64; P. Kulig, "Returning the Whole Employee to Work," *Canadian HR Reporter* (March 9, 1998), p. 20; see also A. Gibbs, "Gearing Disability Management to the Realities of Working Life," *Canadian HR Reporter* (December 2, 2002), p. G7.

40. J. Curtis and L. Scott, "Making the Connection," *Benefits Canada* (April 2003), pp. 75–79.

41. N. Rankin, "A Guide to Disability Management," *Canadian HR Reporter* (March 22, 1999), pp. 14–15.

42. *Staying@Work: Effective Presence at Work*, 2007 Survey Report–Canada (Toronto, ON: Watson Wyatt); "Mental Health Claims on the Rise in Canada," *WorldatWork Canadian News* (Third Quarter, 2005), pp. 15–16; D. Brown, "Mental Illness a Top Concern but Only Gets Band-Aid Treatment," *Canadian HR Reporter* (May 9, 2005), pp. 1, 3; "Mental Health Biggest Workplace Barrier, Women Say," *Canadian HR Reporter* (January 17, 2005), p. 2.

43. P. Weiner, "A Mental Health Priority for Canada's Employers," *Workspan* (January 2009), pp. 91–95.

44. "What Are the Top Challenges You Face in Improving How Mental Health Issues Are Addressed in Your Workplace?" *2008 Mental Health in the Workplace National Survey* (Toronto, ON: Mercer and Canadian Alliance on Mental Illness and Mental Health, 2008), p. 22. Reprinted with permission of Mercer.

45. J. Melnitzer, "Down and Out," *Workplace News* (September/October 2005), pp. 20–23; M. Burych, "Baby Blues," *Benefits Canada* (October 2000), pp 33–35.

46. B. Hayhoe, "The Case for Employee Retirement Planning," *Canadian HR Reporter* (May 20, 2002), p. 18.

47. J. Nunes, "Defined Benefit or Defined Contribution, It's Always Costly," *Canadian HR Reporter* (November 5, 2001), pp. 7, 9.

48. S. Klie, "Little guarantee for Ontario pensions," *Canadian HR Reporter* (May 4, 2009); S. Dobson, "Costs top list of concerns for DB plan sponsors: Survey," *Canadian HR Reporter* (March 24, 2008).

49. A. Scappatura, "DB Plans Endangered," *Canadian HR Reporter* (June 15, 2009); T. Humber, "The Death of the DB Pension," *Canadian HR Reporter* (March 23, 2009); S. Dobson, "Ottawa Provides Pension Relief," *Canadian HR Reporter* (December 15, 2008); D. Birschel, "Alberta and British Columbia Provide Pension Solvency Relief," *Benefits Quarterly*, 25, no. 2 (2009), p. 66.

50. T. Piskorski, "Minimizing Employee Benefits Litigation through Effective Claims Administration Procedures," *Employee Relations Law Journal*, 20, no. 3 (Winter 1994–95), pp. 421–431.

51. A. Rappaport, "Phased Retirement: An Important Part of the Evolving Retirement Scene," *Benefits Quarterly*, 25, no. 2 (2009), pp. 38–50; R. Castelli, "Phased Retirement Plans," *HR Professional* (December 2008/January 2009), p. 23.

52. D. Brown, "New Brunswick Nurses Find Phased Retirement Solution," *Canadian HR Reporter* (September 22, 2003), pp. 1, 12; Y. Saint-Cyr, "Phased Retirement Agreements," *Canadian Payroll and Employment Law News*, www. hrpao.org/HRPAO/HRResourceCentre/LegalCentre/ (accessed July 11, 2005).

53. *Towers Perrin 2004 SERP Report: Supplementary Pensions Under Pressure* (Toronto, ON: Towers Perrin).

54. Ricker, Susan. "Title Versus Salary: What Workers Want." *The Workbuzz*, January 24, 2014

55. Ibid.

56. Ibid.

57. Ibid.

58. Ibid.

59. Elka Maria Torpey, "Flexible Work: Adjusting the When and Where of Your Job," *Occupational Outlook Quarterly*, Summer 2007, pp. 14–27.

60. "Slightly More Workers Are Skirting 9–5 Tradition," *BNA Bulletin to Management*, June 20, 2002, p. 197.

61. The percentage of employers with flextime programs actually dropped from 2007 to 2011, from 58% to 53%. Joseph Coombs, "Flexibility Still Meeting Resistance," *HR Magazine*, July 2011, p. 72.

62. Dori Meinert, "Make Telecommuting Pay Off," *HR Magazine*, June 2011, pp. 33–37. See also Donna Dennis et al., "Effective Leadership in a Virtual Workforce," *Training & Development*, February 2013, pp. 47–49.

63. "Telework Among Full-Time Employees Almost Doubled in the Last Decade, Study Says," *BNA Bulletin to Management*, June 12, 2012, p. 187.

64. Martha White, "One Part Gone: Yahoo Says No to Telecommuting," www. CNBC.com/ID/100492123/, accessed February 25, 2013.

65. See, for example, "Compressed Workweeks Gain Popularity, but Concerns Remain About Effectiveness," *BNA Bulletin to Management*, September 16, 2008, p. 297.

66. Boris Baltes et al., "Flexible and Compressed Workweek Schedules: A Meta-Analysis of Their Effects on Work-Related Criteria," *Journal of Applied Psychology* 84, no. 4 (1999), pp. 496–513. See also Charlotte Hoff, "With Flextime, Less Can Be More," *Workforce Management*, May 2005, pp. 65–66.

67. John Pletz, "Workers, Go Home," *Crain's Chicago Business* 34, no. 8 (February 21, 2011), pp. 2, 14.

68. John Pletz, "Workers, Go Home," *Crain's Chicago Business* 34, no. 8 (February 21, 2011), pp. 2, 14.

69. SHRM, "2003 Benefits Survey," p. 2.

70. "With Job Sharing Arrangements, Companies Can Get Two Employees for the Price of One," *BNA Bulletin to Management* 56, no. 47 (November 22, 2005), pp. 369–370.

71. L. Burger, "Group Legal Service Plans: A Benefit Whose Time Has Come," *Compensation and Benefits Review*, 18 (July–August 1986), pp. 28–34.

72. "Financial Distress Impacts Health and Productivity: Employees Turning to EAP for Help," Shepell-fgi Research Group, 2009 Series, 5, no. 1; A. Scappatura, "EAP Use Soars as Economy Tanks: Study," *Canadian HR Reporter* (March 23, 2009); "Requests for Help through EAP Up Significantly," *Workspan* (February 2009), p. 13.

73. J. Hobel, "EAPs Flounder without Manager Support," *Canadian HR Reporter* (June 2, 2003), p. 7; P. Davies, "Problem Gamblers in the Workplace," *Canadian HR Reporter* (November 4, 2002), p. 17; A. Sharratt, "When a Tragedy Strikes," *Benefits Canada* (November 2002), pp. 101–105.

74. R. Csiernik, "The Great EAP Question: Internal or External?" *Canadian HR Reporter* (August 20, 2007).

75. R. Csiernik, "What to Look for in an External EAP Service," *Canadian HR Reporter* (May 31, 2004), p. 7; D. Sharar, "With HR Chasing Lowest Price,

EAPs Can't Improve Quality," *Canadian HR Reporter* (May 31, 2004), pp. 6, 8; A. Davis, "Helping Hands," *Benefits Canada* (November 2000), pp. 117–121.

76. "100 Best Companies to Work For," *Fortune* (January 2000), http://money.cnn.com/magazines/fortune/fortune_archive/2000/01/10/271718/index.htm (accessed September 4, 2012).

77. "Canada's Top 100 Employers." ISSUU. January 1, 2015. Retrieved from http://issuu.com/ct100./docs/ct100-magazine-2015?e=14200235/9961408.

78. C. Foster, "Workers Don't Leave Problems at Home," *Canadian HR Reporter* (May 7, 2007).

79. S. Dobson, "Is Backup Care Worth the Investment?" *Canadian HR Reporter* (November 3, 2008); D. Brown, "Bringing the Family to Work," *Canadian HR Reporter* (November 6, 2000), pp. 19–20.

80. "Employer-Sponsored Child Care Can Be Instrumental in Attraction and Retention," *Workspan* (January 2009), p. 10.

81. D. McCloskey, "Caregiving and Canadian Families," *Transition Magazine* (Summer 2005), p. 1; B. Parus, "Who's Watching Grandma? Addressing the Eldercare Dilemma," *Workspan* (January 2004), pp. 40–43.

82. "Elder Care to Eclipse Child Care, Report Says," *Canadian HR Reporter* (August 14, 1995), p. 11; A. Vincola, "Eldercare—What Firms Can Do to Help," *Canadian HR Reporter* (June 5, 2000), p. G3.

83. D. Dyck, "Make Your Workplace Family-Friendly," *Canadian HR Reporter* (December 13, 1999), pp. G5, G10.

84.

85. E.E. Kossek and C. Ozeki, "Work-Family Conflict, Policies, and the Job-Life Satisfaction Relationship: A Review and Direction for Organizational Behavior–Human Resources Research," *Journal of Applied Psychology*, 83, (1998), pp. 139–149.

86. B. Ellig, *Executive Compensation—A Total Pay Perspective* (New York, NY: McGraw-Hill, 1982), p. 141.

87. B. Jaworski, "'I'll Have My People Call Your People '" *Canadian HR Reporter* (March 27, 2006).

88. W. White and J. Becker, "Increasing the Motivational Impact of Employee Benefits," *Personnel* (January–February 1980), pp. 32–37; B. Olmsted and S. Smith, "Flex for Success!" *Personnel*, 66, no. 6 (June 1989), pp. 50–55.

89. B. McKay, "The Flexible Evolution," *Workplace News* (January/February 2006), pp. 14–15.

90. Ibid.

91. D. Brown, "Everybody Loves Flex," *Canadian HR Reporter* (November 18, 2002), pp. 1, 11; R. Dawson and B. McKay, "The Flexibility of Flex," *WorldatWork Canadian News* (Fourth Quarter, 2005), pp. 1, 6–13

92. J. Tompkins, "Moving Out: A Look at Comprehensive Benefits Outsourcing," *Canadian HR Reporter* (May 5, 1997), p. 9.

93. N. Chaplick, "Enter at Your Own Risk," *Benefits Canada* (May 2000), pp. 37–39; see also M. Reid, "Legal Aid," *Benefits Canada* (June 2000), pp. 46–48; S. Deller, "Five Hot Survival Tips for Communicating Benefits," *Canadian HR Reporter* (July 13, 1998), pp. 9, 19.

94. C. Davenport, "Employers Twig to Value of Ongoing Pension Communication," *Canadian HR Reporter* (December 16, 1996), p. 33.

Chapter 14

1. D. Brown, "Wellness Programs Bring Healthy Bottom Line," *Canadian HR Reporter* (December 17, 2001), pp. 1, 14.

2. "Injury/Disease & Fatality Statistics." AWCBC/ACATC. Last accessed April 17, 2015, http://awcbc.org/?page_id=14.

3. Association of Workers' Compensation Boards of Canada, *Tables of accepted time-loss injuries/diseases and fatalities-Age, Industry, Jurisdiction*. Accessed at www.awcbc.org/common/assets/nwisptables/all_tables.pdf.

4. H. Bryan, "Attitude Is Everything," *WorkSafe Magazine* (October 2005), p. 18.

5. S. De Léséleuc, "Criminal Victimization in the Workplace," Canadian Centre for Justice Statistics Profile Series (2004), http://downloads.workplaceviolencenews.com/criminal_victimization_in_the_workplace.pdf (accessed September 26, 2011).

6. T.A. Opie and L. Bates, *1997 Canadian Master Labour Guide* (CCH Canada Inc.), pp. 1015–1034.

7. Adapted and modified from: Canada's National Workplace Health and Safety Website, last accessed April 17th, 2015 at http://www.canoshweb.org/Legislation/All; Government of Canada, Labour Program, last accessed April 17, 2015 http://www.labour.gc.ca/eng/health_safety/; OHS Regulation and Related Materials, Work Safe BC, last accessed April 2017, http://www2.worksafebc.com/publications/OHSRegulation/Home.asp?_ga=1.45707811.649093395.1429297238.

8. C.A. Edwards and C.E. Humphrey, *Due Diligence Under the Occupational Health and Safety Act: A Practical Guide* (Toronto, ON: Carswell/Thomson Canada, 2000).

9. N. Keith, "The Omniscient Employer: The Need to See the Unforeseeable," *Workplace* (March/April 2008), pp. 16–19.

10. M. Pilger, "Conducting a Hygiene Assessment," *Canadian HR Reporter* (April 10, 2000), pp. G3, G4; J. Montgomery, *Occupational Health and Safety* (Toronto, ON: Nelson Canada, 1996), p. 97; D. Brown, "Joint H&S Committees: An Opportunity, Not a Nuisance," *Canadian HR Reporter* (October 20, 2002), pp. 7, 10.

11. P. Strahlendorf, "What Supervisors Need to Know," *OH&S Canada* (January/February 1996), pp. 38–40; N. Tompkins, "Getting the Best Help from Your Safety Committee," *HR Magazine*, 40, no. 4 (April 1995), p. 76.

12. J. Grant and D. Brown, "The Inspector Cometh," *Canadian HR Reporter* (January 31, 2005), pp. 13, 17; "It's Time to Wake Up to Health and Safety: Ministry of Labour Increases Number of Inspectors," *Safety Mosaic*, 8 (Spring 2005), pp. 5–6.

13. "Alberta Imposes Record Penalties for OH&S Violations," *Workplace*, www.workplace-mag.com/Alberta-imposes-record-penalties-for-ohs-violations.html (accessed July 16, 2009).

14. S. Klie, "Individuals Targeted under OHS," *Canadian HR Reporter* (March 12, 2007); R. Stewart, "Legal Duties of the Front Line," *Canadian HR Reporter* (March 12, 2007).

15. "Employer Jailed for H&S Violation," *Canadian HR Reporter* (April 8, 2002), p. 2; see also T. Humber, "Putting the Boss Behind Bars?" *Canadian HR Reporter* (April 7, 2003).

16. "Quebec Employer First to Be Criminally Convicted in Death of Worker," *Canadian HR Reporter* (February 7, 2008); "C-45 Conviction Nets $110K Fine," *Canadian HR Reporter* (April 7, 2008).

17. J. Montgomery, *Occupational Health and Safety* (Toronto, ON: Nelson Canada, 1996), p. 34.

18. K. Prisciak, "Health, Safety & Harassment?" *OH&S Canada* (April/May 1997), pp. 20–21.

19. *A Safety Committee Man's Guide*, Aetna Life and Casualty Insurance Company, Catalog 872684.

20. J. Roughton, "Job Hazard Analysis," *OH&S Canada* (January/February 1996), pp. 41–44.

21. M.V. Vyas, A.X. Garg, A.V. Iansavichus, J. Costella, A. Donner, L.E. Laugsand, I. Janszky, M. Mrkobrada, G. Parraga & D.G. Hackam. 2012. "Shift work and vascular events: systematic review and meta-analysis", *BMJ* 2012;345:e4800

22. Felix, S, Top Tactics to Reduce Absenteeism, Benefits Canada, August 27, 2012, Last accessed April 14, 2015 at http://www.benefitscanada.com/benefits/disability-management/top-tactics-to-reduce-absenteeism-31299

23. A. Fowler, "How to Make the Workplace Safer," *People Management*, 1, no. 2 (January, 1995), pp. 38–39.

24. List of unsafe acts from *A Safety Committee Man's Guide*, Aetna Life and Casualty Insurance Company; E. McCormick and J. Tiffin, *Industrial Psychology* (Englewood Cliffs, NJ: Prentice Hall, 1974).

25. E. McCormick and J. Tiffin, *Industrial Psychology* (Englewood Cliffs, NJ: Prentice Hall, 1974), pp. 522–523; David DeJoy, "Attributional Processes and Hazard Control Management in Industry," *Journal of Safety Research*, 16 (Summer 1985), pp. 61–71.

26. E. McCormick and J. Tiffin, *Industrial Psychology* (Englewood Cliffs, NJ: Prentice Hall, 1974), p. 523.

27. A. Campbell, *All Signs Point to Yes: Literacy's Impact on Workplace Health and Safety* (Ottawa, ON: The Conference Board of Canada, 2008).

28. S. Dobson, "Evidence of Link between Literacy, Safety," *Canadian HR Reporter* (December 1, 2008).

29. A. Campbell, *All Signs Point to Yes: Literacy's Impact on Workplace Health and Safety* (Ottawa, ON: The Conference Board of Canada, 2008).

30. "IAPA Wins First Place at International Film and Multimedia Festival," *Workplace* e-newsletter (July 18, 2008).

31. M. Blum and J. Nayler, *Industrial Psychology* (New York, NY: Harper & Row, 1968), p. 522.

32. L. Scott, "Measuring Employee Abilities," *Benefits Canada* (September 2002), pp. 41–49.

33. K. Gillin, "Reduce Employee Exposure to Injury with Pre-Employment Screening Tests," *Canadian HR Reporter* (February 28, 2000), p. 10.

34. M. Shaw, "Rewarding Health and Safety," *Canadian HR Reporter* (December 2, 2002), pp. 19–20.

35. M. Morra, "Fun, with Caution," *Workplace* (March/April 2008), pp. 1; L. Scott, "Measuring Employee Abilities," *Benefits Canada* (September 2002), pp. 41–49.

36. A. Dunn, "Back in Business," *Workplace News* (April 2005), pp. 16–17.

37. Ergomed Solutions, http://ergomedsolutions.com/functionalabilitiesevaluationsp17.php (accessed July 15, 2009); C. Colacci, "Meet Your Return to Work Obligations with a Functional Abilities Evaluation," *Canadian HR Reporter* (April 10, 2000), p. G5.

38. C. Hall, "Sobering Advice," *Workplace News*, 11, no. 10 (November/December 2005), pp. 11–12.

39. *British Columbia (Public Service Employee Relations Commission) v. B.C.G.S.E.U.*, (1999) 176 D.L.R. (4th) 1 (S.C.C.) [*Meiorin*].

40. Policy on Drug and Alcohol Testing, Ontario Human Rights Commission, www.ohrc.on.ca/en/resources/Policies/PolicyDrugAlch (accessed July 16, 2009).

41. D. McCutcheon, "Confronting Addiction," *HR Professional* (June/July 2009), p. 39.

42. D. O'Meara, "Sober Second Chance," *Alberta Venture*, 9, no. 2 (March 2005), http://albertaventure.com/2005/03/sober-secondchance/?year=2005 (accessed September 4, 2012).

43. A. Nicoll, *Time for Action: Managing Mental Health in the Workplace* (Toronto, ON: Mercer Human Resources Consulting), (2008); L. Duxbury and C. Higgins, *Exploring the Link between Work – Life Conflict and Demands on Canada's Health Care System: Report Three* (Public Health Agency of Canada: March 2004).

44. *Mental Health at Work: Booklet 1*. IRSST (Laval University, 2005).

45. *Staying@Work: Effective Presence at Work: 2007 Survey Report:Canada* (Toronto, ON: Watson Wyatt).

46. Ibid.

47. D. Crisp, "Leaders Make the Difference," in A. Shaw, "Toxic Workplaces as Bad as Unsafe Ones," *Canadian HR Reporter* (April 21, 2008).

48. A. Nicoll, *Time for Action: Managing Mental Health in the Workplace* (Toronto, ON: Mercer Human Resources Consulting), (2008).

49. J. Santa-Barbara, "Preventing the Stress Epidemic," *Canadian HR Reporter* (March 8, 1999), p. 19; see also A. Chiu, "Beyond Physical Wellness: Mental Health Issues in the Workplace," *Canadian HR Reporter* (February 26, 2001), p. 4; L. Hyatt, "Job Stress: Have We Reached the Breaking Point?" *Workplace Today* (January 2002), pp. 14, 15, 37.

50. "Health Care Workers Most Stressed," *Canadian HR Reporter* (November 15, 2007).

51. Statistics Canada, "Study: Workaholics and Time Perception," *The Daily* (May 15, 2007).

52. "Is Your Job Making You Sick?" *Canadian HR Reporter* (September 17, 2008).

53. J.W. Simpson, "Psychopaths Wear Suits, Too," *National Post* (May 10, 2006), p. WK6; A. Gill, "The Psychopath in the Corner Office," *Globe and Mail* (May 27, 2006), p. F1; "Push for Productivity Taking its Toll," *Canadian HR Reporter* (November 6, 2001), p. 15; D. Brown, "Doing More with Less Hurts Employees and Productivity," *Canadian HR Reporter* (October 7, 2002), pp. 3, 13; A. Sharratt, "Silver Linings," *Benefits Canada* (March 2003), pp. 51–53.

54. P. Crawford-Smith, "Stressed Out," *Benefits Canada* (November 1999), pp. 115–117.

55. *Stress at Work: Taking Control* (Industrial Accident Prevention Association, 2002); J. Newman and T. Beehr, "Personal and Organizational Strategies for Handling Job Stress: A Review of Research and Opinion," *Personnel Psychology* (Spring 1979), pp. 1–43; see also Bureau of National Affairs, "Work Place Stress: How to Curb Claims," *Bulletin to Management* (April 14, 1988), p. 120.

56. T. Humber, "Stress Attack," *Canadian HR Reporter* (February 10, 2002), pp. G1, G10; M. Shain, "Stress and Satisfaction," *OH&S Canada* (April/May 1999), pp. 38–47.

57. P. Carayon, "Stressful Jobs and Non-Stressful Jobs: A Cluster Analysis of Office Jobs," *Ergonomics*, 37, no. 2 (1994), pp. 311–323.

58. A. Pihulyk, "When the Job Overwhelms," *Canadian HR Reporter* (January 14, 2002), p. 11.

59. MacDonald, Heather A., Victor Colotla, Stephen Flamer, and Harry Karlinsky. 2003. Posttraumatic stress disorder (PTSD) in the workplace: A descriptive study of workers experiencing PTSD resulting from work injury. *Journal of Occupational Rehabilitation* 13, (2) (06): 63-77, http://search.proquest.com/docview/230503070?accountid=11233 (accessed January 22, 2015).

60. "CNW Group." Wounded Warriors Canada. January 14, 2015. Retrieved From http://www.newswire.ca/en/story/1472303/wounded-warriors-canada-announces-launch-of-cope.

61. Grant, Kelly. "Post-traumatic Stress Disorder Doubles among Canadian Forces." The Globe and Mail. August 11, 2014. Retrieved From http://www.theglobeandmail.com/news/national/one-in-six-military-members-have-mental-health-problems-statscan-says/article19990160/.

62. Negrusa, Brighita, and Sebastian Negrusa. 2014. Home front: Post-deployment mental health and divorces. *Demography* 51, (3) (06): 895-916, http://search.proquest.com/docview/1533623904?accountid=11233 (accessed January 22, 2015).

63. P. Kishchuk, *Yukon Workers' Compensation Act Subsection 105.1 Research Series: Expansion of the Meaning of Disability* (March 2003).

64. M. Gibb-Clark, "The Case for Compensating Stress Claims," *Globe and Mail* (June 14, 1999), p. M1; L. Young, "Stressed Workers Are Suing Employers," *Canadian HR Reporter* (May 3, 1999), pp. 1, 6; D. Brown, "Liability Could Extend to Mental Damage," *Canadian HR Reporter* (October 9, 2000), pp. 1, 8.

65. OPSEU Online, "International RSI Awareness Day—February 28, 2006," www.opseu.org/hands/rsi2006.htm (accessed May 18, 2006); J. Hampton, "RSIs: The Biggest Strain Is on the Bottom Line," *Canadian HR Reporter* (February 10, 1997), pp. 15, 19; see also G. Harrington, "Pushing Ergonomics into Place," *Canadian HR Reporter* (April 24, 1995), pp. 11–12.

66. "Prevent Workplace Pains and Strains! It's Time to Take Action!" Ontario Ministry of Labour, www.labour.gov.on.ca/english/hs/ergonomics/is_ergonomics.html (accessed May 25, 2006).

67. S.B. Hood, "Repetitive Strain Injury," *Human Resources Professional* (June/July 1997), pp. 29–34.

68. "Ergonomic Intervention Improves Worker Health and Productivity," *Institute for Work and Health* (December 15, 2003), www.iwh.on.ca/media/ergonomic.php (accessed July 8, 2006); "Ergonomic Intervention Improves Worker Health and Productivity," *Workplace News* (February 2004), p. 16.

69. J.A. Savage, "Are Computer Terminals Zapping Workers' Health?" *Business and Society Review* (1994).

70. "Office Ergonomics and Repetitive Strain Injuries: What You Need to Know," Ottawa Valley Physiotherapy, www.ovphysio.com (accessed May 25, 2006); Occupational Health and Safety Agency for Healthcare in British Columbia, www.ohsah.bc.ca/templates/index.php?section_copy_id=5396 (accessed May 25, 2006); S. Tenby, "Introduction to Ergonomics: How to Avoid RSI—Repetitive Strain Injury," Disabled Women's Network Ontario, http://dawn.thot.net/cd/20.html (accessed May 25, 2006).

71. U. Vu, "Steel Union Gathers Workplace Cancer Data," *Canadian HR Reporter* (June 2, 2008).

72. "Unions Stress Cancer Prevention," *Canadian HR Reporter* (February 28, 2005), p. 2.

73. D. Brown, "Killer Toxins in the Workplace," *Canadian HR Reporter* (April 23, 2001), pp. 1, 12.

74. A. Scappatura, "Enhanced Coverage for Firefighters," *Canadian HR Reporter* (May 18, 2009).

75. "EI Granted in Second-Hand Smoke Case," *Canadian HR Reporter* (May 19, 2003), p. 3; see also M.M. Finklestein, "Risky Business," *OH&S Canada* (September/October 1996), pp. 32–34.

76. T. Humber, "Snuffing Out Smoking," *Canadian HR Reporter* (April 11, 2005), p. 19, 23; *Towards Healthier Workplaces and Public Places* (Health Canada, 2004).

77. C. Hallamore, *A State of Unpreparedness: Canadian Organizations' Readiness for a Pandemic* (Ottawa, ON: The Conference Board of Canada, June 2006).

78. C.C. Cavicchio, "Action Plan for Dealing with a Global Pandemic," *The Conference Board Executive Action Series* (May 2009).

79. C. Hallamore, *A State of Unpreparedness: Canadian Organizations' Readiness for a Pandemic* (Ottawa, ON: The Conference Board of Canada, June 2006).

80. R.A. Macpherson, E. Ringsels, and H. Singh, "Swine Influenza: Advice for Employers Preparing for a Pandemic," *McCarthy Tetrault e-Alert* (April 29, 2009), http://news.mccarthy.ca/en/news_template_full.asp?pub_code=4502&news_code=1066 (accessed April 29, 2009).

81. C.C. Cavicchio, "Action Plan for Dealing with a Global Pandemic," *The Conference Board Executive Action Series* (May 2009).

82. D.J. McKeown and K. Ford, "The Importance of People-Focused Pandemic Planning," *Workplace News* (September/October 2006).

83. *Violence in the Workplace*, Canadian Association of University Teachers (October 4, 2004); W.H. Glenn, "Workplace Violence: An Employees' Survival Guide," *OH&S Canada* (April/May 2002), pp. 26–31.

84. S. De Leseleuc, *Criminal Victimization in the Workplace* (Canadian Centre for Justice Statistics, Catalogue No. 85F0033MIE – No. 013, 2004).

85. "Male Nurses More Likely to Be Assaulted by Patients: StatsCan," *Canadian HR Reporter* (April 16, 2009).

86. S. Dobson, "Sexual Assault Prompts OHS Charge," *Canadian HR Reporter* (December 15, 2008); L. De Piante, "Watch Out for Dangerous Employees," *Canadian HR Reporter* (October 22, 2007); A. Feliu, "Workplace Violence and the Duty of Care: The Scope of an Employer's Obligation to Protect against the Violent Employee," *Employee Relations Law Journal,* 20, no. 3 (Winter 1994/95), pp. 381–406; G. French and P. Morgan, "The Risks of Workplace Violence," *Canadian HR Reporter* (December 18, 2000), pp. 27–28.

87. M.M. LeBlanc and E.K. Kelloway, "Predictors and Outcomes of Workplace Violence and Aggression, *Journal of Applied Psychology*, 87, no. 3 (June 2002), 444–453.

88. L. De Piante, "Watch Out for Dangerous Employees," *Canadian HR Reporter* (October 22, 2007).

89. A. Tomlinson, "Re-evaluating Your Workplace: Is It Safe and Secure?" *Canadian HR Reporter* (February 25, 2002), pp. 3, 12; L. Martin and D. Tona, "Before It's Too Late," *OH&S Canada* (April/May 2000), pp. 52–53.

90. C. Warren, "Healthy Competition Boosts Workplace Wellness," *Workplace News* (November/December 2007).

91. S. Pellegrini, "The Next 25 Years: Wellness," *Benefits Canada* (June 2002), pp. 83–85.

92. J. Taggart and J. Farrell, "Where Wellness Shows Up on the Bottom Line," *Canadian HR Reporter* (October 20, 2003), pp. 12, 15.

93. S. Klie, "Seven Oaks Hospital Relies on Healthy Staff," *Canadian HR Reporter* (October 23, 2006).

94. E. Buffett, "Healthy Employees Translate into Profits," *Canadian HR Reporter* (April 9, 2007).

95. A. Tomlinson, "Healthy Living a Remedy for Burgeoning Employee Absentee Rates," *Canadian HR Reporter* (March 25, 2002), pp. 3, 12.

Chapter 15

1. Compdata Surveys, www.compdatasurveys.com/Products/Compensation.

2. News 4, "Reasons for Turnover," *Canadian HR Reporter,* June 16, 2008. www.hrreporter.com

3. N. Chhinzer and K. Ababneh, "Characteristics of the Unemployed in Canada: Leavers, Losers, and Layoffs," *International Business & Economics Research Journal*, 9, no. 12 (2010), pp. 1–15.

4. Statistics Canada, "Permanent Layoffs, Quits and Hirings in the Canadian Economy 1978 to 1995," Business and Labour Market Analysis Division, www.statcan.gc.ca/pub/71-539-x/71-539-x1995001-eng.pdf (accessed September 26, 2011).

5. W.F. Cascio, *Responsible Restructuring: Creative and Profitable Alternatives to Layoffs* (San Fransico, CA: Barrett-Koehler, 2002).

6. W.F. Cascio, *Costing human resources: The financial impact of behavior in Organizations* (Boston, MA: PWS-Kent, 1991).

7. J. Johnson, R.W. Griffeth, and M. Griffin, "Factors Discrimination Functional and Dysfunctional Sales Force Turnover," *Journal of Business & Industrial Marketing*, 15, no. 6 (January 2000), pp. 399–415.

8. R.W. Griffeth, P.W. Hom, and S. Gaertner, "A Meta-Analysis of Antecedents and Correlates of Employee Turnover: Update, Moderator Tests, and Research Implications for the Next Millennium," *Journal of Management,* 26, no. 3 (June 2006), pp. 463–488.

9. M. Stovel and N. Bontis, "Voluntary Turnover: Knowledge Management Friend or Foe?" *Journal of Intellectual Capital*, 3, no. 3 (2002), pp. 303–322.

10. W.H. Mobley, R.W. Griffeth, H.H. Hand, and B.M. Meglino, "Review and Conceptual Analysis of the Employee Turnover Process," *Psychological Bulletin*, 86, no. 3 (May 1979), pp. 493–522.

11. P.W. Hom and A.J. Kinicki, "Toward a Greater Understanding of How Dissatisfaction Drives Employee Turnover," *Academy of Management Journal*, 44, no. 5 (October, 2001), pp. 975–987.

12. B. Prentice, "When can an employer sue an employee for damages?" Employment Update: January 2013, January 16, 2013, p. 1.

13. *Mass Exodus of Employees, Implied Duties Owed to Employers and the Supreme Court of Canada*, Norton Rose Fulbright, November 10, 2008, accessed at http://www.nortonrosefulbright.com/knowledge/publications/49742/mass-exodus-of-employees-implied-duties-owed-to-employers-and-the-supreme-court-of-canada

14. C. Chan, "Notice Is a Two-Way Street: OCA Upholds $20 Million Award against Departing Employees," *Canadian Lawyer Magazine*, April 16, 2012.

15. S. Norris, and T. Williams, "Healthy Aging: Adding Years to Life and Life to Years," Government of Canada (October 27, 2000), http://dsp-psd.pwgsc.gc.ca/Collection-R/LoPBdP/BP/prb0023-e.htm (accessed September 26, 2011).

16. "Mandatory Retirement Fades in Canada," CBC News (October 18, 2010), www.cbc.ca/news/canada/story/2009/08/20/mandatory-retirementex-plainer523.html (accessed September 26, 2011).

17. Ibid.

18. G. Golightly, "Preparing Employees for Retirement Transitions," *HR Professional* (December 1999/January 2000), pp. 27–33.

19. *1995 Canadian Dismissal Practices Survey* (Toronto, ON: Murray Axmith & Associates).

20. G. Golightly, "Preparing Employees for Retirement Transitions," *HR Professional* (December 1999/January 2000), pp. 27–33.

21. J. Famularo, *Handbook of Modern Personnel Administration* (New York, NY: McGraw-Hill, 1972), pp. 65.3–65.5.

22. N. Chhinzer and K. Ababneh, "Characteristics of the Unemployed in Canada: Leavers, Losers, and Layoffs," *International Business & Economics Research Journal*, 9, no. 12 (December 2010), pp. 1–15.

23. Gorman, Ryan. "'No Excuses, Zero Tolerance': PayPal Exec FIRED after Bizarre Late-night Twitter Rant against Colleagues He Had Known for Less than Two Months." Daily Mail. May 5, 2014. From http://www.dailymail.co.uk/news/article-2620526/No-excuses-zero-tolerance-PayPal-exec-FIRED-bizarre-late-night-Twitter-rant-against-colleagues.html.

24. N.C. MacDonald, "Progressing towards Just Cause," *Canadian HR Reporter* (September 22, 2008).

25. S. Rudner, "Just Cause Termination Still Not Clearcut," *Canadian HR Reporter* (March 23, 2009).

26. D. Bambrough and M. Certosimo, "Worker Fraud Usually Justifies Dismissal," *Canadian HR Reporter* (October 23, 2006).

27. L. Cassiani, "Dishonesty Not Always Enough to Terminate," *Canadian HR Reporter* (August 13, 2001), pp. 3, 6; P. Israel, "Firing an Employee for Dishonesty? Put Things in Context First," *Canadian HR Reporter* (August 12, 2002), p. 5.

28. "Proving Cause for Termination Getting Harder," *Workplace Today* (January 2001), p. 17; L. Harris, "High Standards Allow Employer to Fire Threatening Employee," *Canadian HR Reporter* (October 22, 2001), pp. 8, 10.

29. D. Bambrough and M. Certosimo, "Worker Fraud Usually Justifies Dismissal," *Canadian HR Reporter* (October 23, 2006).

30. A. Britnell, "Stop Employee Theft," *Canadian Business Online* (July 16, 2003), www.canadianbusiness.com (accessed May 29, 2006); J. Towler, "Dealing with Employees Who Steal," *Canadian HR Reporter* (September 23, 2002), p. 4.

31. "Employee theft on the rise: A thorn in the side for retailers says survey," *The Huffington Post Canada*, October 31, 2012.

32. "Air Canada Searches Employee Rooms," *Canadian HR Reporter* (February 10, 2003), p. 2.

33. J. Divon, "Why more employees are stealing from you," *The Globe and Mail*, November 26, 2012.

34. Ibid.

35. Ibid.

36. J. Famularo, *Handbook of Modern Personnel Administration* (New York, NY: McGraw-Hill, 1972), pp. 65.4–65.5.

37. K.S. Cameron. "Investigating Organizational Downsizing: Fundamental Issues," *Human Resource Management*, 33 (1994), pp. 183–188.

38. Ibid.

39. Commerce Clearing House, *Personnel Practices/Communications* (Chicago, IL: CCH, 1992), p. 1410.

40. E.A. Lind, J. Greenberg, K.S. Scott, and T.D. Welchans, "The Winding Road from Employee to Complainant: Situational and Psychological Determinants of Wrongful Dismissal Claims," *Administrative Science Quarterly*, 45 (2000), pp. 557–590.

41. E.E. Mole, *Wrongful Dismissal Practice Manual*, Chapter 7 (Toronto, ON: Butterworths Canada, 1993).

42. K. Blair, "Sports Editor Scores 28-Month Severance," *Canadian HR Reporter* (April 7, 1997), p. 5.

43. J. McAlpine, "Don't Add Bad Faith to Wrongful Dismissal," *Canadian HR Reporter* (May 6, 2002), p. 7; P. Israel, "Cut Down on Lawsuits Just by Being Nice," *Canadian HR Reporter* (November 18, 2002), p. 5.

44. N.C. MacDonald, "Record-Setting Wallace Award Overturned," *Canadian HR Reporter* (September 11, 2006).

45. J.R. Smith, "Top Court Strips Out Damages in *Keays*," *Canadian HR Reporter* (July 14, 2008); T. Giesbrecht, K. McDermott, and K. McNeill, " *Keays v. Honda Canada Inc.*" www.mccarthy.ca/article_detail.aspx?id=4053 (accessed June 27, 2008).

46. M.J. MacKillop, "The Perils of Dismissal: The Impact of the Wallace Decision on Reasonable Notice." Paper presented at the Human Resources Professionals Association of Ontario Employment Law Conference (Toronto, ON, October 1999), p. 18.

47. K. Blair, "Pay in Lieu Just the Beginning," *Canadian HR Reporter* (July 14, 1997), p. 5; see also K. Blair, "Dismissal Damages, Thy Name Is Mitigation," *Canadian HR Reporter* (February 9, 1998), p. 5.

48. M. MacKillop and L. Jessome, "Manage Disability Claims with Care," *HR Professional* (August/September 2005), p. 30; J.M. Carvalho, "$500,000 Punitive Damages Award Shocks Honda," *McCarthy Tetrault Report on Canadian Labour and Employment Law* (September 2005).

49. N.C. MacDonald, "The *Keays* to Punitive Damages," *Canadian HR Reporter* (November 20, 2006); T. Giesbrecht, K. McDermott, and K. McNeill, " *Keays v. Honda Canada Inc.*" www.mccarthy.ca/article_detail.aspx/id=4053 (accessed June 27, 2008).

50. E.E. Mole, *Wrongful Dismissal Practice Manual*, Chapter 3 (Toronto, ON: Butterworths Canada, 1993).

51. H.A.Levitt and V. Michaelidis, "Ex-Employee Granted $800,000 in Constructive Dismissal Case," *Workplace* (March/April 2008), p. 11.

52. J. McApline, "10 Steps for Reducing Exposure to Wrongful Dismissal," *Canadian HR Reporter* (May 6, 2002), p. 8.

53. E. Caruk, "What to Do If a Wrongful Dismissal Action Hits," *Canadian HR Reporter* (May 6, 2002), p. 10.

54. A. Saks, "Engagement: The Academic Perspective," *Canadian HR Reporter* (January 26, 2009).

55. J. Gibbons, *Employee Engagement: A Review of Current Research and Its Implications* (New York, NY: The Conference Board, 2006).

56. *Engaging Employees to Drive Global Business Success: Insights from Mercer's What's Working* TM *Research* (New York, NY: Mercer, 2007).

57. Y. Cohen-Charash and P. E. Spector, "The Role of Justice in Organizations: A Meta-Analysis," *Organizational Behavior and Human Decision Processes*, 86 (November 2001), pp. 278–321.

58. S. Dobson, "'We're Live from the HR Firing Session!'" *Canadian HR Reporter*, Feb 25, 2013, Vol. 26(4), p. 1.

59. A. Silliker, "Is There a Better Way to Close a Store?" *Canadian HR Reporter*, Mar 11, 2013, Vol. 26(5), p. 1.

60. D. Jones, "What If You Held a Survey and No-One Came?" *Canadian HR Reporter* (July 16, 2001), pp. 19, 22.

61. D. Brown, "Getting the Hard Facts in Employee Attitude and Satisfaction," *Canadian HR Reporter* (November 1, 1999), p. 2.

62. A. Massey, "Blogging Phobia Hits Employers," *Canadian HR Reporter* (September 26, 2005), pp. 15, 17.

63. L. Harris, "Staffer Fired after Bad-Mouthing Colleagues, Management in Blog," *Canadian HR Reporter* (September 8, 2008); S.E. Sorenson, "Employee Blogging," *HR Professional* (April/May 2008), p. 16.

64. L. De Piante, "Blogging Guidelines for Employees: A Necessity in the Workplace," *Canadian HR Reporter* (April 23, 2007); S. Crossley and M. Torrance, "Indiscriminate Blogging and the Workplace," *Workplace News* (November/December 2007), pp. 12–13.

65. Based on D. McElroy, "High Tech with High Touch: A New Communication Contract," *Canadian HR Reporter* (April 7, 1997), p. G6.

66. S. Klie, "Blogs Connect CEOs with Employees, Clients," *Canadian HR Reporter* (November 17, 2008).

Chapter 16

1. T.T. Delaney, "Unions and Human Resource Policies," in K. Rowland and G. Ferris (eds.), *Research in Personnel and Human Resources Management* (Greenwich, CT: JAI Press, 1991).

2. S. Klie, "Wal-Mart Closes Union Shop in Quebec," *Canadian HR Reporter* (November 3, 2008).

3. L. Harris, "Union-Proof: How Some Employers Avoid Organized Labour," *Canadian HR Reporter* (October 22, 2007).

4. Based on U. Vu, "Collective Agreement Puts Aboriginals First," *Canadian HR Reporter* (November 6, 2006).

5. R. Morissette, G. Shellenberg, and A. Johnson, "Diverging Trends in Unionization," *Perspectives on Labour and Income*, 17, no. 2, Statistics Canada (Summer 2005); U. Vu, "Low Membership Keeps Unions on the Defensive," *Canadian HR Reporter* (February 13, 2006), pp. 4, 9.

6. C. Hallamore, "Globalization Shifts the Ground in Labour Relations," *Inside Edge* (Spring 2006), p. 14; see also C. Hallamore, *Industrial Relations Outlook 2006: Shifting Ground, Shifting Attitudes* (Ottawa, ON: Conference Board of Canada, 2006).

7. C. Hallamore, *Industrial Relations Outlook 2007: Finding Common Ground through the War for Workers* (Ottawa, ON: The Conference Board of Canada, 2007); S. Klie, "Labour Market Should Unite Business, Unions," *Canadian HR Reporter* (February 27, 2007).

8. L. Harris, "Unions Taking Up the Mantle of Women's Issues," *Canadian HR Reporter* (August 11, 2008); L. Harris, "Youthful Proposition from Unions," *Canadian HR Reporter* (October 20, 2008).

9. H.N. Wheeler and J.A. McClendon, "The Individual Decision to Unionise," in G. Strauss et. al., (eds.), *The State of the Unions* (Madison, WI: Industrial Relations Research Association, 1991).

10. H.S. Farber and D.H. Saks, "Why Workers Want Unions: The Role of Relative Wages and Job Characteristics," *Journal of Political Economy*, 88, no. 21 (April, 1980), pp. 349–369.

11. J. Kelly, *Rethinking Industrial Relations: Mobilization, Collectivism, and Long Waves* (London, UK: Routledge, 1998).

12. C. Fullager and J. Barling, "A Longitudinal Test of a Model of the Antecedents and Consequences of Union Loyalty," *Journal of Applied Psychology*, 74, no. 2 (April 1989), pp. 213–227; A. Eaton, M. Gordon, and J. Keefe, "The Impact of Quality of Work-Life Programs and Grievance Systems Effectiveness on Union Commitment," *Industrial and Labor Relations Review*, 45, no. 3 (April 1992), pp. 592–604.

13. H.N. Wheeler and J.A. McClendon, "The Individual Decision to Unionise," in G. Strauss et. al., (eds.), *The State of the Unions* (Madison, WI: Industrial Relations Research Association, 1991).

14. Shepherdson, David K. *Industrial Relations Outlook 2014: Back to Basics for the Labour Movement*. Ottawa: The Conference Board of Canada, 2013.

15. Ibid.

16. Ibid.

17. Ibid.

18. Ibid.

19. Ibid.

20. Statistics Canada, "Average Hourly Wages of Employees by Selected Characteristics and Occupation, Unadjusted Data, by Province (Monthly)," www.statcan.gc.ca/tables-tableaux/sum-som/l01/cst01/labr69a-eng.htm (accessed July 22, 2013).

21. Statistics Canada, "Average Earnings and Usual Hours by Union and Job Status, 2010," www.statcan.gc.ca/pub/75-001-x/2011004/tables-tab-leaux/11579/tbl03-eng.htm (accessed July 22, 2013)

22. Statistics Canada, "Unionization Rates in First Half of 2007 and 2008," (March, 3, 2010), www.statcan.gc.ca/pub/75-001-x/topics-sujets/unionization-syndicalisation/unionization-syndicalisation-2008-eng.htm (accessed September 26, 2011).

23. L. Young, "Union Drives: Initiated Within, Prevented Within," *Canadian HR Reporter* (November 29, 1999), pp. 2, 14.

24. *Canadian Master Labour Guide*, 16th ed. (Toronto, ON: CCH Canadian, 2002).

25. A.W.J. Craig and N.A. Solomon, *The System of Industrial Relations in Canada*, 5th ed. (Toronto, ON: Prentice Hall Canada, 1996), p. 217.

26. Ibid., p. 218.

27. Ibid., p. 216.

28. J. Peirce, *Canadian Industrial Relations* (Toronto, ON: Prentice Hall Canada, 2000), p. 431.

29. The section on distributive bargaining is based on R.E. Walton and R.B. McKersie, *A Behavioral Theory of Labor Negotiations* (New York, NY: McGraw-Hill, 1965), pp. 4–6.

30. The section on integrative bargaining is based on R.E. Walton and R.B. McKersie, *A Behavioral Theory of Labor Negotiations* (New York, NY: McGraw-Hill, 1965), pp. 4–6.

31. Based on C. Kapel, "The Feeling's Mutual," *Human Resources Professional* (April 1995), pp. 9–13; see also S.D. Smith, "Taking the Confrontation out of Collective Bargaining," *Canadian HR Reporter* (September 10, 2001), pp. 11, 13.

32. U. Vu, "Interest Wanes on Interest-Based?" *Canadian HR Reporter* (February 28, 2006), pp. 6, 9.

33. Bianco, Anthony. "No Union Please, We're Wal-Mart." Bloomberg Business Week. February 12, 2006. Retrieved From http://www.businessweek.com/stories/2006-02-12/no-union-please-were-wal-mart.

34. Vieira, Paul. "Canadian Supreme Court Rules Against Wal-Mart Over Store Closing." WSJ. Retrieved From http://www.wsj.com/articles/canadian-supreme-court-rules-against-wal-mart-over-store-closing-1403883945.

35. J. Peirce, *Canadian Industrial Relations* (Toronto, ON: Prentice Hall Canada, 2000), p. 431.

36. CBA Talks Timeline, http://www.tsn.ca/nhl/feature/?id=9678, accessed June 21, 2013.

37. D. Friend, "NHL Brand Value Dips Thanks To 2012 Hockey Lockout, Say Study," Huffington Press, February 13, 2013, www.huffingtonpost.ca/2013/02/13/nhl-brand-value-drops_n_2675352.html

38. See J.E. Grenig, "Stare Decisis, Re Judicata and Collecteral Estoppel and Labour Arbitration," *Labour Law Journal*, 38 (April 1987), pp. 195–205.

39. Based on M. Gunderson and D.G. Taras, *Union–Management Relations in Canada* (Toronto, ON: Pearson Education Canada, 2001), p. 429; J. Peirce, *Canadian Industrial Relations* (Toronto, ON: Prentice Hall Canada, 2000), p. 431.

40. M. Hebert, "Length of Collective Agreements," *Workplace Gazette*, 7, no. 4 (Winter 2004), p. 27.

41. *Canadian Master Labour Guide*, 16th ed. (Toronto, ON: CCH Canadian Ltd., 2002).

42. M. Hebert, "Length of Collective Agreements," *Workplace Gazette*, 7, no. 4 (Winter 2004), p. 27.

Chapter 17

1. R. Runzheimer and G. Harper, "Workforce Mobility Management Saves Money and Increases Efficiency," *Workspan* (December 2007), pp. 76–81.

2. "Definition of 'Immigrant,'" Statistics Canada (November 2010), www.statcan.gc.ca/pub/81-004-x/2010004/def/immigrant-eng.htm (accessed September 26, 2011).

3. L. Grobovsky, "Protecting Your Workers Abroad with a Global Diversity Strategy," *Canadian HR Reporter* (November 1, 1999), pp. 15–16.

4. "Oil and Water," *Canadian Business* (November 8–21, 2004), pp. 14, 16; "Expect Corruption Overseas," *Canadian HR Reporter* (September 23, 2002), p. 9.

5. R.J. House, P.J. Hanges, M. Javidan, P.W. Dorfman, and V. Gupta, *Culture, Leadership, and Organizations: The GLOBE Study of 62 Societies* (Thousand Oaks, CA: Sage Publications, 2004); G. Hofstede, "Cultural Dimensions in People Management," in V. Pucik, N. Tichy and C. Barnett (eds.), *Globalizing Management,* (New York, NY: John Wiley & Sons, 1992), p. 143.

6. S. Klie, "HR Around the World," *Canadian HR Reporter* (November 6, 2006); K. King-Metters and R. Metters, "Misunderstanding the Chinese Worker," *The Wall Street Journal* (July 7, 2008), p. R11.

7. R. Little, "Foreigners Explore Pros and Cons Behind Vietnamese Work Ethic," http://vietnamnews.vnagency.com.vn/showarticle.php?num=)!SAY080808 (accessed September 4, 2008).

8. A. Yeo, "A Brief Look at the PRC Employment Promotion Law," *Human Resources* (December 2007), pp. 29–31; J. Yan, "A Snapshot of Chinese Employment Law," *Canadian HR Reporter* (November 6, 2006); "China's New Labor Contract Law," *Workspan* (March 2008), p. 12.

9. D. Matthews, *Severance Practices Around the World* . (Philadelphia, PA: Right Management, 2008); G. Avraam, A. Ishak, and T. Appleyard, "Terminating Employees Around the World," *Canadian HR Reporter* (April 6, 2009).

10. "Britain Introduces Corporate Manslaughter Act," *Canadian HR Reporter* (April 16, 2008).

11. A. Macaulay, "Culture, Safety and Privacy Norms Abroad Present Challenges for HR," *Canadian HR Reporter* (November 6, 2006).

12. Discussed in E. Gaugler, "HR Management: An International Comparison," *Personnel* (August 1988), p. 28.

13. Wharton School, "Made in China," *Human Resource Executive Online* (February 26, 2008).

14. "Press Release 2014, Global Expatriates: Size, Segmentation and Forecast for the Worldwide Market." Finaccord. January 20, 2014. Retrieved From http://www.finaccord.com/press-release_2014_global-expatriates_-size-segmentation-and-forecast-for-the-worldwide-market.htm.

15. *2008/2009 Benefits Survey for Expatriates and Globally Mobile Employees* (New York, NY: Mercer, 2009).

16. M. Sim and L. Dixon, "Number of Women Expats Increasing," *Canadian HR Reporter* (May 21, 2007).

17. S. Dobson, "Enticing Employees to Go on Relocation," *Canadian HR Reporter* (May 18, 2009).

18. J. Head, "How Paper Can Protect International Relocations," *Canadian HR Reporter* (March 13, 2006).

19. *2005 Employee Relocation Survey: Domestic, Cross-Border & International Relocations* (Toronto, ON: Canadian Employee Relocation Council, 2005).

20. Ibid.

21. *Global Relocation Trends: Survey Report 2008* . GMAC Global Relocation Services.

22. G.N. Abbott, B.W. Stening, P.W.B. Atkins, and A.M. Grant, "Coaching Expatriate Managers for Success: Adding Value Beyond Training and Mentoring," *Asia-Pacific Journal of Human Resources,* 44, pp. 295–317.

23. G. Insch and J. Daniels, "Causes and Consequences of Declining Early Departures from Foreign Assignments," *Business Horizons,* 46, no. 6 (November–December 2002), pp. 39–48.

24. E. Krell, "Budding Relationships," *HR Magazine,* 50, no. 6 (June 2005), pp. 114–118.

25. "Trends In Global Relocation: Global Mobility Policy & Practices." Cartus. 2014. Retrieved From http://guidance.cartusrelocation.com/rs/cartus/images/2014_Global_Mobility_Policy_Practices_Survey_Exec_Summary.pdf.

26. P. Caligiuri, "The Big Five Personality Characteristics as Predictors of Expatriates' Desire to Terminate the Assignment and Supervisor-Rated Performance," *Personnel Psychology,* 53, no. 1 (Spring 2000), pp. 67–88.

27. J. Selmer, "Expatriation: Corporate Policy, Personal Intentions and International Adjustment," *International Journal of Human Resource Management,* 9, no. 6 (December 1998), pp. 997–1007.

28. Discussed in C. Hill, *International Business: Competing in the Global Marketplace* (Burr Ridge, IL: Irwin, 1994), pp. 511–515.

29. C. Solomon, "One Assignment, Two Lives," *Personnel Journal* (May 1996), pp. 36–47; M. Harvey, "Dual-Career Couples During International Relocation: The Trailing Spouse," *International Journal of Human Resource Management,* 9, no. 2 (April 1998), pp. 309–330.

30. Based on B.J. Punnett, "International Human Resources Management," in A.M. Rugman (ed.), *International Business in Canada: Strategies for Management,* pp. 330–346 (Toronto, ON: Prentice Hall Canada, 1989); L.G. Klaff, "Thinning the Ranks of the 'Career Expats,'" *Workforce Management* (October 2004), pp. 84–87.

31. V. Galt, "World Loves to Milk Canada's Executive Pool," *Globe and Mail* (September 5, 2005), p. B10.

32. S. Cryne, "The Changing World of the Relocation Specialist," *Canadian HR Reporter* (March 8, 2004), pp. 13, 15; G. Reinhart, "Preparing for Global Expansion: A Primer," *Canadian HR Reporter* (March 14, 2005), pp. 14, 17.

33. *Survey 2011 Global Assignment Policies and Practices*, KPMG, p. 9, www.kpmginstitutes.com/taxwatch/insights/2011/pdf/gapp-survey-2011.pdf.

34. Z. Fedder, "Short-Sighted Thinking Shortchanges Short-Term International Assignments," *Canadian HR Reporter* (September 25, 2000), p. 20.

35. S. Cryne, "The Changing World of the Relocation Specialist," *Canadian HR Reporter* (March 8, 2004), pp. 13, 15.

36. J.D. Daniels and L.H. Radebaugh, *International Business* (Reading, MA: Addison-Wesley, 1994), p. 767; Arvind Phatak, *International Dimensions of Management* (Boston, MA: PWS-Kent, 1989), pp. 106–107.

37. A. Bross, A. Churchill, and J. Zifkin, "Cross-Cultural Training: Issues to Consider During Implementation," *Canadian HR Reporter* (June 5, 2000), pp. 10, 12.

38. E.M. Norman, "How Multinationals Doing Business in Asia Can Develop Leadership Talent During a Recession," *Workspan* (May 2009), pp. 35–43.

39. "More Multinationals Embracing Centralized Compensation Structures," *Workspan* (November 2006), p. 10; C. Reynolds, "Global Compensation and Benefits in Transition," *Compensation and Benefits Review* (January/February 2000), pp. 28–28; J.E. Richard, "Global Executive Compensation: A Look at the Future," *Compensation and Benefits Review* (May/June 2000), pp. 35–38.

40. L. Laroche, "Negotiating Expatriate Packages," *Canadian HR Reporter* (November 20, 2000), pp. 15, 19.

41. J. Cartland, "Reward Policies in a Global Corporation," *Business Quarterly* (Autumn 1993), pp. 93–96; L. Mazur, "Europay," *Across-the-Board* (January 1995), pp. 40–43.

42. K. Bensky, "Developing a Workable Global Rewards System," *Workspan* (October 2002), pp. 44–48.

43. Based on KPMG, 2013, Approaches to Compensation for Global Assignment, http://www.kpmg.com/Global/en/IssuesAndInsights/ArticlesPublications/Documents/global-assignment-policies-practices-survey-v6.pdf, last accessed Jan 27, 2015.

44. A. Phatak, *International Dimensions of Management* (Boston, MA: PWS-Kent, 1989), p. 134; see also L. Laroche, "Negotiating Expatriate Packages," *Canadian HR Reporter* (November 20, 2000), pp. 15, 19.

45. K. Abosch, J. Schermerhorn, and L. Wisper, "Broad-Based Variable Pay Goes Global," *Workspan* (May 2008), pp. 56–62.

46. "Expatriates, Families Face Different Stressors than Stateside Counterparts," *Workspan* (October 2008), p. 18.

47. V. Frazee, "Keeping Your Expats Healthy," *Global Workforce* (November 1998), pp. 18–23; see also B. Barker and D. Schulde, "Special EAP Helps Expatriates Face International 'Culture Shock,'" *Canadian HR Reporter* (November 29, 1999), p. 20; L. O'Grady, "Using Technology to De-stress on International Assignment," *Canadian HR Reporter* (September 24, 2001), pp. 8, 12; R. Melles, "Lost in Translation," *Canadian HR Reporter* (March 8, 2004), p. 14; E.C. Heher, "Anticipating the Psychological Effects of Expatriate Life," *Workspan* (May 2006), pp. 54–56.

48. A. Bross and G. Wise, "Sustaining the Relocated Employee with an International EAP," *Canadian HR Reporter* (November 29, 1999), pp. 18, 19, 21.

49. C. Storti, *The Art of Coming Home* (Boston, MA: Nicholas Brealey Publishing, 2001); S. Cryne, "Homeward Bound," *Canadian HR Reporter* (March 9, 2009).

50. "Views of Employees and Companies Differ on International Assignments," *Workspan Focus Canada 2006*, pp. 22–24; L. Stroh, "Predicting Turnover among Repatriates: Can Organizations Affect Retention Rates?" *International Journal of Human Resource Management,* 6, no. 2 (May 1995), pp. 443–456.

51. J. Keogh, "A Win–Win, from Start to Finish," *Workspan* (February 2003), pp. 36–39; D. Brown, "Companies Undervaluing Skills Learned During Relocation," *Canadian HR Reporter* (February 28, 2000), pp. 15, 21; J. Hobel, "The Expatriate Employee Homecoming," *Canadian HR Reporter* (June 1, 1998), pp. G5, G11.

52. D. McCutcheon, "Repatriation: Bringing Home the Troops," *HR Professional* (April/May 2009), pp. 33–34; P. Stanoch and G. Reynolds, "Relocating Career Development," *Canadian HR Reporter* (May 5, 2003), pp. 13, 15; L.M, "Global Talk," *HR Professional* (June/July 2006), p. 12.

53. Global Assignment Policies and Practices: Survey 2013. KPMG. 2013. Retrieved From http://www.kpmg.com/Global/en/IssuesAndInsights/ArticlesPublications/Documents/global-assignment-policies-practices-survey-v6.pdf

54. Reforming the International Mobility Programs. Government of Canada, Employment and Social Development Canada. September 29, 2014. http://www.esdc.gc.ca/eng/jobs/foreign_workers/reform/imp.shtml.

55. S. Lopes and Y. Poisson, "Bringing Employers into the Immigration Debate: Survey and Roundtable," *Public Policy Forum* (2004), www.toronto.ca/metropolis/metropolistoronto2005/pdf/lopesetal_audc.pdf (accessed September 26, 2011).

56. C.C. Miller, L.M. Burke, and W.H. Glick, "Cognitive Diversity among Upper Echelon Executives: Implications for Strategic Decision Processes," *Strategic Management Journal,* 19, no.1 (January 1998), pp. 39–58; S.K. Horwitz and I.B. Horwitz, "The Effects of Team Diversity on Team Outcomes: A Meta-Analytic Review of Team Demography," *Journal of Management,* 33, no.6 (December 2007), pp. 987–1015.

57. Society for Human Resources Management Survey Programme, 2001, p. 16.

58. Statistics Canada, "Earnings Differences between Immigrants and the Canadian-Born—The Role of Literacy Skills," (May 1, 2009), www.statcan.gc.ca/pub/81-004-x/2008005/article/10798-eng.htm (accessed September 26, 2011).

59. G. Picot, and A. Sweetman, "The Deteriorating Economic Welfare of Immigrants and Possible Causes: Update 2005," Statistics Canada, Catalogue No. 11F0019MIE, No. 262.

60. Statistics Canada, "Earnings Differences between Immigrants and the Canadian-Born—The Role of Literacy Skills," (May 1, 2009), www. statcan.gc.ca/pub/81-004-x/2008005/article/10798-eng.htm (accessed September 26, 2011).

61. Yssaad, Lahouaria. "The Immigrant Labour Force Analysis Series: 2008-2011." Statistics Canada. Catalogue No. 71-606-X. Retrieved From http://www.statcan.gc.ca/pub/71-606-x/71-606-x2012006-eng.pdf.

62. Statistics Canada, "Longitudinal Survey of Immigrants to Canada: Process, Progress and Prospects," Housing, Family and Social Statistics Division (October 2003), http://dsp-psd.pwgsc.gc.ca/Collection/Statcan/89-611-X/89-611-XIE2003001.pdf (accessed September 26, 2001).

63. G. Larose and G. Tillman, "Valorizing Immigrants' Non-Canadian Work Experience," (Ottawa, ON: Work and Learning Knowledge Centre, 2009).

64. M. Fernando, "The Non-Accreditation of Immigrant Professionals in Canada: Societal Dimensions of the Problem," *Metropolis* (September 15, 1999), http://canada.metropolis.net/research-policy/conversation/MATAPAPER.html (accessed September 26, 2011).

65. J. Gilmour, "The 2008 Canadian Immigrant Labour Market: Analysis of Quality of Employment," Statistics Canada, Labour Statistics Division (November 23, 2009), www.statcan.gc.ca/pub/71-606-x/71-606-x2009001-eng.pdf (accessed August 11, 2010).

66. Ibid.

67. Ibid.

68. "Progress Report 2010," Foreign Credentials Referral Office, Government of Canada (August 5, 2011), www.credentials.gc.ca/fcro/progress-report2010.asp#bfn07.

69. C. Grondin, "Knowledge of Official Languages among New Immigrants: How Important Is It in the Labour Market?" Statistics Canada (April 2007), www.statcan.gc.ca/pub/89-624-x/89-624-x2007000-eng.pdf (accessed September 26, 2011).

70. Ibid.

71. M. Adamuti-Trache and R. Sweet, "Exploring the Relationship between Educational Credentials and the Earnings of Immigrants," *Canadian Studies in Population*, 32, no. 2 (2005), pp. 177–201.

360-degree appraisal A performance appraisal technique that uses multiple raters including peers, employees reporting to the appraisee, supervisors, and customers.

A

accidental death and dismemberment coverage Employer-paid benefit that provides a fixed lump-sum benefit in addition to life insurance benefits when death is accidental or a range of benefits in case of accidental loss of limbs or sight.

achievement tests Tests used to measure knowledge or proficiency acquired through education, training, or experience.

action learning A training technique by which management trainees are allowed to work full time, analyzing and solving problems in other departments.

advance/reasonable notice Advance written notice required if the employer is going to terminate employment of a worker without cause.

alternation ranking method Ranking employees from best to worst on a particular trait.

applicant tracking systems (ATS) Online systems that help employers attract, gather, screen, compile, and manage applicants.

appraisal bias The tendency to allow individual differences, such as age, race, and sex, to affect the appraisal ratings that these employees receive.

aptitude tests Tests that measure an individual's aptitude or potential to perform a job, provided he or she is given proper training.

arbitration The use of an outside third party to investigate a dispute between an employer and union and impose a settlement.

attrition The normal separation of employees from an organization because of resignation, retirement, or death.

auditory learning learning through talking and listening.

authority The right to make decisions, direct others' work, and give orders.

authorization card A card signed by an employee that indicates his or her willingness to have the union act as his or her representative for purposes of collective bargaining.

B

baby boomers Individuals born between 1946 and 1964.

bad-faith damages Reserved for extreme circumstances in which the employers was untruthful, misleading, or unduly insensitive to the employee in the course of a dismissal.

balanced scorecard A measurement system that translates an organization's strategy into a comprehensive set of performance measures.

balance sheet approach A method of formulating expatriate pay based on equalizing purchasing power across countries.

bargaining unit The group of employees in a firm, a plant, or an industry that has been recognized by an employer or certified by a labour relations board (LRB) as appropriate for collective bargaining purposes.

bargaining zone The area defined by the bargaining limits (resistance points) of each side, in which compromise is possible, as is the attainment of a settlement satisfactory to both parties.

behaviour modelling A training technique in which trainees are first shown good management techniques, then asked to play roles in a simulated situation, and finally given feedback regarding their performance.

behavioural interview or behaviour description interview (BDI) A series of job-related questions that focus on relevant past job-related behaviours.

behaviourally anchored rating scale (BARS) An appraisal method that aims to combine the benefits of narratives, critical incidents, and quantified ratings by anchoring a quantified scale with specific narrative examples of good and poor performance.

benchmark job A job that is critical to the firm's operations or that is commonly found in other organizations.

biographical information blank (BIB) A detailed job application form requesting biographical data found to be predictive of success on the job, pertaining to background, experiences, and preferences. Responses are scored.

blind ad A recruitment ad in which the identity and address of the employer are omitted.

bona fide occupational requirement (BFOR) A justifiable reason for discrimination based on business necessity (that is, required for the safe and efficient operation of the organization) or a requirement that can be clearly defended as intrinsically required by the tasks an employee is expected to perform.

boycott An organized refusal of bargaining unit members and supporters to buy the products or use the services of the organization whose employees are on strike in an effort to exert economic pressure on the employer.

broadbanding Reducing the number of salary grades and ranges into just a few wide levels or "bands," each of which then contains a relatively wide range of jobs and salary levels.

burnout The total depletion of physical and mental resources caused by excessive striving to reach an unrealistic work-related goal.

business unionism The activities of labour unions focusing on economic and welfare issues, including pay and benefits, job security, and working conditions.

C

Canada/Quebec Pension Plans (C/QPP) Programs that provide three types of benefits: retirement income; survivor or death benefits payable to the employee's dependants regardless of age at time of death; and disability benefits payable to employees with disabilities and their dependants. Benefits are payable only to those individuals who make contributions to the plans or to their family members.

capital accumulation programs Long-term incentives most often reserved for senior executives.

career A series of work-related positions, paid or unpaid, that help a person to grow in job skills, success, and fulfillment.

career anchor A concern or value that a person will not give up if a choice has to be made.

career development The lifelong series of activities (such as workshops) that contribute to a person's career exploration, establishment, success, and fulfillment.

career planning The deliberate process through which someone becomes aware of personal skills, interests, knowledge, motivations, and other characteristics; acquires information about opportunities and choices; identifies career-related goals; and establishes action plans to attain specific goals.

case study method A development method in which a trainee is presented with a written description of an organizational problem to diagnose and solve.

caucus session A session in which only the members of one's own bargaining team are present.

central tendency A tendency to rate all employees in the middle of the scale.

certification Recognition for having met certain professional standards. In labour relations, the procedure whereby a labour union obtains a certificate from the relevant LRB declaring that the union is the exclusive bargaining agent for a defined group of employees in a bargaining unit that the LRB considers appropriate for collective bargaining purposes.

change agents Specialists who lead the organization and its employees through organizational change.

Charter of Rights and Freedoms Federal law enacted in 1982 that guarantees fundamental freedoms to all Canadians.

classification/grading method A method for categorizing jobs into groups.

closed shop Only union members in good standing may be hired by the employer to perform bargaining unit work.

coinsurance The percentage of expenses (in excess of the deductible) that are paid for by the insurance plan.

collective bargaining Negotiations between a union and an employer to arrive at a mutually acceptable collective agreement.

collective bargaining agreement (union contract) A formal agreement between an employer and the union representing a group of its employees regarding terms and conditions of employment.

compensable factor A fundamental, compensable element of a job, such as skill, effort, responsibility, and working conditions.

competencies Demonstrable characteristics of a person that enable performance of the job.

competency-based job analysis Describing a job in terms of the measurable, observable behavioural competencies an employee must exhibit to do a job well.

compressed work week Schedule in which employee works fewer but longer days each week.

conciliation The often mandatory use of a neutral third party who has no direct input on the negotiation process to help an organization and the union representing a group of its employees communicate more effectively with the aim of coming to a mutually satisfactory collective agreement.

construct validity The extent to which a selection tool measures a theoretical construct or trait deemed necessary to perform the job successfully.

constructive dismissal When the employer makes unilateral changes in the employment contract that are unacceptable to the employee, even though the employee has not been formally terminated.

content validity The extent to which a selection instrument, such as a test, adequately samples the knowledge and skills needed to perform the job.

contextual performance An individual's indirect contribution to the organization by improving the organizational, social, and psychological behaviours that contribute to organizational effectiveness beyond those specified for the job.

contingent/non-standard workers Workers who do not have regular full-time employment status.

contract workers Employees who develop work relationships directly with the employer for a specific type of work or period of time.

contrast or candidate-order error An error of judgment on the part of the interviewer because of interviewing one or more very good or very bad candidates just before the interview in question.

controlled experimentation Formal methods for testing the effectiveness of a training program, preferably with a control group and with tests before and after training.

craft union Traditionally, a labour organization representing workers practising the same craft or trade, such as carpentry or plumbing.

criterion-related validity The extent to which a selection tool predicts or significantly correlates with important elements of work behaviour.

critical illness insurance The benefit that provides a lump-sum benefit to an employee who is diagnosed with and survives a life-threatening illness.

critical incident method Keeping a record of uncommonly good or undesirable examples of an employee's work-related behaviour and reviewing the list with the employee at predetermined times.

D

data mining Algorithmic assessment of vast amounts of employee data to identify correlations that employers then use to improve their employee-selection and other practices.

data warehouse A specialized type of database that is optimized for reporting and analysis and is the raw material for managers' decision support.

decertification The process whereby a union is legally deprived of its official recognition as the exclusive bargaining agent for a group of employees.

deductible The annual amount of health/dental expenses that an employee must pay before insurance benefits will be paid.

deferred profit-sharing plan (DPSP) A plan in which a certain amount of company profits is credited to each employee's account, payable at retirement, termination, or death.

defined benefit pension plan A plan that contains a formula for determining retirement benefits.

defined contribution pension plan A plan in which the employer's contribution to the employees' retirement fund is specified.

Delphi technique A judgmental forecasting method used to arrive at a group decision, typically involving outside experts as well as organizational employees. Ideas are exchanged without face-to-face interaction and feedback is provided and used to fine-tune independent judgments until a consensus is reached.

developmental job rotation A management training technique that involves moving a trainee from department to department to broaden his or her experience and identify strong and weak points.

diary/log Daily listings made by employees of every activity in which they engage, along with the time each activity takes.

differential piece-rate plan A plan by which a worker is paid a basic hourly rate plus an extra percentage of his or her base rate for production exceeding the standard per hour or per day. It is similar to piecework payment but is based on a percentage premium.

differential or unequal treatment Treating an individual differently in any aspect of terms and conditions of employment based on any of the prohibited grounds.

differential validity Confirmation that the selection tool accurately predicts the performance of all possible employee subgroups, including white males, women, visible minorities, persons with disabilities, and Aboriginal people.

direct financial payments Pay in the form of wages, salaries, incentives, commissions, and bonuses.

disability management A proactive, employer-centred process that coordinates the activities of the employer, the insurance company, and healthcare providers in an effort to minimize the impact of injury, disability, or disease on a worker's capacity to successfully perform his or her job.

discrimination As used in the context of human rights in employment, a distinction, exclusion, or preference based on one of the prohibited grounds that has the effect of nullifying or impairing the right of a person to full and equal recognition and exercise of his or her human rights and freedoms.

discrimination because of association Denial of rights because of friendship or other relationship with a protected group member.

dismissal Involuntary termination of an employee's employment.

dismissal for just cause An employer-initiated termination based on an employee's poor behaviours; in these situations, no severance, reasonable notice periods, or additional payments beyond what the employee has already earned are owed.

distributive bargaining A win–lose negotiating strategy, where one party gains at the expense of the other.

distributive justice Fairness of a decision outcome.

downsizing Refers to an intentional decision made by executives within the organization that involves a reduction of the workforce to improve efficiency or effectiveness of the organization by affecting the work process. Often the term layoff is used to define downsizing in research and organizations.

due diligence Employers' responsibility regarding taking every reasonable precaution to ensure the health and safety of their workers.

E

early retirement buyout programs Strategies used to accelerate attrition that involve offering attractive buyout packages or the opportunity to retire on full pension with an attractive benefits package.

e-learning Delivery and administration of learning opportunities and support via computer, networked, and web-based technology to enhance employee performance and development.

electronic HR (e-HR) A form of technology that enables HR professionals to integrate an organization's HR strategies, processes, and human capital to improve overall HR service delivery.

electronic performance monitoring (EPM) Having supervisors electronically monitor the amount of computerized data an employee is processing per day and thereby his or her performance.

electronic performance support systems (EPSS) Computer-based job aids, or sets of computerized tools and displays, that automate training, documentation, and phone support.

emotional intelligence (EI) tests Tests that measure a person's ability to monitor his or her own emotions and the emotions of others and to use that knowledge to guide thoughts and actions.

employee assistance plan (EAP) A company-sponsored program to help employees cope with personal problems that are interfering with or have the potential to interfere with their job performance, as well as issues affecting their well-being or the well-being of their families.

employee benefits Indirect financial payments given to employees. They may include supplementary health and life insurance, vacation, pension plans, education plans, and discounts on company products.

employee compensation All forms of pay or rewards going to employees and arising from their employment.

employee engagement The emotional and intellectual involvement of employees in their work, such as intensity, focus, and involvement in his or her job and organization.

employment insurance (EI) A federal program intended to provide temporary financial assistance to eligible persons who experience interruption to their work through no fault of their own.

employee opinion surveys Communication devices that use questionnaires to ask for employees' opinions about the company, management, and work life.

employee orientation (onboarding) A procedure for providing new employees with basic background information about the firm and the job.

employee self-service (ESS) Enables employees to access and manage their personal information directly.

employee share purchase/stock ownership plan (ESOP) A plan whereby a trust is established to hold shares of company stock purchased for or issued to employees. The trust distributes the stock to employees on retirement, separation from service, or as otherwise prescribed by the plan.

employee wellness program A program that takes a proactive approach to employee health and well-being.

employer branding The image or impression of an organization as an employer based on the benefits of being employed by the organization.

employment equity program A detailed plan designed to identify and correct existing discrimination, redress past discrimination, and achieve a balanced representation of designated group members in the organization.

employment (labour) standards legislation Laws present in every Canadian jurisdiction that establish minimum employee entitlements and set a limit on the maximum number of hours of work permitted per day or week.

empowerment Providing workers with the skills and authority to make decisions that would traditionally be made by managers.

enterprise-wide/enterprise resource planning (ERP) system A system that supports enterprise-wide or cross-functional requirements rather than a single department within the organization.

environment scanning An assessment of external factors influencing the organizations ability to find and secure talent from the external labour market including economic, competitive, legislative, social, technological and demographic trends.

environmental scanning Identifying and analyzing external opportunities and threats that may be crucial to the organization's success.

Equal pay for equal work Specifies that an employer cannot pay male and female employees differently if they are performing the same or substantially similar work.

equality rights Section 15 of the Charter of Rights and Freedoms, which guarantees the right to equal protection and benefit of the law without discrimination.

equity theory A theory suggesting that people are motivated to maintain a balance between what they perceive as their contributions and their rewards.

ergonomics An interdisciplinary approach that seeks to integrate and accommodate the physical needs of workers into the design of jobs. It aims to adapt the entire job system—the work, environment, machines, equipment, and processes—to match human characteristics.

ethnocentric staffing policy Policies that align wit the attitude that home-country managers are superior to those in the host country.

evidence-based HRM Use of data, facts, analytics, scientific rigor, critical evaluation, and critically evaluated research/case studies to support human resource management proposals, decisions, practices, and conclusions.

expatriate Employees who are citizens of the country where the parent company is based who are sent to work in another country.

expatriate assignment failure Early return of an expatriate from a global assignment.

expectancy A person's expectation that his or her effort will lead to performance.

external equity Employees perceives his or her pay as fair given the pay rates in other organizations.

F

fixed pay Compensation that is independent of the performance level of the individual, group, or organization.

flexible benefits programs Individualized benefit plans to accommodate employee needs and preferences.

flextime A work schedule in which employees' workdays are built around a core of midday hours, and employees determine, within limits, what other hours they will work.

forced distribution method Predetermined percentages of ratees are placed in various performance categories.

formal appraisal discussion An interview in which the supervisor and employee review the appraisal and make plans to remedy deficiencies and reinforce strengths.

Functional Job Analysis (FJA) A quantitative method for classifying jobs based on types and amounts of responsibility for data, people, and things. Performance standards and training requirements are also identified.

G

gainsharing plan An incentive plan that engages employees in a common effort to achieve productivity objectives and share the gains.

geocentric staffing policy Policies that aligned with the belief that the best manager for any specific position anywhere on the globe may be found in any of the countries in which the firm operates.

generation X Individuals born between 1965 and 1980.

generation Y Individuals born after 1980.

glass ceiling An invisible barrier, caused by attitudinal or organizational bias, that limits the advancement opportunities of qualified designated group members.

global nomads Employees who continuously more from country to country on multiple assignments.

globalization The emergence of a single global market for most products and services.

grade/group description A written description of the level of compensable factors required by jobs in each grade; used to combine similar jobs into grades or classes.

grades Groups of jobs based on a set of rules for each grade, where jobs are similar in difficulty but otherwise different. Grades often contain dissimilar jobs, such as secretaries, mechanics, and firefighters.

graphic rating scale A scale that lists a number of traits and a range of performance for each. The employee is then rated by identifying the score that best describes his or her level of performance for each trait.

grievance A written allegation of a contract violation, filed by an individual bargaining unit member, the union, or management.

group life insurance Life insurance provided at lower rates for all employees, including new employees, regardless of health or physical condition.

group termination laws Laws that require an employer to notify employees in the event that they decide to terminate a group of employees.

guaranteed piecework plan The minimum hourly wage plus an incentive for each piece produced above a set number of pieces per hour.

H

halo effect A positive initial impression that distorts an interviewer's rating of a candidate because subsequent information is judged with a positive bias. In performance appraisal, the problem that occurs when a supervisor's rating of an employee on one trait biases the rating of that person on other traits.

harassment Unwelcome behaviour that demeans, humiliates, or embarrasses a person and that a reasonable person should have known would be unwelcome.

hiring freeze A common initial response to an employee surplus. Openings are filled by reassigning current employees and no outsiders are hired.

HR audit An analysis by which an organization measures where it currently stands and determines what it has to accomplish to improve its HR functions.

HR portal A single Internet access point for customized and personalized HR services.

HR technology Any technology that is used to attract, hire, retain and maintain talent, support workforce administration, and optimize workforce management.

HR technology strategy A plan that is aimed at increasing the effectiveness of HR programs, processes, and service delivery by shortening cycle times, increasing customer service levels, reducing costs, and adding new service capabilities.

human capital The knowledge, education, training, skills, and expertise of a firm's workers.

human capital theory The knowledge, education, training, skills, and expertise of an organization's workforce.

human resources information system (HRIS) Integrated systems used to gather, store, and analyze information regarding an organization's human resources.

human resources management (HRM) The management of people in organizations to drive successful organizational performance and achievement of the organization's strategic goals.

human resources planning (HRP) The process of forecasting future human resources requirements to ensure that the organization will have the required number of employees with the necessary skills to meet its strategic objectives.

Human Rights Legislation Jurisdictions specific legislation that prohibits intentional and unintentional discrimination in employment situations and in the delivery of goods and services.

I

immigrant A person residing in Canada who was born outside of Canada (excluding temporary foreign workers, Canadian citizens born outside of Canada and those with student or work visas).

indirect financial payments Pay in the form of financial benefits such as insurance.

industrial engineering A field of study concerned with analyzing work methods; making work cycles more efficient by modifying, combining, rearranging, or eliminating tasks; and establishing time standards.

industrial union A labour organization representing all workers eligible for union membership in a particular company or industry, including skilled trades people.

in-house development centre A company-based method for exposing prospective managers to realistic exercises to develop improved management skills.

incumbent Individual currently holding the position.

insubordination Willful disregard or disobedience of the boss' authority or legitimate orders; criticizing the boss in public.

instrumentality The perceived relationship between successful performance and obtaining the reward.

integrative bargaining A negotiating strategy in which the possibility of win–win, lose–win, win–lose, and lose–lose outcomes is recognized, and there is acknowledgement that achieving a win–win outcome will depend on mutual trust and problem solving.

intelligence (IQ) tests Tests that measure general intellectual abilities, such as verbal comprehension, inductive reasoning, memory, numerical ability, speed of perception, spatial visualization, and word fluency.

interactional justice Fairness in interpersonal interactions by treating others with dignity and respect.

interest arbitration The imposition of the final terms of a collective agreement.

interest dispute A dispute between an organization and the union representing its employees over the terms of a collective agreement.

interest inventories Tests that compare a candidate's interests with those of people in various occupations.

internal equity Employees perceives his or her pay as fair given the pay rates of others in the organization.

intranet A network that is interconnected within one organization using web technologies for the sharing of information internally.

intrinsic motivation Motivation that derives from the pleasure someone gets from doing the job or task.

involuntary turnover Employer-initiated termination of employment, such as dismissal or layoff.

J

job A group of related activities and duties, held by a single employee or a number of incumbents.

job analysis The procedure for determining the tasks, duties, and responsibilities of each job, and the human attributes (in terms of knowledge, skills, and abilities) required to perform it.

job classes Groups of jobs based on a set of rules for each class, such as amount of independent judgment, skill, physical effort, and so forth. Classes usually contain similar jobs—such as all secretaries.

job description A list of the duties, responsibilities, reporting relationships, and working conditions of a job—one product of a job analysis.

job design The process of systematically organizing work into tasks that are required to perform a specific job.

job enlargement (horizontal loading) A technique to relieve monotony and boredom that involves assigning workers additional tasks at the same level of responsibility to increase the number of tasks they have to perform.

job enrichment (vertical loading) Any effort that makes an employee's job more rewarding or satisfying by adding more meaningful tasks and duties.

job evaluation A systematic comparison to determine the relative worth of jobs within a firm.

job evaluation committee A diverse group (including employees, HR staff, managers, and union representatives) established to ensure the fair and comprehensive representation of the nature and requirements of the jobs in question.

job instruction training (JIT) The listing of each job's basic tasks along with key points to provide step-by-step training for employees.

job posting The process of notifying current employees about vacant positions.

job rotation A technique to relieve monotony and employee boredom that involves systematically moving employees from one job to another.

job sharing A strategy that involves dividing the duties of a single position between two or more employees.

job specification A list of the "human requirements," that is, the requisite knowledge, skills, and abilities, needed to perform the job—one product of a job analysis.

just cause An employer-initiated termination based on an employee's poor behaviours; in these situations, no severance, reasonable notice periods, or additional payments beyond what the employee has already earned are owed.

K

kinesthetic learning Tactile learning through a whole-body experience.

KSAs Knowledge, skills, and abilities.

L

labour–management relations The ongoing interactions between labour unions and management in organizations.

labour relations strategy A component of an organization's HR strategy specific to the overall plan for dealing with unions, which sets the tone for its union–management relationship.

labour union (union) An officially recognized association of employees practising a similar trade or employed in the same company or industry who have joined together to present a united front and collective voice in dealing with management.

layoff The temporary withdrawal of employment to workers for economic or business reasons.

Learning management system Special software tools that support Internet training by helping employers identify training needs, and to schedule, deliver, assess, and manage the online training itself

learning organization An organization skilled at creating, acquiring, and transferring knowledge and at modifying its behaviour to reflect new knowledge and insights.

learning portal A section of an employer's website that offers employees online access to training courses.

leave of absence Allows those who may be interested in taking time away from work for a variety of reasons (e.g. personal, educational, etc.) to have a set period of time away from their position without pay, but with a guarantee that their job will be available upon their return.

line authority The authority exerted by an HR manager by directing the activities of the people in his or her own business unit, department, or service area.

line manager A manager who is authorized to direct the work of subordinates and is responsible for accomplishing the organization's tasks.

local A group of unionized employees in a particular location.

lockout The temporary refusal of a company to continue providing work for bargaining unit employees involved in a labour dispute, which may result in closure of the establishment for a time.

lost-time injury rate Measures any occupational injury or illness resulting in an employee being unable to fulfill the work full work assignments, not including any fatalities.

M

maintenance-of-membership arrangement Individuals voluntarily joining the union must remain members during the term of the contract.

management assessment centre A strategy used to assess candidates' management potential that uses a combination of realistic exercises, management games, objective testing, presentations, and interviews.

management by objectives (MBO) Involves setting specific measurable goals with each employee and then periodically reviewing the progress made.

management development Any attempt to improve current or future management performance by imparting knowledge, changing attitudes, or increasing skills.

management game A computerized development technique in which teams of managers compete with one another by making decisions regarding realistic but simulated companies.

management inventories Records summarizing the qualifications, interests, and skills of management employees, along with the number and types of employees supervised, duties of such employees, total budget managed, previous managerial duties and responsibilities, and managerial training received.

management self-service (MSS) Enables managers to access a range of information about themselves and the employees who report to them and to process HR-related paperwork that pertains to their staff.

market-pricing approach An approach usually limited to determining compensation for professional jobs based on values established for similar benchmark jobs in the market

Markov analysis A method of forecasting internal labour supply that involves tracking the pattern of employee movements through various jobs and developing a transitional probability matrix.

mass interview An interview process in which a panel of interviewers simultaneously interviews several candidates.

mediation The often voluntary use of a neutral third party who has direct input on the negotiation process to help an organization and the union representing its employees reach a mutually satisfactory collective agreement.

memorandum of settlement A summary of the terms and conditions agreed to by the parties that is submitted to the constituent groups for final approval.

mentoring The use of an experienced individual (the mentor) to teach and train someone (the protégé) with less knowledge in a given area.

merit pay (merit raise) Any salary increase awarded to an employee based on his or her individual performance.

metrics (workforce analytics) Statistical measures of the impact of HRM practices on the performance of an organization's human capital.

micro-assessment A series of verbal, paper-based, or computer-based questions and exercises that a candidate is required to complete, covering the range of activities required on the job for which he or she is applying.

mixed (semi-structured) interview An interview format that combines the structured and unstructured techniques.

multiple-hurdle strategy An approach to selection involving a series of successive steps or hurdles. Only candidates clearing the hurdle are permitted to move on to the next step.

must criteria Requirements that are absolutely essential for the job, include a measurable standard of acceptability, or are absolute and can be screened initially on paper.

mutual gains (interest-based) bargaining A win–win negotiating approach based on training in the fundamentals of effective problem solving and conflict resolution, in which the interests of all stakeholders are taken into account.

N

National Occupational Classification (NOC) A reference tool for writing job descriptions and job specifications. Compiled by the federal government, it contains comprehensive, standardized descriptions of about 40 000 occupations and the requirements for each.

negligent training Occurs when an employer fails to adequately train an employee who subsequently harms a third party.

nepotism A preference for hiring relatives of current employees.

networking An organized process whereby the individual arranges and conducts a series of face-to-face meetings with his or her colleagues and contacts, plus individuals that they recommend.

nominal group technique A decision-making technique that involves a group of experts meeting face to face. Steps include independent idea generation, clarification and open discussion, and private assessment.

O

occupation A collection of jobs that share some or all of a set of main duties.

occupational health and safety legislation Laws intended to protect the health and safety of workers by minimizing work-related accidents and illnesses.

occupational orientation The theory, developed by John Holland, that there are six basic personal orientations that determine the sorts of careers to which people are drawn.

occupational segregation The existence of certain occupations that have traditionally been male dominated and others that have been female dominated.

open shop Union membership is voluntary and non-members are not required to pay dues.

organizational climate The prevailing atmosphere that exists in an organization and its impact on employees.

organizational culture The core values, beliefs, and assumptions that are widely shared by members of an organization.

organizational structure The formal relationships among jobs in an organization.

organization chart A "snapshot" of the firm, depicting the organization's structure in chart form at a particular point in time.

outplacement counselling A systematic process by which a terminated person is trained and counselled in the techniques of self-appraisal and securing a new position.

outsourcing The practice of contracting with outside vendors to handle specified business functions on a permanent basis.

P

paired comparison method Ranking employees by making a chart of all possible pairs of employees for each trait and indicating the better employee of the pair.

panel interview An interview in which a group of interviewers questions the applicant.

pay equity Providing equal pay to male-dominated job classes and female-dominated job classes of equal value to the employer.

pay grade Comprises jobs of approximately equal value.

pay in lieu of reasonable notice A lump-sum equal to an employee's pay for the notice period provided to employees who cease working immediately.

pay ranges A series of steps or levels within a pay grade, usually based on years of service.

pension plans Plans that provide income when employees reach a predetermined retirement age.

performance analysis Verifying that there is a performance deficiency and determining whether that deficiency should be rectified through training or through some other means (such as transferring the employee).

performance management The process encompassing all activities related to improving employee performance, productivity, and effectiveness.

Personal Information Protection and Electronic Documents Act (PIPEDA) Legislation that governs the collection, use, and disclosure of personal information across Canada, including employers' collection and dissemination of personal information about employees

personality tests Instruments used to measure basic aspects of personality, such as introversion, stability, motivation, neurotic tendency, self-confidence, self-sufficiency, and sociability.

personnel replacement charts Company records showing present performance and promotability of inside candidates for the most important positions.

phased retirement An arrangement whereby employees gradually ease into retirement by using reduced workdays or shortened workweeks.

physical demands analysis Identification of the senses used and the type, frequency, and amount of physical effort involved in a job.

picket Stationing groups of striking employees, usually carrying signs, at the entrances and exits of the struck operation to publicize the issues in dispute and discourage people from entering or leaving the premises.

piecework A system of pay based on the number of items processed by each individual worker in a unit of time, such as items per hour or items per day.

point method A job evaluation method in which a number of compensable factors are identified, the degree to which each of these factors is present in the job is determined, and an overall point value is calculated.

polycentric staffing policy Policies that align with the belief that only host-country managers can understand the culture and behaviour of the host-country market.

portability A provision that employees who change jobs can transfer the lump-sum value of the pension they have earned to a locked-in RRSP or their new employer's pension plan.

position The collection of tasks and responsibilities performed by one person.

Position Analysis Questionnaire (PAQ) A questionnaire used to collect quantifiable data concerning the duties and responsibilities of various jobs.

position replacement card A card prepared for each position in a company to show possible replacement candidates and their qualifications.

pre-hearing vote An alternative mechanism for certification, used in situations in which there is evidence of violations of fair labour practices early in the organizing campaign.

pre-retirement counselling Counselling provided to employees some months (or even years) before retirement, which covers such matters as benefits advice, second careers, and so on.

principle of joint responsibility An implicit and explicit expectation that both workers and employers must maintain a hazard-free work environment and enhance the health and safety in the workplace.

primary sector Jobs in agriculture, fishing and trapping, forestry, and mining.

procedural justice Fairness of the process used to make a decision.

process chart A diagram showing the flow of inputs to and outputs from the job under study.

productivity The ratio of an organization's outputs (goods and services) to its inputs (people, capital, energy, and materials).

profit-sharing plan A plan whereby most or all employees share in the company's profits.

programmed learning A systematic method for teaching job skills that involves presenting questions or facts, allowing the person to respond, and giving the learner immediate feedback on the accuracy of his or her answers.

promotion Movement of an employee from one job to another that is higher in pay, responsibility, or organizational level, usually based on merit, seniority, or a combination of both.

punitive damages Reserved for malicious or outrageous cases in which an employer engages in harsh and vindictive treatment of an employee, or if the employee suffered undue distress from not being given adequate notice of termination.

Q

Quitting/Resigning Voluntary, employee-initiated resignation.

R

ratification Formal approval by secret-ballot vote of the bargaining unit members of the agreement negotiated between union and management.

ratio analysis A forecasting technique for determining future staff needs by using ratios between some causal factor (such as sales volume) and the number of employees needed.

realistic job preview (RJP) A strategy used to provide applicants with realistic information—both positive and negative—about the job demands, the organization's expectations, and the work environment.

reality shock (cognitive dissonance) The state that results from the discrepancy between what the new employee expected from his or her new job and the realities of it.

reasonable accommodation The adjustment of employment policies and practices that an employer may be expected to make so that no individual is denied benefits, disadvantaged in employment, or prevented from carrying out the essential components of a job because of grounds prohibited in human rights legislation.

reasonable cause A complaint about a workplace hazard has not been satisfactorily resolved, or a safety problem places employees in immediate danger.

reasonable notice legislation Laws that require an employer to notify employees in the event that they decide to terminate employees through layoffs (i.e., no just cause). Minimum notice varies on size of the layoffs, with smaller layoffs determining minimum notice based on employee tenure and mass layoffs determining minimumnotice based on total layoff size.

recency effect The rating error that occurs when ratings are based on the employee's most recent performance rather than on performance throughout the appraisal period.

recruiter A specialist in recruitment whose job is to find and attract capable candidates.

recruitment The process of searching out and attracting qualified job applicants, which begins with the identification of a position that requires staffing and is completed when résumés or completed application forms are received from an adequate number of applicants.

red circle pay rate A rate of pay that is above the pay range maximum.

reduced workweek Employees work fewer hours and receive less pay.

regression analysis A statistical technique involving the use of a mathematical formula to project future demands based on an established relationship between an organization's employment level (dependent variable) and some measurable factor of output (independent variable).

regulations Legally binding rules established by special regulatory bodies created to enforce compliance with the law and aid in its interpretation.

relational database One piece of data is stored in several different data files so that information from the separate files can be linked and used together.

reliability The degree to which interviews, tests, and other selection procedures yield comparable data over time; in other words, the degree of dependability, consistency, or stability of the measures used.

repatriation The process of moving the expatriate and his or her family back home from the foreign assignment.

repetitive strain injuries (RSIs) Activity-related soft-tissue injuries of the neck, shoulders, arms, wrists, hands, back, and legs.

replacement charts Visual representations of who will replace whom in the event of a job opening. Likely internal candidates are listed, along with their age, present performance rating, and promotability status.

replacement summaries Lists of likely replacements for each position and their relative strengths and weaknesses, as well as information about current position, perfor mance, promotability, age, and experience.

representation vote A vote conducted by the LRB in which employees in the bargaining unit indicate, by secret ballot, whether or not they want to be represented, or continue to be represented, by a labour union.

request for proposal (RFP) A document requesting that vendors provide a proposal detailing how the implementation of their particular HRIS will meet the organization's needs.

restitutional remedies Monetary compensation for the complainant to put him or her back to the position he or she would be in if the discrimination had not occurred (this includes compensation for injury to dignity and self-respect), and may include an apology letter.

retirees on call A program where retirees can continue to work on a part-time or as needed basis post-retirement.

rights arbitration The process involved in the settlement of a rights dispute.

rights dispute A disagreement between an organization and the union representing its employees regarding the interpretation or application of one or more clauses in the current collective agreement.

role-playing A training technique in which trainees act the parts of people in a realistic management situation.

S

scatter plot A graphical method used to help identify the relationship between two variables.

scientific management The process of "scientifically" analyzing manufacturing processes, reducing production costs, and compensating employees based on their performance levels.

secondary sector Jobs in manufacturing and construction.

selection The process of choosing among individuals who have been recruited to fill existing or projected job openings.

selection interview A procedure designed to predict future job performance on the basis of applicants' oral responses to oral inquiries.

selection ratio The ratio of the number of applicants hired to the total number of applicants.

seniority Length of service in the bargaining unit.

severance package A lump-sum payment, continuation of benefits for a specified period of time, and other benefits that are provided to employees who are being terminated.

Severance pay An additional payout on top of the minimum notice period requirements and only applies if the specific conditions in the applicable jurisdiction are met.

sexual annoyance Sexually related conduct that is hostile, intimidating, or offensive to the employee but has no direct link to tangible job benefits or loss thereof.

sexual coercion Harassment of a sexual nature that results in some direct consequence to the worker's employment status or some gain in or loss of tangible job benefits.

sexual harassment Offensive or humiliating behaviour that is related to a person's sex, as well as behaviour of a sexual nature that creates an intimidating, unwelcome, hostile, or offensive work environment or that could reasonably be thought to put sexual conditions on a person's job or employment opportunities.

short-term disability and sick leave Plans that provide pay to an employee when he or she is unable to work because of a non-work-related illness or injury.

sick leave Provides pay to an employee when he or she is out of work because of illness.

similar-to-me bias The tendency to give higher performance ratings to employees who are perceived to be similar to the rater in some way.

situational interview A series of job-related questions that focus on how the candidate would behave in a given situation.

situational tests Tests in which candidates are presented with hypothetical situations representative of the job for which they are applying and are evaluated on their responses.

skills inventories Manual or computerized records summarizing employees' education, experience, interests, skills, and so on, which are used to identify internal candidates eligible for transfer and/or promotion.

socialization The ongoing process of instilling in all employees the prevailing attitudes, standards, values, and patterns of behaviour that are expected by the organization.

social (reform) unionism Activities of unions directed at furthering the interests of their members by influencing the social and economic policies of governments at all levels, such as speaking out on proposed legislative reforms.

social responsibility The implied, enforced, or felt obligation of managers, acting in their official capacities, to serve or protect the interests of groups other than themselves

staff authority Staff authority gives the manager the right (authority) to advise other managers or employees.

staffing table A pictorial representation of all jobs within the organization, along with the number of current incumbents and future employment requirements (monthly or yearly) for each.

staff manager A manager who assists and advises line managers.

stand-alone system A self-contained system that does not rely on other systems to operate.

statistical strategy A more objective technique used to determine whom the job should be offered to; involves identifying the most valid predictors and weighting them through statistical methods, such as multiple regression.

stock option The right to purchase a stated number of shares of a company stock at today's price at some time in the future.

straight piecework plan A set payment for each piece produced or processed in a factory or shop.

strategy The company's plan for how it will balance its internal strengths and weaknesses with external opportunities and threats to maintain a competitive advantage.

strictness/leniency The problem that occurs when a supervisor has a tendency to rate all employees either low or high.

strike The temporary refusal by bargaining unit members to continue working for the employer.

strategy-based metrics Metrics that specifically focus on measuring the activities that contribute to achieving a company's strategic aims.

strike vote Legally required in some jurisdictions, it is a vote seeking authorization from bargaining unit members to strike if necessary. A favourable vote does not mean that a strike is inevitable.

structured interview An interview following a set sequence of questions.

succession planning The process of ensuring a suitable supply of successors for current and future senior or key jobs so that the careers of individuals can be effectively planned and managed.

supplemental employee retirement plans (SERPs) Plans that provide the additional pension benefit required for employees to receive their full pension benefit in cases where their full pension benefit exceeds the maximum allowable benefit under the Income Tax Act.

supplemental unemployment benefits (SUBs) A top-up of EI benefits to bring income levels closer to what an employee would receive if on the job.

survivor syndrome A range of negative emotions experienced by employees remaining after a major restructuring initiative, which can include feelings of betrayal or violation, guilt, or detachment, and can result in stress symptoms, including depression, increased errors, and reduced performance.

systemic remedies Forward looking solutions to discrimination that require respondents to take positive steps to ensure compliance with legislation, both in respect to the current complaint and any future practices.

T

task analysis A detailed study of a job to identify the skills and competencies it requires so that an appropriate training program can be instituted.

task performance An individual's direct contribution to their job related processes.

team A small group of people with complementary skills who work toward common goals for which they hold joint responsibility and accountability.

team-based job designs Job designs that focus on giving a team, rather than an individual, a whole and meaningful piece of work to do and empowering team members to decide among themselves how to accomplish the work.

team or group incentive plan A plan in which a production standard is set for a specific work group and its members are paid incentives if the group exceeds the production standard.

termination Permanent separation from the organization for any reason.

termination interview The interview in which an employee is informed of the fact that he or she has been dismissed.

tertiary or service sector Jobs in public administration, personal and business services, finance, trade, public utilities, and transportation/communications.

the Rand formula All members of the bargaining unit pay union dues, but employees have the choice to join the union or not.

total employment rewards An integrated package of all rewards (monetary and non-monetary, extrinsic and intrinsic) gained by employees arising from their employment.

tort law Primarily judge-based law, whereby the precedent and jurisprudences set by one judge through his or her assessment of a case establishes how similar cases will be interpreted.

traditionalists Individuals born before 1946.

training The process of teaching employees the basic skills/competencies that they need to perform their jobs.

transfer Movement of an employee from one job to another that is relatively equal in pay, responsibility, or organizational level.

transfer of training Application of the skills acquired during the training program into the work environment and the maintenance of these skills over time.

trend analysis The study of a firm's past employment levels over a period of years to predict future needs.

turnover The termination of an individual's employment with an organization.

U

unclear performance standards An appraisal scale that is too open to interpretation of traits and standards.

underemployment Being employed in a job that does not fully utilize one's knowledge, skills, and abilities (KSAs).

undue hardship The point to which employers are expected to accommodate under human rights legislative requirements.

unintentional/constructive/systemic discrimination Discrimination that is embedded in policies and practices that appear neutral on the surface and are implemented impartially, but have an adverse impact on specific groups of people for reasons that are not job related or required for the safe and efficient operation of the business.

union recognition clause Clarifies the scope of the bargaining unit by specifying the employee classifications.

union security clause The contract provisions protecting the interests of the labour union, dealing with the issue of membership requirements and, often, the payment of union dues.

union shop Membership and dues payment are mandatory conditions of employment.

union steward A union member elected by workers in a particular department or area of a firm to act as their union representative.

unstructured interview An unstructured, conversational-style interview. The interviewer pursues points of interest as they come up in response to questions.

V

valence The perceived value a person attaches to the reward.

validity The accuracy with which a predictor measures what it is intended to measure.

variable pay Any plan that ties pay to productivity or profitability.

vestibule or simulated training Training employees on special off-the-job equipment, as in airplane pilot training, whereby training costs and hazards can be reduced.

vesting A provision that employer money placed in a pension fund cannot be forfeited for any reason.

video conferencing Connecting two or more distant groups by using audiovisual equipment.

visual learning Learning through pictures and print.

voluntary turnover Employee-initiated termination of employment, such as quits, retirement, or resignation.

W

wage curve A graphic description of the relationship between the value of the job and the average wage paid for this job.

wage/salary survey A survey aimed at determining prevailing wage rates. A good salary survey provides specific wage rates for comparable jobs. Formal written questionnaire surveys are the most comprehensive.

want ad A recruitment ad describing the job and its specifications, the compensation package, and the hiring employer. The address to which applications or résumés should be submitted is also provided.

want criteria Those criteria that represent qualifications that cannot be screened on paper or are not readily measurable, as well as those that are highly desirable but not critical.

web-based application An application that can be accessed from any computer connected to the Internet.

wildcat strike A spontaneous walkout, not officially sanctioned by the union leadership, which may be legal or illegal, depending on its timing.

workers' compensation Workers' compensation provides income and medical benefits to victims of work-related accidents or illnesses or their dependants, regardless of fault.

workforce mobility The focus on managing the recruitment, relocation, and retention of employees who complete work-related tasks and activities outside of the core or primary head office or region of the company.

Workplace Hazardous Materials Information System (WHMIS) A Canada-wide, legally mandated system designed to protect workers by providing information about hazardous materials in the workplace.

work sharing Employees work three or four days a week and receive EI benefits on their non-workday(s).

work simplification An approach to job design that involves assigning most of the administrative aspects of work (such as planning and organizing) to supervisors and managers, while giving lower-level employees narrowly defined tasks to perform according to methods established and specified by management.

wrongful dismissal An employee dismissal that does not comply with the law or does not comply with a written or implied contractual arrangement.

Y

yield ratio The percentage of applicants that proceed to the next stage of the selection process.

Subject Index